FRAGMENTED FRANCE

Fragmented France

Two Centuries of Disputed Identity

JACK HAYWARD

OXFORD
UNIVERSITY PRESS

2007

OXFORD
UNIVERSITY PRESS

Great Clarendon Street, Oxford ox2 6DP
Oxford University Press is a department of the University of Oxford.
It furthers the University's objective of excellence in research, scholarship,
and education by publishing worldwide in
Oxford New York

Auckland Cape Town Dar es Salaam Hong Kong Karachi
Kuala Lumpur Madrid Melbourne Mexico City Nairobi
New Delhi Shanghai Taipei Toronto

With offices in

Argentina Austria Brazil Chile Czech Republic France Greece
Guatemala Hungary Italy Japan Poland Portugal Singapore
South Korea Switzerland Thailand Turkey Ukraine Vietnam

Oxford is a registered trade mark of Oxford University Press
in the UK and in certain other countries

Published in the United States
by Oxford University Press Inc., New York

British Library Cataloguing in Publication Data
Data available

Library of Congress Cataloging in Publication Data
Hayward, Jack Ernest Shalom.
Fragmented France : two centuries of disputed identity / Jack Hayward.
p. cm.
Includes bibliographical references and index.

1. France—Politics and government—1789–1900. 2. France—Politics and government—20th
century. 3. France—History—1789–1900. 4. France—History—20th century. 5. National
characteristics, French. 6. Political culture—France—History. 7. France—Intellectual life.
I. Title.
DC58.H295 2007
944—dc22 2006103213

Typeset by SPI Publisher Services, Pondicherry, India
Printed in Great Britain
on acid-free paper by
Biddles Ltd., King's Lynn, Norfolk

ISBN 978–0–19–921631–4

Preface

When, a third of a century ago, I entitled with deliberate derision my book *The One and Indivisible French Republic*, I did not anticipate that any reader who had understood the arguments advanced would take it literally. Hence my choice of *Fragmented France* as the title for this book is partly intended to avoid any such misunderstanding. Their underlying theme remains the same. Just as the earlier volume sought to contrast unitary norm and fragmented reality, this study dwells on the same contradiction, while more explicitly emphasizing the latter rather than the former in its title. Whereas the previous discussion was largely confined to the description and analysis of the institutions and practices of the Fifth Republic, this time the longer historical timescale renders possible a greater extension and depth of both the normative and empirical interpretation suggested. Because of the French compulsive politicization of most aspects of national life, this will be reflected nevertheless in the emphasis adopted. Retrospect interprets the past unavoidably by some implicit or explicit reference to the preoccupations of the present, which have distorting effects that must be guarded against.

The vantage point from which this study of how the French have retreated from an extrovert self-perception as both exceptional in its attributes and a universal model for less well endowed nations into a fearful introspection reflects a lifetime's critical affection for France. It combines the approaches of the intellectual and political historian in terms of the subject matter with interpretations that are shaped by a commitment to a broad based implicit or explicit comparative political science. If readers detect a bias against a militant monocultural, assimilationist conception of nationhood inspired by French republican mythology, they can place the blame upon a preference for pluralism that comes from implicit British assumptions. Because of the focus upon contending conceptions of French national identity, it seemed best to start with an explicit comparison with the implicit when not overt 'other': the Anglo-Saxons before turning more directly to intra-French exclusions.

To take the measure of the French sense of their own identity, it is first necessary to identify two kinds of 'anti-France'. The most obvious kind consists of foreign rivals, exemplified by that spurious conflation, the 'Anglo-Saxons', the counter-identities of England and then Britain until the end of the nineteenth century, thereafter increasingly the USA. The more implicit exemplars of 'anti-France' are fratricidal, all the more abhorrent for that. As Charles de Gaulle notoriously expressed his exasperation: 'How can you govern a country that has 246 varieties of cheese?' Parts I and II are devoted to exploring the cultural, religious, ideological, political, social, and economic components of France's designated internal enemies, as the endeavour to assert unity has struggled to contain where it could not extirpate these dimensions of national dissensus. The 1878 split will not be slavishly adhered to but it conveniently separates the years before the republican form of government acquired a large measure of acceptance from the years when its institutional expression changed from the Third to the Fifth Republic. While the bulk of the discussion will focus upon these internecine, introvert Franco-French conflicts that have left enduring traces even when they have diminished over time, it is preceded by the Anglo-American foreign 'other' against which France has pitted itself, lending an overarching nationalist cohesion to contending fellow countrymen.

I would like to thank the Department of Politics and International Studies of the University of Hull for welcoming me back as a Research Professor at the end of 1998, when I retired as Professor of Politics and Professorial Fellow of St Antony's College, Oxford University. I had previously served for twenty years in the Hull Department, so it proved a congenial environment in which to work without undue distraction on this book. I am grateful to have had the use of the London School of Economics Library, which usefully supplemented the holdings of the Hull University Library. An Emeritus Fellowship from the Leverhulme Trust provided some of the peace of mind and financial support for the research and preparation of the manuscript for publication. I would also like to thank Professor Edward Page, a former colleague in Hull, now of the London School of Economics, with whom I frequently had occasion to discuss the work in progress and who read the first draft in manuscript. Finally I wish to thank the OUP readers for their helpful suggestions, some of which I have adopted in making final revisions.

Jack Hayward
Kirk Ella
2006

Contents

List of Tables

Introduction: The Anglo-American Counter-Identity

In the twenty-first century, national identity has become more than ever an intro-spective subject of intense preoccupation within France because there has been a loss of confidence in the country's capacity to protect its integrity and project its power. The values that have provided its normative legitimacy for two centuries seem unsuited to a world whose intrusive pressures seem increasingly irresistible. As a result the political system's integrative capacity has been impaired and the perennial cross-cutting cleavages, that will be the main subject of our discussion, have become not a source of potential cohesion but of multi-fragmentation. How-ever, the alien 'other' has, from the dawn of French nationalism, been the external counter-identity against which France has pitted itself as a way of uniting its contending fellow countrymen. The most conspicuous foreign rival, exemplified by the spurious conflation 'the Anglo-Saxons', was first England, then Britain until the end of the nineteenth century and thereafter increasingly the USA. So, before exploring the cultural, religious, ideological, political, social, and economic components of France's designated internal enemies, which could sometimes be stigmatized as in collusion with external forces, we need to place them in the con-text of the alternative model that continues to be represented by Anglo-America.

FRANCE AND INIMITABLE BRITAIN

For a thousand years, the rivalry between England and France was marked by a mutual anxiety that the other country was winning the struggle for predominance. After their medieval conflicts, foreign wars and civil wars were a feature of French and English seventeenth-century history, as attempts at royal absolutism were suc-cessful in France and were curbed into limited monarchy in England. As S. E. Finer put it, the two countries travelled in opposite directions. The French government overcame many medieval restraints, whereas in England 'an antithetical political tradition'[1] based upon the Crown-in-Parliament and competitive political parties became dominant after the second Stuart attempt at establishing absolutism was

---

[1] S. E. Finer, *The History of Government from the Earliest Times*, III, 1997, 1335; cf. 1308. The whole of Book IV, Part 2, Chapter 6 on 'The Two Traditions: Absolute versus Parliamentary Monarchy' is worth reading for a comparative historical perspective.

halted in 1688 and despite French-supported Jacobite invasions in the eighteenth century. Although some members of the French elite envied Britain's 'crowned, nobiliar, republic' given cohesion by a united governing class of parliamentary aristocrats at the centre and a provincial squirearchy, this was not the predominant viewpoint.[2]

The preoccupation of the French with what they call the Anglo-Saxons (by which they mean the Anglo-Americans) has a long history based upon an enduring rivalry. The successful Norman invasion of England was the prelude to centuries of warfare, marked by fluctuating fortunes, with Joan of Arc's heroic resistance to an immolation by the English becoming a retrospective symbol of an emerging nation. These conflicts culminated in the revolutionary and Napoleonic Wars, Britain being seen as the main obstacle to the ideological and military hegemony of France. Medieval wars between England (a designation which the French still use interchangeably with Great Britain) and France helped them to become pioneering nation states, while in the late eighteenth century they respectively pioneered the industrial and democratic revolutions.

Despite a continuing colonial rivalry in the nineteenth century, France and Britain periodically fought on the same side thereafter, although working together has proved much more problematic. Following the seventeenth century high point of French power and prestige during the reign of Louis XIV, preoccupation with French decline relative to an increasingly expansionist Britain was a feature of the early eighteenth century. A key factor was that, thanks to parliamentary assertion of financial control after the exclusion of the Stuart dynasty, the persisting problems of mismanaged public finances that continued to plague the French monarchy until the Revolution had been solved in Britain. Preceded by the Glorious Revolution of 1688 that provided their constitutional framework, Britain's increasing trade and wealth, Marlborough's victories, and the influence of Newton's science and Locke's political philosophy prompted growing French interest in all aspects of British life. The Revocation in 1685 of the Edict of Nantes, which had tolerated French Protestantism, led to over 70,000 Huguenots establishing themselves in Britain, promoting greater contact with Continental Europe than previously.

Before examining more precisely the way in which the French defined themselves in ambivalent opposition in characteristics, manners, beliefs, and institutions to the English (as they significantly persisted in describing the British), this obsession was shared in reverse by the British. 'The French wallowed in superstition: therefore the British, by contrast, must enjoy true religion. The French were oppressed by a bloated army and by absolute monarchy: consequently, the British were manifestly free.' 'Under Napoleon, the French reverted in the British imagination to what they had so often seemed in the past: spiritless victims of overpowerful government at home and ferocious exponents of military aggression abroad. Once again, the full barrage of Protestant and libertarian complacency

---

[2] S. E. Finer, 1358; cf. 1356–7. In other countries and in Britain itself 'England' has been widely used as a shorthand for Britain. A. Gamble, *Between Europe and America: The Future of British Politics*, 2003, 18–20.

was brought to bear against the traditional enemy across the Channel.' 'Right until the end of the nineteenth century, in fact, most politicians, military experts and popular pundits continued to see France as Britain's most dangerous and obvious enemy, and for good reason. France had a larger population and a much bigger land mass than Great Britain ... [3] Did the French reciprocate this negative view?

FRENCH ANGLOPHILIA AND ANGLOPHOBIA

Exiles have historically played a disproportionately important part in the international transfer of ideas. The flow of French Protestants to Britain was followed by the reverse flow of British Jacobite supporters of the vanquished Stuarts to France. A particularly influential ambassador for British political ideas was Lord Bolingbroke, a friendship with whom—first in France from 1722 and later during his own exile in England from 1726 to 1728—initially gave Voltaire a momentously favourable impression of Britain, an idealized conception of which he was to popularize. Banished from Paris in 1726 after a short stay in the Bastille, Voltaire chose to go to England because 'It is a country where one thinks freely and nobly, without being constrained by a servile fear'.[4] Allowed to return to Paris in 1729, Voltaire published in 1733 his *Letters concerning the English Nation*, which appeared in French the following year as *Lettres Philosophiques*, getting him once again into hot water. Voltaire escaped arrest by fleeing abroad but copies of his book were burnt by the common hangman in the courtyard of the *Palais de Justice* on the orders of the *Parlement de Paris*. Allowed to return to Paris in 1735, he nevertheless prudently chose to live at a safe distance for the rest of his life to avoid risking imprisonment again in the Bastille.

Censorship could not prevent clandestine editions of his work appearing in France and elsewhere, ensuring that Voltaire's comments on the connection between religious and political liberty and prosperity became commonplace. When he was discussing priestless Quakers or the anti-superstitious scepticism of Locke, he was making the point that, thanks to religious toleration, 'As a free man, the Englishman goes to heaven by whichever way he wishes'.[5] Newton was honoured in his homeland while Descartes was forced to go abroad to write freely. In politics, while England had 'drowned the idol of despotic power in seas of blood', elsewhere (such as France) 'the blood shed for liberty only cemented

[3] Linda Colley, *Britons: Forging the Nation 1707–1837*, 1992, 368, 312, 24–5; cf. 17, 24, 33–5, 250. The French supported the Welsh in the early fifteenth century and the Irish against the English King William at the end of the seventeenth century, the Scottish Jacobites in 1745 and the Irish Wolfe Tone in 1796 against the British.

[4] F. A. Taylor, Introduction to Voltaire, *Lettres Philosophiques*, 1946 edn, viii. On the English and Scottish Enlightenment, see Roy Porter, *Enlightenment: Britain and the Creation of the Modern World*, 2000.

[5] Taylor, 14, Fifth Letter.

servitude'.[6] Voltaire was 'less concerned with telling the truth about England than with presenting to the France of the *ancien régime* by comparison a provocative picture of her own stagnation and incompetence'.[7] So, in praising the British mixed government of King, Lords, and Commons, Voltaire was not only offering the French a preferable political system but one achieved by replacing an absolute by a constitutional monarchy. The English had achieved liberation from a tyrannical Church and priesthood, from despotic Kings and a privileged nobility, freedom of thought from both, as well as equal justice and taxation between commoners and nobility. However, Voltaire did not regard Britain as offering a model that could be followed, later championing enlightened despotism à la Frederick the Great of Prussia or Catherine the Great of Russia in the hope that an alliance between monarchs and philosophers could replace that between monarchs and churchmen. So, because Britain's exceptional virtues were the result of a historical experience that could not be emulated, it could be admired rather than imitated.

French ambivalence towards Britain is captured in a 1790 remark: 'England is our model and our rival, our guiding light and our enemy'.[8] Just prior to the Revolution, it seemed that the French elites having generally idealized and even mythologized many aspects of British manners and practices as popularized in fiction and by travellers, would go on to copy the British political system. The liberal aristocracy imitated the 'milord' style of dress and demeanour, while the calculated informality of English gardens and the sport of horse racing was enthusiastically adopted. English-style clubs multiplied in the early 1780s and it became fashionable to learn English and to use anglicisms. The leading 'Anglomaniac', the Duke of Chartres (who became Duke of Orleans in 1795 and finished on the scaffold as *Philippe Egalité*) was the flamboyant 'embodiment of the excesses of *anglomanie*' in his lifestyle as well as his political predispositions.[9] During the 1820s Restoration years there was another wave of Anglomania, associated in particular with enthusiasm for Shakespeare's plays and Byron's poetry but this was to prove a passing fashion, although the music of Berlioz has perpetuated it for posterity. However, on each occasion there was a nationalist reaction against foreign cultural and political values.

Resentment against the import of alien freedom of thought and press was reflected in the popularization of the pejorative term 'Anglomania' by Fougeret de Montbron in a 1757 book that was republished five years later as *L'Anti-Anglais*. It was a counterblast to the implicit denigration of French arbitrary constraints on freedom that was couched indirectly in praise lavished on Britain, from whence came encouragement to anti-monarchical and anti-revelation propensities. 'Behind their admiration lurks their appraisal, unstated and thus uncensurable, of their own society. England appeared to protect those rights of which

---

[6] Taylor, 23, Eighth Letter.   [7] Ibid. xxii.

[8] J. P. L. Luchet, *Les contemporains de 1789 et 1790*, I, 1790, 56, quoted in Frances Acomb, *Anglomania in France, 1763–1790: An Essay in the History of Constitutionalism and Nationalism* 1950, 2, 121.

[9] Josephine Grieder, *Anglomania in France, 1740–1789*, 1985, 14–16; cf. 10–13, 26–30.

their own government was depriving them: "freedom to speak and to publish".[10] So, while opinion-leading liberal French aristocrats and the 'legal aristocracy' of the *parlements*, who favoured limited monarchy, could deplore the turbulent lack of popular deference that went with a British rejection of caste privilege and the acquisitive primacy of money making and self-interest of the British ruling classes, they envied the freedom from stultifying state surveillance.

Although it is undoubtedly his chapter on the English Constitution which became the most frequently quoted part of Montesquieu's *De l'Esprit des Lois* in the half century after its publication in 1748 because it exemplified the attainment of constitutional liberty, it was virtually exempt of empirical detail, treating Britain as an illustration of his theory of the separation of powers. As he disarmingly put it, 'It is not up to me to examine whether or not the English actually enjoy this liberty. I look no further than to show that it is established by their laws.'[11] By giving a theoretical formulation to English improvisation, Montesquieu offered America and France encouragement in basing their constitutional innovations on first principles. Although his generally implicit comparisons with France praised the British commitment to liberty in politics, religion, and commerce, he warned that it would lose its freedom 'when legislative power will be more corrupt than the executive'.[12] This warning was repeated by later French critics of those who advocated imitating the British system of government—among which one should not number Montesquieu—because they considered that under the Hanoverian monarchy, corruption and patronage had subverted the safeguards against executive 'influence'. It was left to Jean de Lolme, former disciple of his fellow-Genevan Rousseau, no admirer of the British political system, to repair Montesquieu's omission by publishing the first detailed study of British government by comparison with other European governments.

Forced to flee from Geneva, the radical republican de Lolme, having elected exile in London, ironically became the great protagonist of Britain's 'mixed' constitutional monarchy. Published in 1775 and banned in France, *The Constitution of England* nevertheless achieved great popularity in the controversy-suffused 1780s, being exceeded only by Montesquieu's *Esprit des Lois* and Rousseau's *Contrat Social* in attracting the attention of those seeking institutional solutions to France's political predicament. Rather than describing the actual British political system, de Lolme portrayed it as the best and only one able to guarantee both liberty and stability, thanks to the combined resistance of nobility, bourgeoisie, and peasantry to absolute monarchy, culminating in the 1688 Revolution. It was then that 'the true principles of civil society were fully established' and 'it was finally determined that nations are not the property of kings'.[13] While the asylum seeker in Britain

---

[10] Ibid. 119; cf. 120. The earlier title of Louis-Charles Fougeret de Montbron's book was *Préservatif contre l'anglomanie* (ibid. 7 note and 121–2).

[11] Montesquieu, *De l'Esprit des Lois*, edn 1979 I, Book XI, Chapter 6, 304.

[12] Ibid. More generally see J. Dedieu, *Montesquieu et la tradition politique anglaise en France: Les sources anglaises de l'Esprit des Lois*, 1909 and Melvin Richter, *The Political Theory of Montesquieu*, 1977, 9–12, 85.

[13] J. L. de Lolme, *The Constitution of England*, 1775, 1822 edn, 50; cf. 17–19.

concluded his book with a panegyric, declaring that 'Liberty has at length disclosed her nature and genuine principles, and secured to herself an asylum against despotism on the one hand, and popular licentiousness on the other',[14] de Lolme rejected copying Britain outright. Having referred to 'the peculiar *stability* of the executive power of the British crown ... and the advantages that result from that stability in favour of public liberty', he enumerated nine advantages 'peculiar to the English government. To attempt to imitate them, or to transfer them to other countries, with that degree of extent to which they are carried in England, without at the same time transferring the whole order and conjunction of circumstances in the English government, would prove unsuccessful attempts.'[15] The early experience of the French Revolution was to prove him right. However, we must first consider the specific arguments of the opponents of such imprudent imitation to see why the French might regard it as undesirable as well as impracticable.

BRITISH ANACHRONISM AND AMERICAN MODERNITY

Although a highly unfavourable portrayal of America's inhospitable natural and backward human resources had been popularized in the eighteenth century by the leading naturalist Buffon among others, on the political plane a more flattering picture emerged in association with anti-colonialism. The transition from an admiration for imperfect British monarchical liberalism to a perfected American republican liberalism is exemplified by the influential co-editor of the Encyclopaedia, Denis Diderot. Far from an uncritical admirer of the English, he nevertheless shared the belief that the seventeenth century struggle against the Stuart monarchy, culminating in the 1688 Revolution, had bequeathed a right of resistance to oppression that the American colonists had taken to its logical conclusion. While Diderot never abandoned the view that the English had attained an unprecedented measure of freedom at home, it was imperially oppressive, so that 'Insular self-interest has deprived the English of their role as standard-bearers of liberty'.[16] His friendship with the radical Whig MP John Wilkes, vociferous critic of the corruption into which the British parliamentary system had sunk, reinforced Diderot's refusal to consider it as a model. The early influence of Rousseau imparted to him a belief that the general will was the only basis for obedience, so that his brand of republicanism made him a precursor of French

[14] J. L. de Lolme, *The Constitution*, 1822 edn.

[15] Ibid. xvi–xviii, 'Advertisement' of the 1784 edn. More generally, see Jean-Pierre Machelon, *Les Idées Politiques de J L de Lolme, 1741–1806*, 1969.

[16] Anthony Strugnell, 'An Island Race: Diderot's deconstruction of English history' in Frédéric Ogée and Anthony Strugnell (eds), *Diderot and European Culture*, forthcoming. See also Anthony Strugnell, 'Diderot entre la Révolution américaine et le libéralisme anglais', in *Studi settecenteschi*, 11–12, 1988–89, 359–66 and Anthony Strugnell, 'L'Anglais selon Diderot ou la fin d'une manie' in Sylvain Auroux, Dominique Bourel and Charles Porset (eds), *L'Encyclopédie, Diderot, L'Esthétique*, 1991, 89–98. On the unflattering presentation of America in the mid-eighteenth century, see Philippe Roger, *L'Ennemi américain: Généalogie de l'antiaméricanisme français*, 2002, 30–55.

Jacobinism. As he chillingly put it in 1780: 'A nation is only regenerated in a bath of blood'.[17] Despite the Puritan fanaticism which the American colonists had taken with them from England, he regarded them as having established in a purified form the principles of English liberty that had degenerated during the eighteenth century. Although as an opponent of slavery he did not approve the colonists' denial of a freedom to others that they had achieved for themselves, he became an outspoken protagonist of the American Revolution in France in 1778 when France came to its support.[18]

The future Girondin revolutionary republican leader, Brissot, shared both Diderot's retrospective admiration for England's stormy constitutional struggles as the prelude to freedom and his ardent support for the American War of Independence in alliance with France. Brissot co-founded the Gallo-American society in 1787 out of whose discussions emerged his book on the relevance of American experience to France.[19] Other influential admirers of the American rationalization of the historical peculiarities of the British Constitution were Mably and Condorcet. The earlier cosmopolitanism was being replaced by a nationalist repugnance to imitate the traditional enemy; but just prior to the Revolution, Brissot expected a political system on the English model to emerge and had advised the Duke of Orleans on creating an Opposition such as he had observed as an exile in England.[20] Others emphasized the exceptional character of English institutions, notably the prominent journalist Simon-Nicolas-Henri Linguet, 'who recanted his anti-English prejudices after a stay in the Bastille' but remained hostile to a Montesquieu-inspired aristocratic constitutionalism, entitling a chapter of an 1788 book: 'ABSURDITY of the efforts that some would like to make to adopt in France the CONSTITUTION of England'.[21] Another writer described English government as 'impracticable everywhere else', 'their singular constitution (being) admired in Europe, feared in the universe and our eternal enemies'.[22] France represented a modern Rome capable of crushing the modern Carthage, a comparison that was to be revived notably by 1940s supporters of the Vichy regime.

The most influential outright opponents of the British model were the circle around the *philosophe* and Encyclopaedist Baron d'Holbach and the economists known as the Physiocrats. For d'Holbach, like Diderot, seventeenth century Britain's heroic civic virtue had been replaced by corruption and cupidity. But he went further because 'Holbach had reacted violently against everything he had

---

[17] Quoted by Richard Whatmore, *Republicanism and the French Revolution: An Intellectual History of Jean-Baptist Say's Political Economy*, 2000, 31.

[18] Anthony Strugnell, *Diderot's Politics*, 1973, 208–9.

[19] Whatmore, 78–81; cf. J. P. Brissot de Warville, *De la France et des Etats-Unis, ou de l'importance de la revolution d'Amérique pour le bonheur de la France*, 1788.

[20] Accomb, 82–3, 96–7; cf. Brissot's *Testament politique de l'Angleterre*, 1780. See also the abbé Gabriel Bonnot de Mably's critical tract *Observations sur le gouvernement et des lois des Etats-Unis d'Amérique*, 1784 and the Marquis de Condorcet's 1785 pro-American *Lettres d'un bourgeois de New-Haven à un citoyen de Virginie*.

[21] Grieder, 143. His book's title was *La France plus qu'anglaise*.

[22] Ibid. quoting Jean-François Sobry, *Le Mode français, ou discours sur les principaux usages de la nation française*, 1786, 28.

seen or experienced during travels in England'.[23] His attitude was influenced by his friendship with John Wilkes, who took refuge in France in 1764–8 after conviction for seditious libel. (His repeated elections as MP for Middlesex were annulled, although he was eventually able to take his seat and was elected Mayor of London.) D'Holbach supported the Radical programme of extending the franchise (in his case only to citizens by virtue of owning property) annual parliaments and the mandate, not merely the Whig case for reducing Crown powers. However, like Rousseau, d'Holbach rejected British-style party conflict because the republic of virtue would replace conflicting interests with the harmonious general interest. Unity should prevail over plurality; while political parties were 'necessary in the struggle to attain liberty, but once liberty had been secured, opposition should wither away.'[24] Had not Rousseau asserted 'The people of England regards itself as free; but it is grossly mistaken; it is free only during the election of Members of Parliament. As soon as they are elected, slavery overtakes it, and it is nothing. The use it makes of the short moments of liberty it enjoys shows indeed that it deserved to lose them.'[25] The French Revolutionaries, partly in response to the 'new conservative Anglomania' that saw the English Constitution portrayed by de Lolme as a protection of aristocratic privilege, were to outdo Rousseau's objections, Camille Desmoulins boldly proclaiming in 1789, 'We shall go beyond these English, who are so proud of their constitution and who mocked at our servitude'.[26]

While the 'disloyal' Anglophiles had looked to constitutional change to achieve national regeneration, the Physiocrats maintained that this was both unnecessary and undesirable. Whether it was the ruralist economist Quesnay, relying on the sovereign laws of nature enforced by an absolute monarch, or the techno-bureaucrat Turgot, seeking to use state power to carry out far-reaching economic reforms, the English priority accorded to liberty was not theirs. Tocqueville, who blamed them for promoting rationalist administrative centralization, quoted Quesnay as declaring that "any system of opposing forces within a government is highly objectionable", while ' "The present situation in France", Letronne observed complacently, "is vastly superior to that of England, for here reforms changing the whole social structure can be put through in the twinkling of an eye, whereas in England such reforms can always be blocked by the system of parliamentary government" '.[27] True in principle, this assertion proved not to be true in practice, as the termination of Turgot's attempt at reform and the substitution of revolution for reform in 1789 were to demonstrate. Controller General of Finance from 1774 to 1776, Turgot looked to changes in political culture rather than institutions to

---

[23] Acomb, 41.   [24] Ibid. 38; cf. 31–41 and Whatmore, 26–8.

[25] Jean-Jacques Rousseau, *The Social Contract and Discourses*, 1973 edn, Book III, Chapter 15 of *The Social Contract*, 266. However, he had earlier conceded that 'the English ... are nearer liberty than anyone else' (ibid. 192 note).

[26] Camille Desmoulins, *La France libre*, 1789, 69, quoted in Acomb, 121; cf. 104–6.

[27] Alexis de Tocqueville, *The Old Régime and the French Revolution*, 1856, 1955 edn, 159, 161–2. Part Three, Chapter 3 is entitled 'How the desire for reforms took precedence of the desire for freedom'. See also Acomb, 43–50.

revive France, rejecting both democracy and jury trial in favour of relying on an administrative elite. His view of America as having the 'potential to become an ideal physiocratic state' reflected his rationalist utopianism in the French late eighteenth century context.[28] In helping the Americans to win their independence, unreformed France was to ruin herself financially, materially contributing to her own revolutionary outcome. Turgot's leading economist disciple, Dupont de Nemours, implored the admirer of Adam Smith, Jean-Baptiste Say, not to 'imprison yourself in the ideas and language of the British, a sordid people who value a man only by the money he spends.... '[29] But French economists were to take contrasting views of industrial and commercial-centred Britain.

Whereas in Britain the market economy's liberal implications were the aspect of Adam Smith's writings that were most enduringly influential, in France it was the political implications of giving the industrial and commercial classes priority over the landed aristocracy that predominated. Adam Smith's *Theory of the Moral Sentiments* and his *The Wealth of Nations* had a big impact on France, notably his emphasis on the division of labour as part of a theory of value that displaced the Physiocratic emphasis on land as the source of wealth. A former disciple of Turgot, Pierre-Louis Roederer, who was to work first with Sieyès and then for Napoleon, proclaimed in 1797 the '*Wealth of Nations* the most useful of books which has ever been written', and propagated Smith's ideas in the 1790s as presupposing the constitutional prerequisites of wealth creation.[30] It was Sieyès, as a critic of the Physiocrats in the early 1770s, who arrived at a labour theory of wealth which he claimed was confirmed by Smith. However, Sieyès generalized the principle of specialization to cover a theory of representation that was to become influential during the French Revolution.[31] Furthermore, when he wrote his celebrated *What Is the Third Estate?* he made clear that he did not seek his political inspiration from Britain.

While Sieyès was not 'surprised to see a nation, which has only just had its eyes opened, turn towards the English Constitution and accept it as a model in every detail', he condemned it as 'a monument to Gothic superstition',[32] being especially critical of the hereditary second chamber. Although he did not deny that 'this exotic constitution' provided 'a framework of precautions against disorder', praising 'trial by jury, which is the true safeguard of individual liberty', his inordinate optimism led him to conclude that it was not a rational or modern answer to France's needs. Armed with the 'true science of society', 'Let us rise to the challenge of setting up ourselves as an example to the nations.'[33] Rather than the piecemeal empirical reformism that was gradually to transform the aristocratic British political system into a liberal democracy, Sieyès and the dominant French political class thought that they had a comprehensive and immediate capacity to rationalize the political system through an abstract, universal general will rather

[28] Whatmore, 65; cf. 62–7.   [29] Quoted ibid. 38; cf. 37.

[30] Quoted ibid. 8; cf. 7, 76, 172.

[31] Murray Forsyth, *Reason and Revolution: The Political Thought of the Abbé Sieyès*, 1987, 56; cf. 48–52.

[32] Abbé Sieyès, *What Is the Third Estate?*, 1789, 1963 edn, 113.   [33] Ibid. 114–17; cf. 110–11.

than shoddy compromises between private interests represented by political parties, as foreshadowed in 1770 by the Whig Edmund Burke. Interests were identified
with pre-revolutionary privileges rather than freedoms. The pursuit of a uniform
state-guaranteed equality collided with societal particular liberties. The rejection
of pluralism as synonymous with institutionalizing discord in the name of self-
evident, rational unity meant in practice that social conflict could not be managed
and France was condemned to lurch between top-down rationalist imposition and
bottom-up street power. So, it is not surprising that Robespierre could assert: 'As
a Frenchman, as a representative of the people, I declare that I hate the English
people'.[34] Anti-liberal Jacobinism was not a stable alternative to the absolutism of
kings and emperors.

Nor could Sieyès follow Condorcet in his admiration for American federalist polyarchy, which had taken British pluralism to extremes. As French secret
agent to America and arms smuggler Beaumarchais (better remembered for his
subversive plays than his politics) put it, colonial revolt was only to be expected
from these offshoots of 'mixed and turbulent governments like the English royal-
aristocratic-democracy'.[35] When the French came to the assistance of the American Revolution, they were 'not so much friends of American liberty as they were
enemies of Great Britain'.[36] However, Count Henri de Saint-Simon (a pioneer
social scientist like Condorcet) wounded when serving as an artillery officer in
Lafayette's expeditionary force in support of the American colonists, who we shall
encounter again as the 1814 advocate of Franco-British unity, reflected in his
1817 'Letters to an American' on what he had then considered 'the likely consequences for my own country. I now saw that the American Revolution marked
the beginning of a new political era' but he concluded that because of different
circumstances—absence of a dominant religion and a privileged nobility, devotion
to commerce rather than war—'the Americans would establish for themselves a
regime infinitely more liberal and more democratic than the one under which
the peoples of Europe lived'.[37] Anticipating Tocqueville, Saint-Simon argued that
'The Americans who came from England to establish a colony brought along the
political knowledge that the English had acquired after long labour and at the same
time found themselves emancipated from the habits which were bound up with
the social organization which the English had before their revolution and with the
remnants of the old institutions—but this results in the fact that their political
capacity is superior to that of the English'.[38]

---

[34] Quoted by Gérard de Puymège, *Chauvin, le soldat-laboureur: contribution à l'étude des national-
ismes*, 1993, 127. See more generally, Pierre Rosanvallon, *L'Etat en France de 1789 à nos jours*, 1990,
96–9. See also Edmund Burke, *Thoughts on the Cause of the Present Discontents*, 1770.

[35] Quoted in Acomb, 76; cf. Jean-Baptiste Duroselle, *France and the United States: From the Beginnings to the Present*, 1976, 1978, 14–15

[36] Ibid. 72–3.

[37] Quoted from the second 'Letter to an American' in Keith Taylor (ed.), *Henri Saint-Simon (1760–
1825). Selected Writings on Science, Industry and Social Organisation*, 1975, 162–3.

[38] Unpublished 'Examination of the political capacity of various peoples', quoted by Frank E.
Manuel, *The New World of Henri Saint-Simon*, 1956, 281.

RESURGENT ANGLOPHILIA

A much more ardent admirer of British constitutional monarchy and business practices (he wanted to establish a French equivalent of the Bank of England) in preference to those of the American Republic was the Genevan banker Jacques Necker. After visiting England in 1776, he was called upon to repair French public finances by an increasingly desperate Louis XVI. Although excluded from the cabinet as a Protestant, as Finance Minister he caused a sensation in 1781 by adopting the British practice of publishing the budget and generally winning over public opinion in a way that led to his recall in 1789 as a financial saviour but he was put in charge too late.[39] His support for reform under a moderate constitutional monarchy was quickly overtaken by events and he was left to plead from the sidelines for a strong but non-authoritarian government that was not at the mercy of either the legislature or the mob. As against Montesquieu, Necker stressed the interdependence between the executive and the legislature in Britain, which continued to work smoothly even when the King (George III) had taken leave of his senses.[40] Although he realized that the French were unwilling to adopt the 'admirable English model', it was the touchstone of the criticisms that the banker-statesman made in his Swiss retreat from the French revolutionary flight forwards into instability. His praise of British-style government and of ministerial responsibility in particular was to exercise through Benjamin Constant a powerful influence on liberal constitutionalism after the Restoration, so that he has a claim to be regarded as the grandfather of French liberalism.[41]

A much more radical Anglophile critic of the way the Revolution was going, Joseph de Maistre had, pre-1789, both admired Necker's reformist policies and held Whiggish political views. However, events and the influence of the conservative 'Old Whig' Edmund Burke, turned him into a 'counter-revolutionary', with Burke as 'Maistre's anti-Rousseau'.[42] Attacking the abstractions of reason, individualism, and natural rights, as well as the democracy derived from them, he argued that the lesson of English constitutional history was avoiding a priori attempts to establish a rational Constitution from first principles. Historical circumstances had created piecemeal and institutional balance based upon a political culture. 'The real *English Constitution* is this admirable, unique, infallible public spirit which is beyond all praise, which guides everything and saves everything. What is written is of no account whatsoever.'[43]

---

[39] Jean-Denis Bredin, 'Necker et l'opinion publique' in Lucien Jaume (ed.), *Coppet, Creuset de l'Esprit Libéral: Les Idées Politiques et Constitutionnels de Groupe du Madame de Staël*, 2000, 32; cf. 28–34. Coppet was a Swiss chateau just across the French border that became the focus of Madame de Staël's circle of liberal exiles.

[40] Henri Grange, *Les idées de Necker*, 1974, 331–49.

[41] J Christopher Herold, *Mistress to an Age: A Life of Madame de Staël*, 1959, 78–88 and Marcel Morabito, 'Necker et la question de "chef de l'Etat"' in Jaume (ed.) *Coppet*, 46–52.

[42] Jack Hayward, *After the French Revolution: Six Critics of Democracy and Nationalism*, 1991, 49; cf. 46–7.

[43] Joseph de Maistre's *Essai sur le principe générateur des constitutions*, written in 1809 and published in 1814, quoted from Maistre's *Oeuvres Complètes*, 1884, 241–2; cf. 235, 246–7, 265.

Like Burke, Maistre had sympathized with the American Revolution because, unlike the French, the Americans did not start afresh but built on the English constitutional tradition. However, in his vitriolic *Considérations sur la France* of 1797, Maistre scornfully asserted that 'America is often cited to us: I know nothing so provoking as the praise showered on this babe-in-arms; let it grow.' He even confidently predicted that its purpose-built capital—a typical example of rationalist folly—would never materialize. 'It is 1,000 to one that the town will not be built, or that it will not be called *Washington*, or that Congress will not sit there'.[44] He was, of course, wrong on all three counts, which simply goes to show that fatalist reactionaries can sometimes be as disastrously misguided as can optimistic innovators. The conventional champions of the Old Regime, such as the ultra-traditionalist Louis de Bonald, were more dismissive of the British model because 'It deconstructs political society to constitute mercantile society'.[45] The USA were just a more extreme manifestation of liberal commercialism.

The most distinguished member of the liberal wing of French royalism was François-René de Chateaubriand, who sought to impart to France the constitutional procedures and political practices that had given Britain stability and freedom, thereby avoiding both revolutionary government by Assembly and Old Regime or Napoleonic absolutism. His seven years exile in Britain from 1793, reinforced by nearly two years as Ambassador in London in 1822–3, enabled Chateaubriand to acquire a first-hand knowledge of the working of British political institutions. To the ultra-royalist slogan: 'Remain French, do not become English', Chateaubriand replied in his 1814 *Réflexions politiques* that France had shared in the past an English type of government but 'England had merely preceded the general development by a little more than a century'.[46] Although the desire to emulate Britain was not uncommon during the Restoration, he was one of the very few who fully appreciated its implications. He sought to persuade fellow royalists that although Christianity had engendered representative institutions, which alone could reconcile divided Frenchmen, it did not suffice as a foundation for them. As he put it in an 1824 article: 'the age of fictions is over in politics; a government based on adoration, cult and mystery is no longer viable: everyone knows their rights' so the only solution was a 'mixed government', such as the Constitutional Charter granted by Louis XVIII afforded.[47] Chateaubriand did his eloquent best in *De la Monarchie selon la Charte* to explain in 1816 that it would only work if the British principle that 'the King can do no wrong' was accepted, with its consequence of ministerial responsibility. He made clear to his readers that ministers had to be accountable to a parliamentary majority reflecting public opinion (by which he meant the 'enlightened' few that then had the vote). The

---

[44] *Considérations sur la France*, 1797, 1936 edn, 94.

[45] Louis de Bonald, *Théorie du Pouvoir politique et religieuse*, 1796, 118. For Bonald's extended hostile review of Madame de Staël's book on the French Revolution, see *Oeuvres de M. de Bonald*, 1852, 527–93.

[46] Quoted in Aurelian Craiutu, *Liberalism under Siege: The Political Thought of the French Doctrinaires*, 2003, 83 note; cf. 71.

[47] Quoted in Jean-Paul Clément, *Chateaubriand politique*, 1987, 193–4.

government would either have successfully to lead or submissively to follow its parliamentary majority.[48] The only alternatives were the dissolution of parliament or a *coup d'état*, both of which Charles X adopted, precipitating the 1830 Revolution. Chateaubriand's Memoirs expressed at length his eloquent regrets at the failure of his exertions.

While Chateaubriand was in royalist exile in England (along with some 180,000 other refugees from the Revolution), the other great champion of British representative government, Benjamin Constant, was actively assisting Sieyès as a pamphleteer in the attempt to establish it in Paris. He had acquired a lifelong Anglophilia as a 16–18-year-old student in the 1780s at Edinburgh University, then at the height of the intellectual prestige of the Scottish Enlightment. Constant was especially influenced by the political economy of Adam Smith and Adam Ferguson's historical analysis of the development of civil society, with their emphasis on the emergence of commercial life as a self-regulating and self-sustaining process, rather than the intentional result of state action; deriving from Ferguson his seminal distinction between civic republican 'ancient liberty' and intransigently individualistic 'modern liberty'. In Edinburgh he embraced the radical brand of reforming Whig doctrine identified with Charles James Fox, whom he eulogized as 'the most cosmopolitan and therefore the most enlightened man in England ... the most attached to the British Constitution in its purity, that is with all the improvements of which it is capable', adding for good measure that he would prefer to be Fox than George III.[49]

With Necker and his daughter Madame de Staël (whose posthumous book on the French Revolution taught the lessons of British history for France), Constant shared an immense admiration of the British political system, asserting: 'I feel on strong ground when I draw my examples from that dwelling of freedom'.[50] For a while, under the influence of Condorcet, Constant argued in an unpublished work that 'America, disencumbered of nobility and royalty, provides the aptest model for France to imitate'.[51] However, when he decided that constitutional monarchy rather than a republic would provide the best safeguard against absolutism in France, he had reverted by the Restoration to the British model for the head of state, who reigned but left ruling to the government. Although his Whig friends were in opposition and despite the absurdities of its unreformed electoral system, Constant championed the British parliamentary system.[52] Unlike Constant, as was partly reflected in the 1814 Charter, Louis XVIII, who became accustomed to speaking English and reading English newspapers during his 1807–14 exile

[48] See the full text of this work in Chateaubriand, *Ecrits Politiques (1814–1816)*, 2002, 397–537.

[49] Constant's 'Eloge de Sir Samuel Romilly' is quoted in Marcel Gauchet's selection from the works of Constant in *De la Liberté chez les Modernes*, 1980, 683 note; cf. 449. See also Paul Bastid, *Benjamin Constant et sa Doctrine*, II, 1966, 1061–70.

[50] Benjamin Constant, *Réflexions sur les constitutions*, 1814, Chapter 4, 68. See also Germaine de Staël's *Considérations sur les principaux événements de la Révolution Française...*, I, 1818, 15; cf. 323–8 and Volume III generally.

[51] Quoted by Stephen Holmes, *Benjamin Constant and the Making of Modern Liberalism*, 1984, 211.

[52] Preface to *Réflexions sur les constitutions*.

years in England, found the British model acceptable rather than congenial but like Constant he deplored the French lack of a two-party system to make the parliamentary system work properly.

Throughout the Restoration, Constant (to whom we return in Chapter 2) was the leading parliamentary debater of the Independent Left in Opposition, whose figurehead Lafayette delivered the eulogy at Constant's graveside in 1830. Identified with the American Republican model following his heroic intervention in the War of Independence, serving in the expeditionary force which he persuaded the King to send to support the American revolt, Lafayette became Commander-in-Chief of the National Guard in 1789, leading a group dubbed 'the Americans'; he was regarded by Condorcet among others as a potential French Washington.[53] He contributed American-inspired drafts for the 1789 Declaration of the Rights of Man although the principal author was the Anglophile 'Monarchical' Mounier, but as the Revolution took an increasingly radical course, like Mounier before him, he went into exile. The main intellectual protagonist of the American model was Destutt de Tracy (to whom we return at greater length in Chapter 2), a member of the liberal nobility who served in Lafayette's revolutionary army and became his son-in-law. As the leader of the *Idéologues*, he remained committed to republicanism and to the only example of a large republican state, the USA.

After electoral defeat in 1824, Lafayette, as the popular 'hero of two worlds', was invited to America by the US Congress, where his 'royal progress' there in 1824–5 was exploited as 'an act of liberal propaganda' back in France.[54] Nevertheless, following the 1830 Revolution, the opportunity as head of the National Guard to re-establish a republic was missed by Lafayette, who sought to pass off the July Monarchy as a 'royal republic' because he thought France was not ready to adopt his American ideal. His embrace of Louis-Philippe at the Paris Town Hall was caustically dismissed in his memoirs by Chateaubriand with the words: 'The republican kiss made a king'.[55] Lafayette's cult standing rapidly went into decline and with it the associated idealized image of the USA. His death in 1834 was followed a year later by the publication of Tocqueville's *Democracy in America* which offered a more realistic assessment of the USA at a time when the Orleanist regime was more inclined to admire Britain.

The main ideological beneficiaries of the July Revolution were the *Doctrinaires*, who had collaborated with Lafayette and Constant in opposing Charles X but were in a better position to take advantage of his overthrow. Although they shared Constant's admiration for British institutions, his friend Sismondi said of Constant's liberalism that 'In politics, he founded more doctrines than those who

---

[53] Jean-Baptiste Duroselle, *France and the United States: From the Beginnings to the Present*, 1978, 21–3, 35. Condorcet dedicated his 1786 essay *De l'influence de la Révolution de l'Amérique sur l'Europe* to Lafayette. See Elisabeth and Robert Badinter, *Condorcet (1743–1794) Un intellectual en politique*, 1988, 1990, 228.

[54] René Rémond, *Les Etats-Unis devant l'Opinion Française, 1815–1852*, II, 1962, 620; cf. 617–30.

[55] Chateaubriand, *Mémoires d'Outre-Tombe*, 1849–50, IX, 303–4. See also François Ribadeau-Dumas, *La Destinée secrète de Lafayette ou le messianisme révolutionnaire*, 1972, 395; cf. 4–12–15.

have been called doctrinaires'.[56] While they included some remarkable intellectual politicians such as Royer-Collard, Rémusat, and Madame de Staël's son-in-law Victor, Duke de Broglie, the leading luminary and future de facto Prime Minister from 1840 to 1848 was François Guizot, his nickname 'Lord Guizet' conflating his arrogance and Anglophilia. After serving the restored Bourbon monarchy in its more liberal phase, regarding Louis XVIII's Charter as 'a victory of the partisans of the English Constitution' as initially envisaged by the Mounier faction in 1789, Guizot was forced to turn to writing and lecturing, particularly about English history and the rise of representative government.[57] While his main purpose was to suggest that the 1688 Revolution could offer a precedent for France to follow, he argued that this would not have been possible without the earlier Puritan Revolution and Cromwell, with the analogies to the transition from the French Revolution to Napoleon. He went as far as declaring that the English Revolutions had 'succeeded twice. Its authors first founded constitutional monarchy in England; their descendants founded in America the republic of the United States'.[58] However, as a closer observer of the latter, Tocqueville was more inclined to contrast democratic America with aristocratic Britain. He did not accept Guizot's conservative claim that the advent of the middle class to power precluded further democratic advance except in the most gradual and incremental way, nor the repressively illiberal way in which he exercised power.

AMERICA AS A MODERNIZED BRITAIN

A Norman aristocrat by birth and married to an Englishwoman, Alexis de Tocqueville, like his mentor Guizot, had made a close study of English history before he ventured to America. Circumspect in his use of cross-national comparison, Tocqueville eschewed facile analogies. The French 1830 Revolution was a continuation of 1789 not the English 1688 Revolution, heralding debilitating disorder rather than reinvigorating order. As he explained to one of his English correspondents in 1851: 'Sometimes we draw from our own history; sometimes from yours. Sometimes we use the precedent as an example, sometimes as a warning. But as the circumstances under which we apply it always differ materially from those under which it took place, it almost always misleads us.'[59] He traced the historical roots of English liberal political culture to the medieval period, which had freed it from the incubus of France's despotic political culture.

---

[56] Quoted in J. R. de Salis, *Sismondi, 1773–1842: La vie et l'oeuvre d'un cosmopolite philosophe*, 1932, 121; cf. 117–22.

[57] Francois Guizot, *Memoirs to Illustrate the History of My Time*, I, 1858, 35, quoted in Craiutu, 71; cf. 27–39, 72–3. See also J. Egret, *La Révolution et les Notables: Mounier et les Monarchiens*, 1950.

[58] François Guizot, *Histoire de la Révolution d'Angleterre*, 1826–7, 1997 edn, 15, quoted in Craiutu, 101; cf. 27–39.

[59] Seymour Drescher, *Tocqueville and England*, 1964, 171, quoting Nassau Senior, *Correspondance and Conversations of Alexis de Tocqueville with Nassau William Senior from 1834 to 1859*, I, 1872, 255.

In a long letter in 1828 to a friend entitled 'Reflections on English History', Tocqueville wrote that the English '*constitution* was famous already.... Nowhere else in Europe as yet was there a better organized system of free government'.[60] He placed particular explanatory reference upon the 'great feudal maxim "do not tax the unwilling"' as the basis of parliamentary insistence on securing consent to raising taxes, which usually helped to unite Lords and Commons whereas 'in the rest of Europe (they) have been irreconcilable enemies', allowing royal despotism to exploit their divisions.[61] Contrasting the significance of the term 'gentleman' in English and French, he was already arguing in 1833, during his first visit to England, that 'The English aristocracy ... is not in the least founded on birth, that inaccessible thing, but on wealth that everyone can acquire, and this one difference makes it stand, while the others succumb either to the people or to the king.'[62]

Compared to America, England was a hybrid in transition from an acquisitive aristocracy to democracy, although 'English aristocracy will fall more slowly and less violently than in France ... '.[63] As well as praising English incrementalism, gradualism and its allergy to bureaucratic centralization, during his second visit in 1835 Tocqueville admired the subordination of state administration to the Common Law and the ordinary courts, preference for precedent over reason. Foreshadowing his influential attack on administrative law, he notes: 'The necessity of bringing the judicial power into the administration is one of those central ideas to which I am brought back in all my researches to discover what allows and can allow men the enjoyment of political liberty'.[64] Jury trial (as a political instrument of public opinion, not just a judicial procedure), the role of elected local authorities and of voluntary associations, which he had observed in America, he also recognized as underpinning a liberal political culture in England that shaped his analyses and normative judgements.

Regarding the Anglophile and oligarchical July Monarchy as obstinately refusing to recognize the need to democratize, Tocqueville crossed the Atlantic to study a less traditionalist society than Britain, producing his first masterpiece, *Democracy in America*. He admired America for combining generous amounts of liberty and equality, whereas Britain had developed liberty without equality and France had given equality priority over liberty. Nevertheless, unlike Lafayette, who wanted France to imitate America, Tocqueville realized that a culture characterized by a self-interested, self-reliant, and self-disciplined people, able to dispense with strong government, could not simply be transposed to France. However, rather than opposing the English conception of modern liberty as the individualist right of personal autonomy against the Classical collectivist conception of civic duty as Constant had done, Tocqueville sought a pluralist reconciliation between them while being sceptical that it could be achieved in France.

[60] Alexis de Tocqueville, *Journeys to England and Ireland*, 1958, 32.   [61] Ibid. 31; cf. 28–35.

[62] Ibid. 59–60; cf. 67. On the significance of 'gentleman', see also Tocqueville's *The Old Regime and the French Revolution*, 83, 88–9, 135–7.

[63] Ibid. 68; cf. Drescher, 68–9, 123–4.

[64] Ibid. 95; cf. 96–7 and Drescher, 83–7, 221. See also Tocqueville's *The Old Regime*, 285–6 and *Democracy in America*, 1835, 1946 edn, Chapter 15, 203–4.

Having experienced the Second Empire despotism based on a democratic suffrage, Tocqueville transferred his despairing hopes for liberty to Britain, which as early as 1835 he had described as intellectually his second homeland. In contrast to his previous opinion, Britain was not so much aristocratically backward as a pioneer modernizer, capable of reconciling economic advance with political stability and liberty. His second masterpiece, *The Old Regime and the French Revolution*, offers an internal exile's devastating critique of all aspects of French state, society, and politics by implicit or sometimes explicit comparison with Britain, like Burke to whom he was indebted. While not going as far as Madame de Staël, of whom it has been claimed that while 'she regarded America as the ideal, (she) nonetheless clung to England as the model',[65] Tocqueville now emulated that doughty opponent of Napoleon in expressing his identification with how and why Britain had resisted his might. 'It is not the Channel which saves England; it is her spirit, her constitution, above all, her *liberty*. A proud spectacle: *liberty* alone capable of struggling successfully against *revolution*' and its authoritarian successor.[66] 'At the end of his life England was morally and politically, as well as intellectually, his second homeland.'[67]

Although Tocqueville's Anglo-American analyses and liberal values were to make a comeback in the late-twentieth century, they were—but second to those of Constant—to exercise an influence on the founders of the Third Republic Constitution. Edouard Laboulaye, who was to play an active part as a deputy in its adoption in 1875, had published an influential book *Le Parti Libéral* in 1863 in which he poured scorn on the patriots who justified the denial of liberty because 'France is not England, the French are not English'.[68] While admiring Britain, Laboulaye nevertheless followed Tocqueville in arguing that the USA was a better model for France. 'North America is emigrant England, leaving behind in the Old World monarchy, the Established Church, the House of Lords, nobility and privilege: if I may say so it is free England adapted to our weaknesses and prejudices.'[69] However, after the disastrous Second Republic experience with presidentialism, the Third Republic preferred a would-be British-style parliamentarism. A disciple and editor in 1861 of the works of Constant, for thirty years professor of comparative legislation at the *Collège de France*, Laboulaye's book championed Britain's laissez-faire economic policy, its local autonomy (notably in education), judicial independence, and the jury system (especially in press trials). In this respect, like his mentors Constant and Tocqueville, he fitted into

---

[65] Herold, 195.

[66] Alexis de Tocqueville, *'The European Revolution' and Correspondence with Gobineau*, 1959, 113; cf. his 26 March 1853 letter to Henry Reeve in Alexis de Tocqueville, *Correspondence Anglaise*, VI of the *Oeuvres Complètes*, 1954, 143.

[67] Drescher, 223; cf. 222 and Chapter 10 passim. Françoise Mélonio, *Tocqueville et les Français*, 1993, 153, quotes a sardonic 1856 review of Tocqueville's *Old Regime*, referring to those who 'having to write a history of France, always seem to regret not having to write a history of England'.

[68] Edouard Laboulaye, *Le Parti Libéral: Son programme et son avenir*, 1863, 323; cf. v–viii, 120–2, 137–8, 244–6. For his obituary on Tocqueville, see *L'Etat et ses limites*, 1863, 138–201.

[69] *Journal des débats*, 1 October 1859, quoted in Françoise Mélonio, *Tocqueville et les Français*, 1993, 394; cf. 204–5, 213. See also Rémond, II, 851–2.

a long Anglo-American tradition in which adversarial trial and reliance upon the common man to dispense justice, representing society against the state, as well as a free press as a countervailing power to government, were espoused by liberals in France.[70]

The Jury system imported from Britain in 1791 (abolished by Napoleon and subsequently only reintroduced with circumspection) was also ardently championed by Anatole Prévost-Paradol, the leading political journalist of the 1860s, who, like Constant, was really a French Whig. His unbounded admiration for Britain was based on the view that it had liberty and prosperity, aristocracy and democracy, a cheap and free press to expose abuses of power, decentralization and the rejection of abstract declarations of rights which proclaimed principles that were frequently infringed in practice. His *La France Nouvelle* of 1868 was widely read by the 1875 constitution makers, even though the political system they established did not work like the British parliamentary model that many thought they were adopting.[71] The Anglophile liberal legacy of Laboulaye and Prévost-Paradol was perpetuated by Emile Boutmy's *Ecole Libre des Sciences Politiques*, which Laboulaye helped found in 1871 to educate a new republican elite to master mass democracy in the name of the most capable and reconstruct France in the wake of military defeat.

Boutmy was an enthusiast for an elitist, Whig liberalism directly inspired by British constitutional experience. However, successive editions of his 1887 book on *Le développment de la constitution et de la société politique en Angleterre* (based on lectures given at the *Ecole Libre*) showed a decline in his optimism about the working of partisan parliamentary democracy as the oligarchical politics of which he approved gave way to mass politics. Although the degenerative process was slower in Britain than in the USA, the explicitly Burkean view of representation was being corrupted by the new class of politicians emerging from the extra-parliamentary party organizations that had developed to take advantage of universal suffrage. By the beginning of the twentieth century, in books on the political psychology of the British and American peoples, Boutmy's pessimistic assessment was to feed the debate upon the crisis of representative democracy in France that sought to counteract the consequence of popular sovereignty as the basis of political legitimacy generated by the French Revolution. He argued in 1902 that 'any grafts, transplants or propagations from one side of the Atlantic to the other are liable to be sterile. The Constitution of the United States... lends itself neither to piecemeal borrowings nor to full blown imitation.'[72] Because

---

[70] See Lucien Jaume, *L'Individu Effacé ou le paradoxe du libéralisme français*, 1997, 379–405 on the jury and 407–44 on the free press for Britain's liberal influence in France.

[71] Anatole Prévost-Paradol, *La France Nouvelle*, 1868 and his *Essais de Politique et de Littérature*, 1859. See also, on Paradol's anglomania, Pierre Guiral, *Prévost-Paradol (1829–70). Pensée et Action d'un Libéral sous le Second Empire*, 1955, 115–16, 209–10, 494–7.

[72] Boutmy's *Elements d'une psychologie politique du peuple américain*, 1902, quoted by Marie-France Toinet in Denis Lacorne et al., *The Rise and Fall of Anti-Americanism: A Century of French Perception*, 1990, 194; cf. 192–3. More generally, see Gaetano Quagliariello, *Politics without Parties: Moisei Ostrogorski and the Debate on Political Parties on the Eve of the Twentieth Century*, 1996, 6, 18–20, 24–5.

the British model no longer offered a sustainable defence against mass democracy, functional representation of interests was advocated as an alternative basis of legitimacy. Despite the twentieth century creation of consultative Economic and Social Councils, which were also inspired by a Saint-Simonian endeavour to mobilize industrial society and expertize as a counterweight to liberal democracy, these proved inadequate to contain the propensity to populist demagoguery that Boutmy and others anxiously anticipated.

In 1814, at the time of another disastrous military setback, Count Claude-Henri de Saint-Simon, having served with Lafayette in the American War of Independence and then survived imprisonment during the Terror, ephemerally embraced political and economic liberalism, in the process substituting Adam Smith for Newton as offering the solution to Europe's problems. Before finally rejecting the political nostrums that had been discredited since the Revolution, Saint-Simon proposed Franco-British political unity in *On the Reorganisation of European Society*. Written largely by his 'secretary' Augustin Thierry (whose subsequent role is discussed in Chapter 2), it advocated the adoption of British parliamentary government as the best model available. Although extremely vague, a joint Anglo-French parliament under British tutelage would form the nucleus of a European federation. This publication was to be followed by an appeal, 'To all Englishmen and Frenchmen who are zealous for the public good' to promote the scheme but he was persuaded by Jean-Baptiste Say to give up political remedies which had overshadowed French life for thirty years and instead to embark upon the propagation of Say's industrialist political economy.[73]

Say, whose 1803 *Treatise on Political Economy* had marked him out as the leading exponent of Adam Smith's economics and provoked Napoleon's hostility, was commissioned in 1814 by the Restoration government to investigate secretly the British economy. He concluded that Britain should not be copied and as a committed republican preferred the American model. Unlike Constant, who lectured at the same institution (Say had Saint-Simon in his audience) Say did not rely on liberal political institutions to underpin a prosperous commercial society. He regarded Britain's idle aristocratic property owners as denying it liberty and efficiency, being influenced by the Benthamite critique of British government corruption, so the efforts of his grandson Léon Say to portray his as a liberal economist were misleading. He did not share Smith's belief that enlightened self-interest would satisfy society's needs and substituted an emphasis upon industrial production for unproductive consumption. His emphasis on the industrious classes and on the entrepreneur in particular was to achieve great influence through the Saint-Simonians. So the former Saint-Simonian turned Social Catholic, Buchez, reviewing Tocqueville's *Democracy in America* in 1835, could attack the Protestant individualism that meant that 'America is socially

---

[73] Keith Taylor (ed.), *Henri Saint-Simon (1760–1825): Selected Writings on Science, Industry and Social Organisation*, 1975, 130–5. More generally, see Henri Gouhier, *La Jeunesse d'Auguste Comte*, III, 1941.

organised egotism and systematically and legalised evil'.[74] The Swiss economist Sismondi also started in 1803 as an ardent admirer of Adam Smith with his *De la Richesse Commerciale*. A member of Madame de Staël's Coppet circle and closely associated with Constant, he was much closer during the Restoration and July Monarchy to Anglophobe Say, rejecting laissez-faire capitalism for undermining social solidarity. However, against Say and Saint-Simon, Sismondi attacked over-production that British industrialism had caused leading to cyclical unemployment and poverty for many, criticizing British political economy on the evidence of British economic experience. While not abandoning support for the market economy, he stressed the need for regulatory correction of its undesirable side effects that anticipated later socialist writers.[75]

Socialist exiles in Britain often turned out to be its sternest critics from a mixture of horror at social and economic inequality and of allergic nationalism. In contrast to the aristocratic dominance admired by the liberals, a Flora Tristan in her 1840 *Promenades dans Londres ou l'aristocratie et les prolétaires anglais* and Louis Blanc in his 1866 *Letters on England* described it in the latter's words as the 'classic land of inequality'.[76] However, the most vitriolic attack came in Ledru-Rollin's *De la decadence de l'Angleterre* of 1850, which comprehensively damned all British institutions: political, social, judicial, ecclesiastical, educational, in a country 'enslaved by the greed and self-interest of its aristocratic class'.[77] While these critics focused on the exploitation of the working classes by a privileged aristocracy, the historian Michelet was especially horrified at the elimination of the peasantry in England. More generally, he argued that 'Liberty without equality, unjust and impious liberty is nothing else than the absence of sociability in society. France wants liberty through equality' and as such 'England explains France, but by opposition' and was an 'anti-France'.[78] This was to become the dominant Republican view outside a shrinking liberal elite of the aristocracy and upper-middle class.

Tocqueville's neglect of American economic activity was criticized by the former Saint-Simonian Michel Chevalier, who was commissioned by Interior Minister Thiers in the mid-1830s to study US railways, a development which ex-Saint-Simonians were to promote in France as we shall see. He stayed two years and sent back letters that were published in the *Journal des débats* before appearing as a book, being widely read and quoted at the time. He was 'convinced that France would learn from and follow the US example' generally.[79] We shall encounter

[74] Quoted by Guy Sorman in Lacorne et al., 214. More generally on Say see Whatmore, 3–6, 17, 39, 146–53, 160, 170, 174, 183, 195–201 and Hayward, *After the French Revolution*, 84–6. Say's critical *De l'Angleterre et des Anglais* was published in 1816.

[75] Jean-Jacques Gislain, 'Sismondi, penseur critique de l'orthodoxie économique' in Jaume (ed.), *Coppet*, op. cit., 75–98; cf. de Salis, *Sismondi* and Jaume, *L'Individu Effacé* 483–8.

[76] Louis Blanc, *Letters on England*, II, 1866, 16.

[77] Jeremy Jennings, 'Conceptions of England and its Constitution in Nineteenth Century French Political Thought' in *The Historical Journal*, XXXIX/I, 1986, 82; cf. 81–3 on Tristan, Blanc, and Ledru-Rollin.

[78] Ibid. 83, quoting Michelet's 'Introduction à l'histoire universelle' and *Le Peuple*.

[79] Rémond, I, 376–7; cf. 331 and Duroselle, 68–72. See also Jeremy Jennings 'Democracy before Tocqueville: Michel Chevalier's America', *Review of Politics*, Summer 2006, 398–427.

Chevalier again as the co-architect of the Cobden-Chevalier Treaty promoting freer trade between France and Britain as part of the Second Empire's move in a liberal direction during the 1860s, recalling Saint-Simon's flirtation with economic liberalism nearly half a century earlier. Reviewing Bagehot's *The English Constitution*, Chevalier also effusively praised English political institutions as the bulwarks of liberty.[80]

Despite Tocqueville's admiration for British liberty, he was scandalized by the increasing number of indigents dealt with by the administratively centralizing Royal Commission on the Poor Law Report, leading to an 1834 Act. His pessimistic 1835 *Memoir on Pauperism* was prompted by this evidence of the insecurity resulting from a competitive market economy pioneered by Industrial revolution in Britain, as well as by the work of Catholic social investigators influenced by Sismondi. Viscount Villeneuve-Bargemont's three volume *Christian Political Economy or Research on the Nature and Causes of Pauperism in France and in Europe* of 1834 was followed in 1840 by Eugène Buret's *On the Poverty of the Working Classes in England and France*, which suggested that the Protestant pursuit of profit had led to the increasing misery of the proletariat before others, such as Karl Marx, took up the critique of the social consequences of Britain's Industrial revolution. However, Sismondi's call for a social economy counterpart of political economy was not heeded by mainstream French economists.[81]

Against Maistre, who had dismissed liberalism as merely Protestantism in politics, the Liberal Catholicism of Count Charles de Montalembert was closer to that of Chateaubriand, who had traced the origins of representative government back to medieval Christianity. After initially supporting Louis-Napoleon's 1851 coup, Montalembert looked to British aristocratic liberalism as a model for checking despotic power in France, just as he opposed Papal claims to infallibility in the name of his advocacy of a *Free Church in a Free State*.[82] Anglophilia and elitist liberalism were also perpetuated on the Catholic Right-Centre by Duke Victor de Broglie, son-in-law of Madame de Staël. Aspiring to achieve a 'French 1688', as de facto Prime Minister in 1835–6 he tried to enforce post-George III British-style parliamentary government against Louis-Philippe who sought to be his own Prime Minister. Looking back on his role in drafting the Constitutional Charter of 1830, his periods as Prime Minister in the 1830s and French Ambassador in London shortly before 1848, he declared: 'I loved England like the ultramontanes love Rome: it was my second homeland.'[83] The political career of the Broglie

[80] Chevalier, 'La constitution d'Angleterre' in *Revue des Deux Mondes*, LXXII, 1867, 529–55.

[81] Cheryl B. Welch, 'Tocqueville's resistance to the social' in *History of European Ideas*, XXX/I, 2004, 88–90.

[82] This was the title of his 1863 book. In 1855 he had published an optimistic assessment, *De l'avenir politique de l'Angleterre*. Born in London of an émigré father and Scottish mother, Montalembert wrote of Britain that 'it would have been even better for us to imitate than to admire'. (Quoted in Robert Gibson, *Best of Enemies: Anglo-French Relations since the Norman Conquest*, 1995, 188). See also Jaume, *L'Individu Effacé*, 217–19; cf. 195, 210–12, 227–8.

[83] Quoted by Jean-Pierre Machelon, 'Victor de Broglie et les *Vues sur le Gouvernement de la France*' in Jaume (ed.) *Coppet*, 188; cf. 187–98. See also Alain Laquièze, *Les Origines du Régime Parlementaire en France (1814–1848)*, 2002, 102–3; cf. 123, 262, 271–3.

political dynasty effectively ended with Duke Albert de Broglie, Madame de Staël's grandson, who led an ultra-conservative Orleanist liberalism to defeat in the 1870s and resigned himself to the Third Republic. Writing before he became its founder in the 1870s, Adolphe Thiers sadly reflected that 'in France kings cannot make concessions and the people cannot be patient. Consequently, the regime that suits England so well appears in France only to demonstrate its impossibility.'[84]

The visits of Edward VII to Paris and President Loubet to London in 1903 put on a formal footing the cautious steps towards the establishment in 1904 of an *Entente Cordiale* based on a comprehensive settlement of Anglo-French colonial rivalries involving an imperial exchange of British domination in Egypt for French domination in Morocco. (Ironically, the last Anglo-French military–colonial entente involved the attack on Suez in 1956, motivated on the French side primarily to protect its hold on Algeria.) The *Entente* was transformed into an alliance by the German attack on Belgium in 1914 and it survived the dissensions over the 1919 Versailles Treaty. In the 1936 crisis, precipitated by Hitler's remilitarization of the Rhineland, and the Munich crisis of 1938, weak French governments followed with cowardly relief a British policy of appeasement. 'The occupation of the Ruhr in 1923 taught France that unilateral action against Germany was too risky an enterprise. Thenceforward she tried to keep in step with Britain.'[85]

While France and Britain fought the First World War as allies of comparable weight, the occupation of France from 1940 to 1944 meant that when Charles de Gaulle maintained in London a diminutive French presence alongside Churchill's Britain, the imbalance could not be gainsaid. The 16 June 1940 desperate Anglo-French union proposal improvized to keep France from capitulating, in which de Gaulle played an active part, was rejected with contempt by the defeatist French government—Pétain called it 'union with a corpse'—precipitated Prime Minister Reynaud's resignation and Pétain's takeover. (Reynaud had said at a Cabinet meeting on 12 June that 'it is impossible to conceive of France's future without the friendship and support of the Anglo-Saxon World'.[86]) Nevertheless, with invaluable help from Churchill and against the opposition of US President Roosevelt, de Gaulle was able resolutely to reassert the role of France as a world power by the end of the Second World War. Showing the ingratitude of the strong, this did not prevent him from single-handedly blocking British entry into the European Economic Community (EEC) in 1963 and 1967, especially because she

[84] Thiers letter of 1850, quoted in J. P. T. Bury and R. P. Tombs, *Thiers 1797–1877: A Political Life*, 1986, 128.

[85] Anthony Adamthwaite, 'Reactions to the Munich Crisis' in Neville Waites (ed.), *Troubled Neighbours: Franco-British Relations in the Twentieth Century*, 1971, 179.

[86] Quoted by P. M. H. Bell, 'The Breakdown of the Alliance in 1940' in *Waites*, 209. At the time of the 1956 joint Suez adventure, Prime Ministers Guy Mollet and Anthony Eden discussed reviving the 1940 scheme for an Anglo-French Political Union on Anglophile Mollet's initiative but the British government was unenthusiastic about this as well as Mollet's fallback suggestion that France join the Commonwealth! P. M. H. Bell, *France and Britain, 1940–1994*, 155–8. On the abortive 1940 Anglo-French Union proposal, see General de Gaulle, *Mémoires de Guerre*, I, 1954, 80–4, François Kersaudy, *Churchill and de Gaulle*, 1981, 70–3 and Jean Lacouture, *De Gaulle. The Rebel*, 1890–1944, 1990, 202–5.

was too close—he would have said subservient—to her transatlantic fellow Anglo-Saxons to be part of a 'European Europe', which without Britain would continue to be dominated politically by France. The Second World War had demonstrated that Churchill's Britain would always defer to Roosevelt's America and nothing changed thereafter.

While most of the Fourth Republic politicians had initially looked to Britain for a lead, reflected in the signing of the 1947 Anglo-French Dunkirk Treaty that was primarily an anti-German alliance and the 1948 Brussels Treaty against the Soviet Union, these were quickly overtaken by the American-dominated creation in 1949 of the North Atlantic Treaty Organisation (NATO). Furthermore, British reluctance to engage in the European integration process of the 1950s was momentously anticipated in a 1949 Cabinet paper by Foreign Secretary Bevin: 'we should not involve ourselves in the economic affairs of Europe beyond the point at which we could, if we wished, disengage ourselves.... We must remain, as we always have been in the past, different in character from other European nations and fundamentally incapable of whole-hearted integration with them.'[87] France therefore turned to Germany as her principal political ally, with whom she could be the senior partner, and the Suez fiasco of 1956 ensured, as a former British Ambassador to Paris put it, that 'The days of the *Entente* based on British leadership were over'.[88] The return of de Gaulle to power and a politically and economically reinvigorated Fifth Republic, while Britain had gone into relative decline, set the scene for de Gaulle's condescending rebuff to the belated British applications to join the European Community.

That there was also an underlying historical resentment is revealed by an exchange between de Gaulle and Paul Reynaud, with whom he had worked closely in the 1930s and who had appointed him a minister in his 1940 wartime government. Appalled at de Gaulle's treatment of France's friend and ally in vetoing British EEC entry in January 1963, he wrote him a long letter of protest. When he received a reply, the envelope contained nothing... but on the back in de Gaulle's hand were the words: 'If absent, forward to Agincourt (Somme) or Waterloo (Belgium).'[89] Revenge for unforgiven defeats (he could have added the victory of Churchill's ancestor Marlborough at Blenheim (Bavaria) perpetuated in the French nursery rhyme *Malbrouck s'en va en guerre*), which de Gaulle remembered with most of his countrymen, was a more deep-seated sentiment than the anti-liberalism which has overlaid but not wholly displaced it. Later we shall see how the USA—resistance to whose hegemony became a focus of de Gaulle's action in the 1960s—replaced Britain as arch counter-identity in the twentieth century.

---

[87] Quoted in Alan Bullock, *Bevin*, III, 734.   [88] *The Memoirs of Lord Gladwyn*, 1972, 285.

[89] Recounted by Lord Gladwyn in the special issue on 'De Gaulle and Great Britain' in *Espoir: Revue de l'Institut Charles de Gaulle*, No 43, Juin 1983, 20. On the 1940 desperate attempt to establish an Anglo-French Union, see Francois Duchêne, *Jean Monnet. The First Statesman of Interdependence*, 1994, 76–83 and Jean Lacouture, *De Gaulle: I, The Rebel, 1890–1944*, 1990, 202–4. During the Second World War, the Resistance hero Pierre Brossolette said of de Gaulle: 'The General must be constantly reminded that our enemy number one is Germany. If he followed his natural inclination it would be the British'. Quoted by Kersaudy, *Churchill and de Gaulle*, 186.

Most of the protagonists or antagonists of British and more generally Anglo-American liberal, cultural, political and economic institutions, and values will crop up in the main body of what follows. In his retrospective contrast between the French 'Jacobin' or more strictly statist and rationalist conception of politics with the piecemeal and pluralist Anglo-American one, Pierre Rosanvallon suggested that despite its attractions for liberal elites, the British influence has not been the dominant one principally because of the identification of countervailing forces with dismembering discord to which France was prone, so that political parties and civil society were not stabilizing but potentially or actually subversive.[90] In later chapters, we shall have frequent occasions to verify the pertinence of this line of argument. However, in the twentieth century, the USA rather than Britain became the foreign embodiment of anti-France, despite its attractions to the mass French public rather than the elites who had previously been drawn to Britain.

So, we now turn to the tendency of the French to define their declining status as measured against the American model and anti-model of a desirable culture, economy, society, and polity, when the USA emerged as the hegemonic world power.

THE AMERICAN ANTITHESIS

Just as Britain had been *par excellence* the counter-identity that enabled the French elites to define a partly imagined, changing, contested, self-conscious sense of their exceptional identity, after the Second World War the USA became the reference point for expressing French hopes and forlorn fears about their shrinking prestige and diminishing distinctiveness.[91] Obnoxious America, with which France felt no sense of kinship, subsumed an enfeebled 'perfidious Albion'.[92] However, by 2000, Britain had reversed its relative decline and its GNP exceeded that of France and the Channel Tunnel, finally built after an agreement in January 1986 signed by Prime Minister Thatcher and President Mitterrand, meant that physically if not psychologically, France and Britain were less separate.[93] Nevertheless, Britain remained wedded to its 'Anglo-Saxon' counter-identity, and was as such regarded as the subservient extension of an alien, intrusive economic liberalization that

---

[90] Pierre Rosanvallon, *La Monarchie Impossible*, 1994, 7. More generally, see his *Le sacre du citoyen: Histoire du suffrage universel en France*, 1992, 2001 edn, 200–3, 283–6, 597 and his *Le Modèle Politique Français: La société civile contre le jacobinisme de 1789 à nos jours*, 2004, 165–6, 182–3.

[91] Richard F. Kuisel, *Seducing the French. The Dilemma of Americanisation*, 1993, 4–6.

[92] See W. Alison Phillips, 'The Legend of Perfide Albion' in *Edinburgh Review*, 1920, 143–65. See also H. D. Schmidt, 'The idea and slogan of 'Perfidious Albion', *Journal of the History of Ideas*, 1953, xiv/4, 612.

[93] An initial agreement in July 1966 to build the Channel Tunnel between Prime Ministers Wilson and Pompidou was followed by a Treaty between Prime Minister Heath and President Pompidou, unilaterally cancelled by Prime Minister Wilson in January 1975 and revived by Prime Minister Thatcher in 1981 at a Franco-British summit with President Mitterrand. It was finally opened on 6 May 1994. See P. M. H. Bell, *France and Britain, 1940–1994: The Long Separation*, 1997, 231–2, 253–5, 285–7.

remained normatively anathema to most French people. National identity, despite the fratricidal quarrels between its constituent anti-Frances, continues to define France's shrinking exceptionalism by opposition to the 'Anglo-Saxons'. The French path to anti-Americanism requires elucidation if we are to comprehend its nature.

In 1812 Britain went to war with the USA and France—much more disastrously—with Russia. Far from making war on the USA, France had decisively supported it militarily in winning independence from Britain. Nevertheless in the twentieth century the French switched Anglo-Saxon counter-identities. They substituted the earlier extrovert view across the Channel with one across the Atlantic as reinforcement of the introvert preservation of their national identity. By the beginning of the century, although Britain's status as the hereditary enemy was sustained by colonial rivalry, it was needed as a counterweight to Germany, making an *Entente Cordiale* expedient. However, the superpower status of 'perfidious Albion' as the repellent focus of French jealousy was increasingly taken by an overbearing USA, the senior partner in the Anglo-Saxon tandem. Anxious about its own loss of world power standing and cultural leadership, with which its sense of national identity was bound up, it has not been so much transatlantic linguistic, economic, and military intrusion that prompted many from the Extreme Right to the Extreme Left, as well as many in the Centre, to see America as the diabolical exposure of French relative decline. French intellectuals in particular were enraged at the displacement of France's civilizing mission by America's modernizing mission, with its more plausible claim to universality, particularly because of its attractions to mass publics in both France and worldwide.

Rather than gratitude for US rescue in two world wars and protection from the Soviet threat during the cold war, resentment predominated. Context coloured the form this reaction took, the late 1940s through the 1950s being characterized by anti-US neutralist and pro-communist sentiment, while the 1960s were marked by the Gaullist assertion of national independence. Although the 1980s had a greater emphasis on US indifference to Third World poverty and the 1990s on condemnation of neoliberal economic globalization, by the beginning of the twenty-first century indifference to its impact on escalating environmental problems and condemnation of its imperialist interventionism came to the fore. Nevertheless, the anti-American phenomenon has been, with ups and downs, a permanent feature of the French response to the challenge to its self-respect, self-sufficiency, and residual ambition.

The demonizing of the Anglo-Saxons was rooted in the decisive French choice of giving counter-myth precedence to their idealized Gallo-Roman past over their deprecated Frankish-Germanic origins, with its consequent predominance of the state over society, of law over custom, of the sovereign centre over the insubordinate periphery. By contrast, the English resistance to royal absolutism in the seventeenth century was rooted in championing 'Saxon freedom' against 'Norman tyranny'. 'The eighteenth century English view of the Anglo-Saxons was a mythical one produced by two centuries of religious and political conflict and reinforced by the image of the Germanic peoples that originated with Tacitus', Roman *Germania* being the source for the Whig view that the Anglo-Saxons were a race of freedom-loving tribes, who imparted this attribute to Englishmen.[94] Popularized by Rapin-Thoyras in his *Histoire d'Angleterre* of 1727–38, by Boulainvilliers in his championing of English parliamentarism as a way of reviving France's ancient Gothic government, and then by Montesquieu, this commonplace was enthusiastically adopted in New England, where the 'Real Whigs' saw themselves as the Puritan successors of the Levellers whose democratic aspirations had been quelled by Cromwell. Future US President Thomas Jefferson was obsessed with Anglo-Saxon language and history. He popularized the view that pre-Conquest natural rights, elective monarchy, local self-government, and trial by jury had been corrupted by post-Conquest English government. So, 'in the very act of revolution the revolutionary generation believed they were reinforcing their links with their Anglo-Saxon ancestors while separating from the government of Great Britain'.[95] In the nineteenth century, the myth of a specific Anglo-Saxon English people was imperially extended to the worldwide English-speaking peoples, while in America it generously embraced the Celtic Irish, German, and Scandinavian immigrants, all others being expected to conform to the dominant culture of the original English settlers. By the mid-nineteenth century, encouraged by the fiction of Walter Scott and the romantic history of Thomas Carlyle, white Anglo-Saxon Protestants, born Anglo-Saxons but bred Americans, regarded themselves 'as a separate, innately superior people who were destined to bring good government, commercial prosperity and Christianity... to the world'.[96]

Tocqueville, who pioneered the view that the USA exemplified modernity, eschewed the anachronistic reference to Anglo-Saxons in *Democracy in America*. Still, the Norman aristocrat pointed out in his chapter on the English 'Origin of the Anglo-Americans, and its importance in relation to their future condition' that 'not an opinion, not a custom, not a law, I may even say not an event, is upon record which the origin of that (American) people will not explain', sweepingly asserting that it was 'the key to almost the whole work'.[97] The New England Puritans had taken with them into exile the democratic and republican principles voiced in the Civil War Putney debates, together with older attachments to freedom of association, local autonomy, and parliamentary legislation. Because in America, unlike Europe, 'the township was organised before the county, the county before the State, the State before the Union', although formal colonial subordination to the British monarchy prevailed, 'the republic was already established in every township'.[98] In words particularly directed to his fellow countrymen, pathologically prone to oscillate between despotism and

[94] Reginald Horsman, *Race and Manifest Destiny: The Origins of American Racial Anglo-Saxonism*, 1982, 15; cf. 4–12.

[95] Ibid. 23; cf. 15–22, 28. On the British radical's desire to reimport its 'buried treasure' in America, see Jonathan Freedland's *Bring Home the Revolution: The Case for a British Republic*, 1999, 14; cf. 241 and Chapter 9 passim.

[96] Ibid. 1–2; cf. 4, 38–41, 63–5, 160–3, 168–9, 219–20, 226, 302.

[97] Tocqueville, *Democracy in America*, Chapter 2, 30. On Tocqueville and England, see above, 16–17. See also Seymour Martin Lipset, *American Exceptionalism*, 1996, 18.

[98] *Democracy in America*, 38; cf. 128 and Chapter 5 passim.

anarchy, Tocqueville spelled out the momentous implications of his prefatory remark that 'in America I saw more than America... The image of democracy itself... to learn what we have to fear or to hope from its progress.'[99] 'The general principles which are the groundwork of modern constitutions—principles which were imperfectly known in Europe, and not completely triumphant even in Great Britain, in the seventeenth century—were all recognised and determined by the laws of New England: the intervention of the people in public affairs, the free voting of taxes, the responsibility of authorities, personal liberty, and trial by jury were all positively established without discussion. From these fruitful principles consequences have been derived and applications have been made such as no nation in Europe has yet ventured to attempt.'[100] However, the French, more inclined to teach than to learn lessons from others, were reluctant to emulate a profoundly alien democratic experience. Having been unable to learn the lessons of English political experience, they were unwilling to accept guidance based upon American institutional innovation.

Until Bryce's *American Commonwealth* (published in 1888 but not translated into French until 1901–2), Tocqueville offered the only searching analysis of American democracy at a time when anxieties about the implications of universal suffrage were widespread among French elites. While warning of the dangers of majority tyranny, he explained that unlike anti-pluralist France, the USA accepted that conflicting interests were natural and that thanks to decentralization and politically independent judges exercising judicial review, the dangers of unlimited power were checked by countervailing powers. In particular, he argued that carried over to America from England, 'the jury is pre-eminently a political institution' because 'manners are the only durable and resisting power in a people.... Thus the jury, which is the most energetic means of making the people rule, is also the most efficient means of teaching it to rule.'[101] More significant in the longer run was his attack on centralizing uniformity promoted by the French Revolution and Bonapartism, the French 'at once teaching the world the way to win freedom, and the way to lose it'.[102] Wanting to be led even more than to be free, democracies in Europe, more than America, risked succumbing to a paternalistic but totalitarian government, a word he groped for but did not find: 'the old words despotism and tyranny are inappropriate: the thing itself is new'.[103]

The failure in 1848 by Tocqueville as constitution-maker to establish American bicameralism and presidentialism in the Second Republic, still less an American-style Supreme Court, was followed by that of Laboulaye in the preparation of the Third Republic Constitution, frustrated by the 'French idolatry of power'.[104] Even for those like Gambetta, who did not desire a concentration of executive power, the USA was not a model. It was left to Laboulaye to pursue by public subscription the idea of erecting a Statue of Liberty in New York, proposed in 1865

[99] Ibid. 16.   [100] Ibid. 37.   [101] Ibid. 211, 214.
[102] Ibid. 576; cf. Chapter 34 passim.   [103] Ibid. 579; cf. 576–81.
[104] Françoise Mélonio, *Tocqueville et les Français*, 1993, 78; cf. 74–9, 204–6; Philippe Roger, *L'Ennemi Américain: Généalogie de l'antiaméricanisme français*, 2002, 141–4; cf. 204–5, 238.

and intended to commemorate the centenary of US independence in 1876. It was only installed in 1886, notably because the Americans were reluctant to pay for the plinth! Despite the hope that it would symbolize liberal French admiration for American democracy, waning enthusiasm in France and US indifference meant that the imaginative gesture was ineffective. The 1889 erection of a replica statue on the banks of the Seine in Paris could not overcome the fact that when America took the Statue of Liberty to its heart, it ceased to be associated with the French donors.[105]

If liberal republicans were to desert Tocqueville and the American model for the disorganized delights and manoeuvres of government by Assembly, this was in part because they refused to accept the two-party system which made American and British democracy work effectively. Both Prosper Duvergier de Hauranne during the July Monarchy and his son Ernest in the early years of the Third Republic had argued in its favour, based on the British and American experience respectively. Before being elected to the Chamber of Deputies in 1871, Ernest Duvergier de Hauranne had observed the US Civil War on the spot, as well as the effects of the 1867 widening of the suffrage in Britain by the Second Reform Bill. In his 1873 book *La République Conservatrice* he advocated the 'opportunism' practiced by American political parties as the means of steering democracy in a liberal, non-revolutionary direction. Parties would be encouraged to converge on the centre at the expense of extremes of Left and Right. Although parliamentary defenders of the Third and Fourth Republics were to converge, they failed—as we have seen—to form two parties alternating in government, while the extremes refused to wither away.[106] The prevailing view was that in France the state was self-sufficient. It did not need political parties capable of linking state to society, still less to transmit impulses from society to a state that reserves to itself the right to impart impetus to society. Since the Revolution, Anglo-American partisan representation has in France been delegitimized as denying national unanimity and threatening civil war, but instead of achieving consensus or even duality it has resulted in enduring factionalism and party multipolarization.

Whereas Britain and France had fought eight wars between 1689 and 1815, prompted in part by their transatlantic colonial rivalry, there were no wars with the remote USA, whose independence had been saved by French military intervention in 1778.[107] When the USA returned the compliment in 1917—Colonel Stantion declaring, in words usually incorrectly attributed to the commander of the American expeditionary force General Pershing, 'Lafayette, here we are' when laying a wreath on his tomb—more than a century of relative indifference seemed to have ended.[108] There had been a number of popular anti-American diatribes, although nothing on the impressive scale of Tocqueville's favourable

---

[105] Roger, 141–8, 181; cf. Duroselle, *France and the United States*, 80–1.

[106] Quagliariello, *Politics without Parties*, 67–74; cf. 57–62 on Tocqueville. Laboulaye's more circumspect views on the importation of American electoral practices into France were expressed pseudonymously in *Paris en Amérique par le docteur René Lefebre, Parisien*, 1874, 100–52, cited in Quagliariello, 76.

[107] Duroselle, 1–2, 15–23.   [108] Roger, 341–2; cf. 395.

view. From the anti-democratic, traditionalist Right, the 1876 *Les Etats-Unis contemporains* was notable particularly for Le Play's preface, which proclaimed: 'Since the publication of the Social Contract, Tocqueville's book has had the greatest influence on our destinies. ... Let us not forget the errors of La Fayette and Tocqueville. ... '[109] Far from being a democracy, the 'Yankees' were a disguised aristocracy claimed a former protagonist the neo-Jacobin Frédéric Gaillardet in 1883, hiding their 'manifest destiny' imperialism under the nominally isolationist and defensive Monroe Doctrine of 1823.[110] By 1897, Edmond Dumolins in *A quoi tient la supériorité des Anglo-Saxons?* detaches the barbarian and entrepreneurial USA that was economically overtaking civilized and staid Britain, identifying the Anglo-Saxons essentially with the Yankees as the future threat.[111] This polemic was rapidly reinforced by the 1898 impact on French opinion of the defeat of a European nation in the Spanish–American War[112] at the end of the nineteenth century and the *Entente* with Britain at the beginning of the twentieth century. As the years passed, Britain was increasingly seen as the junior cousin of the USA within the Anglo-Saxon family rather than vice versa.

Engels had anticipated as early as 1845 the switch in the relative weight within Anglo-American capitalism and in 1872 Marx shifted the headquarters of the failing First International to New York. Whereas the utopian socialists had attempted to set up communist communities in America in mid-century, by 1903 when Paul Lafargue, Marx's son-in-law, published *Les Trusts américains*, American business corporations, personified by John D. Rockefeller and his Standard Oil Company, had become the embodiment of finance capitalism. The 1 May 1886 Chicago strike for the 8-hour working day (with four strikers being executed for involvement in the ensuing violence), assumed great symbolic importance, being adopted in France as the annual celebration of the class struggle,[113] remaining a day for mass worker demonstrations long after the specific demand had been achieved. While reformist and revolutionary socialists could agree on such piecemeal improvements, their attitude to the USA was very different. Although the reformists were impressed by the standard of living of American workers, the revolutionaries regarded American capitalism as an augury of what was to come in Europe, allowing them to ignore present realities in favour of escapist prognostications about an ever-receding future.

Liberal conservative publicists based in Sciences Po, like its founder Boutmy and one of its most popular professors André Siegfried, might had been expected in that haven of elsewhere neglected Tocqueville to be pro-America but they were critical when not hostile. If the USA was accepted by Siegfried as having succeeded Britain as the 'leader of the white race', he had great pessimism about its capacity to assimilate the vast numbers of ethnically diverse immigrants it was absorbing. 'There is no American race, although the Americans as a whole pride themselves

---

[109] Quoted in Mélonio, 231; cf. 229–30.   [110] Roger, 149–54, 163–6, 176, 185–9.
[111] Ibid. 233–7; cf. 263–4.   [112] Ibid. 179, 191–200, 211–12.
[113] Ibid. 182, 294–302, 316, 324–5, 329–34. See also Jacques Portes, *Fascination and Misgivings: The United States in French Opinion, 1870–1914*, 2000, 377–87.

on their original stock, which was Anglo-Saxon and inherently Protestant.'[114] Quoting Israel Zangwill's melting pot metaphor—'America is God's crucible, the great melting pot where all the races of Europe are melting and reforming'— Siegfried took a less optimistic view of 'Americanisation, which imposed the strictly Anglo-Saxon outlook to an extent that will probably not continue in the future'.[115] As assimilation was very much a French preoccupation, Siegfried's view, in a 1927 book that became the most readable reference work on the USA in France until the 1950s, proved very influential. Condemning American culturally regressive materialism and standardization, as well as its bewildering religious pluralism (strange comment for a Protestant to make) Siegfried concluded: 'To America the advent of the new order is a cause for pride, but to Europe it brings heart-burnings and regrets for a society that is doomed to disappear'.[116]

In Chapter 16 of *America Comes of Age*, entitled 'America, creditors of the world', Siegfried described how the USA had been transformed by the First World War from Europe's debtor to her creditor, leading to acrimonious arguments over France's war debt. Whereas the French were determined—against Anglo-American urging of leniency—that thanks to draconian reparations 'Germany will pay', the American attitude was that 'France must pay' for the aid it had received, leading to 'Uncle Sam' being dubbed 'Uncle Shylock', allowing an additional anti-Semitic allusion to the anti-Protestantism that flourished from Maurras to Mounier. Coupled with the post-Woodrow Wilson isolationist foreign policy pursued by the USA in the 1920s, starting with non-ratification of the Versailles Peace Treaty and rejection of the League of Nations, the 1929 Depression and its after-effects led France to cease paying its debts to the USA.[117]

From the interwar years the negative stereotype of 'the cowboy who has struck it rich'[118] conflated the earlier identification of Americans with cultural shallowness, crass consumerism, and intrusive modernism in popular books like Georges Duhamel's chilling *America the Menace: Scenes from the Life of the Future*. Faced with the dilemma of simultaneously attaining American prosperity while retaining the French way of life, the USA was 'both a model and a menace' of the coming mass society, with its standardized products from Ford and Hollywood. Differentially between and within the elites and the general French public, they responded by 'resistance, selective imitation, adaptation, and acceptance' as shaped by 'Gallic preconceptions, anxieties, aspirations, and sense of self-identity'.[119] A defeatist, defensive consensus, orchestrated mainly by intellectuals, of which the most virulent was *Le Cancer américain* by Robert Aron and Arnaud Dandieu in 1931,

---

[114] André Siegfried, *America Comes of Age: A French Analysis*, 1927, 3 in Chapter 1 entitled: 'The Ethnic Situation. Will America remain Protestant and Anglo-Saxon?' More generally, see Chapter 27.

[115] Ibid. 10; cf. 145.   [116] Ibid. 347; cf. 345–50. See also Roger, 273–88, 404–5, 534–41.

[117] Duroselle, 121–9 and Roger, 350–1, 393–5, 398–415. Ironically, it was Woodrow Wilson that attracted the most hostility. See in particular Charles Maurras, *Les Trois Aspets du Président Wilson, La Neutralité: L'Intervention, L'Armistice*, 1920. See also a book by J. L. Chastanet, *L'Oncle Shylock*, 1927.

[118] Portes, 419.

[119] Richard F. Kuisel, *Seducing the French: The Dilemma of Americanisation*, 1993, x, xii; cf. 1–11. Duhamel's book was published in 1930 in French and translated in 1931.

pilloried all aspects of American life in the name of French civilization. In a nation wracked by internecine conflicts, 'anti-Americanism was what least divided the French'.[120] American reality was comprehensively and hysterically distorted by prejudiced perception.

During the Second World War the USA 'became accustomed to the exercise of an unprecedented degree of meddling in internal French affairs' and once the intransigent de Gaulle was out of the way, US leaders were used to Fourth Republic politicians frequently coming cap in hand to seek financial and military support that fostered arrogant contempt in the USA and humiliated resentment in France.[121] Until the advent of Pierre Mendès France as Prime Minister in 1954 put an end to the colonial war in Indo-China (previously sold to the Americans as an anti-communist struggle) and still more de Gaulle's return to power in 1958 and the end of the Algerian War, weak French governments accepted their dependence upon the USA. It was only thanks to Monnet that, owing to his planned allocation in France of Marshall Plan aid, the French retained a measure of control over the use of the resources provided. Furthermore, although pervasive American pressure was intrusive, it was often ineffective but with France as a political battle-ground with Soviet Russia (assisted by the PCF) it was vital to support political allies, who after 1954 came to be regarded as 'hostile allies'.[122] A French attempt in 1950 to create with Britain and the USA 'a three-power directorate for NATO that would institutionalize France's claim to be a world power' was repeated in vain by successive French governments until de Gaulle's failure to achieve it led to his expulsion of US forces from France.[123]

The year of 1954 marked the US refusal of the insistent French request for direct military intervention to save her troops at Dien Bien Phu, opposition to French withdrawal from Indo-China (in contrast to Britain whose Foreign Secretary Anthony Eden played a key role in the Geneva peace settlement) and the rebuff of French rejection of the European Defence Community (EDC). What has been accurately described as the 'patronizing attitude that prevented Washington from ever treating the French as equals' is reflected in the exasperated comment by the US Ambassador to Paris in 1954: 'With Anglo-Saxon generosity and credulity we have more ardently espoused the cause of European integration than its origina-tors, the French'.[124] Resentment in France against the consumerist manifestations of the American way of life was only exacerbated by the President of the Coca-Cola Company, who provocatively vaunted his drink as 'the "essence of capitalism" in every bottle'.[125] Nevertheless, 'Indirect American influence has proven much more pervasive in French life than the direct and clumsy attempts to determine the direction of politics. . . . The story of post-1958 American influence on France

---

[120] Roger, 354; cf. 353–63, 542–3. Future admirer of Mussolini and author of a lenient *Histoire de Vichy*, Robert Aron published in 1935 *Dictature de la liberté*, accusing New Deal America of being a totalitarian capitalism (ibid. 509–11).

[121] Irwin M. Wall, *The United States and the Making of Postwar France, 1945–1954*, 1991, 34; cf. 90, 159, 189.

[122] Ibid. 298; cf. 6–7, 186–90, 303–4.   [123] Ibid. 193.   [124] Ibid. 174; cf. 286, 304–5.

[125] Quoted ibid. 113; cf. 121–5.

is that of cultural diffusion rather than political or economic tutelage',[126] although the former is often confused with the latter.

The hostile politico-cultural reaction to the invasion of American comics, crime novels, and gangster films, provoked paroxysms of outrage as manifestations of '*racketeering*, nothing less than capitalist competition by other means' in the words of a Communist polemicist.[127] Presented as its mass propaganda counterpart to besmirch the popular 1948–52 Marshall Plan of economic aid, it was particularly in the cinema industry that the most assertive cultural patriotism was exerted. French films having suffered relative to Hollywood during the First World War and never recaptured their previous hold, the Vichy years were an interlude during which anti-American culture offered protection not only against its films but against 'judaeo-negro-american jazz'.[128] After the 1940–4 interlude in which the BBC was listened to by many, partly to hear Free French broadcasts, the end of the Second World War led to massive inroads of American films into the French market and between 1946 and 1953, 43 per cent of French film viewers were watching them. Desperate attempts by governments of the Fourth and Fifth Republics to contain the influx, reflected in the general hostility to hyper-modernization that had been captured in Chaplin's much admired *Modern Times*, but could be ridiculed as a fear of Mickey Mouse, have proved to be an ineffective cinematic Maginot line.[129]

Once silent films became talkies, linguistic contamination accentuated cultural colonization by a 'cocacolic civilisation' in the vituperative best-selling diatribe by Etiemble *Parlez-vous franglais?* preaching resistance against subservience to France's American 'protectors' through the indiscriminate adoption of Americanisms.[130] Cultural protectionism by bodies like the *Office du Vocabulaire français*, were aimed at asserting French cultural exceptionalism, but successive governments sought to ensure that in international commercial negotiations, films in particular were not treated as goods like any others.[131] In 1966, de Gaulle established a *Haut Comité de la langue française*, followed in 1984 by Mitterrand's *Comité consultative de la langue française*, reflecting the presidential equation of national identity with linguistically induced cultural unity.

---

[126] Roger, 306–7.

[127] Vladimir Pozner, *Les Etats-Désunis*, 1948, 161, quoted in Roger, 560. More generally on Communist mobilisation against cultural subversion by the Americans, see Roger, 555–61.

[128] Robert Paxton, 'Anti-Americanism in the Years of collaboration and Resistance' in Denis Lacorne, Jacques Rupnuk and Marie-France Toinet (eds), *The Rise and Fall of Anti-Americanism*, 1990, 61; cf. 55–60.

[129] Roger, 550–67.

[130] Etiemble, *Parlez-vous franglais?* 1964, especially 231–7, Part 4, Chapter 1 and Part 5, Chapter 1. Etiemble had left France for America in 1937, intending to become an American citizen but found the American way of life intolerable (292). See also Cyrille Arnavon, *L'Américanisme et nous*, 1958. For a more sympathetic linguistic analysis of the interchange between the French and English languages see Henriette Walter, *Honni soit qui mal y pense: L'incroyable histoire d'amour entre le français et l'anglais*, 2001.

[131] Roger, 573 note; cf. 439–43, 484–9. French is a protectionist language, unlike English which is a free trade language.

The Second World War led initially to a close relationship between France and Britain, while after the French defeat the close personal relationship between de Gaulle and Churchill prevented the flame of Fighting France from being extinguished. Roosevelt's America remained on the sidelines, cultivating links with Vichy France that were to continue in an equivocal form even after the USA and Germany were at war. Because of Britain's increasing dependence on America, as well as Anglo-French colonial rivalry, especially in the Middle East, the Churchill–de Gaulle relationship came under increased strain. De Gaulle's fear that the Anglo-Saxons would deprive his country of its independence by taking over direct responsibility for a liberated France led to acrimonious relations, despite public acknowledgement of the sacrifices they were making to achieve her liberation. De Gaulle's exasperating intransigence vis-à-vis his benign Anglo-American Allies proved far more effective in protecting French national interests than Pétain's ineffectual subservience towards the ruthless German Occupation. Although Britain was clearly playing second fiddle to America, with Churchill's assistance and despite US reluctance, recognition as a victor entitled to a top table place on the United Nations Security Council and with much of its pre-war status restored were secured before he resigned as head of the French Provisional Government in January 1946. However, de Gaulle's resentment against perceived Anglo-American infringements of French sovereignty fuelled his 1960s rejection of British entry into the European Community and expulsion of US/NATO forces from French soil.

During the cold war years, international politics permeated French attitudes, suffering from the hurt pride of a liberated secondary power subordinate to the liberating superpower, being treated by US leaders as in permanent eclipse. Irritation at mass low culture's inroads that threatened an economically poorer but culturally richer country where it was far better to live was not confined to the intellectuals or to the Communists and Gaullists. Concerned above all to avoid war with the Soviet Union, the neutralist left-wing Catholics of *Esprit* not only 'denounced the Marshall Plan and NATO for incorporating Western Europe into an American protectorate' but 'coca-colonization' as symbolic of corruption of consumer taste by advertising in the service of profit.[132] The hysterical hyperbole in which its editor Jean-Marie Domenach indulged is shown in a 1960 article on 'The American Model'. It made the claim that 'the American state is liberal but American society is totalitarian; it is possibly the most totalitarian in the world.'[133] At a time when France was vainly striving to retain its own colonial empire, the obsession with American satellization—political, economic, and cultural—took the derisory form of attempts to ban coca-cola in the early 1950s, partly in the interests of winegrowers, who by the end of the century would be more worried by loss of markets to other international wine competitors. Fury at the imbalance of power and fear of being precipitated into war led Sartre's *Temps modernes* and Beuve-Méry's *Le Monde* to adopt a censorious neutralism that systematically denigrated and resented France's ally America more than the

---

[132] Kuisel, 42; cf. 52–3, 68–9.   [133] Ibid. 116; cf. 108.

Table 0.1. Which side should France support in the event of war?

	USA (%)	USSR (%)	Neither (%)
September 1952	36	4	55
September 1957	15	3	62

Source: Duroselle, *France and the United States*, 185.

Soviet Union.[134] As the Table 0.1 shows, while larger minorities of French public opinion preferred the USA to the USSR, majority sentiment was massively neutralist.

FROM INCOMPATIBILITY TO SEMI-DETACHMENT

The advent of the Fifth Republic, owing to a settler-army supported uprising in Algeria, was in part precipitated by US pressure on weak French governments to make peace with the rebellion. The resulting change of regime led to a Gaullist switch of emphasis from the ideological and cultural anti-Americanism of the 1950s to the avoidance of integration into NATO and the European Community and the economic domination of American inward investment. Thanks to the fact that American forces in Germany protected France from the Soviet Union, de Gaulle was painlessly able to expel them. De Gaulle's tactical and strategic anti-Americanism led to his non-Communist Left opponents becoming less hostile to the USA, despite earlier resentment at US pressure to establish a EDC, which was defeated in the French parliament in 1954 and the Suez misadventure in 1956 opposed by the USA. Nevertheless, when de Gaulle vetoed British entry into the European Community in 1963, Maurice Duverger argued in *Le Monde* that the real 'Trojan horse' was not Britain but 'neocolonial' economic penetration by US multinational firms.[135] When President Giscard d'Estaing adopted a 'regulated liberalism' in the 1970s, it was roundly condemned by Left Gaullist protectionists like former Industry Minister Jean-Marcel Jeanneney and especially former Foreign Minister Michel Jobert as 'doctrinaire liberalism' acting in a 'sprit of national capitulation'.[136] The Left was also split between the nationalist protectionism of future Socialist Minister Jean-Pierre Chevènement and the competitive modernizing future Prime Minister Michel Rocard, the latter's supporters being castigated by the former's faction as the 'American Left'.

---

[134] Ibid. 55–68; Roger, 423–5, 431–3, 567–72.

[135] *Le Monde*, 10 January 1963, quoted in Kuisel, 168; cf. 139. On de Gaulle's 1963 rejection of British application to join the European Community, see Lacouture, *De Gaulle*, III, 326–39.

[136] Quoted by Denis Lacorne, in Lacorne et al., 152; cf. 149–56.

However, protectionism could only fight a case-by-case rearguard action because the European Community refused to curb US inward investment that surged from the early 1960s. So, despite an exceptional hostility to having French firms dwarfed by the sheer size of their ruthless American 'multinational' competitors and the humiliation of French backwardness being exposed, well before the end of the twentieth century French governments were eagerly seeking to preserve French control. Reluctant pragmatism prevailed to avoid becoming uncompetitive and bypassed as Jean-Jaques Servan-Schreiber had pointed out in *The American Challenge* which sought preservation of France's technological capacity by a combination of imitating the USA and European collaboration, Americanizing so as not to be run by Americans. Going further, former *Express* journalist Jean-François Revel could in 1971 condemn both 'archaic and authoritarian' Gaullism and 'the Left's anti-Americanism as a symptom of its own paralysis'.[137] The survival of these attitudes in July 2005 was illustrated by the uproar from all quarters at the rumoured threat of a takeover by American Pepsi Co. of Danone, France's food products national champion, described as an industrial Chartres Cathedral prompting a call by Prime Minister Villepin for 'economic patriotism'. This was treated with appropriate derision by the *Canard Enchaîné* as painting yoghurt in the national *tricolore* colours. It stressed the nationalistic contradiction with pride in the French takeover of foreign companies: 'France for the French' but non-France as well. The 1970s provisional shift in opinion away from anti-Americanism can be shown by comparing polls from the preceding and succeeding decades. When asked in April 1968 to identify the people who least resembled the French, the Americans with 43 per cent and British with 22 per cent headed the responses. By 1984, 44 per cent declared themselves pro and 15 per cent anti-American, while 39 per cent were pro and 20 per cent anti-British. As former neutralist, *Le Monde*, in a 1984 survey of 'Uncle Sam's French' put it: 'anti-Americanism made little sense because France was Americanised', the *Canard Enchaîné* having bewailed in 1977: 'there is no modern way of being French'.[138] Socialist Culture Minister Jack Lang's attempt in the early 1980s to revive attacks on anti-humanist US cultural imperialism in a spirit of 'cultural Jacobinism' did not elicit the anticipated support from intellectuals, while the purportedly Gaullist government of Jacques Chirac started negotiations for the establishment of a Euro Disneyland which was eventually opened outside Paris in 1992. The 1986–8 Chirac government's flirtation with American-style economic liberalism nevertheless constrained it within a framework of selective state control and public opinion continued to show reservations often amounting to

---

[137] Kuisel, 200; cf. 160–7, 178–84, 203–10, 216. See also Richard Kuisel, The American Economic Challenge: De Gaulle and the French' in Robert Paxton and Nicholas Wahl (eds), *De Gaulle and the United States*, 1994, Chapter 9. See Chapter 7 on Servan-Schreiber. Revel's book was entitled *Without Marx or Jesus: The New American Revolution has Begun*. For the counter-argument, see Claude Julien, *L'Empire Américain*, 1968.

[138] Quotations and polls reported in Kuisel, 219, 225, 271, 275. See also Hoffmann, *Decline or Renewal?*, 335–44. Ironically, as the French Right-wing elites were becoming temporarily more attracted to liberalism, American Left-wing intellectuals were increasingly addicted to neo-Marxism.

repugnance towards favouring private entrepreneurs and deregulated market forces, often reflected more in words than deeds.[139]

FOR AND AGAINST ANTI-AMERICANISM

French ambivalence towards the USA, with anti-Americanism predominating, is vociferously conveyed in 2003 polemics by two combative French intellectuals, Emmanuel Todd and Jean-François Revel, representing rival conceptions of anti-France. Todd is not a typical French intellectual, having been educated in Cambridge, where he acquired a commitment to British empiricism. However, his onslaught on US imperialism—once a protector, now a predator—concludes with the doubly implausible if flattering assertion that Britain could end 'American hegemony with one blow by choosing to cast its lot with Europe.'[140] Todd asserts that her declining economic, military, and ideological power means that 'the United States simply does not have what it takes to be a true empire.... First, its power to constrain militarily and economically is insufficient for maintaining the current levels of exploitation of the planet; and second, its ideological universalism is in decline...'[141]

Following on Roosevelt's New Deals from 1950 to 1975, as problem solver, US 'positive imperialism'—exemplified by the Marshall Plan—has become a problem, 'a superpower living from hand to mouth'.[142] Owing to massive trade deficits and escalating indebtedness, 'America has become a sort of black hole... absorbing merchandise and capital but incapable of furnishing the same goods in return...'[143] This fragility is military as well as commercial and financial. Using the examples of Afghanistan and Iraq, Todd claims that 'The real America is too weak to take on anyone except military midgets. By provoking all these secondary players, it can at least affirm its global role'.[144] The pseudo-superpower is an arsonist—firefighter, behaving with unilateralist irresponsibility, and recklessly impetuous when engaging in 'theatrical micromilitarism'.[145] 'The elevation of terrorism into a universal force institutionalising a permanent state of war across the globe' arises because 'America requires a minimum level of global disorder in order to justify its politico-military presence in the world'.[146] Todd unconvincingly claims that 'A large part of the Muslim world is already in the

---

[139] For two views that reflect the French mid-1980s flirtation with liberalism see Suzanne Berger, 'Liberalism reborn: the new liberal synthesis in France' in Jolyon Howarth and George Ross (eds), *Contemporary France*, Volume I, 1987, Chapter 5 and Diana Pinto, 'The Atlantic influence and the mellowing of French identity', ibid. volume II, 1988, Chapter 6. For a more up-to-date analysis see Vivien A. Schmidt, *The Futures of European Capitalism*, 2002, 271–82.

[140] Emmanuel Todd, *After the Empire: The Breakdown of the American Order*, 2002, 2003, Eng. edn, 190; cf. xvi–xvii, 15. For a searching discussion of why Britain has not chosen Europe over America, see Andrew Gamble, *Between Europe and America: The Future of British Politics*, 2003, especially Chapter 5 on 'Anglo-America'.

[141] Todd, 77.   [142] Ibid. 90; cf. 1, 5, 67.   [143] Ibid. 123; cf. 15, 71.
[144] Ibid. 132.   [145] Ibid. 134; cf. xviii, 133, 142–4.   [146] Ibid. 3, 57.

process of finding a new peaceful equilibrium', and women 'throughout the Arab world are in the process of emancipating themselves through contraception'.[147] Because 'The theme of France's little universalist music is faint indeed without the power of Russia as amplifier', Todd—like de Gaulle—looks to Russia as 'a counterweight to American military influence and a secure supply of its energy requirements'.[148] This is his forlorn hope of overcoming the 'voluntary servitude' of Europe's 'tributary ruling classes'.[149]

A master of irony and derision, based on an acute analysis of French psycho-pathology, Revel ridicules the paradoxical claim that 'America's success derives entirely from her abysmal inferiority'.[150] 'America largely owes her unique super-power status today to Europe's mistakes... in our thinking and our will to act,' which have facilitated American unilateralism.[151] Revel attacks 'French political and cultural narcissism' based on megalomaniac aspirations to become a 'global leader', prompting them to 'take their phobias as guiding principles'.[152] Returning to his 1970 theme in *Without Marx or Jesus*, Revel had predicted that 'The great revolution of the twentieth century will turn out to be the liberal revolution', owing to American-driven economic globalization, so 'The principal function of anti-Americanism has always been, and still is, to discredit liberalism by discrediting its supreme incarnation'.[153] Fearing the extinction of a 'French cultural exception-alism (which) has never existed', national vanity cannot countenance the waning of French *rayonnement* 'whose function is to shine down and warm the entire planet'.[154]

Castigating the criminal disorder exemplified by car burnings, passed off with euphemistic reference to 'incivilities' until the riots of 2005 forced the political class to take seriously 'the superdelinquency of immigrant offspring, in their *banlieu* ghettos, Revel blamed 'officially sanctioned illegality'.[155] Setting aside the prevailing political correctness as the mask for political and economic neglect, Revel argued that France had failed to achieve America's success as a melting pot. Instead, it was attacked as tolerating a multicultural diversity alien to the formal commitment to French republican uniformity. He argued that Muslim hatred of France was 'largely the product of an educational ideology that, on the pretext of honouring minority identity and promoting egalitarianism, has denied North Africans access to French culture, without preventing them from losing their own', with the result that they have behaved like outlaws.[156] Encouraged by Muslim religious schools that have been 'centres of anti-French fundamen-talist propaganda', the jihadists have extended their hatred of liberalism (shared with European anti-globalists) into a hatred of Western civilization itself.[157] Less

---

[147] Ibid. 39, 51.   [148] Ibid. 155, 147.

[149] Ibid. 99, 98. For a splenetically excessive expression of French cultural anti-Americanism, see Jean Baudrillard, *America*, 1988.

[150] Jean-François Revel, *Anti-Americanism*, 2003, 19; cf. 25, 146.

[151] Ibid. 16, 18; cf. 170, 176.   [152] Ibid. 44–6.   [153] Ibid. 13, 12.

[154] Ibid. 105, 122.

[155] Ibid. 89, 98. More generally, see Christian Jelen, *Les Guerres des rues*, 1998.   [156] Revel, 95.

[157] Ibid. 99; cf. 123, 128–9.

sweeping and vitriolic denunciations of the French incapacity to assimilate its Muslim immigrants have been made by others. Anti-Americanism has obsessively persisted despite the wave of public sympathy following the spectacular al-Qaida terrorism inflicted on the Great Satan. While the Editor of *Le Monde*, Jean-Marie Colombani's response to the 11 September 2001 attack on the New York twin towers was to proclaim resoundingly in an editorial: 'We are all Americans',[158] the French rapidly reverted to their predominantly elite hostility. This was despite ever-increasing economic interdependence, and the attraction of US culture and resignation to the prevalence of the English language in their dealings with the outside world. The Iraq fiasco confirmed the worst French suspicions.

Resentment against American domination coupled with the sense of national decline from a self-image of superiority, has cut across both Left and Right. Loss of leadership in the European Union and the insubstantial post-colonial imagined community of *Francophonie* have resulted in the French being bereft of their pretentious international standing and a globophobic inclination to seek foreign culprits, with the USA as the prime scapegoat. Linguistically, 'English is seen as merely a version of American', while the recourse to the term Anglo-Saxon leads to the condemnation of 'a non-existent, monolithic imagined identity, represented as a united, dominating presence'.[159] Like Britain, France has, since the Second World War, been compelled to understand the implications of the drastic reduction in its power. To assert right without might has a hollow ring. However, France has found it far more difficult than its fellow ex-imperial power, Britain, to accept—albeit with an ambivalent combination of repugnance, resignation, and enthusiasm—that the American 'other' has become an inseparable part of its own identity. A retreat into inaction is not credible, so even unwelcome options have to be considered.

Having explained at length France's Anglo-American counter-identity, we turn to the lengthier complexities of her identity, doing so with the intimacy of a semi-insider but the detachment of a semi-outsider. The aspiration is that this duality has made it possible to go beyond stereotypes of how the French have understood themselves, instead emphasizing what regarding themselves as exceptional (are not all nations?) has obscured from their self-perception.

---

[158] *Le Monde*, 12 September 2001; cf. Jean-Marie Colombani, *Tous Américains?*, 2002. *Le Monde* began publishing a weekly supplement in English from *The New York Times*. More generally on the phenomenon, see Paul Hollander (ed.), *Understanding Anti-Americanism: Its Origins and Impact at Home and Abroad*, 2004, especially Introduction and Chapters 1 and 2.

[159] Dennis Ager, *'Francophonie' in the 1990s: Problems and Opportunities*, 1996, 171.

Part I

The Unfinished Revolution, 1789–1878

1

French Identity: The National Search for Retrospective Legitimacy and Unanimity

The composite nature of French identity, in which diversity predominates over unity, emerges from retrospective self-evaluative interrogations of what constitutes France and the French nation as a society, a state, and a political regime. Historically, it has been the state that has been used by those who have successively controlled the government to counteract the fissiparous forces of French society by recourse to centralized authority. While this political thrust has come to be identified with the revolutionary myth of France as a 'one and indivisible republic', the impetus was much older than its Jacobin manifestation. Pierre Nora, in a study of 'state memoirs', whose purpose was to 'base on personal accounts of the past the national legitimacy of the present'[1] (and one might add the future) picked out three myths of national unity conveyed in them, after three great national crises. Following the Fronde seventeenth-century civil war, there were Louis XIV's memoirs, although Richelieu's *Testament* is arguably a better exemplar (albeit not cast as a memoir) of the coming of absolute monarchy. After the late eighteenth-century revolution, Napoleon's memoirs reflect the establishment of the countervailing power of an integrated state administration to stabilize the democratic turbulence on firm bureaucratic foundations, as well as the nostalgia for national military glory. Following the devastating 1940 defeat, de Gaulle began the process of restoring national self-respect and reconstructing France's political regime that he was to complete after 1958 with the establishment of the Fifth Republic.[2]

In seeking to digest a divisive history and demonstrate the emergence of a consensual political culture, Nora explicitly chose to emphasize symbols rather

---

[1] Pierre Nora, 'Les Mémoires d'Etat. De Commynes à de Gaulle' in Nora, *Les lieux de mémoire*, II, *La Nation*, 1986, 360. I agree with the criticism levied by Steven Englund's 'The Ghost of Nation Past' (*Journal of Modern History*, LXIV, June 1992, 299–320, that Nora's monumental defence of the perennial myths of the French nation and republic should be approached critically and not reverentially. Nevertheless, the results of his enterprise will be selectively used to examine what Englund calls 'the central vaults of French historical consciousness' (300), the reinterpretation of the past by selective reference to the retrospectively legitimizing preoccupations of the present, through the perspective of memory. In this way the French reaffirmation of their own identity can be seen against the Anglo-American counter-identities. For another critical review of Nora's enterprise, see H. T. Ho Tai, 'Remembering Realms: Pierre Nora and French National Memory' in *The American Historical Review*, 106/3, June 2001, 909–22. For a more favourable assessment of Nora's 'attempt to capture the processes through which a complex national identity is formed and transmitted' see Stefan Collini, *English Pasts: Essays in History and Culture*, 1999: 53; cf. 50–8.

[2] Nora, 'Les Mémoires d'Etat, 390.

than realities. So, in answering the question of how to write its national history, he replied: 'the multiple excursions of its history and its forms of existence have no meaning other than a symbolic one.... That the Nation and France could appear to be synonymous and derive from a selfsame unitary approach is one of France's singularities, incarnation of the national model....'[3] This messianic would-be universalist model came under increasing strain in the second half of the twentieth century. Gaullism took its nationalist–statist variant to one extreme and the French Communist Party took its revolutionary–statist version to the other extreme.[4] So many French people have been Communists or Gaullists from the 1920s to the 1990s but both ideologies have receded fast into the museum of imploded guides to political rectitude. The protagonist of eternal France has at least bequeathed a viable set of political institutions and personified national unity, integrating the Right firmly into the Republic. While the Communist Party played an unintentional part in integrating the workers into the Republic, its legacy has been eclipsed more completely through guilt by servile association with the Soviet Union. So, despite reliance upon the historical inevitability of their victory, the Stalinist-style comrades made a smaller contribution than did the *compagnons* of de Gaulle.

CONTESTED ORIGINS AND EMBLEMS

If the symbolic search for retrospective national legitimacy is to be pursued to its mythical historical roots, we must return to the Gauls, who have—apart from the comic strip triumph of Astérix—been banished from French history. Although the Third Republic primary school textbooks had taught generations of children to believe in 'our ancestors the Gauls', with the cult of Vercingétorix symbolizing glorious defeat, it was the inglorious Vichy regime's adoption of the double headed axe or *francisque* as its symbol and the linking of Pétain with Vercingétorix that discredited this myth of unifying consanguinity and culture. References to Gallo-Romans and a pseudo-Trojan ancestry (in substitution for barbarian and rustic Gauls by recourse to legendary genealogy) were replaced in the fifteenth century by turning back to the Gauls.[5] However, in the early eighteenth century, Boulainvilliers controversially fixed the starting point of French history at the conquest of Gaul by the outsider aristocratic Franks, who reduced the insiders to serfdom, his thesis being perpetuated by Montesquieu, Mably, and Montlosier. The latter argued in 1814 that the French monarchy, with the help

---

[3] Nora, 'Comment écrire l'histoire de France', ibid. III *Les Frances*, Volume I on 'Conflits et Partages', 1992, 22; cf. 24, 30.

[4] Nora 'Gaullistes et Communistes', ibid. 348–50, 379, 382–3. On the tendency of an 'ideology of memory' to 'reconstruct an idealized or demonised past', see Henry Rousso, *The Haunting Past: History, Memory and Justice in Contemporary France*, 2002, 12, 7; cf. 16.

[5] Krzysztof Pomian, 'Francs and Gaulois', ibid. III/I, 43–8, 65; cf. Colette Beaune, *The Birth of an Ideology: Myths and Symbols of Nation in Late Medieval France*, 1991.

of the enfranchised Third Estate, descendants of the Gauls, had degraded the Frankish nobility. However, Sieyès had in 1789 declared class war on the nobility on behalf of the Third Estate, which was followed in the 1820s by the liberal counter-attack on Montlosier by the historians Augustin and Amédée Thierry and François Guizot. Nevertheless, subsequent historians, such as Fustel de Coulanges denied that the Gauls were a nation, lacking both political and ethnic unity, so that France could not authentically trace its origin to true born Frenchmen.[6]

However, the Gaulish link was symbolically perpetuated by reference back to the Roman pun linking *gallus* with its Latin meaning, cockerel. While the Carolingian and Capetian kings had adopted the *fleur de lis* as their symbol and it appeared on royal money in the early twelfth century, it was foreign attempts at ridicule that eventually persuaded the propagandists on behalf of the Valois kings to take up the *coq gaulois* and this practice persisted, Louis XIV being especially partial to the cockerel emblem. Although the French Revolution popularized it, notably on its coins, Napoleon preferred in 1804 a more aggressive bird, the eagle. The Restoration returned to the *fleur de lis* but the July Monarchy ordered the cockerel to be incorporated into the flags of the National Guard and it was increasingly used on official documents. The Second Republic formally readopted the cockerel, and after the return of the eagle during the Second Empire, the cockerel was once again incorporated into the official seal of the Third, Fourth, and Fifth Republics. Although it symbolically survived in some stamps and sports, the cockerel's rural association has ceased to have much significance in urbanized France.[7]

A more enduring emblem of France, the *tricolore*, was initially improvised in 1789 by Lafayette, as head of the new National Guard, who needed a rallying flag for his civic troops. He did so by incorporating the white flag of the royal guards into the blue and red flag of the Paris militia. It was a year later, at the 14 July 1790 *fête de la Fédération*, that the *tricolore* became the visual symbol of national unity, in a ceremony orchestrated by Lafayette, its inventor and promoter. Carried victoriously onto the battlefields of the revolutionary and Napoleonic wars, the *tricolore* was banned during the Bourbon Restoration but revived in 1830 when, following the July Revolution, Lafayette 'anointed' Louis-Philippe by giving him a *tricolore* flag, symbolizing republican support for constitutional monarchy. (Lafayette and Louis-Philippe had both fought under the *tricolore* in the pre-Jacobin revolutionary army.) In 1848, the poet-politician Lamartine prevented the socialist revolutionaries from replacing the *tricolore* with the red flag (although as a compromise a red rosette was temporarily added) and thereafter it remained the national flag. Following the failure to restore the monarchy in the 1870s, it was the national celebration of 14 July 1880 that symbolically conjoined in the cult of the flag the army and the republic.[8]

It was also in 1880 that it was decided to emblazon the revolutionary triadic slogan, 'Liberty, Equality, Fraternity', on the front of all public buildings, although

---

[6] For detailed references, see Pomian, 67–81.

[7] Michel Pastoureau, 'Le Coq Gaulois' in *Les lieux de mémoire*, III/3, 584.

[8] Raoul Girardet, 'Les Trois Couleurs: Ni blanc, ni rouge' in *Les lieux de mémoire*, I, 1984, 8–33.

it would have been more accurate to substitute fratricide for fraternity. Mona Ozouf has pointed out the irony of 'liberty' appearing on prisons, 'equality' on schools and universities and 'fraternity' on police stations and immigration offices.[9] At first the duo liberty and equality predominated but by 1792 an embattled Republic gave official encouragement to the proliferation of the intimidating slogan proclaiming 'Unity; Indivisibility of the Republic; Liberty, Equality, Fraternity or Death'. The Directory replaced 'fraternity' with 'order', Napoleon and Louis-Napoleon contented themselves with 'Liberty, Public Order', while the July Monarchy reversed them into 'Order and Liberty'. Preoccupation with maintaining order was not absent from the Second Republic, which asserted: 'the Republic has Liberty, Equality and Fraternity as its principles, and Work, Family, Property and Order as its foundations'.[10] The liberal Third Republic was happy to put 'liberty' first but the anticlericals wished to replace 'fraternity', evoking Christian echoes, with the secular notion of solidarity, championed by a leading Radical Léon Bourgeois.[11] A turn of the century school teacher, one of the 'black hussars of the Republic', expressed the message clearly: 'To be a republican is to be determined to apply the motto of our Republic, by making liberty the greatest good of all, equality through merit alone and of fraternity an indefectible solidarity'.[12] With such unachievable ideals, the French Republic ensured that its work would never be completed as it strove to attain them.

That other great national symbol, the *Marseillaise*, began life as a battle hymn of the French Republic but was quickly elevated into a national and then international anthem of liberal revolutionaries in 1848, before another French anthem, the *Internationale*, composed in 1888, became an explicitly global counterpart from the end of the nineteenth century. Improvised by Rouget de Lisle in April 1792, the *Marseillaise* was adopted by the Convention in 1793 as the official anthem, having freed its author from the prison to which he had been consigned. Napoleon was not keen on it but it resurfaced during the 100 Days, prompting Rouget de Lisle to comment: 'Things are going badly.... They are singing *The Marseillaise*'.[13] The Old Guard sang it to no avail at the battle of Waterloo. Banned during the Restoration (when Rouget de Lisle was in 1826 imprisoned for debt) it was sung on the barricades in the July 1830 Revolution. It inspired Delacroix's celebrated painting of Liberty leading the people, explicitly referring to the *Marseillaise* and Rude's striking sculpture of the soldiers departing for the front on the Arc de Triomphe in the early years of a July Monarchy increasingly inclined to regard it as subversive by association with the democratic republic. Reinstalled

---

[9] Mona Ozouf, 'Liberté, Egalité, Fraternité' in *Les lieux de mémoire*, III/3, 584.

[10] Quoted ibid. 627 n. See also 586–613.

[11] Jack Hayward, 'The official social philosophy of the French Third Republic: Léon Bourgeois and Solidarism' in *International Review of Social History*, VI/I, Spring 1961, 19–48.

[12] Quoted in Ozouf, 620; cf. 618–19.

[13] Michel Vovelle, 'La Marseillaise: La guerre ou la paix' in *Les lieux de mémoire*, I, 105; cf. 85–107, 122–3. The harpsichordist Sylvie Pécot has argued in *Edelman: le musicien guillotiné*, 2002, that the musical inspiration for the *Marseillaise* was a piano sonata by the revolutionary composer Jean-Frédéric Edelman, executed in 1794.

as the national anthem in 1879 by a more confident Third Republic, it came into its own as a mobilizing military symbol with the First World War, the remains of Rouget de Lisle being reburied in the Invalides on Bastille Day 1915.[14] Although the sanguinary sentiments of the *Marseillaise* are now a source of embarrassment, it continues to be a potent national affirmation of an enduring assertive will.

The French Revolution's ambition to 'make a *tabula rasa* of the past' (to quote the first stanza of the *Internationale*) was inspired by an Enlightenment rationalist repudiation of a past that was still very present. The contrast with the English seventeenth-century revolutions seeking to restore past rights infringed by would-be absolute monarchs (Charles I and James II) is striking. France had long since had an absolute monarchy and when it was overthrown, this was in favour of an absolute republic. The institutional instability of permanent revolution derived from trying to ground government on an act of political will that failed because it had no firmer foundation. The result was a perpetuation of conflict without consensus, leading to a desperate flight forwards, denying a past that refused to be consigned to oblivion.[15] The Revolutionaries' determination to rationalize by starting afresh took many forms. The change to the decimal system survived in weights and measures. However, the attempt to apply the same principle to the calendar only lasted a little over twelve years. It was abolished in 1806 by Napoleon, without ever having displaced the Gregorian calendar except in official usage.[16] The symbolic innovations were often frustrated by inertial realities as stubborn practice prevailed over the audacious assertion of new principles. Prospective legitimacy proved to be altogether a more problematic enterprise than relying on tenacious custom. The futuristic pursuit of progress encountered territorial, institutional, and human realities that selected, modified, or repelled would-be ruptures of historic continuity.

TERRITORIAL FRAMEWORKS OF REFERENCE

There are many Frances, nations and republics within the shifting territorial boundaries of France. The secular process of state and nation-building and rebuilding has involved the reaffirmation and redefinition of founding myths, some of which we have already encountered. Sentimental loyalty predominates

---

[14] Vovelle, 124–5; cf. 117–18 It had been intended to bury Rouget de Lisle in the *Panthéon* but because this required a law and parliament was not in session, the Invalides was chosen. See Avner Ben-Amos, *Funerals, Politics and Memory in Modern France, 1789–1996*, 2000, 209–12. That North African mass immigration had not been adequately integrated was symbolized by the scandal of young Algerians booing the *Marseillaise* at a France-Algeria football match in September 2001.

[15] François Furet, 'L'Ancien Régime et la Révolution' in *Les lieux de mémoire*, III/I, 113–19, 138. For a useful selection of essays by Furet and others on its historiography, see Gary Kates (ed.) *The French Revolution: Recent Debates and New Controversies*, 1998.

[16] Bronislaw Baczko, 'Le calendrier républicain. Decréter l'éternité' in *Les lieux de mémoire*, I, 46–7; cf. 38–78.

over rational self-criticism in what are sensitive matters constitutive of French self-perception.

The antiquity of France's national frontiers invited the claim that they were natural, leading on to the assertion that they were imprescriptible and inalienable. By the twelfth century, although all France's internal frontiers were contested, they were more or less precise and by the end of the thirteenth century the kingdom's frontiers were not just one boundary among others. 'And the more time passes, the advance of royal justice, royal taxation and royal armies impart to the kingdom's frontiers an increased importance.'[17] By the sixteenth century, France's frontiers were the limits of royal sovereignty, regarded (although this may be more a matter of retrospective legitimization by premature nation-building historians) as 'inviolable and sacred'.[18] With Louis XIV in the seventeenth century, France attained its territorial limits. Frontiers were regularized by treaty in the eighteenth century, yet the use of the expression 'natural frontier' was still very unusual. The revolutionary wars quickly provoked a controversy in January 1793, with Danton arguing that France's natural limits were restrictively defined by rivers, mountains, and the Atlantic, while Robespierre and St Just took a more expansionist view. This subsequently led via the principle of popular sovereignty to that of national self-determination, hence the need for a plebiscite to ratify the annexation of Savoy and Nice by Napoleon III as the price of assisting Italian unification.[19]

It was not until after the notion of France as a 'hexagon' was popularized by Buisson in the wake of universal primary education by his 1887 Educational Dictionary that it began to be commonplace to describe the country in terms of a symmetrical geographical form. Through the lessons it offered to thousands of primary school teachers, the Dictionary reached millions of schoolchildren.[20] However, Eugen Weber attributes the neglect to map the country to a French preference for abstract words not images and among images for a flag rather than a map. He dates the first map of France as probably 1525 but such maps were thereafter confined to a privileged few. The 1809 *Atlas Napoleon* was a series of partial maps of France and the War Ministry Chiefs of Staff were only prompted to commission a map following the 1870 defeat. In the 1860s, schoolchildren never saw maps enabling them to locate their *département* and the Bruno *Le Tour de la France par deux enfants* (which sold 3 million copies between 1877 and 1887 and 200,000 copies annually until 1901) did not have a map among its many illustrations until its 1905 edition.[21] Even the *Guide Michelin* of 1900 had no map of France.

[17] Bernard Guenée, 'Des limites féodales aux frontières politiques' in *Les lieux de mémoire*, II/2 21; cf. 12–26.

[18] Ibid. 27; cf. 26.

[19] Daniel Nordman, 'Des limites d'Etat aux frontières naturelles' in *Les lieux de mémoire*, II/2, 35–55.

[20] Eugen Weber, 'L'Hexagone' in *Les lieux de mémoire*, II/2, 98. See also Pierre Nora, 'Le Dictionnaire de Pédagogie de Ferdinand Buisson: Cathédrale de l'école primaire' in *Les Lieux de mémoire*, I, 353 ff.

[21] E. Weber, 100–8. But see ibid. 334. On the importance of *Le Tour de la France* see the chapter by Jacques and Mona Ozouf, 'Le Tour de la France par deux enfants: Le petit livre rouge de la République' in *Les lieux de mémoire*, I, 191–321.

The loss of Alsace-Lorraine to Germany, as well as confusing the hexagon image, provoked a controversy between the prominent French historian Fustel de Coulanges and the German historian Theodor Mommsen in October 1870. The Frenchman, who taught at Strasbourg University until that year, declared: 'It may be that Alsace is German by race and language. But by rationality and patriotic sentiment it is French'.[22] Generalizing, Fustel de Coulanges asserted: 'What distinguishes nations is neither race nor language. Men feel in their hearts that they are one people when they share a community of ideas, interests, affections, memories and hopes'.[23] In similar vein, the Breton historian Ernest Renan wrote in 1871 to another German, attacking the idea of race-based nations as a 'scientific error' leading, he prophetically warned, to 'wars of extermination' and emphasizing that nations were practically constituted by consent, what he called a decade later in a celebrated lecture 'a daily plebiscite', even though it has been calculated that 95 per cent of French people acquire their citizenship involuntarily from place of birth or parents.[24]

The late nineteenth-century extension of the French Empire blurred the hexagon image and it was only after the post–Second World War loss of empire that it became popular. So, paradoxically, it was when the territory had largely retreated to the confines of metropolitan France that the hexagon represented reality.[25] However, the new context of increasing integration into the European Community meant that the hexagon was a piece in a larger jigsaw puzzle that was expanding rather than shrinking. In his lecture on the nation, Renan had already anticipated that France would become part of a European Confederation in the next century.[26]

When the urge to reduce French diversity to unity has proved implausible, there has been a tendency to represent it dualistically. Territorially, this has particularly taken the form of polarization between centre and periphery or the north–south divide. Before the Revolution, peripheral France was culturally, linguistically, legally, and administratively differentiated. While Latin was the learned language, French struggled to assert its predominance over regional languages. Alsatian, Basque, Breton, Catalan, Corsican, Flemish, and Occitan survived well into the twentieth century, with the uneducated rural population often only speaking their local dialect until the late nineteenth century.[27] The north–south divide reflected

---

[22] Quoted by Jean-Marie Mayeur, 'Une mémoire-frontière; l'Alsace', in *Les lieux de mémoire*, II/2, 67; cf. 77–93 on the German annexation.

[23] Quoted by D. Nordman, *Les lieux de mémoire*, II/2, 5608. For a convincing critique of the Braudelian conception (in his iconic *L'Identité de la France*, 1986, 1988–90 Eng. edn) of 'the French as simply the continuation of their ancestors', see Gérard Noiriel, *The French Melting Pot: Immigration, Citizenship and National Identity*, 1988, 1996 Eng. edn, 40; cf. 29–44.

[24] Renan's Sorbonne lecture *Qu'est-ce qu'une Nation?*, 1882. See also Patrick Weil, 'Immigration, nation et nationalité: regards comparatives et croisés', *Revue Française de Science Politique*, 1994, 323. More generally, see Alec Hargreaves, 'Multiculturalism' in Christopher Flood and Laurence Bell (eds), *Political Ideologies in Contemporary France*, 1997, Chapter 7.

[25] E. Weber, 110–13.   [26] Renan, *Qu'est-ce qu'une Nation?*, 28.

[27] Maurice Agulhon, 'Le Centre et la Périphérie' in *Les lieux de mémoire*, III/I, 826–7 and Eugen Weber, *Peasants into Frenchmen: The Modernization of Rural France, 1870–1914*, 1977, Chapter 6, 'A Wealth of Tongues'.

many ancient polarities. The Gallo-Roman southern contrast with the Frankish-Celtic north bequeathed an enduring difference between the strong private property and paternal authority of Roman Law with the north's more egalitarian customary law until the Revolution. The heretical, poetic, and poorer south was crushed in the thirteenth century by the anti-Albigensian crusade but the religious wars of the sixteenth century, culminating in the 1685 revocation of the tolerant Edict of Nantes, left significant Protestant enclaves in certain parts of the south.[28]

The difficulties experienced in establishing effective regions are partly due to the destruction of provincial particularisms by the Revolution, determined to rationalize the old irregularities and to standardize the heterogeneities. Inspired by a geometrical urge towards uniformity that dictated a *tabula rasa* approach, the authors of a would-be 'rational utopia' were compelled to compromise with historico-geographical realities. A symbolic rupture with the incrementalist legacy of the past quickly reverted to using the old provincial boundaries as a starting point and improvising compromises with local notables and deputies who knew the situation on the ground. The territorial reorganization was motivated by the need to accommodate administrative practicality, electoral representation, and the fiscal crisis. Citizens needed to be able to reach the new administrative centre in a day's travel but the choice of *département* capital was influenced by other considerations, such as the suspicion of domination by larger towns in a predominantly rural society. Taxation assessments were allocated from Paris, calculated on estimates of *ancien régime* tax yields, subsequently subdivided by local councils. Girondin-federalist resistance to Parisian imposition has prompted a misleading stress upon Jacobin political centralization, whereas the administrative Napoleonic centralization through prefects and sub-prefects has been of greater significance for the bulk of the population. The Restoration and the July Monarchy provided greater scope for the influence of local notables, with the *département* becoming the locus of negotiations between local political and administrative elites. The Third Republic, in retrospect, marked the apogee of this style of politics. By the Fifth Republic, the *département* was recognized as obsolescent in size and inappropriate to its functions but regionalist reform was obstructed by the entrenched local elites.[29]

We now turn successively to the controversial dead heroes and the interlocking contested religious, military, and educational institutions through which the French have fashioned a national identity.

NATIONAL HEROES: DIVIDED EVEN IN DEATH

While we may consider that Auguste Comte was overstating the matter when he asserted in the early 1850s that 'the living are always and increasingly governed fundamentally by the dead', nevertheless, we cannot deny the pertinence

---

[28] Emmanuel le Roy Ladurie, 'Nord-Sud' in *Les lieux de mémoire*, II/2 118–39.

[29] Marcel Roncayolo, 'Le Département' in *Les lieux de mémoire*, III/1, 885–917. See also Jacques Revel, 'La Région', ibid. 852–31.

of his remark.[30] The French like to immortalize some of their most distinguished countrymen, whether by election to the French Academy (an ephemeral defiance of death) or burial in the *Panthéon*. What might be regarded as, and doubtless was, intended to promote national unanimity has in fact provided an illustration of the divergence. While the literary quarrels can be dismissed as academic, the question of who should be installed (or removed) from the *Panthéon* is of far greater symbolic importance. It is a striking demonstration of how difficult it is to achieve national reconciliation since the Revolution because of the lack of consensus in beliefs and values. The historic burial place of the French kings since 1271 being in St Denis Basilica, the Revolution had to find an alternative location for its illustrious and meritorious dead. The primary school personification of French monarchy, Charlemagne, appropriately enough for a Germanic ruler, is buried at Aix-la-Chapelle (Aachen). In the last fifty years, he has been redesignated as a forerunner of European Union. Napoleon, who identified himself with Charlemagne, is buried in the *Invalides*, considered suitable for a military genius. Joan of Arc, the heroine appropriated by the Catholic Right and Extreme Right (although writers like Voltaire and Bernard Shaw portrayed her as a victim of the Church), has no burial place but is identified both with Rouen where she was burnt at the stake and her statues in Paris and Orléans. She became an anti-Marianne,[31] the personified symbol of the Republic.

The death in 1791 of Mirabeau, a brilliant parliamentary orator and a controversial champion of constitutional monarchy, prompted the conversion of the Church of Sainte-Geneviève into a pantheon in which to lodge him. It was intended to become a republican sanctuary in which the French nation could worship itself through the cult of its 'Great Men', not merely expressing its gratitude but celebrating them as glorious examples to all citizens. However, in 1794 Mirabeau's body was removed and replaced with that of Marat but when the Directory in turn ejected Marat and sought to reinstall Mirabeau in 1797 his body could not be found![32] The shifting political criteria that intervened in deciding those worthy of apotheosis meant that no final judgement was possible, unlike Westminster Abbey—the example that was imitated—which has avoided such partisan to-ings and fro-ings in the monument to heroic national memory.

Voltaire and Rousseau were 'pantheonized' in 1791 and 1794, respectively, reflecting the Revolution's changing priorities from the apostle of anticlericalism and tolerance to the protagonist of a populist conception of sovereignty. The desire of resurgent republicanism to flaunt its prestigious intellectual progenitors led to the 1878 commemoration of the centenary of their death, with much

[30] Auguste Comte, *Système de Politique Positive*, Mathias ed., II, 1851–4, 363. Comte secularized the Catholic catalogue of saints with a Positivist Calendar of benefactors of humanity. August Comte, *Calendrier positiviste, ou système général de commémoration publique*, 1849.

[31] See Maurice Agulhon, *Marianne into Battle: Republican Imagery and Symbolism, 1789–1880*, OUP, 1983 and Agulhon, *Marianne au pouvoir: Imagerie et la symbolique républicaines de 1880 à 1914*, 1989. See also Robert Morrissey, 'Charlemagne' in *Les lieux de mémoire*, III/3, 632–70 and Michel Winock, 'Jeanne d'Arc', ibid. 676–729.

[32] Ben-Amos, op. cit. 30–1 cf. 25, 48–9. See also Mona Ozouf, 'Le Panthéon. L'Ecole normale des morts' in *Les lieux de mémoire*, I, 150, 156–63.

greater prominence accorded to Voltaire, a more comfortable official philosopher for the militantly anticlerical Third Republic than the deist Rousseau. As such, it was vainly but bitterly opposed by the clerical Right, spearheaded by Bishop Dupanloup. It is calculated that over a 200-year period, Voltaire's complete works were published 6 times more often than those of Rousseau, so it was natural that the centenary was commemorated for propagandist purposes with a 1,000 page selection of his writings, with a quarter devoted to his sulphurous views on religion and the Church.[33]

Pantheonizing Jean Baudin and Victor Hugo presented instructive uses of two contrasting opponents of the Louis-Napoleon *coup d'état* of December 1851. Baudin died heroically on the barricades, proclaiming—in response to the anti-parliamentary criticisms of deputies being paid—'I shall show you how one dies for 25 francs a day'—while Hugo went into a nearly twenty-year exile from which he launched his vitriolic condemnations of the Second Empire. As a reminder of the illegitimate origins of that regime, some republicans located with difficulty Baudin's intended grave, making speeches promising to avenge his death, and subsequently starting a national subscription to erect a monument there. This provocation led the government to indict the organizers of the subscription and seize the newspapers publicizing it. At the subsequent trial, defence lawyer Léon Gambetta made his reputation as an opponent of the regime, while 'Baudin came to represent all the martyrs who had died resisting Louis-Napoleon'.[34] Baudin's remains were transferred to the *Panthéon* at the centenary of the French Revolution in 1889. Hugo's entry into the *Pantheon* at his death in 1885 coincided with its reversion from being a Church (a decision of Louis-Napoleon) to the Republican mausoleum for its 'Great Men'. On his return to Paris in 1870, he had declared: 'Citizens, I said that I would return with the Republic. Here I am', so the use of his prestige to facilitate the realization of the republican campaign could be regarded as his posthumous vengeance on 'Napoleon the Little'. His grandiose civil funeral provided excellent propaganda for the secularist cause.[35]

While the Third Republic is especially associated with the use of the *Panthéon* for promoting republican values, by the time of the Fifth Republic it had been deserted as a frigid repository of dead heroes ... until President Mitterrand attempted imaginatively to restore its symbolic hold on the national memory. On the day of his inauguration (21 May 1981), he intercalated a ritual gesture in the *Panthéon* between a left-wing public demonstration and subsequent festivities by placing emblematic Socialist red roses on the tombs of Jean Jaurès, Jean Moulin, and Victor Schoelcher. They symbolized respectively socialist unity, the Second World War Resistance and the 1848 liberation of slavery in the French Empire. This use of the *Panthéon*, accomplished in the first flush of the attainment of

---

[33] Jean-Marie Goulemont and Eric Walter, 'Les centenaires de Voltaire et de Rousseau: Les deux lampions des Lumières' in *Les lieux de mémoire*, I, 392–3; cf. 381–420. See also Ben-Amos, op. cit. 34–7, 49–50.

[34] Ben-Amos, op. cit. 97; cf. 96, 189, 27–9.

[35] Avner Ben-Amos, 'Les funérailles de Victor Hugo: Apothéose de l'événement spectacle' in *Les lieux de mémoire*, I, 473–516.

power after nearly a quarter of a century in opposition, did not enjoy the same success when, following the pantheonization of Jean Monnet in 1988 as architect of European integration, Mitterrand selected another trio to be honoured at the bicentenary of the Revolution in 1989. Although Condorcet, the philosopher-mathematician and martyr of the Terror and the scientist-educator Monge were uncontroversial, the choice of the Abbé Grégoire, protagonist of the Civil Constitution of the Clergy, displeased the Catholic Church.[36] While Mitterrand's successor, Jacques Chirac, arranged for the pantheonization of the writer and Gaullist Minister André Malraux in 1996, it is unlikely that the *Panthéon*'s vocation as a symbolic republican sanctuary will retrieve in the early twenty-first-century context of disenchantment with politics and especially its practitioners, whatever popularity it may have once enjoyed.

Street names and statues provide a more generalized, open-air way of commemorating and celebrating a multiplicity of worthies and mediocrities than the highly selective *Panthéon*. In the case of street names, the switch from the medieval initiative of local inhabitants to central state monopoly came with absolute monarchy from the early seventeenth century, although the glorification of individuals only really developed in Paris street nomenclature in the late eighteenth century. However, it was with the French Revolution that the ideological and pedagogical function of attributing first the names of Voltaire, Rousseau, and Mirabeau and then a host of others to Paris squares, bridges, and streets, assumed assertive significance. (Reversion to old names came more quickly in the provinces as revolutionary fervour dissipated.) Successive changes of regime led to 'debaptization' of numbers of Paris street names, adding and subtracting to the national historical compendium as the political tide changed direction. Local patriotism ensured that greater honour was accorded to local worthies, with less susceptibility to the fluctuations of political fortunes and the clash of political cultures. The pre-1914 Third Republic was the heyday of both politically motivated street naming and statue installation. At first Thiers, Gambetta, and Hugo enjoyed priority in the number of avenues, boulevards, bridges, and squares named after them, joined later by Jaurès and Pasteur, Clemenceau and Briand. Among contemporary writers, Anatole France and Emile Zola owed their prominence in street nomenclature as much to their political role as to their works, while Voltaire was better acknowledged than Rousseau. By 1978, de Gaulle was way ahead of Napoleon.[37]

'Statuomania' was essentially a nineteenth-century phenomenon, with its apogee from the 1880s to the First World War. Pre-1870, statues were mainly of royal sovereigns and military heroes, whereas post-1870 cultural heroes were meritocratic writers, artists, and scientists as well as politicians, who took the decisions. Monumental sculptures in the centre of Paris required the approval of the Minister of the Interior, acting on the advice of the Prefect of Paris. Choice of the site necessitated the approval of the Paris City Council, which

[36] Ben-Amos, *Funerals, Politics and Memory in Modern France 1789–1996*, 370–3.
[37] Daniel Milo, 'Le nom des Rues' in *Les lieux de mémoire*, II/3, 287–307.

voted subsidies, whose amount varied with its judgement of the importance of the person concerned. Location of a statue often raised problems of political sensitivity, quite apart from the conformity of the artistic style with the architectural context. Zola's statue was shifted several times between 1907 and 1924, ending up in the Avenue Zola, while Captain Dreyfus—whom he had championed—was refused a place near the Ecole Militaire, owing to military susceptibilities. More surprisingly, Napoleon's statue was shifted from the Vendôme column, via the suburb of Courbevoie, to storage and finally to the *Invalides*, where he had been reburied in 1840. After the First World War, a combination of the previous proliferation commemorating mediocrities and the decline of republican enthusiasm, made the passion for elevating statues seem anachronistic. The Vichy regime took the opportunity to settle retrospective scores by melting down some seventy-five statues of Third Republic celebrities, leaving many empty pedestals.[38] The second half of the twentieth century had a more prosaic reason for shifting or removing statues: the growth of traffic necessitated clearing away obstructions. The consumer durable motor car now enjoyed priority over the pedagogical and propagandistic public figures that had been intended to remind the people of illustrious exemplars of their national past.

The year of 1840 was marked symbolically by the apotheosis of the July Revolution ten years earlier with the erection of the Bastille column and the return of Napoleon's remains for interment in the *Invalides*. When the decision to erect the column (with a crypt for reburial of 504 combatants) was taken in 1831, the link with the 1789 Revolution represented by the Bastille site seemed appropriate. However, by 1840, its location in a working class Paris that had become hostile aroused official apprehension.[39] Nevertheless, its inauguration, with the participation of an unreliable National Guard, to the sound of Berlioz's stirring and solemn *Symphonie funèbre et triomphale*, played by hundreds of musicians, and watched by over 200,000 people, was an impressive success for the July Monarchy celebrating its advent. Surmounted by the allegorical figure of Liberty, it symbolized the liberalism of 1789, which by 1840 had lost much of its impetus.

Encouraged by this achievement, Prime Minister Thiers, prompted by the intention of a British MP to propose the return to France of Napoleon's remains from St Helena, persuaded King Louis-Philippe that Guizot, the French Ambassador in London, should negotiate the transfer. As a historian of the Revolution and Empire, Thiers was an ardent admirer of Napoleon. However his bellicose Middle Eastern policy, that threatened war with the reconstituted British-led anti-Napoleon coalition, led the pacific Louis-Philippe to dismiss him. The king went ahead with the project, seeing the advantage in flattering a chauvinistic public opinion, by being associated with the military glories of Napoleon,

[38] June Hargrove, 'Les statues de Paris', in *Les lieux de mémoire*, II/3, 243–78. See also Maurice Agulhon, 'La "statuomanie" et l'histoire' in *Ethnologie française*, VIII, 1978, 145–72.

[39] Ben-Amos, *Funerals, Politics and Memory*, 65–8.

embodiment of the Romantic hero which he could never be. The *Invalides* was chosen for the interment because, having been created by Louis XIV, it had been used by Napoleon to link the military exploits of Monarchy, Revolution, and Empire. Although the July Monarchy was able to exploit the return of Napoleon's remains without the risk of reviving Bonapartism, of which Lamartine presciently warned, the institution of universal suffrage by the Second Republic allowed Louis-Napoleon to emerge out of the Pandora's box opened by Louis-Philippe. The tomb was only completed in 1861, when it was inaugurated by the Emperor. The 'Napoleonic Pantheon' subsequently became the most visited Paris monument.[40]

As well as playing the role of promoting national integration, as was the case with the July column and Napoleonic reinterment, we have seen that the illustrious dead could be utilized for subversive purposes in the case of Baudin during the Second Empire. There had been earlier examples during the Restoration, in which pro-Republican students had played an active part. They attempted to repeat this tactic in December 1830 at the funeral of Benjamin Constant, vainly seeking to take him to the *Panthéon* for burial. More successfully, the bodies of the demonstrators killed at the start of the February 1848 Revolution were used to arouse sections of the people of Paris to overthrow the July Monarchy.[41] Civil funerals, subversive of the role of the Catholic Church, went back to the Revolution and prompted controversy around the deathbeds of celebrities. The civil funeral of former priest Lamennais in 1854 and of the redoubtable antitheist Proudhon in 1865 encouraged freethinkers and republicans to find in Freemasonry a substitute for Church ceremonial, while such funerals also provided opportunities for political orations and ' "seditions collections" made on behalf of the families of political prisoners'.[42]

During the Third Republic, state funerals were deliberately utilized to promote the regime's maximalist core values of secularism, patriotism, and republicanism. 'Making the dead great man stand for the Republic solved the problem of representing an abstract regime in a palpable manner...the only instance when the regime could use for its benefit the royal doctrine of the two bodies: a human, perishable body, and a metaphorical one, signifying the eternal values of the Republic'.[43] Of the eighty-two Third Republic state funerals, thirty were of politicians, twenty-three of military men, and twenty were of writers, scientists, and musicians. Thiers's death at the height of the 1877 political crisis led to a highly politicized funeral for the first President of the Third Republic. A leading member of the 363 deputies whose no confidence motion decisively challenged the

---

[40] Jean Tulard, 'Le retour des cendres' in *Les lieux de mémoire*, II/3, 82, 92–108. See also Ben-Amos, *Funerals*, 70–9.

[41] Ben-Amos, *Funerals*, 92 and Chapter 3 passim. See also Louis Blanc, *Histoire de Dix Ans*, II, 174–7 and Paul Bastid, *Benjamin Constant et sa Doctrine*, 1966, 479–83.

[42] Ben-Amos, 121; cf. 114–22, 131–3.

[43] Ibid. 143; cf. 138–9. For the royal doctrine, see Ernst Kantorowicz, *The King's Two Bodies: A Study in Medieval Political Theology*, Princeton University Press, 1981.

monarchist President MacMahon's attempt to reverse the republican tide, Thiers rendered sterling 'posthumous service to the republicans'.[44] The man who had pitilessly crushed the Paris Commune attracted a crowd of over half a million people to his religious funeral and his electoral address became the principal republican campaign manifesto, as well as being used in many posters and pamphlets. He was rewarded after the Republican triumph by having his name given to nearly 100 streets and squares.[45]

Subversive use of funerals could come from the Right as well as from the Left. In 1899, at the height of the Dreyfus Affair, the state funeral of President Félix Faure provided an opportunity for a populist nationalist Paul Déroulède to try to provoke the army into overthrowing the Third Republic and institute a direct election of the President,[46] an unsuccessful anticipation of the 1958 advent of the Fifth Republic. The use of Hugo's funeral in 1885 to support the Republic when it was still establishing itself, following on the centenaries of Voltaire and Rousseau in 1878, have already been mentioned. They show how 'The writer became a sort of prophet, having exceptional moral force and the power to envision the future, thus enabling the Republic to proclaim itself to be the fulfilment of his visions'.[47]

What has been stated about the political motivation underlying the use to which the *Panthéon* has been put is true more generally of French museums. The conversion of the *Louvre* royal palace into a national gallery of fine art by the Revolution, further enriched by Napoleon with treasures looted by conquest, is a spectacular example of the propagandist–pedagogical cultural function of museums. What is specific about French museums is 'their close link with central government and their pedagogical aim. Museums were born in France as a result of the nationalization of the property of the king, of the émigrés and of the clergy' at the Revolution.[48] Subsequently, 'The museum tends to become the location of a cult in which the nation worships itself through works of genius', even though many of these—as in the *Louvre*—are of foreign origin.[49] The preservation and promotion of French cultural identity is more specifically the function of the National Archives and National Library as guardians of collective memory. In their case the chronology is that 'the Revolution collects and sets out the principles; the July Monarchy organizes the practice, after which progress is slow and the resources devoted to them are inadequate for the rest of the century'.[50]

[44] Ben-Amos, *Funerals*, 187; cf. 169, 174–86.

[45] Ibid. 187–8. See also Henri Malo, *Thiers 1797–1877*, 1932, 586–95.

[46] Ben-Amos, *Funerals*, 197–203. On the circumstances of Faure's death, see 198, 124 note.

[47] Ibid. 241; cf. Chapter 8 passim.

[48] Françoise Mélonio in *Lumières et Liberté: Les Dix-Huitième et Dix-Neuvième Siècles*, Volume III of Jean-Pierre Rioux and Jean-François Sirinelli (eds), *Histoire Culturelle de la France*, 1998, 274.

[49] Ibid. 274. See also Jean-Pierre Babelon, 'Le Louvre: Demeure des rois, temple des arts' in *Les lieux de mémoire*, II/3, 200–6.

[50] Mélonio, 283.

THE PERSONIFICATION OF THE PEOPLE

The inclusive character of the notion of the people purports to transcend all distinctions but in the course of the French Revolution a process of successive exclusions made it not a consensual concept but a weapon in a series of political confrontations. At first Mirabeau, following Rousseau, included the whole population in the people versus the king. The 'people-nation' was narrowed down to the Third Estate by Sieyès, excluding the aristocracy and the clergy, with leadership of the commoners being held by the intellectual bourgeoisie. The rich bourgeoisie were excluded by Robespierre and especially Babeuf and the people were confined to the poor by Jacques Roux and the *Enragés*. Power no longer came from God to the monarch but from popular sovereignty to the government. However, Rousseau caused enduring controversy by arguing that the people should exercise sovereignty directly, destabilizing successive attempts at representative government. Jacques Julliard comments that 'Never perhaps in the history of political regimes has a new system been approached with principles that were so incompatible with its very existence'.[51]

By separating the productive from the idle, Sieyès started a process of exclusion that was developed by Saint-Simon and subsequently by socialists generally in the nineteenth and twentieth centuries. Liberal conservatives like Guizot adopted a different basis for exclusion. Democracy, like aristocracy, based fitness to exercise power on birth, not on the capacity to rule. The latter necessitated restricting the suffrage to those fit to exercise it, which achieved its apotheosis in the July Monarchy, with Guizot as de facto Prime Minister from 1840 to 1848. A less exclusive liberalism was championed by Benjamin Constant, who confined popular sovereignty to public affairs, excluding broadly defined private affairs from political interference. From the institution of universal suffrage in 1848, the working classes were politically integrated into the nation but remained socially excluded for another century. In vain did Michelet reject class conflict in the name of the predominantly peasant people, liberated by the Revolution and representing national unity. Against his friend Proudhon, who had declared that 'Property is theft', Michelet optimistically asserted that if so, France had 25 million thieves.[52] However, his peasant and artisan-based ideal of a society of small-scale property owning democrats was to be a long time coming in an increasingly urbanized and industrialized society.

John Stuart Mill admired Michelet's imaginative focus on 'the everyday plebian mind of humanity' but criticized him for 'pushing that ordinary artifice of modern French composition, the personification of abstractions, to an almost startling extent'.[53] The personifying of the Republic in the female symbol of Marianne was an attempt to infuse emotional veneration into an abstraction. It began life

[51] Jacques Julliard, 'Le Peuple' in *Les lieux de mémoire*, III/1, 196; cf. 185–95.

[52] Ibid. 205; cf. 197–211. See also Lionel Gossman, 'Jules Michelet and Romantic Historiography' in *Between History and Literature*, 1990, 181.

[53] John Stuart Mill, 'Michelet's History of France' in *Dissertations and Discussions*, 1857, 139, 180. This essay first appeared in the *Edinburgh Review*, January 1844.

in 1850 as a piece of polemical, counter-revolutionary sarcasm in the Languedoc area of southern France, where it was being used as a password by secret society conspirators in defence of the Second Republic Constitution from the impending *coup d'état* by Louis-Napoleon. It was popularized by the republican Félix Pyat in the mid-1850s and 'from this time onwards there was a general acceptance of the personification of the Republic as a female allegory, a woman with the name of Marianne who was the object of an affection that sometimes reached quasi-religious proportions'.[54] By the mid-1860s, Proudhon, in seeking to promote a cross-class alliance, was arguing that 'the cause of the peasants is the same as that of the industrial workers; the *Marianne* of the fields is the counterpart of the *Sociale* of the cities'.[55] The attractive feminine face of the Republic, 'Symbol of symbols...the effigy of Marianne, in plaster, marble and bronze began to pro-liferate without any official bust having been imposed upon local authorities'.[56] So the Left's idolization of Marianne (a popular first name that was attached to the 'Goddess of Liberty' in a red Phrygian cap) became the secular substitute for the Right's idolization of the Virgin Mary. Although Michelet had sought to popularize Joan as a patriotic, consensual national heroine, by the turn of the century the Right adopted Joan of Arc as their anti-Marianne, with the *Action Française* and subsequently the Vichy regime emphasizing patriotic anglophobia as well as her rural, uneducated connotation, against the urban intellectual Left.

ROMAN CLERICALISM: A COMPREHENSIVE
AND PERVASIVE CHURCH

France's relationship with the Roman Catholic Church provides an important part of the explanation of a pivotal paradox of French identity: that it is both exceptional and universal in character. Retrospectively tracing France's claim to be the 'eldest daughter of the Church' back to the baptism of the Frankish King Clovis in 496, following the collapse of the Roman Empire, René Rémond explains that this event became 'considered as the baptism of the nation'.[57] While many centuries were to elapse before the French could credibly be argued to constitute a nation, the link between the French crown and Roman Catholicism provided an association between national specificity and religious universality. The myth of France's prior evangelization, followed by the claim in the early twelfth cen-tury by the Capetian kings that France had succeeded Israel as the home of God's chosen people, inspired the self-perception of France as the disinterested

---

[54] Maurice Agulhon, *Marianne into Battle*, 129; cf. 9–10, 112–19, 125–7.

[55] Agulhon, 130, quoting Proudhon's posthumous *De la Capacité Politique des Classes Ouvrières*, 1865.

[56] Jean-Pierre Rioux, 'Laïcisations, massifications, sécessions, 1885–1918' in Rioux and Sirinelli (eds), *Histoire Culturelle de la France*, IV, 1998, 19. See also Michel Winock, 'Jeanne d'Arc' in *Les lieux de mémoire*, III/3, 709–22.

[57] René Rémond, 'La Fille Ainée de l'Eglise' in *Les lieux de mémoire*, III/3, 550; cf. 541, 548, 551, 569.

instrument of Providence. 'Even when secularized, it is from this certitude that comes the deeply rooted conviction in French culture that France's actions are relevant to all humanity'.[58] Roman Catholicism inspired both the repression of threats to national unity from the Albigensian and Protestant challenges, as well as subsequent international claims to a colonial civilizing mission and the right to humanitarian intervention. However, although Roman Catholicism became a foundation of emerging national unity prior to the Revolution, it subsequently was the storm centre of intranational dissension.[59]

The revolutionary severance of the unity of Church and State loosened the clerical grip over the French people, which had been weakening in the eighteenth century. However, religious observance had until then been almost universal. Spiritually and physically, the Church's hold was all embracing in daily life. The priest kept the parish register, so he recorded births and deaths; furthermore religious marriage was a binding contract. 'Primary education was almost wholly under clerical control, and rudimentary social services very largely so'.[60] The Church, consisting of some 170,000 men and women, owned about 8 per cent of the land, mostly through monastic orders. However, signs of dechristianization surfaced, such as the decline in wills providing for masses for the dead, the fall in religious publications, 'rising illegitimacy and bridal pregnancy, and the first signs of systematic contraception within marriage'.[61] Towns were in the forefront of dechristianization, which affected men rather than women, the young rather than the old and was already geographically distributed in a way that remained familiar in the nineteenth and twentieth centuries. Although about a quarter of the clergy were of upper class social origin, the nobility and bourgeoisie were less inclined to attend church and were increasingly attracted to deist masonic lodges.

In the rural areas, superstition prevailed because the 'peasants saw religion as the only means whereby they might manipulate a largely hostile world. ... '[62] The clergy attempted to Catholicize the unavoidable superstitions and saints. 'God was far away. The saints were near ... and every malady was the province of a particular saint'.[63] However, in seeking to separate the sacred from the profane and by their cultivation of fear rather than hope, damnation and the devil were given priority over heaven and God. Through their intrusion into private life, notably by exploiting feminine deference in the confessional to regulate sexual behaviour, the priesthood acquired an unpopularity exacerbated by their reputation for rapaciousness in extracting fees for their services, notably at burials.[64] An apparently comprehensive and pervasive Church control over French society was disrupted irretrievably by the Revolution. 'Too much blood was spilt in the 1790s, too many atrocities committed by both sides, for either to forgive or forget' for nearly two centuries. 'The Catholic clergy would spend much of the nineteenth century trying to reestablish in France the kind of religion that had dominated

[58] Ibid. 560; cf. 558.   [59] Ibid. 541–2.

[60] Ralph Gibson, *A Social History of French Catholicism, 1789–1914,* 1989, 2; cf. 1.

[61] Ibid. 7; cf. 2–8.   [62] Ibid. 18; cf. 10–17.

[63] Eugen Weber, *Peasants into Frenchmen: The Modernization of Rural France, 1870–1914,* 1977, 347.

[64] Ibid. 345–6, 357–9, 365; cf. Gibson, 18–27.

before 1789', with some success in the first half of that century but ultimately in vain.[65]

Initially, the Revolution did not challenge either religion or the Church's centrality to social life. The *cahiers de doléances'* criticisms of the Church were mainly financial, reflecting the grievances of the often poorly paid parish priests against their opulent hierarchical superiors. 'About one *cahier* in four envisaged using part of the Church's wealth to solve the problem of the national debt that had led to the calling of the States-General in the first place, but only 2 per cent of them wanted total expropriation.'[66] Their discontent led to a crucial alliance between many of the First Estate priesthood and the Third Estate commoners that resulted in radical control of the National Assembly, where the former got more than they bargained for between August 1789 and April 1790. 'In very short order, the National Assembly abolished the tithe without compensation, nationalised the whole of Church property, abolished the contemplative and mendicant orders and forbade the taking of religious vows, and turned down a proposal that catholicism be declared the State religion.'[67] The sale of Church property created 'a landowning bourgeoisie with a powerful vested interest in preventing any attempt in the nineteenth century to restore the *ancien régime*, and in particular the power and wealth of the Church.'[68]

In July 1790, a momentous step was taken towards state control over the Church with the establishment of the Civil Constitution of the Clergy. The incompatibility between popular sovereignty and clericalized religion meant that far from the priests choosing the bishops, both of them were to be elected by 'active' citizens. The National Assembly decided on 27 November 1790 that all paid clergy must swear a loyalty oath to the Civil Constitution or be dismissed. Only seven bishops and just over half the parish clergy took the oath, in revulsion against secular state intrusion into hierarchical religious authority. Nonjurors varied widely in number, with 4 per cent in the Var but 90 per cent in the Bas-Rhin and the Vendée, foreshadowing the map of religious fervour well into the twentieth century. In March 1791 the Pope responded by condemning the Civil Constitution of the Clergy as well as the principles of the Revolution and reaffirming that royal power came from God.[69]

The struggle was sharpened when in June 1791 Louis XVI fled. He left behind incriminating documents, justifying his flight on religious grounds and proclaiming his intention to return and restore traditional religion. The resulting association between counter-revolution and the refractory clergy was reinforced once the 1792 outbreak of war led to the latter as émigrés being identified with the foreign enemies. Most of the 32,500 refractories were deported. On 20 September 1792, following the massacre of some 250 priests, the Legislative Assembly secularized the registration of births, marriages, and deaths, which became the responsibility of mayors. It also provided for divorce, a decision reversed in 1816 but reintroduced in a much more restrictive form in 1884. The Vendée insurrection of

---

[65] Gibson, 30.   [66] Ibid. 31; cf. 32–3.   [67] Ibid. 34.   [68] Ibid. 35
[69] Ibid. 36–40.

March 1793, precipitated by conscription, was defeated by the end of the year but a guerrilla war dragged on until 1796. 'This was not simply a war of countryside against town, or of peasant against bourgeois; it was often these things as well, but its general character was that of an exceptionally bitter war of religion'.[70] More generally, there was a close correlation between areas with a high proportion of refractory priests and counter-revolutionary support.

The Thermidorians in 1794–5 reversed the Jacobin assault on the Catholic religion and the attempt to replace it with a Rousseauist-cum-rationalist secular religion. The suspension of Catholic worship was replaced by religious toleration. A decree of 21 February 1795 proclaimed: 'the Republic neither recognises nor finances any religion; it guarantees the free exercise of all religions'.[71] This liberal dispensation led to a revival of traditional church services thanks to the rapid return of emigré priests but it was Napoleon who established a Concordat with the Pope in 1801. Envisaging religion as an instrument of social and political control, Napoleon secured the right to choose all bishops and vet their choice of parish priests, who had to take an oath of loyalty to the government. The Pope, in ending the schism, accepted the loss of Church property and the priority of civil over religious marriage. The ecclesiastical legitimacy this agreement conferred on the political authorities survived until the 1905 separation of Church and state. However, the Concordat could not conceal the post-revolutionary reality: 'French people were no longer automatically Catholic, simply by the fact of being French'.[72]

MASS MILITARIZATION: CONQUEST, CONSCRIPTION, AND PROTECTING PUBLIC ORDER

Whereas in mid-nineteenth century France the army and the Church were the twin military and spiritual pillars of the established order, the revolutionary and Imperial decades had identified the army not with repression at home but with foreign conquest. It was a destabilizing force, aimed at overthrowing monarchies in the name of the rights of the people. The old, aristocrat-officered standing army, in which commissions were purchased, had formed an exclusive subculture divorced from the nation. The existence of a compulsory militia lottery, with such numerous exemptions that it was the peasantry that supplied the rank and file, augmented an unpopularity which was compounded by the recruitment of foreign mercenary contingents. Although the Revolution sought to rely on a volunteer army, this quickly proved inadequate as the Republic became embroiled in war and had to improvise a 'mass levy'. Subsequent recourse to military conscription 'created nearly as much contention as the Revolution's religious policies and political upheavals'.[73] What was then and since presented as a 'nation in arms'

---

[70] Ibid. 51; cf. 49–53. [71] Ibid. 46; cf. 43–4. [72] Ibid. 55; cf. 47–9, 54.
[73] Isser Woloch, *The New Regime: Transformations of the French Civic Order, 1789–1820s*, 1994, 380; cf. 381ff.

turns out on closer inspection to have been a militarily successful but divisive enterprise.

The need to move from an emergency mobilization to permanent conscription was underlined by mass evasion of the call-up in 1793, estimated at 40 per cent. This created 'a huge outlaw population', supplemented by desertion, which enjoyed the support of families and local communities unwilling to lose the services of their young men.[74] Although the conscription pill was sugared by an ideological invocation of the army's role of civic education (which was later to become of practical importance in unifying French society), the immediate priorities were practical. The 1798 Jourdan Law subjected unmarried men of 20 to 25 to selective call-up (an uncovenanted incentive to marriage) and abandoned the practice of hiring replacements which was popular with the middle classes. Napoleon initially tried to decentralize conscription, with Prefects subdividing departmental quotas by commune, recruitment becoming the responsibility of appointed mayors. The latter proved unreliable and so by 1806 a centralized system was established. Napoleon justified replacements on the grounds that 'Among a people whose existence is based on the inequality of wealth, it is essential to allow the rich to buy substitutes'.[75] (The Restoration adopted an even more permissive replacement policy, averaging some 15 per cent in the 1820s.)[76] Despite the running sore of desertions, the rigour of Napoleon's conscription system in overcoming the resistance of French society deluded him into believing he could continue to fight the Allies after 1813 and indirectly led to his downfall. Discredited for a few years, the memory of past glories, embellished by an 1823 masterpiece of political propaganda, Las Cases' *Mémorial de Sainte-Hélène*, helped restore him as a popular hero.[77] The state-building and society-unifying function of conscription was a legacy that was, with ups and downs, to last until its abolition at the end of the twentieth century.

A more ephemeral innovation of the Revolution was the spontaneous emergence after 14 July 1789 of the National Guard. This civic militia elected its own officers and was only subject to a lax civilian discipline. Commanded by Lafayette at the start of two revolutions, 1789 and 1830, it quickly evolved into a territorial home guard, allowing the army to venture abroad. With conscription, the army absorbed much of the National Guard but it re-emerged with the Restoration when approximately 5 per cent of the Paris population served in it. Predominantly bourgeois in composition, it showed itself to be politically unreliable at a military review in 1827, leading to its dissolution by ordinance. Although its arms were not collected, the former National Guard did not play an active role in the July 1830 Revolution.[78] Excessive casualness on the part of Charles X, despite the warning by his commander in Paris Marshal Marmont, meant that with only 11,000 troops at his disposal, the army was boxed in by barricades and overwhelmed by the

[74] Isser Woloch, *The New Regime: Transformations of the French Civic Order, 1789–1820s*, 1994, 387; cf. 386, 391, 412–13. See also A. Forest, *Conscripts and Deserters: The Army and French Society During the Revolution and Empire*, 1989.

[75] Antoine Thibaudeau, *Bonaparte and the Consulate*, 1908, quoted by Woloch, 399; cf. 390–404.

[76] Woloch, 425.   [77] Tulard, 'Le retour des cendres', op. cit. 88–92.

[78] Louis Girard, *La Garde Nationale, 1814–1871*, 1964, 7–9, 42–9, 64–6, 116, 146–8, 159–62.

revolutionary crowds. The class character of the three-day civil war in Paris is illustrated by an on the spot observation. 'While the top floors of houses poured shot and stones on the guardsmen, residents of the lower floors freely offered them refreshments and shelter, a reflection of the characteristic distribution of tenants in Parisian apartment houses, which put the well-to-do on the lower floors, the poor on the top'.[79]

The army and the National Guard were used in the early years of the July Monarchy to defend the regime from the Republicans who felt cheated by a conservative constitutional monarchy which was not what they had fought for. The fear that Lafayette was aspiring to be a Republican Lord Protector, caused him to be eased out of his command at the end of 1830 and thereafter the regime of the Absolute Bourgeoisie felt secure. However, the National Guard consisted largely of people without political rights. In 1848, only a quarter of the elected officers and non-commissioned officers had the vote, so that in his hour of need Louis-Philippe was not protected by the National Guard.[80] Nevertheless, the regular army came to the bourgeoisie's rescue in 1848, notably in the June Days, whereas the Paris National Guard fought on both sides and the provincial National Guard helped defeat the insurgents.

Hitherto concerned with making money and regarding the army as an unproductive and destructive force in what should be a pacific, commercial society, the business bourgeoisie turned with gratitude to the armed forces to protect private property and the hierarchical social order from subversive disruption and destruction. The army officers, who retained their contempt for the bourgeoisie, even though they were now much less aristocratic, were willing to be used as bastions of established order, more out of political passivity than a desire to intervene. So, despite the reluctance of most senior officers to play an active part in Louis-Napoleon's December 1851 *coup d'état*, they quickly accommodated themselves to the Second Empire. The unreliable National Guard played no part on either side in the *coup* and narrowly escaped being abolished.[81] The role of the army in repressing disorder meant that 'the mystique of the army becomes inseparable from the mystique of order', a force to contain revolution at home rather than to promote revolution abroad.[82] This meant that when the Left revived, antimilitarism joined anticlericalism in the attack upon the twin pillars of the established disorder. However, it was unable to halt the outbreak of the First World War.

Ironically, it was disastrous defeat in the 1870 Franco-Prussian War that made the armed forces a supreme national symbol and restored their prestige. The mass public support for a *revanche* to reverse national humiliation and to retrieve the loss of Alsace-Lorraine fostered a vehement patriotism. The defeat of Gambetta's

---

[79] David H. Pinkney, *The French Revolution of 1830*, 1972, 122; cf. 108–25.

[80] Girard, 192–3, 201, 212–3, 220–2, 229. See also Jean Lhomme, *La Grande Bourgeoisie au Pouvoir (1830–1880)*, 1960, 116–19.

[81] Ibid. 337–40; cf. 283–8, 311–21. More generally, see Raoul Girardet, *La Société Militaire dans la France Contemporaine, 1815–1939*, Part I, 1953.

[82] Girardet, 31; cf. 26–33.

1870 attempt to revive a Jacobin nation in arms led to reliance upon a disciplined conscript army, the male national common denominator, to retrieve France's honour. Although the army leadership was discredited by the Dreyfus Affair in the late 1890s, the colonial rivalries of the first decade of the twentieth century revived the prospect of war and public support for the army. The First World War carnage pushed mass militarization to its logical conclusion. Afterwards, war memorials were inaugurated in virtually every French commune.[83] On 11 November each year, the nation paid homage to the citizens who died for their country rather than to the army, with ex-servicemen's associations playing a leading role. A ministry for ex-servicemen was established and survived until the end of the twentieth century, when it was absorbed into the Defence Ministry. By then, the republican nationalism that had inspired the soldiers of 1914–18 but failed to motivate those of 1940 had long since dwindled into a pretext for lobbying on behalf of ex-servicemen.

The 'democratization of war' and the fact that 'about a quarter of the French soldiers who died in the Great War were either not buried at all or buried in unidentified graves and reported missing' prompted the commemoration of the Unknown Soldier.[84] Although the initial inclination was to bury the Unknown Soldier in the *Panthéon*, this was strongly opposed by the ex-servicemen. 'The Temple of Great Men was a closed, sombre, and rarely frequented monument, where the Unknown Soldier would be one among many, some of whom were second-rate figures. This unique war hero deserved to rest alone under the Arc de Triomphe, an open and elevated structure that dominated Paris and was situated in the heart of a busy and modern part of the city, where his memory would be kept alive'.[85] A right-wing government was happy to yield because the *Panthéon* was associated with left-wing celebrities such as Zola, while the Arc de Triomphe's military and Napoleonic associations were politically more acceptable. From 11 November 1923, a daily ceremony of relighting the flame with 'a minute of silence, a sort of secular prayer' was instituted.[86] Thereafter, 'The tomb became a place where the popular and the official cults of the dead soldiers coalesced, thus turning the arch into a focal point of the national identity, more than the *Panthéon* (too much on the Left) and the *Invalides* (too Bonapartist).[87]

LANGUAGES, LITERACY, AND EDUCATION

The vehemence with which official French spokesmen bewail the decline of the international status of the French language betokens both its importance for national identity and symbolic worldwide prestige. Conscious that the rearguard battle to support *Francophonie* is becoming a lost cause, owing to the innovation of French usage by what is dismissed as 'airport English' as well as the displacement

---

[83] Antoine Prost, 'Les monuments aux morts, culte républicain? Culte civique? Culte patriotique?' in *Les lieux de mémoire*, I, 195–222.

[84] Ben-Amos, *Funerals*, 215–16.   [85] Ibid. 219–20.   [86] Ibid. 223.   [87] Ibid. 224.

of French as the medium of international diplomacy and business, its protagonists take refuge in recalling its past glories.[88] Paris as the focus of French cultural leadership, offering literary, artistic and ideological models that attracted widespread admiration, has lost it primacy. To explain why this decline is particularly dramatic in France, we have to consider the political and ideological origins of the preoccupation with education and the centrality of the controversies it has aroused. To do so, we have to investigate the struggle to impose French throughout France to achieve cultural unity but first we must turn to the supranational sixteenth-century origins of educational conflict in the Reformation and the Counter-Reformation.

For Protestantism, education in general and literacy in particular was enshrined as the way of achieving both eternal salvation and worldly success. 'Luther made necessary what Gutenberg had made possible; by placing the scriptures at the centre of Christian eschatology, the Reformation turned a technical invention into a spiritual obligation'.[89] In reaction, the Counter-Reformation developed elementary schools to provide Catholic education, supplementing the catechism taught by the parish priest. 'In the *Ancien régime* village, the schoolmaster had to be approved by the ecclesiastical authorities (primarily by the parish priest) but he was generally chosen by the inhabitants of the village or their representatives'.[90] The state confined itself to helping the Church combat heresy. This changed with the Revolution, when the state challenged the Church's use of education for purposes of ideological and political control, 'a source of power whose exercise must be neither abandoned or even shared'.[91] Like the Church, the Revolutionaries believed that society could be shaped through the minds of the young, so education could not be neutral. The duality was expressed as the inculcation of either obedience or of freedom. 'By laying upon it a preeminent function, the Revolution placed it at the centre of the national political debate for over a century; the Church being an old hand at the game, followed without the slightest effort'.[92]

However, in retrospect it can be seen that 'the Revolution had done nothing to change the elementary school. All it did was to propose a republican catechism in place of the Church catechism....'[93] Its inordinate ambitions were frustrated by lack of finance and its ephemeral duration. Impecunious state school teachers had to wait for the Guizot Law of 1833 to receive a small salary and often inadequate

---

[88] See the extracts from a lecture by Alain Decaux of the Académie Française entitled 'La survie du français, cause nationale' in *Le Monde* 17 October 2001, 19. See also Marc Fumaroli, *Quand l'Europe parlait Français*, 2001.

[89] François Furet and Jacques Ozouf, *Reading and Writing: Literacy in France from Calvin to Jules Ferry*, 1977, 1982 Eng. edn, 59; cf. 60, 308.

[90] Ibid. 66; 60–7.

[91] Ibid. 302. See the abbé Grégoire report on universalizing the French language reprinted in Michel de Certeau et al., *Une politique de la langue*, 1975.

[92] Furet and Ozouf, 98; cf. 2.

[93] Ibid. 98. As the arch counter-revolutionary and theocrat Joseph de Maistre put it: 'To exercise the kind of supremacy that belongs to it, France has been given a dominating language'. ('Fragments sur la France' in *Oeuvres Complètes*, I, 1884, 489.)

accommodation, compelling them to supplement their income with other jobs. A low status and unskilled teaching profession (no proof of competence was required until 1816) only began to be transformed after Guizot's insistence that each *département* establish a primary teacher training college for men. (Women had to wait another half century.) A Protestant, Guizot's motivation was his sense that far from being a cause of subversion as Catholic reactionaries now feared, education could be reinforced as an instrument of social control. In a circular to school teachers on the implementation of the 1833 Law, he asserted: 'Universal elementary education shall henceforth be the guarantee of order and social stability'.[94]

Until elementary education was seen as having practical value, which it only did gradually in rural France, sending children to school was regarded as depriving parents of their labour. However, conservatives saw its political function as indoctrination of deference to existing authorities, while Radicals regarded its purpose as educating voters to use universal suffrage. When they received the vote in 1848, more than half the men were illiterate. At the 1866 census, one-third were still illiterate and in 1901 over 15 per cent were so recorded.[95] Poor mass education was blamed for the political failure of the Second Republic and the military failure of the Second Empire, so under the Third Republic elementary education was charged with teaching citizenship and patriotism preparatory to undertaking military service. In spreading this message, *Le Tour de la France par deux enfants* by the wife of the philosopher Alfred Fouillée (using the evocative pseudonym G. Bruno) and Ernest Lavisse's *Première année d'histoire de France* (history having been introduced into the curriculum) played a particularly important part.[96] Politics displaced religion as the decisive formative influence, so that by the end of the nineteenth century 'General literacy claimed two sets of victims, the parish priest and old people, by robbing the former of the secret of their prestige and the latter of their memory'.[97]

Motivated by a desire to spread French to communicate information and propaganda, as well as to promote national unity from the Revolution, linguistic diversity was seen as an obstacle to be overcome. For the majority of the population, especially in rural and peripheral France, the mother tongue was the local dialect, not French. Backwardness in the achievement of literacy was attributed especially to this language barrier. While this is true, other factors such as reliance upon oral tradition and poverty were formidable contributory factors. Most of all, there was, notably in Western Brittany, a 'sweeping rejection of a culture, going well beyond mere rejection of literacy in a language that is felt to be foreign. Seen thus, low levels of literacy in certain regions where minority languages were spoken may be viewed as an expression of resistance first to monarchic centralization, later to Jacobin unification, as the rejection of that ideology of a homogenized

[94] Furet and Ozouf, 121; cf. 115021, 131, 136, 142–4.   [95] Ibid. 125, 329.

[96] E. Weber, *Peasants into Frenchmen*, 331–6. See also Pierre Nora, 'Lavisse, instituteur national. Le "petit Lavisse", évangile de la République' in *Les lieux de mémoire*, I, 247–86 and Jacques and Mona Ozouf, *Le Tour de la France par deux enfants*, ibid. 291–317.

[97] Furet and Ozouf, 314.

humanity which was the cement of the national community'.[98] The Catholic clergy supported minority languages, while Protestant pastors promoted the use of French but in the former case it was more a matter of reflecting rather than leading local linguistic resistance.[99] The delayed education of women was indirectly important because they increasingly spoke in French to their children. Once the resistance receded, with the time lag of a century, the French language could play the role set out by the integrationist Republicans of the 1790s. The Ferry legislation of the 1880s, instituting free, non-confessional and compulsory education thus consecrated a universal literacy that had already largely been achieved.[100]

Having initially concentrated upon the turbulent historical experience that motivated the French search for an elusive consensus around a legitimate authority, we now turn to the diversity of intellectual interpretations of that contested experience, in which pride of place is occupied by the French Revolution. Institutionalized in successive Republics, successive revolutions have been elevated into the increasingly inclusive manifestation of an integrative French political culture. We should, however, bear in mind that the selective nature of historic memory has meant that the past has been interpreted by reference to the preoccupations of the present, always restarting from a shifting end.

The 1880s, notably with the 2 October 1888 decree requiring identification documents for foreigners and the 1889 Naturalization Law defining the borderline between those included within national identity and those excluded from it, took the issue into the sphere of police procedures.[101] These became an even more controversial matter a century later when immigration was exploited by the National Front, as we see at the end of Chapter 8.

---

[98] Ibid. 298; cf. 282–93, 296–7. For a moving account of a Breton's revolt against subjection to a linguistic steamroller, see Morvan Lebesque, *Comment peut-on être Breton? Essai sur la Démocratie française*, 1970.

[99] E. Weber, *Peasants into Frenchmen*, 82–9, 310–18; cf. 72–3

[100] Furet and Ozouf, 45; cf. 46.

[101] Noiriel, *The French Melting Pot*, 56; cf. Chapter 2, 'The Card and the Code'.

2

Intellectual Interpretations and Projections of the French Revolution

While it is tempting to trace the origin of the conflated national sense of cultural singularity and universal vocation to the French Revolution, we have already seen that France's much earlier claim to be the 'eldest daughter of the Church' had simultaneously grounded national specificity and religious universality.[1] However, the Revolution prompted secular attempts to close the wounds it had inflicted by establishing new founding myths. Of all of these, whether Catholic reactionary, Anglophile liberalism, scientist ideology, political economy, positivism and Doctrinaire liberalism, it was the providentialist historians that came into their own in the mid- and late-nineteenth century, that sought most explicitly 'to produce the nation by imparting to it a common memory'.[2] The problem was that it was precisely its memories that perpetuated national disunity. The substitution of history for religion as the means of inculcating a common political culture was pioneered in the early and mid-nineteenth centuries, notably by Augustin Thierry and Jules Michelet, but came into its own during the Third Republic. In 1895, the historian Lavisse could compare the history teacher to the priest officiating at his altar.[3] The historian's supreme task was to be mobilize the national master myths in the service of his country.

The superimposition of a spurious unity upon an empirical plurality was facilitated by a national inclination towards a formalistic priority accorded to abstract principle over actual practice. However, we should not assume that in reality rather than rhetoric the French did not sometimes actually move from practice to theory. Pierre Rosanvallon has convincingly argued that in the matter of parliamentary government, Restoration France sought to adopt British-style accountability of the government to parliament, tentatively groping its way towards the individual and collective responsibility of ministers. While 'parties' were too informal and shifting to be worthy of the name, nevertheless they tried to adopt the notions of Majority and Opposition in the Westminster manner. As in Britain in the early nineteenth century, the exercise of the royal prerogative was still a constitutionally controversial issue, except that in France, Charles X

---

[1] See Chapter 1. On tracing the feeling of cultural singularity to the Revolution, see Françoise Mélonio, '1815–1880', in Antoine de Baecque and Françoise Mélonio, *Lumières et Liberté: Les Dix-Huitième et Dix-Neuvième Siècles*, Volume III of Rioux and Sirinelli (eds), *Histoire Culturelle de la France*, 192.

[2] F. Mélonio, 262; cf. 193, 265.   [3] Ibid. 261.

pushed his extensive interpretation of his powers to the point of provoking the 1830 Revolution. Initially, matters were confused by the fact that the ultra-royalist majority sought to use parliamentary pressure to push Louis XVIII to adopt more extremist positions, while the liberal Opposition defended his prerogative for equally tactical reasons as a restraint on the ultras. They switched roles in 1827 when the ultras lost their majority in the Chamber of Deputies. Rosanvallon, following Barthélemy, maintains that 'the Revolution bequeathed to modern France its intellectual foundations, the Empire forged its administrative system and the Restoration and the July Monarchy gave her political institutions, perhaps more precisely the spirit of those institutions' as they developed under the Third and Fourth Republics.[4]

Nevertheless, the French addiction to comprehensive abstract principle and allergy to the piecemeal compromises that have made British parliamentarism work so differently from that of France, is due in no small measure to castigating these inclinations as intellectually disreputable. The tendency to regard Descartes as the quintessential French philosopher is indicative of the superiority accorded to rationalist deductive clarity over empirical inductive content. Identified as one of France's 'Great Men', Condorcet proposed that Descartes' remains be lodged in the *Panthéon* but this was never done because of clerical and right-wing hostility. It was the *Idéologue* Destutt de Tracy who launched the idea of a methodology-based French school of philosophy whose supreme exponent was Descartes. Like Tracy, many of the other proponents of a unifying national philosophy whom we shall mention subscribed to this view. Thus, the eclectic Victor Cousin and the Doctrinaire François Guizot placed him at the fountainhead of modern civilization and used their influence—especially during the July Monarchy—to make Descartes the enduring official philosopher of the French University and State.[5] Saint-Simon and Auguste Comte also regarded 'French philosophy' as personified by Descartes but his rationalism was anathema to the Catholic Traditionalists, to whom we shall turn before considering more mainstream representatives of French thinking following the Restoration reaction against the Revolution.

ANTI-REVOLUTIONARY ROMAN CATHOLICISM

The perverse traditionalist interpretation of the Revolution was that it was a providential product of divine determinism. By rejecting monarchy and Church, it would reinforce them by reaction to the institutionalized revolution against temporal and spiritual authority that had begun with the Protestant Reformation.

---

[4] Pierre Rosanvallon, *La Monarchie Impossible: Les Chartes de 1814 et de 1830*, 1994, 9; cf. 65. See also Joseph Barthélemy, *L'Introduction du gouvernement parlementaire en France sous Louis XVIII et Charles X*, 1904.

[5] François Azouvi, 'Descartes' in *Les lieux de mémoire*, III/3, 735–53. See more generally, François Azouvi, *Descartes en France: Histoire d'une passion nationale*, 2002.

The Catholic Church had been the bulwark of order by inculcating obedience. Against the attack of the Enlightenment philosophers, the Catholic traditionalists defended dogma, superstition, and even the Inquisition, Maistre claiming that had the latter not been abolished, it could have stopped the Revolution.[6] As the great theophobe Proudhon declared in his *Idée générale de la Révolution* (1851), 'When, fifty or sixty years ago, catholic and monarchist absolutism was about to descend into the tomb, it made a supreme effort. It was then that it produced its most illustrious apologists, de Maistre, Bonald, Chateaubriand and Lamennais'.[7]

The most trenchant and in the longer term influential exponent of clericalist anti-revolution was Joseph de Maistre, notably in his 1797 *Considérations sur la France*. Seeing history as a struggle between Christian good and secular evil, Maistre formulated a God-centred conception of nature and society. Turning seemingly all–conquering rationalism against itself, he maintained as early as 1793 that 'just as in religion there is a point where faith must be blind, so in politics there is a point where obedience must be the same, and that the mass of men is made to be led, that reason itself teaches distrust of reason, and that the masterpiece of reasoning is the discovery of the point where one must stop reasoning.'[8] An ardent admirer of Edmund Burke's *Reflections on the Revolution in France*, he shared his view that 'man is by his constitution a religious animal',[9] so divorced from God, men could only destroy, not create. However, Maistre could not share the Anglican Burke's disassociation of Protestantism from any share of responsibility in the French Revolution. Instead, he united politics and religion in a duality of Papal Church and monarchical state, the latter based upon the former for its authority.[10]

Maistre quickly grasped that far from being an ephemeral phenomenon, the French Revolution had permanently changed the context within which political activity would take place. So, despite his theocentric standpoint, he adopted an empirical and pragmatic approach, trusting to practical experience rather than the abstract deduction from first principles favoured by the rationalist revolutionaries in their headlong experiments with institutional engineering. 'If the foundation is purely human, the building cannot stand; the more men who have been involved in its construction, the more deliberation, science and *especially writing* they have devoted to it...the more will the institution be fragile'.[11] Constitutional

---

[6] Cyprian B. Blamires, *Three Critiques of the French Revolution: Maistre, Bonald and Saint-Simon*, unpublished D.Phil. thesis, Oxford, 1985, 89; cf. 52–9.

[7] Quoted in Pierre Haubtmann, *P-J Proudhon: Genèse d'un Antithéiste*, 1969, 123.

[8] Joseph de Maistre, *Lettres d'un Royaliste savoisien à ses compatriotes*, quoted by Richard A. Lebrun, *Joseph de Maistre: An Intellectual Portrait*, 1988, 126. I shall concentrate on Maistre because I agree with Cyprian Blamires: 'Much of what Bonald said was said better by Maistre', op. cit. 8.

[9] Edmund Burke, *Reflections on the Revolution in France*, Clarendon Press edition of *Select Works*, 1888, 107.

[10] Robert Triomphe, *Joseph de Maistre: Etude sur la vie et sur la doctrine d'un matérialiste mystique*, 1968, 138–9. For a detailed comparison of Burke and Maistre, see J. P. Cordelier, *La Théorie Constitutionnel de Joseph de Maistre*, 1965, 72–94.

[11] Joseph de Maistre, *Essai sur le principe générateur des constitutions politiques*, 1814, quoted from his *Oeuvres Complètes*, I, 1884, 299; cf. 243–4, 265–6.

improvisation could change words but changing things was much more difficult. 'Man' was an abstraction and the Rights of Man, like the proclamation of Liberty, Equality, and Fraternity, were exercises in rhetoric with little impact on reality. Society was a natural not a contractual fact and appeal to the 'people' was just another forlorn abstraction.[12] While revolutions were caused by abuses, these 'cost infinitely less than revolutions'.[13] Experience had shown 'irrational' hereditary monarchy to be the most stable and satisfactory form of government. Albert Hirschman, in his study of *The Rhetoric of Reaction*, was able to illustrate his argument by reference to Maistre as an advocate of its main themes: the perversity, futility, and jeopardy of attempts at purposive action. Perversity refers to the counterproductive results of innovation; futility to the illusion of change; jeopardy to the threat to other desirable achievements.[14]

Maistre anticipated that Napoleon was both the incarnation of an ongoing revolutionary process and yet would regenerate an effete monarchy. Napoleon's humiliation of the papacy and destruction of the Holy Roman Empire, ruthlessly subordinating the Roman Catholic Church to the secular power of the French state, had discredited the Gallicanism favoured by Maistre's fellow protagonist of political clericalism, Bonald. Maistre instead asserted papal infallibility in his *Du Pape*, an extremely influential work that went through some forty editions and reprints, culminating in the consecration of this principle by the First Vatican Council of 1870. The most vigorous protagonist of ultramontane Catholicism in mid-nineteenth-century France, the journalist Louis Veuillot, wrote to his son in 1847: 'God made me a Catholic. M. de Maistre made me a Roman.'[15]

Maistre's appeal to theocracy derived partly from his lucid scepticism about the survival of the Bourbon Restoration. He had great contempt for the 1814 Charter of constitutional monarchy, describing it as a 'soap bubble' incapable of founding political stability, being a fragile compromise between the Divine Right of Kings and the Rights of Man. Louis XVIII did not take kindly to Maistre's claim that he was not sitting on the throne of his ancestors and that the Revolution had not lost its impetus despite its royal veneer.[16] Moderation was not to the taste of the author of *Considérations sur la France*, which was described by Lamartine as 'thought out by an exterminating mind and written in blood', who was subsequently to elevate

---

[12] See Jean-Yves Le Borgne, *Joseph de Maistre et la Révolution*, 1976, 121–7; cf. 105, 132–3, 157.

[13] Letter of 1803 quoted in Lebrun, 182.

[14] Albert O. Hirschman, *The Rhetoric of Reaction: Perversity, Futility, Jeopardy.* 1991, 7 and passim.

[15] Quoted in Lebrun, 261; cf. 239–40, 269. See also C. Latreille, *Joseph de Maistre et la Papauté*, 1906. With his habitual remorseless resort to deductive logic, Maistre wrote in 1814 to the King's favourite Blacas; 'No public morality or national character without religion, no European religion without Christianity, no Christianity without Catholicism, no Catholicism without the Pope, no Pope without his supremacy.' Quoted by Fernand Baldensperger, *Le mouvement des idées dans l'émigration française, 1789–1815*, II, 1924, 244.

[16] See the quotations and comments in Jack Hayward, 'Maistre: the Compleat counter-revolutionary?' in Hayward (ed.), *After the French Revolution: Six Critics of Democracy and Nationalism*, 1991, 60–1, Chapter 3 passim.

the executioner into the supreme agent of social order.[17] Maistre shared the ultra-royalist view that 'Any Constitution is a regicide'.[18]

After Maistre's death in 1820, Lamennais continued for a decade the Catholic anti-revolutionary campaign, notably in *De la religion considérée dans ses rapports avec l'ordre politique et civil* of 1825–6, equating democracy with atheism, materialism, instability, corruption, and despotism.[19] He then abandoned theocracy and from the 1830s became first a liberal and then a socialist. It was Bonald, first as a deputy and then as a peer, who during the Restoration became 'the oracle of the ultra-royalist party', while Chateaubriand (where *Génie du christianisme ou Beauté de la religion chrétienne* of 1802 enjoyed a great vogue during the Napoleonic Empire and the Restoration) after serving as Ambassador and Foreign Minister, became increasingly convinced of the inevitability of liberal democracy.[20]

Maistre's influence extended well beyond the Catholic milieu. He had a major impact upon Auguste Comte, imparting a strong authoritarian bent to positivism of which he was first the scientist and then the dictatorial exponent. As Proudhon caustically put it: Comte 'ruins his case in damning the Revolution…he only required a little more consistency to reconstruct the whole of Catholicism'.[21] Charles Maurras, a disciple of Comte, who became the leader of the extremist nationalist *Action Française*, was one of Maistre's leading monarchist disciples, promoting historical continuity into a methodological dogma.[22] His active support for the collaborationist Vichy regime helped to discredit both his ideas and those of Catholic traditionalism, so that Maistre can now be regarded as truly a 'prophet of the past'.[23]

LEARNING BRITISH CONSTITUTIONAL LESSONS: PROTESTANT LIBERALISM

The Chateau de Coppet, on the Genevan side of the Swiss border with France was, in the years just before and after 1800, the focus of a culturally cosmopolitan salon in which a nucleus of Anglophile, Protestant, politically active intellectuals exercised an anti-authoritarian influence over enlightened European public opinion.

[17] Alphonse de Lamartine, *Souvenirs et Portraits*, I, 1874, 188; cf. 189. On the executioner, see Joseph de Maistre, *Soirées de St Petersbourg* in Jack Lively (ed.), *The Works of Joseph de Maistre*, 1965, 192.

[18] Quoted in Pierre Rosanvallon, *La Monarchie Impossible*, 25, from Jean-Denis Lanjuinais, *Constitutions de la nation française*, I, 1819, 70.

[19] Dominique Bagge, *Les Idées Politiques en France*, 1952, 275–82.

[20] G. de Bertier de Sauvigny, *La Restauration*, 3rd edn, 346; cf. 347 and Jean-Paul Clément (ed.), *Chateaubriand politique*, 1987.

[21] Haubtmann, 207, quoting Proudhon's *De la Justice dans la Révolution et dans l'Eglise*, 1858.

[22] Francis Bayle, *Les idées politiques de Joseph de Maistre*, University of Lyon doctoral thesis, 1944, 23–6, 138. See also Michael Sutton, *Nationalism, Positivism and Catholicism: The Politics of Charles Maurras and French Catholics 1890–1914*, 1982, Chapter 1 passim, 121, 139, 291 and Louis Dimier, *Les Maîtres de la Contre-Révolution*, 1907.

[23] Pierre-Simon Ballanche, *Oeuvres*, III, 259.

Its key figures were the Swiss banker Jacques Necker, his daughter Germaine de Staël and her lover, the political philosopher Benjamin Constant.[24] From the last years of Louis XVI's reign, when Necker as Finance Minister attempted to rescue the public finances, whose inextricable problems were precipitating revolution, through the vicissitudes of the revolutionary decade, on to the Napoleonic Empire, they argued the case for importing liberalism on the British model. Forced into exile from the Paris to which they sought to impart their convictions, like Maistre—but for diametrically opposed reasons—they did not exercise the direct political influence to which they aspired because their message was unwelcome to mainstream French political culture.

Necker, as we mentioned in the Introduction, was Finance Minister from 1777 to 1781 and from 1788 to 1790. He was forced to resign on three occasions—in July 1789 his departure was brief, being recalled after the fall of the Bastille—but was unable to persuade Louis XVI of the need for the reforms he proposed. Despite his public standing as potential financial saviour of France, amounting in 1789 to 'neckromania', he was excluded from the King's Council of Ministers because of his heretical religion, which reduced his ability to control events. Without the support of either the king or the deputies of the Third Estate, Necker was in office but not in power.[25] Deprived of the capacity to act, he exchanged the role of statesman for commentator on the need for a strong but non-despotic executive. While rejecting the vogue for rationalist constitutional engineering epitomized by Sieyès, Necker's grasp of English constitutional history led him to choose it as a model. At a time when the earlier Anglophilia of Voltaire and Montesquieu had been submerged by an Anglophobia arising from both the American War of Independence, and an anachronistic second chamber and corrupt House of Commons, Necker admired the British political system for pragmatic reasons. 'Perfection would be secured by a Government whose Constitution would be able to maintain the laws of property, order and liberty, without itself being able to infringe them. And this perfection seems to me to be represented by the political Constitution of England'.[26] Unlike Montesquieu, he saw the efficient secret of British institutions as the collaboration not the separation of powers, ensuring an effective state authority, unlike the government by assembly which was the French Revolution's version of legislative sovereignty. His analysis was subsequently developed by Madame de Staël and Benjamin Constant.[27]

Ironically, this politically inseparable pair of protagonists of liberalism joined with Sieyès in supporting Napoleon Bonaparte's 1799 *coup d'état* 'to overthrow the tottering Directory before either the Jacobins or the royalists had a chance to

---

[24] Simone Balayé, 'Âme et unité de Coppet' in Lucien Jaume (ed.) *Coppet, Creuset de l'Esprit Libéral*, 14–15 and Alain Laquièze, 'Le modèle anglais et la responsabilité ministérielle selon le Group de Coppet', ibid. 167.

[25] Jean-Denis Bredin, 'Necker et l'opinion publique', ibid. 29; cf. 25–40 and J. Christopher Herold, *Mistress to an Age: A Life of Madame de Staël*, 1959, 78–88.

[26] Jacques Necker, *Du pouvoir exécutif dans les grands états*, II, 1792, 356, quoted by Louis Lacchè (ed.), 138 note; cf. Alain Laquièze, 'Le modèle anglais', ibid. 159–61.

[27] Lacchè, 147–8 and Laquieze, 161–2.

overthrow it'.[28] They quickly came to rue their illusion that Napoleon could be domesticated into a British-style constitutional monarch when Napoleon showed his true dictatorial colours. Fearing her influential salon as the focus of intellectual and conspiratorial opposition to his desire for total subordination, he exiled Madame de Staël from Paris, having failed to buy her subservience as he had that of so many ex-revolutionaries and aristocrats. He asked his brother to find out what she wanted, to which Madame de Staël proudly replied: 'it's not a question of what I want but of what I think'.[29] Ably supported by Constant, she retreated to Coppet, which after 1804 attracted the liberal opposition to Napoleonic tyranny from all over Europe. As she wrote retrospectively, 'I cried, not for liberty, which had never existed in France, but for the hope of liberty'....[30]

Madame de Staël had thought of giving her influential reflections on the French Revolution the subtitle: 'and English political institutions in their application to France'.[31] She could not praise too effusively 'England that we have ceaselessly commended as a model to French legislators, accusing them whenever they have departed from it.'[32] Since 1688, by grafting the new onto the old, improvement had been achieved without violence. Peaceful changes of government were possible because of the existence of a government and an opposition party, bolstered by a free press and public opinion.[33] She reiterated earlier arguments in favour of Protestantism as an undogmatic cultural underpinning of English liberty in contrast with 'catholicism that decides everything by authority and considers kings as equally infallible as popes when they are not at war with each other'.[34] Admiring English decentralization for socializing many people into citizen participation in local affairs, she regretted that France had rejected federalism in 1795 but recognized that it 'was not in harmony either with the character or the habits of the nation'.[35] However, she briefly contrasted illiberal, collectivist ancient liberty which maximized popular political involvement, with individualist modern liberty which guaranteed citizen privacy from government intervention[36]—a distinction that was to become famous as developed by Constant. Instead of classical direct democracy, Madame de Staël championed representative government in the hands of 'the best', which she equated with educated property owners. Democracy would have to await mass education and presumably mass property ownership.[37]

---

[28] Herold, 212.

[29] Ibid. 215; cf. 213–14 and Madame de Staël, *Dix années d'exil*, ed. by Simone Balayé, Bibliothèque 10/18, 1966 and Simone Balayé, *Madame de Staël: Lumières et Liberté*, 1979, 88–90; cf. 112, 115.

[30] Madame de Staël, *Considérations sur les principaux événements de la Révolution Française*, II, 1818, Part 4, 237.

[31] Balayé, *Madame de Staël*, 239.

[32] Madame de Staël, *Considérations*, III, 158; cf. 166–8, 210, I, 15.

[33] Ibid. 221, 226–9, 241–3, 262.

[34] Ibid. 177. See her earlier advocacy of Protestantism as a state religion in *Des Circonstances Actuelles quie peuvent terminer la Révolution et des Principes quie doivent fonder la République en France*, Lucia Omacini (ed.), 1979, 227–34.

[35] *Considérations*, II, 153; cf. III, 113, 164.   [36] *Des Circonstances Actuelles*, 111–12.

[37] Ibid. 170; cf. 12, 160–1, 167–9. See also 'Note on property', ibid. 45–8.

This combination of meritocracy and plutocracy was to come into its own, in a very conservative form, during the July Monarchy.

Germaine de Staël's intimate partnership with Benjamin Constant in promoting liberalism in France began under the anti-Jacobin Directory and defined itself during the Empire against Napoleon. She hoped he would play the direct political role that was denied to her as a woman. He was to do so as an opposition parliamentarian, mainly during the Bourbon Restoration, even as constitution maker during Napoleon's '100 Days', but never as minister like her father had been. The representative government, which he championed in his writings did not allow him to play the full part to which he aspired, so he expressed his views in speeches and journalism which provided a 'parliamentary education to liberal France' based on his admiration for the British practice he had observed at first hand.[38] Purged from the pseudo-parliamentary *Tribunat* by Napoleon in 1802, when free political debate was no longer in season and only regimented intellectuals were tolerated, during the Restoration Constitutional Monarchy he endeavoured to import British-style parliamentary practices, notably the idea of a loyal Opposition, which never took hold in France. Constant saw his task as teaching the French how to become politically free, to realize Madame de Staël's forlorn hope quoted earlier. However, liberalism has always found the majority of French people allergic to its precepts.

Despite his Huguenot ancestry, Constant only acquired French nationality when Geneva was annexed by France. He was always an incorrigible cosmopolitan, but his particular affinity with British values can especially be traced to the eighteen months he studied at Edinburgh University in 1783–5. His freethinking was reinforced by his Protestant background that inclined him towards a religious pluralism that placed religious freedom far above religious authority, with its predilection to dogmatism and intolerance. He was scathing about those (of whom Thiers was to become a prominent exemplar after 1848) who while themselves unbelievers thought there should be religious restraints upon the 'weak and disarmed' working classes on behalf of the powerful and rich idle classes for whom such constraints were unnecessary.[39] It was a persecuting Catholicism that promoted scepticism, as force in the service of faith marshalled courage in support of secular free thought.

Even before Constant's momentous encounter and partnership with Germaine de Staël, his Scottish education had predisposed him to make the liberal separation between state and society and to regard individual rights as the protection of civil society against state intrusion. However, thanks to her introducing him to all those who counted in Directory politics and through the frequentation of her salon, Constant was able to show his polemical talents, which he quickly did in his pamphlet *De la Force du Gouvernement Actuel et de la necessité de s'y rallier* that quickly enjoyed a great success, provoking Maistre's *Considérations sur*

---

[38] Joseph Barthélemy, *L'introduction du régime parlementaire en France*, 184.
[39] Constant, *Principes de Politique*, 1815, in *Oeuvres*, Pléiade (ed.), 1124–5, cf. 1220–2, 1229–30.

la France.[40] Concerned to stabilize the new regime by 'ending the Revolution', Constant argued that to try to reconstruct everything meant despotically dragging opinion along in the name of liberty in a repeated tyrannical use of force in which crimes followed errors. To avoid lurching between apparent anarchy and actual despotism, Constant advocated strong but limited government. In reaction against the Terror, the royalists did not appreciate that 'counter revolution would itself be a new revolution'.[41] As he later wrote: 'The extremes not only touch but follow each other. One exaggeration always produces its contrary exaggeration'.[42] Because the mass population above all wanted peace to pursue their personal pleasures, it was up to their representatives to create the political stability to make this possible.

So Constant adopted Sieyès's distinction between the many passive citizens content to enjoy their private freedoms and the few active citizens who would represent them. Although he had followed Condorcet in arguing that humanity was progressing towards equality, until property was spread to all it would be the minority of property owners who held political power. He argued that it would only be a divisive privilege if property did not change hands, while the propertyless would use the vote to redistribute property instead of acquiring it by work.[43] Constant supported a lowering of the property qualification during the Restoration and was not against majority rule so much as misrule in the name of the majority. In a parliamentary speech in 1829, he reminded the Right, who feared majority tyranny, that 'whenever there has been tyranny in France for the last forty years, it was minorities that governed.'[44] However, quite apart from the fact that all are sometimes in the minority, in words that anticipate J. S. Mill's *On Liberty*, Constant argued that 'The assent of the majority is by no means sufficient in all cases to legitimate its acts.... It will be no more legitimate, even if the whole nation approves less the citizen it oppresses.'[45]

While liberalism subsequently became generally identified in France as the doctrine justifying *grand bourgeois* hegemony, under Napoleon 'Liberalism gradually became the doctrine of a minority on the defensive, struggling, without the support of public opinion, for a few principles'.[46] It was in opposition, first to popular sovereignty exercised by assembly government and then by one-man rule, that liberals rejected any unlimited power. Constant sagely observed that 'Today it is an illusion to call on the mass of citizens to exercise sovereignty. The people can only be slaves or free; it never governs.'[47] Further, the interests of government and the governed were not identical and being more remote from everyday reality,

---

[40] Etienne Hofmann, *Les 'Principes de Politique' de Benjamin Constant: Genèse d'une oeuvre et l'évolution de la pensée de l'auteur (1789–18)*, I, 1980, 128; cf. 111–20 and Kurt Kloocke, *Benjamin Constant: Une biographie intellectuelle*, 1984, 61–9.

[41] *De la Force du Gouvernement*, 1796, 21; cf. 4–5.

[42] *De l'Esprit de Conquête et de l'usurpation dans leurs rapports avec la civilisation européenne*, 1814, in *Oeuvres*, 1057.

[43] Hofmann, II, 201–9, 221–4, 238.

[44] Constant *Ecrits et Discours Politiques*, Pozzo di Borgo ed., 1964, 140. But see 167.

[45] *Principes de Politique* in *Oeuvres*, 1105; cf. Hofmann, II, 53.

[46] Hofmann, I, 211–12; cf. 189–191.

[47] Hofmann, II, 421; cf. *Principes de Politique* in *Oeuvres*, 1104, 1109.

government took longer to discover its mistakes and to correct them, so the rights of the individual must be protected from their representatives who may borrow the name of liberty in order to pervert it. 'When the individual is nothing, the people is nothing'.[48]

Constant spent most of the First Empire writing the works that he subsequently mined for publication during the Restoration when he could do so more freely, rushing parts of them out as circumstances dictated. As Napoleon's power collapsed, Constant belied his name but not his principles by supporting first Bernadotte, ex-republican general and Prince-inheritor of the Swedish crown, then the Restoration of Louis XVIII, before—at Napoleon's request—writing a liberal Constitution dubbed the 'Benjamin' during the 100 Days.[49] Prudently absenting himself after Waterloo for a year in London, where he published his renowned autobiographical novel *Adolphe*, he returned to France, first writing articles in the liberal press and then seeking and securing election to parliament, where he sat on the extreme Left. He attacked the ultra-royalist majority, describing them to his election agent in 1820 in scathing terms. 'All the insolence of provincial nobility, all the ignorance of court nobility, all the fury of counterrevolutionaries, all the greed of titled beggars, as well as the determination to listen to nothing and the inability to understand anything....'[50] He became the spokesman but not the leader of the liberals. Constant made some 250 speeches in the Chamber of Deputies (more than 120 between March 1819 and August 1822 when he lost his seat) combining British debating style such as he had observed in the House of Commons with French clarity of exposition.

In 1818–19 Constant gave public lectures on 'The fundamental maxims of the English Constitution', although the most celebrated is the one comparing Ancient and Modern Liberty based on his earlier writings. In his 1814 *Réflexions sur les constitutions*, Constant explicitly stated that the English Constitution had been his model: 'I have not sought originality: in many matters I have not diverged from the English Constitution. I have explained why what existed in England was good rather than proposing something new.'[51] He particularly advocated following the British-style monarch who—separate from the government—could exercise a neutral authority capable of arbitrating between the conflicts natural in a free society without degenerating into arbitrary power. Because of the principle that 'the King can do no wrong', ministerial responsibility could be enforced. This presupposed what did not exist in France: 'a cohesive government, a stable majority and an opposition clearly separated from that majority', with elections called if the majority ceased to exist.[52]

[48] Hofmann, II, 460; cf. 75–6, 384, 463–6.

[49] Paul Bastid, *Benjamin Constant et sa Doctrine*, 1966, 255–87. It was Montlosier who coined the name 'Benjamine', ibid. 286. Lasting only from 3 to 23 June 1815, this shortest lived French Constitution could be dubbed the June Constitution. Constant supported Bonaparte in 1799 and 1815 to avoid the return of the Bourbons, having been his resolute critic in between.

[50] Quoted in Stephen Holmes, *Benjamin Constant and the Making of Modern Liberalism*, 1984, 221.

[51] Quoted in Paul Bastid, *Sièyes et sa pensée*, 1939, 1970, 2nd edn, 561.

[52] *Principes de Politique* in *Oeuvres*, 1177; cf. 1113–18, 1171–8.

More fundamentally, he regarded Britain as the freeist country in Europe, especially because of its free press and rule of law, supplemented by the jury system that refused to enforce unjust laws, so that one might ask where, 'if Britain had been subjugated by Napoleon, he could write, speak, think, breathe.'[53] He was a particularly ardent advocate of the fundamental importance of the press in sustaining political freedom and pilloried the consequences of its subordination. 'It is the long privation of a free press that has rendered most French credulous, anxious, ignorant and as a result ferocious. ... In all that is called the excess of freedom I only recognise the education of servitude.'[54] More generally, Constant admired British pluralism, reflected in local autonomy, as against French central-ization, being willing to go further in a federalist direction.[55] He favoured British freedom of trade and its opposition to the slave trade, against which he made numerous speeches in the 1820s. Steering a course between over-politicization and over-privatization, for Constant 'liberal man is a part-time citizen',[56] who has the freedom to express an insubordinate individuality. The nominally liberal July Monarchy did not accept this intransigent commitment to liberty.

IDEOLOGY AS A SCIENCE OF POLITICS

Like the liberals Constant and Staël, the *Idéologues* identified most closely with the anti-Jacobin and anti-Bourbon Directory of 1795–9. They sought to impart to the revolutionary ideals a rationalist and scientific basis, making them a political extension of the intellectual revolution of the eighteenth century. They looked for their inspiration to Locke, Turgot, Condorcet, and Condillac and prepared the way for the positivism of Comte. Condillac provided them with a determinist-materialist systematic substitute for Christianity, while Condorcet's rationalism and belief in progress and political socialization by education made him the last of the Enlightenment *philosophes* and the pioneer *Idéologue*. Unlike the liberals, they countenanced the notion of enlightened despotism, reflected in Turgot's pre-revolutionary assertion: 'Give me five years despotism and France will be free',[57] a sophism which many were subsequently to emulate.

Whereas the leading Revolutionaries were lawyer-orators like Mirabeau, Danton, and Robespierre, the *Idéologues* were scientists and men of letters, not demogogues but pedagogues, preoccupied with educating the people for democ-racy. Narrowly escaping death (unlike Condorcet) when imprisoned during the

---

[53] *Principes de Politique* in *Oeuvres*, 1177; cf. 1113–18, 1171–8. See also Bastid, *Benjamin Constant*, 928–55 and Mary S. Hartman, 'Benjamin Constant and the Question of Ministerial Responsibility in France, 1814–15' in *Journal of European Studies*, VI, 1976, 248–61.

[54] Constant, *De l'Esprit de Conquête* in *Oeuvres*, 1028; cf. 1607–11, 1214, 1240–2.

[55] Hofmann, II, 134, repeated in *Réflexions sur les Constitutions*, 153.

[56] *Principes de Politique* in *Oeuvres*, 1188–93.

[57] Holmes, 129. For a more extended discussion, see Jack Hayward, 'Constant: part-time citizenship and constitutional freedom' in Jack Hayward, *After the French Revolution*, Chapter 5.

Terror, Destutt de Tracy and ex-abbé Daunou rejected the identification of the people with the least educated, so that as Daunou put it, 'no one had the right to be wiser than the people'.[58] Their explicit elitism—reflected in a dual education system for the ruling elite and the ruled mass population—meant that they lacked popular support when Napoleon, whom they helped to power in 1799, rounded on them as subversive intellectuals. Although they rightly feared that the uneducated were unready for political participation, to restrict the suffrage to the educated (not property owners, as the Restoration and July Monarchies did) was a recipe for unpopular democracy.

Destutt de Tracy, who coined the term ideology in 1796, had risen to the rank of colonel prior to the Revolution, as a member of the liberal nobility closely connected to the Court. Elected to the Estates General in 1789, he was subsequently second-in-command of the cavalry in Lafayette's army but refused to follow him into exile. Arrested during the Terror, he wrote in prison: 'I hope to prove by facts what Locke and Condillac have shown by reasoning, that morality and politics are susceptible of demonstration.'[59] The Thermidor coup saved him from trial two days later, his hair having gone white by the time he was released in October 1794. He had become closely associated with the Condorcet salon frequented by many of those who belonged to the Academy of Moral and Political Sciences established in October 1795 on Daunou's proposition. (Daunou was the main author of the Directory Constitution of 1795.) His most intimate intellectual friend was the physician and physiologist Cabanis and 'ideology' was an attempt to substitute a rigorous 'science of ideas' for metaphysics.

Like Cabanis, Tracy and his fellow *Idéologues* served as the Directory's 'intellectual brains trust', mobilizing science in the fight for the Republic and against royalism and clericalism.[60] When the Directory failed to achieve political stability, they followed Sieyès in turning to Napoleon Bonaparte in the hope that at best he would be a French Washington, at worst an enlightened autocrat restraining the agitators who were rousing the manipulable mob. As Cabanis peremptorily asserted: 'Choices must be made not at the bottom, where they are necessarily made badly, but at the top where they are necessarily made well'.[61] Thanks to the Sieyès–Bonaparte coup, democracy had been purged of its defects: 'the ignorant class no longer exercises any influence either on the legislature or on the government; consequently no more demagogues. All is done for the people and in the name of the people. Nothing is done by it under its unthinking guidance.'[62]

---

[58] Quoted in Georges Gusdorf, *La Conscience Révolutionnaire: Les Idéologues*, Payot, 1978, 67 note. See also, on Turgot's disciple Condorcet, Shirley M. Gruner, *Economic Materialism and Social Moralism: A Study of the History of Ideas in France from the Latter Part of the Sixteenth Century to the Middle of the Nineteenth Century*, 1973, 27–33.

[59] Quoted ibid. 302; cf. 294–300.

[60] Quoted by Emmet Kennedy, *A Philosophe in the Age of Revolution: Destutt de Tracy and the Origins of 'Ideology'*, Philadelphia, 1978, 37; cf. 29–36.

[61] Ibid. 72; cf. 32–3, 46–7.

[62] Cabanis, *Oeuvres Philosophiques*, II, 1956 edn, 474 quoted in Thomas E. Kaiser, *The Idéologues: From Enlightenment to Positivism*, Harvard, Ph.D. dissertation, University of Michigan microfilm, 270.

However, this would-be republican elite was quickly relegated to the impotent Senate and Tribunate which Sieyès was allowed to fill with those such as Constant and Daunou, Cabanis, and Tracy, as well as the economist Jean-Baptiste Say. Ideology acquired, thanks to ideophobe Bonaparte, a pejorative sense, as he railed—once the first signs of opposition manifested themselves—against 'windbags and *Idéologues*. They have always fought the existing authority.... Always distrusting authority, even when it was in their own hands, they always refused to give it the indispensable force needed to resist revolutions....'[63] When they ventured into politics their scientific speculations were in practice subversive of his statecraft, so he purged most of them in 1802. In 1801 he had already replaced 'ideological' subjects, that is moral and political sciences, in the new *lycées* with military training. Church influence at all levels of education was increased. Napoleon reorganized the Institute, abolishing the class of Moral and Political Sciences, Tracy being transferred to 'Language and French Literature'! On 20 May 1801, slavery had been restored in French colonies, after having been abolished by the Girondins with *Idéologue* support, so the illiberal tide was flowing powerfully. Scientists collaborated with the authoritarian regime enthusiastically and with servility and when Napoleon became hereditary emperor Lagrange declared: 'All things considered, I prefer hereditary power because it is considered the simplest way of resolving problems'.[64] In his commentary on Montesquieu's *Esprit des Lois*, begun in 1806 (but only published in French in 1819 after Napoleon's fall, although it appeared anonymously in translation in America thanks to Jefferson), Tracy dismissively observed that a hereditary monarch was as absurd as a hereditary coachman or cook![65]

Tracy was one of the senators who set up a Provisional Government in April 1814, headed by Talleyrand, to secure the deposition of Napoleon. He helped draft a Constitution which—against his opposition—provided for hereditary monarchy, predicting that 'what ruined the Stuarts will ruin the Bourbons'.[66] He did not rally to Napoleon during the 100 Days—unlike Constant—so he kept his place in the Chamber of Peers, where increasing blindness made him inactive. He presciently wrote to his son (Lafayette's son-in-law) in 1829: 'I consider it certain that we are headed towards a second revolution ... we experienced counterrevolution from 1799 to 1814 and then the revolution recommenced and has continued ... I feel that I am at the end of 1791'.[67] Old, almost blind, he was nevertheless present at the 1830 barricades, disenchanted with the conservative turn of the July Monarchy. Tracy ceased attending the Chamber of Peers in 1831. Influenced by Smith and especially Say in his belief that 'Industrial entrepreneurs are really the

---

[63] Ibid. 475, quoted in Kaiser, 224–5.

[64] Quoted in Kennedy, 89; cf. 80–1, 189. Daunou, main author of the 1795 Constitution, was asked to write a constitution overnight by Bonaparte, after the Brumaire coup. See F. R. Picavet, *Les Idéologues*, 1891, 402.

[65] Kennedy, 103; cf. 104–5.

[66] Quoted in Brian W. Head, *Ideology and Social Science: Destutt de Tracy and French Liberalism*, 178.

[67] Letter in May 1814 to Maine de Biran, quoted in Kennedy, 222; cf. 219–20.

heart of the body politic and their capital is its blood', his attack on idle *rentiers* and his rejection of metaphysics link him with Saint-Simon and August Comte, while Marx adopted the concept of ideology as an inverted representation of bourgeois reality.[68] Guizot, Tracy's successor in the Academy, delivered a disparaging criticism of his ideological theory of knowledge, promoting instead the quietist eclecticism of Cousin and regarding both the *Idéologues* and liberals like Constant as subversive once he was in power.

A REPUBLICAN POLITICAL ECONOMY

Much closer to the *Idéologues* than to the political liberals was Jean-Baptiste Say, the most widely read economist between Adam Smith's 1776 *Wealth of Nations* and J. S. Mill's 1848 *Principles of Political Economy*. A combination of Smith's intellectual influence and the failure of the Directory to achieve a state reorganization of economy and society led Say to separate economic from political analysis. As he wrote at the start of his 1803 *Treatise on Political Economy*: 'Until Smith's work, Politics, which ought to be understood as the science of government, was confused with Political Economy, which shows how wealth is created, distributed and consumed. . . . Wealth is independent of the nature of government. Under all forms of government a state can prosper if it is well administered. We have seen absolute monarchs enrich their country and popular councils ruin theirs. The structure of public administration itself only indirectly and accidentally influences the formation of wealth, which is almost entirely the work of individuals.'[69] His disillusion with political action is reflected in his 1800 utopian essay *Olbie*: 'The greatest revolutions are not political revolutions' because all that happens is that 'Authority changes hands but the nation stays the same'.[70] Political and constitutional reform had to be preceded by behavioural and cultural change linked with the development of an industrial society.

Although, like Constant and the *Idéologues*, Say had initially favoured the Sieyès-Napoleon 1799 overthrow of the Directory, like them he quickly came to regret it. Having rebuffed an attempt by Napoleon to co-opt him, Say was excluded from the Tribunate in 1804 and spent the next ten years as a cotton textile manufacturer. After the Restoration he remained pessimistic, expecting the Bourbons to accentuate clericalism and a reactionary attitude towards industrial development. Like his fellow Protestant Constant, he lectured at the *Athenée Royale* until 1819, an attentive Saint-Simon being encouraged to launch his journal *L'Industrie* in which he not only accepted Say's separation of politics from economics but characteristically exaggerated it into a fully fledged economic determinism.

---

[68] Quoted in Kennedy, 317.   [69] Ibid. 199; cf. 200–4, 337–9, 343–5.

[70] Jean-Baptiste Say, *Traité d'économie politique*, I, i–ii as quoted in Richard Whatmore, *Republicanism and the French Revolution: An Intellectual History of Jean-Baptiste Say's Political Economy*, 2000, 148–9.

Although remembered among economists primarily for his theory of markets, Say was searching for an empirically based generalization to underpin his republican politics and thought he had found it in Bentham's utility principle which made a virtue of the pursuit of self-interest. So, while he separated economics from politics, it was the better to achieve a social scientific basis for the emerging industrial society in which the entrepreneur, not the mercantilist, interventionist state, would play a pivotal role as the prototypical productive citizen displacing the idle aristocrat. For Say, as for Tracy and Saint-Simon, 'the entrepreneur is the central figure in the economy. He is the universal mediator. He mediates between the landlord and the capitalist, between the scientist and the manual labourer, between the various suppliers of productive services among one another, and between producers and consumers.'[71]

While it was the *Idéologue* Pierre-Louis Roederer who in 1795 launched the industrialist analysis that challenged the interests of the landowners and *rentiers*, it was his friends Say and Tracy, after Roederer's co-option by Napoleon, that developed it. The propaganda campaign, started in 1817, on behalf of industrialism and industrialists popularized by Saint-Simon, was conducted both by *L'Industrie* and *Le Censeur Européen* whose staff were in the same building. The editors of the latter were the economists Charles Comte (who first met Say in 1814 and later became his son-in-law) and Charles Dunoyer. Augustin Thierry, who as his secretary until 1817 had steered Saint-Simon first in the direction of political and then economic liberalism, influenced the editors of *Le Censeur Européen* before joining them, running the journal when they were imprisoned for infringing the press laws.[72] (We shall return to Thierry when considering the *Doctrinaires*.) The woollen textile entrepreneur and *Doctrinaire* deputy Ternaux, who used his influence to secure Say's appointment to the first chair of industrial economics, was persuaded by Saint-Simon (for whom he was a major source of financial support) to get Rouget de Lisle to compose the *Chant des Industriels* that was performed in 1821 in the hope that it would attain the popularity of his *Marseillaise*.

THE INDUSTRIAL AND POSITIVIST COUNTER-REVOLUTION: SAINT-SIMON AND COMTE

In commenting on Saint-Simon's ambitious 1817 programme, *Le Censeur Européen* cautioned that 'The men who control industry have no ideas or they

---

[71] Quoted in Kaiser, 222 from *Olbie*, 97–8.

[72] Ephraim Harpaz, 'Le "Censeur Européen": Histoire d'un journal Industrialiste', in *Revue d'Histoire Economique et Social*, Part I xxxvii, 1959, 188–91, 194–8, 203–6, 213 and Elie Halévy *L'Ere des Tyrannies*, 1938, 31–40. Dunoyer, 'Notice historique sur l'industrialisme' in *Revue Encyclopédique*, February 1829 was republished in his *Oeuvres*, III, 1870, 178–84. See also Michael James, 'Pierre-Louis Roederer, Jean-Baptiste Say and the concept of *industrie*' in *History of Political Economy*, IX/4, 1997, 457–65.

have erroneous ones. The men who have ideas own no industries.'[73] Saint-Simon saw it as his pre-eminent task to make the industrialists and bankers conscious of their historic role as the new aristocracy, once the idle nobility had been eliminated.[74] The associated priority was to substitute the scientists (to whom he later added the artists) for the ignorant clergy as the spiritual unifiers of a conflict-ridden society. With the *Ecole Polytechnique* as a model, Saint-Simon and Comte looked to a new class of engineers, combining spiritual and practical capacities, to organize a harmonious society in which industrialists and proletarians would be productive partners; the minimal administration of matters of common interest by the large Paris banks replacing government commands, thereby bringing an end to the revolutionary process.[75] The Revolution's negative functions had been to clear the ground of debris of the theological and metaphysical past, to make way for the positive order based upon applied science, which would lead to unending progress. What constituted 'science' for Saint-Simon, however, changed our time, with Cabanis's physiology displacing Newtonian gravitation, to be in turn replaced by Bichat's functionally specialized organicist physiology and then social engineers, with final despair culminating in the pseudo-religion of New Christianity. (It was more new than Christian.) It was left to Comte to devise the methodical, hierarchical system that was more plausible than the successive prophetic aspirations of Saint-Simon, fulfilling the urge to achieve a unified, universal scientism in the service of technocracy.

After fighting in the American War of Independence, Saint-Simon took advantage of the Revolution to speculate in nationalized land, amassing a fortune which he subsequently squandered in acquiring a multitude of scraps of speculative scientific knowledge. Arrested during the Terror, he emerged as an opponent of aristocratic and ecclesiastical privilege. From 1798 he was seeking the comprehensive intellectual foundation for rule by a meritocratic elite but relying upon uninstructed intuition and a smattering of science through talking to scientists and superficial reading of Condorcet and the *Idéologues*. Lodged opposite the *Ecole Polytechnique*, the dilettante Saint-Simon uncritically sampled its intellectual fare, leading to an extravagant conception of the potentialities of science and technology in the management of society. The results were simplistic, grandiose, crackpot schemes...until his acquisition of two secretaries, Augustin Thierry from 1814 and then Auguste Comte from 1817. They imparted for the ten years from 1814–24 a serious structure to his disjointed speculations, using his macro-political ideas as a springboard for their own influential personal contributions to French post-revolutionary thinking. Similarly, after Saint-Simon's death in 1825, it was the Saint-Simonians that developed what came to be Saint-Simonism.[76] They

[73] *Le Censeur Européen*, III, 1817, 206, quoted in Frank E. Manuel, *The New World of Henri Saint-Simon*, 1956, 197; cf. 325, 330–1.

[74] Manuel, 250–1.

[75] Friedrich Hayek, *The Counter-Revolution of Science: Studies on the Abuse of Reason*, 1955, 133, 137.

[76] Henri Gouhier, *La Jeunesse d'Auguste Comte et la formation du positivisme*, II, 1933–41, 1964, 2nd edn, 344–7.

subsequently went off in different directions, some developing socialist interpretations, while others spearheaded French financial and industrial capitalism. This is to oversimplify the significance of Saint-Simon's successive enthusiasms because as a precursor, 'his writings again and again gave an uncanny impression of one who had a hurried preview of the next hundred years history and, excited, confused and only half understanding, tried to set down disjointed fragments of what he had seen'.[77]

From Saint-Simon's 1802 'Religion of Newton', via his 'New Christianity' of 1825, through to Comte's Religion of Humanity, these dogmatic champions of scientism sought to synthesize the analytically separate sciences, resulting in what T. H. Huxley called 'Catholicism minus Christianity'.[78] Most explicitly in his 1826 'Considerations on the Spiritual Power', Comte described Maistre's ultra-authoritarian *Du Pape* as offering 'the most systematic, profound and precise exposition' of the priority of doctrinal communion over the economists' purported harmony of interests. Only by recourse to religion could the conflicts between industrialists and workers, farmers and industrialists and all with bankers, be overcome and by extension regulate economic and political international relations to prevent warfare.[79] It was this view that led Saint-Simon and Comte to abandon the liberal focus upon wealth creation in favour of a secularized version of Catholicism which gave priority to preserving order.

In 1816, Saint-Simon launched his periodical *L'Industrie*, adding in 1817 its slogan: 'Everything by industry; everything for it'. Alongside the liberal weekly *Le Censeur*, (later *Le Censeur Européen*) for which his secretary wrote from 1817 when he left to become the liberal banker-politician Laffitte's parliamentary secretary and speech writer, Augustin Thierry gave the first expression to 'industrialist' ideas in an article asserting: 'A Nation is nothing but a large scale industrial enterprise',[80] defined by common interests, not by language or national frontiers. *L'Industrie* was financially backed by France's leading industrialist, textile manufacturer Ternaux and the richest banker and Governor of the Bank of France Laffitte. The latter was the epitome of the self-made new bourgeois meritocracy, whose hold over the government derived from its reliance upon bankers to fund its debts. Laffitte had lent very large sums to Louis XVIII and the future Louis-Philippe in 1815 and saved the Stock Exchange from financial collapse in 1818 but the post-Revolution 1830 crisis led to his bankruptcy owing to bad debts and his political career as Louis-Philippe's Prime Minister in 1830-1 was short-lived. Saint-Simon deserved support as a propagandist on behalf of banker power; he wanted business to take over the state rather than the state to take over industry.[81] However, in *L'Industrie*'s successor *Le Politique*, Saint-Simon—perhaps under

[77] E. H. Carr, *Studies in Revolution*, 1950, 2.

[78] Quoted by Hayek, 184, 184; cf. Manuel, 122–4 and Chapter 9 on 'The Religion of Science'.

[79] *The Crisis of Industrial Civilisation: The Early Essays of August Comte* (ed.), Ronald Fletcher, 1974, 239–44, cf. 219–20, 229–34.

[80] Quoted in Gouhier, III, 137, cf. 144–64.

[81] Ibid. III Supplement, 123–9; cf. 11–20, 228 and Maurice Lévy-Leboyer, *Les Banques Européenes et l'Industrialisation Internationale dans la première moitié du XIXe siècle*, 1964, 483.

Comte's influence—began to detach himself from his liberal allies, declaring that the problem was how 'to end the liberal enterprise with which we began in 1789', although he remained committed to industrialism, with councils of industrialists attached to each ministry.[82] His prestige in liberal circles increased following his 1820 trial and acquittal for exacerbating class conflict in a notorious article on the productive bees and parasitic drones but in his last years Saint-Simon in disillusion turned his attention to improving the lot of the proletarians.

By 1820, a youthful Auguste Comte was emerging from Saint-Simon's intellectual spell and expounding his own dogmatically determinist ideas, although without the later colossal 'self-conceit' that meant that 'As his thoughts grew more extravagant, his self-confidence grew more outrageous', culminating in 'Comte's frenzy for regulating'.[83] However, even in his 1820 'Brief Appraisal of Modern History', he argued that military leaders would be replaced by industrial leaders who would direct not command, the people not being subjects but partners under the guidance of 'capacity and capital'. 'All the participants were in fact co-workers and partners, from the humblest workman to the richest manufacturer and the ablest engineer.'[84] The engineers would provide the applied link between the scientists and the industrialists who would organize society. By 1824 Comte had parted company from Saint-Simon, going on to develop the positivist sociological system that was to exercise great influence in the latter half of the nineteenth century.

His leading disciple and popularizer was Emile Littré, who—after they broke over Comte's support for the 1851 *coup d'état* by Louis-Napoleon—combined a liberal conservatism with a Comtian scientism stripped of its authoritarian religiosity. His secularist and elitist republicanism, which influenced the Opportunist leaders of the 1870s and 1880s, Gambetta and especially Ferry, revived the legacy of Condorcet and the *Idéologues*. He argued that only through accepting the Republic as a determinist historical fact would France emerge from the infernal dualism of revolution and counter-revolution by reconciling order and progress. He prescribed a period of prudent 'republican apprenticeship' based upon a pragmatic synthesis of science and democracy under elitist guidance.[85] This meant adopting a parliamentary form of government that was anathema to Comte but which the Third Republic consolidated, following the Restoration and July Monarchy partial accommodation of this British model to French political culture. Anti-parliamentary, 'Catholicism without Christianity' perpetuation of Comtian positivism was championed by Charles Maurras even before the Dreyfus

----

[82] Quoted in Gouhier, III, 206; cf. 232 and Manuel, 288–93, 327.

[83] J. S. Mill, *Auguste Comte and Positivism*, 1865, 130, 196; cf. 181. More generally see Keith M. Baker, 'Closing the French Revolution: Saint-Simon and Comte' in François Furet and Mona Ozouf (eds), *The Transformation of Political Cultures 1789–1848*, 1989, 324–37.

[84] *The Crisis of Industrial Civilization*, 14; cf. 102–3.

[85] E. Littré, *De l'établissement de la Troisième République*, 1880, 195–7; cf. 466–73, 485 ff. See also Littré, *Conservation Révolution Positivisme*, 1852, 1879, 2nd edn; Claude Nicolet, *Idée Républicaine en France, 1792–1924*, 1982, 200–17; Sudhir Hazareesingh, *Intellectual Founders of the Republic: Five Studies in Nineteenth Century French Political Thought*, 2001, Chapter 1.

Affair led him to join with Henri Vaugeois in the creation of *L'Action Française* in 1899, to which we return later.[86]

THE DOCTRINAIRES: THIERRY, ROYER-COLLARD, AND GUIZOT

Whereas Comte had sought to subordinate politics to a determinist philosophy of history as a post-revolutionary way of restoring order, the bevy of 1820s historians who followed in the wake of Madame de Staël, confronted by the Restoration's attempt to turn the clock back, argued that the Revolution was the culmination of a long historical process characterized by the rise of the bourgeoisie in association with the emergence of the modern state. Unlike Comte, the liberal historians did not reject the Revolution as a wholly critical episode that had to be replaced by a positive reconstruction of French society. Nor were they content with a purely institutional solution, France having fruitlessly experimented with eight constitutions between 1789 and 1814 to stabilize the polity.

Not will nor artifice, but social determinism and rationality served by pragmatic men of government experience were necessary to move from the destructive liberalism of the 1820s, associated with the resistance to a reversion towards absolute monarchy by the insurrectionary *Charbonnerie*, to the authoritarian and repressive conservatism of most of the July Monarchy, the reign of the Absolute Bourgeoisie. A strong and assertive upper-middle class-dominated government control was necessary rather than the non-interventionist, limited government advocated by the political liberalism of Constant and the entrepreneurial industrialism of Say. The democratic impetus, having destroyed divine right and hereditary privilege, had to be curbed because universal suffrage would lead to the domination of quality by quantity. Reason having displaced God, it was only those who had the rational capacity to govern who should exercise power as an exclusive political class. Reason as self-evident truth would be matched by merit as the self-evident, legitimate superiority of the capable.

The early 1820s were marked by 'a prolonged, far ranging debate between the liberals and ultra-royalists, which dominated the Chamber of Deputies, the press and pamphleteering for several years'.[87] This intellectual upsurge was precipitated by the ultra-royalist attempt to reverse not merely the compromise Constitutional Charter but all the social and political changes that had both prepared the way for the Revolution and were developed and consolidated by the republican changes of the 1790s as well as by Napoleon. The counter-revolution that was attempted between the 1820 assassination of the heir to the throne and the overthrow of

---

[86] See Sutton, Chapter 1 and Charles Maurras, 'Auguste Comte' in *Minerva*, 1902, 17–204, reprinted in *L'Avenir de l'Intelligence*, 1905.

[87] Larry Siedentop, *Tocqueville*, 1994, 22. The whole of Chapter 2 on 'The Great Debate of the 1820s' is an excellent discussion of the intellectual role of the *Doctrinaires*, despite a tendency to read back into his predecessors some of Tocqueville's democratic presuppostions. He unaccountably ignores the role of Thierry.

Charles X in 1830 prompted an ideological polarization that led the *Doctrinaires* to propose a historical defence of the irreversible transformation which rendered the ultra-royalist exertions futile. Lacking the roots of the Bourbon Restoration, the protagonists of its successor regime sought to trump its Legitimist claims by an appeal to a deep-seated social analysis of French history. The leading exponents of this militant doctrine were the historian-conspirator Augustin Thierry, the philosopher-parliamentarian Royer-Collard and the historian-statesman Guizot. Together, they formed 'a bourgeois advance guard committed to providing its party and class with a clearer consciousness of itself, its origins and its mission.'[88] In conjunction with other historians born in the 1790s—Mignet, Thiers, and Michelet—they placed the Revolution in perspective as a centuries old class struggle between the bourgeoisie and the aristocracy capable of inspiring confident resistance to counter-revolution.

As we saw earlier, Augustin Thierry, when initially associated with Saint-Simon, produced a book *On the Reorganisation of European Society* in 1814 in which they proposed the union of Britain and France on the British model of parliamentary government as the nucleus of a European federation. From Saint-Simon, Thierry probably learnt to take a broad view of historical dynamics, emphasizing the role of what he called in the first of his *Letters on the History of France* (published as articles in 1820 and as a book in 1827) 'the most numerous and most neglected part of the nation.'[89] His history-from-below emphasis upon impersonal society rather than great statesmen led him to regard French history from the twelfth century as the slow advance of self-governing communes, based on the urban bourgeoisie, that culminated in 1789, and with the seventeenth-century English Revolution anticipating the later French triumph of the industrious over the idle. Thierry defined his standpoint by reaction against Montlosier's massive 1814, ultra-reactionary and ultra-aristocratic *De la monarchie française*, emphasizing the secular conflict between the conquered revolutionary Third Estate and the counter-revolutionary First Estate. The nation, personalized in the King, with the help of the Church had created a transcendent absolutism but the decapitation of the King led to history being henceforth identified with, and personalized in, the French nation. In place of monarchical history as a succession of kingly reigns that was a 'continuous lie', Thierry substituted a history of the French people, the Third Estate being descended from the slaves in ancient Gaul.[90]

Because the Charter was being subverted from 1821 by the Villèle government that replaced the consensual royalism of Decazes, Thierry took part in what a fellow conspirator Pierre Leroux called the 'great conspiracy of adolescent

[88] Marcel Gauchet, 'Les *Lettres sur l'Histoire de France* d'Augustin Thierry' in *Les lieux de mémoire*, II/1, 250.

[89] Ibid. 270; cf. 266–9. See also Hayward, *After the French Revolution*, 79.

[90] Quoted by Lionel Gossman, 'Augustin Thierry and Liberal Historiography', Chapter 4 in *Between History and Literature*, 1990, 89; cf. 88–100. See also Gauchet, 264–9, 285–8, 293–4, Gouhier, III, 72–9 and R. N. Smithson, *Augustin Thierry: Social and Political Consciousness in the Evolution of a Historical Method*, 1972, 15–20 and Chapters 3–5 passim.

liberalism', the *Charbonnerie*.[91] Faced with restrictive press, security and electoral laws directed against a disloyal Liberal opposition, a generation of reformists, revolutionaries and post-1830 reactionaries plotted the violent overthrow of the Bourbons. Future Saint-Simonions Bazard, Buchez, and Leroux as well as republicans like the figurehead Lafayette and Carrel (supported by disgruntled half-pay soldiers) were joined among others by Victor Cousin, the eclectic official philosopher of the July Monarchy. Cousin, one of twelve Sorbonne Professors dismissed in 1820, had described the Declaration of the Rights of Man effusively as 'the holiest, the most beneficent document to have appeared on earth since the Gospel.'[92] (Ironically, the conspiracy also contributed the first three ministers of justice, a minister of the interior, a prefect of police, and distinguished prosecuting attorneys to the security of the July Monarchy.[93]) The execution of the 'Four Sergeants of La Rochelle' in 1822 inspired Auguste Blanqui to become a professional revolutionary to avenge their martyrdom which he witnessed at the age of 17.

Thierry, whose increasing blindness may have accentuated his post-1830 conservative liberalism, never repudiated his previous extralegal activities. The initial failure of direct revolutionary action bore practical historiographical fruit in his writings and those of Guizot. After all, 'the conspiratorial and pre-insurrectionary outburst of 1820–2, this prodigious movement of cultural secession by civil society, when study, ideas, books become the chosen instrument of political action ... in an indirect battle that does not have power as its target but the foundations of its legitimacy,'[94] bequeathed through Thierry a class conflict conception of history explicitly acknowledged by Karl Marx,[95] who was to apply it to the French struggles of 1848 and 1871.

Royer-Collard and Guizot were more typical *Doctrinaires*, studiously shunning conspiracy in the 1820s. 'No one could have predicted that the Royer-Collard of 1814 would, in 1830, have acquiesced in the overthrow of legitimism; yet the sequence of events drove him to an opposition upon which he entered with grave disquiet.'[96] A Girondin lawyer who served in the Directory parliament, he became a convert to constitutional monarchy and secret adviser to the future Louis XVIII in 1797. He taught the history of philosophy under Napoleon as a Sorbonne

[91] Alan B. Spitzer, *Old Hatreds and Young Hopes: The French Carbonari Against the Bourbon Restoration*, 1971, 275 quoting P. Leroux, *La Grève de Samarez*, I, 1863, 363. More generally, see G. de Bertier de Sauvigny, *La Restauration*, 3rd edn, 1974, 180–3.

[92] Quoted in Peter McPhee, *A Social History of France, 1780–1880*, 1992, 114 cf. 115.

[93] Spitzer, 9; cf. 2–8, 17–39, 219–24, 230–64. On the military conspiracy, see ibid. 119–28, 170–5, 254–7.

[94] Gauchet, 293; cf. 283–5.

[95] Gossmann, 102, quoting a letter of Marx to Engels of 27 July 1854. While acknowledging a pre-1789 split between the bourgeoisie and proletariat, Thierry argued that thereafter national unity had been achieved and class conflict analysis was no longer relevant (ibid. 104–5). He was upset by the 1848 Revolution because it showed that the July Monarchy had not ended the process of class conflict (ibid. 113–4).

[96] Harold J. Laski, 'The Political Theory of Royer-Collard', Chapter 4, in *Authority in the Modern State*, 1919, 1927 edn, 316.

colleague of Guizot who lectured on history; in the early Restoration they both worked as senior administrative officials. However, the reactionary turn of the Restoration led him to deploy his formidable skill as a parliamentary orator to defend the Charter which 'was for him a touchstone by which the rightness of all action might be tested. He looked upon it as the crystallised experience of the whole of French history.'[97]

While he denied that the Chamber of Deputies represented the nation, which would logically lead to a republic with a single chamber elected by universal suffrage, his conception of power shared between King, Peers, and Commons would avoid the dangerous concentration of power in either King or parliament. Freedom of the press and religion, protected by judicial independence, would ensure the capacity to resist oppression but once these constitutional safeguards were threatened by Charles X, Royer-Collard went into vociferous opposition. He presented the hostile Chamber of Deputies address to the King that provoked the parliamentary dissolution which foreshadowed the 1830 Revolution. When the July Monarchy and his former ally Guizot as Interior Minister interfered with the press and centralized power, reducing citizens to *administrés*, he again went into opposition, as did his pre-eminent disciple Tocqueville, who we shall encounter again.

Like Royer-Collard, Guizot vainly hoped that the Constitutional Charter would provide the basis for an enduring compromise between the Old Regime and the Revolution. Dismissed from the Council of State in 1820 and between 1822 and 1828 from his professorship, he took to journalism and historical writing in which the English experience, culminating in the 1688 Revolution, became his model, as we saw in the Introduction. He generalized and developed Thierry's historical analysis of French experience but as against him and Royer-Collard, Guizot praised the process of centralization as part of the orderly subordination of society to the state and put this to stern illiberal practice in the 1830s and 1840s when he was in power.

Guizot refused to refer to the sovereignty of the people, only to the 'sovereignty of number'. He rejected democracy, which Royer-Collard described in 1831 as 'naturally violent, warlike, spendthrift'.[98] As Guizot declared in a 1837 parliamentary speech (to whose circulation in 30,0000 copies over 200 deputies subscribed) 'as in 1830, I want, I seek, I bend all my efforts to secure the political preponderance of the middle classes in France, the final and complete organisation of the great victory that the middle classes have won over privilege and absolute power from 1789 to 1830.'[99] With 1830 as the end of history, he was disappointed that the middle class, out of unenlightened self-interest, was more inclined to follow his exhortation to enrich themselves than to organize themselves into an effective counter-revolutionary political party. However, his biographer Douglas Johnson

---

[97] Harold J. Laski, ch. 4 in *Authority in the Modern State*, 1919, 1927 edn, 290; cf. 309.

[98] Speech quoted in Pierre Manent (ed.), *Les Libéraux*, II, 1986, 131.

[99] Speech quoted in Pierre Rosanvallon, *Le Moment Guizot*, 1985, 179; cf. 181–5. On the 'sovereignty of number', ibid. 85 note.

has argued that 'The French middle classes eventually proved their resilience. The history of the nineteenth century as a whole shows that the French Revolution did produce social stability and the French possessive classes were never deprived of their economic and social power.'[100]

As we shall see, these rival yet overlapping interpretations of the Revolution were taken up subsequently by many historians: secular and anti-Jacobin republicans like Michelet and Quinet; socialist republicans like the former Saint-Simonians Buchez and Leroux, as well as pro-Jacobins like Louis Blanc, to be followed by the more ecumenical Jean Jaurès; liberal conservatives, pre-eminently Tocqueville and, much later by Raymond Aron; conservative nationalists like Fustel de Coulanges and Taine. Literature contributed many insightful social witnesses, notably Chateaubriand, Stendhal, Balzac, Flaubert, and Zola, who pilloried the social aspirations of the bourgeoisie whose advent had been acclaimed by the *Doctrinaires*, while the poets Hugo, Lamartine and even Baudelaire took an active part in politics, influenced by their views of the First Republic and participating directly in the Second Republic. Painters' visual portrayals of the successive revolutions as well as their more indirectly political representations of French society, particularly Delacroix, Daumier, and Courbet, will be discussed. The musical dimension, most spectacularly exemplified by the *Marseillaise* and the *Internationale*, has already been touched upon but will unfortunately be neglected. Together with their successors, they will all contribute to filling out the role of committed intellectuals in shaping post-revolutionary French political culture in the nineteenth and twentieth centuries by the influential way they presented controversial issues both to unify and perpetuate divisions in French society. Such is the changing context within which protagonists of the contending components of a composite national identity endeavoured to become leaders of opinion by making sense of France's turbulent experience.

[100] Douglas Johnson, *Guizot: Aspects of French History, 1797–1874*, 1975, 85.

3

Tensions and Trajectories: The Constituents of French Exceptionalism

The paradoxical claim to be both exceptional and exemplary has many aspects so that the aspirations and interpretations associated with the French Revolutions from 1789 to the 1870s have aroused numerous and diverse attempts at emulation within and outside France. Successive disintegrations of state sovereignty during the 1789–99 decade were repeated in 1814 and 1815, 1830, 1848, 1851, 1870, and 1871. This turbulence suggested that sections of the ruled had successfully called the bluff of their rulers, assisted by squabbles among the latter. Under the pressure of socio-economic and cultural-ideological changes, state power had either to be reorganized or transferred to new rulers to contain and manage these changes. The ruled did not collectively become rulers and democracy became in practice a counter-revolutionary set of procedures to achieve this purpose more effectively. Although it took less perspicacious liberal conservatives longer to recognize this fact, Tocqueville sought, in his *Democracy in America*, to teach his countrymen its relevance for them.

Liberals had been worried by the process through which revolutions to achieve freedom had quickly degenerated into despotisms. We shall see how they attempted to disassociate democracy as a bottom-up legitimization of political authority from the top-down exercise of governmental power, reserving the latter to those fit to take decisions. While this required devising an electoral process and institutional arrangements to transmute the principle of popular sovereignty into the practice of elite rule, it was also necessary to emasculate the revolutionary potential to disrupt the substitution of the one for the other. To prevent comprehensive and unexpected upheaval, it was necessary to undertake timely piecemeal reform. As Charles Dunoyer put it in 1815: 'There is only one way for peoples to prevent major revolutions; it is to adapt themselves to a state of wisely regulated permanent revolutions.'[1]

The Restoration exhortation to transmute revolution into evolution failed in France because the attempt by the 1820s reactionary Right to reverse the achievements of the 1789 Revolution irretrievably polarized the political class and public opinion. The minimalist reforms of the July Monarchy did not offer a dynamic conservatism capable of preventing destabilization by making substantial, albeit

---

[1] 'Des révolutions en général', *Le Censeur*, III, 1815, 43 quoted in Gouhier, III, 17, who also quotes a similar reference to 'permanent revolution' by Charles Comte in *Le Censeur*, IV, 1815, 42.

incremental, changes. As Proudhon pointed out in his 'Toast to the Revolution' at a Socialist banquet in October 1848, the social revolution was the fourth in a continuous movement. After the Christian religious revolution of fraternal equality before God had come the Renaissance and Reformation assertion of the freedom of the mind, followed by the late eighteenth-century proclamation of equality before the law and the constitutional limitation of power. '... The starting point of each revolution is an earlier revolution ... so it follows that revolution is permanent and that strictly speaking there are not several revolutions but only one and the same perpetual revolution'.[2]

Because revolution was a continuing process, it could not be ended as so many had vainly sought to do, an end which, in 1848, the institution of universal suffrage was believed by many to have finally achieved. For Proudhon, permanent revolution meant a libertarian rejection of state socialism in favour of decentralized and autonomous associations and communes, recalling the ephemeral French 'municipal revolution' of 1789, not the 'class dictatorship of the proletariat' which Marx advocated in his 1850 *Class Struggles in France*.[3] Louis-Napoleon's 1851 overthrow of the Second Republic brought these contrasting hopes of a continuing revolutionary impetus to an abrupt halt. The 1871 Paris Commune marked a last attempt to achieve a Proudhonian permanent revolutionary regime, while the 1917 Bolshevik Revolution—nominally installing a Marxist proletarian dictatorship—rapidly subordinated the Russian proletariat to a one-party dictatorship of professional, permanent 'revolutionaries', such as we shall see Blanqui had sought to achieve from 1830 to 1871.

RIVAL FRENCH CONCEPTIONS OF POLITICAL REPRESENTATION

Elections were not a novelty in revolutionary France but their pre-democratic character needs to be stressed. They were a feature of both early elective French monarchy and of the choice of bishops but the former was a formality and the latter was unanimous and by acclamation. The key feature that separated such 'elections' from their democratic counterpart is that the latter represents individuals treated as equals, not communities. Differences in ability are deliberately ignored and the social bond is based on this presupposed equality. This revolutionary rejection of the corporatist privileges of the past meant that the hierarchy of inequalities as the basis of social integration was replaced by an extension of equal civil rights into equal political rights.[4] Universal suffrage did not become a controversial issue until the July Monarchy and democratic

---

[2] *Le Peuple*, 17 October 1848 and Proudhon, *Idées Révolutionnaires*, 1849, 255.
[3] Karl Marx and Frederick Engels, *Selected Works*, I, 1962, 22–3; cf. 110, 117.
[4] Pierre Rosanvallon, *Le sacre du citoyen: Histoire du suffrage universel en France*, folio edn, 1992, 12–17; cf. 347–41.

inclusiveness was only extended to most adult males after the 1848 Revolution, even though Extreme Left Parisian Republicans favoured postponing elections until the mass of peasant provincial voters were deemed fit to vote free from clerical and aristocratic constraints. Before then, the vote was restricted in various ways during the Directory, Restoration, and July Monarchy, or manipulated to give the illusion of mass support under Napoleon.

The pre-eminent French theorist of representation was the abbé Sieyès. He derived his inspiration from the division of labour expounded by Adam Smith, extending it into political specialization as a more refined, rational, and efficient basis for taking decisions than crude, direct democratic government. While citizenship should be inclusive, to provide a legitimate basis for government, professionalization was indispensable through the election of representatives more capable than the generality of citizens to act in the general interest. Furthermore, to govern a large but unified state, a Rousseauist direct democracy was neither possible nor desirable. As he put it, in his immensely influential *What Is the Third Estate?*, it was necessary to establish '*government by proxy*... it is no longer the *real* common will which is in operation, but a *representative* common will.'[5] In a society devoted to prosperity though work and not conquest through war, idle aristocrats need not be represented either in a National Assembly or a Second Chamber. 'Do not ask what is the appropriate place for a privileged class in the social order. It is like deciding on the appropriate place in the body of a sick man for a malignant tumour that torments him and drains his strength. It must be *neutralised*.'[6] In words that bluntly anticipate the Restoration arguments of Thierry and Guizot, Sieyès declared that the Third Estate which had hitherto been 'nothing' should be recognized as 'everything'.[7]

Sieyès' achievement was to separate the legitimizing 'national will' as the source of all legality from deliberation and decision that were to be confided to the assembly of its representatives, who were not mandated by the voters but free to exercise their enlightened judgement.[8] Thus power was ceded by a system of indirect election to the few who were the real electors. Expected for the first time to vote as individuals and not simply endorse collectively their traditional leaders, the mass of Frenchmen were unprepared for their new role. The result in the 1789–99 decade was that 'There were no electoral campaigns, nor avowed candidates, no platforms', so it is not surprising that 'elections in the revolutionary period remained a mixture of irrationality and manipulation' by organized minorities.[9] Because representation was not intended to reconcile opposed interests but to reflect 'the unified interest of a unified nation... the organisation of

---

[5] Abbé Sieyès, *What Is the Third Estate?*, 1789, 1964 edn, 122. Italics are in the original. See the excellent Chapter 7 in Murray Forsyth, 'The means of the new state: the representative system.' in *Reason and Revolution: The Political Thought of the Abbé Sieyès*, 1987 Also see William H. Sewell, Jr., *A Rhetoric of Bourgeois Revolution: The Abbé Sieyès and 'What Is the Third Estate?'*, 1994.

[6] Sieyès, 174; cf. 110–12, 161–5, 173. Italics in the original.   [7] Ibid. 51; cf. 58.

[8] Ibid. 126; cf. 124–8, 148–9.

[9] Patrice Gueniffey, 'Revolutional Democracy and the Elections' in R. Waldinger et al., *The French Revolution and the Meaning of Citizenship*, 1993, 92, 96.

competition within each district would weaken the legal fiction that each deputy represented the entire nation. . . .'[10] So political parties, such as existed in Britain, were anathema, equated with factions hostile to the general interest. The daunting unpredictability of the political advent of a mass of citizens was to be controlled by an educated and leisured elite minority at the cost of alienating the majority by reducing their participation to symbolic legitimation of the actions of their betters.

In a rapid response to Lafayette's draft July 1789 Declaration of Rights, Sieyès proposed his Exposition of the Rights of Man and Citizen in which he made his momentous distinction between passive civil and active political rights. 'All the inhabitants of a country ought to enjoy within it the *passive* rights of a citizen; all have a right to the protection of their persons, of their property, of their liberty, etc., but all do not have a right to take an active part in the formation of the public powers; not all are *active* citizens'.[11] Passive citizens included women, children, foreigners and those who did not pay direct taxes and consequently were not 'true shareholders of the great social enterprise'.[12] There was also to be a residence qualification in the constituency for at least a year. Domestic servants were also excluded as lacking independence. More stringent qualifications were required of those seeking the right to be eligible, reducing those electable to a fraction of even the active citizens. While conceding that excluding half the population by denying women the vote was yielding to prejudice, Sieyès asked rhetorically of the 'lower classes . . . who are citizens by right, but never in fact . . . who would dare to consider it wrong that they should be excluded . . . from the exercise of political rights?'[13]

Electable citizens were reduced in practice to property owners, even though it was pointed out, this would have excluded the likes of Rousseau! It was claimed the eligible were not meant simply to be taxpayers, but landowners on the ground that the only producers of wealth were those who owned its source: land, a Physiocrat view not shared by British economists. Thus in 1791, only 1 per cent of the 4.5 million active citizens (out of a population of 26 million) were proprietorial citizens entitled to be elected, while in 1795 of the 6 million active citizens, only some 30,000 were eligible to belong to the political class.[14] The Restoration was in 1817 to institute direct election of Deputies and to increase somewhat the propertied who were eligible, while drastically restricting the numbers entitled to vote: 72,000 in 1814 and 241,000 in 1845. Necker in 1802 described indirect election as a fictional filtration that prevented the people from identifying with their government, while the liberal Charles de Rémusat was retrospectively even more forthright about the Restoration electoral system. 'Indirect election, invented to give the masses participation in political elections, was an artifice aimed at rendering illusory something approximating to universal suffrage, simultaneously democratic and mendacious, that might mask the domination of minorities and

---

[10] Patrice Gueniffey in Waldinger et al., 1993, 99.

[11] Forsyth, quoting Sieyès' *Exposition*, 117–18.   [12] Ibid. 118.

[13] Ibid. 162; cf. 154 quoting Sieyès, *Observations sur le rapport du comité de Constitution concernant la nouvelle organisation de la France*, October 1789.

[14] Rosanvallon, *Le sacre du citoyen*, 254; cf. 57–68, 108–10, 317–19.

dupe the multitude by popular appearances.'[15] Thus was a mockery made of the equality proclaimed in 1789, as principle and practice spectacularly parted company and privilege was restored. Camille Desmoulins could bitterly claim that 'The real active citizens were those who took the Bastille' but this did not prevent their de facto exclusion from the political process. So, they were to return to revolutionary action in 1830 and 1848, as the 'real country' reminded the 'legal country' of its existence in no uncertain terms.

In any case, most of the newly enfranchised did not bother to exercise their right to vote. 'In Paris in 1791 only 17,200 out of 81,200 electors voted and only 200 out of 946 delegates. . . . In 1792 only 700,000 of the national electorate of 7,000,000 voted. In the referenda on the successive constitutions between one-third and five-sixths of the electorate abstained'.[16] Furthermore, 'Under the Republic corruption, fraud, intimidation and violence were practiced by the candidates of all factions and their supporters; even when the law provided for secret voting electors were often made to vote publicly in the presence of a mob whipped up by the faction that was strongest locally; electors with the wrong views were prevented from voting. . . . In each assembly one of the first tasks of the triumphant factions was to unseat some members of the minority on the grounds that they had violated the electoral laws or were unworthy to represent the nation . . . Both the Republic and the Empire made a mockery of the electoral process'.[17] Napoleon offered the French manhood suffrage minus liberal democracy. During the early years of the Restoration, even with a very restricted franchise, a low turnout persisted; one-third did not vote in 1817. However, in the bitter conflicts at the end of the 1820s, abstention declined sharply, particularly because of liberal campaigns, falling below 20 per cent. Under the July Monarchy turnout was regularly between 75 and 85 per cent. With manhood suffrage, the percentage turnout 'during the Second Republic ranged from 65 to 84, under the Second Empire from 63 to 82 and under the Third Republic from 69 to 85'.[18]

The year after the establishment of the National Guard in 1789 to maintain internal order, a decree confined membership to active citizens but radicalization of the Revolution and war in 1792 led to membership being extended to passive citizens. However, the total number was reduced to a third, those judged able to bear the cost of service—the rest being placed in reserve—with the intention of confining the election of National Guard officers to those who could be relied upon to defend private property. The irony of a much larger electorate for the National Guard than for the Chamber of Deputies made it less reliable as a defender of the political regime and by splitting the middle classes, contributed to the 1840s agitation to extend the suffrage that preceded the 1848 Revolution.[19] The lower middle class was not content to protest without sharing in the rights of the upper middle class.

---

[15] Ibid. 276, quoting from an unpublished part of Rémusat's *Mémoires de ma vie*. See also, ibid. 243–7, 271–83.

[16] Peter Campbell, *French Electoral Systems and Elections since 1789*, 1958, 57.   [17] Ibid.

[18] P. McPhee, *A Social History of France*, 265; cf. Rosanvallon, *Le sacre du citoyen*, 284–6.

[19] Rosanvallon, 118–24, 357–63.

The Revolution had instituted election not only of National Guard officers but of the judiciary and clergy as well. At the 1790 municipal elections, nearly a million men were elected in what has been called a 'vast exercise in grass roots democracy', 'providing a training-ground for a new rural elite', even though the newly enfranchised voters generally remained deferential.[20] The right to vote in local elections under the July Monarchy was much wider than for parliament, so that apprenticeship for post-1848 manhood suffrage was taking place. In addition to the 4 million who voted in National Guard officer elections, 3 million voted in local elections as provided by a 1831 Law prepared by Guizot. This ensured a political socialization of about half the adult male population in the countryside and about 15 per cent in the large towns. The turnout at these local elections was 56 per cent in 1834 and 55 per cent in 1837.[21] However, we should bear in mind that mayors were appointed by the King and they played their part in the corrupt and manipulative practices of the administration which we discuss later. Furthermore, although the July Monarchy doubled the size of the parliamentary franchise, it was still a landlord-dominated electorate, while as we shall see, many of those elected were placemen. So, France's democratic apprenticeship was limited until spectacularly accelerated in 1848.

DISMANTLING FEUDALISM AND POLITICAL DESTABILIZATION

The conspicuous fiscal, financial, and political bankruptcy of the feudal and monarchical Old Regime at the end of the 1780s led to recall of the representatives of the French people who had not met since the early seventeenth century. Mass pressure requiring precipitate action resulted from a disastrous 1788 harvest, with riots prompted by hunger. Because inaction was no longer an option, 'the only way to prevent the people from taking the law into their own hands was for others to do so',[22] although neither the activist elements in the people or their representatives could forget that a recurrence of direct action was always possible. Rural insurrections were succeeded by Parisian popular militancy which destroyed the inert old order without replacing it with a stable new order. The King's dismissal of Necker, his only non-aristocratic minister, on 11 July 1789 provoked a popular uprising in Paris and successful assault on the Bastille, bolstering the authority of the National Assembly and leading to a Paris city government susceptible to popular pressure. The represented made clear that popular protest by food riot had become a potentially permanent part of the political process for intervention by the Parisian 'crowd'.[23] The years after 1789 were to show that the hopes aroused by peasant resentment against feudal privileges such as seigneurial extraction of

[20] Peter M. Jones, *The Peasantry in the French Revolution*, 1988, 176, 266; cf. 178.

[21] Rosanvallon, *Le sacre du citoyen*, 284–6.

[22] William Doyle, *Origins of the French Revolution*, 1980, 167.

[23] Ibid. 191. See also the classic study by George Rudé, *The Crowd in the French Revolution*, 1959 and Georges Lefebvre, *The Great Fear of 1789: Rural Panic in Revolutionary France*, 1932, 1973 Eng. edn.

harvest dues and exemption from the tax (the *taille*) to which all others were subject, were to spread to all the governed. The inability to satisfy the impatient expectations of rapid relief from centuries of oppression was to ensure a prolonged period of political instability.

The legislative task of dismantling 'the prerogatives, perquisites and privileges attaching to lordship' was complex.[24] The apparent abolition at a stroke of the seigneurial regime of feudal dues on 11 August 1789 was quickly followed by proposed indemnification that left the peasantry feeling cheated. Their grievances were not the prime concern of the lawyer-dominated Assembly, intent on protecting private property rights. 'The indirect system of elections ensured that, virtually to a man, the deputies of the Third Estate were lawyers, officials and men of property'.[25] Rural unrest and seigneurial resistance were only overcome by ending redemption payments by decree in August 1792 in a context of political and military crisis that necessitated honouring 'the rhetorical promises of August 1789'.[26] An incidental consequence of the voting preconditions for active citizenship meant that 'the residential qualification prevented absentee landowners from interfering in the political life of the village'.[27] The 'municipal revolution' in the countryside produced unremunerated mayors and rural councils that were usually 'a makeshift assembly of semi-literate peasants deliberating in the open air', with extensive responsibilities but without the resources effectively to fulfil them.[28] The peasants having often refused in 1789–90 to pay taxes, the new local authorities were required to apportion and collect direct taxes, carry out public works, and maintain local order through control of their National Guard. Calling taxes 'contributions' instead of 'impositions' did not prevent attempts to evade the land tax that replaced the *taille* and/or the new version of the old poll tax.[29]

However, although the violent resistance of peasants in the south and west of France was partly tax inspired, the Civil Constitution of the clergy (discussed later) and resistance to conscription were more important. Counter-revolutionary resistance in the southern Massif Central to the 7 March 1793 decree requiring equal division of inheritance between offsprings was prompted by this area's Roman Law tradition of primogeniture but was quickly repressed. The fanatically Catholic and royalist uprising elsewhere was provoked by conscription and a dechristianization campaign. It led to an ideological-cum-class war between peasants and rural artisans, led by the local nobility, versus 'patriots' who were generally urban middle-class professionals holding local government office, who had often purchased confiscated 'national property'. The Vendée uprising was brutally repressed at the command of Jacobin deputies such as had been sent on a mission to impose the will of Paris on 'federalist' provinces. This campaign of Terror led to an anti-Jacobin White Terror in 1795–7, with the murder of 'patriots' and constitutional priests, encouraged by the return of aristocratic émigrés and refractory priests.[30]

As 6 per cent of the army had deserted in the first half of 1793, all single males of 18–25 years of age were conscripted in what was called an emergency

---

[24] Jones, 87; cf. 81–5.   [25] McPhee, 34.   [26] Jones, 92; cf. 103–23.   [27] Ibid. 174.
[28] Ibid. 179; cf. 168–73.   [29] Ibid. 181–91.   [30] Ibid. 207–47.

'mass levy' or 'nation in arms'. This not only disorganized the labour force but produced a large number of outlaws. However, conscription became permanent as France remained at war. Resistance continued to be a problem, so that 'By 1798, many parts of the West, the Massif Central and the Pyrenees were virtually ungovernable.'[31] In the revolutionary and Napoleonic years of 1792–1815, it is estimated that over a million Frenchmen died as a result of civil or foreign wars. Despite the elite privilege of paying for replacements, resistance to the call-up was a major problem under Napoleon and in the first decade of the nineteenth century there were large numbers of anti-conscription disturbances, increasing after the invasion of Spain. By 1810, there were some 160,000 deserters. Growing conscription pressures after massive military losses in Russia and increased taxation meant that in 1810–14, 'many regions of France again became virtually ungovernable.'[32] The Restoration initially abandoned unpopular conscription but revived it in 1818 in a more modest form, with especially generous arrangements for replacements, which in the 1820s averaged 15 per cent.[33]

Another major source of economic and political instability was the adoption of a paper currency, *assignats*, at the instance of another Genevan banker Etienne Clavière—the great rival and successor of Necker as Finance Minister—in the early 1790s. The intention was to increase national credit, backed by the confiscated 'national property', and pay off the national debt.[34] (Arrested in June 1793 with other Girondin ministers, Clavière committed suicide in December 1793.) However, as a result of an inflationary overissue of the paper currency, the *assignat* fell to 36 per cent of its face value in June 1793 and to 22 per cent by August. It was replaced by a metallic currency in 1798 but full stabilization awaited Napoleon's creation of the Bank of France in 1800 and the return to the franc.

Compared to Britain's industrial and social revolutions of the late eighteenth and early nineteenth centuries, political and cultural revolutions left French society relatively undisturbed. While 'about 20 per cent of land changed hands as a result of the expropriation of the church and émigrés' and peasant holdings increased from about one-third to two-fifths, 'nobles remained at the pinnacle of landholding', still the major source of wealth and prestige in an inegalitarian society.[35] Equality of rights before the law was a mockery for the mass of the rural and urban destitute, swelled periodically at times of economic crisis by unemployed farm labourers and workers. Greater uniformity in taxation, administrative centralization and internal free trade coexisted with cultural and linguistic diversity and a mainly peasant and artisan economy well into the nineteenth century.

Although feudalism had been abolished, the old nobles and new notables continued for a while to remain pre-eminent economically, socially, and politically.

---

[31] McPhee, 77; cf. 58.   [32] Ibid. 90; cf. 88–93.

[33] On conscription, see Chapter 13 of Isser Woloch, *The New Regime: Transformations of the French Civic Order, 1789–1820s*, 1994.

[34] Whatmore, 86–93; cf. 10–11, 78–81.   [35] McPhee, 102, 105; cf. 93–100.

The Napoleonic nobility was dominated by army officers (59 per cent) and higher civil servants—a functional aristocracy. However, the monarchical and imperial aristocracy could not turn the clock back because it had never been a political class like its English counterpart. It was 'too numerous, too poor, too exclusively military, too lacking in political rights, and insufficiently keen to acquire them'.[36] It took the 1830 Revolution to install the propertied bourgeoisie as the dominant political class, a result which 1789 had failed to achieve. It could then pursue the liberal programme of 'ending the revolution by political liberty and founding political liberty through representative government'.[37] However, the social base of the new regime was too narrow: it was not only anti-aristocratic and anti-working classes but excluded the lower middles classes and too many members of the able but insufficiently wealthy liberal professions.

CLASS CONFLICTS

We have seen that the rise of the middle classes to power in the name of the whole French people had been aggressively asserted by Sieyès in 1789 and was retrospectively traced from the middle ages by Thierry. The enemy had been the aristocracy (which had escaped the taxation imposed on the rest of the French without representation) but the egalitarian implications of revolutionary principles were rapidly applied to class conflict between the bourgeoisie and the mass of the poor by Gracchus Babeuf in the 1796 Conspiracy of the Equals. Against the exponents of a vulgar Marxism, François Furet pointed out that 'in our history, class consciousness is a legacy of the Revolution before being a product of industrial development...the new post-revolutionary power declares itself to be a middle class government. So it believes itself entitled to exclude from the fruits of victory those who had achieved it...thereby designating as the new enemy of the revolution the class that had confiscated for its benefit the people's insurrection: the bourgeoisie. The idea of class thus becomes the epicentre of revolutionary culture, with the bourgeoisie henceforth succeeding the nobility as its scapegoat'.[38] While the Restoration saw an attempt to reassert aristocratic control of government, the army, the administration, the judiciary, and the episcopate, the July Monarchy marked the resurgence of the upper middle class as the new ruling class, seeking to exclude the victors of 1830 from a share of the spoils, as their predecessors had done after 1789. How far is this popular analysis of a *juste milieu* Orleanist rule by the bourgeoisie supported by the evidence?

As early as 1937, Sherman Kent's study of *Electoral Procedure under Louis-Philippe* demonstrated that dominance by landowners of both the electorate and the elected was characteristic not only of the Bourbon Restoration but of the July

---

[36] Charles de Rémusat, *Politique libérale ou fragments pour server à la défense de la Révolution française*, 1860, 439. On the Napoleonic nobility see Christophe Charle, *Les hauts fonctionnaires en France au XIXe siècle*, 1980, 56.

[37] Rémusat, 275.   [38] François Furet, *La Révolution, 1770–1880*, 1988, 341.

Monarchy as well. He began by enunciating the general proposition: 'Electoral legislation tends to differ from all others in one striking way. It is the one kind of lawmaking which most perfectly represents the selfishness of its creators'.[39] In the revolutionary Chamber of Deputies elected prior to the overthrow of Charles X in 1830, 'the great landed estates which furnished more than half the voters, furnished as well only a trifle less than half the eligibles'.[40] Although the 1831 Electoral Law doubled the number entitled to vote, it was only 2.4 per cent of adult males, rising to 2.8 per cent in 1846. 'Between 82 and 90 per cent of the voters derived their livelihoods from one of the many forms of agriculture; between 3 and 5 per cent belonged to the new class of industrial entrepreneurs; between 5 and 9 per cent came from the commercial group and between 2 and 4 per cent from the liberal professions'.[41] While 25,000 were qualified to be elected, the nucleus of the political class consisted of about 4,000 candidates and some 1,000 who were successful. Deputies were unpaid so mainly the leisured rich and the holders of government sinecures could afford to stand. . . . 'A landlord, particularly were he an absentee landlord, had more time at his disposal than the businessman.'[42] Despite the Doctrinaire rhetoric of government by the capable, citizenship was confined not to the meritocratic few but to the plutocratic and proprietorial few who had little need to nurse their constituencies, ignoring them between elections.

In 1960 the economist and economic historian Jean Lhomme forcefully argued that although the landed aristocracy had been politically dominant until 1830, thereafter 'History offers few examples of as rapid and complete a disappearance.'[43] While 77 ultra-royalists excluded themselves from the Chamber of Deputies by refusing to take the oath of allegiance to Louis-Philippe and the hereditary Second Chamber was replaced by a constitutional aristocracy based on life peerages in 1831, it was not so much in parliament that the upper middle class acquired power. Lhomme concedes that between 30 and 43 per cent of members of parliament were government officials: magistrates, army officers, and administrative officials. He dwells on the fact that the first two Prime Ministers, Laffitte and Casimir-Périer were bankers. Laffitte (who we have already encountered) was a Regent of the Bank of France from 1809 to 1831, until he became bankrupt, Governor of the Bank from 1814 to 1820 and Prime Minister from 1830 to 1831. (Laffitte was significantly made Governor of the Bank of France a week after convincing Marshal Marmont to capitulate to the Allies on 31 March 1814.) Through their control of the Bank of France (the Preface to whose constitution was written by Napoleon, who took shares in it) the *grande bourgeois* dynasties, as well as securing favourable legislation, notably in relation to railway development (of particular interest to the Rothschild Bank), asserted their control over

---

[39] Sherman Kent, *Electoral Procedure under Louis-Philippe*, 1937, 7; cf. 8.

[40] Ibid. 15; cf. 10–12.   [41] Ibid. 54; cf. 25, 50–3.

[42] Ibid. 58; cf. 25, 56. See also Christophe Charle, *A Social History of France in the Nineteenth Century*, 1991, 1994 edn, 18–19. For an interesting comparison, see Adolphe Jollivet, *Examen du système électoral anglais depuis l'acte de réforme, comparé au système electoral français*, 1835.

[43] Lhomme, 37; cf. 36–42, 71.

France.[44] The money-minded Louis-Philippe and Guizot, his Prime Minister from 1840 to 1848 (who was not himself corrupt but employed corruption systematically to secure political support), ensured that the interests of the *grande bourgeoisie* were accorded exclusive attention. For Lhomme, what united the upper middle business class was much more important than what divided it.

A much more circumspect view was provided by André-Jean Tudesq in his detailed and authoritative 1964 study of *Les Grands Notables en France* in the 1840s. He pointed out the divisions not only between the landed aristocracy and the *grande bourgeoisie* but also between Catholics and Protestants, with the July Monarchy being a 'golden age of French Protestantism', as led by Guizot they took up positions abandoned by the Catholic ultras.[45] Like Lhomme, Tudesq emphasized the importance of public officials in parliament, with the resulting fusion of politics and administration to compensate for the lack of public support. However, he dwelt on the continuing power—especially in the provinces—of those who controlled the major means of production: land. While there was some overlap between a Catholic Legitimist aristocracy on the one hand and a Protestant Orleanist *grande bourgeoisie* on the other, there was also some absorption of the former by the latter, although much more slowly than in Britain with its less caste-like class system.[46] Tudesq's findings were used by Alfred Cobban to argue that 'The businessmen's regime disappears from sight beneath the weight of evidence' and that the predominant socio-economic group consisted of an aristocracy of landowners and rentiers who often combined proprietorship with financial, industrial and especially official positions.[47] The Higonnets, in their study of the French Chamber of Deputies in 1846–8, demonstrated the continuing numerical importance of the nobility: 'More than one-third of the deputies were aristocrats', so 'it remains obvious that the July Monarchy was not a "bourgeois monarchy"'.[48] As aristocrats usually had an army and landowning background, 'the great majority of deputies had no connection with the business world'[49]—a view we have already encountered in Kent's earlier study.

The policy issue of free trade versus protectionism also offers an insight into the class character of the July Monarchy government. Free trade was a minority view, championed by shipping interests (especially Bordeaux), by ex-Saint-Simonian journalists, notably Michel Chevalier (who did not achieve success until the Cobden-Chevalier Treaty of 1860) and economists such as Frédéric Bastiat, who was General Secretary of the Free Trade Association. Protectionism was

[44] Ibid. 42–123. See on Bank of France, J. S. G. Wilson, *French Banking Structure and Credit Policy*, 1957, 271–3. See also Jean Bouvier, *Les Rothschild*, 1967, especially Chapter 6.

[45] André-Jean Tudesq, *Les Grands Notables en France (1840–1848): Etude historique d'une psychologie sociale*, I, 1964, 124; cf. 121–5.

[46] Ibid. 113, 127, 335–9, 365–6.

[47] Alfred Cobban, 'The "Middle Class" in France, 1815–48' in *French Historical Studies*, V/1, Spring 1967, 49; cf. 44–51.

[48] Patrick and Trevor Higonnet, 'Class, corruption and politics in the French Chamber of Deputies, 1846–48' in *French Historical Studies*, V/2, Autumn 1967, 207; cf. 209.

[49] Ibid. 208; cf. 209.

predominant, being supported by the landowners, the majority of Chambers of Commerce and most industrialists, notably the ironmasters who feared British competition. Anti-British chauvinism was reflected in most of the press.[50] Compared to Britain, French liberalism was more timid in economic policy as well as being more exclusive in its politics. It also reflected the divisions of interest and ideology within the middle classes.

While the peasants and middle classes were the main beneficiaries of the severance of private property rights from Old Regime privileges through the abolition of seigneuries, venal offices, and tithes, the skilled artisans suffered from the Revolution's abolition of guilds and corporations. A Lockean labour theory of property that became the new orthodoxy made no sense to the labouring propertyless who observed those who possessed property without engaging in labour and alone enjoyed the privilege of full citizenship rights. The artisans clung tenaciously but in vain to their official status as exercising a lifelong '*profession* which denoted a solemn public declaration or vow.'[51] While their journeymen brotherhoods had generally been illegal, through the *compagnonnage* they formed a federated mutual aid community across occupations, as itinerant artisans—especially hatmakers, shoemakers, saddlers and cutlers, and later building workers—moved in search of employment. In 1791, in quick succession, the National Assembly abolished corporations (the d'Allard Law) and then the right to form 'coalitions' of workers and employers (the Le Chapelier Law) 'passed enthusiastically after only the most cursory discussion'.[52] The skilled artisans of Paris formed the hardcore of the *sans-culottes* who radicalized the Revolution in a desperate attempt to seek political expression of 'the moral collectivism of the pre-revolutionary corporate mentality'.[53] Although frustrated in the 1790s, this revolutionary response of those who came to see themselves as a proletariat was to revive in the early 1830s after disillusion with another recourse to political solutions to their predicament.

Living standards and working conditions deteriorated in the first half of the nineteenth century, reducing incomes to little more than was necessary to meet the most basic needs of food and rent. Excluded from a political process capable of regulating market forces and subject to repression of their efforts to outlaw machinery, raise wages, and shorten the working day, the skilled artisans turned to mutual aid and provident societies, as well as clinging to the backward-looking, illegal *compagnonnage* associations for support. More constructively, instead of resisting new machinery, an ephemeral 1830 newspaper—*L'Artisan, journal de la classe ouvrière*—advocated producer cooperatives run by associated workers, 'The most numerous and the most useful class of society', identified with the whole people.[54] This practical expression of freedom of association took up ideas

---

[50] Tudesq, II, 615–27.

[51] William H. Sewell, J., *Work and Revolution in France: The Language of Labor from the Old Regime to 1848*, 1980, 35; cf. 119–38, 145.

[52] Ibid. 89; cf. 86–91, 100. The Le Chapelier Law described the former 'masters' as 'entrepreneurs' (ibid. 140).

[53] Ibid. 113; cf. 105–12.   [54] Ibid. 198; cf. 195–202.

propagated notably by the ex-Saint-Simonian Philippe Buchez, who recognized that such producer cooperatives were only appropriate in trades where skilled labour rather than large amounts of capital was required. Elsewhere, Buchez advocated the government regulation of wage rates.[55] Strikes were often associated with attempts to establish worker cooperatives and led to Lyon silk weaver Mutualist risings of 1831 and 1834. The latter was provoked by the March 1834 Law restricting the right of association. Like similar protests in Paris it was repressed with the utmost brutality.[56] The July Monarchy was to pay with its life for this repression in 1848.

The years immediately before and after the 1830 Revolution were times of falling wages and rising prices, a context in which the 'proletariat' emerges as a distinct social class. In particular, the 1831 insurrection of the Lyon silk workers was recognized as heralding this phenomenon, not merely by socialists but by a perceptive right-wing journalist like Saint-Marc Girardin who witnessed it in person. 'The Lyon sedition has revealed a serious secret, that of the internal struggle in society between the class that owns and that which does not own. Our commercial and industrial society has its festering infection like all other societies: that ulcer is the workers... Each manufacturer lives in his factory like planters in the colonies among their slaves, one against a hundred.... The Barbarians that threaten society are not in Caucasia or the Tartar steppes: they are in our suburbs and in our manufacturing towns.'[57] In 1801 the neologism 'proletarian' had already been defined as the propertyless and accompanied with the comment: 'Woe to a nation divided into two necessarily hostile classes, that of the property owners and the proletarians'.[58] Whereas the 1789 Revolution had asserted the individual's civil and political rights, dissatisfaction with the 1830 Revolution led to the demand for collective, social, and economic rights for the underprivileged. Socialism challenged liberalism as the ideology of the working classes seeking to have an equal share in French society by reducing or even ending their de facto exclusion.

In the 1840s, the associationist ideas that were formulated in the early 1830s attracted favourable attention from Socialists like Louis Blanc, Etienne Cabet, and Pierre-Joseph Proudhon, who were briefly to come into their own in 1848. In particular, Louis Blanc's succinct *Organisation du Travail* (which first appeared as articles in 1839 and in successive and expanded editions in 1840, 1841, 1847, 1848, and 1850) captured the public imagination. He blamed private property and unregulated competition for the degrading physical and moral conditions in which poverty stricken workers were living, as depicted in detail by Villermé in his survey of working class life. Whereas Villermé portrayed 'a brutalized proletariat, wallowing in filth, stupefied by alcohol' as the reason for the perpetuation of

---

[55] Ibid. 202–4.   [56] Ibid. 208–17.

[57] Saint-Marc Girardin, article in the *Journal des débats* of 8 December 1831, quoted by Rosanvallon, *Le sacre du citoyen*, 334 from *Souvenirs et réflexions d'un journaliste*, 2nd edn, 1873, 144–7.

[58] Louis Sebastien Mercier, *Néologie ou Vocabulaire des mots nouveaux*, II, 1801, 380, quoted by Rosanvallon, *Le sacre du citoyen*, 337.

poverty, the socialists sought a way out of this deplorable situation.[59] They argued that because, working in small-scale workshops, they could exercise control over production, it was natural that skilled workers should believe themselves able to replace the capitalist wage system through their combined efforts.[60] Whereas Blanc emphasized the need for state intervention to help the worker cooperatives, the Buchez-influenced worker journal *L'Atelier* stressed worker self-help. This heroic option was unlikely to be successful except among the printers (Proudhon was one) who enjoyed strong craft cohesion and high wages and educational standards.[61]

Blanc's campaign for a 'right to work' came to the forefront of 1848 revolutionary policy when his attempt to secure state support for 'social workshops' was distorted into the establishment of relief work for the unemployed in 'national workshops'. The counter-revolutionary closure of these workshops in June 1848 precipitated four days of outright class warfare, when the Paris workers fought for what they regarded as their rights. Fifteen thousand insurgents were killed and twelve thousand imprisoned or deported by a reactionary Republic and Louis Blanc would soon be compelled to go into a twenty-year exile in England. The failure of both state support and insurrection inspired Proudhon to set up a People's Bank to provide credit for producer associations but his arrest for slandering President Louis-Napoleon led him to wind it up for fear that it would be run in a collectivist manner by others. Few worker associations survived the post-December 1851 *coup d'état* and they only revived in the 1860s with official tolerance. This new mood was reflected in the workers 'Manifesto of the Sixty' whose efforts were celebrated and theorized by Proudhon in his posthumously published *De la Capacité Politique des Classes Ouvrières* that inspired the French founding members of the First International. However, the hope that producer associations of workers 'could accumulate capital, outcompete and eventually absorb private enterprise peacefully and gradually' only briefly survived the bloodletting of the 1871 Commune.[62] Thereafter, the divided minority of organized workers turned either to the Marxists led by Jule Guesde or to the anarcho-syndicalists of the *Bourses du Travail* and C.G.T. who radicalized Proudhon's legacy through placing their hopes in the general strike.

ROMAN CATHOLICISM AND GALLIC SECULARISM

The struggles to declericalize France from the latter half of the eighteenth to the late twentieth century, when the strife ceased because neither side any longer had the strength and fervour to pursue it, made nonsense of any attempt clearly to separate spiritual from temporal life. Until the earlier twentieth century, particularly

---

[59] Sewell, 230; cf. 223–34.

[60] Bernard H. Moss, *The Origins of the French Labor Movement, 1830–1914: The Socialism of Skilled Workers*, 1976, 19; cf. 14–18.

[61] Ibid. 40; cf. 34–8.   [62] Ibid. 69; cf. 43–71.

in the countryside, religion was of pervasive importance in the daily lives of most people, with ostentatious public rituals predominating over private belief. Popular religion in France has been described as 'an unholy mixture of paganism, peasant magic and half-baked Christian doctrine...Catholicism provided the framework wherein rural households and, by extension, whole villages and parishes could affirm their collective identity'.[63] Into a context in which the laity was reduced to a passive subordination to clerics, the radical reform of July 1790, creating the Civil Constitution of the clergy, was bound to prompt reservations and outright hostility by this drastic intrusion into traditional practices. The lay election of bishops and priests, who became salaried state officials, amounted to an urban and deist-inspired cultural revolution. Many ecclesiastical posts were abolished, dioceses redistricted to coincide with the new *départements* and small urban parishes eliminated. The peasants prevented this last process in rural parishes, refusing 'the closure of their churches and burial grounds under any circumstances' as tantamount to destruction of their cultural identity.[64]

The sweeping reform of religious institutions was imposed in all parishes by the swearing of an oath of allegiance to the nation, constitution and king in early 1791. Despite papal condemnation in May 1791 (antagonized by the loss of his territories in southern France), a few bishops and about half the parish priests took the oath. The Roman Catholic Church was split by the imposition of state control, with a constitutional priesthood, ranging from about 10 per cent in Brittany to over 80 per cent in the Alps and the Var. 'The expulsion of non-juring clergymen from their livings and the closure of chapels' meant that 'In many parts of the West....there was no one to say Mass on Sundays, no one to baptise the new-born, no one to bury the dead.'[65] By 1796, there were only about 15,000 priests for 38,000 parishes.[66] The Republican attempt to reduce Sunday to a day like any other ended on 1 January 1806 when Napoleon restored the Gregorian calendar, having reconciled himself with a subordinate Church by the 1801 Concordat, with bishops becoming episcopal prefects.

Despite the effects of the Bourbon Restoration, the nobility and Church never fully recovered their pre-revolutionary social authority and cultural dominance in most of France. Nevertheless, the priests sought to instil docility in their flock, asserting the priority of reverent piety over the critical intellect and equating sexuality with sin. As part of a tendency to turn their back on a hostile modern world, 'The French clergy was absolutely obsessed with the idea that irreligion and immorality were being propagated essentially by the written word'.[67] So great was the fear of literacy that 'The mission preachers of the Restoration organised sessions of book burning, and bishops' Easter letters later in the century regularly called for such purification by fire'.[68] The impoverished secular primary school-teacher, obliged to teach the catechism to his pupils, was subordinate to the parish priest and the mayor. His *revanche* only came from the 1880s, when the Third

---

[63] Jones, 193.   [64] Ibid. 204; cf. 197–203.   [65] Ibid. 201; cf. 197–9, 215–16.
[66] McPhee, 74–5; cf. 43–5.   [67] Gibson, 97; cf. 94–8.   [68] Ibid. 233.

Republic improved both his status and his income, enabling the rivalry for local influence to be conducted on more equal terms.

The close alliance between throne and altar, especially in the reign of Charles X (1824–30) meant that one could not attack the one without attacking the other. However, the Church–State alliance was challenged from the Right by two incendiary polemicists, the maverick Count de Montlosier and the theocratic priest Lamennais. The former rejected ecclesiastical domination on behalf of the feudal nobility, while the latter attacked the Gallican bishops in the name of Papal authority of which Maistre had earlier been the protagonist. Lamennais succeeded in splitting the clergy, Montlosier the aristocracy and royalists, to the delight of liberals like Stendhal. The resounding anticlerical articles and pamphlets of the Gallican Montlosier focused particularly on the Jesuits (who were in the 1840s to attract the hostility of Michelet and Quinet) for interfering excessively in the political and private lives of Frenchmen and women.[69] The subject of many conspiracy theories, the Jesuit Order, which had been dissolved in France in 1764 and by the Pope generally in 1773, was re-established in Rome in 1814 and in France in 1815. It quickly increased in numbers from 91 in 1815, to 456 in 1828, 1,209 in 1850, and 2,658 in 1870. The Jesuits, themselves generally recruited from elite social backgrounds, shaped the Catholic elite, notably the army officers of St Cyr and the *Ecole Polytechnique*, also exploiting the 1850 Falloux Law to become active in secondary education. Officially dissolved in 1880 by the anticlerical republicans, the Jesuits crept back into France, numbering 3,868 when they were expelled again in 1901.[70]

VARIETIES OF PARLIAMENTARY AND ELECTORAL RIGHT AND LEFT

The fiction with a future that partisan political differences, whether ideological or organizational, can be reduced to the duality of Right and Left, originated with the Revolution. Foreshadowed by the split on 23 August 1789, over article 10 of the Declaration of the Rights of Man and the Citizen concerning religious freedom, it was reinforced by the constitutional debate over the issue of royal power between 28 August and 11 September 1789. The Assembly discussed whether the king should have a veto over the decisions of the people's representatives. As was the practice in the Estates General, the nobility sat on the left side of the chamber, the commoners or Third Estate in the centre and the clergy on the right side. When it came to the vote on the issue, the commoners voted against, the clergy in favour, with the nobility split. To simplify counting votes (which was done by members

[69] Robert Casanova, *Montlosier et le Parti Prêtre*, 1970, an extended introductory essay and selection of texts.

[70] Gibson, 109–15; cf. Stanley Mellon, *The Political Uses of History: A Study of Historians in the French Restoration*, 1958, 153–88.

standing and sitting) the pro-veto nobility crossed the floor to sit on the right with the clergy, while the commoners and the anti-veto nobles grouped themselves on the left. This seating arrangement was not perpetuated in the early revolutionary Assemblies: the 'Left' representatives sat on the upper seats and were known as the 'Mountain', while the 'Right' sat on the lower seats and were known as the 'Marsh'.[71]

For a while, use of the Left/Right terminology was rare, as the Extreme Left increasingly pushed the Left towards the Right in the successive Constituent, Legislative, and Convention assemblies. Thermidor 1794 restored the early duality but a deliberate attempt was made to counteract it, out of a concern to avoid polarization, with a suggestion that seating should be decided monthly by drawing lots![72] According to the Rousseauist conception that prevailed, only an individual or the general will could be represented and so political parties were regarded as illegitimate. The perpetuation of a semantic polarization had to contend with the actual complexity of the views of the representatives that were not susceptible to dualist simplicity. In vain pursuit of a unanimist general will, an anarchy of shifting factions created a turbulent attempt at government by assembly that handed power successively to a Committee of Public Safety, a Directory, a First Consul and finally an Emperor. The French paradoxical combination was 'a traditionally strong politicisation with chronically weak political organisations'.[73]

After the 1789 false start, the Restoration ironically seemed to confirm the Left/Right duality thanks to the ultra-royalists who sat on the Right of the Chamber of Deputies. As Gauchet puts it, 'it was the worst enemies of the Revolution who would complete its work'.[74] However, the 'Constitutional', moderate Centre-Right, who supported both the Charter and the dynasty, were victorious in the 1816 elections over the ultra-Right who supported the dynasty but not the Charter. After the 1817 elections, the liberal Left created a parliamentary group of 'Independents' who supported the Charter but not the dynasty. So the centrist governments were opposed on both Right and Left, which was also to be an important feature of the politics of the Third and Fourth Republics. Well might Louis XVIII deplore the lack of a British-style confrontation between a government and an opposition party, writing in 1820 to his former Prime Minister Decazes (who had leaned on the Left-Centre in 1818 and on the Right-Centre in 1819): 'Oh Tories, oh Whigs, where are you?'[75]

So, despite the revolutionary and counter-revolutionary dichotomy, the Parliament represented a spectrum of shades of opinion. Extremist theorizing was contrasted with moderate parliamentary practice: 'It is not in relation to ideologues that one acts but in relation to them that one defines oneself.'[76] The fluidity of parliamentary groupings during the July Monarchy meant that the transfer of the

---

[71] This paragraph is largely borrowed from Jack Hayward, *After the French Revolution: Six Critics of Democracy and Nationalism.* 1991, 39–40.

[72] Marcel Gauchet 'La Droite et la Gauche' in *Les lieux de Mémoire*, III/1, 401; cf. 395–402.

[73] Ibid. 442; cf. 416–19.   [74] Ibid. 402.   [75] Ibid. 403.   [76] Ibid. 435.

parliamentary partisan terminology to the mass public came about slowly. It was only with manhood suffrage in 1848 that the Red versus White electoral bipolarization between 'social democrats' and reactionaries briefly simplified political controversy before the catch-all Bonapartism of the Second Empire again negated parliamentary and electoral dualism.

ADMINISTRATIVE CENTRALIZATION AND THE SLOW RISE OF MERITOCRACY

While the Revolution standardized and Napoleon reinforced the system of nation-building state centralization, Tocqueville pioneered the demonstration that democracy and despotism constructed the integrated administration of France from monarchical survivals of the Old Regime. Writing in the Second Empire, he claimed that, a century earlier, the Physiocrat-formulated central monopoly of rationality led logically to comprehensive centralization. This standpoint only found its full expression in Sieyès's demand that France be made into a '*single whole*, uniformly submitted in all its parts to the same legislation and a common administration' to make 'all the peoples that divide it into a single nation'.[77] The liberal Tocqueville, reflecting on his country's post-revolutionary experience, disconsolately concluded that 'it was this desire of combing freedom with the servile state that led during the last sixty years to so many abortive essays of a free regime followed by disastrous revolutions.'[78]

The Old Regime was characterized by three administrative features which were adapted to the requirements of nineteenth-century France. First, although the purchase and inheritance of positions (notably judicial ones) introduced in the fourteenth century, officialized in the seventeenth century, was abolished, nepotism, co-optation, and patronage ensured that it took a long while for merit to replace family connections, wealth, and partisan loyalty as the formal criterion of administrative recruitment in practice, although these factors remained indirectly and informally of importance. Second, the royal commissioners—notably the Intendants and councillors of state—the direct crown servants removable at will, were resurrected by Napoleon in the shape of the Roman-styled Prefects and a powerful Council of State. With ups and downs, these two institutions have been pillars of central control by the Centre, imposing as best they can uniformity over the provincial periphery. Third, the fusion of political and administrative functions of senior officials was only gradually and partly dismantled, the nineteenth century being punctuated by purges of public servants judged unreliable by a new regime or a new government. Techno-bureaucracy, although it too was rooted in pre-revolutionary engineering corps, only slowly and partially

---

[77] Quoted in G. G. Van Deusen, *Sieyès: His Life and His Nationalism*, 1932, 85–6, 95.

[78] Alexis de Tocqueville, *The Old Régime and the French Revolution*, 1856, 1955 edn, 168; cf. Part 2, Chapters 2–6; 158–63, 167–9.

established depoliticization as a feature of French public administration. The minister's private staff (*cabinet ministériel*) which has been such a feature of French government since the early nineteenth century, also had its predecessor in the *entourage* of the King's ministers.[79]

Centuries of incremental encroachment of the Parisian centre over traditional provincial autonomy and failures in 1770s and 1790s to reform public administration meant that at the onset of the Revolution, 'There was great overlapping of functions, unclear divisions of responsibility, and a general lack of internal control' in the central ministries seeking to administer the 'mad mosaic of fiscal, legal and administrative jurisdictions into which France was divided'.[80] The impetus for increased overall coordination came from the need to coerce these competing authorities and corporate privileges into some semblance of public order, replacing the tiny court administration of lawyer-clerics and court aristocrats owing personal allegiance to the King, with more numerous officials answerable to the new regime. The Revolutionaries were suspicious, despite purging the administration, and would have preferred to dispense with it. However, particularly with the mass mobilization for war from 1792, they had to content themselves with controlling its expansion and subjecting it to close scrutiny. Ministers were directly supervised by parliamentary committees that sought to confine them to the strict implementation of legislation.[81] The judiciary—feared as a potential countervailing power—was excluded from cases involving the administration, establishing an enduring French tradition of separate administrative law.

The end of Jacobin attempts, through the Public Safety and General Security committees of the Convention, to create a politicized 'counter-bureaucracy to ensure surveillance of the ministerial bureaucracy', was followed under the Directory by an attempt to stabilize, streamline, and depoliticize public administration.[82] It began to acquire the characteristic features of a bureaucracy: emphasis upon experience, efficiency, and reliability rather than ideological conformity. Thanks to the Directory, much of what is regarded as the Napoleonic bureaucracy was already in place before his seizure of power. Overall coordination was organized through a General Secretariat and especially its Central Bureau. Some ministries also had a line Secretariat General but in others the minister relied on his personal staff or Private Bureau.[83] However, political appointments, patronage, and nepotism prevailed in an atmosphere in which fear of royalist subversion and disloyalty meant that bureaucratic stability had to await the regimented authority of Napoleon Bonaparte, with its hierarchical chain of command, his Council of State, his Prefects, and Ministry of Police.

Although the increased number of officials supported the ideal that public service offered a career open to the talented, the social background of senior civil servants makes clear that meritocracy was largely a myth and has in practice

---

[79] See the early chapters of *Origines et Histoire des Cabinets des Ministres en France*, 1975, 5–34.

[80] Clive H. Church, *Revolution and Red Tape: The French Ministerial Bureaucracy, 1770–1850*, 1981, 20–21.

[81] Ibid. 47–53, 71–8.   [82] Ibid. 90; cf. 94–143.   [83] Ibid. 147–56, 164, 179–282.

since remained so for the vast majority of senior officials. While the First Republic's *Ecole Polytechnique* of 1794 (as well as the teacher training *Ecole Normale Supérieure*) was intended to be meritocratic, we have seen that the effort by Destutt de Tracy to make it a model for public service education was rejected. The attempt under the Second Republic to create a School of Administrative Education by an ex-Polytechnician and Saint-Simonian Education Minister, Hippolyte Carnot, similarly failed to establish a techno-bureaucratic training allied with equality of opportunity.[84] This was repeated in the 1870s when Carnot's proposal was blocked by the Third Republic's Jules Ferry, who preferred Boutmy's liberal model of the *Ecole Libre de Sciences Politiques*.[85] It became the main source of France's ruling elites and even after the 1945 creation of the *Ecole Nationale d'Administration*, 'Sciences Po' has continued to be the main source from which France's top officials, and by mobility into business and politics its interlocking directorate, has been recruited. A self-perpetuating oligarchy of school made men, to whom a veneer of technocratic specialization was added to the general culture acquired from their elite social upbringing, became a prominent feature of the interface between French government, economy and society.[86] The results of competitive civil service examinations challenged competitive democratic elections as the road to decision-making influence and power.

The Royal Intendants, the instrument of Richelieu's centralization of power, had been the personal representatives of the King as the Prefect was to be of Napoleon when he turned for inspiration to absolute monarchy. In reaction against the Revolution's rather anarchic efforts to establish local self-government and abolition of the Intendants—'If they were efficient they defied the Government, if they were inefficient they endangered the safety of the State'—Napoleon insisted on an official, residing in each *département*, subject to instant recall, to govern in his name.[87] Under the Prefect, sub-Prefects administered the *arrondissements* and the appointed Mayors the communes; above him were the Ministers of the Interior and Police, with Paris, as the perennial source of unrest, having its own Prefect of Police. On 11 March 1800, the Minister of the Interior (Napoleon's brother Lucien Bonaparte) issued an instruction to the Prefects that they were to overcome divisions between Frenchmen and show that 'the Revolution is finished, that a profound gulf separates for ever what has been from what is'.[88] This pious hope oft-repeated for a century after the Revolution's inception was to prove beyond

[84] Vincent Wright, 'L'Ecole d'Administration de 1848: un échec révélateur' in *Revue Historique*, January 1976, CCLV/1, 21–42, and Howard Machin and Vincent Wright, 'Les élèves de l'Ecole d'Administration de 1848–1849' in *Revue d'Histoire Moderne et Contemporaine*, October 1989, XXXVI, 605–39. See also Paul Carnot, *Hippolyte Carnot et le ministère de l'Instruction Publique de la IIe République*, 1948, especially Chapter 14. Lamartine and Ledru-Rollin from the Provisional Government were appointed to Chairs at the Ecole but never lectured. William Fortescue, *Alphonse de Lamartine: A Political Biography*, 1983, 159–60.

[85] Dominique Chagnollaud, *Le Premier des Ordres: Les hauts fonctionnaires (XVIIIe-XXe siècle)*, 1991, 137–40; cf. 107, 127–32.

[86] Christophe Charle, *Les Hauts Fonctionnaires en France au XIXe siècle*, 1980, 28–9, 33–51.

[87] Brian Chapman, *The Prefects and Provincial France*, 1955, 16; cf. 12–19.

[88] Quoted ibid. 26; cf. 23–5.

even the capacity of Prefects formally endowed with supreme local power but subordinate to central authority.

In addition to compiling and extracting resources for Napoleon's military conquests, the Prefects devoted attention to developing the local public infrastructure: roads and bridges, schools and hospitals, and barracks and prisons. Preserving order (notably against conscript resisters) was a major task, as it had ceased in many parts of the country during the revolutionary decade. Parliamentary representation having been emasculated, it was the Prefect who became the means of conveying local public demands to Paris and winning support from the locally influential notables for the regime. His role was even more political than administrative, although from the Restoration until the Second Empire the nature of the Prefect's political duties changed with the emergence of a representative political system. As the electorate expanded—and particularly after manhood suffrage— the Prefect's function as electoral agent of the government became increasingly onerous and under the Third Republic ineffective, despite the myth of the all-powerful Prefect nurtured by Republicans when in opposition, especially during the Second Empire. Nevertheless, various dubious devices were used by Prefects and sub-Prefects (many of whom themselves went into parliament as government supporters) selectively to help or hinder voters, from pressure on public employees to manipulation of electoral registers and bribery to crippling the Opposition press with prosecutions, to ensuring that the dead voted ... for the right candidate! Prime Minister Casimir-Périer bluntly instructed the Prefects in 1831 that 'the Government will not be neutral in the elections, nor does it desire the administration to be so. The Government insists, however, that the electoral law be executed with the most rigorous impartiality. At the same time, the Government wishes it to be known that the distance between administrative impartiality and administrative indifference is infinite. The Government is convinced that its continuance in office is vital to the interests of the Nation.'[89]

Such official electoral management was perfected and systematized by Minister of Interior Persigny during the Second Empire and taken for granted. Already under the July Monarchy, even so conservative a liberal as Royer-Collard was horrified at the reduction of citizens to *administrés*. 'Centralisation has not arrived with its head erect, with the authority of a principle; rather it has developed ... as a necessity. ... That is how we have become an *administered* people, under the control of irresponsible civil servants, themselves centralised through the power of which they are agents.'[90] By the Second Empire, however, centralization was defended in principle even by an ex-Socialist liberal such as Dupont-White in the name of a uniform rule of law. 'In France the path of progress resides in centralization ... France can effectively gather its thoughts only in the capital, and its strength only in government.'[91] The remoteness of centralization was seen as

[89] Quoted ibid. 35; cf. 33–7.

[90] Quoted in Amable de Barante, *La vie politique de Royer-Collard*, II, 1861, 131.

[91] Charles Dupont-White, *La centralisation*, 1860, 347, quoted in Sudhir Hazareesingh, *From Subject to Citizen: The Second Empire and the Emergence of Modern French Democracy*, 1988, 204. See also Sudhir Hazareesingh, *Intellectual Founders of the Republic*, 104–7.

a positive virtue by a Bonapartist councillor of state in 1868. He defined centralization as 'a government far removed from the men it governs. This distance is
necessary so that the law can be fair and impartial....'[92] However, this obsessive
official centralization could not change the local habits that led to 'tacit collusion'
between most prefects who wanted a quiet life and the local notables and field
services of the various ministries, jealous of their autonomy, who resisted the
instructions, circulars, and decrees emanating from Paris. While administrative
structures were centralized, reality was decentralized because of the superposi-
tion of four traditions: semi-feudal traditional aristocratic and clerical notables;
intervention by local deputies; imperial hierarchy; and fragmented, self-centred
field services. So, even 'Under the Second Empire, one cannot speak of a single,
coherent and indivisible administration....'[93]

During the Restoration, the revived role of the aristocracy was attacked by
a liberal deputy, General Foy, for appointing incompetent members of the
leisured class to official positions, accounting for 70 per cent of Prefects and
40 per cent of subordinate staff. He roundly declared in the Chamber of Deputies
in 1821: 'aristocracy in the nineteenth century is the league, the coalition of
those who wish to consume without producing, live without working, know
everything without learning anything, appropriate all honours without deserving
them, occupy all posts while being incapable of carrying out their functions,
that is aristocracy....'[94] Nearly a quarter of Restoration Prefects were deputies
and others became peers, leaving their *départements* for the duration of the parliamentary session. Because of 'the substitution of a parliamentary regime for
a monolithic military dictatorship...politics intruded at every stage and level
of an administrative career. Political patronage was necessary for appointment,
survival, promotion, even a pension'.[95] The July Revolution resulted in a 'massacre' of senior officials recalling that of 1815: only 5 per cent of the Prefects
remained in post or returned later, while half of the sub-Prefects were replaced.[96]
This marked the retreat of the Legitimist nobility from state administration but
not diplomatic service, allowing a partial bourgeois takeover. It was the era *par
excellence* of the deputy civil servant, accounting for nearly half the Chamber of
Deputies. 'The government sought to control politicians by giving them office,
while *fonctionnaires* sought election as an unparalleled means of advancement.'[97]
However, in 1842, the Left-Centre only narrowly lost a vote in the Chamber of
Deputies to exclude most government officials from parliament. This politico-
administrative symbiosis produced a narrow, closed elite that was unable to
withstand the popular resentment that ignited the 1848 Revolution. It was only
a century after 1789 that the Revolution's meritocratic ambitions at last began
to have a major impact, as the educational reforms and expansion of the 1880s

[92] Edouard Boinvilliers, *Paris souverain de la France*, 1868, 19, quoted in Hazareesingh, *From Subject to Citizen*, 38.

[93] Vincent Wright, 'Administration et politique sous le Second Empire' in *Procès-Verbaux de l'Académie des Sciences Morales et Politiques: Institut de France*, May 1973, 295; cf. 289–96.

[94] Quoted in Nicholas Richardson, *The French Prefectoral Corps, 1814–1830*, 1966, 4; cf. 6–9.

[95] Ibid. 131; cf. 16, 37–8.   [96] Ibid. 127–8; cf. 70–2.   [97] Church, 298; cf. 297–9.

started to have a significant effect on recruitment to some elite institutions such as *Polytechnique*.

In judicial affairs, the 1789 Revolution had replaced the royal, aristocratic, and clerical courts by a national system of elected Justices of the Peace providing accessible and cheap adjudication but Napoleon halved their number and supplemented election with co-optation. He installed a hierarchy with a key role for state prosecutors analogous to the repressive functions of the Prefects, combined with the duty of protecting private property. As judges were often ex-prosecutors rewarded for their loyal service, it reinforced 'the perpetual confusion in nineteenth century France between service of the state and that of the government of the day.'[98] Because French court procedure allowed the defendants and their lawyers in political trials to persuade the jury (an import from England) to acquit, the Criminal Code gave the Prefect the function of empanelling the jury and the government could shift the trial to a more politically reliable area.[99] This did not prevent juries from sometimes responding to the eloquence of the advocates of the accused or sympathetic public opinion.

NATIONALITY, NATURALIZATION, AND ASSIMILATION

Prior to the Revolution, if one lived in the kingdom, one was deemed to be French by virtue of owing personal allegiance to the king. One's national identity was principally defined territorially by where one was born or resided, known as *jus soli*. Until national identity became identified with citizenship, there was no problem about foreign subjects loyally serving the monarchy in the army or church, in government or finance as Necker did in the two latter capacities, although his Protestantism was a handicap. However, 'the revolutionary notion of the sovereignty of the nation implied that they be excluded from such roles'.[100] While continuing to define nationality in political terms, it was allegiance to the Revolution through the swearing of a civic oath that replaced subjection to the king. The revolutionary constitutions placed increased emphasis upon French parenthood (*jus sanguinis*) in the context of war, coupled with increasing hostility towards foreigners, sympathisers having initially been welcomed with open arms in the cosmopolitan climate of 1789–92.

The ideological contradiction between universal human rights and exclusion of foreigners was in practice resolved against inclusiveness if only because otherwise the French nation would have been geographically boundless. However, the rejection of ethnicity or religion as criteria of nationality (Protestants and then Jews

---

[98] Charle, *Les Hauts Fonctionnaires*, 135; cf. 121–5, 132–4 and McPhee, 83.

[99] Spitzer, *Old Hatreds and Young Hopes*, 149–50. On Jury trial during the Revolution and First Empire, see Woloch, *The New Regime*, Chapter 12.

[100] Michael Rapport, *Nationality and Citizenship in Revolutionary France: The Treatment of Foreigners 1789–99*, 2000, 29; cf. 32–3, 78, 85–7, 329–34 and Patrick Weil, *La France et ses étrangers*, 1991, 458–62.

were accepted as citizens) and the rapid abandonment of a 1794 attempt to impose linguistic unity as unworkable because it would in particular have excluded Alsace and Brittany from the French nation, meant that the proclaimed legal equality of citizens and the universalist symbolism of the 1789 Declaration of the Rights of Man and the Citizen preserved a more assimilationist conception of nationality. So, although in 1792 the Legislative Assembly conferred French citizenship upon eighteen distinguished foreign luminaries—including Joseph Priestley, Tom Paine, and Jeremy Bentham—implying that 'Nationality was not a matter of birth or culture, but a state of mind', Tom Paine elected a deputy, spent nearly a year in prison during the Terror for his Girondist affiliations.[101] The proximity of international fraternity and the guillotine was, not only in his case, too close for comfort.

That national assimilation required more than loyalty to the Republic was made clear by the 1804 Civil Code, which gave priority to the blood-ties of *jus sanguinis* while remaining silent on the subject of naturalization. However, in a context of declining birth rate and increasing immigration, the feeling that resident foreigners were taking advantage of their status, notably to avoid military service, led to an 1851 Law insisting that a child born in France of a foreigner born in France was French.[102] Confidence in the country's capacity to assimilate immigrants into republican values and the national identity later led to a further stage in the transition from nationality as a royal prerogative to a political right and then a citizen duty.

Under Napoleon, administrative discretion in dealing with foreigners displaced human rights. Whereas pre-revolutionary passports had been issued to foreigners to facilitate their exit from the country and in 1792 passports were introduced for those leaving Paris, which required a certificate of their civic loyalty, passport control over foreigners became much more systematic. Furthermore, a domestic passport, the *livret*, such as had existed under the Old Regime, was required to secure manual employment, as part of the Police State surveillance pioneered by Napoleon, some features of which survived into the late twentieth century.

The revolutionary ideal of equal human rights, incompatible with Louis XIV's *Code Noir*, had particular difficulty in dealing with the West Indian slave colony of San Domingo, which revolted in August 1791. The complicated and heroic story of this slave insurrection and its leader Toussaint L'Ouverture has been recounted by C.L.R. James in *The Black Jacobins*, from Girondin improvised liberation, to the 1794 Jacobin decree formally freeing the slaves as equal citizens living in a French territory, to the 1802 reintroduction of the *Code Noir* and slavery and the deliberate death of Toussaint in a French prison in 1803.[103] (His followers successfully achieved their independence as Haiti in 1804.) The fact that William Wilberforce and Thomas Clarkson, leaders in the British fight against the slave trade, were among the select group of foreigners accorded French citizenship in 1792, is

---

[101] Rapport, 138; cf. 27, 40–1, 172, 189–93, 202.   [102] Weil, 466–72.

[103] C. L. R. James, *The Black Jacobins: Toussaint l'Ouverture and the San Domingo Revolution*, 1938, 1980 edn. Lamartine, who campaigned against slavery during the July Monarchy and was in a position to secure its abolition in 1848, was the author of a drama *Toussaint Louverture*.

indicative of the Revolution's sympathy for the abolitionist cause. Once the slave trade revived after the British blockade during the Napoleonic Wars, the agitation from 1814 by the *Société des Amis des Noirs* (lead founders in 1787 were Sieyès and Condorcet) involved Madame de Staël and her brother. Benjamin Constant was the campaign's leading spokesman in parliament in the 1820s, its supporters consisting mainly of Protestants and liberal Catholics. Anti-abolitionism was led by the slave trading ports, especially Nantes and Bordeaux. British naval captures of French slave trading ships caused diplomatic tensions that only ended with the 1830 Revolution, after which reciprocal rights of search of suspect merchant ships was agreed. As a result, the French slave trade almost ceased.[104] Despite Tocqueville's 1845 parliamentary speech claiming that the French revolutionary principle of equality had priority in the abolition of slavery, it was British practice that had secured its application in her Empire from 1833. So, it was not until the 1848 Revolution that slavery in the French Empire was itself abolished. The race barrier to assimilation has proved more difficult to overcome.

LIBERAL PLURALISM: ANGLOPHILIA AND ANGLOPHOBIA

Consciousness in mid-eighteenth-century France that Britain was fast overhauling her in trade and economic development, required an explanation. Voltaire's answer, as we saw in the Introduction, was that her prosperity was due to the 1688 Revolution that had restrained the monarch's political interference. Much more than the circumspect Montesquieu's *The Spirit of the Laws* (1748), it promoted what was called 'Anglomania' in which a 'mixed' parliamentary government that favoured commercial society was both praised and criticized.[105] Rousseau's criticisms of British government were counteracted by Jean de Lolme's *The English Constitution* (1771), although its circulation was officially restricted in France. However, as the effects of early industrialization on living and working conditions in the English towns were observed by visitors such as Tocqueville, admiration for English freedom and political institutions was combined with horror at the impact of industrial society upon the mass population. Although elite Anglomania proposed Britain as a model of the desirable future, it was also regarded as an economic and political rival to be feared. French constitutional monarchy marked a post-revolutionary and post-Napoleonic high point of British influence upon French political institutions. But, as Rosanvallon puts it, 'To illuminate national idiosyncrasies, the starting point is the fact that there is *both* a Jacobin and a British

---

[104] Serge Daget, 'The Abolition of the Slave Trade by France: the decisive years 1826–1831' in David Richardson (ed.), *Abolition and Its Aftermath: The Historical Context, 1790–1916*, 1985, 141–62. See also Tudesq, *Les Grands Notables en France* II, 834–46.

[105] Whatmore, 39–46, who notes that the term 'anglomania' was coined by L. C. F. de Montbron in *Préservatif contre l'anglomanie*, 1757. More generally, see Josephine Grieder, *Anglomania in France 1740–1789: Fact, Fiction and Discourse*, 1985, F. Acomb, *Anglophobia in France 1763–1789*, 1950 and Tudesq, *Les Grands Notables en France*, II, 762–80. See also Introduction.

spirit in French institutions'.[106] In the tension between these two trajectories, the former has generally predominated over the latter, especially when Jacobin republican culture was reinforced by Roman Catholic religious culture and Napoleonic administrative culture.

Having been appointed in 1797 as 'Commander of the Army against England', as First Consul in 1803, having reopened hostilities with Britain, Napoleon wrote from Boulogne: 'The Channel is a mere ditch and will be crossed as soon as someone has the courage to attempt it.' Adopting fashionable historical analogies, he reminded the French that 'Rome destroyed Carthage', a maritime-commercial state. He popularized the disdainful characterization of Britain as a shopkeeper nation, having read Adam Smith's Wealth of Nations remark that 'To found a great empire for the sole purpose of raising up a people of customers, may, at first sight, appear a project fit only for a nation of shopkeepers.' However, in the comments recorded by Montholon at St Helena, a chastened Napoleon declared: 'either fight England or share the world with her. The second alternative is the only possible one in our day.'[107]

Although Cromwell's role in mastering the English Revolution fascinated Guizot, it was the parallels between English history and French developments, via Napoleon and the Restoration, that impressed French liberals, who were to see the 1830 Revolution as her 1688 and not to understand 1848, which should not have happened. On the English model, the revolutionary process should have been over.[108] To return to 1789 and make it a successful 1688, they supported the King's improvised 1814 Charter which his authoritarian brother Charles X abominated, uncompromisingly asserting: 'I would prefer to saw wood rather than be a king like the Kings of England.'[109]

While a Franco-British Union (such as we saw in Chapter 2 was naively advocated by Saint-Simon and Thierry) was not acceptable, many in the early Restoration were attracted to English institutions as a model for France. Anglophile liberal aristocrats, notable the Madame de Staël circle, particularly admired the deference accorded to their British counterparts who had succeeded in stemming the egalitarian and democratic tide that threatened to swamp them in France. This was made possible because 'In England, the power of capital has succeeded, almost without interruption, the territorial power of feudalism and has done so in the same hands.'[110] However, because British practice had been a product of historical development rather than political will, it was not directly imitable. Nevertheless,

---

[106] Pierre Rosanvallon, *La Monarchie Impossible: Les Chartes de 1814 et de 1830*, 1994, 7; cf. 8.

[107] Quotations from Robert Gibson, *Best of Enemies*, 150–1, 172–4. The Adam Smith citation comes from Book 4, Chapter 7 of the *Wealth of Nations*. See also Jean-Hérold Paquis, *L'Angleterre comme Carthage*, 1944.

[108] Rosanvallon, *Le Moment Guizot*, 321. See also François Furet, *La Révolution, 1770–1880*, 308 and Furet, 'L'Ancien Régime et a Révolution in *Les lieux de mémoire*, III/1, 126, 130. The official philosopher of the July Monarchy, Victor Cousin, wrote in the Preface to the second edition (1833) of his *Fragments Philosophiques*: 'The July Revolution is nothing else than the English Revolution of 1688'.

[109] Quoted in B. de Sauvigny, *La Restauration*, 269; cf. 270.

[110] Baron Prosper de Barante, *Des communes et de l'aristocratie*, 1821 quoted in Lucien Jaume, *L'Individu effacé ou le paradoxe du libéralisme français*, 1997, 293 cf. 291–5, 302–5.

through a decentralization of power to local notables and the creation of a Second Chamber based not on heredity but on life peerages (implemented by the July Monarchy) it was vainly hoped to come closer to a Britain that owed its open elite more to commercialism and early industrialization, its individualist values to Protestantism and its social integration to the voluntary association that provided a civil society with scope for participation by the general public.

An *Entente Cordiale*—Louis-Philippe's phrase for the official *rapprochement* between France and Britain—symbolized by his returning in 1844 Queen Victoria's 1843 visit to France had been prepared by Prime Minister Guizot's close friendship with Lord Aberdeen, the British Foreign Secretary who replaced the hostile Palmerston. Louis-Philippe especially welcomed Victoria's initiative because of his sulphurous reputation in European royal circles as 'king of the barricades'.[111] Like Guizot, a former French Ambassador to Britain, Louis-Philippe's Anglophilia and pacifism was reinforced by the intermarriage of both royal families with the house of Saxe-Coburg Gotha. However, despite the Restoration fashion among the happy few for Walter Scott's novels and Shakespeare's plays, Anglophobia remained deeply rooted. Because a dogmatic Catholic and authoritarian France was allergic to all these deep-seated liberal features of British life, the importation of a deformed parliamentary system based on restricted suffrage supplemented by a stifling, repressive administration, could not defuse democratic pressures by reformist gradualism. So, although July Monarchy politicians like Rémusat could dream of living under 'English government in French society' and Guizot could write at the end of his life that he had 'almost two fatherlands', France and England,[112] it proved impossible to make British political institutions work in the same way in France. When the Third Republic tried again, it reverted to a more staid, two chamber version of the First Republic's government by assembly. French exceptionalism stubbornly reasserted itself.

[111] David Pinkney, *Decisive Years in France, 1840–1847*, 1986, 128–38.

[112] Rémusat's *L'Angleterre au XVIIe siècle*, I, 10, is quoted by Jaume, 349 note and Guizot's 1874 letter to Henry Reeve is to be found in *Life and Letters of Henry Reeve*, II, 223, quoted by Douglas Johnson, *Guizot*, 441.

4

Enduring Conflicts and Elusive Consensus

We shall now explore in greater detail the tensions that have been touched on in the trajectories of development in the century between the French Revolution and the Third Republic's consolidation thanks to the victory of its most ardent protagonists. We shall consider how far a peasant and artisan dominated rural economy can be said to have retarded her political and economic modernization. Next, we shall turn our attention to the middle and working classes, as France became an increasingly urbanized industrial society, with the resulting consequences for socio-economic and political leadership and conflict. Then, we shall examine the struggle between secularism and clericalism, notably their rivalry to socialize the mass population through primary education and the leaders through elite education. This chapter concludes with a discussion of the role of politically committed historians, novelists, poets, and painters in reflecting and shaping the ideological and social conflicts in the run up to the Third Republic. In their different ways, they exemplify the fact that anti-France was at least as much the enemy within as the Anglo-Saxon external rival.

A PREDOMINANTLY 'PEASANT' POPULATION

It is difficult to resist using the compendious term 'peasant' for what was a very diverse category of people. But does one mean all those involved in cultivating the land or only self-sufficient farmers? The narrower definition would not only involve excluding the increasing number of landless farm labourers and farm servants but also rural artisans who were usually part-time farmers. It is estimated that in the 1780s landless labourers were on average 30 per cent of the total, with peasants in the strict sense averaging 55 per cent, while landowners and tenant farmers employing labourers accounted for the remaining 15 per cent. However, the term peasant misleadingly 'conveys an image of homogeneous, subsistence-oriented and closed communities'.[1] In a broad sense, just prior to the Revolution, the peasantry amounted to about two-thirds of the French population but in some sense owned about one-third of the land. The Republican-inspired myth, promoted notably by Michelet, that the Revolution created a class of freehold peasant proprietors cannot be sustained because 'peasant land ownership was well

---

[1] McPhee, A *Social History of France*, 153; cf. 11.

entrenched before 1789. . . . All the revolution did was to accelerate existing trends, but the transformation was scarcely dramatic because the quantity of property changing hands represented only a small percentage of the total land surface of the country'.[2]

Although agrarian violence did prompt the August 1789 abolition of feudalism, the peasants were nevertheless attached to their traditional rights. Pre-revolutionary campaigns by royal officials against the customary, collective rights of the peasantry to grazing, gleaning, and wood cutting on the common land as unproductive were resisted by the mass of poor peasants to whom they were even more important than ownership. Despite liberal attempts to overcome this opposition to proto-capitalist farming, the 1791 Rural Code achieved a compromise largely preserving peasant rights from enclosure and increasing subsistence farming. The sale by auction of property seized from the Church and émigré nobility was mainly financially motivated. Only briefly in 1793–4 was the land sold not to bourgeois speculators rather than in smaller lots 'to fulfil the Jacobin dream of a republic of property owners'.[3] However, because the speculators subsequently resold the land piecemeal to the peasants and because, unlike their English counterparts, French landlords were generally rentiers, the peasants came to own or rent more of the land. The result was greater equality in the distribution in land ownership because of the high agricultural population densities of the underemployed using little capital relative to labour.[4] Only with rural depopulation from the mid-nineteenth century did a slow motion agricultural revolution belatedly occur.

In his *Peasants into Frenchmen*, Eugen Weber, following Robert Redfield, takes a broader view of the pre-modern 'peasant, for whom agriculture is a way of life, not a profit-making enterprise, and the farmer, who carries on agriculture as a business'. . . .[5] The relationship of these pre-modern peasants to urban society was one of mutual incomprehension. The Revolution's normative endeavour to impose an ideal of integrated national unity, condemning traditional diversities as intolerable imperfections, was impeded for decades by stubborn reality in much of the country. Writers like Balzac, Flaubert, Stendhal, and Zola described the peasantry as largely uncivilized aliens to French language and culture, more like their beasts than human beings. Such stereotypical simplifications of a much more complex diversity, with different parts of the country moving at variable speeds from locality to nationality, were exemplified in the 1850 survey of rural populations by the liberal economist brother of the revolutionary Blanqui. Unlike Auguste, who dichotomized his countrymen on class lines, Adolphe's duality was between town and country. More than in other countries, he had observed 'Two different peoples living on the same land a life so different that they seem foreign

---

[2] Jones, *The Peasantry*, 124; cf. 253   [3] Ibid. 154; cf. 155–66, 258, 266.

[4] Patrick O'Brien and Caglar Keyder, *Economic Growth in Britain and France 1780–1914: Two Paths to the Twentieth Century*, 1978, 189–90; cf. 138–9.

[5] Eugen Weber, 117, referring to Robert Redfield, *Peasant Society and Culture*, 1956, 27.

to each other, though united by the bonds of the most imperious centralization that ever existed'.[6]

The intrusion of urban modernity and national authority manifested by officials demanding taxes and requiring military service, as well as enforcing harsh laws against the begging to which many were reduced by penury, was generally unwelcome. However, the Revolution's conferment of the right to hunt was doubly precious, as a source of food and a pleasure that the game laws had denied the peasantry.[7] (Its symbolic status has been such that attempts from the late twentieth century to protect wildlife led to the creation of a political party to preserve the freedom to hunt whose presidential candidate proved capable of attracting over 4 per cent of the vote in 2002.) Popular indifference towards national electoral politics, which we have discussed, derived from the fact that they seemed too abstract and remote from routine rural concerns and could be left to local notables. As the canal and rail communications improved, peasant protest riots against local food shortages and price variations ceased, along with local tax revolts, which instead became national issues in the second half of the nineteenth century. Before the politically polarized 1877 general election, many opposition commune councils were dissolved and their mayors dismissed, showing the impact of national political contention upon local politics. After 1877, when mayors were elected by commune councils, local politics seemed much more relevant and politicization could become more general and sustained than the ephemeral Second Republic surge in participation in some parts of France.[8] Nevertheless, they continued to take a personalized rather than a partisan form until well into the twentieth century.

Before rural exodus and farm mechanization led to a double loss of customers, craftsmen that serviced the peasants were an integral part of the countryside community. The mass of artisans, self-employed or with only one apprentice, or employee, sustained the post-revolutionary craftsmen-centred economy characterized by 'the little unit, the little man, the little goal' that preserved social stability as well as providing an opportunity for upwards social mobility.[9] Until a capitalist-centred, mass production economy displaced them, artisans mainly produced one-off articles for specific customers. Before the 1870s, artisans were still twice as numerous as industrial workers and proud to be their own masters. Itinerant artisans were important purveyors of new ideas to the peasant communities, including radical political ideas, while those who stayed put often provided a focus for discussion with clients, especially when also operating a shop or café.[10] Although the larger enterprises coexisted for a time with the craftsmen,

[6] Weber, 9; cf. 5–10, quoting Adolphe Blanqui, 'Tableau des populations rurales en France en 1850' in *Journal des Economistes*, XXVIII, 1851, 9–13.

[7] Weber, 249; cf. Jones, 249.

[8] Weber, 274 and Chapter 15 on 'Peasants and Politics' more generally. For the view that Weber tends to post-date the shift from rural apoliticization, see McPhee, 161–2, 221–2, 267.

[9] J. E. Sawyer, 'Strains in the Social Structure of Modern France' in E. M. Earle (ed.), *Modern France*, 1951, 304.

[10] Weber, 221–6.

the unsentimental pressures of competition allowed a few artisans to become entrepreneurs but the rest lost their independence as workers in the expanding industrial and service sectors.

AN URBANIZING AND INDUSTRIALIZING SOCIETY

Initially factories—except in textiles—tended to increase rather than reduce the number of skilled craftsmen, so that 'For the better part of the nineteenth century, artisans remained the dominant sector of the urban working class, numerically, politically and culturally.'[11] The census modestly defined towns as anything with a population over 2,000, accounting for 20 per cent of the total at the end of the eighteenth century. They consisted mainly of artisans and public officials in market towns servicing their hinterland administrative centres, while others were primarily administrative centres or mono-industrial towns. Between 1801 and 1951, the larger towns expanded faster than the average population increase of 26 per cent: Paris doubled to a million people, while of towns between 50 and 100,000, Marseille grew by 76 per cent, Lyon by 62 per cent and Bordeaux by 44 per cent.[12] Although French industrialization and urbanization were much more gradual than in Britain, it is questionable whether France can be regarded as relatively backward. It was different, with the relative importance of craft production of furniture and jewellery in Paris, silk in Lyon, and porcelain in Limoges being exemplars of a French specialized comparative advantage in higher value products.[13]

The 1791 Le Chapelier Law, as enforced by an 1804 Law against unions of producers, was much harsher for workers than employers: three-month imprisonment for the former and one month or a fine for the latter, who had the collective action benefit of Chambers of Commerce. Although workers could circumvent repression through illegal but tolerated *compagnonnages* journeymen brotherhoods, the Civil Code discriminated against them. Until it was repealed in 1868, article 1781 'stated that in a dispute about wages, the word of the master was to be preferred to that of the worker in the absence of written records—just as article 1716 stated that in a dispute about rent, the word of the landlord was to be preferred to that of the tenant.'[14] At a time of rapidly increasing rents, the conflict between landlord and tenant was important enough to rival that of worker and employer. The biased economic liberalism of the July Monarchy is reflected in the 1835 comment by Prefect Charles Dunoyer: 'if society is not master of the property of those who possess something, it is under no obligation to those who possess nothing.... Society owes everybody justice and protection: it owes nobody lucrative employment, education or bread in default of work.'[15] More

---

[11] Sewell, 157, cf. 153–7.   [12] Ibid. 150.

[13] Ibid. 153. See also O'Brien and Keydar, 15–22, 178.   [14] Zeldin, I, 199; cf. 203.

[15] Charles Dunoyer paper presented to the Institute quoted from Irene Collins (ed.) *Government and Society in France 1814–1848*, 1970, 153–4.

offensively, Granier de Cassagnac defined the proletariat in 1837 as including workers, beggars, thieves, and prostitutes.[16]

If male urban workers were the poorly clothed victims of low wages, insanitary housing, and short life expectancy, the conditions of female workers were worse. In 1866, 28 per cent of women workers were domestic servants, 21 per cent employed in garment making, and 20 per cent in textiles, all poorly paid. 'In Paris in 1846, 12.8 per cent of babies were abandoned (compared to 3 per cent of all of France) almost all of them from among the 32 per cent of children born outside marriage....'[17] Fear of contamination by venereal disease led to the registration of prostitutes in licensed brothels but a similar number were unregistered. Proudhon's provocative dichotomy in *La Pornocratie* of women between housewives and harlots, as well as neglecting the large numbers of nuns, ignored the fact that working-class women might be compelled by poverty to move between these categories. McPhee points out that by 1880, one-third of 'the non-registered prostitutes and mothers of abandoned children were former domestics, and behind these figures were harrowing individual stories of sexual exploitation by employers' and subservience to the whims of housewives.[18] The public façade of bourgeois moralizing and ostentatious respectability could not conceal the cynical toleration of vice.

While the 1830 Revolution marked the accession of the upper middle class to positions of power and the 1848 Revolution finally abolished aristocratic titles, the aristocrats continued to be important long after the July Monarchy. 'Many of them went into industry and finance. Thirty per cent of the directors of railway companies in 1902 were noblemen, 23 per cent of those of the large steel and banking companies.'[19] This contributed to the conservative slant that French liberalism took in the nineteenth century as the upper middle class supplemented economic with political power. Ironically, it was the propaganda of the radical followers of Saint-Simon (who we saw was successively a champion of economic liberalism and then technocratic industrialism) in the early 1830s that pilloried liberalism as the ideological enemy associated with the bourgeoisie. Instead of being the virtuous industrious class, it was castigated as synonymous with the greedy rich exploiting the poor proletarians. Abel Transon, in an 1830 lecture to *Polytechnique* students, described this new class of oppressors as being epitomized by the 'rentier, capitalist, proprietor, BOURGEOIS', who had confiscated the 1830 Revolution for their sole benefit.[20] Many ex-Saint-Simonians who were *polytechniciens* became active promoters of the railways and banking not only in the July Monarchy but especially during the Second Empire, Saint-Simonism becoming part of its ideology thanks to Louis-Napoleon having had a Saint-Simonian mentor and continuing to sympathize with their industrialist ideas. While Emile Péreire was important in

---

[16] Adolphe Granier de Cassagnac, *Histoire des Classes Ouvrières et des Classes Bourgeoises*, quoted by Johnson, *Guizot*, 77.

[17] McPhee, 147; cf. 202.　　[18] Ibid. 202; cf. 123, 142–3, 205.

[19] Zeldin, I, 405; cf. 123, 142–3, 205.

[20] Abel Transon, *De la religion Saint-Simonienne*, 1830, 50, quoted in Shirley M. Gruner, *Economic Materialism and Social Moralism*, 1973, 144, cf. 140–5.

both these activities, notably in association and then rivalry with Baron James de Rothschild, Michel Chevalier, *polytechnicien*, journalist, and lecturer in the Collège de France, continued the work of propaganda but this took a strong liberal turn, leading in 1860 to the free trade Cobden-Chevalier Treaty between Britain and France.[21]

In contrast to the mass of small-scale family firms, motivated by a desire to achieve a comfortable and secure retirement, the new industrialists and bankers were not merely seeking to maximize profit but to acquire social status and political influence. Although less economically significant than the mass of textile firms, iron and steel dynasties like the Schneiders and de Wendels were more socially and politically significant. 'In the nineteenth century the majority of iron masters were nobles. Iron was the one respectable industry... Under the July Monarchy the richest men in fourteen departments were iron masters and they enjoyed proportional political influence. The large firms all had their representatives in parliament.'[22] The links between banks and industry, such as the Crédit Lyonnais and silk manufacture, or with trade, like Rothschilds, which was not only important in railways but had a virtual monopoly of tea imports, were also frequent, while Léon Say (grandson of Jean-Baptiste Say) would combine a prominent political career with being president of the Decazeville Coal Mine Company and Vice-president of the Rothschild-owned Northern Railways.

The business–political upper middle class networks that were built up over the July Monarchy and Second Empire came to maximum power in the 1870s and 1880s. Their business ties were supplemented by personal and family links, frequenting the same *salons*, writing for and reading the same newspapers, which gave them an ideological and cultural cohesion; bankers and industrialists rubbing shoulders with liberal economists, prominent journalists, and business lawyers. Their intellectual mouthpiece was the *Journal des Économistes*, they were well ensconced in the Académie des Sciences Morales et Politiques and the Académie Française, while the quality press was dominated by the *Journal des Débats* (controlled by Léon Say in the 1870s and 1880s) read by the most influential people and for whom the leading liberal intellectuals wrote. In the 1870s the posts of ministers of finance, agriculture, trade, and public works were almost entirely held by businessmen of the political Right, Centre, and Left-Centre, with banking and railway connections being especially important. Inaugurating the *Hautes Etudes Commerciales* business school established by the Paris Chamber of Commerce in 1881, Léon Say, then President of the Senate (who was Finance Minister for four years between 1872 and 1882) could expand on Guizot's 'Enrich yourselves' by exhorting his audience to 'Enrich France'.[23]

Conspicuous among those who enriched themselves under the July Monarchy were the railway speculators. Although the state corps of *Ponts et Chaussées* had

---

[21] Arthur L. Dunham, *The Industrial Revolution in France 1815–1848*, 1955, 58–60. See also Maurice Wallon, *Les Saint-Simoniens et les chemins de fer*, 1908.

[22] Zeldin, I, 74–5.

[23] Jean Garrigues, *La République des hommes d'affaires, 1870–1900*, 1997, 89; cf. 15, 26, 53–105.

played the leading role in expanding the network of royal administrative roads into a nationwide local network, its attempt to retain control over the ownership and construction of railways lacked the necessary governmental support and public investment funds, exacerbated by parliamentary bickering motivated by the promotion of constituency interests. The compromise 1842 Law laid down that the government would provide the land and the roadbed but lease the operations to private companies, having decided that the main lines would radiate from Paris. (Louis-Napoleon increased the leases to ninety-nine years.) Using his financial resources and government connections, James de Rothschild—in association with other bankers—took control of the Northern Railway, while the less profitable Paris–Lyon–Marseille line was run by a company headed by Paulin Talabot, in association with other ex-Saint-Simonians. James de Rothschild boasted in 1840 that he frequently met all the ministers. If he did not like their policies, he went to the king, who he could see whenever he wished as he managed his personal finances. The king often acted on his advice, notable in getting rid of Thiers in 1840 because of his warlike Egyptian policy.[24]

The 1879 Freycinet Plan launched another great surge in railway building to stimulate the economy and unite the country when the Republicans took political control. This was done in association with a massive programme of improvements in the transport infrastructure generally. It allowed the Third Republic to attract the support of the provincial lower middle classes and sections of the peasantry that would stand it in good stead as the new political leaders displaced the older bourgeois elites.

CLERICALISM AND SECULARISM

Anticlericalism is characteristic of countries where Roman Catholicism has used the secular power to domineer over both personal and family life as well as acting as a state within the state. It adopts the liberal separation of the public and private spheres and seeks to confine the Church to the latter domain. Clerical interference with freedom of thought and behaviour, both in children's indoctrination as well as in the family life of adults, is rejected, while subordination to papal authority is regarded as a supranational challenge to national independence. Although known from the eighteenth century as 'Voltairianism', it acquired the name anticlericalism in 1852 because of the Church's support for Louis-Napoleon's *coup d'état* as he had restored the Pope's temporal power in the Vatican by overthrowing the Roman Republic in 1849. Ironically, its use spread especially after his 1859 military intervention to support Italian unity against Pope Pius IX, being reinforced by hostility to the 1864 papal Syllabus of Errors and the 1870 proclamation of papal

---

[24] Jean Bouvier, *Les Rothschild*, 1967, 113–14; cf. Chapters 5 and 6. Balzac based the central figure in his novel *La Maison Nuncigen* on James de Rothschild (ibid. 56). See also Dunham, 68–78 and David H. Pinkney, *Decisive Years in France, 1840–1847*, 1986, 27, 35–7.

infallibility.[25] Anticlericalism was not anti-Christian and Protestantism was an ally not a clerical enemy.

The term secularism brings out the fact that it is not merely a negative response to clericalism but an affirmation of freethinking rationalism against dogmatic faith and of modern science against superstitious religion. Initially, it was the 'enlightened' nobility that applauded anticlerical satires such as Molière's *Tartuffe* and Don Basilio in the plays of Beaumarchais. They were attracted to deism as practised in Masonic lodges, whose 210,000 members in some 600 lodges in the 1780s included many 'enlightened' bourgeois. But after the Revolution, it was the middle-class professions, notably doctors and lawyers, that were attracted to an anticlericalism that the aristocracy was abandoning as subversive of traditional hierarchy. The business bourgeoisie, allergic to the Catholic rejection of capitalist values, became detached from the Church in the first half of the nineteenth century. After the 1848 Revolution a section of the bourgeoisie, led by Thiers, while personally remaining sceptical, saw the Catholic Church as a bulwark in defence of private property and tactically supported the clericalism that flourished during the Second Republic and Second Empire. The Church support for Thiers' bloody repression of the 1871 Paris Commune marked a further stage in the secularization of the working classes. The workers, who had not until then been anticlerical, moved in that direction because of the alliance of Church and State. Together with large sections of the male bourgeoisie, they provided the electoral support for the anticlerical programme of the Third Republic, which relied on the spread of state primary school teachers as the agents of secularist socialization. However, the workers were increasingly attracted to a socialist anticlericalism that attacked the Church's collusion with exploitative employers.

The foundations for this anticlericalism were laid by the Restoration's replacement of Napoleon's state control of the Church with Catholicism as the state religion and government at the service of the Church, whose zealous new lower-class clergy rejected their bishops' Gallicanism in favour of theocracy. While Napoleon's institution of the baccalaureat examination survived, the Revolution's *École Normale Supérieure* was abolished in 1822 as areligious and only re-established after the 1830 Revolution. Lamennais expounded their extremist view with remorseless logic in 1825. 'Without the Pope, no Church; without the Church, no Christianity; without Christianity, no religion and no society' and his book was banned for his pains.[26] However, the Minister for Ecclesiastical Affairs and Public Education pushed through a purge of primary and secondary education, which was supplemented by rechristianization missions in the countryside. In 1826, a law prescribing capital punishment for the supernatural crime of sacrilege was passed but not implemented.

[25] René Rémond, *L'Anticléricalisme en France de 1815 à nos jours*, 1976, 9–11; cf. 14–15, 23–6, 51–2, 124–5.

[26] B. de Sauvigny, 311; cf. 300–24, quoting Felicité de Lamennais, *De la religion considérée dans ses rapports avec l'ordre politique et civil*, 1825. See also Collins, 45–61.

The reactions against this orgy of clericalism led in the July Monarchy to a reassertion of state control over education and a virulent anti-Jesuit campaign by Michelet and others inspired by the counterpart of the clerical anti-Freemason myth. Michelet also castigated the Church's hold over women, who flooded into religious orders in the nineteenth century. While in 1880, some 30,000 men (including 3,245 Jesuits) were in religious orders, 'In the first 80 years of the century, nearly 400 successful new female orders were established, and some 200,000 women entered the religious life. At the apogee of recruitment, in the late 1850s, perhaps 1 girl in 12 who did not marry entered a religious order.'[27] The Pope having proclaimed the immaculate conception in 1854, Marianism was reflected in the proliferation of statues of the Virgin Mary into the early years of the Third Republic, the feminizing religiosity of love assuming greater importance than the earlier religion of fear. The continuing political alliance with the Right was reflected in the Church organized mass pilgrimages in a vain effort to rally support before the crucial 1877 elections that shifted power to the anticlerical republicans.[28]

It was to be a long haul before they substituted freethinking education for the inculcation of passive obedience. For a start, until 1816 no teaching qualifications were required and even in the late nineteenth century most teaching nuns had no qualifications and were better at imparting piety than knowledge. Impecunious primary school teachers, living and teaching in an insalubrious schoolroom, had usually to make ends meet by doing another job such as gravedigger or act as town crier. They sometimes collected their fees in kind not cash. Rote learning predominated, stressing the capacity to recite the catechism.[29] From 1816 each commune was required to provide single sex primary education, if the parents so wished, for those who could not afford to pay. In 1828, four million out of five and a half million children between the ages of 6 and 15 nevertheless did not go to school.

It took the further impetus imparted by Guizot's 1833 Primary Education Law to reduce the number of communes without a primary school to about 6,000. The status of teachers was raised by payment of a modest salary and the requirement that each *département* or groups of *départements* should establish a teacher training college, which increased from 21 in 1830 to 47 in 1848. They were the secular answer to the seminary. However, many teachers remained semi-literate. Because Guizot wished to combine the stabilizing influence of state and Church, pride of place was given to moral and religious instruction and 'Every class shall begin and end with prayers.... On Sundays and Feast Days the pupils shall be taken to Divine Service.'[30] Reading and writing in French (to overcome local dialects) and arithmetic were also taught, while from age 10, elementary

---

[27] Gibson, 105; cf. 118,122; cf. McPhee, 209. See also Jules Michelet, *Du prêtre, de la femme et de la famille*, 1845.

[28] McPhee, 241, 260–2.   [29] E. Weber, 304–7; cf. McPhee, 231.

[30] 1834 decree quoted in Collins, 130; cf. 127–34 and Pinkney, *Decisive Years*, 65–8, 80–4; Félix Ponteil, *Les Institutions de la France de 1814 à 1870*, 1966, 117–31, 251–60. Also Antoine Prost, *Histoire de l'Enseignement en France 1800–1967*, 1968, Chapter 6.

geography and history—especially of France—were added. While seven types of punishment, ranging from black marks to temporary expulsion were specified, corporal punishment was forbidden. The school year generally lasted only from two to five winter months, so that the children could help in agricultural work, sweep chimneys, or beg.

At the mercy of the local parish priest and mayor, the schoolmaster was supposed to teach the use of reason—Guizot's touchstone—to an unreasonable people judged unfit to vote. When universal suffrage came in 1848, it produced a reactionary parliamentary majority which rejected Carnot's ambitious plans for primary education as a preparation for democratic citizenship, the counterpart of his National School of Administration for government officials.[31] The key figure was the leader of the 'Party of Order', Adolphe Thiers, who persuaded the ardent Catholic Count de Falloux to become Education Minister in the 1849 Barrot government in return for promising support for pro-Church educational reform. He chaired the extra-parliamentary commission that prepared legislation that intensified the conflict over education that lasted into the 1980s. 'Although known as the Loi Falloux, it could well have been called the Loi Thiers.'[32]

Thiers' motivation was correctly described as seeking to defend the social and political order with the help of gendarmes in cassocks. Worried that the Carnot plans would have given a free rein for anti-priest, socialist schoolmaster agitators, Thiers clearly separated primary education for the poor working classes and secondary education for the propertied middle classes. All that the potentially dangerous—if educated above their station—working classes needed was reading, writing, counting, and religious instruction and acceptance that 'inequality is the law of God', for to go further for the poor was 'to light a fire under an empty pot'.[33] Schoolmasters should be subordinated to Prefects to ensure that they were 'humble and submissive'. However, for secondary education—reserved to the middle classes—only imposed religion was desirable or possible. Nevertheless, in the spirit of Napoleon—Thiers was concurrently writing a 20-volume history of the Consulate and Empire—the authorized Church schools should also be subjected to state control, to ensure that subservience to government and private property was not subverted by either Jesuits or Socialists.

As Thiers was the prime inspiration and proponent of the 'Falloux Law', it is not surprising that he not only acquired the lifelong friendship of Dupanloup, Bishop of Orleans and leading advocate of clericalism; he was described by a cardinal as the 'saviour of religion'.[34] As he also supported the 1849 French military expedition to Rome that restored the Pope's temporal power, Thiers had made full amends for his earlier anticlericalism, like many freethinking members of the frightened propertied classes. The Falloux 1850 legislation, amended in 1854, duly

[31] Paul Carnot, *Hippolyte Carnot et le Ministère de l'Instruction Publique*, 1948, Chapter 3.

[32] J. P. T. Bury and R. P. Tombs, *Thiers 1797–1877: A Political Life*, 1986, 120. The Comission's members included Cousin, Dupanloup and Montalembert.

[33] Ibid. quoting Georges Chenesseau (ed.), *A l'origine de la liberté de l'enseignement: la Commission extra-parlementaire de 1849*, 1937, 39–40.

[34] Bury and Tombs, 120–2. See also Henri Malo, *Thiers 1797–1877*, 1932, 400–6.

subjected the schoolmaster, as he had been under Napoleon and the Restoration, to the Prefect, who appointed and could dismiss him. However, even more important, it allowed the Church to penetrate secondary education of the elite. The middle classes after 1848 welcomed the Church's teaching that social inequality was divinely ordained and that poverty was a punishment inflicted on the sinful and the spendthrift. In addition to local authorities, some businessmen, notably the heads of the mining and textile firms in the North, subsidized the clergy as an instrument of social control.[35] The Falloux Law reduced the role of teacher training colleges, admission to which was by nomination of the mayor and parish priest instead of competitive examination. This marked a setback for Guizot's faith in reason in favour of revelation as the best protection of the social order. Initially, the political leader of the Catholics, Count de Montalembert, supported Louis-Napoleon's coup, because he had 'for three years rendered incomparable services to the cause of order and of Catholicism', for 'the party of Catholicism against the revolution'.[36] However, whereas the unbelieving Thiers saw the Church as politically useful to the state, Montalembert moved against Louis-Napoleon because he wanted to free the Church schools from state monopoly control, arguing by 1863 for *The Free Church in the Free State*.[37] Nevertheless, liberal Catholicism was an awkward elitist tandem and it was the anti-liberal Catholicism of the journalist Louis Veuillot which attracted mass support.

The Liberal Empire of the 1860s saw the emergence of the *Ligue de l'Enseignement* which, together with many freemasonry lodges, played a key part in promoting not only secularized free and compulsory education but republicanism that triumphed in the Third Republic. The key figure was Jean Macé, an 1848 social democrat who had taken refuge as a teacher in an Alsace school after the 1851 coup and wrote a number of didactic children's books in which he couched his republican propaganda. Facilitated by the more tolerant political context of the Liberal Empire and the activities of educational organizations like the Society for Elementary Instruction and the Polytechnic Association (created by its students) and with help from Protestant Alsatian industrialists, Macé launched the *Ligue* in 1866, the year he became a freemason. He prudently avoided politics, rapidly attracting support, notably from freemasons, not only individually but from lodges.[38] Although the freemasons were locked in an internal controversy over deism in the 1860s and early 1870s, many of them played an active role in the shift towards secularism and republicanism that was to make anticlericalism such a salient feature of Third Republic politics. It was no accident that the Grand Orient's abandonment of the deist reference to the Grand Architect of the Universe coincided with the Republican electoral triumph in 1877.

[35] Gibson, 200–5. See also Prost 150–1, 172–82, Ponteil, 336–43 and Georges Duveau, *Les Instituteurs*, 1961, 88–90; cf. 31, 56–60.

[36] Quoted in Katherine Auspitz, *The Radical Bourgeoisie: The Ligue de l'Enseignement and the Origins of the Third Republic, 1866–1885*, 1982, 26.

[37] Lucien Jaume, *L'Individu effacé*, 210–37, 251–4.

[38] Auspitz, 51–88. See also Sudhir Hazareesingh and Vincent Wright, *Francs-maçons sous le Second Empire*, 2001, 128–9, 184 and the Introduction.

THE COMMITTED HISTORIAN AND POLITICAL CULTURE

Although, as we shall see, the committed intellectual did not emerge fully fledged until the end of the nineteenth century, the ground was prepared well before, especially by exceptionally gifted historians, writers of fiction and poetry, painters, and caricaturists. The Restoration had an unprecedented appetite for history, stimulated by the experience of the Revolution and Empire, the availability of historical archives, the new habit of parliamentary debate, and the impact of Romanticism, which promoted but distorted historical interpretation. Anti-revolutionary diatribes by Legitimists were countered with liberal defences of the Revolution. The disabused verdict of a leading participant, Talleyrand, was characteristically sceptical. 'If historians strive to discover the men to whom they can give the honour or attribute the blame of having caused, or directed, or modified the French Revolution, they will be wasting their time. It had no authors, nor leaders, nor guides.'[39]

However, the Restoration historians did seek in the French Revolution both an understanding of France's past and an augury of France's future. They combined a Romantic reassessment of national history that was impassioned and subjective with a determinist conception that reassuringly identified it with the inevitable rise and triumph of the middle classes treated as synonymous with the nation. They were not detached professional historians but prominent political actors, Guizot and Thiers more than Thierry and Mignet. However, they all admired the early anti-feudal liberal Revolution of 1789–91 and condemned the Jacobin Terror that followed in 1793–4, misleadingly identifying the latter with a popular revolt against the middle classes, although the Socialists would enthusiastically embrace this interpretation. Socialist historians Buchez and Louis Blanc accepted the view that the Revolution marked the determinist victory of the bourgeoisie in a class war with the aristocracy. However, whereas the liberal historians thought that was the end of history, the Socialists argued that class conflict had been resumed between the middle and working classes. The despair of a refuted determinist is reflected in Thierry's 1850 comment on the shattering effect of the 1848 Revolution on his philosophy of history. 'I no longer understand the history of France, the present has turned upside down my ideas about the past and with all the more reason it has overturned my ideas about the future.'[40] Like the Catholic Romanticism of Chateaubriand, who had hoped that the Christian past could be perpetuated, the Liberal Romantic determinists were doomed to disappointment in their belief that the struggle for freedom was over.

The most emblematic, prolific, and influential of the next generation of historians was Jules Michelet, who attained under the Third Republic the status of national ideologist. As early as his 1828–9 lectures, Michelet had asserted that

---

[39] Quoted in Duff Cooper, *Talleyrand*, 1932, 1934 edn, 70.

[40] Quoted in Ceri Crossley, *French Historians and Romanticism: Thierry, Guizot, the Saint-Simonians, Quinet and Michelet*, 1993, 60; cf. 8, 30–3, 53, 68 and François Furet, *La Gauche et la Révolution au milieu du XIXe siècle: Edgar Quinet et la Question du Jacobinisme, 1865–1870*, 1986, 12, 31.

'France is the true centre of Europe' but it was the 1830 Revolution that revealed to him that Paris would teach France and Europe the Revolution's lessons. Furthermore, he personified them as figments of his fertile imagination.[41] In his 1831 *Introduction to Universal History* (which he confessed could have just as readily been called *Introduction to French History*) he proclaimed: 'France has a centre. One and identical for centuries, she should be regarded as a person who lives and moves', a 'living organism' that had absorbed and assimilated its diverse components.[42] 'France owes the English a great debt. It was England who taught France to know herself' thanks to their incessant conflicts.[43] Appointing himself spokesman for the French people, the construction of whose united national consciousness he traced in his 17-volume *History of France* (1833–69) interrupted by his 7-volume *History of the French Revolution* (1847–53), Michelet argued that it had been liberated from subjection to Church and king by the Revolution. In *The People* (1846) he asserted the French people's historic role as 'saviour of the human race.... Only France has the right to project herself as a model, because no people has merged its own interest and destiny with that of humanity more than she'.[44] *Excusez du peu ...*

Edgar Quinet placed religion even more firmly in the centre of his historical analysis than Michelet, regarding the French loyalty to Roman Catholicism as having frustrated the fulfilment of France's messianic mission of applying the Revolution's embodiment of Protestant Reformation principles. Having helped to popularize the myths of the Revolution and Napoleon, he saw the 1830 Revolution as an incomplete democratic revolution. Recourse to Louis-Philippe had been intended to prevent another Jacobin 1793 by an 'improved 1789 on the model of the English 1688'[45] but this misfired, converting Quinet into a republican. Hostility to the prevailing materialism led him to emphasize the importance of religion for political culture. A *Collège de France* colleague of Michelet, both being deprived of their posts under the July Monarchy because of their anticlerical lectures, Quinet became a deputy in 1848 and took part as a National Guard colonel in the June Days repression. Hostile to the 1851 *coup d'état*, he went into exile and pessimistically concluded that in France, since the Roman victory over the Gauls, freedom was always defeated and always adjourned. His attack on Robespierre and the Terror's attempt to establish freedom through dictatorship helped disassociate republicanism from the guilt attached to Jacobinism. As such, it assisted those like Jules Ferry to develop the case for the Third Republic in the 1860s and implement it in the 1870s.[46]

Like his Restoration predecessors, Alexis de Tocqueville's history of the Old Regime was written with a political purpose: to demonstrate that France's inability to achieve a stable and free political system was due to the entrenched legacy of absolutism. Unlike Guizot, from whom he learnt to see French history in long-run

---

[41] Quoted in Gossman 172; cf. 167, 220.
[42] Quoted in Gauchet, 'Les *Lettres sur l'Histoire de France*' in *Les lieux de mémoire*, II/1, 303; cf. 305.
[43] Quoted in Robert Gibson, *Best of Enemies*, 32.   [44] Quoted in Gildea, 138.
[45] Furet, *La Gauche et la Révolution*, 13.
[46] Ibid. 31–4, 78–83; cf. Furet, *La Révolution*, 461–2 and Crossley, Chapter 5 on Quinet.

determinist terms, he did not regard the 1830 Revolution as a permanent resting place. As early as August 1830, he wrote that he doubted the middle classes' capacity to resist the movement for change: 'Already the lower classes treat them as a new aristocracy'.[47] The year of 1830 was the end of an act in an ongoing play, enacted by the class conflict that Guizot had identified as a historical driving force, but which he sought in vain to halt as a politician. As Tocqueville recollected in 1850, the exclusive triumph of an exiguously demarcated middle class was based upon 'the statutory exclusion of all beneath them and the actual exclusion of all above'.[48] Putting private enrichment first, the absolute bourgeoisie condemned itself to mediocrity in the defence of proprietorial privilege.

Having published the first volume of *Democracy in America*, which—in contrast with the liberals like Madame de Staël and Constant or the doctrinaires Guizot and Thierry—he thought was a better guide to the future than Britain, Tocqueville wrote to his English translator in 1837: 'I came into the world at the end of a long revolution which, after destroying the old state, had not succeeded in creating anything durable....I was living in a country which for forty years had tried out everything and settled permanently on nothing, so I had few illusions.'[49] Ten years after, in late 1847, as a member of the liberal opposition in the Chamber of Deputies, he prepared a draft manifesto, warning: 'The time will come when the country will find itself once again divided between two great parties. The French Revolution, which abolished all privileges and destroyed all exclusive rights, has allowed one to remain, that of property. Let not the proprietors deceive themselves as to the strength of their position, nor think that the rights of property form an insurmountable barrier because it has not as yet been surmounted.'[50] In a prophetic parliamentary speech one month before the February 1848 Revolution, Tocqueville again warned of an impending political struggle between the haves and the have-nots that would bring about 'sooner or later...a most formidable revolution...we are at this moment sleeping on a volcano...the earth is quaking once again in Europe'.[51]

Postponing his acute and acerbic explicit analysis of the Second Republic and (implicitly) of the Second Empire, Tocqueville's book on *The Old Regime and the French Revolution* reversed his earlier Guizot-inspired socio-political explanation giving societal factors priority over the state. In the light of his 1848–51 experience, Tocqueville now emphasized the secular monarchical administrative centralization that was reinforced by Napoleon, so that 'Paris *was* France'.[52] The nobility had been subservient to the centralizing monarchy in return for privileges, rather than allying itself with the increasingly rich and assertive middle classes, as in Britain. 'Thus the nobles, who had refused to regard the bourgeois

---

[47] Quoted by Edward Gargan, *Alexis de Tocqueville: The Critical Years, 1848–51*, 1955, 11. More generally see Jack Hayward, *After the French Revolution*, Chapter 6.

[48] *The Recollections of Alexis de Tocqueville*, 1893, 1959 edn, 2; cf. 9

[49] A. de Tocqueville, *Oeuvres Complètes*, IV, *Correspondance Anglaise*, I, 1954, 37–8.

[50] Tocqueville, *Recollections*, 10.   [51] Ibid. 12–13.

[52] Alexis de Tocquiville, *The Old Regime and the French Revolution*, 1856, 1955 edn, 72; cf. Part 2, Chapters 2–7.

as allies or even fellow citizens, were forced to envisage them as their rivals, before long as their enemies, and finally as their masters.'[53] However, 'the bourgeois ended up by being as isolated from the people as any nobleman' and in defence of their privileges accepted subservience to authoritarian government.[54] The socialist historians Philippe Buchez, Etienne Cabet, and Louis Blanc as well as Karl Marx pushed this class critique even further but in their admiration for Jacobinism reinforced what Tocqueville denounced as a 'slave mentality'.

Tocqueville's emphasis upon administrative centralization of the state-centred historical process could no longer suffice after 1848 because the revolutionary impetus had not been halted. So he now added a cultural-ideological dimension to his argument by emphasizing the authority attained by philosophic and literary writers as leaders of public opinion from the mid-eighteenth century, bent on a radical restructuring of all the social and political institutions of the country. Like Burke, Tocqueville attacked their rationalist addiction to holistic, simplistic, abstract generalization, divorced from practical political experience. 'Our revolutionaries had the same fondness for broad generalisations, cut-and-dried legislative systems, and a pedantic symmetry; the same desire to reconstruct the entire constitution according to the rules of logic and a preconceived system instead of trying to rectify its faulty parts. The result was nothing short of disastrous; for what is a merit in the writer may well be a vice in the statesman and the very qualities which go to make great literature can lead to catastrophic revolutions.'[55] The post-revolutionary writers of the early nineteenth century were more circumspect leaders of opinion. Their influence upon the national interpretation of its own recent history was indirectly conveyed through novels rather than didactically like their Enlightenment predecessors or their historian contemporaries.

LITERATURE, THE ARTS, AND POLITICAL CULTURE

Four of France's major writers of the early and mid-nineteenth century—Chateaubriand, Balzac, Stendhal, and Flaubert—either wrote explicitly about political and social issues or these concerns were so infused in their fiction that they had an indirect impact upon both elite and mass political culture. Of her poets, Lamartine and Hugo (more briefly Baudelaire) in their prose, poetry, and direct involvement in politics exercised a combination of ephemeral and more enduring influences, which in their case were less hostile to the changes that France was undergoing. Of her painters, works of David, Delacroix, Courbet, and Daumier made explicit reference to contemporary political and social matters, although in Daumier's case it was his caricatures rather than his paintings that are especially relevant. Other writers, such as Alexandre Dumas, were more prolific

---

[53] Ibid. 135.   [54] Ibid. 136; cf. 137.

[55] Ibid. 147; cf. 138–42, 150–2. More generally, see Daniel Mornet, *Les Origines Intellectuelles de la Révolution Française*, 1933.

and popular (his *Three Musketeers* and *The Count of Monte Cristo* have continued to attract a wide readership) but they tell us less about the evolution of French society than those discussed here.

Chateaubriand was the most Romantic of the four writers picked out and the most directly involved in politics. By his origins a traditionalist aristocrat and Catholic, he caused a literary sensation in 1802, after returning from exile in England, with the publication of *The Genius of Christianity*. A brief rapprochement with an admiring Napoleon led to an ephemeral diplomatic career that he was to resume in the Restoration, becoming Minister of Foreign Affairs in 1823–4. However, his main writings were those of a political polemicist from 1814, championing the Bourbon Restoration as a pamphleteer and journalist and by his speeches as a Peer in parliament. Nevertheless, during his 1793–1800 years in English exile, he acquired an enduring admiration for representative political institutions, which would be an antidote to Bonapartist despotism. Tracing the representative system to its ecclesiastical origins, he sought to convince the reactionary champions of the old order that elected representatives were not a subversive foreign import.

Chateaubriand and Constant converged from diametrically opposed directions to become the leading Restoration protagonists of constitutional government, purveyed respectively to the reactionary Right and the liberal Left as the Duke de Broglie put it. Chateaubriand's *Monarchy According to the Charter* of 1816 was most unwelcome to his ultra-royalist political friends, and he lost his ministerial position and pension as a result. His liberal views were also reflected in his critique of the Revolution for sacrificing liberty to equality. His *Memoirs Beyond the Grave*, his greatest literary work, predicted the demise of the restless, improvized Orleanist monarchy, the future of France being a republic.[56] While such views commended themselves to his relation Tocqueville, they were anathema to Balzac who wrote in 1833 of Chateaubriand: 'He is the most dangerous servant that the Bourbons have had. . . . I admire his talent but I dislike his political conduct. . . .'[57]

Royalists were much more comfortable with the novels of Balzac. As he put it in his 1842 preface to the *Human Comedy*: 'I write by the light of two eternal truths: Religion, Monarchy, two necessities proclaimed by contemporary events and back towards which any writer with common sense should try to bring our country.'[58] In novels that systematically covered private and political, provincial and Parisian life, inspired by a social zoology derived from the naturalist Buffon, Balzac combined history and social criticism, declaring with pseudo-modesty: 'French society was to be the historian, I was only the secretary.'[59] As he wrote

---

[56] Jean-Paul Clément, *F. R. de Chateaubriand: De l'Ancien Régime au Nouveau Monde. Ecrits politiques*, 1987 and Chateaubriand, *Mémoires d'Outre-Tombe*, posthumously published in 1848–50, 1973 edn. Chateaubriand just lived long enough to witness the coming of the Second Republic.

[57] Letter quoted in Edmond Biré, *Honoré de Balzac*, 1897, 132.

[58] Balzac, *La Comédie Humaine*, 7–9.

[59] Ibid. 7; cf. 16. The childless marriage of Adolphe Thiers to the fifteen-year-old daughter of the financier Dosne who had helped him financially in 1830—gossip said he was marrying the daughter of his mistress—'was echoed in the marriage of Balzac's ambitious and unscrupulous character Rastignac

to his future wife of his *Human Comedy*: 'I will have embraced a whole society in my head'.[60] However, behind the description of the multitude of characters and passions that peopled his novels, lay their 'hidden meaning': the 'twin principles of Catholicism and monarchy' necessary systematically to 'repress the depraved tendencies of man' in the service of social order.[61] Balzac admired Napoleon without being a Bonapartist because he personified strong but illegitimate government. However, he aspired to achieve with his pen what Napoleon had achieved with the sword and was described by a late-nineteenth-century novelist as 'our literary Napoleon'.[62]

From his earliest Restoration writings, Balzac championed primogeniture, the Jesuits and the Vendée uprising, which marked him out as an ultra-royalist. In *Le Départ*, about Charles X going into exile, he asserted: 'a king is the country incarnate; a hereditary king is the seal of property, a living contract between all those that own and those that do not. A king is the social keystone'[63]. . . . However, the Orleanist monarchy was not authentic, a view reflected in his most political novels. Thus in his *Country Doctor* of 1833, through his mouthpiece Dr Benassis, he warned: 'The triumph of the bourgeoisie over the monarchical system will increase the number of the privileged in the eyes of the people; the victory of the people over the bourgeoisie will be the inevitable effect of this change. If this turbulence comes, it will be through a limitless suffrage extended to the masses.'[64] (Although Balzac regarded elections as dangerous, this did not prevent him from standing unsuccessfully for election in 1831, 1832, and 1834, finally in 1848.) In the *Village Priest* of 1839 Balzac argued that those who wish to fragment ownership would claim that 'perpetual property is a theft'[65] and sure enough in 1840 Proudhon published his *What Is Property?* to which he replied 'Property is theft'. By 1849, the outright advocate of political and religious absolutism, while remaining a monarchist, could agree with a friend: 'Louis-Napoleon is a ladder to lift us out of the gutter of the Republic'. . . [66]

Balzac was only one of many writers who recoiled with horror from the increasing class conflict that they observed, initially resulting in a predominance of the bourgeoisie, with the prospect that this would in turn be followed by that of the working classes. In Balzac the bourgeois appears in many guises, notably that of enrichment through the purchase of confiscated Church and émigré property, making it possible to achieve elevated social status and political power. However, 'Increasingly, bourgeois became a dirty word, used by different people to categorise their enemies: it meant the exploiter for the socialist, the master for the servant, the civilian for the soldier, the man of vulgar taste for the artist, the

---

who, like Thiers, had come from the provinces to conquer Paris'. J. P. T. Bury and R. P. Tombs, *Thiers*, 1986, 50.

[60] Quoted in Biré, 75.   [61] Balzac, *La Comédie Humaine*, 7–9.

[62] Quoted in Biré, 69. See Chapters 2 and 3 for his discussion of Balzac's novels dealing with Napoleon.

[63] Quoted in Biré, 128; cf. 102–9, 123–4.   [64] Quoted in Biré, 169; cf. 136–49, 174, 178–80.

[65] Quoted in Biré, 172.

[66] Quoted in Biré, 182. More generally, see Ronnie Butler, *Balzac and the French Revolution*, 1983.

capitalist for the penniless.'[67] A liberal like Stendhal was scathing about those who equated liberty with the Right and intelligence with the capacity to make money. In an 1825 pamphlet, the habitué of the *Idéologue* salon of Destutt de Tracy attacked the Saint-Simonians on behalf of the 'thinking class' for regarding businessmen as heroes worthy of admiration, compared to genuine heroes like Washington and Lafayette.[68]

However, Stendhal was as stern a critic of the Church and the aristocracy as he was of the bourgeoisie. Having served in Napoleon's armies in Italy and during the disastrous Russian campaign, he was well equipped to provide a much admired description of the battle of Waterloo in *The Charterhouse of Parma* a novel which Balzac described as worthy of Machiavelli. Both his earlier *The Red and the Black* of 1830 and *Lucien Leuwen* left unfinished in 1835 had heroic ambition as a focus, reflecting the Napoleonic nostalgia that tempted Stendhal to try, unsuccessfully, to write a biography of his hero. Instead, he concentrated upon the social and political climber in the Restoration and the July Monarchy in an unheroic era, reflecting the hostility felt by the able but excluded. Although rewarded by his liberal friends with a minor consular post in Italy after 1830, Stendhal resented serving a corrupt and politically manipulative regime which repelled him. He expressed the imaginative transposition of his political insights in three great novels. '*Le Rouge et le Noir* shows the political mechanism perceived from below, from without; only its consequences are seen. *Lucien Leuwen* places the observer inside the political machine; it is a guided tour of the inner works...with *La Chartreuse de Parme* we are above the spectacle; we have a dizzying downwards view, total and terrifying.'[69]

In *Lucien Leuwen*, which was initially to have been called *Leuwen or the Student Excluded from the Ecole Polytechnique*, Stendhal stayed close to contemporary reality. The first sentence makes clear that his hero was dismissed for having taken part in 'one of the famous days of June, April or February 1832 or 1834', that is the anti-regime insurrections.[70] As well as describing the insidious and pervasive administration's pressures on the electorate, the novel makes derogatory comments on the political and business *arrivistes* that were in charge under the July Monarchy. '...Since July, the banks are running the State. The bourgeoisie has replaced the Faubourg Saint-Germain (i.e. the Bourbon elite) and the banks are the nobility of the bourgeois class.'[71] He singles out Jacques Laffitte by name— the first of the two banker—prime ministers, with Casimir-Périer, in 1830–2— and asserts: 'the king only loves money...a government cannot get rid of the Stock Exchange but the Stock Exchange can get rid of the government.'[72] Like Balzac before and Flaubert after him, Stendhal—without sharing their reactionary

---

[67] Zeldin, *France*, I, 20

[68] Stendhal (Henri Beyle), *D'un Nouveau Complot Contre les Industriels*, 1825, 1972, 10–15. More generally, see Stendhal's posthumous *Souvenirs d'égotisme*, 1983 edn, especially 75–7, 90.

[69] Maurice Bardèche, *Stendhal romancier*, 1947, 417 quoted in Robert Alter and Carol Cosman, *Stendhal: A Biography*, 1979, 228.

[70] Stendhal, *Lucien Leuwen*, 1973 ed, 9; cf. x.   [71] Ibid. 664   [72] Ibid. 665; cf. 664, 719.

views—transcended the mediocre reality of his times. Despising the prevailing materialism, he remained loyal to ideals that were beyond reach.

Even more than Balzac and Stendhal, Flaubert was determined to fit his fictional characters into a historical context, being convinced, that 'Historical people are more interesting than those of fiction,'[73] as he wrote apropos of his novel *Sentimental Education*. Notorious because of *Madame Bovary*, being tried—and acquitted—of indecency, Flaubert became increasingly misanthropic and pessimistic about giving the vote to the mass population, exemplifying mass mediocrity. He considered that just as shareholders voted according to the number of their shares, the same principle should apply in politics—not the infinite stupidity of one man, one vote. For him, democracy was a bad joke. As he wrote to democratic socialist George Sand in 1871, 'The numerous mass is always idiotic. I have few convictions but I believe this strongly.'[74] The French Revolution had destroyed divine right monarchy and hereditary aristocracy; the 1848 Revolution had discredited the bourgeoisie and the people generally, which was compounded by the 1871 Paris Commune. This civil war reminded him of his revulsion against the June Days of 1848 and prompted him to vent his exasperation with the people's unfitness for any share in political power.

He expressed this especially in his exercise in 'political education', the unfinished *Bouvard et Pécuchet* (planned in 1872 and published in 1881 a year after his death) and his *Dictionary of Accepted Ideas*, also incomplete and published as an appendix to his novel. 'I will vomit over my contemporaries the disgust I feel for them' was his deliberate intention.[75] The pivotal Chapter 6 of *Bouvard et Pécuchet* deals with the Second Republic in a way that reflects no credit on any of the participants—revolutionaries, 'moderates', and reactionaries—their gullibility vying with their brutality. Having satirized anticlericalism in the person of the pharmacist Homais in *Madame Bovary*, he turned on clerical oppressive intervention in the shape of abbé Jeufroy in *Bouvard and Pécuchet*. *The Dictionary of Accepted Ideas* (which was to have as its subtitle 'Encyclopedia of Human Stupidity') reflected his view that 'the average intelligence of the Frenchman is inadequate; he is narrow minded and easily taken in because he thinks he is competent....'[76] The Thiers government of 1871–3 was acceptable precisely because it had no principles. Flaubert did not share the Third Republic's belief in education, writing to the more sanguine George Sand in 1871: 'Free and compulsory education will only increase the number of imbeciles. ... The whole dream of democracy is to raise the proletarian to the level of bourgeois stupidity. The dream is partly achieved' ...[77] If one seeks a more enthusiastic and optimistic view of the democratic age one has to turn to the poets, who reacted very differently to the 1848 Revolution.

[73] Flaubert's *Correspondance*, III, 405, quoted in Antoine Compagnon, *La Troisième République des Lettres, de Flaubert à Proust*, 1983, 308–9.

[74] Flaubert, *Correspondance*, IV, 44, quoted by Compagnon, 292–3; cf. 271.

[75] Flaubert, *Correspondance*, IV, 167, quoted by Compagnon, 282.

[76] Flaubert, *Correspondance*, III, 99, quoted by Compagnon, 280.

[77] Flaubert, *Correspondance*, IV, 44, quoted by Compagnon, 304.

The poetic French protagonists of Romanticism, first Chateaubriand at the turn of the century and then in the early 1820s Lamartine, with his *Poetical Meditations* and Hugo in his *Odes*, were strongly associated with royalism and Catholicism. However, the arrogant oppressiveness of the ultras in politics and religion led them in new directions, so that by 1830 Hugo in his preface to *Hernani* could describe romanticism as 'liberalism in literature'.[78] Lamartine pursued a diplomatic career in the 1820s but his poetry with the help of literary and political friends—including Chateaubriand and Hugo—secured his election to the French Academy just before the 1830 Revolution. He resigned from the diplomatic service and pursued a political career, without belonging to any political faction and presenting his supra-partisan views with calculated ambiguity. Asked where he would sit in the Chamber of Deputies, he evasively replied: 'On the ceiling'.

Lamartine had become a deputy in January 1833 and was re-elected in the general election of June 1834. Following his support for Social Christianity until Lamennais' spectacular break with the Catholic Church, he was attracted to the 'New Christianity' of Saint-Simonism, which he interpreted as 'the application of Christianity to political society, the legislative implementation of human brotherhood. From this standpoint I am a Saint-Simonian', adding in the Political Summary at the end of *Voyage en Orient*, that 'The proletarians...will be a source of unrest in society until socialism has replaced odious individualism'.[79] Lamartine was attracted to the idea of establishing a 'Social Party' in 1834 by an ex-Saint-Simonian and ex-Fourierist, Jules Lechevalier, who founded a circumspect *Revue du Progrès Social* with Lamartine's financial backing. Among the 20–30 deputies that Lamartine hoped to attract to his 'party' was the future deputy Tocqueville, with whom he had discussed launching a political review having a social and moral slant. He was more successful with the journalist Emile de Girardin who was elected as a deputy in 1834 and launched the pioneering *La Presse* newspaper in 1836 but Girardin never stayed long in any political position. Under pressure, Lamartine asserted that his Social Party 'is not yet a party, it is much more, it is an idea'.[80] For the rest of the 1830s Lamartine hoped that the 'Social Party' could be a vehicle for his eclectic political ambitions (he turned down ministerial offers, holding out for Foreign Affairs or the Interior), but it never became much more than a one-man band because of his all too transparent self-centred opportunism.

Having memorably asked in 1839: 'Is France a nation which is bored?' by 1843 Lamartine rejected the July Monarchy in general and the Guizot government in particular, rallying to the Left parliamentary opposition. Between 1843 and 1946 he wrote his 8-volume idealistic vindication of the 1789 Revolution, *Histoire des Girondins*, whose publication in 1847 aroused immense public interest and helped prepare the way for the 1848 Revolution. Speaking frequently during the banquet campaign launched by the regime's opponents, Lamartine demanded

---

[78] Bertier de Sauvigny, *La Restauration*, 358; cf. 353–7.

[79] A. de Lamartine, *Voyage en Orient*, 1835, 1875 edn, II, 150–1 and Conclusion. See also C. Maréchal, *Lamennais et Lamartine*, 1907, 313.

[80] William Fortescue, *Alphonse de Lamartine: A Political Biography*, 1983, 87; cf. 86–8, 112–14.

radical and comprehensive reforms calculated to win him the popularity in republican quarters that he craved. The early post-revolutionary months in 1848, when he headed the Provisional Government (as well as being Foreign Minister) gave him the scope to deploy the effusive oratory and heroic posturing that served him well in opposition but lost all credibility after the June Days bloodletting. He is remembered for the symbolic victory of securing the adoption of the *tricolore* in preference to the Red Flag, playing—like Lafayette in 1830—the role of calming republican militancy. He received the highest personal vote in the April 1848 general election, where he was returned in 10 *départements* but the June conflict exposed the hollowness of his consensual rhetoric. The public and Assembly turned first to General Cavaignac and then to Louis-Napoleon. His decisive October 1848 speech in favour of the direct election of the President, asserting that even if the people chose unwisely, its will had to be respected, paved the way for Louis-Napoleon, Lamartine only receiving a derisory vote in the December 1848 election.[81] The poet's political credibility had finally been exhausted and the people had not returned his compliment.

Unlike Chateaubriand and Lamartine, Victor Hugo never, even ephemerally, became a minister but his life reflected a characteristically French transfer into political status of literary prestige. He was a peer from 1845 to 1848, an elected Member of Parliament from 1848 to 1951, political exile from 1851 to 1870, deputy in 1871 and finally senator from 1876 until his death in 1885. He pursued his literary and political careers simultaneously, using his leadership of the French Romantic movement to exercise political influence. His political standpoint changed dramatically over the years, moving from the early 1820s Royalist Right to the Republican Left during his Second Empire exile, with the Second Republic as the watershed, after which his literary stature augmented his political significance. However, from 1832 his liberalism was conspicuously reflected in his principled opposition to the death penalty (as opposed to the decision to end it only for political offences, to save the four ministers tried for provoking by their *coup d'état* the 1830 Revolution), a humanitarian attitude he shared with Lamartine. Against Maistre who regarded the executioner as the guardian of social stability, Hugo—anticipating his 1862 defence of the underdog in *Les Misérables*—castigated retention of capital punishment for the criminal poor.[82] His play *Le roi s'amuse* having caused uproar at the *Comédie Française* in 1832, further performances were banned and Hugo challenged the arbitrary decision on the ground that the Charter had abolished censorship. Napoleon having deprived the French of liberty, offering them instead military glory, Hugo argued in vain that as the July Monarchy could not provide the latter, it should offer them the former. He warned prophetically that the government would otherwise take advantage of the subsidence of the 1830 revolutionary libertarian surge to outlaw public freedom

[81] André-Jean Tudesq. *L'élection présidentielle de Louis-Napoléon Bonaparte: 10 décembre 1848*, 1965, 109; cf. 108 and Raymond Huard, *Le suffrage universel en France 1848–1946*, 1991, 41–2. See also Alexis de Tocqueville, *Recollections*, 118; cf. 117, 123–4 and Fortescue, 164–87, 243–8.

[82] See the extract from Hugo's preface to the 1832 edition of *Le Dernier Jour d'un condamné*, 1829, in Victor Hugo, *Ecrits politiques*, 2001, 45–78.

of the press and the performance of plays.[83] Hugo lost his case and draconian theatrical and press censorship was imposed in 1835.

During the rest of the July Monarchy, Victor Hugo supported the Orleans dynasty and then the presidential candidature of Louis-Napoleon in 1848. However, he quickly became disenchanted with the reactionary turn of his policies, opposing the French armed restoration of clerical government in Rome. He was especially incensed by the Jesuit interference in elections, legislation, and education, attacking the 'school of despotism' whose hostility to free thought and speech would promote 'not France's future but Spain's past'.[84] In a sensational speech in the 1850 debate on the Falloux Education Law, Hugo castigated the 'clerical party' for seeking to impose ignorance through a revived Inquisition, a journalist protagonist, Louis Veuillot having declared: 'We need a coercive institution; some sort of inquisition, not the name if you will, but the thing.'[85] Hugo championed a secular, free, and compulsory primary education, as well as the separation of Church and State. Uproar was caused by his speech against the reduction of the electorate by a third in 1850, warning parliament not to abandon 'the exchange of the right of revolt against the right to vote'.[86]

Hugo was the author of a proclamation on 3 December 1851, vainly calling on the army not to support the *coup d'état* and was one of the sixty-six deputies proscribed for their pains. From his 1851–70 exile, most of which was spent in the Channel Islands, issued forth a stream of diatribes against what he called Louis-Napoleon's crime. The two vitriolic publications of 1852 which had the most impact were his collection of poems *Les Châtiments* and his pamphlet *Napoléon-le-Petit*. The former is remembered especially for his anticlerical condemnation of 'Le *Te Deum* du 1 janvier 1852' celebrating the Church's support for overthrow of the Second Republic, while Hugo castigated in *Napoléon le Petit* 'the orgy of order', establishing a 'caricature' of the First Napoleonic Empire.[87] The pamphlet briefly set out the Republican programme that was advocated in the 1860s and very partially implemented by the Third Republic. While the separation of Church and State was achieved, more radical suggestions like elected judges, replacement of the army by a citizen militia and of administrative centralization by semi-autonomous communes were never adopted. Hugo rejected the offer of an amnesty in 1859, continuing to personify the exiled opposition to Napoleon III and championing the United States of Europe, with Paris as its capital, Europe being a 'sublimated France'.[88] His death in 1885 was the occasion, as we mentioned earlier, of the restoration of the *Panthéon* as the resting place of Republican heroes, in which he took his unquestioned place.

The Second Republic, which marked such a watershed in Hugo's politico-literary life, was an even more explosive interlude in the life of Baudelaire.

[83] Hugo, *Ecrits politiques*, 130; cf. 116–36.

[84] Quoted in Rémond, *L'Anticléricalisme*, 141; cf. 133–42.

[85] Hugo, *Ecrits politiques*, 130: cf. 116–36.   [86] Ibid. 145; cf. 137–58.

[87] Ibid. 183–4; cf. 177–93. Hugo first used the phrase 'Little Napoleon' in his 17 July 1851 speech against the revision of the Constitution (ibid. 354–5).

[88] Ibid. 238; cf. 237–43, 265, 291.

Remembered above all as the disenchanted poet of *Les Fleurs du Mal*, Baudelaire was also the street fighter of February and (on the side of the insurgent workers) in June 1848, as well as possibly the resistance to Louis-Napoleon's coup in December 1851. His political commitment and rejection of 'art for art's sake' owed much to his resentment, as a *déclassé* dandy against bourgeois society, to his friendship with the worker–poet Pierre Dupont (remembered particularly for his 'Le chant des ouvriers' and alongside whom he fought in June 1848), and to his enthusiasm for the incendiary ideas and political stance of Proudhon. He read and took notes from Proudhon's 1846 *System of Economic Contradictions* and in 1848–9 was a disciple, retaining his admiration ever after his post-1851 detachment from overt political preoccupations. One of Proudhon's remarks that would have appealed to him was 'The mass murders of monopoly have not yet found their poets'.[89] He also shared Proudhon's all-out attack on religion, proclaiming 'God is Evil' because God's world is hell on earth.[90] To the end of his life, Baudelaire remained an aesthetic revolutionary with a rather splenetic, self-destructive emphasis upon demolition and despair.

Baudelaire had earned his living in the 1840s partly by art criticism, which led him into contact with painters like Delacroix and Courbet, as well as the caricaturist Daumier. In 1846, when he produced an early tribute to the quintessentially anti-bourgeois Daumier in his 'Quelques caricaturistes français', Baudelaire prefaced his 'Salon de 1846' with a dedication 'Aux bourgeois' expressing his ironic derision. 'You are the majority—in number and intelligence; so you are power, which is justice. Some of you are learned, some landed; the glorious day will come when the learned will become landed, and the landed learned. Then your power will be complete, and no one will protest against it.'[91] His 1849 attempt to communicate his enthusiasm for Proudhon to Delacroix met with a rebuff but in Courbet he found a more receptive ear. Courbet painted Baudelaire in 1849 and included him in his iconic, retrospective *The Studio* (to which we shall return) while 'Baudelaire drew Courbet on a sheet of caricatures'.[92] However, their close friendship proved to be ephemeral. Baudelaire revolted against Courbet's determination to push his theoretical Realism to extremes, seeing it as a domineering attempt to impose a personal style on painting generally.[93] More fundamentally, Baudelaire remained a Bohemian social outcast, who was unsure of which side in the class war he was on, whereas in their opposed ways Delacroix and Courbet did know.

---

[89] T. J. Clark, *The Absolute Bourgeois: Artists and Politics in France 1848–1851*, 1982, 167, quoting P. J. Proudhon, *Système des contradictions économiques*, 1846, 1923 edn, I, 269.

[90] Clark, 168, quoting *Système des contradictions économiques*, I, 384.

[91] Charles Baudelaire, *Oeuvres Complètes*, 1961, 874–6. See also Clark, *The Absolute Bourgeois*, 142–4, 161–3. On Delacroix as a protégé of Thiers, see Bury and Tombs, *Thiers*, 49, 153.

[92] T. J. Clark, *Image of the People: Gustave Courbet and the 1848 Revolution*. 1982, 23; cf. 74–6 and *The Absolute Bourgeois*, 124–5. Courbet's Portrait of Baudelaire is reproduced in *Image of the People*, 55.

[93] Clark, *Image of the People*, 30, 52. On Sartre's criticism of Baudelaire for fleeing political commitment, see Jean-Paul Sartre, *Baudelaire*, 1947, 1949 Eng. edn.

Although in 1848 it appears that Delacroix briefly considered a companion piece to his symbolically powerful 'Liberty guiding the People' portrayal of the 1830 Revolution, to be called 'Equality on the Barricades of February', it never materialized. Having suffered under the July Monarchy by having 'Liberty' hidden away by a government reluctant to be reminded of its revolutionary origins, he had to be content in 1848 to have it shown in Lyon. However, in the 1830s, Thiers as minister had commissioned him to paint murals in both chambers of Parliament and Delacroix acknowledged that the conservative Thiers was the only public personality ever to have helped his career as a painter. In revulsion against the socialist-worker revolutionaries, he retreated into a private world, painting fruit, flowers, and then the murals of the Church of Saint-Sulpice. He now looked to Louis-Napoleon to protect social order. In disgust, Victor Hugo declared: 'Delacroix, reactionary in his ideas, romantic in his talent, was in contradiction with his own works. ... In my violent and frequent discussions with Delacroix. ... I told him that his opinions were diametrically opposed to his painting: he agreed with me, and said his painting was a turpitude.'[94]

There was a very different reaction to the betrayal of the 1830 Revolution from Daumier in association with Charles Philipon, who became the most visually damaging and verbally subversive opponents of the July Monarchy. Prior to the Third Republic's revival of corrosive political caricature, the years 1830–5 witnessed the most explosive and talented output, associated with the relaxation of censorship, such as had occurred in 1789–92 and from 1814 to 1820. What imparted its exceptional impact to the Philipon–Daumier duo was the close collaboration achieved between verbal and visual satire purveyed through the press, Philipon usually providing the captions and Daumier—and others, such as Grandville—producing the lithographs. Testimony to their achievement is provided by a contemporary British observer who declared that *La Caricature* and *Le Charivari* were a more powerful force than both chambers of parliament, while a leading historian of the July Monarchy referred to 'an insurrection by drawing, regicide by pencil'.[95] If it is thought that the reference to regicide is excessive, a week before the Fieschi *machine infernale* attempt to assassinate the king on 18 July 1835, *Le Charivari* had included a snippet announcing that 'His Majesty has not once been assassinated today'.[96] The repression of press freedom silenced political caricature until 1848 but not before Philipon produced his most effective portrayal of Louis-Philippe's head as pear-shaped, which frequently reproduced in Parisian graffiti, 'came to symbolize the king's entire body and then his system of government'.[97]

Jean-Baptiste Daumier was a close observer of the bourgeois and the proletarian but remained a lifelong artisan, resentful of the inroads of industrialization

[94] Quoted in Clark, *The Absolute Bourgeois*, 126; cf. 124–41.

[95] Paul Thureau-Dangin, *Histoire de la Monarchie de juillet*, I, 1884, 426 and Henry Bulwer-Lytton, *France: Social, Literary, Political*, I, 1834, 72, both quoted by David S. Kerr, *Caricature and French Political Culture 1830–1848: Charles Philipon and the Illustrated Press*, 2000, 4, 6; cf. 1–3, 63–4.

[96] Kerr, 115; cf. 114–16.   [97] Ibid. 85; cf. 36, 45 note, 83–4, 142, 144, 179.

that was destroying the culture and status of his class, proudly reasserting their traditional skills, inclined to be radical and even revolutionary.[98] Unlike Philipon and Grandville, Daumier did not fight in the July 1830 uprising but like the former he was subsequently imprisoned for his satirical work as a caricaturist. After Balzac quickly abandoned editing *La Caricature*, disliking its increasing political radicalism and Grandville became disillusioned with republican politics, it was Daumier who emerged as its leading caricaturist, illustrating the captions by 'the republican party's unofficial artistic impresario', Philipon.[99] This was especially true of his Robert Macaire series of lithographs in which the swindler was made to symbolize the sleazy side of the get-rich-quick July Monarchy. Daumier also made a series of grotesque clay busts of leading Orleanist politicians that were then used as models for lithograph caricatures both individually and collectively, for example in the ministerial bench depicted in 'Le Ventre législatif' of 1834.[100] That year of Paris and Lyon unrest was marked by another masterpiece, the lithograph depicting the massacre of sleeping citizens in rue Transnonain.[101] From Daumier's prolific *oeuvre*, two more works must be specifically mentioned: his magnificent painting of 'The Republic', presented in an 1848 competition for which he was encouraged to enter by his friend Courbet, and the sculpture 'Ratapoil', which personified the jaunty and menacing Bonapartist activist in 1850 and prompted Michelet to get down on his knees and tell Daumier that 'he had done more for Republicanism with that one invention than the rest of the politicians put together.'[102] When the Republicans at last took control of the Third Republic in 1878, the pension of an old and blind Daumier was doubled by his grateful admirers.

Daumier frequented the Brasserie Andler at which many of the avant-garde artists who were associated with Courbet and Realism met to drink, eat, and talk. They included not only Realism's leading theoretician, the art critic Jules Champfleury, but painters like Corot, the poets Baudelaire and Dupont, the radical journalist and future Communard comrade, Jules Vallès and sometimes Proudhon. Realism was a defiant description for those who rejected the conventional art exemplified in the annual sale which gave the selection jury

---

[98] Clark, *The Absolute Bourgeois*, 100–03.

[99] Kerr, 66; cf. 23–4, 30–2, 40–3. Like Grandville, Daumier shared with Balzac a physiological approach to portraying and caricaturing society's human zoo. Balzac launched a series of 423 portraits in 8 volumes between 1839 and 1842, *Les Français peints par eux-mêmes*. See Pierre Rosanvallon, *Le Peuple Introuvable*, 290–3. Ridiculing provincial life was common, e.g. Balzac's *Scènes de la vie de province* and Pierre Durand's *Physiologie du provincial à Paris*, 1842, illustrated by Gavarni.

[100] Reproduced ibid. 159; cf. 160–4. They are displayed in the *Musée d'Orsay*.

[101] Reproduced ibid. 112; cf. 110–13. Thiers, who as Minister of Interior, personally took part in the repression, was identified with it and an investigation covering up the Transnonain killings (Bury and Tombs, 53–4) as he was later to be with the much more sanguinary repression of the 1871 Commune.

[102] Clark, *The Absolute Bourgeois*, 103; cf. 105 'The Republic' is reproduced on page 83 and 'Ratapoil' on page 152. Clark explains the probable source of the name Daumier invented: a conflation of General Rapatel, recalled to crush the June 1848 uprising and General Hautpoul, who became War Minister in 1849. Clark also sees a possible inspiration in a poem given at the time by Baudelaire to Daumier, 'Le Vin des Chiffonniers', especially a Bonapartist ragpicker (ibid. 116).

great power over painters through their influence over the award of official prizes and the public purchases that favoured religious and historical subjects rather than portraits and landscapes. In the catalogue manifesto for his 1855 one-man show, Courbet protested that 'The title of realist has been imposed on me as that of romantic was imposed on the men of 1830'.[103] He was uneasy because the name did not reflect his subjective revolutionary concern to change rather than copy the objective world. Whereas the anti-bourgeois literary realism of a Balzac had been politically reactionary, in Gustave Courbet's case realism was associated with an anarcho-socialism that he shared with his fellow Franc-Comtois Proudhon. His 1850 picture of the madcap Fourierist proselytiser Jean Journet—who interrupted meetings of Hugo and Lamartine among others—'setting out for the conquest of Universal Harmony' and modelled on the popular image of the Wandering Jew, and perhaps the artisan *compagnon* in search of work, reflected, as Baudelaire had spotted, Courbet's own utopian aspiration to save the world.[104] Like Hugo, Lamartine, and Baudelaire, Courbet had been touched by the Saint-Simonian ambition of the artist as the prophetic guide of humanity, not the self-effacing practitioner of art for art's sake.

Like Proudhon, Courbet in June 1848 was an agonized spectator of the tragic civil war but, as he asserted in 1851, he was 'not only a Socialist, but a democrat and a Republican as well; in a word a supporter of the whole Revolution, and above all, a Realist, that is to say a sincere lover of genuine truth'.[105] Abandoning his earlier admiration for Fourierism, Courbet's self-conscious self-description as an artisan-painter warmed to Proudhon's claim that manual work was man's defining characteristic and title to nobility. In his 'The Painter's Workshop, a True Allegory Summarising a Period of Seven Years in my Life as an Artist' usually known as the Studio and covering the years 1847–54, Courbet included Baudelaire, Champfleury, and Proudon on the right side as sometime friends of Realism, while the figures on the left represented those he abominated ideologically.[106] Courbet was also inspired by Proudhon's libertarian assertion of the artist's personal freedom and rejection of government authority, in art as in all else, as incapable of comprehending genius. From Proudhon's imprisonment during the Second Republic, a great mutual admiration developed that culminated with the collaboration in 1863–5 leading to the posthumous publication of Proudhon's *On the Principle of Art and Its Social Destination* in which he described Courbet's 'The

---

[103] Quoted in Jack Lindsay, *Gustave Courbet: His Life and Art*, 1977, 138; cf. 44, 120. See also Courbet's 1861 manifesto, ibid. 171–2.

[104] Clark, *Image of the People*, 21–2, 32; cf. Lindsay, 71–3, 119. The picture of Journet is reproduced in Clark, 28.

[105] Quoted in Clark, *Image of the People*, 28, from a 19 November 1851 letter cited in G. Riat, *Gustave Courbet, peintre*, 1906, 93–4.

[106] James Henry Rubin, *Realism and Social Vision in Courbet and Proudhon*, 1980, 8–9, 19–23, 30–4, 131. See also Lindsay, 130–4.

Stone-Breakers' of 1849 as the first socialist painting.[107] It was followed by other great Realist paintings: 'Firemen going to a fire', 'Burial at Ornans' and 'Peasants of Flagey returning from the Fair'.

The collaboration was prompted by the uproar caused in 1863 by Courbet's anticlerical painting of drunken priests entitled 'Return from the Conference'. Proudhon had intended to write a pamphlet defending this painting that was called the 'Curés' for short but was encouraged by Courbet to produce a much more wide-ranging work. Courbet inundated Proudhon with frequent letters of advice in the hope that 'we shall at last have a treatise on modern art along the lines I have indicated, corresponding to Proudhonian philosophy'.[108] The unfinished but extended analysis of the relationship of the radical artist to society delighted Courbet but he was dismayed at the premature death of his protagonist, 'The nineteenth century has lost its pilot.... We have no compass and humanity and the Revolution are adrift. I am in a state of moral prostration and discouragement such as I have only felt once before in my life (on 2 December [1851], when I went to bed and vomited for three whole days).'[109]

However, worse was to come. The police reported Courbet's presence at the 1868 anniversary of Proudhon's death, indicating that he had joined the First Socialist International (whose French contingent were mainly Proudhonians) but it was the Paris Commune of 1871 that got Courbet into hot water bedevilling the rest of his life. He was President of an unofficial artist's committee that recommended in 1870 getting rid of the column in Place Vendôme surmounted by a statue of Napoleon as a Roman Emperor, on the grounds that it was devoid of artistic value and offensively militarist. (In July 1833, Thiers—who was to repress with brutality the 1871 Commune—had inaugurated the replacement of Napoleon's statue on the Vendôme column.) Courbet was elected to the committee that took up the question of the Vendôme column and decided it should be demolished and he was present when this was done. On the Versaillais reoccupation of Paris, Courbet went into hiding but was arrested, sentenced by military tribunal and imprisoned for six months in addition to the three months he had already served. Thereafter his life was one of exile in Switzerland to escape the vindictiveness of the French government that insisted that he personally pay for the re-erection of the Vendôme column. Its minions seized and sold off all his pictures and property they could lay their hands on, including his portrayal of 'Proudhon and Family' which he had painted after Proudhon's death, because his subject had always obstinately refused to sit for it.[110]

On his election to the Paris Commune, Courbet sent a *profession de foi* to Jules Vallès, proudly asserting: 'I have always been concerned with the social question

---

[107] Lindsay, 59; cf. Proudhon, *Du Principe de l'art et de sa destination sociale*, 1865, 236 ff.

[108] Alan Bowness, 'Courbet's Proudhon' in *The Burlington Magazine*, CXX, No 900, March 1978, 126; cf. 123–8, quoting a letter in Riat, 209. See also Lindsay, 181–5.

[109] Quoted in P. Haubtmann, *Proudhon, 1855–65*, 308. See also Lindsay, 197, 205–7.

[110] Lindsay, Chapters 14–18 passim.

and its related philosophies, pursuing a path parallel to my comrade Proudhon'.[111]
As his sometime friend Baudelaire had put it, Courbet believed that like great art,
its criticism should be 'partial, passionate and political'.[112] He died in 1877, just
as the Republicans were coming to power but it was not to be quite the Republic
to which Courbet had aspired. Social conflicts persisted and political consensus
remained elusive.

---

[111] Quoted by Bowness, 123, from P. Courthion, *Courbet raconté par lui-même*, II, 1950, 47.
[112] Rubin quoting Baudelaire's *Salon de 1846* from Baudelaire, *Art in Paris, 1845–62*, 1965, 44.

5

A Liberal Democratic Republic Struggles to be Born, 1814–78

The 1789–99 revolutionary decade telescoped and tried out all the institutional frameworks that the French were to recapitulate in the nineteenth century, so that they could all claim some share in its normative legacy. Far from being a 'bloc' as Clemenceau controversially claimed, the Revolution was not one and it was divisible. The two versions of constitutional monarchy and a Bonapartist despotism, as well as an ephemeral attempt at Jacobin dictatorship and a much more extended exercise in republican government by parliamentary assembly, could all seek to borrow some virtue and legitimacy from association with the historic break with the Old Regime. So, it is not surprising that ultra-royalist attempts to revive the pre-1789 regime would destabilize the Bourbon Restoration and restart in slower motion the struggle to end the revolutionary process by establishing a consensual liberal democracy. This continued to prove elusive for reasons that we began to explore in Chapter 4.

Turning now to the more specific causes of dissensus, we first investigate the problems associated with representing the people prior to and after manhood suffrage, before discussing partisanship without parties, fractionalism of the Right, Centre, and Left. Then the pressures from above and resistance from below will be examined: the representation of the people, plebiscites, and parliamentary institutions; an intrusive central administration in pursuit of comprehensive and uniform control; the struggle for freedom of the press in a context in which it was treated by governments as subversive of the established institutions. Despite the pervasive nationalism, the temptation to damn opponents as explicitly or implicitly anti-France proved difficult to resist.

FROM REGIME INSTABILITY TO GOVERNMENT INSTABILITY

Whereas the British approach to the practical reconciliation of liberalism and democracy was to introduce the people's participation through the gradual extension of the suffrage into liberal representative institutions, the French approach was to substitute for royal sovereignty, an undifferentiated nation embodying a rationalist abstraction dubbed the general will. British pluralism, based on the countervailing power of private interests to curb royal power, was rejected as accepting ongoing conflict, whereas French monism was alone capable of producing general rules that expressed the purported unity of the nation, issuing in an orderly uniformity. Instead of an untidy historically derived empirical diversity, the French revolutionaries—after an initial Anglophile phase—elevated to supremacy an abstract entity, the nation, converting the general will—which Rousseau had made the legitimizing basis of the political community—into the foundation of legislative authority in a Republic.[1]

Of the anti-liberal implications of the attempt to put this rationalist principle into practice, the one that concerns us here is the problem of how to represent individuals of the one and indivisible nation. Elections, hard upon the virtual manhood suffrage at the outset, were indirect, allowing the predominantly irrational and illiterate mass electorate to be mediated by their betters, prior to the outright restriction of the electorate and eligibility. This left unresolved the problems of popular sovereignty expressed by revolutionary mobs, whose appetite could not be appeased by abstractions, as well as the relation of government action to legislative decisions. The sources of persisting instability of political regime lie in these practical difficulties derived from theoretical presuppositions elevated to the status of ideological dogmas.

How could the unanimous people, as the conceptual source of political legitimacy, be institutionalized? When all social and territorial diversities are denied as the source of disreputable privilege and inequality, an abstract legal fiction of unity is superimposed on actual differences. But a complex society cannot be simplified by an ingenious formula. Citizenship identity came from belonging to a nation that could not meet except through representation in a parliament claimed Sieyès. Indirect election would allow those qualified for the representative function to import into the democratic process an essential meritocratic component argued Roederer. 'Government by the best' quickly became equated, during the Directory, with property owners, notably by Boissy d'Anglas. When this equation of merit with property had been elaborated and implemented during the July Monarchy, 'Guizot incarnates in almost caricature form this degradation of eminence into banal class power'.[2] In a desperate effort to overcome by rhetoric the deception involved, for all practical purposes, through reducing the abstraction 'people' to the propertied bourgeoisie, Michelet personified France and the French people into a mystical unity, emulated by the poet–politicians Lamartine and Hugo.[3] However, the revival of a Saint-Simonian call in 1832 and 1848 for separate representation for 'proletarians' in the 1863 Manifesto of the Sixty for working class candidates, given eloquent support in Proudhon's 1865 *Political Capacity of the Working Classes*, challenged the fiction of a classless nation whose representation could be safely left to the self-designated best people.[4]

---

[1] P. Rosanvallon, *Le sacre du citoyen*, 131, 204–13, 217, 220–7, 234–5.

[2] P. Rosanvallon, *Le Peuple Introuvable: Histoire de la représentation démocratique en France*, 1998, 53; cf. 12–17, 31–54.

[3] Ibid. 57–8; cf. 30. In addition to Michelet's *Le Peuple*, 1846, see Paul Villaneix, *La Voie royale: Essai sur l'idée du peuple chez Michelet*, 1971.

[4] Rosanvallon, *Le Peuple Introuvable*, 67–96.

The foundation myth of abstract unanimity led in 1791 to both the abolition of guilds and corporations and a decree forbidding political parties, both promoted by Le Chapelier. Thus both economic and political representative organizations were almost simultaneously rejected. A former Saint-Simonian turned Second Empire dignitary, Michel Chevalier, in presenting the 1864 Bill allowing trade unions to be formed, described the Le Chapelier elimination not merely of compulsory but voluntary associations of workers as 'the fundamental error of the Revolution'.[5] It took the industrial and political leaders of the working classes decades to achieve weak and fragmented organizational expression, as we shall see. For the present, we shall concentrate upon the vicissitudes of parliamentary representation, taking up the story where we left it at the end of the revolutionary decade with Bonaparte's seizure of power from legislators whose factional disputes over tactics provided an opportunity for a reassertion of personalized executive control.

On the eve of his fall from imperial power in 1814, Napoleon addressed the Legislature in characteristically forthright fashion: 'You say you are the representatives of the people, you are not ... I am the only representative in France. Five million voters have successively elected me Consul, Consul for life and Emperor. If there is an authority or individual in France who can say as much, let him come forward.'[6] During the transition to dictatorship, parliament could discuss and reject but not propose or amend legislation. This was the function of the Council of State handpicked by Napoleon, who chaired the meetings at which draft Bills were discussed. He also appointed and dismissed ministers at will. All this was in sharp reaction to the attempt at government by Assembly in the revolutionary decade. The membership of the three chambers of parliament were selected by Sieyès, Napoleon, and Talleyrand and when speeches were made, notably by Constant, criticizing Bills, Napoleon's anger at the unbearable insolence of the 'vermin who have got under my skin' led to critics being purged.[7] Napoleon also invented a new technique of constitutional amendment, the *senatus-consultum*, which in 1802 enabled him to become Consul for life and reorganize parliament. Ironically it was the hitherto tame Senate and Legislative Body, led by Talleyrand at the head of a Provisional Government (assisted by Minister of Police Fouché), that deposed Napoleon in 1814. It was military defeat that was decisive, as in 'France only events are allowed to vote.'[8]

The Restoration Constitutional Monarchy—in reaction against the First Empire's rubber stamp parliament—revived the idea of representation but with an electorate of merely 1 per cent of the population, with only some 15,000 people qualified to stand as candidates. Unlike the much admired British parliament, Restoration France had difficulties in seeing politics as a competition for office

---

[5] Ibid. 133; cf. 176.

[6] Quoted in Adrien Dansette, (ed.), *Vues politiques de Napoléon*, 1939, 46.

[7] Irene Collins, *Napoleon and His Parliaments, 1800–1815*, 1977, 44; cf. 10–32, 41–7, 62–81, 147–9.

[8] Unattributed remark mentioned by Madame de Staël, quoted in Marcel Gauchet, 'Constant, Staël, et la Révolution Française' in François Furet and Mona Ozouf (eds), *The Transformation of Political Culture, 1789–1848*, 1989, 171.

between a majority party supporting the government and a minority party in opposition, seeking to persuade the electorate to switch their votes to ensure a change of parliamentary majority and government, although in 1800 (not a good time to point this out), Madame de Staël had indicated that 'it is through opposition that the English acquire the necessary talents to become ministers'.[9] Despite the efforts of Constant on the Liberal Left and Chateaubriand on the Royalist Right to promote a dualistic political polarization, the members of the Restoration parliament showed little inclination to accept even minimal party discipline. Only in 1830, when Charles X violated the constitutional Charter which Louis XVIII had improvised under pressure from the victorious Allies to fill the political vacuum left by the defeat of Napoleon, did polarization take place and it led to the revolutionary overthrow of the regime.

After Louis XVIII's return in 1815, 'Europe witnessed the curious spectacle of a restored monarch attempting, rather feebly, to defend his old enemies from those who were determined to avenge his wrongs.'[10] Not to infringe the principle of divine right, the equivocal Charter (a backward-looking name, perhaps inspired by English *Magna Carta*) was unilateral in form—the king set the limits to his own power—but a compromise in content. Thus, article 6 stated that all religions were protected but article 7 proclaimed Roman Catholicism the state religion. Louis XVIII lent credence to the liberal view of the Charter as a contract between the king and the nation by swearing to remain faithful to and defend it in his speech opening parliament in March 1815. A struggle quickly developed between the vociferously reactionary, ultra-royalist majority, elected in the wake of Napoleon's 100 Days comeback and the pro-ministerial minority, supporting the moderate government in which the key role until 1820 was played by Interior Minister Decazes, the royal favourite. Ironically, the ultra-royalists for tactical reasons, being in the majority, established the *principle* of collective ministerial responsibility to parliament (article 13 of the Charter) but in *practice* none of the eight governments between 1814 and 1830 was removed by a parliamentary vote of no confidence. They disintegrated or were dismissed by the king. The six dissolutions of parliament were not an appeal to the electorate to settle a conflict between the government and parliament but exercises of the royal prerogative, which ultimately proved fatal to the regime in 1830 when used by Charles X, who had contempt for the Charter.[11]

His brother, Louis XVIII, the last French king to die while still on the throne, tried to separate the role of the monarch from that of the Prime Minister, writing to Decazes in 1820 that 'it is not the king who is the keystone, it is the President of the Council of Ministers'.[12] Governments were small with only six or seven

---

[9] *De la Littérature*, II, 1800, 124, quoted by Jean Starobinski, 'Benjamin Constant: comment parler quand l'eloquence est épuisée' in Furet and Ozouf (eds), 193.

[10] Duff Cooper, *Talleyrand*, 1932, 1934 edn, 284.

[11] P. Rosanvallon, *La Monarchie Impossible: Les Chartes de 1814 et de 1830*, 1994, 87–9; cf. 48–50, 71–81. See also G. de Bertier de Sauvigny, *La Restauration*, Chapters 4–5, 8–9, 16 passim and Chateaubriand, *De la Monarchie selon la Charte*, 1816.

[12] Bertier de Sauvigny, *La Restauration*, 270; cf. 196.

ministers: Foreign Affairs, Interior, Finance, Justice, War, Navy, and Police. More ephemerally, there were ministers of Ecclesiastical Affairs and of Commerce. The Prime Minister combined his office with one of the others—either Foreign Affairs or Finance. Lengthy Cabinet meetings were held three times a week in the king's presence. Louis XVIII often fell asleep at the Wednesday meeting at which he presided, while the ministers read and wrote letters when matters not concerning their department were being discussed. During the later years of the Villèle premiership of 1822–8, he often worked directly with Charles X, only consulting his colleagues formally, without fixed dates for Cabinet meetings. Thereafter, Charles X tried to govern himself, leading to the dangerous identification of king and government that Louis XVIII had wisely avoided. Under Polignac's premiership in 1829–30, there were long meetings four times a week, with the king—present at two of the four—persistently intervening.[13]

In the absence of disciplined political parties, the Restoration Chamber of Deputies was dominated by the landed nobility on the Right and attempts by the government to secure a reliable majority by combining membership of parliament and public employment. Prefects, councillors of state, and army officers were elected either before appointment or appointed after election. Nevertheless, the Deputies developed procedures for detailed budgetary control that set the pattern for well over a century. The House of Peers had little power or prestige, being packed with supporters as governments changed. It consisted of the rejects of all the political regimes France had tried for the preceding quarter of a century. Its members, unlike Deputies, were paid. The political legitimacy of the Deputies was itself limited, not merely by the very restricted suffrage but by the electoral process. Election meetings were forbidden and programmes were frowned upon as pandering to the voters. The Prefects fraudulently manipulated the electoral register to eliminate opponents and aid supporters. Civil servants were, on pain of dismissal, required to vote for government candidates.[14] Nevertheless, the king's partisans lost the elections of 1827 and 1830. His attempt to override the electoral verdict, with the ultra-royalists openly calling for outright dictatorship and the king saying he would not make Louis XVI's mistake of retreating, led to the overthrow of the Bourbon monarchy.

THE 1830 REVOLUTION AND THE JULY MONARCHY

However, parliament played only a timid part in the 1830 Revolution. It was the press—led notably by Thiers and the *National*—that prompted resistance to the ordinances that *inter alia* curbed the press. The press called for passive resistance and a refusal to pay taxes as a protest against arbitrary government. It was the Parisian skilled workers and artisans, especially in the building trades and printers (who had a direct incentive) in the context of economic depression, with

---

[13] Ibid. 271–4.   [14] Ibid. 289–91, 296–9; cf. 247–9, 252–61.

their own agenda concerning pay, prices and banning of labour-saving machinery, whose armed insurrection was decisive. The defeatist parliamentary opposition offered no leadership until after victory was achieved. It was then that the banker Laffitte, who had funded the *National*, whose home became the headquarters of the Opposition, helped by the fast footwork of Thiers, who persuaded the unheroic Louis-Philippe to 'choose between a crown and a passport'.[15]

To fill the power vacuum as 'King of the French' on terms approved by the Chamber of Deputies', Guizot, Constant, and two others drafted a parliamentary proclamation commending Louis-Philippe to the French people as a constitutional ruler, while the new monarch assured Lafayette—who had rallied the National Guard to his support—that he offered 'a popular throne surrounded by republican institutions.'[16] The Charter was hastily redrafted by Guizot and others in a liberal direction: parliament shared legislative power with the king, National Guard Officers elected up to the rank of captain, press censorship ended, as was Roman Catholicism as the official state religion. The liberal conservative aim was to achieve as much continuity as possible, despite the change of dynasty. The workers, who fought on the barricades in 1830, demonstrated how a tiny minority in Paris could change the regime before most of the country was aware of the fact.[17] Yet they did not themselves profit from their ephemeral alliance with the liberal middle classes.

Lacking popular support, the new regime relied upon a close collusion between political, administrative, and—to a lesser extent—economic power. 'Probably at no other time did France experience so thorough a purge of the higher officers of state so rapidly'.[18] In 1 month, Interior Minister Guizot removed all but 7 Prefects; the Justice Minister replaced 437 magistrates in 4 months; all the generals commanding the 19 military districts were removed. Forty-seven of the Mayors in the fifty largest cities were evicted, businessmen frequently replacing noblemen. Former imperial civil and military officials were often appointed but in the top army posts nobles replaced nobles, under the oversight of the king's sons. Diplomats remained an aristocratic preserve. Suspicion of bishops and archbishops as pro-Legitimist prompted an 1831 Prefect's report that eleven were hostile, twenty-five favourable, and fifty uncertain. Half the Peers resigned, new ones were created, and 120 deputies either resigned their seats or were invalidated. 'The "Revolution of the Job-seekers" brought thousands into the streets not to man the barricades but to besiege the ministries' in search of appointments.[19] Many supplicants were disappointed but Protestants disproportionately took the positions abandoned by Catholic ultras with the prominent role of Guizot

[15] Quoted in Pinkney, *The French Revolution of 1830*, 146; cf. 85–98, 127–39, 255–64.

[16] Pinkney, 163; cf. 157–62, 185–95.

[17] Rosanvallon, *La Monarchie Impossible*, 109–20 and James Rule and Charles Tilly, 'Political process in revolutionary France 1830–32' in John M. Merriman (ed.), *1830 in France*, 1975, 66–70.

[18] Pinkney, *The French Revolution of 1830*, 277.

[19] Ibid. 284; cf. 276–93. See also André-Jean Tudesq, *Les Grands Notables en France*, I, 378, 436–40 and McPhee, *A Social History of France 1780–1880*, 118–19.

especially giving the July Monarchy the appearance of a 'golden age of French Protestantism'.[20]

By the end of 1830, the Revolution had been mastered by a new politico-administrative elite. Symbolically, the four Polignac ministers who had signed the ordinances were found guilty but sentenced to life imprisonment (not served) whereas the mob demanded death. The crowds that mourned the death of that true liberal Constant and turned his funeral into a political demonstration with the cry 'To the Pantheon' were not satisfied either. Most important of all, Lafayette, who commanded the National Guard, was no longer indispensable and his resignation was secured, while the hardline Casimir-Périer in early 1831 replaced the more liberal Laffitte.[21] Attempts to repeat the worker eruption into politics of the 'real country' were repelled forcefully in Paris and Lyon by 1834 and conservative Orleanism organized its control through what Guizot called the 'legal country': the few who could vote and the fewer who were eligible.

Lacking party organization to mobilize support, the Orleanist governments relied heavily on the administration. In Chapter 3 we quoted Prime Minister Casimir-Périer's instruction to the Prefects not to be neutral in elections and a few years later the Interior Minister wrote to the Prefect of the Manche that he should actively support the official candidate against Tocqueville because 'prudence insists that the electors should not be left to their own political convictions'.[22] Official candidatures had been inaugurated during the First Empire but during the July Monarchy their selections and promotion, from manipulating the electoral register to campaign management, was a primordial prefectoral duty. Dependent on the government that appointed and could remove them, the Prefects and sub-Prefects had 'limitless opportunity for dishonest practice' which they exercised without respect for the law.[23] Such manipulation was facilitated by the small electorate, with many closely contested elections won by five or fewer votes, with four-fifths winning on the first ballot. The use of secret public funds to bribe voters and administrative pressure to browbeat the press was a feature of elections, supplemented by a flood of pamphlets. Voters were few enough to be bribed with government jobs, as well as promises to build or repair local schools, churches, hospitals, and other public works. The secrecy of the ballot was circumvented by getting government officials or the beneficiaries of subsidies to identify themselves by marking their ballot papers.[24] Nevertheless, it has been pointed out that many pro- and anti-government candidates relied mainly upon their local prestige and in 1846 more than a third of the winners were 'elected unopposed or with more than two-thirds of the vote'.[25] Successive defeats of the reformist opposition parliamentary groups, culminating in 1846, demonstrated

---

[20] Tudesq, *Les Grands Notables*, I, 125.

[21] Pinkney, *The French Revolution of 1830*, 318–24, 337–68.

[22] Quoted by Sherman Kent, *Electoral Procedure under Louis-Philippe*, 108–9.

[23] Ibid. 86.   [24] Ibid. 77, 96–7, 107–29. See also Bury and Tombs, 84, 88.

[25] Patrick and Trevor Higonnet, 'Class, Corruption and Politics in the French Chamber of Deputies, 1846–48'. *French Historical Studies*, V/1, Spring 1967, 212; cf. 213–16.

that they could never win with an exclusive electoral suffrage that confined the 'legal country' to the landed proprietors and wealthy businessmen.

The implosion of the July Monarchy was provoked not only by its narrow electoral base (which was less than a third of Britain's after the 1832 Reform) but by a monarch who refused to be merely a figurehead. Thiers, who saw Louis-Philippe as a French version of what William III's successors became, had in 1830 popularized his distillation of British Whig doctrine into the slogan: 'The king reigns but does not govern' but he failed to persuade Louis-Philippe to behave like his conception of a constitutional monarch. The king enjoyed the support for this personal intervention of Guizot, de facto Prime Minister from 1840 to 1848, who maintained that the throne was not an empty chair.[26] Tocqueville, who had warned that France was 'sleeping on a volcano', added later that Louis-Philippe 'resembled the man who refused to believe that his house was on fire, because he had the key to it in his pocket'.[27] Nominally liberal institutions had resulted in 'a preponderance of Royal power which verged upon despotism'.[28] Having been denied the vote, the lower-middle class National Guard did not come to the aid of the king who temporized and then abdicated out of defeatism rather than necessity when insurrection occurred.

THE 1848 REVOLUTION AND THE SECOND REPUBLIC

This was precipitated by the banquet campaign of 1847–8, used as a substitute for banned public meetings and for demonstrations championing the widening of the electorate, although only the republicans advocated manhood suffrage. However, as Tocqueville feared, the campaign escalated into a violent confrontation. In an economic context of harvest failure and a slump following railway speculation, the appeal to non-middle class political participation by the dynastic opposition led to more than they had bargained for: the Republic.[29] Cheated of victory in 1830, the republicans—led by journalists from *Le National* and *La Réforme*—formed a Provisional Government headed by Lamartine, to avoid the same fate. It was postponed but not avoided because after the elites recovered from their initial consternation, they turned manhood suffrage into a counter-revolutionary bludgeon, with the help of the clergy in the rural areas. As predicted by Chateaubriand, rootless Orleanism may have prepared the way for democracy but most of the newly enfranchised voters were not ready to support its republican advocates.

Despite attempts to postpone elections, a Constituent Assembly was precipitately elected because as Tocqueville put it, 'they neither knew how to make use of universal suffrage (sic) nor how to do without it' and unlike the revolutionaries of 1789, they could not abolish tithes and aristocratic privileges or divide the land

---

[26] Bury and Tombs, 41. The phrase 'The king reigns but does not govern' was first used by the Grand Chancellor of Poland in 1605. I thank Edward Page for drawing this to my attention.

[27] *The Recollections of Alexis de Tocqueville*, 9, 12; cf. 10–14.   [28] Ibid. 9.

[29] Ibid. 16–17, 98–9; cf. Tudesq, II, 981–4, 1028, 1054–6 and Bury and Tombs, 89–95.

among the peasantry to attract support.[30] An explosion of long repressed freedom led to hundreds of ephemeral newspapers and political clubs being launched; slavery was abolished, as was capital punishment for political offences, along with the unpopular salt tax. There was an 84 per cent turnout to the 23 April election, with 566 of the 851 Deputies elected being former monarchists and 285 republicans. The days of the Provisional Government were clearly numbered and its demise was precipitated by the 21 June decree to disperse the 100,000 unemployed attached to the emergency work creation National Workshops. What ensued in June was described by Tocqueville as 'a struggle of class against class, a sort of Servile War' in which the despairing workers fought leaderless (Blanqui was already in prison).[31] The reunited middle classes, out of fear of the Paris proletariat, bloodily repressed it with the army, sections of the National Guard and volunteer provincial, peasant troops. It was therefore apposite that the term reactionary came into general use in 1848, with preserving order taking priority over all other considerations. The dominant factions in the Constituent Assembly became known as the 'Party of Order'.

As was to occur again with the Third Republic, the fate of the Second Republic was in the hands of people opposed to it: monarchists had a parliamentary majority and the president was a Bonaparte! However, those who wished to replace the Conservative Republic were divided between alternative regimes: Legitimist and Orleanist monarchy as well as Bonapartism. We have seen that Louis-Napoleon emerged as overwhelming victor in the December 1848 presidential election, preparatory to restoring the Empire by *coup d'état* in December 1851. Secure in the knowledge of unorganized mass support for personality not party, he outmanoeuvred the *notables* led by Thiers, who in 1850 had declared that 'the Republic... is of all governments that which divides us least'.[32] By 'us', he meant the ruling classes, divided by dynastic loyalties. When the issue once again came to the fore in the 1870s, Thiers was a provisional President of the Republic (whose repression of the 1871 Paris Commune recalled the June Days of 1848). He had said bluntly to the republicans in 1850: 'If it lasts, you will not govern it, and it will only last because of that.'[33] As we shall see, although he was ousted by the monarchist majority in 1873, Thiers contributed to the foundation of a conservative Third Republic that was able successfully to resist attempts at regime change for seventy years.

However, in 1850 he and the *notables* played into Louis-Napoleon's hands, reducing the electorate by a third, provocatively explaining that the dangerous part of the population, 'the vile multitude', inclined to vote for the Social Democrats, should be denied the vote.[34] Although Thiers successfully stampeded the

---

[30] *Recollections*, 105; cf. 106. The 1848 Revolution instituted *manhood* suffrage.

[31] Ibid. 150; cf. 107 and Chapters 9 and 10 passim. For Karl Marx's 1850 description and interpretation, see 'The Class Struggles in France 1848 to 1850' in Karl Marx and Frederick Engels, *Selected Works*, I, 1962 edn, 139–63.

[32] Quoted in Bury and Tombs, 123.   [33] Ibid.

[34] Ibid. 124; cf. 126 and Malo, *Thiers*, 405–6. See also Raymond Huard, *Le suffrage universel en France, 1848–1946*, 1991, 51–9; cf. 23.

parliament into abandoning manhood suffrage, Louis-Napoleon, who narrowly failed to secure the restoration of manhood suffrage on 4 November 1851, had the last laugh with massive support in a December 1851 plebiscite to legitimate his *coup d'état* by over 7 million votes to 641,000. He had purged the army command of pro-parliamentary officers and Thiers—in anticipation of a forthcoming coup—had failed to persuade parliament to give its president the right to requisition troops for its protection. For his pains, Thiers was one of those arrested and banished, giving him ample leisure to complete his *History of the Consulate and the Empire*, with less emphasis upon Napoleon's military genius and explicit criticism of one-man despotism. Some isolated acts of heroic resistance did not prevent the voters being taken like 'a flock to the abattoir' (Hugo dixit) or the regime from enjoying popular support until military defeat brought its downfall as it had that of his uncle.

THE SECOND EMPIRE, 1852–70

The survival of the Second Empire came from paternalistically giving the people what they were judged by their rulers to need rather than allowing them any control over how decisions were made, except to approve them after the event. 'If one concentrates on the parliamentary history, the foreign policy or the court intrigues of the Second Empire, one would be inclined to conclude that this was a reign so muddled in its objectives and so blundering in its actions that it has not permanent significance in French history,.... The importance of the Second Empire lies elsewhere. It was a catalyst in the meeting of democracy and centralisation.'[35] Zeldin's stress upon the Bonapartist contribution to establishing a populist statism is only acceptable with reservations. The Second Empire did give voters the experience with manhood suffrage elections that was to enable them to become less easily manipulable during the Third Republic. Taking advantage of the fact that most French liberals were generally hostile to manhood suffrage, Louis-Napoleon revived his uncle's recourse to plebiscites in combination with the Restoration and July Monarchies' use of top-down administrative pressure and patronage to secure the passive public support sought, not the bottom-up public participation advocated by the republicans in the name of popular sovereignty. When the liberals and republicans coalesced to preserve the Third Republic, they compromised with an elitist democracy.

Without effective political parties to organize opposition, the voters—especially in the countryside—were at the mercy of administrative manipulation. This took several forms. Systematic gerrymandering was used to split urban constituencies, to which substantial numbers of voters from rural areas were added. The ability to campaign was restricted and the press was muzzled. Promotion of official candidates took advantage of widespread but not universal peasant deference towards government sponsorship, especially when this was accompanied with a scattering

---

[35] Zeldin, *France*, I, 521; cf. 510–11.

of public largesse to secure clientelist loyalty. Placing a different connotation on Hugo's characterization of the voters as a flock of sheep quoted earlier, the wife of a Bonapartist minister—welcoming the regime's electoral victory in 1857—proclaimed: 'universal suffrage had to populate the country either with wolves or with sheep; praise be given to the countryside where there are only sheep'.[36] The people were fobbed off with being the legitimizing source of power and were to content themselves with being passive recipients of its arbitrary activities. Most of them appeared to be content with this arrangement.

Louis-Napoleon actively chaired Cabinet meetings, steering discussion, and taking the final decisions. The Legislature met for only three months each year. It could not initiate legislation (the prerogative of the Council of State, as in the First Empire) and its amendments could be ignored. Its president from 1854–65 was the Duke de Morny, Talleyrand's grandson and Louis-Napoleon's illegitimate half-brother. Of an Orleanist disposition, he did what he could to promote parliament's role, which did increase as the Second Empire was liberalized in the 1860s. The regime's opponents concentrated their fire on the corrupt profiteering associated with the ambitious public works programmes, notably the railway construction boom and Haussmann's reconstruction of the centre of Paris, discussed later. Gambetta joined in the task of discrediting the regime by drawing attention to its *coup d'état* origin. He made his reputation in the 1868 trial of journalists who had launched a subscription for a memorial to Baudin, a deputy killed at an 1851 barricade. As late as the May 1870 referendum on the liberalized parliamentary system to be established, 7.3 million voted in favour and 1.5 million against. Only humiliating defeats in the 1870 Franco-Prussian war, with the capture of an overconfident Emperor, brought the downfall of a regime that had previously enjoyed majority public support. Following Napoleon III's 1873 death in English exile, the 1879 death of the Prince Imperial, fighting in a British uniform in the Zulu War, finally destroyed hopes of a Bonapartist restoration, although its populist political culture proved more enduring.

THE 1870s VICTORY OF THE THIRD REPUBLIC

Regime change took the form of leading republicans proclaiming the Republic at the Paris Town Hall, as in 1848, this time without violence. A Provisional Government of National Defence was improvized, in which Gambetta—a would-be latter-day Danton—became first Interior Minister and then War Minister, having escaped by balloon from encircled Paris, to organize a forlorn resistance to the Prussian invaders after the main French armies had capitulated. However, it was the policy of securing peace on Bismarck's terms—unconditional surrender,

[36] Quoted in Sudhir Hazareesingh, *From Subject to Citizen: The Second Empire and the Emergence of Modern French Democracy*, 1998, 51; cf. 26–8, 46–9, 267. On gerrymandering see Huard, 83–4. See more generally Theodore Zeldin, *The Political System of Napoleon III*, 1958.

annexation of Alsace-Lorraine and continued occupation until reparations were paid—that prevailed, securing overwhelming endorsement at the quickly organized election of February 1871, with only nine days between its announcement and polling.

If Gambetta had personified the pursuit of war, Thiers emerged as the personification of peace at the Prussian price. With multiple candidatures possible, he was elected on twenty-six departmental lists, an exploit never exceeded before or since. He was then almost unanimously chosen as 'Chief of the Executive Power of the French Republic' by an Assembly in which monarchists constituted a large majority because the Bonapartists had caused the war and the Republicans had failed to win it. The former Orleanist, who during the Second Republic, as we have seen, declared that a Conservative Republic was the least divisive political regime, set about solidifying a precarious de facto Republic, with constitution-making postponed. It was time once again to make rather than write history. The illegitimate upstart southerner had the task of preventing both ideological extremes—the Legitimist and Orleanist Right and the Republican Left—from destroying his fragile, pragmatic institutional compromise.

Thiers had to deal first with the insurrection in Paris which had voted in February for patriotically continued war and had 175 battalions of armed National Guards at the disposal of the Extreme Left leadership chosen at elections on 16 March 1871. However, the Commune lacked any effective authority and the National Guards were reluctant to do more than defend their own *quartiers*. Thiers, who had moved government from its Bordeaux retreat to Versailles, ordered the withdrawal of the Paris garrison, deliberately leaving the capital to the insurgent Commune. Civil War quickly ensued in April, a draconian peace treaty was signed with Bismarck on 10 May, followed by the defeat and summary mass executions of some 20 to 25,000 Communards in the 'bloody week' of 21–8 May. Denounced by the Pope as 'men escaped from hell', 38,578 Communards were arrested (only a tenth of the denunciations received), 10,137 were convicted, half of whom were deported to New Caledonia, testimony to the even greater class hatred generated by the spring 1871 conflict compared to June 1848. The Tuileries Palace and Town Hall had been destroyed but 'In the conflict between France and her arrogant capital, Paris was at last beaten. And if universal suffrage was to have its way, it was as necessary to dethrone Paris as to dethrone Bonaparte or Bourbon.'[37] As a result, Thiers was detested in radical Paris but not in the conservative provinces that had supplied first the votes and then the troops to retrieve control of the capital. With some 300,000 written denunciations to process, it took nearly a decade for the arrests and court martials of Communards that dragged on to be concluded by an amnesty. Meanwhile, Thiers turned his attention towards checkmating the supporters of the three dynasties that had ruled France, intending to play on their divisions until a pro-Republican majority could be elected.

---

[37] D. W. Brogan, *The Development of Modern France [1870–1939]*, 1940, 1967 edn, 74; cf. 55–63, 72–3 and Zeldin, *France*, I, 737–44.

Despite cunning use of his parliamentary skills to steer a middle course—'I oscillate, my ministers see-saw'[38]—Thiers was in a weak political position once he secured the early evacuation in March 1873 of the German occupation forces on rapid payment of reparations with the help of the French bankers headed by Alphonse de Rothschild. He was no longer indispensable and the Right-Centre, headed by Duke Albert de Broglie, suspected that he would try to frustrate their desire to restore monarchy. Thiers did not have a parliamentary major-ity due, in part, to his own refusal to take the organizational steps to acquire one. 'It is striking that Thiers, the great advocate of parliamentary government, had never tried hard to create his own party in parliament', having declared in his November 1872 message to the Assembly: 'the Republic is a contradiction in terms if, instead of being the government of all, it is the government of a party.'[39]

The obsession with rhetorical unity was the counterpart of Thiers' description, in an 1872 Assembly speech, of France as 'a country which may be called a universal contradiction, where everybody is divided on everything'.[40] There, in a nutshell, we have the fundamental institutional cause of both past regime instabil-ity and the governmental instability that dogged the country during the enduring Third Republic. An inability to accept the practical pluralistic consequence of their liberal principles was a feature of an illiberal political culture shared by most of the political class throughout the nineteenth century. Gambetta was a conspicuous exception but he did not succeed in uniting the Left into a single party within a two-party system. The wilful incapacity to create the party basis for the regime he so much admired in Britain meant that, when Thiers sought to speed up constitution-making to allow the reactionary Assembly to be dissolved and was defeated, he felt obliged to resign in May 1873. The way was open for the institutionalization of unstable government by Assembly . . . except that it was further exacerbated by an unrepresentative Senate, the parting legacy of the 1871 Assembly to its successors.

Whereas Thiers had wanted a strong President, the Right led by Broglie—having curbed the President's power—in the name of the Assembly's sovereignty chose as his successor Marshal MacMahon, who could be relied upon gracefully to give way if monarchy was restored. Meanwhile, the new President declared in a May 1873 message to the Assembly that it was where power resided; he was only its delegate. He called on Broglie to form a coalition government, which reflected the disorderly partisans of order who had helped him remove Thiers. It consisted of three Legitimists, three Orleanists, a Bonapartist, and a Conservative Republican. The anti-Republican strategy was shattered by the uncompromising October 1873

[38] J. P. T. Bury, *Gambetta and the Making of the Third Republic*, 1973, 127; cf. 120.

[39] Bury and Tombs, 230. On Thiers' role in 1870–73 see ibid. Chapter 11. See also Odile Rudelle, *La République Absolue 1870–1889*, 1982, 18–29 and Daniel Halévy, *La Fin des Notables*, 1930. In his 1872 introduction to a new edition of *The English Constitution*, 55. Bagehot explained why, lacking party support and the dissolution power, Thiers as a strong head of the executive was 'the exception of a moment; he is not the example of a lasting condition'.

[40] Bury, *Gambetta and the Making of the Third Republic*, 88.

letter from the Bourbon Pretender Chambord, reiterating in substance his January 1872 assertion that 'nobody, on any pretext, will induce me to consent to become the legitimate King of Revolution'.[41] Anticipated symbolically by his July 1871 manifesto refusing to abandon the White Flag, this virtually amounted to abdication. In the hope that an Orleanist Restoration would be possible once Chambord died, Broglie secured an extension of MacMahon's presidential term to seven years—an arrangement that survived into the Fifth Republic, only being replaced by a five-year term for the 2002 election. In a political context in which the Republicans were making sweeping by-election gains and were to win the departmental and municipal elections in the autumn, the Broglie government fell on a vote of no confidence in May 1874. By November 1874, the Republicans had increased their Assembly numbers from 120 in 1871 to 340, only 20 short of a majority.[42]

Until 1874, the Republicans had been disinclined to accept the Assembly's constituent power, pressing instead for a dissolution, confident that they would win the ensuing election. However, despite warnings from Louis Blanc on the Old Left that implicitly to accept the Assembly's right to draw up a constitution was to end up at best with a Conservative Republic, Gambetta, and the bulk of the Republicans, together with some Orleanists who were willing reluctantly to accept a Republic if it was Conservative, carried the day. After indecisive votes proposing a pseudo-British style parliamentary system based on two Chambers, prompted by fear that a Bonapartist revival calling for an appeal to the people was gathering pace, the Assembly by one vote (carrying the Wallon amendment by 353 to 352 votes) brought an end to four years of political manoeuvring.

Wallon also formulated the compromise on the Senate's composition that Gambetta, cunningly designating it the 'Grand Council of the Communes', persuaded most of the Left to accept. This meant abandoning their lifelong principled opposition to a Second Chamber, quite apart from one that weighted its membership decisively and enduringly in favour of rural voters. In vain, Louis Blanc melodramatically but accurately complained that it meant 'the stifling of the big towns by the small, of the small by the villages, of the villages by the hamlets. It was the defeat of day by night.'[43] This was the price extracted by the Centre; to perpetuate the conservative character of the Republic, a role the Senate played throughout the life of the Third Republic. Tactically, it was a masterly demonstration of Gambetta's pragmatic opportunism by contrast with the fatal intransigence of a Chambord. Strategically, it crippled the Republic's capacity to innovate and contributed to making France the stalemate society it subsequently became.

Having completed its constitution-making with improvised expedients destined to last because they were provisional, the Assembly made way for elections, having

---

[41] Quoted Bury 80; cf. 30–1, 36, 153 note, 172–4.

[42] Ibid. 210–17; cf. 174–5. By-elections were especially numerous because of the need to replace the many candidates elected in several constituencies simultaneously.

[43] Ibid. 237; cf. 202–4, 220–34, 240–3 and Rudelle, 35–8, 43–5.

rejected the list system that Gambetta had championed as conducive to the creation of disciplined political parties. Gambetta as leader of the Republican Union failed to prevent a Radical breakaway led by Louis Blanc or to persuade Ferry, leader of the Republican Left to unite, Ferry disingenuously claiming that 'The real way to remain united, really united, is to stay distinct.'[44] Although the right-wing candidates carried the Senate, the Left swept the Chamber of Deputies, Republicans winning 340 seats to 155 for the Right (including 94 Bonapartists) and 35 for the Centre, following a lively campaign. MacMahon, chosen by Broglie as a figurehead he could manoeuvre, may not have been 'the most stupid man in the army' (General Changarnier dixit) or 'the most worthless, incapable and imbecile of Frenchmen' (Gambetta dixit) but he was woefully ill-equipped to handle the political dilemmas that confronted him.[45] Ignoring the voters by refusing to call on the most prominent Republican leader, Gambetta, he asked a moderate Republican political associate of Thiers, Dufaure, to form a government. Keeping out an unwelcome strong Prime Minister subsequently became a frequent practice of presidential power.

Unable to reconcile the demands of the deputies with those of the President, Dufaure resigned at the end of 1876 on defeat in the Senate, to be replaced by another moderate, tightrope walker, Jules Simon. Despite equivocally stressing to the deputies his republicanism and to the senators his conservatism, Simon was forced to accept a motion insisting on the subordination of bishops who were engaged in political agitation put by Gambetta, who launched his resonant slogan: 'Clericalism? There is the enemy'. Simon's capitulation on the issue of jury trial for press offences was used by the President as a pretext to get rid of him, a headstrong act that was treated as an unconstitutional violation of the principles of ministerial responsibility to parliament and parliamentary sovereignty.[46] The scene was set for a decisive confrontation between the republican deputies and a pro-monarchist President who had himself been elected by parliament and was regarded as attempting a semi-Restoration without a king.

The 1875 constitutional laws had seemed to reduce the Republic to humdrum proportions but MacMahon's attempt to impose his authority prompted a heroic response from the republican deputies. MacMahon prorogued parliament prior to dissolution and appointed a government headed by the austere and electorally unattractive Broglie and consisting mainly of senators. Gambetta countered with a protest of 363 deputies from all 4 republican groups on 18 May 1877 that self-consciously emulated the 221 who had in 1830 opposed the Polignac ordinances, insisting that the President respect the constitution and not exercise a supremacy to which he was not entitled. In terms of public campaigning, the field was left

---

[44] Quoted in Bury, 292; cf. 253–5, 289–95, 321.

[45] Bury, *Gambetta*, 153 note, 287, 396–7. Daniel Halévy reports that, visiting a hospital and encountering a victim of typhus, MacMahon commented: 'Ah, typhoid fever. I have had it: one either dies or remains an imbecile for life'. (*La République des Ducs*, 1937, 291; cf. 322–3.)

[46] Bury *Gambetta*, 377–99. On the Dufaure and Simon premierships, see Halévy, *La République des Ducs*, 225, 251–80. See also Brogan, 131–3.

open to the republicans, the President's supporters regarding such vulgar activities as beneath their dignity. Gambetta deliberately cast the debate as one between the 'sons of 1789' and aristocrats like Broglie who wished to restore a clericalist monarchy. Broglie rapidly replaced the head of the police, 484 prefects and sub-prefects, 184 magistrates, 381 justices of the peace, and 83 mayors in the hope that classic recourse to administrative pressure, including a crackdown on newsvendors, would swing the election his way. The acrimonious interpellation on the composition of the Broglie government, which had just asked for a dissolution, prompted a frequently interrupted speech of over 2 hours by Gambetta, widely distributed throughout the country. At the end of a 3 days debate on 19 June, a vote of censure was passed by 363 against 158.[47]

The republicans, determined to locate state power in the hands of parliament not the president, achieved an ephemeral but potent unanimity against what they regarded as a surreptitious attempt to restore the Old Regime. They organized committees to collect funds from business, to direct press strategy by Parisian newspaper editors and to disseminate propaganda with the slogan 'Send back the 363'. Despite the prosecution of hundreds of newspapers, newsvendors, bookshops, and even cafés, the republican message was distributed by volunteer activists. While he had accepted the Republic and democracy out of fatalism rather than conviction, Thiers was happy to join in another 1830 press and deputy-led campaign, a reassuring figure who had repressed the Commune and liberated the country, personifying the fears and aspirations of the middle classes, who could replace MacMahon as President of the Republic. Although he died a month before the October election, Thiers' funeral massively demonstrated public support for the republican cause. He was buried in the Père Lachaise cemetery, where the Communards he had repressed made a last heroic stand, which is still commemorated annually by the Left.

It was Gambetta who led the campaign against a divided Right that was reluctant to mobilize the clergy on its behalf because of the unpopularity of clericalism. On 15 August, he ended his speech with a memorable warning to President MacMahon, 'When France has spoken with her sovereign voice ... it will be necessary to submit or resign.'[48] Gambetta was prosecuted for insulting the President and sentenced to three months imprisonment and a fine but the case was dropped on appeal by the post-electoral government, when MacMahon was first obliged to submit to parliament and later to resign. Ferry had presciently warned in a less celebrated speech of 12 June 1877 that MacMahon's gamble would upset the balance of the Conservative Republic, giving way to a 'Convention Republic', with state power monopolized by parliament.[49]

After the republicans lost forty seats but won a smaller majority, Broglie's attempt to hold on to office by securing a vote of confidence in the Senate was rejected by its president, amounting to a tactical acceptance of the pre-eminence of the deputies elected by manhood suffrage. However, on future occasions

[47] Bury, *Gambetta*, 400–12.   [48] Ibid. 421; cf. 414–28 and Halévy, 284–303.
[49] Quoted in Rudelle, 56; cf. 54–8.

(against Léon Bourgeois in 1896 and Léon Blum in 1937) the Senate would cause the downfall of weakened governments retaining a majority in the Chamber of Deputies. MacMahon's attempts to find a personally acceptable alternative government failed in the face of the deputies' refusal to vote the budget, spearheaded by the Chairman of the Budget Committee: Gambetta. Fear of a *coup d'état* led Gambetta to turn to his old 1870 contacts with some senior army officers (notably General Gallifet, later to play a notable role as War Minister during the Dreyfus Affair) who promised support. He knew that although most generals favoured a *coup*, the army was split and from the rank of colonel downwards most were pro-republican. The Senate's refusal to accept a second dissolution and the problematic recourse to a proclamation of martial law forced MacMahon not only to accept Jules Dufaure as Prime Minister but his choice of Ministers of War, Navy, and Foreign Affairs. On 14 December 1877, MacMahon was obliged to sign a message to parliament, drafted by the new government, declaring that he accepted the people's decision: in a parliamentary republic, ministers not the president were responsible for decisions. The triumph of parliamentary over personal power was sealed by the Republicans winning a Senate majority in January 1879, quickly followed by the anticlimax of MacMahon's resignation over the enforced retirement of generals regarded as unreliable by the republicans. The 'harpooned whale' had finally expired after an inglorious lingering demise.[50]

Not Gambetta but Jules Grévy (who had wanted to avoid having a President in 1848), chosen by a joint meeting of both Chambers of parliament, succeeded MacMahon as President of the Republic. Nor did Gambetta become Prime Minister. However, he received the consolation post of the presidency of the Chamber of Deputies. He was too oratorically radical for the conservatives and too prudently conservative in action for the Radicals, as well as ostentatiously disposed to being a real leader. As early as 1871, the *Radical* newspaper had written of a Gambetta speech: 'He has principles, but principles that he subordinates to their opportuneness'.[51] Five years later, the Communard journalist Henri Rochefort coined the epithet 'Opportunist' to describe those, like Gambetta, who wished to delay indefinitely an amnesty for the Communards until the 'opportune time'.[52] Gambetta responded in a speech to his Belleville electors during the 1876 campaign, arguing that his opportunist policy 'consists in only committing oneself completely to a question when one has the country incontestably with one'.[53]

His personal magnetism was both his strength and his weakness. It was his strength to cultivate mass public support and continue to carry with him the working class voters who had originally elected in 1869 the admirer of Proudhon. But in a parliamentary-centred republic his popularity was feared despite his tactical moderation, so the republican coordinating committee, behind which Gambetta had been the guiding hand, established after the 1877 election, was quickly disbanded in January 1878. The pleasures and poisons of a parliamentary system rejecting broad-based and disciplined political parties, affording unlimited

---

[50] Bury, *Gambetta*, 440; cf. 434–5, 441–61 and Rudelle, 58–60.
[51] Quoted in Bury, *Gambetta*, 75.   [52] Ibid. 299.   [53] Quoted ibid. 325.

scope for factional intrigues and derisory ambitions, institutionalized government instability, with ministerial posts shuffled within a self-perpetuating oligarchy. This nightmare was not the regime of which republican idealists had dreamed, for which they had schemed, a *mystique* that had been debased into a *politique*. In unscrupulous hands, opportunism was to degenerate quickly into *arrivisme* and corruption.

With the republicans firmly in command, it was not only time for 80-year old Dufaure (who had first held ministerial office in 1839) to give way to more ardent protagonists of a republican Republic. It was decided to make yet another purge of the administration. By the end of December 1877, all but 1 Prefect and 267 sub-Prefects had been replaced, as was the secretary-general at the Elysée. Of the 130 contested elections, 77 were invalidated in 1878, of which 67 were later won by republicans. Attempts to prosecute the Broglie government (again an analogy with the Polignac ministers in 1830) petered out, as it would logically also have involved persecuting MacMahon. However, systematic resort to the spoils system in January 1879, with each minister bringing a list of people to be replaced, pushed MacMahon to the limit of endurance. He threatened resignation at a Cabinet meeting, declaring: 'Removing magistrates and prefects I am prepared to agree but Generals, no. I prefer to leave rather than to accept that. If I have remained in office for a year and swallowed so many bitter pills, it is solely to protect the army.'[54] The government refusing to retreat, MacMahon resigned.

As we have seen, the recourse to what a socialist deputy, following the electoral victory of the Left in 1924, brutally demanded: 'All the posts, rightaway', was not a new phenomenon. The spoils system was intended not merely to reward supporters but to provide state-based electoral agents and loyal officials to carry out government policy. The destabilizing effects of a systematic recourse to patronage and politicization will be our next concern, senior civil servants not providing the counterweight to partisan flux that might have been expected. More fundamentally, it was only in the late nineteenth and early twentieth centuries that Gambetta's sensational 1872 speech turned—in part—from prophecy into reality. He asked whether 'after having tried many forms of government, the country was turning to another social stratum in order to experiment with the Republican form? Yes, I foresee, I feel, I announce the coming and presence in politics of a new social stratum....'[55] Before examining in a later chapter how far this partial democratization took place, we must first examine how the state's servants had fared since the Revolution.

ELITE POLITICIZATION AND ADMINISTRATIVE INSTABILITY

Until the post-1880 relative regime stability allowed public officials to acquire a greater degree of depoliticization, the close interrelationship between politics and administration disrupted the continuity associated with the notion of

---

[54] Halévy, 402; cf. 399–405.　　　[55] Quoted in Bury, *Gambetta*, 114–15.

bureaucracy. An interlocking politico-administrative directorate based on the cumulation—successive or simultaneous—of political and administrative office, resulted in purges of senior officials when power changed hands. Recruited from a similar, restricted elite background, election and selection were not alternative but complementary routes to the exercise of power, so it was natural that the impact of change would be felt both by politicians and officials. However, the effects were not uniform across the administration and varied between regimes, although the Old Regime left enduring marks on the greatly expanded public services created by the revolutionary and Napoleonic mass mobilizations to deal with civil and foreign wars.

The pre-1789 French civil service had been direct servants of the king in a context of court politics. His personal and patrimonial style of authority was reflected in the way ministers in Paris organized their own staffs as well as the role of the provincial Intendants used to bypass unreliable venal officials. Nepotism and patronage dominated recruitment, while policing Paris was a prime preoccupation. The initial effect of 1789 was to generalize the election of officials of importance as a democratic corrective to royal abuse of arbitrary power but with the struggles for political control from 1792 and the organization of the war effort, the central administration grew from about 700 in 1788 to some 6,000. Coordination was sought through the Convention's Committee of Public Safety which had a staff of over 100 by the end of 1793.

After the Jacobin dictatorship was decapitated, central political power was deliberately dispersed and under the 1795–9 Directory a measure of very relative political stability was achieved, allowing the government machine to begin to acquire the centralized, hierarchical, streamlined character that Napoleon was to build upon once he took over and imposed a pyramidal chain of command.[56] Although everyone rejected neutrality and expected unreserved loyalty, most officials were content to serve their changing political masters, so it was not necessary to purge the administration in 1799 as so frequently occurred in the next eighty years. The 1790 subordination of the judiciary to the government, whose legislation and administration were immune to judicial review, as well as the Ministry of Police established by the Directory to control Paris and deal with subversion, were destined to impart a police state dimension to all subsequent regimes, which underlines why the French both look to the state for support but resent its repressive propensities.

'Statist, powerful, centralised, hierarchically-structured, ubiquitous, uniform, depoliticised, instrumental, expert and tightly controlled; such were the dominant features of the Napoleonic administrative model.'[57] However, Vincent Wright went on to point out how none of these features was ever fully imposed despite Napoleon's pursuit of comprehensive and unlimited control. Louis XIV having

---

[56] Church, *Revolution and Red Tape* exaggerates the extent to which bureaucracy was established by the Directory but is a mine of information.

[57] Vincent Wright, 'The Administrative Machine: Old Problems and New Dilemmas' in Peter A. Hall et al. (eds), *Developments in French Politics*, 1990, 116.

turned the old nobility into courtiers, Napoleon turned the new notables into servants of the state. The prefectoral successors of the Old Regime Intendants have often been regarded as exemplifying the ideal type in the wake of Napoleon's St Helena reflections where he asserted that 'The Prefects, with all the authority and local resources which they embodied... were themselves micro-Emperors (*Empereurs au petit pied*)...', a myth which Wright did his best to dispel in the context of the Second Empire.[58] However, despite much discussion of the need for decentralization, in so far as the Prefects deconcentrated centralized power, they reinforced control over the 'administered'. As Odilon Barrot, one of their liberal critics put it, 'It is the same hammer that strikes but the handle has been shortened.'

Although the local military commander exercised a share of coercive power and the bishop exercised spiritual authority, the Prefect had control over the police and political appointment of departmental and commune councillors, using appointed mayors to promote the election of the government of the day's official candidates. Unlike the July Monarchy, when the Prefects—in consultation with the Interior Minister—decided which of the candidates should be supported, during the Second Empire the Prefects took the initiative in selecting and promoting clearly designated official candidates, securing the Minister's approval of their choices in most cases. While in practice the Second Empire Prefects could not follow the advice of the bombastic Second Republic Interior Minister who wrote to his Prefects: 'You ask what your powers are: they are unlimited. Agent of a revolutionary authority, you are also revolutionary', they could effectively manipulate local politics.[59] They consulted their sub-Prefects and mayors, a prime concern being to win over important local notables and avoid the election of irreconcilable Legitimists, Orleanists, and Republicans. Those selected were presented as government candidates purporting to represent the whole nation, not party candidates. This top-down approach contrasts with both the Second and Third Republics, when the Bonapartists—along with other partisans—relied upon local electoral committees to choose and campaign for candidates.

The key links in the network of elite mobilization were the mayors in rural areas, in everyday contact with the voters. Unlike the clientelism of the pre-manhood suffrage years, it was now necessary not just to provide posts for a few political friends but to offer mass benefits. The financial dependence of most communes on government favours allowed scope for negotiating aid for local improvements in exchange for supporting official candidates. In carrying out his side of the bargain, the mayor could rely on the local schoolmaster, constable, tax collector, postman, licensed innkeeper, and tobacconist to spread propaganda by word of mouth and by putting up posters. The government sent all voters, together with their electoral card, a ballot in the name of the official candidate; his rivals had to produce

---

[58] Emmanuel de Las Cases, *Mémorial de Sainte-Hélène*, 1823, 1961 edn, 527. For Wright's criticism of this myth, see Bernard Le Clère and Vincent Wright, *Les Préfets du Second Empire*, 1973, 133, 160.

[59] Georges Weill, *Histoire du Parti Républicain en France [1814–870]*, 1928, 217; cf. 216–18; Zeldin, *The Political System of Napoleon III*, 1958, 1971 edn, 10–26.

and distribute their own ballots. Such practices helped ensure large parliamentary majorities for Louis-Napoleon's supporters, assisted by the self-defeating decision of many Legitimists and Republicans to abstain in protest.[60]

It would be wrong to assume that—as portrayed by their critics—outside the larger towns, the Prefects had things very much their own way. Concerned to attract not merely mass support but to win over local elites, the Prefects had to ensure wherever possible good relations with those who were influential, particularly as many of them combined being departmental councillors with holding office in Paris. 'During the Second Empire, two-thirds of ministers, three-fifths of Councillors of State and over four-fifths of deputies were departmental councillors', with many ministers, senators, and deputies becoming presidents of the departmental council.[61] Such a cumulation of local and national office—which has remained both an enduring counterweight to centralization and its reinforcement—gave those generally elected for longer periods than the Prefects kept their post and able to influence their appointment and occasionally removal, the capacity to curb inclinations to omnipotence. This was especially true of the liberal last years of the Second Empire, when the Prefect could no longer dismiss mayors and schoolmasters who campaigned against official candidates. The regime's opponents lost elections less because of the Prefects' intervention than owing to their own division.

The Prefect of Paris deserves special mention. He was more important than many ministers, especially in the years from 1853–69 when Baron Georges Haussmann was in command. Selected by the Interior Minister for his 'cynical brutality... full of audacity and cunning, capable of pitting expedient against expedient, setting trap for trap', Haussmann would alone be capable of overcoming the opposition to reshaping Paris as Louis-Napoleon desired.[62] Similarly to some of the Presidents of the Fifth Republic—notably Mitterrand—the Emperor had set his heart on pushing through a number of major architectural and town planning projects for the capital. He saw Haussmann almost daily—the Emperor preferred transacting important affairs through bilateral dealings rather than in Cabinet—only formal business going through the Interior Minister.

To ensure political as well as administrative control, Haussmann prevented the establishment of an elected Paris municipal council and doubled the area he controlled by extending the capital's boundaries to pre-empt the potential threat from the industrial workers living there. With the help of unorthodox financial methods (the bourgeoisie disliking being taxed for the provision of public services), he left his enduring imprint on the appearance of Paris. The Rue de Rivoli, Les Halles, the Bois de Boulogne, the Etoile, and the Opera are only some of his more spectacular achievements. Although many of his majestic boulevards were

---

[60] Zeldin, *Political System*, 74–6, 80–7, 108, 112, 159–60.

[61] Le Clère and Wright, 136; cf. 133–8, 270–2.

[62] Quoted in J. M. and Brian Chapman, *The Life and Times of Baron Haussmann: Paris in the Second Empire*, 1957, 57; cf. 55–8.

flanked by monotonous buildings, this was because he did not have the assistance of a major architect. His financial expedients were the cause of his downfall, pilloried in 1868 by Jules Ferry in his *Comptes fantastiques d'Haussmann*, although his forceful style did not fit into the liberal context of the Second Empire's twilight. 'He, rather than Louis-Napoleon, epitomized the authoritarianism, the panache, the contempt for legality which led the Second Empire to the brink of disaster', an overweening self-confidence that came to an end with military defeat.[63] When Victor Hugo returned to France in 1870, much of the Paris he had described in *Les Misérables* (written during his exile) had been demolished and reconstructed by prefectoral fiat.

As government expanded out of its traditional regal functions of foreign affairs and warfare and the domestic functions of finance and justice, the Interior Ministry—successor of the King's Household—spawned a succession of specialist ministries: Commerce, Public Works, and Agriculture. The division directors in these ministries were in post (like Haussmann) for long periods, longer than their ministers, running the ministry with the help of their more specialized bureau heads. During the Second Empire, 6 directors lasted more than 20 years, 6 between 16 and 20, 21 between 11 and 15, 44 between 6 and 10, so that 40.5 per cent stayed in post over 6 years. Their capacity to control policy was to increase with the greater instability of ministers during the Third Republic. By 1901, the average duration of directors was 15 years in Agriculture, over 11 in Education, 10 in Interior, 8 in Commerce, 7 in Colonies, over 6 in War and in Navy, 6 in Public Works but between 5 and 6 in Finance and the Foreign Office, and 5 years in Justice.[64]

In the repeated administrative purges that took place in the nineteenth century, the Council of State was second only to the Prefectoral Corps, because they were both close to political power and exercised highly political functions. During the authoritarian First and Second Empires, the Council of State worked with the Emperor not only to prepare legislation and decrees but subsequently to interpret their application. However, during the parliamentary regimes (Restoration, July Monarchy, and Third Republic) the reassertion of the role of elected representatives as legislators significantly reduced the Council's role to administrative justice and general regulation of the administration. Nevertheless, like the Prefects, the councillors of state survived attempts to abolish them by making themselves indispensable to the powers that be. As Vincent Wright pertinently observed, the purges 'By focusing on men saved the institutions'.[65] The Council had shown that on occasion it could criticize the executive, as it did in relation to the budgetary

---

[63] Quoted in J. M. and Brian Chapman, 1957, 242; cf. 71, 142, 250.

[64] Christophe Charle, *Les hauts fonctionnaires en France au XIXe siècle*, 1980, 177–8. The Second Empire figures come from Vincent Wright, 'Les directeurs et secretaires généraux du Second Empire' in *Les Directeurs des ministères en France*, 1976, 57.

[65] Vincent Wright, 'La crise de 1871–1880' in *Administration et parlement depuis 1815*, 1982, 55; cf. 56. More generally, see Vincent Wright, *Le Conseil d'Etat sous le Second Empire*, 1972 and Charle, *Les hauts fonctionnaires*, 202–4, 207–12. On administrative purges from 1814–1880, see the statistical analyses in Dominique Chagnollaud, *Le Premier des Ordres: Les hauts fonctionnaires (XVIII-XX siècle)* 1991, 73–87 and Pierre Rosanvallon, *L'Etat en France de 1789 à nos jours*, 1990, 75–81.

aspects of Haussmann's schemes,[66] so even in the imperial years it played the role of administrative juridical watchdog. The Finance Inspectorate developed more slowly during the Restoration and Orleanist parliamentary regimes, as budgetary control became a more central feature of both parliamentary and government activity. However, it subsequently went from strength to strength, equalling the Council of State in its standing as the socio-economic functions of government expanded, with their consequences for public expenditure and taxation, thanks to being the state's financial watchdog.

During the Restoration and July Monarchy, small *cabinets ministériels* developed, consisting often of trustworthy family and friends, to assist the minister. Sometimes they were seconded officials, journalists, or former/future deputies, reflecting the administrative, communication, or parliamentary aspects of the executive's work respectively. They were paid out of 'secret funds' at the disposal of each minister—a practice that continued until abolished in 2002 by Prime Minister Jospin. Gradually, one of the two to three members acquired the title of *chef de cabinet*. A particularly influential example from 1840–8, Alphonse Génie held this post in Guizot's *cabinet*, acting as his confidant in political affairs and election agent, in addition handling dealings with the other ministers, the parliamentary supporters, and the press.[67] As well as supervizing civil service and judicial appointments, Génie distributed the 'secret funds' that helped to give Guizot the reputation of an honest man presiding over a corrupt system. It became the practice for service in a *cabinet* to lead to appointment to the Council of State or Prefectoral Corps, despite such fast track favouritism being a flagrant violation of the meritocratic principle in the appointment and promotion of officials. By now, we should have become accustomed to habitual divergence of practice from principle in France.

Counteracting hostile press criticism and subsidizing supportive newspapers was an important function of both the line and staff officials, conscious of the need to shore up fragile regimes and governments. So, the destabilizing role of the press must be considered as a countervailing force both to arbitrary and authoritarian propensities to the abuse of public power, as well as a challenger to the legitimacy of the constitutionally established authorities.

THE PRESS: POLEMICALLY SUBVERSIVE VERSUS GOVERNMENT PROPAGANDIST PROP

The oscillation between long periods of repressive censorship and prosecution and ephemeral orgies of uninhibited free for all, characterized by reassertions of government control after explosions of unrestrained and irresponsible libertarianism,

---

[66] Chapman and Chapman, 142–9.
[67] André-Jean Tudesq, 'Les Chefs de Cabinet sous la Monarchie de Juillet: L'exemple d'Alphonse Génie' in *Origines et Histoire des Cabinets de Ministre*, 43–9; cf. 39. See also Pierre Guiral, 'Les Cabinets Ministériels sous le Second Empire', ibid. 55–63.

has been an enduring feature of French public life inaugurated by the 1789 Revolution. 'In newspapers, songs, plays and broadsheets, the period 1789–92 was the great age of savage satire, especially licentious attacks on political opponents, because of the ending of political censorship at a time when popular literature was already distinguished by obscene mockery, anticlericalism and political slander.'[68] With news distributed by hundreds of street sellers and rumour spread by word of mouth, the incendiary articles by a Desmoulins, a Hébert and a Marat led the first two to the guillotine and the last to assassination in the political hothouse that was Paris. The Jacobins in practice restored censorship of press and plays in 1793 and while the Directory proclaimed the constitutional right to publish freely, by 1797 fears for the regime's survival led to the simultaneous arrest and trial of the printers and editors of thirty-two Paris newspapers, with the death penalty (never applied) for advocating overthrow of the government or the restoration of monarchy.[69]

In January 1800, Napoleon personally decided to reduce the seventy-two Paris newspapers to thirteen, which were subjected to police supervision. One of the Bertin brothers who edited the *Journal des débats* was arrested in 1801 and deported to Elba for three years and then exiled to Italy. As Emperor in 1804, Napoleon decided further to reduce the number of authorized Paris newspapers to four, one being allowed in each provincial department under prefectoral supervision. Even when waging war far from Paris, Napoleon continued to read the newspapers and repeatedly instructed Police Minister Fouché to warn any editor who did not offer unreserved support that his paper would cease to be authorized. Disliking the word 'debate' in the title of the *Journal des débats*, he forced it to change to *Journal de l'Empire* and then in 1811 confiscated it. When he had seized power in 1799, he had expressed his fear of the subversive capacity of a free press: 'If I give the press free rein, I will not remain in power for three months'.[70] Censorship directed against thought crime ensured that liberal critics like Madame de Staël and Benjamin Constant were silenced, along with many less notorious or resolute critics.

Louis XVIII followed the revolutionary habit of proclaiming the principle of press freedom (article 8 of the Charter) and then restricting it in practice. Repression of its abuse took the form of prior authorization and censorship, editors being responsible for depositing a copy of their paper daily with the censors. Guizot was one of those appointed as a censor, remaining as we shall see an advocate and practitioner of government control. An early confrontation with Constant took place in 1819, Guizot producing a Bill requiring caution money to keep the press in 'enlightened' hands. The tightening of press censorship and increase of penalties following the murder of the Duc de Berri led not merely to liberal papers ceasing publication but also Chateaubriand's decision to scupper

---

[68] McPhee, *Social History of France*, 48; cf. 61.

[69] René Mazedier, *Histoire de la Presse Parisienne*, 1945, 46–7; cf. 40–3.

[70] Quoted in Jean-Marie Charon and Jean-Luc Pouthier, 'La Presse' in Jean-François Sirinelli (ed.), *Histoire des droites en France*, II, 1992, 134. See also Mazedier, 49–58.

his *Conservateur*. Because prosecutions—notably for disparaging the Church—had frequently failed because juries acquitted, the Villèle government of 1822–7 ended jury trial for press offences. It used the surreptitious tactic of buying out the shareholders of dissident newspapers and the overt financial pressure of increasing stamp duty, postal charges, and maximum fines. The ensuing outcry, led by the *Journal des débats*, was followed by Villèle's downfall after the 1827 elections.[71]

Newspapers had four closely printed small format pages, with modest solely subscription circulations and without advertising. They were expensive, so the less wealthy clubbed together or read them in cafés. Opposition papers—notably the *Journal des débats* and *Le Constitutionnel*—were able to print criticism through their reports of parliamentary proceedings.[72] Despite attempts to control the press, the circulation of Opposition newspapers usually exceeded those supporting the government by over 3 to 1. This was supplemented by the sophisticated pamphlets of Paul-Louis Courier and the popular songs of Béranger promoting the cult of Napoleon especially among the illiterate and semi-literate, which landed him in prison. (However, he had the last laugh as they were sung on the 1830 barricades.) When, in 1829, Bertin of the *Journal des débats* was acquitted after pleading that he had only criticized the *use* of the royal prerogative, the king's authority was further undermined. This line of attack was developed in *Le National*, launched in 1830 with Thiers, Mignet, and Carrel as editors. Using the analogy with the English Glorious Revolution of 1688, they argued that a king that violated the Charter could be replaced by one who respected it. In the battle against the Polignac government's fatal ordinances suspending press freedom, *Le National* and the press generally played a pivotal role in organizing protests and agitation but it was others that did the fighting. However, Thiers and *Le National* were able to steer the Revolution in an Orleanist direction, publishing on 31 July an article justifying avoidance of an outright republic by its sanguinary associations and presenting the Orleanist *fait accompli* as a 'republic disguised by monarchy through representative government'.[73]

The July Monarchy rapidly demonstrated, first in the Press Law of December 1830, reinforced in 1835, that once again the press freedom promised in principle (article 7 of the revised Charter) meant subordination in practice. Jury trial was restored but selection by lot was replaced by prefectoral selection in the provinces. Stamp duty was retained, as was caution money, albeit reduced. Shortly before his death, Benjamin Constant spoke forcefully in the Chamber of Deputies against this backsliding. 'When the days of peril dawned, the press preceded us onto the battlefield, braving exile and death before us. At its call, the people armed itself; we came after the people, and the miraculous trio of the press, the people and we overthrew tyranny.... With the press, there is sometimes disorder; without the press there is always servitude as well as disorder because unlimited power

---

[71] Irene Collins, *The Government and the Newspaper Press in France 1814–1881*, Chapters 1–5.
[72] Bertier de Sauvigny, *La Restauration*, 293–5.
[73] Charles Ledré, *La Presse à l'assaut de la Monarchie, 1815–1848*, 1960, 117; cf. 18, 55–7, 60–1, 96–9, 106–22 and Collins, *The Government and the Newspaper Press*, 55–8.

becomes mad.'[74] The Casimir-Périer government of 1831–2 stepped up the number of prosecutions for press offences. A particular target was the Republican *Tribune*, hauled before the courts 111 times by the end of 1834, with heavy prison sentences and fines that killed it in 1835. The editors of four newspapers had 'special quarters in the prison of Sainte-Pélagie, they were there so often'.[75] While Philipon's satirical *La Caricature* was frequently seized and prosecuted for its ridicule of the political class generally and the king in particular, juries frequently acquitted him. Nevertheless, he spent thirteen months in prison between 1832–3, although he continued to edit his paper there.[76]

The Fieschi attempt to kill Louis-Philippe in July 1835 had been preceded a week before by an imaginary dialogue in *La Caricature* between the king and Thiers, ridiculing rumours of threats to Louis-Philippe's life, as mentioned in Chapter 4.[77] So, it was naturally a victim of the stringent libel law that was rushed through parliament, aimed at destroying the seditious republican and Legitimist press, *inter alia* requiring prior approval of caricatures. Treason trials for bringing the king into contempt or advocating overthrow of the regime were switched from juries to the Chamber of Peers. Caution money and fines were substantially raised and organizing public subscriptions to pay fines was forbidden. As Interior Minister in 1835 and as Prime Minister from 1840–8, Guizot was to instrumentalize the press on behalf of government deemed to monopolize rational truth. The uninspiring provincial newspapers were controlled by the Prefects, 'ordering mayors to subscribe to them and buying copies to send free to electors...'[78] France was a long way from the liberal aspirations of 1830, as censorship in defence of established order was reimposed and official propaganda actively promoted.

The clampdown on the political press provided an opportunity for a less committed cut price press with advertising, inspired by British practice, that was pioneered in France by Emile de Girardin with *La Presse*, launched in 1836 with a massive publicity campaign. (Guizot is alleged to have surreptitiously funded a rival paper from public funds, supplemented with the promise of peerages.) The serialization of novels melodramatizing the poor, criminals, and social outcasts was copied by rivals such as the *Journal des débats*, publishing Eugène Sue's *Mystères de Paris* in 1841 and Dumas' *Comte de Monte Cristo* in 1845. The political press survived frequent lawsuits. The *National*'s editor Armand Carrel was killed in a duel with Girardin in 1836 but under his successor it conducted a campaign for the extension of the suffrage that was to culminate in the months preceding the 1848 Revolution. In the absence of effective political parties, the republican press, aided and abetted by the satirical press, discredited the July Monarchy. Without playing as active a role as in 1830 when it was directly threatened, the press, persecuted but not silenced by the Guizot government, contributed to the build-up

[74] Quoted by Jean Starobinski, 'Benjamin Constant: comment parler quand l'éloquence est épuisée' in Furet and Ozouf (eds), *The Transformation of Political Culture, 1789–1848*, 198.

[75] Collins, *The Government and the Newspaper Press*, 77; cf. 62–80.

[76] Kerr, *Caricature and French Political Culture*, 58, 71–3, 81–2, 90–2.

[77] See Chapter 4.

[78] Collins, *The Government and the Newspaper Press*, 86; cf. 77–8, 82–4.

to the Second Republic but waited until Louis-Philippe's abdication to come out openly for the revolution and thereby acquire posts in the new Republic. However, Michelet's cautionary 1848 comment was apposite: 'The press does not reach the people.... It leaves most women catholic, it leaves most men bonapartist.'[79]

Most of the 1835 press legislation was abrogated but caution money was only suspended and was reduced but restored in the August 1848 press laws that reinstated much of the previous libel law. Almost all the 450 or so newspapers that had been launched had in any case not survived more than a few days or weeks. Although Proudhon raised the caution money for *Le Peuple* by public subscription, Lamennais was forced to close his *Peuple constituent* with valedictory eloquence: 'Silence au pauvre.'[80] In the presidential election campaign, Louis-Napoleon had less press support than his main rival General Cavaignac, although the papers of Girardin, Hugo, and Thiers were on his side. The mass of voters were not influenced by the press but this did not stop subsequent crackdowns. At the *coup d'état* of December 1851, the police occupied the offices of the main Paris newspapers and ensured their silence during the subsequent plebiscite. In the provinces, the Prefects censored, suspended, or suppressed hostile newspapers. A February 1852 decree reinforced prior authorization (rarely granted until 1860), doubled caution money, increased stamp duty and restored postal charges. Jury trial was abandoned and penalties increased. Newspapers were forbidden to publish parliamentary reports (other than official bulletins) and accounts of press trials. Finally, no drawing could be published without authorization of the Prefect of Police—perhaps a tribute to Daumier whose caricatures ridiculing Louis-Napoleon had appeared in *Le Charivari*.[81]

Administrative and financial pressure, backed by judicial repression worked effectively, prompting the papers that survived to engage in prudent self-censorship. Lively clerical versus anticlerical polemics were an exception until the 1868 Press Law abandoned prior authorization and administrative control in the context of a liberalized Second Empire. By contrast with the high minded Republican press, a new weekly made a spectacular impact: Henri Rochefort's *La Lanterne*. The ironic opening sentence of its first issue in May 1868 has remained famous. 'In France there are 36 million subjects, without counting the subjects of discontent.'[82] Its sales rapidly climbed to 500,000 but his personal attacks on the Emperor and the Catholic religion led to him being sentenced to a heavy fine and 13 months imprisonment. He escaped to Brussels from where copies were smuggled into France. Elected deputy in 1869, he served briefly in the Provisional Government of 1870, was elected to and quickly resigned from the February 1871 Assembly, became a Communard, was transported, escaped, and later amnestied,

---

[79] Quoted by Nicolas Roussellier 'La culture politique libérale' in Serge Berstein (ed.), *Les Cultures politiques en France*, 2003 edn, 81. See also Collins, 88–101. On Emile de Girardin, see Mazedier, 92–8. For circulation figures and details of press legislation during the Restoration and the July Monarchy, see Ledré, 236–45.

[80] Collins, *The Government and the Newspaper Press*, 106; cf. 102–5.

[81] Ibid. 107–19, 122 note, 123–131.

[82] Alexandre Zévaès, *Henri Rochefort le pamphlétaire*, 1946, 43; cf. 45–9.

returned to active journalism in *L'Intransigent* in the 1880s, culminating in his support for the populist General Boulanger, ending his life as a nationalist anti-Dreyfusard. The sulphurous Rochefort, by starting on the Extreme Left and ending on the Extreme Right, showed how easy it was for the extremes to touch. The contrast could not be greater with Gambetta (both members of the 1870 Government of National Defence), who avoided compromising himself with the Commune and used his newspaper *La République Française* in the 1870s patiently to build up public support for a middle of the road parliamentary regime.

We should not be surprised that caution money was abolished in October 1870 and restored in July 1871. Thiers having initially repressed the monarchist, Bonapartist, and extreme Left press, Prime Minister Broglie, under President MacMahon, used the Prefects mainly against radical republican newspapers. At the height of the confrontation in May–December 1877, 2,500 prosecutions on every conceivable charge were launched, especially against the provincial press. The republican majority quickly amnestied all recent press offences but it was not until July 1881 that new legislation replacing forty-two previous press laws was enacted despite Girardin, chairman of the parliamentary committee, favouring total freedom. 'There were to be no more prosecutions for the vague offence of inciting to hatred and contempt of the government, for attacks on the idea of property, on freedom of worship, on the respect due to the laws.... '[83] Trial by jury was restored, but in the drastically reduced list of offences remaining figured insulting the President of the Republic, although Clemenceau ridiculed out of existence a proposed offence of insulting the Republic.

Given the importance of a free press in a liberal democracy, it looked as though its emergence, despite being through a prolonged and difficult process, had been successfully accomplished. However, the problems were far from over in a non-consensual republic combining socio-economic stalemate, political instability, and cultural effervescence in a cocktail of continuity and change. Exploring these complexities will be the concern of Part II.

---

[83] Collins, *The Government and the Newspaper Press*, 182; cf. 164–83.

Part II

Selective Memory and Stalled Self-Scrutiny since 1878

Introduction to Part II

It was Ernest Renan, in his famous 1882 lecture *What is a nation?*, who argued that forgetting those features of past history that did not facilitate creating a sense of national unity was an indispensable part of supporting it. What Robert Gildea more than a century later called 'a studied forgetfulness' or 'collective amnesia', sought selectively to substitute a mythical collective memory for 'competing collective memories' and to construct a spuriously integrated political culture and national identity that denied the legitimacy of rival claims to their share in a plural community.[1]

The most memorable and sophisticated late twentieth-century exercise in achieving this ambitious purpose was attempted by a large team of historians headed by Pierre Nora, when the myth was becoming increasingly difficult to sustain convincingly. While purporting to eschew national self-celebration in a nostalgic cult of piously retrieved heritage and collective memory, Nora and his associates have been criticized for resuscitating the 'teleological nationalism of Lavisse, as embodied in his 27-volume early twentieth century *Histoire de France*.[2] In his extended essay on Ernest Lavisse's magnum opus, Nora points out the continuity with Romantic early mid-nineteenth-century predecessors such as Michelet, who institutionalized the nation incarnated in its history. They shared an 'obsessive cut of the fatherland ... and the particular truth of the nation.'[3] Nora did not conceal his admiration. 'Beyond doubt, no history has made a comparable effort to weld the monarchical past with the present republic; to impart to the national adventure its coherence and exemplary significance', providing 'the mirror in which France has continued to recognise itself.'[4]

In his caustic review of *Les Lieux de mémoire*, Steven Englund compares Nora to Lavisse—publicist, pedagogue, professor if not the master of educational policy like his forerunner—in their use of multiple positions of intellectual authority to respond to a national identity crisis by his defence of past revolutionary myths concerning 'the universality and perenniality of "La Nation"'; adding that Nora shows his cunning by 'tacitly implying—indeed defending—traditional

---

[1] Robert Gildea, *The Past in French History*, 1994, 1996 edn, 10–12, 340.

[2] Julian Jackson, 'Historians and the nation in contemporary France' in Stefan Berger, Mark Donovan, and Kevin Passmore (eds), *Writing National Histories: Western Europe since 1800*, 1999, 243; cf. 11, 241–2.

[3] Pierre Nora, 'L'Histoire de France de Lavisse' in *Les Lieux de mémoire*, II/6, 332; cf. 327, 352.

[4] Ibid. 363–4.

"national" orthodoxy by seeming to question it.'[5] In discharging his reverential if rueful state—serving function, Nora normatively minimizes the acknowledged enduring French social and political divisions, while deploring a 'classical heritage irretrievably slipping away' in practice.[6] To flatter a sentimental public demand, Nora and many of his associates engage in mythmaking aimed at promoting national consensus in which the 'Republic' is both all-embracing and synonymous with the French nation but in fact the normative disguise and legitimation of French statism. The result is 'the personification, and reification, of the concept of "the nation" as a sort of eternal representational given, a nineteenth century ideal projected back onto fifteen centuries of French history' that 'seems to operate according to a kind of Law of the Conservation of Sanctity: the sacred may be relocated, even transformed, but not lost.'[7] Because republican political culture is now consensual, it ceases to play its assimilative role effectively in a multicultural French society as the ongoing Muslim headscarves affair of 1989 exemplified. However, the French Republican tradition has always restricted French incorporation into the national community on condition that other identities are abandoned or restricted to private life, not displayed in public, as the law banning in schools ostentatious religious headgear in 2004 reasserted forcefully. The bicentenary commemoration of the revolution in 1989 had ominously suggested that 'France's future is fated to become an endless series of memories of memories', a country locked into retrospection.[8]

The desperate search to deny Franco-French disunity has been repeated after each crisis that cruelly exposed it. During the last century, the Dreyfus Affair, the Vichy regime, and to a lesser extent the Algerian War, all exemplify this pivotal phenomenon of French political culture. The Dreyfus Affair and Algerian War will be discussed in due course but the way in which the Vichy experience has been handled will be singled out here as exemplification of the fact that in France 'memory is a structuring of forgetfulness',[9] in which official memory strives to suppress the truth and substitute its manipulation of the past in the pursuit of national pseudo-reconciliation.

The Vichy regime of 1940–4, following military defeat and increasing collaboration with Nazi Germany, was estimated to be 'directly responsible for the imprisonment of 135,000 people, the internment of 70,000 suspects (including numerous political refugees from central Europe) and the dismissal of 35,000 civil servants'. Its officials 'abetted the deportation of 76,000 French and foreign Jews, fewer than three per cent of whom survived. They also worked to send 650,000 workers to Germany as conscript labour and waged unremitting battle against the Resistance and all other opponents of the regime'.[10] More than

---

[5] Steven Englund, 'The Ghost of Nation Past' in *Journal of Modern History*, LXIV, June 1992, 302, 311; cf. 300–1.

[6] Ibid. 304; cf. 302–3.   [7] Ibid. 311, 31; cf. 315–19.

[8] Jackson, 249; cf. 244–8, 300. See also Jeremy Jennings, 'Citizenship, Republicanism and Multiculturalism in Contemporary France' in *British Journal of Political Science*, xxx/4, October 2000, 575–98.

[9] Henry Rousso, *The Vichy Syndrome: History and Memory in France since 1944*, 1991, 4.

[10] Ibid. 7.

defeat and foreign occupation, the civil war at home and in the colonies—in Africa and Syria, Vichy and Free French soldiers fought and killed each other— has had a more permanently searing effect on the national consciousness because it reinforced enduring dualities. Although some 10,000 French collaborators were summarily executed, mainly before Liberation, only 1,500 of the 169,000 subsequently tried were executed; those sentenced to prison or national degradation in 1945 were more harshly treated and the 1951 and 1953 amnesties rehabilitated many of those condemned in the aftermath of the Second World War. 'A political victory of the Right, the amnesty was a missed opportunity for the nation to remember.'[11]

Assisted by Robert Aron's sympathetic 1954 *Histoire de Vichy* and de Gaulle's calculated amnesia (opportunistically dismissing the Vichy regime as 'null and void' and claiming that France liberated itself in his *Mémoires de Guerre*, which also began to appear in 1954), the process of historic exorcism was illustrated by de Gaulle proclaiming in 1959 during a visit to Vichy: 'The past is finished. Long live Vichy! Long live France! Long live the Republic!'[12] It was left to isolated French specialists such as expatriate Stanley Hoffmann and American historian Robert Paxton to demythologize the Vichy years and scandalize—with the help of a film like *The Sorrow and the Pity* of Marcel Ophuls—before the French public was forced to listen to the rattling of the skeletons in its national cupboard. Hoffmann subsequently answered the question: 'What myths have the French developed in order to appease their consciences and restore their self esteem?' which Henry Rousso's study of *The Vichy Syndrome* posed. Rousso had shown 'how the French chose to believe that Vichy had been the creation of a small group of rather wicked (but still more misguided than evil) men, that the crimes committed were crimes of the Germans and of very small bands of collaborators and that most of the population has resisted the Occupation in some degree ... By and large, French elites agreed, either out of compassion and a fervent desire to bury an ugly past or out of self-interest to avoid embarrassing scrutiny; and the general public, which deep down knew that the myth was a cavalier interpretation of reality, pretended that it was indeed the truth.'[13]

Rousso's book would not have been possible without Robert Paxton's heretical *Vichy France: Old Guard and New Order* of 1972, which displaced Robert Aron's exculpatory minimization of Vichy's perfidies as well as relativizing de Gaulle's maximization of the role of the Free French and the Communist exaggeration of Resistance heroism. Paxton (relying mainly on German sources, being denied access to French ones) demolished four presuppositions of Robert Aron's apologia. First, Vichy initially volunteered cooperation with the German occupation beyond the demands made upon it, notably in its persecution and subsequent deportation of Jews. Secondly, Pétain's metaphorical defence at his 1945 trial that

---

[11] Ibid. 54; cf. 51–3.   [12] Ibid. 73; cf. 17, 33–9.

[13] Hoffmann, Foreword to Rousso, vii-viii. See also the reprint of earlier explorations of the Vichy Regime from 1956 onward in Part 1 of Stanley Hoffmann's *Decline or Renewal? France since the 1930s*, 1974.

he remained in France to 'shield' her rather than continue the fight abroad as other governments did, had in fact not secured more favourable treatment. The main reason for the armistice was to implement a reactionary 'national revolution' to transform the French state and society on the back of the belief that Nazi Germany would win the war and create a European New Order. Thirdly, it was not true that Vichy played a 'double game', secretly negotiating with the Allies... because the Germans were kept informed! In particular, there was especially strong Anglophobia because of wartime exacerbation of long-standing colonial rivalry. Fourthly, Vichy's policy of neutrality within a Hitlerite Europe was based upon voluntary 'state collaboration', bitterly opposed to de Gaulle, the Resistance and their Soviet Allies, resulting in a wait-and-see attitude in tune with majority public opinion. So, from the 'original sin' of the June 1940 Armistice onward, the conduct of the Vichy authorities, despite their divisions, was dictated not by necessity but 'partisan opportunism.'[14] Paxton's book provoked a flood of academic studies, assisted by a 1979 Law easing public access to national archives and institution of a thirty-year rule. It was sustained by the entry of contemporary history into the school curriculum, so that by the 1980s Paxton's interpretation dislodged Aron's in the text books.[15]

That this educational reform was influential in modifying the predominant myths is evident from the widespread ignorance and distortion of public perceptions of the past revealed by opinion polls. Fifty three per cent of French people in 1976 did not know who had headed the French state in 1940–4. Asked in 1980 whether Pétain and de Gaulle had played confrontational or complementary roles, 42 per cent said they were opposed, 31 per cent said they were complementary, and the remaining twenty-seven did not know. The measure of retrospective support for Marshal Pétain is reflected in a 1980 poll in which 56 per cent blamed the Third Republic for France's defeat and 53 per cent regarded the Armistice as a good thing and 10 per cent a very good thing.[16] This reflects what has been called 'Marshalism', rather than approval of the 'national revolution', much less positive collaboration with Nazi Germany.

Following the discredit of public authority associated with the May 1968 'events' and after de Gaulle's death in 1970, the 'cultural time bomb' of repressed memory was detonated by *The Sorrow and the Pity*, a 1971 film about the Occupation, concentrating not on the Germans but on the French civil war and on Vichy's neglected anti-Semitism. Offering an unheroic counter myth to the Gaullist— Communist heroic myths, this deliberate work of demystification was banned from TV for ten years until 1981 (when Mitterrand became President) by a head of broadcasting who had been in the Resistance, because he said the film 'destroys myths that the people of France still needs'.[17] Censorship delayed the revelations' diffusion but increased their impact. The re-emergence in the 1970s of accounts of the Jewish genocide, after the long reluctance to speak the unspeakable, led

---

[14] Robert O. Paxton, *La France de Vichy, 1940–1944*, 2nd edn, 1997, 30; cf. 9–18, 65–6, 284.
[15] Rousso, 265–9; cf. 252–5 on the scandal initially caused by Paxton's book.
[16] Ibid. 278–95.   [17] Ibid. 110; cf. 98–113.

to a polemical orgy, exacerbated by pseudoscientific negationist provocations denying the existence of Nazi gas chambers and dismissing Anne Frank's diary as a post-war forgery. Long delayed court cases for crimes against humanity revived neglected memories.

The extradition to France for crimes against humanity of the SS leader in Lyon, Klaus Barbie, in 1983 led to a 1987 trial which concentrated upon the deportation to their death of forty-three Jewish children from Izieu, that is on anti-Semitism not on anti-Resistance. The showing of a Lanzmann film, *Shoah*, at the same time 'probably had a far bigger impact than the Barbie trial'.[18] The 1981 revelation of former Prefect Maurice Papon's role in the deportation of Jews from Bordeaux, a nauseating example of 'state collaboration' by French officials, was to lead to a long delayed trial, conviction and imprisonment until he was released on questionable health grounds. The Papon case pinpointed 'the scandal of Vichy: that senior civil servants of the republican state could have, without any great qualms or misgivings, long obeyed a regime under Nazi command...and that after the war, they could have pursued administrative advancement under the reinstated republic....'[19] It was not until 1995 that President Chirac symbolically accepted responsibility on behalf of the French state for the acts perpetrated during the Vichy regime, an acknowledgement that had always been stubbornly rejected by both de Gaulle and Mitterrand.

It is from this perspective of a selective memory that had been distorted by a stalled self-scrutiny (that also applied to the 1954–62 Algerian War) that the heady years of the Third Republic, the patchy record of the Fourth Republic, and the achievements of the Fifth Republic will need to be exposed. We shall then turn from the contending anti-Frances within to the anti-France of the threat to the social model that was synonymous with French identity from alien social liberalism. As a leading opponent of multiculturalism bluntly put it during the Muslim headscarves controversy, but with much more general application: 'The French version of democracy is the republic. It is not the Anglo-Saxon model. It is necessary to defend this version because (the French) model is superior, I believe, to the one that prevails in America and England.'[20]

---

[18] Ibid. 215; cf. 148–61, 199–211.

[19] Pierre Birnbaum, *The Idea of France*, 1998, 2001, 151; cf. 149–62. See more generally Marc Olivier Baruch *Servir l'Etat français*, 1997. Between 1944 and 1951, 'men moved from prison cells into boardrooms and from ineligibility to ministerial office' comments Richard Vinen, *Bourgeois Politics in France, 1945–1951*, 1995, 1–2.

[20] Quoting Alain Finkielkraut from *Libération*, 7 November 1989, by Birnbaum, *The Idea of France*, 230; cf. 228–9, 238.

6

Institutional Immobilism, Ideological Ferment, and Reluctant Socio-Economic Modernization

While the shock of military defeat and civil war at the start of the 1870s and the establishment of what proved to be a long-lived Third Republic during the decade did create significant discontinuities with the French past, it will be argued in the rest of this book that François Furet's provocative claim that the French Revolution was completed by the end of the 1870s cannot be sustained. It was Thiers's hope to halt the revolutionary process, to whose history he had contributed by the age of 30 a widely-read 10-volume liberal interpretation. In his seventies, he ended his political career as a constitutional monarchist by helping to institute a conservative republic, having in the process succeeded in taming the French Revolution.[1] However, the man who was accurately described by Walter Bagehot in 1852 as 'an adroit and dexterous intriguer'[2] did not succeed in establishing a parliamentary regime with strong and stable government, a failure that was to bedevil both the Third and Fourth Republics before de Gaulle in 1958 was to take advantage of another regime crisis to amalgamate an imported Anglo-parliamentarism with a traditional Franco-authoritarianism.

Bagehot as early as 1872 predicted that because Thiers boasted that he was not the head of a party, 'He is the exception of a moment; he is not the example of a lasting condition.'[3] However, the problem was less personal than a matter of a French political culture that had 'long been enslaved to authority' and in which 'Every Assembly is divided into parties, and into sections of parties' locked in uncompromising conflict.[4] Parliamentary government in France would not work on the British model because, 'as a sovereign it is unstable, capricious and unruly.... The experiment of a strictly Parliamentary Republic—of a Republic where the Parliament appoints the Executive—is being tried in France at an extreme disadvantage, because in France a Parliament is unusually likely to be bad, and unusually likely also to be free enough to show its badness', with the result that 'the Assembly would be always changing its Ministry.'[5]

---

[1] François Furet, *La Révolution, 1770–1880*, 1988, 493–4.

[2] Walter Bagehot, *Bagehot's Historical Essays*, 1971 edn, 416.

[3] Walter Bagehot, *The English Constitution*, 1867, Introduction to the 1872 Nelson edn, n.d., 55; cf. 54.

[4] Ibid. 53, 51–2.   [5] Ibid. 52–3.

A NEW POLITICAL CLASS

The French Third Republic created a doubly indirect democracy in which, first, the representatives of manhood suffrage substituted their will for that of the people by overthrowing popular leaders between elections or denying them office, and second, established a powerful indirectly elected Senate as a further bulwark against the results of elections which decided who would govern.[6] After having forced the resignation of a popular Thiers in 1873, the parliament in the 1880s defeated Gambetta and Ferry and prevented General Boulanger from converting electoral popularity into political power. Lacking a party system able to provide the electoral link between the people and the politicians, the latter were able to manoeuvre to their heart's content at each government reshuffle. In anticipation of the Republicans' conquest of the Senate in 1879, thanks to their gains in the local elections that determined the composition of the second chamber's electoral college, Gambetta could eulogize the 'Grand Council of the Communes', repudiating the traditional republican commitment to a single chamber. The Senate subsequently asserted the power to force the resignation of governments that lacked its confidence.

The two chambers were happy to agree in 1879 to return parliament back to Paris from Versailles, avoiding tiresome train journeys during the parliamentary sessions. Another symbolic act was to vote full amnesty for the 1871 Communards, so that post-civil war reconciliation could allow the new national holiday on 14 July 1880 to be celebrated in national unity.[7] However, the decisive defeat of Gambetta in 1882 (followed shortly after by his death) who had relied in vain upon extra-parliamentary popularity and the prevalence of Ferry's conservative republic which was elevated above manhood suffrage, politically equipped the Third Republic with strong brakes but a weak engine. The secularist political class successfully acted to avoid a mass electorate threatening ordered society in the absence of a hereditary monarchy and aristocracy bolstered by a militantly clerical Church that was losing its grip on society.

Ninety years after Bagehot's emphasis on political turmoil and looking back with hindsight on the Third Republic, Stanley Hoffmann instead stressed the pride of place accorded to protection of the country's socio-economic equilibrium. Guided by a peculiar style of authority combining an aspiration after strong government with a fear of authoritarianism, post-revolutionary stability was purchased at the cost of relative stagnation, leading to what he dubbed the 'stalemate society'. 'The organisation of their state was such that an effective executive, clear-cut economic or social alternatives, and a strong party system could not emerge. Parliament was supreme but immobile.... The decision of Léon Gambetta and his friends to woo the peasants rather than the urban workers was of decisive importance in disassociating the Republic from "disorder"'.[8] The new political

---

[6] See Odile Rudelle, *La République Absolue*, 84–5, 90–2, 101–3, 281–5.

[7] Bury, *Gambetta's Final Years*, 162–9. On the ephemeral Gambetta government, see ibid. 285–315.

[8] Stanley Hoffmann, 'Paradoxes of the French political community' in Hoffmann et al., *France: Change and Tradition*, 1963, 15.

class sought to underpin the lack of political consensus by crafting a partial social consensus based upon protection of a provincial, rural society under the leadership of a bourgeoisie open meritocratically to lower middle-class talent.

In the Third Republic, the new professional political class came particularly from the educated middle classes rather than the propertied rich of noble birth. They consisted predominantly of provincial lawyers, senior civil servants, *Polytechnique* engineers, doctors, and journalists, with some bright, poor young scholarship boys, but rentiers and businessmen remained important. Political provincialization counterbalanced administrative centralization in Paris but peasants and farmers were almost completely absent. Southerners, with their distinctive accents, were considered intruder *arrivistes* on the make. Future ministers had generally married socially and financially above their station, with their choice of father-in-law being more important than of wife in a careerist matrimonial strategy. Most future anticlerical ministers had received a Catholic childhood education modified subsequently by the secular *lycée*. University education was dominated by law, with the reverence for private property being fostered by 'the analysis and commentary of the civil code almost perceived as revealed truth', the acquisition of advocacy skills being useful in political debate and law-making.[9]

The political career of barristers was facilitated by the complementarity of their political notoriety and acquisition of their professional clientele. Under the Restoration, July Monarchy and the Second Empire, this had allowed Opposition barristers such as Dufaure and Grévy to make a name for themselves, while under the early Third Republic future Prime Ministers like Waldeck-Rousseau and Viviani, or future Presidents of the Republic like Poincaré and Millerand tended to alternate their legal and political roles. In a system of government by Assembly, conspicuous, spellbinding oratorical success was the acknowledged stepping stone to ministerial office. Gambetta, who made his legal reputation under the latter-day Second Empire, was the supreme exemplar of the use of eloquence to impress juries, parliament, and the public. His closest collaborator grandiloquently proclaimed: 'French eloquence has filled the world with its resonance... every single political or social reform is born at the rostrum. It has given wings to all generous ideas and doubled the seductive power of chimeras. Whenever it has been silent, humanity has seemed speechless.... To describe both the good and the evil it has caused, it would be necessary to recount French history of the last century.'[10] While this may have been a plausible claim at the end of the nineteenth century, professionalization was to eliminate eloquence as the number of lawyers declined, the length of parliamentary speeches was curbed from 1926, and the mass media became the predominant form of political communication after the Second World War.

---

[9] Jean Estèbe, *Les Ministres de la République, 1871–1914*, 108; cf. 22–49, 73–89, 99–112. The Minister of Justice in 1848 declared that because the courts protected property, it was important that judges should own some (ibid. 118).

[10] Joseph Reinach, *L'Eloquence française depuis la Révolution jusqu'à nos jours*, 1894, 1 quoted by Jean-Pierre Rioux, 'Le Palais Bourbon: De Gambetta à de Gaulle' in *Les lieux de mémoire*, II/3, 487; cf. 501, 508–13. See also Estèbe, 114–18.

Businessmen accounted for a third of ministers between 1871 and 1914; for half of them their business links preceded ministerial office, while the other half were co-opted into business afterwards. The 1871–7 governments resembled meetings of Boards of Directors, although there was a decline of business presence thereafter. However, under the Opportunist Republicans, Léon Say and Maurice Rouvier were conspicuous examples of political–business linkages. Grandson of Jean-Baptiste Say, Léon Say was the personification of liberal conservative republicanism. As a young man he fought against the June insurgents in 1848; during the Second Empire, he provided Jules Ferry with the financial arguments against Haussmann's fanciful budgeting of the rebuilding of Paris and championed free trade, later becoming Finance Minister and President of the Senate. Say, who had organized finance for Freycinet's massive 1878 public infrastructure investment plan, as the political spokesman of the railway interests (mentioned in Chapter 4) refused to join the Gambetta government which proposed to nationalize the Paris-Orléans Railway Company.[11] Maurice Rouvier was President of the Chamber of Deputies Budget Committee for nine years and Finance Minister in eight separate governments. Insider trading relating to the Panama scandal led to his exclusion from office between 1892 and 1902 but he made a comeback as Finance Minister and then Prime Minister in 1902–6. Paul Doumer, President of the Senate, who was elected President of the Republic in 1931, had combined being Vice-President of the powerful UIMM Metallurgical Trade Association with the presidency of the Railway Products Trade Association before the First World War. More generally, firms linked with public companies and banks attracted political appointments.[12]

From the late 1870s, many of the big businessmen migrated to the Senate from the Chamber of Deputies. The Senate resisted successive attempts to adopt a progressive income tax, Say playing a leading part in blocking this demand by Gambetta and subsequent advocates, notably the Radical Joseph Caillaux, who took up the cause in 1907 and secured its adoption in 1914. Before then, the Budget Committee of the Chamber of Deputies in 1886 adopted the principle of an income tax but the attempt to implement it in 1896 led to the fall of the Léon Bourgeois Radical government owing to Senate opposition. The Senate's obstruction and amendment of the 1884 Trade Union Law, delaying abolition of the worker's passbook until 1890, adoption of industrial accident legislation until 1898, the 10-hour working day until 1900 and worker pensions until 1910, was clearly motivated by the conservative, business-oriented bias of its composition.[13]

Jules Grévy was the first French President of the Republic to complete his first (but not his second) prescribed term of office thanks to his cunning in combining a disposition to prevent governments from asserting effective authority with a determination surreptitiously to steer the state. He was able to delay Gambetta's advent to office and then manoeuvre behind the scenes for others to demolish

---

[11] Jean Garrigues, *La République des hommes d'affaires*, 26–34, 155–61, 211–26. See Chapter 4.

[12] Estèbe, 166–81.

[13] Garrigues, 261–82. The business daily *Le Temps* asserted in 1896 that income tax is 'something anti-French and contrary to the customs and genius of the nation'. Quoted in R. D. Anderson, *France, 1870–1914*, 1977, 98.

his government. A significant early power struggle was over Gambetta's attempt to exclude Grévy from Cabinet meetings. They compromised, Grévy presiding at one of the two weekly meetings, while he did not attend the other, chaired by the Prime Minister.[14] With Gambetta out of the way, Grévy used the absence of a disciplined majority in the Chamber of Deputies to avoid a parliamentary leader such as Jules Ferry establishing a tradition of strong prime ministerial authority because he lacked the extra-parliamentary popular and press support of a Gambetta. Ferry might have become a strong presidential successor to Grévy when the latter was forced to resign in 1887 after re-election but the hostility from the Right because of his anticlericalism and from the Left because of his conservatism led to the election of Sadi Carnot, grandson of the first and son of the second revolutionary Carnot. As Clemenceau, who was determined to secure Ferry's defeat put it, 'He is not very impressive but he bears a republican name'.[15]

Grévy had in 1848 denied the need for a President of the Republic and Clemenceau in the 1880s carried on that republican tradition by pressing for a constitutional revision to abolish both the presidency and the Senate. Determined to radicalize the Republic, Clemenceau decided to democratize the army by securing the appointment of his protégé General Boulanger as Minister for War in 1886 to carry out the necessary reforms: in particular purging anti-republicans from the ranks of senior officers.[16] This was to lead to the most serious threat to the survival of the regime, whose studied avoidance of charismatic leaders was to open the way for a populist adventurer. Promoted by Paul Déroulède, leader of the Patriots League, as 'General Revanche' who would win back Alsace-Lorraine from Germany, celebrated by the popular songwriter Paulus as the man on horseback at the 14 July 1886 military review in his catchy hit *En revenant de la revue*, Boulanger began to see himself as the latest in the line of French national saviours. Orchestrated from May 1886 by a brilliant journalist, the ex-scourge of the Second Empire and Communard returned from exile Henri Rochefort, Boulanger's sweeping electoral popularity became a threat and he was excluded in 1887 from the Rouvier government. Jules Ferry sounded the alarm against 'this Bolivian-style general, audacious demagogue, seductive orator, infatuated politician, dangerous comedian who traverses France in triumph ... an immense vanity ... an unlimited ambition.'[17] To save the threatened regime, Ferry called in August 1887 for the creation of a Conservative Party relying on a Right-Centre parliamentary majority extending rightward from the Opportunists and excluding the Radicals, to support the Rouvier government.[18]

With the republicans divided and profiting from the support of the monarchists and Bonapartists (who hoped he would play the restoration role of the English General Monck in 1660) Boulanger's supporters launched a campaign based on

[14] Bury, *Gambetta's Final Years*, 268, 299; cf. 103. See also Rudelle, 62–3, 68–9.

[15] Rudelle, 193; cf. 71–2, 188–92.

[16] Ibid. 74–6, 164–5; Michel Winock, *Nationalisme, antisémitisme et fascisme en France*, 1992, 299–300.

[17] Letter to his brother of 2.7.86, quoted by Rudelle, 168–9.   [18] Rudelle, 171–2; cf. 173–9.

the slogan: 'Dissolution, Revision, Constituent Assembly'.[19] Taking advantage of the opportunity to launch Boulanger's candidature at each by-election, they provoked the government into retiring Boulanger from the army, which left him free to campaign openly, securing public sympathy as both hero and victim, despite coming off worse in a duel with the civilian Prime Minister Floquet. Mobilizing universal suffrage against the closed parliamentary politics of an introvert political class, Boulanger's electoral triumph in Paris on 27 January 1889 marked the high point of his campaign but in its wake he refused to countenance a violent seizure of power that would probably have succeeded. One of his disconsolate supporters declared: 'Five past twelve. Boulangism has been in decline for five minutes.'[20] It never recovered from this failure of dictatorial nerve.

In 1889, the Parliamentary Republic showed that although it governed ineffectively, it could defend itself successfully against the irresolute Boulanger, the weakest component of Boulangism. Threatened with prosecution he fled to Belgium with his mistress (on whose grave he was subsequently to commit suicide). Any hope of a thorough revision of the 1875 Constitution was buried but parliament adopted an electoral reform forbidding multiple candidatures, whose plebiscitary propensities had been exploited so successfully by Boulanger, who had threatened to stand in all constituencies in 1889. In any case he had become ineligible, tried as a subversive and politically killed by ridicule. The fear aroused by this fiasco nevertheless ensured that thereafter republicanism in France would be identified with government by Assembly.[21] Having achieved a measure of political stability, the Third Republic returned to the task of shoring up the stalemate socio-economic system on which its long-term survival depended.

RETREATING FROM RURALISM IN SLOW MOTION: PEASANTS AND ARTISANS

The gradual colonization of the peasant countryside by bourgeois towns slowed down by protection of the peasantry by tariffs, tax exemptions, and subsidies, eroded the parochial mentality that had prevailed for centuries. As modernity made its presence felt, as the everyday concerns of jobs and goods, roads and markets became less predominantly local, a concurrent process of politicization took place, spearheaded by the election of mayors by their commune councils. Competitive mass partisan politics displaced the traditional authority of the landlords, who had confined politics to a very few socio-economic and cultural superiors. For the bulk of the peasantry, contact with the world beyond their village was mediated indirectly through officials—the mayor, schoolteacher, priest, postman, and rural policeman—or through the local innkeeper or shopkeeper. The local inn or café was a focus for political communication, which partly accounts for

---

[19] Rudelle 202; cf. 196–202.   [20] Winock, 309; cf. 307–10 and Rudelle, 205–32, 249–50.
[21] Winock, 310–12 and Rudelle, 247–56.

the association of drink with political propaganda, especially at election time, a feature of a widened suffrage by no means confined to France or rural areas. Rural politics was highly personalized. Local rivalries rather than ideological conflicts providing the transition from an introvert, hierarchically managed consensus to an extrovert, egalitarian contention, one in which national and even international concerns increasingly intruded into the daily lives of the peasantry.[22]

The reversal of the Second Empire's modernizing incursion into free trade came quickly under the Third Republic, with Thiers reviving protectionism in the 1870s, Jules Ferry (to protect textiles in his Vosges constituency) in the 1880s and Jules Méline (to protect agriculture and textiles) in the 1890s. In parliament, the farm lobby outnumbered the free traders, although the latter had the vocal support of economists and the liberal *Journal des débats*. Méline was as much the personification of protectionism as Léon Say had earlier been of free trade, but by the time of the Méline tariff of 1892, free trade was regarded as 'a utopia of Anglophile liberals'.[23] Although Méline was influentially assisted by the *Comité des forges* metallurgical lobby and the textile lobby, his main support came from the Society of French Farmers. The price paid for preserving the French peasantry— although the number of farm labourers declined from nearly three million in 1848 to about one million in 1946—was that from the 1890s to the 1950s, 'A crucial sixty years were allowed to pass in which the problem of adapting [the peasantry] to industrial society was purposely neglected.'[24] The economic difficulties postponed led to increasing peasant unrest in the 1930s, which continued after the Vichy interlude well into the 1960s and beyond, although with decreasingly virulent and sporadic vehemence and violence. The frustration at inadequate political influence commensurate with their numbers did not diminish as the process of agricultural depopulation accelerated in the second half of the twentieth century, when paradoxically their political influence increased with the European Common Agricultural Policy.

The transmutation of the appellation 'peasant' from a pejorative term of contempt to a positive approbation came after the First World War, just as 'all the virtues associated with a healthy, rooted, traditional rural culture' were perceived to be in decline and disintegrating.[25] The time lag in French modernization has been associated by Paxton with four myths that constitute an increasingly implausible identification of France as an exceptionally peasant nation in an industrialized world. First, 'France is not itself without a large peasantry'. Second, 'even areas not particularly suitable for agriculture should be farmed' for territorial reasons because, third, 'the land is not beautiful unless it is cultivated.' Unfarmed land is deemed to revert to desert. Fourth, farming is not solely for profit but a way of life. This involves subsuming under the peasant umbrella an agribusiness which

---

[22] Eugen Weber, *Peasants into Frenchmen*, Chapter 15 passim. More generally, see Laurence Wylie, 'Social change at the grassroots' in Hoffmann et al., *France: Change and Tradition*, 159–234 and for a case study Wylie, *Chanzeau: A village in Anjou*, 1966.

[23] Garrigues, 245; cf. 232–44.   [24] Zeldin, I, 174–5; cf. 170–6.

[25] Robert Paxton, *French Peasant Fascism: Henry Dorgères's Greenshirts and the Crises of French Agriculture, 1929–1939*, 1997, 176; cf. 75–7.

has progressively bulldozed out of existence the very peasant distinctiveness on which the French mythology has been grounded.[26] The ephemeral Peasant Front movement of the mid-1930s that sought government intervention to support falling farm prices, combined electoral, pressure group, and direct action tactics. Anticipating the Vichy Peasant Corporation in its demand for corporatism in substitution for a market economy in disarray, it was prepared to try to organize a tax strike, for which there were many signatories but few who carried out their threat. In contrast to this right-wing manifestation, the Left organized strikes in the wake of the Popular Front victory of 1936, also involving the occupation of farms, which were met with government repression as well as strong arm strike-breakers from the Dorgères Greenshirt movement.[27]

Such conflicts exposed the hollowness of the myth of peasant unity but there was also a conflict between the farm organizations that provided practical purchasing and marketing services for their members and the purely protest organizations such as the Greenshirts, with their more than symbolic pitchforks. The former were seeking increased semi-official involvement in public decision-making, which was to take the form of closed producer control, backed up by the state to render it compulsory. The insider status they sought was to be satisfied under Vichy, when the Peasant Corporation was the most effective of all its corporatist innovations. Whereas these structures were dismantled with the downfall of Vichy, the corporatist assertion of producer control by farm leaders survived in the post-war practice of co-management of farm policy, even more successfully than industrial businessmen were to ensure that industrial policy planning was to be an industrialists' policy. Dorgères remained an outsider, even though he bequeathed a direct action legacy that allowed militant farmers to alternate collaboration and coercion in extracting concessions from the authorities.[28]

Before the mid-twentieth century onset of the agricultural revolution, bringing in its train a double loss of customers through the rural exodus and farm mechanization, the craftsmen that serviced the peasants (not to be identified with the much larger number of artisans located in rural areas, who were less directly affected) were an integral part of the country community. They were well adapted to the economic system then prevailing and had a great deal in common with the semi-subsistence peasantry, who formed as separate a category from the large-scale capitalist farmer as artisans did from the industrialist. However, the blow fell later and with greater brutality in the farm sector and the consequences on the artisans who were dependent upon it are clear from the dramatic fall in their numbers since the Second World War. From over 80,000 workshops in 1945, their number had decreased by about 50 per cent to 43,777 by 1962.

The sluggishness of the process of French urbanization ensured that the indispensability of the artisan was underpinned in over 30,000 semi-rural, micro-communes. Although the consequent 'swarm of small units' was economically irrational, it served a number of important social functions, notably the preservation of social stability coupled with opportunities for upwards social mobility.

---

[26] Robert Paxton, 1997, 181–4.   [27] Ibid. 84–90, 129–33.   [28] Ibid. 126–9, 138–48, 169–73.

The values associated with this type of socio-economic structure were production-centred and functionalist, not market-centred and capitalist. A job well done rather than pecuniary gain gave the stamp of legitimacy to economic activity.[29] The victims of the new, technologically advanced predators were to feel indignant at the destruction of a socio-economic system with virtues which could not be reduced to the vested interests of a multitude of petty craftsmen and shopkeepers.

The small-scale artisan enterprise is characterized by a number of peculiar features. In addition to the criterion of the number of workers employed, there are a large number of other aspects which differentiate it from big business. First, there is the type of product. Traditionally, articles are produced one at a time, to suit a particular customer. Second, the level of technology tends to be less advanced, associated with a low energy input. Thirdly, there is a lower rate of capital investment per worker because of a greater dependence on self-financing. Fourthly, though its rate of profit may be high, the artisan enterprise has a lower and less stable volume of profit than its bigger brethren. Fifthly, it tends to produce for a local market and is increasingly threatened by monopsony from a particular client which deprives it of the feature which for many artisans represents the very *raison d'être* of their activity: preserving their independence. Finally, artisan enterprises tend to have a high birth rate and death rate. The feature attributed to all private business—risk—as the justification for profit, is much more relevant to the forerunner of modern business than to the large-scale corporation whose protagonists most frequently deploy the argument. To the proprietor-producer, his income is the gross profit of the firm. He may keep his enterprise going even if it yields him no 'interest' or 'profit' and only a tiny wage. However, below a certain income, he must go out of production.

The artisan is a semi-proletarian proprietor working in a micro-enterprise. Of the four criteria which Raymond Aron has used to detect the existence of capitalism,[30] three: the private ownership of the means of production, profit seeking, and the market economy are compatible with the prevalence of a predominantly artisan economy of small-scale entrepreneurs, either self-employed, independent producers or operating modest family firms. It is only with the increase in the size of the firm resulting in a separation between employers and employed that the transition is made from the craftsmen-centred economy predating the Industrial revolution to the capitalist-centred economy that succeeded it. The process by which the entrepreneur ceased to take an active part in the productive process alongside his journeymen and apprentices was prolonged and gradual, especially in France. There, as with the impact of the agricultural revolution, the full force of change did not make itself felt until after the Second World War. The increasing pressure towards modernization provoked violent unrest among social classes that had hitherto been regarded as law-abiding and respectful of their social superiors,

[29] D. S. Landes in E. M. Earle (ed.), *Modern France*, 1951, 340–9. See also C. P. Kindleberger, *Economic Growth in France and Britain, 1851–1950*, 1964, 115–63.

[30] Raymond Aron, *Dix-huit leçons sur la Société Industrielle*, 1962, 111.

content in the modest station which they occupied in the traditional status hierarchy. The outbreak of Poujadism in the early 1950s, in which the forgotten class of artisans surfaced into the glare of publicity and political concern, represented the forlorn counter-attack of the small shopkeepers and artisans upon large-scale industrial and commercial enterprise and the state agents who were in league with them. The agony of the French peasantry evoked a similar response a decade later.

Before the First World War, the artisans had been neglected for a number of reasons. First, it was difficult to secure adequate information about them (still a serious problem) because of the diversity and dispersion of the craft sector. Secondly, the relatively uneducated and inarticulate character of the artisan group and its inability to throw up effective leaders meant that its voice was seldom heard. Some trades were better able to provide leadership, such as shoemakers and more recently hairdressers. However, the major factor was lack of time; only those employing wage earners being able to devote their energies to promoting the general interests of their trade or of artisans as a whole. Thirdly, the craft sector was widely regarded as old-fashioned and condemned to shrink into insignificance with the development of large-scale manufacturing. However, this led politicians to exploit their fears, fourthly, by promising to give them tax privileges and protection from competition. Fifthly, the bigger firms, who often shared the same family-centred values as the artisans, preferred like rentiers to enjoy the profit surplus that accrued from preserving a large number of high-cost marginal producers. Both business and the 'Independent', that is Conservative politicians thus found it in their interest to preserve a large artisan and shopkeeper class as a bulwark against the working classes whose trade unions emerged as much more powerful organizations after the First World War. The interwar years saw the creation of the official and unofficial artisan organizations which were to represent one wing of the lower middle-class movement which sought to defend itself from the threats of 'big business' and 'big labour'. The desperation and exasperation of this group was to find its spokesman in Pierre Poujade, who, in a reformulation of Sieyès's famous slogan on behalf of the revolutionary Third Estate, modestly declared: 'What are the shopkeepers and artisans? Nothing. What should they be? Everything.'

Because artisan production is frequently combined with retailing functions, especially in the food trades, it was customary, before the creation of Craft Chambers in the interwar years, for artisans to belong to the local Chamber of Commerce. Many still belong to both but a feeling that their particular interests were not being adequately protected by the Chambers of Commerce led to a desire to secure separate representation. Despite the competition between artisans and shopkeepers, class interests and values unite them against other classes. In 1955, Pierre Poujade struck a responsive ideological and sociological chord when he proclaimed that together they represented the backbone of the 'free middle class'. In his eulogy he asserted that 'Occupationally, the highest expression of the blooming of the individual personality is without doubt craftsmanship and when one says craftsmanship one should subsume under this heading the small shopkeeper'.[31] However, Poujadism in its explosive 1950s phase was merely taking up a theme that had been developed in the 1930s and 1940s, in response to what was feared by the lower middle classes as a threat of proletarianization. Following the Popular Front victory of the Left in 1936, a number of middle-class movements—including a revival of Maurice Colrat's pioneer Middle Class Defence Association of 1907—eventually combined in 1936 into the General Committee of Middle Class Unions and the General Confederation of Middle Class Associations which attracted right-wing artisan organizations. Their aim was to give the group that linked capital with labour the same say in the nation's affairs as labour and capital enjoyed separately.[32] Again, after the left-wing resurgence in 1945–7, the National Committee of Middle Classes Liaison and Action (CNCM) attracted the support of the two leading artisan organizations.

The Vichy regime abolished the artisan unions but its corporatist structures strengthened the weak pre-war organizations. They nevertheless retained a strong sense of being treated as social pariahs by the civil service and big business. In a country where large firms often did not declare a fifth of their profits for tax purposes, artisans and shopkeepers did not declare over half of theirs because fiscal fraud might be the difference between survival and bankruptcy. In the post-war era of modernization, the previous celebrations of the small went out of fashion. 'As an economic fact, the old independent entrepreneur lives on a small island in a big new world; yet as an ideological figment and a political force he has persisted as if he inhabited an entire continent. He has become the man through whom the ideology of utopian capitalism' is perpetuated in 'the rhetoric of competition'. Yet, unless the much abused government protects him from the reality of competition and the tidal waves of technological innovation and market forces, he cannot survive to celebrate the virtues of the property-owning democracy. However, the process by which society, the economy, and the polity are being increasingly bureaucratized, with power and property being increasingly centralized, are converting what was a ladder to upwards mobility into a treadmill. Small businessmen remain useful to big business as 'shock troops in the battle against labour unions and government controls.'[33]

POLITICIZED INDUSTRIAL RELATIONS, TRADE UNIONS, AND STRIKES

The prolonged coexistence of a diversity of working classes was due in part to the fact that the shift to mass production after the 1880s that accelerated

---

[31] *Fraternité Française*, February 1955, 4 quoted in Stanley Hoffmann, *Le Mouvement Poujade*, 1956, 210. More generally, see Steven M. Zdatny, *The Politics of Survival: Artisans in Twentieth-Century France*, 1990, 170–7.

[32] A. Desquerat, *Classes Moyennes Françaises*, 1936, 205; cf. 197–211.

[33] C. Wright Mills, *White Collar: The American Middle Classes*, 1951, 1959 edn, 20, 34, 58.

during the First World War had limited and delayed effects on the earlier worker organizations. Unskilled workers were largely unorganized and the trade union movements were diffused in a large number of local bodies dominated by skilled workers. The endeavour jealously to preserve occupational autonomy and craft status meant that until the end of the nineteenth century France experienced 'incomplete proletarianization'.[34] Employer hostility to recognizing the existence, much less negotiating with trade unions, meant that the latter retained an outlaw mentality, while appealing in practice to the officials and ministers of the Third Republic to intervene as a way of compensating for their own weakness.

The 1884 Law legalizing trade unions (for which Waldeck-Rousseau has received more credit than he deserved) excluded civil servants, prohibited political involvement and required friendly society functions to be kept separate, while the right to strike was restricted by judicial interpretation of breach of contract. Suspicious unions only registered slowly. Resentment of former artisans, reduced to semi-skilled work, was associated with the decline of shoemaking, hatmaking, furniture, and glassmaking workshops, although artisans survived in the building and printing industries. Industrial federations were established by the printers in 1881 and in the railways and mines in 1883, followed by many others from the 1890s, but they were small and shaky organizations: 'full of dissolutions, false starts, schisms, and crippling rivalries'.[35] As it was very difficult to collect union dues, only one or two paid officials ran the national headquarters of these early trade unions.

Nevertheless, the increase in worker organizational capacity led to militant mobilization by anarcho-syndicalist inspired leaders of artisan mentality in the years from 1880 to 1910, resulting in a large increase in strike activity. This was a response to the fact that 'the only real law in French labour relations appears to be the law of the jungle', characterized by sporadic and arbitrary government intervention and 'no collective agreements to resolve day-to-day grievances' in individual firms.[36] Because private employers generally refused to bargain with weak trade unions, strikes and public demonstrations were less an attempt to coerce employers than to prompt government intervention (notably by seeking conciliation through the Prefect to pressure reluctant employers to concede an agreement), but his recommendations could be ignored. Threatened and actual violence (in 3 per cent of demonstrations between 1890 and 1914) was used in the hope that such intervention would correct the imbalance of power with the employers. Fearing loss of workplace control, the employer refusal to negotiate, and the sacking of strike leaders (regarded as leading mutinies) was motivated by determination to protect absolute employer authority symbolically from worker or state intrusion, not simply to increase profit. Although in the period 1906–10,

---

[34] Gérard Noiriel, *Workers in French Society in the Nineteenth and Twentieth Century*, 1986, 1990 Eng. edn, 5; cf. 9, 24–5, 33.

[35] Edward Shorter and Charles Tilly, *Strikes in France, 1830–1968*, 1974, 167. See also Zeldin, I, 206–9.

[36] Shorter and Tilly, 24, 27.

during the strike-breaker premierships of Clemenceau and of the former advocate of the general strike Aristide Briand, the government's prime concern to preserve public order took precedence over their general wish to restore industrial peace, the Commerce Minister and then Socialist Alexandre Millerand in the 1899–1902 Waldeck-Rousseau government sided with the unions against the employers. Prefects and ministers sometimes even threatened to withdraw troop protection to exert pressure on employers to compromise. The embittered behaviour of both sides in class conflict, precipitating, during and following strikes, was 'determined more by cultural reflexes and responses than by structural features in the economy and society'.[37]

The split in the Left between reformists and revolutionaries cut across the division between political socialists using indirect electoral-parliamentary methods of achieving power and trade unionists relying upon industrial direct action. Within the trade unions, the Marxists led by Jules Guesde overcame the reformists in the mid-1880s but used the unions mainly for political propaganda, so the militant workers turned to the trades council *Bourses du Travail*. These were initially labour exchanges, set up in the wake of the legalization of trade unions, the Radicals establishing the Paris *Bourse* in 1886, which was initially controlled by the Possibilist socialists (see Chapter 9). The anarchists and the Allemanist Socialist faction quickly took it over in 1891, to bypass the rival political factions by advocating the insurrectionary general strike. This was controversial in trade union circles because, quite apart from the Guesdists who wanted the political wing of the worker movement to be in command, influential leaders like Fernand Pelloutier and Aristide Briand favoured a peaceful general strike that achieved victory by simply paralyzing production and transport. The Guesdists were defeated and absorbed into the General Confederation of Labour (CGT) in 1895, while a National Federation of *Bourses du Travail* was established in 1902. The latter's membership—which increased from 34 to 83 *Bourses* between 1895 and 1902—was promoted by the provision of selective benefits. In 1902, the industrial federation-based CGT amalgamated with the territorially based *Bourses*, keeping the former's name but adopting the latter's programme in the 1906 Amiens Charter. However, one should bear in mind that in 1906 the CGT had only about 200,000 members or 'less than 3 per cent of the industrial working class'.[38] The recently amalgamated (1905) Socialists in the SFIO, French Section of the Workers (Second) International, meant that the dualistic character of the Left was underlined, even though the most reformist elements in both were in a minority, the Amiens Charter being the CGT's rejection of the SFIO's claim to be the senior partner.

The peak trade union organization was misleadingly impressive because it lacked both unity and financial resources in the years before the First World War.

---

[37] Ibid. 44–5; cf. 26–43, 378. On Millerand's role in the Waldeck-Rousseau government, see Pierre Sorlin, *Waldeck-Rousseau*, 1966, 462–78.

[38] Moss, *The Origins of the French Labor Movement*, 150; cf. 20–3, 136–54. See also Fernand Pelloutier's posthumous *Histoire des Bourses du travail: Origine, institutions, avenir*, 1902, with a Preface by Georges Sorel.

The CGT had only a tenth of the income of the Printers Union; the Roubaix textile union had five times the income of the Textile Federation and the Pas-de-Calais miners union was far stronger financially than the Coalminers Federation. 'Low though subscriptions were ... it was seldom that ... more than a small proportion was ever paid. The federations could not offer attractive benefits: only the printers had a fund for funeral and sickness benefits and only they and the mechanics offered unemployment pay. ... Many federations promised strike pay, few of them ever paid it. ... The worker continued to trust only the small local union where he was individually known.'[39] There were some 5,000 local unions, usually very small, having on average about 100 members. So, it was in the trades council *Bourses* that French workers felt greatest solidarity compared with the weak and remote industrial federations. 'Though subsidised by the (local) authorities, nearly all of them were run by revolutionaries, who frequently used these subsidies to attack the government. They managed to do this because many municipalities at this time were captured by socialists. ... '[40]

It was the journalist disciple of Proudhon, Fernand Pelloutier, who, from 1896 to 1901 (the year of his early death)—'one of the very few bourgeois leaders of an exclusively working class movement'—gave a vigorously anarcho-syndicalist impetus to the Federation of the *Bourses*.[41] The objectives he set were first to provide practical benefits to the workers: unemployment pay, accident and illness pay, and an employment exchange. Secondly, the workers were to be prepared for the role of managing their own affairs by popular education in association with the cooperatives through the 'People's Universities' at the turn of century. Thirdly, the *Bourses* were to be centres of propaganda. Fourthly, they would coordinate opposition to hostile legislation and support strike action. As we see in Chapter 9, his influence reinforced the worker scepticism about parliamentary reform of conditions of work, their rejection of class conciliation and their hostility to the state.[42] Pelloutier's successor, Yvetot, placed the emphasis instead on revolutionary and antimilitarist propaganda, with the result that many *Bourses* lost or renounced the public subsidies that were necessary to providing attractive selective benefits.

Strike surges were related to the political context, either because they looked to a favourable government in 1899–1900 to arbitrate in favour of the workers (while being enthused by general strike rhetoric) or were provoked by the 1906 Lens coalmine disaster killing 1,200 miners and because they resented the Clemenceau government's refusal of the schoolteachers right to join the CGT in 1906. Furthermore, CGT attempted to use 1 May 1906 to win an 8-hour workday and guaranteed weekly rest day but was beaten back by Minister of Interior Clemenceau, who needed right-wing parliamentary support. This was because Jaurès and the Socialists, under doctrinaire pressure from the Second International, refused to

---

[39] Zeldin, I, 240–1; cf. 239, 256–7.   [40] Ibid. 244–5; cf. 243–6.   [41] Ibid. 247.

[42] Ibid. 248–9; cf. 250–2. See also Jacques Julliard, *Fernand Pelloutier et les origines du syndicalisme d'action directe*, 1971 and J. E. S. Hayward, 'The Cooperative origins, rise and collapse of the "Universités Populaires"' in *Archives Internationales de Sociologie de la Coopération*, IX, January–June 1961, 3–17.

continue the support which, as we shall see, they had offered the 1902–5 Combes government.

The 1919–20 strikewave, also prompted by a 1919 CGT general strike demand for immediate application of the 8-hour working day law adopted by the Clemenceau government, was followed in 1920 by a disastrous railway strike, in which Briand—as he had in 1910—arrested union activists and threatened to mobilize the strikers into the army, in what was widely seen as a post-Bolshevik revolutionary context. In 1936, the electoral victory of the Popular Front led to the factory occupation and sit down strikes of June, involving many previously non-unionized, semi-skilled factory workers. The lesson the workers learnt from these strike surges was that even a weak trade union movement could, on favourable occasions, win significant gains: the 1900 Law on an 11-hour day in manufacturing; the 1906 Sunday rest Law and creation of a separate Ministry of Labour; the 1919 Eight hour Law; the 1936 Matignon Agreements on collective bargaining, shop stewards, and wage increases.[43]

The two decades from 1892 to 1911 marked a major attempt to develop the general strike as a mobilizing myth to bring about the abrupt replacement of capitalism by a generalized system of worker control of the economy. Formulated and popularized by Pelloutier and Briand, especially in 1892–5, it displaced in the trade union movement the reliance on the conquest of power favoured by the Socialist parties, either by reformist parliamentary means as championed by Jean Jaurès or by violent revolution, of which Jules Guesde was the leading protagonist. While the larger unions—the coalminers, railway workers, printers and textile workers—were inclined to a realistic gradualism, they were outvoted at CGT trades union congresses by the smaller unions who claimed that an assertion of revolutionary will would produce victory at a stroke. As a result, 'the revolutionary agitation remained largely the monopoly of trades quite incapable of implementing their threats.'[44] It was never made clear by who and when a general strike would be called, reflecting reliance upon a spontaneous upsurge of the workers engaged in class struggle. The anarcho-syndicalist bluff was called in 1908 when the CGT stumbled into, rather than calling for, a one-day general strike which was a complete fiasco.

The myth of the general strike had been a central feature of Georges Sorel's *Reflections on Violence* that was published first as articles in 1906 and then in book form in 1907. He dogmatically asserted that 'By employing the term "myth" I ... put myself in a position of refusing all discussion with people who wish to subject the general strike to detailed criticism and who accumulate objections against its practical possibility.... A myth cannot be refuted since it is, at bottom, identical to the convictions of a group' and so, he claimed, unrelated to its outcome. 'No failure proves anything against socialism, as it has become a work of preparation; if it fails, it merely proves that the apprenticeship has been insufficient; they must set to work with more courage, persistence and confidence

---

[43] Shorter and Tilly, Chapter 5 passim. See also Zeldin, I, 274–82.
[44] Zeldin, I, 221; cf. 218–45.

than before....'[45] So defined a myth becomes illusory proof against the repeated rebuffs of experience, to which the Extreme Left was subsequently to show it was addicted, rhetorically consoling itself for a de facto defeatism. Léon Jouhaux, who took over the leadership of the CGT in 1909, which he was to hold for nearly forty years, moved the union to an increasingly reformist position from the First World War and the failure of another general strike in 1920, leaving it to the communists (who broke away to form the CGTU in 1921) to subordinate trade unionism to the dictates of their party.

WOMEN'S RIGHTS

At the beginning of the nineteenth century, the inferior status of women had been systematized in the Napoleonic Civil Code, notably by compelling them to adopt their husbands' surnames. The decline of domestic service and the entry of women into factory work—especially textiles—combined with the decreasing hold over them of the Catholic Church and the impact of secular education, paved the way for feminism. The utopian socialist Charles Fourier had coined the term in the early nineteenth century but it was the Saint-Simonians who popularized the idea in the 1830s. The republicans wanted to constitutional-ize marriage, so that 'the home would become a nursery of citizens, a school for democracy.'[46] George Sand championed the right to divorce, not the right to vote, but divorce was only legalized again in 1884. Her mentor, the former Saint-Simonian Pierre Leroux, in 1851 introduced the first Bill to give women the vote... in local elections, without success. There was a decline in religious fervour among women as a result of the anticlerical offensive, promoting creation in 1901 of the League of French Women (200,000 members in 1914), and the Patriotic League of French Women in 1902 (600,000 members in 1914), as men contended with priests for control of their womenfolk over matters such as birth control.

During the Third Republic, the Radicals were reluctant to give women the vote because of their fear of clerical influence over them, while the Right feared that it would threaten male supremacy. In 1919, the Chamber of Deputies voted in favour of female suffrage by 344 to 97, an acknowledgement of women taking over many male jobs during the First World War, but the Senate rejected it then and subsequently... until de Gaulle instituted it in 1944 after the Second World

---

[45] Georges Sorel, *Reflections on Violence*, 1907, 1999 edn, 21, 29, 31; cf. Chapter 4. See also Jacques Julliard, *Clemenceau briseur de grèves*, 1965 and on Clemenceau's combination of repression and conciliation of the CGT, see David R. Watson, *Georges Clemenceau: A Political Biography*, 1974, 172–6, 200–2, 381–3.

[46] Philip Nord, *The Republican Moment: Struggles for Democracy in Nineteenth Century France*, 1995, 243; cf. 251.

War.[47] Only then was the treatment of women as minors rejected, although the feminization of election to political office was very slow in coming thereafter. After President Giscard's appointment of a junior minister for women's rights in 1974, it was President Mitterrand who in 1981 appointed the first full such minister, only for it to be abolished by Prime Minister Chirac in 1986, indicating continuing opposition to correcting the institutionalized inequality of women. However, women became leaders of minor parties like the Greens (Dominique Voynet) and the Trotskyist Lutte Ouvrière (Arlette Laguiller) and in 2006 Ségolène Royal emerged as the popular Socialist contender for the 2007 presidential election.

Family allowances played a very important role in the twentieth-century development of the French Welfare State, equalizing incomes between families rather than between individuals. It reflected a Catholic and natalist emphasis that was pursued actively by the Third Republic, reinforced under Vichy and continued in the Fourth and Fifth Republics. The family has remained a more proximate institution in France than Britain, despite the fact that in the last quarter of the twentieth century the number of marriages (increasingly postponed) nearly halved while the number of divorces nearly doubled and the number of single parent families (mainly unmarried mothers) has rapidly increased.[48] There has, however, been a seamy side to the extramarital relations between the sexes in France.

Proudhon had in *La Pornocratie* scandalized the feminists by proclaiming that the role of a woman was to be either housekeeper or harlot. Prostitution was controlled to avoid public offence (importunate soliciting being compared with begging) and for health reasons. 'Prostitutes were placed outside the law but were required to register with the police and to work in closed and discreet brothels to control the spread of syphilis and to make public thoroughfares more "respectable". No controls were placed on their clients.'[49] The number of official brothels in Paris increased until the mid-nineteenth century and then declined because of increased competition from full-time or part-time street prostitutes. The latter were blamed for the fact that by the end of the nineteenth century some 15 per cent of deaths were caused by syphilis, which partly explains the encouragement given by priests, teachers, and parents to young men to have early recourse to brothels. The prevailing sense of national decadence in *fin-de-siècle* France reflected this degenerate state of public morality.

Asserting women's rights has involved a confusing combination of a demand for republican equality with men—although the term parity is more frequently used—together with the asserting of specificity, notably in the matter of birth control. The role played by Simone Veil as Minister of Health in courageously

---

[47] Zeldin, I, 345–60. See also Gibson, *A Social History of French Catholicism*, 183–7. For a general survey see Siân Reynolds, 'Women: distant vistas, changed lives' in Chapter 6 of James McMillan (ed.), *Modern France*, 2003.

[48] On French family allowance policy see Susan Pedersen, *Family, Dependence and the Origins of the Welfare State: Britain and France, 1914–1945*, 1993, Chapter 5. On the French family see the excellent Chapter 6 and pp. 252–4 of Henri Mendras, *La France que je vois*, 2002, 2005 edn.

[49] McPhee, 78–9.

pushing through the 1975 legalization of abortion, that was strongly opposed by the Roman Catholic Church, both ensured vilification in the mid-1970s but an enduring popularity for her courageous stand thereafter. Although the progress of political parity has been championed particularly by the Socialist Party and the Left generally (by contrast with its earlier resistance motivated by the influence of clerical political guidance on women voters) and enshrined in the 2000 Law in parliamentary, regional and local elections, following a 1999 amendment to the Constitution's preamble, the usual disjuncture between the resounding affirmation of principle and the reluctant and patchy practice continues to prevail. Nevertheless, the process of change continues, although the theorizing and activities of the feminist movements as such have had only a marginal significance in the steps towards rectifying inequality through positive discrimination.[50]

THE ADVENT OF NEW PROVINCIAL, PROFESSIONAL ELITES

While the peasantry and artisans were struggling to survive the effects of economic modernization and encroaching urbanization, while the working classes were failing to organize themselves effectively either to bargain collectively, coerce their employers or to secure satisfaction of their demands by the politicians they elected, what was happening to the new men to whom Gambetta had looked to take charge of the Third Republic? This was the golden age of the liberal professions, associated with a substantial increase in the number of lawyers, doctors, and journalists. Lawyers regarded their self-governing profession as a 'school for liberal statesmanship', cultivating 'independence of mind, eloquence in defence of principle, devotion to self-government', so that 'It was a cliché of the day that the *Palais de Justice* was but a step from the *Palais Bourbon*.'[51] Opportunities for lawyers increased with the massive purge of the judiciary in 1879–83. Meritocratic practices displacing aristocratic values, 'the political system put these professions in a strategic position. By restoring the strength of provincial life, the Republic placed these decentralized professions in the position of intermediaries, indispensable to every type of representational process, political, associative and cultural.' Election to parliament 'became a means of social ascent for the provincial bourgeoisie', with lawyers alone constituting 32 per cent of deputies and 47 per cent of ministers between 1871 and 1914.[52] They exercised their influence as individuals in an era when political parties and pressure groups, when they existed, were not able to fulfil a mediating role effectively. To finance electoral campaigns and other political expenses, it was often necessary for men of independent means to rely on their personal wealth.[53]

[50] David Howarth and Georgios Varouxakis, *Contemporary France: An Introduction to French Politics and Society*, 2003, 95–8.
[51] Nord, 116, 119.
[52] Charle, *A Social History of France in the Nineteenth Century*, 169; cf. 170–7, 202; cf. 204.
[53] Ibid. 204.

The impact of meritocracy in the senior civil service upon the previous practice of co-optation can be measured following the republican purge at the end of the 1870s. 'For example, 40.9 per cent in the Second Empire were sons of high officials while the proportion was only 6.6 per cent in 1901: the percentage of Councillors of State on the same dates fell from 37.8 per cent to 9.3 per cent.'[54] *Pantouflage* (the slipping out of public sector posts into the private sector) increased at the turn of the century, with self-made businessmen being increasingly supplemented by engineers trained in the *Ecole Polytechnique* and *Ecole Centrale*, as well as more specialized engineering schools. 'In 1905, there were two *Polytechnique* graduates over forty in the private sector for every one in the State service.'[55] The French fascination with technocratic specialists persisted despite a sceptical engineer-businessman's assertion: 'There are three ways to ruin, gambling, women and engineers; the first two are more pleasant but the last is more certain.' Nevertheless, the engineers have had some spectacular successes to their credit, such as TGV trains, Ariane satellites, and the modernization of telecommunications. Credential-giving elite schools have, through their apparently competitive selection procedures, created a 'state nobility' that reproduced the old co-optation by linking into interdependent sources of power and prestige, birth and merit, public service, and private profit.[56]

From the eighteenth century, France has been convinced that the state should train its own specialist officials outside the universities, regarded as insufficiently practical and mainly politically Left inclined in the twentieth century. Governments have preferred to rely upon specialist post-entry training, stressing experience applied to the tasks of public service, provided under their own control. In 1945, this tradition was extended from the engineering *grandes écoles* of *Polytechnique, Mines* and *Ponts et Chaussées* to the competitive recruitment and training of administrators in the *Ecole Nationale d'Administration* (ENA). With an annual output of about a hundred officials (by the end of the twentieth century amounting to a total of some 5,000) they fill the top civil service generalist positions, ranging from the Finance Inspectorate and Council of State to the civil administrators in the ministries.

As the bulk of these recruited externally come from the Paris *Institut d' Etudes Politiques* (*Sciences Po*), democratizing recruitment has made little progress, perhaps because the privileged castes who are the system's beneficiaries are content to co-opt to a self-perpetuating meritocracy. This co-option is facilitated by the large part played in both *Sciences Po* and ENA training by senior civil servants in what has been called 'state socialization'.[57] The close ties developed in the years spent in these elite institutions do not merely advance the careers of senior officials inside and outside the public services; they mitigate the rigid compartmentalism

---

[54] Ibid. 207.   [55] Ibid. 209; cf. 197–9.

[56] Pierre Bourdieu, *The State Nobility: Elite Schools in the Field of Power*, 1989, Eng. edn, 1996, 9–11, 335, 375. See also Christophe Charle, *Les Elites de la République (1880–1900)*, 1987, Chapters 1 and 3. The sceptic was Auguste Detouef in *Propos de O.L. Barenton, confiseur*, 1926.

[57] Jean-Michel Eymeri, *La fabrique des énarques*, 2001, especially Chapter 2. See also Ezra Suleiman, *Elitès in French Society: The Politics of Survival*, 1978, especially Part 2.

of French administration at the top of the hierarchy but not in the crucial middle ranks of the ministries.

Legitimizing privilege through education was supplemented by the matrimonial stakes. Marrying into rich business families was attractive to senior civil servants, with property dispositions in the marriage contracts giving financial considerations concerning the size of the dowry priority over personal attraction. With land having lost a quarter of its value between 1880 and 1900, the rich were not generally landlords as had been the case during the July Monarchy but financial speculators from the Second Empire. 'In 1848 only about 5 per cent of money left at death was in shares, while 58 per cent was in land or houses.'[58] By 1900, 31 per cent was in shares and only 45 per cent was in land or houses. However, the new businessmen had to reckon with the entrenched wealth of the mythologized '200 Families', the largest shareholders in the Bank of France entitled to attend its annual meeting, who elected the 15 Regents, often from the same families for generations.

The republican takeover of the parliamentary majority led to the development of a stereotype of the deputy as characterized by 'the grossness of the provincial, the incompetence of the *déclassé* and the corruption of the venal.'[59] While Balzac and Stendhal had provided unflattering portraits of politicians during the July Monarchy, Flaubert had indulged his anti-democratic sentiments in portraying their Second Republic successors and Zola those of the Second Empire, the Third Republic provoked an outpouring of anti-parliamentary hostility to the lower-middle-class southerners who had come up to Paris to acquire fame and fortune. 'Liars, dirty, talkative and superficial, such are the southerners who invade Paris.'[60]

The caricature career of the perspiring, aspiring republican meritocrat was someone from a poor family, who with a scholarship acquires the education to teach philosophy in a provincial and then Parisian *lycée*, becomes a deputy, minister and then President of the Chamber of Deputies. This was the prototype portrayed by Barrès, notably in *Leurs figures* which followed the 1892 Panama scandal (see below) while Jules Lemaître's play *Le député Leveau* preceded it. It did not help to correct the impression of widespread corruption when a prominent politician implicated in the Panama scandal, Maurice Rouvier (who had been Finance Minister four times between 1888 and 1892 and was to be Prime Minister twice subsequently), could plead, 'What I have done, all politicians worthy of the name have done before me.'[61] For Barrès, the regime survived thanks to a political class of mediocrities who combined all the vices and closed their eyes to those of others. They were unfit to govern, concentrating upon pleasing their constituents by satisfying their petty requests.[62] The behaviour of the *arriviste* class of professional politicians lent sufficient credence to the diatribes to which they were treated for the resulting discredit to sap the legitimacy of the Third Republic that

[58] Zeldin, I, 59; cf. 53–61.

[59] Jean Estèbe, 'Le Parlementaire' in Sirinelli (ed.), *Histoire des droites en France*, III, 329.

[60] Ibid. 330; cf. 324–8.   [61] Quoted in Zeldin, I, 583; cf. 570–82, 590.

[62] Estèbe, 'Le Parlementaire', 328, 331–6.

had begun under such promising auspices. It exposed the hollowness of much of the idealistic rhetoric of its protagonists.

By 1914, when *La République des Camarades* was published, disenchantment with parliamentary democracy was prevalent. Rather than the vociferous diatribes of the extremes of Right and Left, it was the perceptive mockery of Robert de Jouvenel that revealed how far cynicism had been prompted by parliamentary malpractices. On ideology, he produced the telling precept: 'There is less difference between two deputies, of whom one is a revolutionary and the other is not, than between two revolutionaries, of whom one is a deputy and the other is not.'[63] Party programmes were not meant to be implemented because this would dispose of proposals that one had championed for many years. This helped to explain why it had taken so long to legislate in favour of the income tax. The Radicals, once they had implemented their anticlerical programme, had lost their *raison d'être*. So, 'Stagnation is perhaps the only practical way of remaining loyal to one's principles.'[64]

Lacking disciplined political parties, when politicians were not simply pandering to their clientele to secure re-election, they were seeking ephemeral ministerial office for its own sake. The same cards were reshuffled as inert governments came and went, although the 1899–1909 years were exceptionally characterized by the active three year governments of Waldeck-Rousseau, Combes, and Clemenceau. This meant that the more things superficially changed the more they remained the same. The interwar years were to reinforce the discredit that the 1940 abdication in favour of Marshal Pétain was to consummate. Partial rehabilitation only came after the further parliamentary abdication to Charles de Gaulle in 1958.

ANTICLERICALISM: THE SEPARATION OF CHURCH AND STATE

It was a feature of late nineteenth-century French politics to designate an enemy, whether it was Gambetta in 1877 quoting Alphonse Peyrat's slogan 'Clericalism? There is the enemy!' to prolonged applause or Adolphe Willette, an anti-Semitic candidate in the 1889 elections, proclaiming: 'Judaism, there is the enemy!' Revenge on the Catholic Church for supporting the anti-republican Right led in 1880 to the expulsion of the Jesuits despite protests by the Pope and the French bishops, as well as the resignations of many magistrates and army officers, although the other religious orders were treated somewhat more leniently. Exemption of clergy from compulsory military service was another controversial issue in the 1880s but the main anticlerical onslaught came under the Combes government of 1902–5 over the issue of the separation of Church and State in the wake of the Dreyfus Affair.

Ironically, whereas the Church's anachronistic political alliance with monarchy and empire in the nineteenth century had led it to lose touch with many religious

[63] Robert de Jouvenel, *La République des Camarades*, 1914, 17.   [64] Ibid. 58; cf. 57–9.

Frenchmen (if not Frenchwomen) especially of the working classes, independence from state institutional and financial support compelled the clergy to develop closer links with the laity. In the process, the Roman Catholic Church acquired greater self-reliance and public esteem, while preserving its hierarchical structure. It successfully resisted the potentially disintegrating pressures of legislation aimed to compel it to become more pluralistic, developing instead its own social movements, notably Catholic Action and its various off-shoots for youth, students, and women, as well as a Catholic trade union movement, the CFTC. In modernizing itself, the Church corrected its out of date image. 'The myth that France was pious and Catholic before the Revolution was invented by modern conservatives idealising the middle ages.'[65] Yet it was precisely because of the actual diversity of beliefs, territorially and over time, in matter of mass piety, church attendance and superstition, that ecclesiastical authority had to be asserted and reaffirmed. However, after the vain Vichy attempt to turn the clock back, there was no return to ardent Third Republic anticlericalism. Although religious conformity was restricted from the mid-twentieth century to a shrinking minority of practising believers, the reinvigorated remnant represented a more accurate reflection of genuine religious belief than the nominal, superficial mass adhesion of earlier times.

The Church's emphasis upon the faithful taking communion at Easter was because it was the hallmark of submission to clerical authority. While for many men religious conformity was confined to baptism, marriage, and burial (with only a conspicuous few choosing, like Lamennais, Michelet, Proudhon, Gambetta, and Hugo, to have a civil burial) the 'residual Catholicism' of the first communion was a nearly universal rite of passage into adulthood. However, the motivation was often not religious because 'you could not normally get a job without it . . .'[66] Preparation for the first communion required extended attendance at catechism classes and until the Ferry secularist educational legislation of the early 1880s a basic duty of the primary schoolteacher was to provide a minimum religious instruction by rote learning. Because all French regimes sought to reinforce their shaky political legitimacy through the educational system, 'for most of the (nineteenth) century literacy came to French children in a religious form; it was the change in the kind of indoctrination given in schools, not the expansion of literacy itself, that weakened the Catholicism of the generation that grew up between Jules Ferry and the First World War.'[67]

The Third Republic was anxious to use secularist education to provide itself with popular support from loyal citizens not disloyal believers. The ground having been prepared by Jean Macé's Education League, the Ferry Laws established free primary state education (1881) and made it compulsory for those aged between 6 and 13. Clergy were replaced as teachers by 'the black Hussars of the Republic', first for boys, later for girls. Although Ferry called on them to be neutral in their teaching, the textbooks they used were not impartial. This was especially

---

[65] Zeldin, II, 984; cf. 983–6, 1024–6.
[66] Gibson, *A Social History of French Catholicism*, 166; cf. 159, 163–7, 213–4, 222–3.
[67] Ibid. 234; cf. 130.

important in the course on 'Moral and Civic instruction', a secularist, rationalist counterpart catechism, while the teaching of history stressed that the Republic was the culmination of the French Revolution. Crucifixes were removed from schools and hospitals. Taken in conjunction with the 1880 ending of a day of rest as compulsory and the re-establishment of the right to divorce, the official anticlerical campaign was in full swing. Even architecture was called upon to play its part, with pseudo-Renaissance Town Halls vying for visual prominence with Gothic Churches and the Eiffel Tower elevated into a secular riposte to the Sacré Coeur.[68]

Whereas corporate religious congregations (of which there were 3,216, grouping nearly 200,000 men and women) had alone been unregulated and untaxed for a century after the Revolution's draconian restriction of freedom of association, the 1901 Law on Association denied them this right. Regarded as closed corporate states within the state, owing allegiance to a foreign Pope and embodying the illiberal repression of individuality and sexuality, they were anathema to the free-thinkers. Ferry had blocked an attempt in 1883 by his Interior Minister Waldeck-Rousseau to legislate on freedom of association, fearing it would hamper his aim of excluding the clergy from a secularized educational system. As such, it reflected the illiberal face of anticlericalism that biased Ferry's partisan programme of reform. From 1879 the Council of State was very restrictive in granting requests by religious congregations to establish schools and Ferry's attempt to exclude them from education provoked the bishops into launching a national petition that secured 1.3 million signatures, while almost half the departmental councils expressed their hostility. Ferry, who declared 'My goal is a society without a God and without a King', responded to the clerical counter-attack by decreeing in 1880 that those congregations that had not received official recognition would cease to be tolerated.[69] Nevertheless, between 1878 and 1901 the number of pupils taught in private Catholic schools doubled and a third of primary pupils in Paris were in such schools; the Catholic share of all secondary education for boys increasing from 32 to 42 per cent between 1887 and 1898. Passive resistance in the meantime did not prevail against this latter-day manifestation of St Just's denial of freedom to the enemies of freedom, which was regarded by most of the public with indifference, but some army officers resigned rather than disperse rioters.

The schools question apart, both the clerical and anticlerical camps had strong incentives to avoid continued conflict, so the ecclesiastical leaders in Rome and especially in France, as well as the anticlerical political leaders, predominantly supported the preservation of the status quo. The reason was their common opposition to pluralism and their desire to retain the traditional alliance of the spiritual and temporal powers. From the standpoint of the politician in office, the power to control ecclesiastical appointments and to curb the propensity of

[68] Claude Langlois, 'Catholiques et Laiques', in *Les lieux de mémoire*, III/I, 154–9. See also J. E. S. Hayward, 'Educational Pressure Groups and the indoctrination of the Radical Ideology of Solidarism' in *International Review of Social History*, VIII/I, 1963, 1–14.

[69] Quoted in Harvey Goldberg, *The Life of Jean Jaurès*, 1962, 39. Jean-Pierre Machelon, *La République Contre les Libertés?*, 362; cf. 352–78, 382–5, 394–5. See also Gibson, 128–33.

clerics to engage in political interference of a hostile nature, was very attractive. The cost incurred: protecting an established church aligned with one's political enemies and providing the salaries of some of its clergy seemed cheap. From the viewpoint of the Church, the advantages of the bargain were clear to the hierarchy, the Vatican and the bishops, who saw the link with the French state as a bulwark of their authority. However, the more extremist rank and file on both sides sought to destroy this collusion between the political and religious establishments, because they wanted either to eradicate ecclesiastical influence over the minds of the people or use the Church's influence to restore the monarchy or revive a hitherto straitjacketed religious fervour.

By 1891 Pope Leo XIII, conscious that 'The Republic had become identified in the minds of its friends and enemies with hostility to the Church' wanted to separate the 'Church of France from the corpse of monarchy'.[70] Seeking French support against the Italian government which had severely curtailed the Papacy's temporal power, he issued an encyclical breaking the traditional link between throne and altar in favour of accepting the de facto government. Although what came to be known as the Rallying to the Republic was not received with enthusiasm in Catholic circles, it was formally obeyed. However, it left scope as we shall see for Maurras and the *Action Française* to resuscitate the link between royalism and the more intransigent Catholics. The Radicals were suspicious, prompting Léon Bourgeois's famous question when forming his 1895 Cabinet: 'You accept the Republic, Gentlemen, that is understood, but do you accept the Revolution?'[71] While some anticlericals, convinced that the Catholic Church was a declining force, believed that without state support it would wither away, the predominant view was that preserving state control over a still powerful Church meant that the Napoleonic Concordat should be retained and its supervisory power over clerical appointments applied rigorously.

The government's nominations of bishops under the Concordat were informally discussed in advance with the papal nuncio (ambassador in Paris). 'In practice, the French *Direction des Cultes* maintained a list of suitable candidates which it based on the various recommendations it received from civil servants, members of parliament, and certain of the more Republican bishops.'[72] However, the resulting appointments were very mixed. In 1896 (when Emile Combes was serving as Minister of Cults in the Bourgeois government), of 86 bishops and archbishops, only nineteen were regarded by the government as satisfactory, thirty-eight were hostile and twenty-nine were considered unreliable. Government also had the right to approve but not nominate the 42,000 state-paid priests, which allowed it to suspend salaries if a cleric was considered guilty of improper conduct, particularly interference in elections. 'Between 1881–92, 1,217 salaries were suspended for periods of varying length', while between 1891 and 1902,

---

[70] Denis Brogan, *The Development of Modern France*, 1940, 1967 edn, 257.

[71] Quoted in Albert Thibaudet, *Les idées politiques de la France*, 1932, 129.

[72] Maurice Larkin, *Church and State after the Dreyfus Affair: The Separation Issue in France*, 1974, 48.

sixteen bishops were deprived of their salaries for a year on average.[73] An uneasy truce prevailed until a confrontation between a less accommodating Pope Pius X and a more intransigent Prime Minister in the person of Combes brought about a separation that neither deliberately sought.

Destined for the priesthood but denied final religious orders, Combes developed his single-minded republican and anticlerical beliefs in opposition to the Second Empire. He became a country doctor, rising from the ranks as a local provincial notable successively as mayor, chairman of the departmental council and senator in the early years of the Third Republic. In contrast to Waldeck-Rousseau, who 'did not estimate the soundness of his policy by the extent and bitterness of the opposition it provoked among the "enemies of the Republic"..., Combes took a simple view of his duties; he was a delegate of the (parliamentary *Délégation des Gauches*) majority for a special purpose, the extirpation of the clerical menace'.[74] So his inquisitorial enforcement of Waldeck-Rousseau's 1901 Law against the religious orders provoked Catholic outrage. However, he was content to intimidate the Vatican by the threat of separation while using state control to suffocate the French Church. He suspended the salaries of four times as many clergy as had Waldeck-Rousseau, including those of an archbishop and eleven bishops.

The Church-State break was precipitated in 1904 by a vehement protest by Pope Pius X against the visit of President Loubet to the King of Italy, who was deemed to have usurped the Church's capital, Rome. Enraged at such interference in French foreign policy (the visit was intended to detach Italy from a German-led Triple Alliance), Combes responded by withdrawing the French Ambassador to the Vatican and placing separation on the political agenda. Diplomatic difficulties were compounded by the Pope's refusal to accept Combes's nominations to bishoprics and the determination to force the resignation of two bishops who had sought the Prime Minister's protection. Pius X had concluded that his predecessor's policy of rallying to the Republic was a failure and that separation would allow him sole control of the appointment of bishops and reinvigorate a Church that had been too dependent upon the state. So, when separation was legislated, he provocatively asserted in his 1906 encyclical *Vehementer nos* that the Roman Catholic Church was 'an unequal society...composed of two categories of people: the pastors and the flock.... The mass has no other duty than to let itself be led and, like a docile flock, to follow its pastors.'[75] The Separation Law's attempt to bypass the Church hierarchy and give control of its property to religious associations of believers was rejected as an attempt to impart an alien Protestant-style pluralism into Catholic Church affairs and surreptitiously promote schism.[76]

Although Aristide Briand is given most of the credit for steering the Separation legislation through parliament, thanks to his charm and skill at negotiating

---

[73] Ibid. 54; cf. 50–8.

[74] Brogan, 363; cf. 361–4 and Malcolm O. Partin, *Waldeck-Rousseau, Combes and the Church: The Politics of Anti-Clericalism, 1899–1905*, 1969, 158, 163–9. For a general survey see Maurice Larkin, 'Religion, anti-clericalism and secularization' in McMillan (ed.), *Modern France*, Chapter 8.

[75] Gibson, 57; cf. Pontin, Chapters 10 and 11 passim.   [76] Larkin, 170–7.

compromises, the substance of the law was inspired by the Protestant President of the League of Human Rights, Francis de Pressensé, who became a Socialist in the course of playing an embattled part in the campaign to rehabilitate Dreyfus. An essential role was also played by Jean Jaurès, who steered the Socialist and Radical parliamentary support towards less vindictive legislation than they would have wished, calling it 'the greatest reform to be attempted in our country since the Revolution.'[77] The three deserve the credit for avoiding the First Republic's mistake of secularizing the churches and expelling thousands of priests. Nevertheless, 'Church services were treated as public meetings, but that meant asking for authorization, which the Pope forbade the clergy to do, and the simple remedy was found of abolishing the last restrictions on the right of public meeting for everybody', a welcome liberal victory from an unexpected direction.[78] As Minister of Cults in the Clemenceau government faced with the refusal of the clergy under papal interdict from accepting associational control of churches, Briand left them to the parish priests to avoid further controversy, while Clemenceau suspended the inventories of church property that had provoked anti-desecration riots, a rather more emollient response to violence than he adopted when it was perpetrated by workers.

Presbyteries and Episcopal palaces were taken over but although the former were often leased back to the priest, who might even be treated as a rent-free caretaker, the palaces generally became public museums or libraries. The problem of public support for the upkeep of churches was initially confined to those classed as cultural or historic monuments but Maurice Barrès persuaded Briand to give the same aid to all churches built before 1800. However, the 42,000 parish priests were dependent upon diocesan collections and their ensuing poverty led to a halving of ordinations between 1901 and 1913. The return of Alsace-Lorraine in 1918, which had remained under the Concordat when absorbed into Germany, retained this status. The general practice developed of the appointment of all bishops only being made by the Pope after consulting the French government, a neat reversal of the Concordat arrangement. In 1924, once again thanks to Briand's negotiating skills, the Papal ban on what were now called diocesan associations was lifted, because they were controlled by diocesan clergy and chaired by the bishop.[79]

The Combes government was brought down in 1905 by the discreditable *Affaire des fiches*, in which it was revealed that his War Minister General André had authorized the systematic collection of information about army officers, suspected of subversive sympathies, nurtured by their predominantly Catholic education and royalist inclinations. (We earlier encountered General Boulanger's attempt to deal with this problem in the 1880s as War Minister. We return to this attempt to republicanize the officer corps in Chapter 10.) The symbiosis between the officer corps and the Catholic Church, conveyed by a phrase popularized by Clemenceau—the alliance between 'the sword and the holy water sprinkler'—was

---

[77] Quoted ibid. 142; cf. 108–16, 142, 145, 207–10 and Goldberg, 293–301.   [78] Brogan, 377.
[79] Larkin 152–7, 193–5, 207–12, 217–22.

sustained by the fact that the armed forces and the diplomatic corps in particular were the careers for which the Jesuit *Ecole Ste Geneviève* and the Marianist *Collège Stanislas* successfully destined many of their pupils. Although the failure of the army to respond to an 1899 attempt by Déroulède to use the funeral of the President of the Republic to persuade it to seize power might suggest its loyalty to the regime, in fact the problem of anti-regime divisions between an authoritarian republican like Déroulède and royalist army officers might be nearer the truth. However, the resulting fear of a *coup d'état* prompted the surveillance of the views of the military in the context of the Dreyfus Affair to which we turn shortly.

The use of the *Grand Orient* Masonic network to provide secret information about the views and behaviour of army officers exacerbated matters, the Freemasons playing the role in Catholic demonology that the Jesuits did among the secularists. Opposition to the Second Empire had begun a process of Masonic radicalization that by the start of the twentieth century led to a substantial ideological overlap of the lodges with Radical and Socialist Party members, so recourse to the Masonic network to assess political reliability was a tempting supplement to the reliance on prefectoral reports. These had been used to provide information on the political and religious views of candidates for sensitive appointments and promotions in the civil service (especially the Ministry of the Interior) and judiciary (especially the Council of State). Combes gave a classic formulation in his June 1902 circular to the Prefects: 'while you owe justice to everyone... keep your favours for those who have unmistakably proved their fidelity to republican institutions'.[80] An obsessive pursuit of guarantees of political loyalty was the mark of a political system unsure of the reliability of its own public servants, whose leaders were convinced that the very existence of the Republic was in danger.

Anti-Masonic conspiracy theory, which went back to the French Revolution for which the Freemasons were happy to accept undeserved credit, was encouraged by a flood of Catholic-inspired propaganda. Between 1880 and 1885, twenty-four anti-Masonic books and twenty-three anti-Masonic pamphlets were published, fourteen by priests, and five by bishops.[81] In an 1884 encyclical, the Pope had denounced Freemasonry for political promoting anti-Christianity. This onslaught was given impetus in the 1890s and early 1900s by the large number of ministers who were Freemasons. All of Combes's ministers were Masons, as were a significant minority of deputies and senators in 1902. Forty per cent of ministers between 1891 and 1914 were Freemasons, with a peak in the 1902–6 legislature when it reached 60 per cent. Fourteen Prime Ministers were Masons between 1871 and 1914, holding office for half those years, but the most frequently held posts were Labour, Trade, and Agriculture—not Education and Interior as is often

---

[80] Ibid. 139; cf. 94–7 and Maurice Larkin, *Religion, Politics and Political Preferment in France since 1890: La Belle époque and Its Legacy*, 1995, Parts I and II passim. On Freemasonry, see Mildred J. Headings, *French Freemasonry under the Third Republic*, 1948 and Philip Nord, *The Republican Moment*, Chapter 1. For the Second Empire, see Sudhir Hazareesingh and Vincent Wright, *Francs-Maçons sous le Second Empire: Les Loges provinciales du Grand Orient à la veille de la Troisième République*, 2001, Introduction.

[81] Robert F. Byrnes, *Antisemitism in Modern France*, 1950, 126–7.

presumed. With conspicuous but inactive exceptions like Gambetta, Ferry and Léon Bourgeois, most leading masons were secondary political figures. Leading Third Republic personalities like Waldeck-Rousseau, Clemenceau, Briand, and Poincaré were not Freemasons.

However, if 'One becomes a Freemason, one is born a Huguenot.'[82] Suspicion of Protestants dated back to the Reformation but the Third Republic allowed them more often to occupy prominent positions, not merely in banking as previously, but in politics and government. The first fully Republican government was headed by a rather colourless Protestant, Waddington (of Anglo-Dutch extraction), with five out of nine ministers sharing his religious culture. Orthodox Protestants had tended to be Orleanist Conservatives, like Guizot, but the Liberal Protestants were more inclined to become republican like the Pelletans, father and son. Even those who were unbelievers, like the first nominally 'Protestant' head of state since Henry IV expediently converted to Catholicism, Gaston Doumergue, in 1924, remained loyal to their Protestant political culture. Their greater cosmopolitanism, in particular, led them to occupy the Finance and Foreign Ministries, four becoming Prime Minister, heading ten governments for a total of seven years between 1879 and 1914. They played an important back-room role in formulating the Third Republic's education programme and in the universities. Active in the Masonic movement, they took a prominent part in the pro-Dreyfus campaign and in the League of the Rights of Man.[83] However, whatever the affinities between anti-protestantism and anti-Semitism, the latter dwarfed the former in its range and venom.

ANTI-SEMITISM AND THE DREYFUS AFFAIR

After the end of the seventeenth century religious wars, there was little mass anti-Semitism in Europe until the 1880s. Although the 50,000 French Jews (nine-tenths living in Alsace-Lorraine) were emancipated as equal citizens by the Revolution on the understanding that they became fully assimilated, Jews had played no significant part in it, so the anti-revolutionary Right at first did not blame them but the Freemasons. Napoleon imposed a consistory system on Protestants and Jews to represent and police them but the Restoration revived pre-revolutionary anti-Jewish legislation. Jews lost many of their civil rights and with the reimposition of Catholic religious tests, Jews were expelled from the universities, liberal professions were barred to them, so the more enterprising retreated to the Stock Market and finance which was to cause them more grief when they succeeded too well.

---

[82] Estèbe, *Ministres de la République*, 220; cf. 207–19.
[83] Ibid. 198–207. On Eugène Pelletan, see Sudhir Hazareesingh, *Intellectual Founders of the Republic: Five Studies in Nineteenth-century French Political Thought*, 2001, 169, 173, 181–2, 194, 288–9. More generally on Liberal Protestantism, see Nord, *The Republican Moment*, Chapter 5.

The July Monarchy was more favourable to its tiny Jewish minority but the prominence of the Rothschild bank stirred up anti-Semitism on the Left. Fourier described Jews as 'the incarnation of commerce' and his disciple Toussenel in *Les Juifs rois de l'époque* (1845) went much further. He also asserted 'Who says Jew says Protestant', linking them in his anti-capitalist diatribe. The Second Republic in 1848 once again treated Jews as equal citizens, liberating them from legal discrimination and during the Second Empire some appeared to prosper by serving it as virtual 'Court Jews'. Although 60 per cent of Jews died as paupers in pre-1870 Paris, 'In the theatre, in literature and in literary criticism, in the press, in scholarship, in law and medicine, and in Republican politics ... French Jewry ... produced a number of leaders ... out of proportion to the relative number of Jews in France'.[84] The ensuing jealousy and resentment fed the late nineteenth-century surge of anti-Semitism among elites for whom Jews were intrusive rivals. After the annexation of Alsace-Lorraine, large numbers of Jews patriotically migrated, particularly to Paris, where half of them lived by 1872, with the rest concentrated in the larger provincial cities.

Racist ideas had been developed in 1850s France by Count Gobineau and criticized by Ernest Renan, a considerable Semitic scholar, whose sceptical investigations into the origins of Christianity had made him 'one of the most influential and detested, men of his generation.'[85] Catholic anti-Semitism was promoted by Gougenot de Mousseaux's *Le Juif, le judaïsme et la judaisation des peuples chrétiens* (1869) with Jews using liberalism and Freemasonry to rule the world. Nevertheless, French anti-Semitism was more influenced by, than influential on flourishing Central and Eastern European anti-Semitism. The term was coined by a German pamphleteer in 1879 (Wilhelm Marr) and taken up by Prussian and Austrian conservatives and then in Poland and Russia, from whence late nineteenth-century pogroms produced an influx of impecunious Jewish immigrants that helped ignite French anti-Semitism. The numbers, wealth, and influence of French Jews were greatly exaggerated by French anti-Semites for their polemical purposes. 'Counting Jews was a favourite pastime ... anti-Semitism was busy counting and multiplying them to prove the danger to public life from their domination.'[86] As Jean-Paul Sartre was later to put it, 'If the Jew did not exist, the anti-Semite would invent him', fiction exceeding fact in monstrous measure.[87]

A major 1882 financial failure of an ostentatiously Catholic bank, the *Union Générale*, precipitated the paroxysm of Judaeophobia that engulfed France in the 1880s. Started in 1878 by an ardent royalist and Catholic former Rothschild employee, its shares increased fivefold in value by January 1882, thanks to imprudent financial speculation. The year 1881 was an ominous one of depression in French agriculture, with a heavily curtailed public works programme and volatile

[84] Byrnes, 76–7, 95–7, 111, 118–21 and Michel Winock, *Nationalisme, antisémitisme et fascisme en France*, 1990, 126–7, 187–93.

[85] Byrnes, 48; cf. 112–14.

[86] Nelly Wilson, *Bernard-Lazare: Antisemitism and the Problem of Jewish Identity in Late Nineteenth Century France*, 1978, 71.

[87] Jean-Paul Sartre, *Réflexions sur la question juive*, 1946, 115, quoted in Byrnes, 92; cf. 79–90.

Stock Market. Seen as the Catholic champion against Jewish-Protestant financial hegemony and preparing to launch a propaganda campaign against anticlericalism, its failure was blamed on 'the Jews' in general and Rothschild in particular, although subsequent judicial investigation revealed the *Union Générale* to have been a victim of its own speculative attempt to buck a falling Stock Market in a context of economic depression.[88] The crash inspired several novels, notably Zola's *L'argent* (1891), with the banker Gundermann being modelled on Rothschild, and *Nemrod et Compagnie* (1892) by George Ohnet, a prolific best-seller writer of the 1880s and 1890s.[89] The stereotype odious and alien Jewish financier was popularized in novels by Paul Adam, *L'Essence du soleil. Roman social sur l'or des juifs*, Paul Bourget's *Cosmopolis* and Guy de Maupassant's *Mont-Oriol*, to mention only three of the most striking examples of fictional anti-Semitism.

Much the most scurrilous stimulant to anti-Semitism in France was *La France Juive* (1886), which a novelist friend Alphonse Daudet only persuaded a publisher to issue at author's expense. Its author Edouard Drumont was an obscure journalist (who had worked for a newspaper owned by the Jewish banker Pereire) of nostalgic nationalist and credulous Catholic views. His sustained diatribe argued that the Jews had been the principal and perennial cause of the misfortunes of 'Aryan' France. 'After asserting that every Protestant was half-Jew and that Protestantism was only a Jewish device for re-entering Christian society, he disclosed the sly hand of the Jews and Freemasons in the ejection of the Jesuits, the execution of Louis XVI and the victorious coalition against Napoleon.'[90] Drumont's calculated compendium of all the accumulated anti-Semitic French phobias achieved his provocative purpose, being popularized by the press controversy it stirred up, selling more than 100,000 copies before the end of 1886 and 150,000 within a year. His apoplectic anti-Semitism was spiced with scandalous anecdotes, calculated to arouse his readers, about the business and political elites, in which the Panama scandal of 1892–4 played a pivotal part.

The Panama Canal Scandal was by far the largest speculative financial disaster in memory to ruin French investors, many of them modest in their resources if not their expectations, who trusted Ferdinand de Lesseps, renowned for building the Suez Canal. However, he badly miscalculated the construction costs and the resulting need to secure frequent infusions of more capital led to paying increasing sums to journalists and those in the know not merely for favourable publicity but for their silence. Money desperately needed to build the Panama Canal was frittered away in a system of blackmail and corruption of politicians, engulfing those that received bribes like Rouvier and the former President Grévy's brother, or those like Clemenceau because he had received money for his newspaper *Justice* from one of the swindlers, Cornelius Herz. Panama itself 'became one vast gambling hell and the three most flourishing industries were brothels, gaming

[88] Byrnes, 130–5. See Jeanine Verdès-Leroux, *Scandale financière et antisémitisme catholique: Le Krach de l'Union Générale*, 1969.

[89] Byrnes, 106–9.

[90] Byrnes, 138, cf. 140–7. On the theatre as a virulent vector of anti-Semitism from 1880 to 1945, see Chantal Meyer-Planteureux, *Les Enfants de Shylock ou l'Antisémitisme sur Scène*, 2005.

houses and coffin manufacture'.[91] Despite desperate attempts to stifle the political fallout from the scandal, information was leaked to Drumont's recently founded *Libre Parole*, who made use of it to fuel his anti-Semitic, anti-capitalist, and anti-parliamentary campaign although it subsequently transpired that he had solicited and secured a loan from Herz for his spendthrift follower the Marquis de Morès. At the trials of the Directors of the Panama Company, several including de Lesseps and Eiffel (of Eiffel tower fame) were sentenced to prison but all the politicians—apart from one who confessed—went scot free. However, Clemenceau—who was spuriously attacked as an agent of the British Foreign Office as well as for his link with Herz—not merely failed to vindicate his reputation as a marksman by not killing Déroulède in a duel but lost his seat at the 1895 general election.[92]

All these demonstrations of the unsavoury workings of the economic and political system played into Drumont's unscrupulous hands. His explosive publications succeeded in fusing Christian anti-Judaism, popular anti-capitalism, and modern racism, enveloped in a simplistic mobilization of the fear of modernity which the Jew was deemed to personify. Catholic traditionalism, nationalism and what Bebel called 'the socialism of imbeciles' led Drumont to suggest that class conflict could be ended by confiscating Jewish property, having for this purpose multiplied the number of Jews tenfold. He blamed the 'Italian Jew Gambetta' (one of his many lies) for anticlericalism, his militant anti-Semitism dating from his fury at the Ferry legislation of 1880–1. The largest circulation (200,000) *Petit Journal* newspaper serialized *La France Juive* in 1892 and some industrialists presented free copies to local priests. His subsequent books, notably *La Fin d'un monde*, published in 1889 (the centenary of the French Revolution) were all bestsellers, unleashing an anti-Semitic flood of thirty-five books and twenty-three pamphlets before the end of that year. Although Pope Leo XIII denounced Drumont's anti-Semitism (whose newspaper *La Libre Parole* from 1892 worked with the Assumptionist *La Croix* to oppose the Pope's *Ralliement* policy), Drumont's main supporters were rural Catholic priests. Most provincial Catholic newspapers supported his anti-Semitic campaign, as did *La Croix*, which was widely read by Catholics.

Drumont upset some of his reactionary supporters by attacking bourgeois exploitation. As his leading disciple Jacques de Biez, Vice-President of the ephemeral French Antisemitic League (1889–90) prophetically told a reporter in 1889: 'We are National Socialists because we attack international finance so that we may have France for the French'.[93] Another active convert, the Marquis de Morès, was more successful in linking some of the Catholic petty bourgeoisie and Paris Meat Market butchers in early 1890s streetfighting, but like his mentor found this combination—leading him to be described as 'the first National Socialist'—difficult to sustain.[94] Only after the First World War were such ideas implemented

[91] Brogan, 270; cf. 269–73.

[92] Ibid. 280–5. More generally, see Jean Bouvier, *Les Deux Scandales de Panama*, 1964, 7–10, 140–98. Clemenceau and Drumont had an equally harmless duel in 1898.

[93] Byrnes, 164; cf. 151–5, 180–6, 234, 273, 298–9, 334–5 and Winock, *Nationalisme*, 80–1, 101, 118–37. See also Pierre Pierrard, *Juifs et Catholiques français*, 1970.

[94] Byrnes, 225–42, 252; cf. Winock, *Nationalisme*, 138–42.

by Hitler in Germany. In pre-war France, the various anti-Semitic movements were unable to establish an effective unified organization.

Because of the immense actual and symbolic impact of the Dreyfus Case epitomizing Franco-French dissensions that went well beyond the specific phenomenon of anti-Semitism, we need to examine in some detail its successive detonations. In 1894, Captain Alfred Dreyfus, from a wealthy, conservative and ultra-patriotic Jewish/Alsatian family that had opted for France in 1871, devoted to his prospering army career, was arrested on suspicion of betraying military secrets to the German military attaché in an unsigned document claimed to be in his handwriting. He was court-martialled and found guilty on the strength of biased and shaky evidence the defence counsel was denied the right to contest. The War Minister, General Mercier, impelled by a frenzied press campaign that aroused mass hysteria, had pronounced Dreyfus guilty before his trial. He was humiliated by being ritually degraded at a military ceremony, stripped of his rank, and sentenced to life imprisonment in solitary confinement on Devil's Island.

Two major developments in 1896 begin to reopen the case and turn it into the Dreyfus Affair. An assimilated Jew, Bernard-Lazare, who had published in 1894 a book on *Antisemitism, Its History and Causes*, which was admired for its frankness even by anti-Semites like Drumont and Maurras, became convinced of Dreyfus's innocence because of the implausibility of the allegations against him. His demonstration in *A Judicial Error: The Truth on the Dreyfus Affair* aroused vitriolic press hostility, from the Extreme Right, against a Jewish traitor, to the Extreme Left, because of Dreyfus's privileged class and military background. He was not prosecuted owing to official fear of reopening the case but was subjected to death threats and lost his job as a journalist. However, within the War Ministry's Counter-Espionage Statistical Section, Major Picquart (an Alsatian of anti-Semitic views) discovered evidence implicating a chronically impecunious Major Esterhazy of selling information to the German military attaché and that the 'secret dossier' used against Dreyfus contained no evidence. For his pains, Picquart was posted to Tunisia by the Chiefs of the General Staff who refused to reopen the case. To avoid doing so 'the Army went to extraordinary lengths, to the point of committing perjuries, forgeries and illegalities.'[95] These included imprisoning Picquart, who was eventually reintegrated into the army, promoted General and even became War Minister in the 1906 Government headed by that ardent Dreyfusard, Clemenceau.

Although Esterhazy was court-martialled on 11 January 1898, he was acquitted while Picquart was arrested. This provoked the second detonation. Persuaded by the arguments deployed by Bernard-Lazare and the Protestant Vice-President of the Senate from Alsace, Scheurer-Kestner, Emile Zola had already written an article in November 1897 devoted to the latter's stand, ending with the

[95] Nelly Wilson, *Bernard-Lazare*, 119; cf. 94–7, 102–7, 113–48, 164, 187, which is an exceptionally perceptive study within an immense literature on the subject. See also Guy Chapman, *The Dreyfus Case*, 1955 for a blow by blow account and Pierre Birnbaum, *L'Affaire Dreyfus, La République en péril*, 2002.

momentous words: 'Truth is on the march and nothing will stop it'.[96] Enraged by the farcical state-managed Esterhazy acquittal, Zola wrote a vitriolic letter to the President of the Republic, published in Clemenceau's newspaper *L'Aurore*, whose 300,000 copies on that day had on the front page the title chosen by Clemenceau: *J'accuse*. Beginning quietly, the long article culminated in a series of blunt accusations against the past and present War Ministers, Chiefs of the General Staff and the courts martial for organizing a judicial crime. Deliberately seeking to reopen the Dreyfus Case in the name of the French Declaration of the Rights of Man and against an odious anti-Semitism, Zola declared that he awaited prosecution.[97]

Unable to ignore this provocation, the government nevertheless succeeded in circumscribing the Zola trial in February 1898 to the accusations concerning the Esterhazy court martial, thereby preventing the Dreyfus Case proper being reopened. To ensure a guilty verdict against Zola the Chief of the General Staff de Boisdeffre threatened to resign if the Army's leaders were not implicitly trusted.[98] Zola (to whose literary role we turn in Chapter 7) was found guilty with the help of forged evidence and sentenced to a heavy fine and a year's imprisonment, going into exile in England to avoid arrest. To cries of 'Down with Zola! Death to the Jews! Up the Army', anti-Semitic riots, prompted by the national and provincial press, broke out in some thirty towns, but with particular violence in Algeria.

On both sides, the press campaign was waged with vigour, Clemenceau alone devoting some 600 articles to the Dreyfus Affair. Celebrated authors were mobilized. 'At no stage in the history of the press have so many writers contributed regularly to the press in one capacity or another. There is hardly a name in the world of letters which cannot also be found in the daily press.... Sensationalism, muck-raking, smear-campaigns, bribery, corruption, extortionate offers of publicity or pressures for silence, all these things were rife.'[99] What had been true in the early 1890s apropos of the Panama scandal became even truer in the late 1890s with the Dreyfus Affair. Just as Clemenceau took up journalism actively after he was excluded by the voters from the parliamentary rostrum, Jean Jaurès—who was initially sceptical about the claims of Dreyfus's innocence, used newspaper articles to argue in earnest the revisionist case after his electoral defeat in 1898. Fear of the electoral consequences of supporting the revision of the Dreyfus trial had dissuaded even those parliamentarians inclined to do so. Most Socialist leaders abstained from actively campaigning. This was backed up by the additional argument in their case that they had no part in an intra-bourgeois conflict and should concentrate on specifically working class issues in the name of Socialist unity. Jaurès was left to conduct a personal campaign in articles and public speeches but the third detonation was to come by a conjunction of his presentation of the evidence and revelations from within the War Ministry.

---

[96] Emile Zola gave the collection of his 1897–1900 articles on the Affair this title, first used in an 1897 *Figaro* article, *La Vérité en Marche*, 1901, 1923 edn, 10.

[97] Ibid. 91–3; cf. 73–93 for the full text of Zola's Letter to Félix Faure. On Clemenceau's journalistic campaign on behalf of the revision of the Dreyfus trial, see Watson, *Georges Clemenceau*, 145–55.

[98] Guy Chapman, 195; cf. Chapter 9 passim.   [99] Nelly Wilson, 30–1.

In 1898, the new civilian War Minister Godefroy Cavaignac (son of the Republican general who repressed the June Days fifty years before) who had in 1892 been active in securing investigation of the Panama scandal, inadvertently reopened the Dreyfus Case in an attempt to clear it up to his satisfaction by confirming the Captain's guilt. A thorough examination of the papers revealed a forgery concocted to prove Dreyfus's guilt and resulted in the suicide of the perpetrator, Lieutenant-Colonel Henry, who had played a key role in preventing the case against Dreyfus being dropped in 1894 by leaking it to Drumont. When the obstinate and credulous Cavaignac refused to acknowledge the implications for the innocence of Dreyfus, he resigned.[100] Before the results of the Cavaignac-instigated investigations became public, Jaurès, determined to demonstrate the innocence of Dreyfus began a series of articles in *La Petite République* from 10 August to 20 September 1898 that were collectively published as *Les preuves*. Zola having gone into exile, Jaurès took up the task of arousing public opinion, combining pity for a victim of injustice with anger at the military High Command's systematic falsifications in covering up its initial error. Henry's suicide and Esterhazy's admission of guilt as the author of the document sent to the German military attaché added extra impetus to the final words of Jaurès' concluding article. 'Daylight for justice! Daylight for revision (of the Dreyfus trial) for the salvation of the innocent, for the punishment of the guilty, for the education of the people, for the country's honour.'[101] After all the ill-merited protestations about the honour of the army, Jaurès was drawing attention to a more elevated and comprehensive sense of honour.

Discussion of the clash of the League of the Rights of Man, established in June 1898, with Déroulède's revived League of Patriots and much more influential League of the French Fatherland, established in January 1899, is postponed to Chapter 7, where we discuss the political commitment of intellectuals aroused by the Dreyfus Affair. Despite anti-Jewish riots in 1898 and Drumont's election as Deputy for Algiers, almost all French Jews adopted a resigned attitude to anti-Semitism. However, the journalist Theodore Herzl, who came from Vienna to report on the 1894 Dreyfus trial and witnessed the anti-Jewish crowd hysteria at his degradation ceremony, concluded that if assimilation could not work in the land of the Rights of Man, it was necessary to create a Jewish state, publishing his momentous call for Zionism in 1896.[102] Meanwhile, the decision of the Court of Appeal annulling the 1894 court martial was followed in 1899 by a retrial that resulted—against the evidence—in a 5 to 2 condemnation of Dreyfus to 10 years imprisonment, 'with extenuating circumstances'! To spare Dreyfus further incarceration, he sought and received a Presidential pardon but had to wait until 1906 for his full rehabilitation. It had taken twelve years for his innocence to be officially acknowledged. When Zola's ashes were transferred to the Panthéon

---

[100] Guy Chapman, Chapter 10 passim. See also Brogan, 305–9.

[101] Eric Cahm (ed.), *Oeuvres de Jean Jaurès: Les Temps de l'affaire Dreyfus (1897–1899)*, I, 691; cf. 451–7. See also Léon Blum, *Souvenirs sur l'Affaire*, 1935, 134–6 and Goldberg, *The Life of Jean Jaurès*, 217–23, 236, 240.

[102] Nelly Wilson, 205–13, 222–4.

by the Clemenceau government in 1908, in the resulting French Action agitation, Dreyfus who was present to honour his illustrious advocate was shot and wounded but his would-be assassin was acquitted by the jury!

The violent threats from the Right and fear of a military *coup d'état* created an atmosphere of civil war, with Déroulède being acquitted of conspiracy to overthrow the government and President Loubet being physically assaulted. This led to establishment of a government of Republican Defence headed by Waldeck-Rousseau, in whom some of the Republican firmness of Gambetta lived on. Anxious at official inertia, he had attacked his predecessor for not standing up to the conspiratorial Right by reasserting Republican legality. To crackdown on military subversion and indiscipline, he appointed as War Minister, General Gallifet, who had mercilessly repressed the Paris Commune but was willing to purge the High Command because of his contempt for their political intrigues. The Prime Minister and War Minister, settled matters between them, including the decision to secure a pardon for Dreyfus to defuse the issue. Waldeck-Rousseau, who was also Interior Minister, suppressed the nationalist, royalist, and anti-Semitic leagues, their leaders Déroulède and Jules-Napoléon Guérin being arrested and sentenced, the former to banishment for ten years and the latter to ten years in prison.[103]

The anti-regime Right was by no means a spent force, winning control of the Paris Municipal Council in 1900. Of greater ideological significance, the failure of Déroulède and the ineffectiveness of the elitist League of the French Fatherland prompted Charles Maurras (who justified of Henry's forgery to incriminate Dreyfus as a fabrication in a good patriotic cause), in 1898 to create the Union for French Action, to pursue a nationalist, anti-Semitic, and anti-parliamentary programme with renewed vigour.[104] Maurras' mistake was to do so in the name of a reactionary royalism which was a lost cause. Nevertheless, French Action was to exercise a powerful ideological influence for nearly half a century, until guilt by association with the Vichy regime decisively discredited it. The Extreme Right was to re-emerge as a political force in Le Pen's National Front as we see in Chapter 8.

---

[103] Pierre Sorlin, *Waldeck-Rousseau*, 391–422.

[104] Eugen Weber, *Action Française: Royalism and Reaction in Twentieth Century France*, 1962, 40–2; cf. 5, 17–19, 23–4, 27–8. For a sound review of the whole history of the subject, see Michel Winock, *La France et Les Juifs: De 1789 à nos jours*, 2004.

7

Adversaries: Partisan Intellectuals and Polarized Political Culture

The post-revolutionary polarization of French political culture, in which ideological compartmentalization led to a dialogue of the deaf between people committed to different convictions, ensured that despite desperate attempts to impose uniformity, disputes over irreconcilable issues have been a salient feature of the nineteenth and much of the twentieth centuries. Tocqueville inaugurated the view that the mid-eighteenth century 'men of letters' and *philosophes*—the forerunners of the intellectuals—gave a particularly abstract and literary twist to adversarial politics in France. His aristocratic class, that had been accustomed to rule under an absolute monarch, was confronted by an elite not of birth but of talent. While 'others held the reins of government, they alone spoke with accents of authority.... Their very way of living led these writers to indulge in abstract theories and generalizations regarding the nature of government, and to place a blind confidence in these.... Quite out of touch with practical politics, they lacked the experience which might have tempered their enthusiasms. Thus they completely failed to perceive the very real obstacles in the way of even the most praiseworthy reforms, and to gauge the perils involved in even the most salutary revolutions.'[1] They projected their literary propensities into the political arena, not as deferential courtiers but as assertive, activist critics, imparting a distinctively contentious argumentativeness not confined to political controversy in France. As can be perennially verified by the style of verbal duelling at any public discussion, 'interruptions are vital to the spirit of French conversation because contention is as characteristic of it as sociability.'[2] A chairman that attempts to restrain the participants would be regarded as imposing an odious authority recalling that of pre-revolutionary absolutism.

While Voltaire established the public role of the writer as having the independent standing to pronounce on religious and philosophical as well as literary matters and to campaign for the rehabilitation of injustices, he prudently avoided direct criticism of state authorities. After the Revolution, writers felt free to include political pronouncements as part of their claim to assert universal truths. As we have seen, this was notably true of Chateaubriand, Saint-Simon, Comte, and Balzac. However, no one attained Victor Hugo's symbolic national

---

[1] Alexis de Tocqueville, *The Old Regime and the French Revolution*, 140; cf. Part 3, Chapter 1 passim.
[2] Priscilla P. Clark, *Literary France: The Making of a Culture*, 1987, 121; cf. 126, 133.

status or capacity through visionary rhetoric to reach a democratic society's mass audience for the 'dramatisation of higher truths'.[3] Initially presenting Romanticism as 'liberalism in literature' just before the 1830 July Monarchy, he went on after the fall of the Second Republic to prophesy further social revolutions in the wake of a post-revolutionary literature. As the poetic high priest of the Republic in exile, Hugo claimed that 'words are the Word and the Word is God', setting an intellectual fashion in believing that words were tantamount to acts.[4]

The Second Empire's official quietist orthodoxy was exemplified by Désiré Nisard, Professor of Eloquence at the *Collège de France* and Director of the *Ecole Normale Supérieure* from 1857 to 1867. 'The man of genius in France is he who says what everybody knows. He is only the intelligent echo of the crowd.'[5] Avoiding originality was not Hugo's conception of the writer's function. After returning from exile, Hugo personified the moralistic public fusion of literary and political roles that set an idealized standard to be emulated in the Third Republic. However, Zola, thanks to the inherent drama of the Dreyfus Affair, and in the Fourth and Fifth Republics Jean-Paul Sartre, through his didactic plays and deliberately exhibitionist political postures in the cold war years, became identified with the use of intellectual prestige and cultural authority to promote a political cause, just as Flaubert exemplified the avoidance of public political commitment and the retreat into an egocentric aestheticism.

INTELLECTUAL COMMITMENT ON THE LEFT

What distinguished the advent of the politically committed intellectuals in the 1890s from their illustrious predecessors was that hitherto the phenomenon had been an individualistic and not a collective manifestation. Although from 1892, when both Maurice Barrès and Léon Blum had used the term intellectual to describe the aesthetic-cum-political advance guard identified especially with the anarchists, to whom—like many writers and artists—they were ephemerally attracted, it was not until Zola's *J'accuse* and his trial that a resounding individual *prise de position* ignited a controversy that quickly led Barrès and Blum to take opposing sides. The year of 1898 was the moment at which the collective self-recognition and affirmation of those with a cultural vocation to communicate their views on the values of the polity and society became manifest.

The intellectual label spread very quickly, thanks to various expressions of commitment: petitions, open letters to the press, and the creation of the League of the Rights of Man, quickly followed by the riposte of the League of the French Fatherland. The former's Central Committee was dominated by University

---

[3] Priscilla P. Clark, 1987, 152.

[4] Ibid. 150, quoting *Les Contemplations*, 1856. See also 145, 151, 155–6.

[5] Quoted by Zeldin, *France*, II, 64. For a perceptive and authoritative account of French intellectuals that draws on most of the same sources as this chapter but appeared after it was written, see Stefan Collini, 'The peculiarities of the French', Chapter 11 in *Absent Minds: Intellectuals in Britain*, 2006. He also refers to Herbert Luthy's 'The intellectuals—IV: France' in *Encounter*, August 1955, 5–15.

Professors and those associated with the *Ecole Normale Supérieure*, ambiguously combining the defence of universal principles with left-wing loyalties. Its membership increased from 8,000 at the end of 1898 to 60,000 in 1904 and has actively survived into the twenty-first century. The elitist League of the French Fatherland, with support from twenty-five of the forty members of the *Académie Française* and the *Institut de France* was initially much more successful in recruiting a mass membership of several hundred thousand but it declined very rapidly after the right-wing defeat at the 1902 general election, the running thereafter being made by Charles Maurras's *Action Française*.[6] With some success, the nationalist Right identified the internationalist Left as anti-France.

What Barrès derisively dubbed the Manifesto of the Intellectuals, which had some 1,200 signatories seeking to arouse public support for a retrial of Dreyfus, transmuted Zola's personal outcry into a collective expression of enlightened, educated opinion. Although there were celebrities among them like Anatole France and Zola, as well as future celebrities like André Gide and Marcel Proust, the bulk of the signatories were lesser known journalists, writers, university and secondary teachers as well as students, often recruited by personal acquaintance within the Latin Quarter of Paris where most of the relevant institutions were located. The Dreyfusards secured their support mainly from the humanities and natural science faculties at a time when science was displacing literature as a substitute moral authority for religion, although even there they represented a minority. The anti-Dreyfusards were dominant in the law (ironically, given the issue of injustice involved) and medical faculties of the Sorbonne and more generally in provincial universities, where they were closely linked to other elites, whereas in Paris intellectuals were sufficiently concentrated to attain a self-conscious autonomy from the wider Church and State Establishment. The mention of their institutional status alongside their signature by the Dreyfusards was deliberately intended to invoke a countervailing authority to that of the army and government, even of public prejudice.[7]

Although Zola's spectacular provocation in 1898 was a powerful catalyst in the emergence of a self-conscious group, in the preceding decade the literary advance guard had become increasingly restive under official censorship, preparing the way for the systematic, political involvement of intellectuals. Abandoning art for art's sake indifference, politicians and writers increasingly took a radically critical line that brought them into conflict with public authority. The War Minister's threat

---

[6] Pascal Ory and Jean-François Sirinelli, *Les Intellectuels en France de l'Affaire Dreyfus à nos jours*, 1986, 6–9, 19–25. For a good general review see Venita Datta, *Birth of a National Icon: The Literary Avant-Garde and the Origins of the Intellectual in France*, 1999.

[7] Christophe Charle, *Naissance des 'Intellectuels', 1880–1900*, 1990, 142–6, 152–4 and Christophe Charle, 'Academics or Intellectuals? The Professors of the University of Paris and Political Debate in France from the Dreyfus Affair to the Algerian War' in Jeremy Jennings (ed.), *Intellectuals in Twentieth Century France: Mandarins and Samurais*, 1993, 102–7. The Dreyfusard intellectual elite saw the need to educate the easily duped mass public, hence the ephemeral surge in adult education. See Lucien Mercier, *Les Universités Populaires: 1899–1914: education popuaire et mouvement ouvrier au début du siècle*, 1986.

to ban Lucien Descaves' anti-militarist novel *Sous-offs* led fifty-four writers to sign a protest in December 1889, which attracted the support not merely of Zola but the future anti-Dreyfusard Barrès, whose anti-parliamentary play *Une journée parlementaire* was banned. Barrès was also a signatory to the protest of over 120 journalists and writers against the prison sentence inflicted on the anarchist Jean Grave for his 1893 book *La société mourante et l'anarchie* at a time when it was anarchist deeds, rather than the words which could be construed as inciting them, that were a public preoccupation. Although Zola refused to sign, fearing guilt by association, the future pioneer champion of Dreyfus, Bernard-Lazare did so, having been attracted to the anarchist cause by a hatred of social injustice.[8]

So, in the years preceding 1898, collective public protest by writers had begun to be recognized as a legitimate way of challenging official decisions. However, the defence of freedom of expression did not succeed in mobilizing the intellectuals to move from a disinterested position to making an explicit commitment by seeking to exert political influence in the way that the condemnation of Dreyfus did. Nevertheless, to shift what have since come to be known derisively as the 'chattering classes' from being marginal if superior in self-esteem to mainstream bourgeois society, it took more than a precipitating, dramatic event. The lycée educated, who had acquired with a smattering of philosophy an overweening intellectual self-confidence, provided an underpinning for self-assertive political involvement. More specifically, there was an institutional basis for the emergence of the intellectuals, as well as a political context that was propitious to their activities, although in the process what began as a mystique was exploited for political purposes.

While lawyers were especially prominent in the political leadership of the Third Republic, providing such notable Prime Ministers as Ferry, Waldeck-Rousseau, Poincaré, and Briand, they did not play an active part in the Dreyfus Affair, although the right-wing Law Schools sided with the anti-Dreyfusards. The *Ecole Libre des Sciences Politiques* was not actively involved in the Dreyfus controversy, although Anatole Leroy-Beaulieu, Boutmy's successor as Director in 1906, had been an early Catholic Dreyfusard. Thibaudet saw the Dreyfus Affair as essentially a struggle between an aristocratic and hereditary military corps of successors and a meritocratic intellectual corps based on personal achievement, pointing out that most of the students of the *Ecole Normale Supérieure* (ENS) had secured their place thanks to state scholarships after serious competition.[9] The librarian of the ENS from 1889, Lucien Herr, himself a product of republican meritocracy, played a key role in the 1890s, recruiting an active minority of *Normaliens* to supporting both socialism and the Dreyfus cause. With the active assistance of Charles Péguy, whose bookshop was a rallying point for the Dreyfusards, Herr used his incomparable network among intellectuals and politicians, such as Jaurès and Blum, to engage in tireless propaganda, directly and through his disciples, in favour of what Péguy was later to condemn as 'the intellectual party'. As Péguy, who physically

[8] Christophe Charle, *Naissance des 'Intellectuels'*, 97–137.
[9] Albert Thibaudet, *La République des Professeurs*, 1927, 1979 edn, 121–3; cf. 33–4.

confronted the disruptive anti-Dreyfusards in defence of pro-Dreyfusard lecturers and in street battles, laconically put it: 'Herr was in command of the republican forces on the days when there was no fighting, I took over on the fighting days.'[10]

Charles Péguy broke with Herr over the latter's subordination of the moralistic and idealistic priorities of the Dreyfus Affair to the partisan and tactical preoccupations of a Socialist Party struggling to attain unity. Ending his association with the intellectual cooperative publisher-bookshop which depended on financial support secured by Herr, Péguy, having given up his academic career for proselytization, in 1900 launched a fortnightly review with the slogan: 'the Revolution is moral or nothing.'[11] Supported by a small group of close associates, including Georges Sorel and his syndicalist disciples Edouard Berth and Hubert Lagardelle, who were developing a virulent critique of politicized intellectualism, as well as Julien Benda, who was to become a leading protagonist of depoliticized intellectualism, Péguy used his *Cahiers de la Quinzaine* to attack electoral parliamentarism as prostituting a sacred act, with the result that, as practised in France, it was a vicious system. In three pamphleteering essays (1906–7) he also castigated the politicization of French higher education by the appointments made to chairs at the Sorbonne, particularly that of Emile Durkheim, thanks to the political influence of 'the intellectual party',[12] a subject to which we shall return.

Although Péguy never went as far to the Right as Sorel and his disciples, with whom he broke in 1912 out of loyalty to Julien Benda over the issue of anti-Semitism, and who were to take their hostility to parliamentary democracy to extremes, his cult of Joan of Arc and anticipation of war with Germany led him increasingly towards a Catholic nationalism that ended with his death on 5 September 1914 as a hero at the battle of the Marne. He never assimilated anti-capitalism to anti-Semitism, which led a Drumont and a Bernanos to equate a socialist Catholicism with anti-Judaism. As he idiosyncratically made clear in 1912: 'I am more and more against anti-Semitism.... If people want to start the *Affaire Dreyfus* again, we will set to work.... I'm on the side of the Jews, because with the Jews I can be the sort of Catholic I want to be, with the Catholics I couldn't.'[13] Péguy remained a champion of a supra-political spiritual power, attached to a pristine mystical Republic that had not been corrupted by exposure to sordid electoral debasement or the eloquent pacifism of Jaurès who he had venerated in the 1890s and who was murdered on 31 July 1914 shortly before Péguy himself was killed, both early victims of the First World War. Péguy's posthumous

---

[10] Quoted in Daniel Halévy, *Péguy and Les Cahiers de la Quinzaine*, 1918, 1946 Eng. edn, 45; cf. 31, 41, 44. Daniel Halévy helped collect signatures for the petition that became known as the Manifesto of the Intellectuals. See also Ory and Sirinelli, 56–7. Despite its splenetic attacks on many of his former friends by an informed insider who swung to the far Right during the First World War, see Hubert Bourgin, *De Jaurès à Léon Blum: L'Ecole Normale et la Politique*, 1938, especially 104–18, 131–3 on Herr and 189–97, 201–2 on Jaurès.

[11] Halévy, *Péguy*, 59; cf. Chapter 6 passim.   [12] Compagnon, 35, 120–6.

[13] Quoted Halévy 171–2; cf. 62–6, 92–6 and Michel Winock, *Nationalisme, antisémitisme et fascisme en France*, 408. See also M. Adereth, *Commitment in Modern French Literature*, 1967, Chapter 2.

influence, notably on the Catholic Left in general and from the 1930s through *Esprit* in particular, proved to be far greater than in his lifetime.

Georges Sorel, an atypical anti-technocrat product of *Polytechnique*, who retired early as a civil engineer, theorized his anti-intellectualism from an anarcho-syndicalist standpoint. Signing the 1898 Dreyfusard petition for retrial, he also published an essay on 'The Socialist Future of the Trade Unions' arguing that the fundamental social division was between the parasitical intellectuals and the productive manual workers, the former exploiting parliamentary politics to achieve dictatorial power over the latter. Based upon a combination of heterodox Marxism with a strong infusion of Proudhonism, Sorel achieved fame thanks to his *Reflections on Violence*, with the myth of the general strike as its centrepiece. His main targets were the reformist socialist intellectuals who had 'embraced the profession of thinking for the proletariat'.[14] A particular bugbear was Emile Durkheim, a quintessential intellectual who advocated the incorporation of the trade unions to overcome class conflict, whereas Sorel sought the exclusive emancipation of the workers through their unions.

However, when Sorel lost faith in the revolutionary capacity of the proletariat, owing to the failure of the general strike and the influence of Henri Bergson's anti-rationalism and Gustave Le Bon's crowd psychology, he turned to a more powerful opponent of liberal democracy, nationalism, which Sternhell has called a national socialism without the proletariat.[15] While this led a disciple like Hubert Lagardelle eventually into becoming a Vichy minister, Sorel himself—despite a flirtation with Maurras's French Action—was more attracted after the First World War by Lenin's Bolshevik Revolution than Mussolini's corporatist fascism, despite the latter's similar transition from revolutionary syndicalism. What they all shared was a determination to destroy the liberal bourgeois society which in Sorel's case left him almost indifferent to whether the Third Republic succumbed to the Extreme Left or the Extreme Right.

In the wake of Zola's *J'accuse* and the Manifesto of the Intellectuals, the most striking confrontation over the issue of the role of the intellectuals was between the leading literary critic and editor of the anti-Dreyfusard *Revue des Deux Mondes*, Ferdinand Brunetière and the future leading Sorbonne sociologist and editor of the more obscure *Année Sociologique*, Emile Durkheim, then a Bordeaux Professor, who was secretary of the local branch of the League for the Defence of the Rights of Man. Brunetière, a haughty Academician, in an article 'After the Trial', condemned 'one of the most ridiculous eccentricities of our time—I mean the pretension of rising writers, scientists, professors and philologists to the rank of supermen.' He went on to justify hostility to the Jews, Protestants, and Freemasons, who were partly themselves responsible for this arrogance because of their 'dominant' role in education, politics, and administration. Having championed the army as 'the keystone of social equilibrium' and national unity,

---

[14] Georges Sorel, *Reflections on Violence*, 1908, 1999 edn, 129; cf. 155–6, 280. See also Sorel, *Matériaux d'une théorie du prolétariat*, 1919, 1929 edn, 89, 92, 94, 98, 132–3.

[15] Zeev Sternhell, *Neither Right nor Left: Fascist Ideology in France*, 1983, 1996, 17–18, 80–1; cf. 71–9.

Brunetière attacked the arrogant intellectuals who appealed to scientific truth as the way of placing themselves above the law; 'when intellectualism and individualism reach this degree of self-infatuation, one must expect them to be or become nothing other than *anarchy*....'[16]

Durkheim's riposte took its stand on impeccable liberal principles. 'There is no reason of state which can excuse an outrage against the person when the rights of the person are placed above the state.'[17] Arguing that intellectuals required authority to be rationally based and exercised justly, he went on: 'Accustomed by the practice of scientific method to reserve judgement when they are not fully aware of the facts, it is natural that they give in less readily to the enthusiasms of the crowd and to the prestige of authority.'[18] He then moved from defence to attack. 'Not only is individualism distinct from anarchy; but it is henceforth the only system of beliefs which can ensure the moral unity of the country.'[19] Individualism was Christian in its roots and had become the foundation of social cohesion. 'Thus the individualist, who defends the rights of the individual, defends at the same time the vital interests of society'[20] which was especially true of France as exemplified by the Dreyfus case. However, the subsequent battle between Left and Right, as well as controversy over whether intellectuals should be politically committed or detached, was not conducted by social scientists but primarily by creative writers of fiction in their novels and especially their polemical journalism.

THE LITERARY LEGACY OF THE DREYFUS AFFAIR

(a) *The Left*: Emile Zola's *Vérité* and Anatole France's *Monsieur Bergeret à Paris* were novels that dealt with the Dreyfus Affair, the latter conveying in a more subtle way the atmosphere at the time. France had held a sinecure post in the Senate Library from which he resigned in 1890 after the chief librarian complained that he had not catalogued a book in eight years. His involvement in the Dreyfusard campaign heralded active involvement in politics as a fellow-traveller of the newly born French Communist Party after the First World War, during which he had adopted a strongly patriotic standpoint. Winner of the Nobel Prize for literature in 1921, he wrote in a 1922 article in *L'Humanité*: 'we thought that we were dying for the homeland; we were dying for the industrialists.'[21] Although the Communist Party was initially delighted to use this emblematic intellectual for their propagandist purposes, he moved away from the increasingly sectarian PCF shortly before his death in 1924. The nihilist Surrealists, who were to have a complicated relationship with the PCF, published a very hostile pamphlet on

[16] Ferdinand Brunetière, *Revue des Deux Mondes*, 15 March 1898, 445; cf. 428–46, quoted from Steven Lukes, 'Durkheim's "Individualism and the Intellectuals"' in *Political Studies*, XVII/I, March 1969, 17–18. See also Compagnon, 37, 64–5, 69–70, 331.

[17] Quoted in Lukes, 22.   [18] Ibid. 25.   [19] Ibid.   [20] Ibid. 27.

[21] Quoted in Yves Santamaria, 'Intellectuals, Pacifism and Communism: The Mandarins and the Struggle for Peace (1914–53)' in Jennings, *Intellectuals in Twentieth Century France*, 121.

that occasion, entitled 'A corpse'.[22] Anatole France's awkward relationship to the Communists foreshadowed the predicament of many writers of later generations in the twentieth century, resulting in vociferous or silent exit from the party.

Romain Rolland had taught Péguy at the *Ecole Normale Supérieure* and his revolutionary plays *Quatorze Juillet* and *Danton* were published by Péguy in the wake of the Dreyfus Affair. Rolland's popular *Jean-Christophe* novels helped to keep the struggling *Cahiers de la Quinzaine* going before the First World War but it was the September 1914 publication from his self-imposed Swiss exile of his anti-militarist article with the title of his 1915 collection *Above the Battle* that brought Rolland to the forefront of political controversy. Influenced by Gandhi, he condemned the political, religious, and cultural leaders for what he saw as a repudiation of European civilized values, only to be attacked by other writers like Anatole France and André Gide as a traitor.[23] After the war he was criticized by Henri Barbusse (who had made his reputation with his antiwar novel *Le Feu*, based upon his frontline experience) from the Communist Left for his idealist refusal to condone the methods of the Soviet dictatorship but by the 1930s they were allies in their hostility to fascism. The new international situation led Rolland and many other fellow-travelling intellectuals to consider that with all the Soviet Union's faults it was an indispensable ally in the united anti-fascist front.[24]

André Gide was another celebrated writer who had a troubled relationship with the PCF and the Soviet Union. Having earlier been attracted to membership of French Action, a 1925 visit to the Congo led him to write a resounding attack on colonial exploitation in Africa. His Protestant background imparted a strong moralistic attitude, which in the early 1930s led him to sympathize with communism. But, as he wrote after his visit to the Soviet Union: 'It is to the truth that I attach myself: if the Party deserts it, at the same moment I desert the Party.'[25] His *Return from the Soviet Union* (recalling his anti-colonial *Return from the Congo* a decade earlier) substituted reality for the anti-fascist abstraction of his previous admiration. Conformist indoctrination, the personality cult of Stalin, pervasive fear and lies, repressive dictatorship, worker exploitation were denounced, provoking the PCF to heap opprobrium on Gide, who could no longer be a useful dupe in the service of party propaganda.[26]

A much more radical and tempestuous rapprochement with communism was achieved by the Surrealists, the poets Louis Aragon and Paul Eluard becoming much more servile adherents of the French Communist Party than its foremost theoretician André Breton could ever be. An early 1920s breakaway from the anti-art and anti-militarist Dada movement, the Surrealists initially retained much of its scandal for scandal's sake nihilism and anarchic individualism, making a

---

[22] Ibid. 123. See also David Caute, *Communism and the French Intellectuals 1914–1960*, 1964, 36, 75–7.

[23] Caute, 64–5 and Halévy, *Péguy*, 29, 72–4. See also Ory and Sirinelli, 71–5.

[24] Caute, 80–1, 104–5, 130; cf. 59, 74–5, 79 and Henri Barbusse, *Manifeste aux intellectuals*, 1927.

[25] Quoted Caute, 238; cf. 237–9.

[26] Ibid. 125, 238–41. See also François Furet, *Le Passé d'une illusion: Essai sur l'idée communiste au XXe siècle*, 1995, 470–7.

derisive practice of treating trivialities with monumental seriousness. Recourse to hypnotic sleep and the importance attached to the ensuing dreams, automatic writing and a freewheeling lifestyle were expounded in the 1924 Surrealist Manifesto ambitiously advocating 'changing life', a seductive theme that was to resurface in 1968 among university students and in the Socialist Party propaganda in the run up to the 1981 presidential election.

When the Surrealists sought salvation from solitude and the human predicament in revolution and the Communist Party, they tried in vain to use this positive outlet in the service of their Surrealist dreams rather than the reverse. Salvador Dali, who took sexual liberation and Freudianism to extremes, continued to be an irrepressible manifestation in his paintings and provocative pronouncements on systematizing contradiction through the paranoid-critical method, of the subversive determination to shock bourgeois convictions and conventions, without giving a damn about Marxism. However, in 1925 the Riff colonial war in Morocco was the issue that convinced the movement's leaders by 1927 that political commitment to the Communist Party was unavoidable. Only then could they satisfy their obsessively anti-bourgeois yearning for both an abstract association with the proletariat and the Comintern as well as the Soviet Union, where the socialist intellectual utopia of an anti-capitalist society appeared to have actually been attained. They did so despite the prevailing sectarian and anti-intellectual character of the late 1920s bolshevizing PCF and the increasingly repressive nature of Stalinist Russia. Accordingly, their periodical changed its title from 'Surrealist Revolution' to 'Surrealism in the service of Revolution'.

'Intellectually, it was a curious period. Intellectuals abandoned the Party before 1927 as Trotskyists. Surrealists joined the Party in 1927 often as semi-Trotskyists, while the Trotskyists denounced them as irresponsible idealists.... Over and above this mêlée was a Party more or less indifferent as to whether the intellectuals came or went.'[27] The PCF was solely interested in the Surrealists—like the Existentialists after the Second World War—in so far as they contributed to discrediting and disintegrating the bourgeois class and system. The PCF made sure—if it was ever a plausible danger—that there was no prospect that the self-realization through revolution practised by the Surrealists could contaminate the working classes. Despite the brutal assertions of literary terror represented by the imposition of Stalinist socialist realism, the Surrealists unrealistically hoped that by affirming and reaffirming their loyalty to the Communist political, economic, and social programme, they could enjoy a licence to express their views in areas innocent of Marxist dogma. (It is hard to think of something aesthetically more antithetical to surrealism than socialist realism.) The Association of Revolutionary Artists and Writers established by Breton in 1930 was used by the Communists against him in 1935 in the name of their monopoly mastery of the revolutionary ideology which it had been created to propagate.

Of all the ex-Surrealists, it was Louis Aragon—Breton's unofficial second-in-command, aspiring to a Benjamin Constant's combination of political, literary,

---

[27] Caute, 98; cf. 95–9, 206.

and amorous fame—who was to play the most outspoken political role in France, after his enforced departure—under Soviet pressure—from the movement. He achieved prominence in 1932 when he was prosecuted for inciting soldiers to disobedience and for provoking murder in his poem *Red Front*. Calling for a proletarian revolution which would *inter alia* involve a massacre of Socialist deputies in general and the murder of Léon Blum in particular, Aragon's extravagance was nevertheless exonerated by Breton on the grounds of poetic licence. A protest against his trial (which never took place because the prosecution was dropped) was supported by numerous French and foreign celebrities—Matisse, Picasso, Thomas Mann, and Federico García Lorca among others—but André Gide and Romain Rolland refused to do so.[28] Relations with the Pacifist Rolland had been bad for years, Eluard contributing the phrase 'If you want peace, prepare for civil war' to a Surrealist pamphlet entitled 'Mobilization Against War is not Peace'.[29]

Aragon's increasing servility to the Communist Party, after he had accepted censorship by it following his 1930 visit to Moscow, led to a break with Breton and Surrealism in 1932. Thereafter, he went to the limits of apostasy, embracing the role of uncritical propagandist to attain personal fulfilment in poetic self-abasement in return for the adulation of the party faithful.

'My party has restored to me my eyes and my memory.

My party has made me understand the meaning of the contemporary world.

My party, my party, thank you for your lessons.'

Not only in his poetry, but in a series of long-winded novels under the general title of 'The Real World', culminating in the six volume *Les Communistes*, Aragon now substituted a pedestrian Socialist Realism for imaginative Surrealism.[30] He went on to laud in the most sycophantic terms Stalin and the PCF leader Thorez in prose and poetry. Aragon commissioned Picasso (who had joined the PCF in 1944) to produce the propagandist 'dove of peace' with which his committed art was for a time as much identified as his Guernica painting powerfully symbolized his protest against the brutalities perpetrated by the anti-Republican and foreign fascist auxiliaries in the Spanish Civil War.

Breton switched to Trotskyism from 1935 and in 1938 published a manifesto 'For an Independent revolutionary Art' written with Trotsky.[31] By the time Breton went into an American retreat during the Second World War, Surrealism as such had shot its bolt. However, the waves from the enormous aesthetic splash it had made continued to wash through the medium of film (especially in the wake of the Buñuel-Dali films *An Andalusian Dog* of 1929 and *The Golden Age* of 1930), the painting for a while of Picasso, the sculpture of Giacometti, the photographs of Man Ray. Surrealism was an example of the powerful attraction of Paris to foreign visual artists and writers, France earlier assimilating into its title to impressionist splendour Van Gogh and Sisley alongside Monet and Renoir.

---

[28] André Thirion, *Revolutionaries without Revolution*, 1972, 1975, 298–302; cf. 139, 164, 177.

[29] Ibid. 325; cf. 324.

[30] Caute, 220–2, 324–6, 332–3. For a more favourable view of Aragon, see Adereth, Chapter 3.

[31] Thirion, 330, 339–401.

In his interwar novels on the early attempts at Communist revolution in China, *The Conquerors* and *The Human Condition*, as well as in *Hope*, his novel about the Spanish Civil War in which he took part as a pilot, André Malraux projected the image of the intellectual hero as man of action. His Communist sympathies were ruptured by the 1939 Pact between Soviet Russia and Nazi Germany but it was only after his role as a colonel commanding the Alsace-Lorraine Brigade in the 1944 capture of Strasbourg that he emerged in 1945 as a Gaullist Minister of Information, ardent member of his RPF party from 1947 and then his Minister of Cultural Affairs from 1959 to 1969. As he wrote in 1948, his disillusion with Communism came with the realization that Russian nationalism had replaced proletarian internationalism. Explaining how an 'anti-France' intellectual could become a French nationalist, he declared: 'We had believed that in becoming less French a man becomes more human. Now we know that he simply becomes more Russian.'[32] During the first decade of the Fifth Republic, Malraux used his position as Minister to promote the spread of cultural activity to as many people as possible throughout France in *Maisons de la Culture*, demonstrating that he had not abandoned a component of the programme of the 1930s Popular Front.

Another writer on whom the 1939 switch of Soviet alliances had a major impact was Paul Nizan, a fellow *Ecole Normale* student with Jean-Paul Sartre, who later developed the idea of political commitment borrowed from Nizan. In the mid-1920s, Nizan was briefly active in French Action and then Georges Valois' fascist movement (discussed in Chapter 8) but he became a Communist after his conversion to Marxism. Novelist and journalist, he made his initial reputation with his 1932 polemic *The Guardogs*, an argument for political commitment by joining the PCF, in explicit opposition to Julien Benda's defence of detachment by the secular intellectual clergy discussed later. For Nizan, the intellectuals had taken over the clergy's function of status quo spiritual supporters of the bourgeoisie and the state. They had shown this by supporting the First World War carnage and capitalist exploitation. Nizan asserted that an apolitical attitude was excluded; one must side either with the bourgeoisie or the proletariat, so he chose to denounce the illusions fostered by the former in the name of the latter. The vocation of the left-wing intellectual was to be a professional revolutionary. However, when war came, shortly after the Soviet–Nazi alliance, he resigned from the PCF and wrote in a letter: 'The only honour which is left to us is that of understanding.'[33] Ostracized by his former party comrades, Nizan, who died in the Dunkirk battle of 1940, was only rescued from oblivion by his *Normalien* friend Sartre.

The prestige of French literature in the aftermath of the Second World War was great, with five Nobel Prize winners: Gide (1947), Mauriac (1952), Camus (1957), the poet Saint-John Perse (1960), and Sartre in 1964, who refused the honour. Jean-Paul Sartre was not as subservient to the Communist Party as Aragon but

[32] Quoted ibid. 245; cf. 242–7.

[33] Quoted in David L. Schalk, *The Spectrum of Political Engagement*, 1979, 72; cf. 49–67. See also Schlomo Sand, 'Mirror, Mirror on the Wall, Who is the true intellectual of them all? Self-images of the intellectual in France' in Jennings, *Intellectuals*, 47–9. Serge Halimi, author of *Les Nouveaux chiens de garde*, 1997, prefaced a new edition of Nizan's *Les Chiens de garde* in 1998.

not as critical as Péguy had been of the Socialist Party. Sartre used his influential periodical, *Les Temps Modernes*, launched in 1945, to popularize Nizan's idea of political commitment as an intellectual duty to support a mythologized working class. Published as *What Is Literature?*, Sartre's articles took the anti-Benda line that it was treason not to be partisan. He claimed in the opening article that 'The "committed" writer knows that words are action. He knows that to reveal is to change'. In his concluding article, Sartre pontificated: 'Everyday we must take sides in our life as a writer... because literature is in essence a taking of position.'[34]

The political involvement of intellectuals had been prompted in the 1930s by the rise of Nazism and the Spanish Civil War but it was Sartre who popularized it, thanks to linking the Existentialist vogue with Marxism. Although Existentialism was popularly associated with frequenting the cafés and nightclubs of St German des Prés rather than abstruse philosophy, the association with Marxism—again in its most vulgarized form—provided a political outlet in the PCF, the party of the working class. As Sartre portentously asserted in 1957: 'Marxism is an all-inclusive whole reflecting our age. No one can go beyond it.' Because writers were members of the bourgeoisie, 'we must be its gravediggers, even if we run the risk of burying ourselves along with it.'[35] Although 'the fate of literature is bound up with that of the working class', writers should not join the PCF because 'The politics of Stalinist Communism is incompatible in France with the honest practice of the literary craft.'[36]

Sartre was frequently attacked for his moralistic reservations by the Communists, as was former Communist Albert Camus, who finally and acrimoniously parted company with him in 1951 over the publication of *The Rebel*. In this book Camus refused to associate human emancipation with what Trotsky had called in 1922 Communist 'fellow travelling', while Sartre and his partner Simone de Beauvoir continued generally to side first with Soviet and then Chinese Communism. Neither Sartre nor his followers were disposed to change despite the devastating 1955 philosophical attack by Maurice Merleau-Ponty (co-founder with Sartre of *Les Temps Modernes*) in *Adventures of the Dialectic*.

Until the mid-1970s exposure by Solzhenitsyn of the enduring Stalinist *gulag* finally dissipated the blinkered delusions of most of the French intellectuals, Sartre retained a hegemonic hold over their minds, because although he claimed that 'we are writing against everybody', he gave priority to his hostility towards the bourgeoisie and the USA. As has been pointed out, 'for Sartre, the Soviet actions had no bearing on the legitimacy of the Communist project' because it

---

[34] Jean-Paul Sartre, *What Is Literature?*, 1948, 1967 edn, 13, 206. In his 1948 play *Les Mains Sales*, Sartre argued that politically committed intellectuals must get their hands dirty. Adereth links this with Péguy's comment: 'Kantism has pure hands, but this is because it has no hands.' Adereth, 162; cf. 161–3. However, Sartre never resolved in practice the Benda dichotomy between intellectual integrity and political commitment. See Rod Kedward, *La Vie en Bleu, France and the French since 1900*, 2005, 364; cf. 365, 367.

[35] Sartre, *What Is Literature?*, 186. The 1957 quotation is from an interview of Sartre by Olivier Todd, *The Listener*, 6 June 1957, cited in Adereth, 144.

[36] Sartre, *What Is Literature?*, 187, 189; cf. 195–6.

was correct in theory even if wrong in its practices.[37] From 1946 to 1969, Sartre had been the most frequent signatory to the manifestos (there were 488 during the de Gaulle presidency, 1958–69) that the Dreyfus Affair had popularized as a militant intellectual activity, dutifully followed by Simone de Beauvoir.[38] She made her independent impact with her feminist book *The Second Sex*. For his part, in the 1970s Sartre moved from committed writing to risking imprisonment by engaging in provocative illegal action. This was the ultimate implication of Sartre's substitution of the uncommitted 'swine' for the religious sinner as the embodiment of the inactive individual.

With the evaporation of both the prospect of revolution in France or the triumph of Soviet Communism abroad, French intellectuals deserted the PCF and ceased to engage in fellow travelling in front organizations, notably peace movements. Following his death in 1980, no intellectual of stature could replace the emblematic Sartre in his semi-detached role of lending respectability to the Communist cause out of deference to its proletarian legitimacy, although sociologist Pierre Bourdieu vainly attempted to emulate Sartre's role on the Left. Alignment with PCF policy out of bourgeois guilt in not identifying oneself with the vanguard party of the working class ceased to be an imperative for increasingly sceptical intellectuals as the working classes diversified in character and the PCF gave increasing signs of senility. Rather than switching their allegiance, most fellow travellers simply abandoned political commitment, no longer being intimidated by accusations of betrayal. Whereas at the PCF railway junction travellers had always been coming and going, from the 1980s many left and very few came. Once they had lost their faith in an inevitable historical process, intellectual dissidents could no longer stomach 'a type of prefabricated speech, repetitive, closed, ending the debate from the start, providing others with a fully constituted truth, transmitted by a stereotyped vocabulary' which constituted PCF speak.[39] The attractions of partisan political commitment disappeared once the myth of class-based revolutionary change had been exposed as a delusion.

(b) *Intellectual Commitment on the Right*: Despite his exaggerations, Sternhell was correct to emphasize that intellectual anti-liberalism traversed both the Left and the Right, prompted by anti-capitalism and hatred of the bourgeoisie, coupled with a contempt for the working of Third Republic parliamentary democracy.

---

[37] Tony Judt, *Past Imperfect: French Intellectuals, 1944–1956*, 1992, 122; cf. 123. See Sartre, *What is Literature?*, 196; cf. 197. See also Sartre's 'A Plea for Intellectuals' of 1972, included in his *Between Existentialism and Marxism*, 1983. More generally, see David Drake, *Intellectuals and Politics in Postwar France*, 2002, 3–5, 24–33, 57–9, 94–5 and Caute, 247–59. On the Sartre–Camus polemic, see Olivier Todd, *Albert Camus: Une vie*, 1996, 564–7, 571–4. Trotsky's 1922 coining of the term fellow-traveller was used in his *Literature and Revolution*, 1923 as pointed out by Yves Santamaria, 'Intellectuals, Pacifism and Communism' in Jennings (ed.), *Intellectuals in Twentieth Century France*, 118 and Chapter 6 passim.

[38] Jean-François Sirinelli, *Intellectuels et passions françaises: Manifestes et petitions au XXe siècle*, 1990, 9–10 and Ory and Sirinelli, 205. Simone de Beauvoir's volumes of autobiography and her novel. *The Mandarins* portray one view of the world of the committed intellectual in the post-war years.

[39] Georges Labica in 1980, quoted in Sudhir Hazareesingh, *Intellectuals and the French Communist Party: Disillusion and Decline*, 1991, 250, an excellent analysis of the decomposition of the PCF.

As we shall see, 'From the period of Boulangism right up to the time of the Collaboration, the French Left never ceased to augment the ranks of the Right-wing and even extreme Right-wing parties of the prefascist and already fully fascist movements.'[40] The mass nature of an industrializing, democratizing society was exploited by advocates of a conjunction of the anti-liberal ideologies of national-ism and socialism, rejecting the cosmopolitanism and centrist politics that were hallmarks of the established bourgeois order. As early as 1890, in his anarcho-socialist phase, Maurice Barrès was demanding a purge of the liberal democratic poison afflicting French society. In an article on 'The struggle between capitalists and workers', Barrès claimed that since the Revolution, 'the bourgeoisie has con-stantly called on the revolutionary energy of the popular classes with the secret purpose of subjugating them.'[41] The Dreyfus Affair, which was the occasion for social and liberal democrats to unite in defence of individual rights and the parlia-mentary Republic, led Barrès to switch from the anti-Establishment revolutionary Left to the anti-Establishment, revolutionary Right. It was supplemented with an anti-Semitism derived from Jules Soury's pseudoscientific antithesis between Aryans and Semites.

He had already prepared for his move by his Boulangism in the late 1880s (he was elected a Boulangist deputy) but with the army in the firing line during the Dreyfus Affair, republican nationalism swung sharply to the Right. Barrès made his impact both as a prolific novelist and as a journalist. His three 'national energy' novels of 1897–1902 each focused on sensitive political issues. *Les Déraci-nés* concentrated on those uprooted from Lorraine by the Franco-Prussian War but also satirized the meritocratic, pro-Dreyfusard professor-politician anti-hero personified by Paul Bouteiller, epitome of the 'Professors' Republic'. *L'Appel au soldat* dealt with Boulangism, while *Leurs Figures* concentrated on the Panama scandal and parliamentary corruption. In *Scènes et doctrines du nationalisme* of 1902, Barrès described the Dreyfusard intellectuals as 'platform anarchists' 'who show a criminal complaisance in their intellect, who treat our generals as idiots, our social institutions as absurd and our traditions as unhealthy.'[42] The only truth was 'French truth'. He followed this with another trilogy inspired by the prepa-ration for *revanche* against Germany: *Au service de l'Allemagne*, *Colette Baudoche*, and *La Colline inspirée*. His mystical evocation of soil and cemeteries to prompt xenophobia was combined with presentation of the army as a model of authority and discipline but his obsession with Joan of Arc allowed him to add a Catholic dimension.

Barrès's almost daily hyperpatriotic articles in *L'Echo de Paris* were read by many army officers, preparing them by frequent brainwashing before and during the First World War to make the ultimate military sacrifice.[43] Becoming president of the League of Patriots on the death of Déroulède in 1914, Barrès devoted 269

---

[40] Sternhell, *Neither Right nor Left*, 15.

[41] Quoted ibid. 107; cf. 37–43, 230. More generally, see Barrès, *L'ennemi des lois*, 1893.

[42] Maurice Barrès, *Scènes et doctrines du nationalisme*, 1902, 208.

[43] Yves-Marie Hilaire, 'L'ancrage des idéologies' in Sirinelli (ed.), *Histoire des droites en France*, I, 523–8 and cf. Ory and Sirinelli, 41–2, 48–50, 67.

articles to the war in 1915 alone, his chronicles of the First World War filling 6,000 pages in 14 volumes. His bellicose propaganda led him to be described as 'the nightingale of carnage' by the pacifist Romain Rolland. (The First World War rallied many ex-Dreyfusard intellectuals to the nationalist cause, in part a testimony to the effectiveness of the patriotic pressure exerted on them to avoid imputations of being anti-France.) However, Barrès was the literary protagonist of a populist nationalism, not its theoretician, whose principal exponent was Charles Maurras, a royalist not a republican.

Deaf from age 14 (which contributed to him abandoning his Catholic faith), Maurras relied mainly upon journalism to convey his views, although he was also a spellbinding public speaker. Like Barrès, his political obsessions derived from his literary opinions although in his case these were not Romantic but Classical, combined with Comtian positivism. Religious, political, and artistic individualism were rejected as exemplified by the Reformation, the Revolution, and Romanticism. He claimed that late nineteenth-century France owed its decadence to liberal democracy, whose purveyors were foreigners (he preferred the Athenian term 'metics'): Jews, Protestants, and Freemasons. French factional disputes would be ended by restoring the monarchy that had unified France. To achieve this required 'creating a conspiratorial mentality' if necessary by a *coup d'état*, Maurras declaring at the height of the Boulangist agitation in 1888: 'We are all a little Bonapartist'.[44] However, his anti-democratic views upset the Bonapartists and his anti-parliamentary views repelled the Orleanists.

Nevertheless, his *Enquête sur la Monarchie* of 1900 revived what seemed a lost cause. His slogan that politics took priority over everything was based on the claim that the Republic was the cause of most things wrong with France. A mythomaniac who transmuted his presuppositions into dogmas, it was Maurras 'whose power of argument, of sophistry, of tenacity, served to give an appearance of life to the dead monarchy and who provided a framework of political doctrine' for most right-wing critics of the Third Republic.[45] Explicit reactionary elitism was given populist impetus by nationalism and anti-Semitism, with the temporal power of the Catholic Church—but not the spiritual message of Christianity—providing an institutional counterpart to monarchy. His Provençal background encouraged support for decentralization, while his economic doctrines were derived from La Tour du Pin's corporatism, both consistent with nostalgia for the Old Regime. Violence was necessary to achieve order, so subversion by propaganda provocative of civil war was emphasized. Right-wing students and brawlers were recruited to sell the *Action Française* newspaper and became known as 'the King's Newsvendors', forerunners of the fascist strong-arm squads in Italy and Germany during the interwar years. Symbolic acts of violence, such as slapping Prime Minister Briand at the inauguration of a Jules Ferry statue in 1910, as well as opportunistic support for worker strikes, upset mainstream conservative royalists and led the

---

[44] Quoted in Eugen Weber, *Action Française: Royalism and Reaction in Twentieth Century France*, 1962, 15; cf. 9–14 and Hilaire, 529–33.
[45] Brogan, *Development of Modern France*, 366; cf. 367–8.

Pretender to the throne temporarily to disown his turbulent partisans. Increasingly, the focus was on the leadership of Maurras, not on royalism.[46]

Léon Daudet (son of the celebrated novelist Alphonse) was the *Action Française*'s most effective public speaker and polemicist, 'a more coherent Rochefort, a less solemn Drumont....'[47] The Daudets enabled the organization's newspaper to become a daily in 1908, with the help of a legacy from a Bonapartist ex-courtesan of the Second Empire. However court costs and fines led to chronic financial difficulties, requiring semi-continuous subscription campaigns, the Pretender preferring to subsidize less compromising newspapers like the *Gazette de France*. An attempt to forge an alliance with the 'yellow trade union' strike-breakers led by Pierre Biétry, founder of an ephemeral Socialist National Party, failed in 1908, despite Daudet, like Drumont, playing the anti-Semitic card: 'You give us the king and we'll give you the Jews!'[48] Other attempts to secure worker links through a short-lived alliance with Sorel and former anarcho-syndicalists in the so-called 'Proudhon circle' of 1911–12 and in the early 1920s by Georges Valois, who broke with Maurras in 1925 to form a fascist party, demonstrated the inability to secure mass support for fear of putting off its traditionalist Catholic clientele and business advocates of corporatism.

However, in 1926, more seriously, *Action Française* was banned to Catholics by Pope Pius XI and seven of Maurras' books were placed on the prohibited Index. For a decade it had been regarded as a scandal that a militantly pagan Maurras, using Catholics opportunistically for his political purposes, should be tolerated but when it came, the condemnation prompted leading Catholic intellectuals like Georges Bernanos and Jacques Maritain to defend Maurras. Eleven out of seventeen Cardinals, who were pro-*Action Française*, temporized while the two million strong National Catholic Front vacillated. Despite papal insistence that dissociating political and spiritual authority was unacceptable, the faithful were inclined to follow the Pope's unwelcome instructions in the letter rather than the spirit. Nevertheless there were serious losses for both *Action Française* (which lost nearly half its readers between 1925 and 1928) and Catholic Action because membership of both was incompatible, although priests often gave absolution to members and readers of *Action Française*.[49] *La Croix* could no longer recruit support for Maurras' organization and the fight against liberalism and modernism could not openly be pursued jointly.

In the 1930s, Maurras relied upon his defamatory newspaper articles to further his incendiary views, calling for the extirpation of those who disfigured France. His invective was directed especially at vilifying the Jewish Socialist leader Léon Blum, amounting to incitements to murder. Following a physical attack on Blum in February 1936, the government decreed the dissolution of the *Action Française*

---

[46] Weber, 30, 53–63, 68–70.   [47] Brogan, 369.

[48] Quoted Weber, 71; cf. 44–9, 69–72. The 'yellow unions' acquired their name from 'the yellow strips of paper with which their office at Montceau-les-Mines repaired the windows broken by striking miners' (ibid. 69).

[49] Weber, 219–44. Christian burial was not refused in 1936 to the historian and AF polemicist, Jacques Bainville (ibid. 247; cf. 245.)

organization and its violent 'newsvendors' offshoot but by then they were already in decline. Maurras was himself sentenced to three and then eight months imprisonment for his incitement to murder, which he served in comfort. He continued to publish his slanderous insinuations and vituperations, describing the Blum Popular Front government within a brief article as 'idiots, fanatics, deserters, crooks, pederasts, traitors, prostitutes, and assorted species of the animal kingdom'.[50] When in 1937 the royal Pretender disassociated himself from the authoritarianism and anti-Semitism of *Action Française*, it hurt him more than Maurras, who was now in the futile and paradoxical position of not merely wanting a Catholic Church without Christ but a monarchy without a king. None of these divergences between theory and practice prevented Maurras from being elected to the French Academy in 1938, reflecting the right-wing views of the majority of its membership.[51]

The supreme irony was that when France was defeated in 1940, Maurras not only took refuge in blaming the Jews for the Second World War but accepted subordination to Germany by a Vichy regime that was welcomed as victory for the Counter-Revolution. His doctrines were widely diffused particularly among military officers and especially during the first year of the 'National Revolution' but Vichy was influenced more in its rhetoric than in its practice. However, the fact that the Collège de France, Sciences Po, and the Universities generally removed their Jewish colleagues without demur can in part be attributed to the intellectual anti-Semitism he had remorselessly purveyed. When he wrote in February 1941 of 'the Divine Surprise', Maurras was referring even more to Marshal Pétain's advent than to the fall of the Republic. 'Without it ever being actually said, Pétain took the place of a king, and to Pétain the royalists transferred the loyalty they had heretofore reserved for the Pretender'.[52] Maurras formally rejected both Resistance and Collaboration (fiercely denouncing the former as agents of London and Moscow but soft-pedalling reservations about the Germans), while in practice accepting with resignation Pétain's de facto collaboration. The *Action Française* slogan 'France alone' conveyed the introvert isolation of his standpoint. As Maurras wrote in as late as May 1944, 'if the Anglo-Americans win, this would mean the re-emergence of Masons, Jews, and all the political personnel eliminated in 1940'.[53] Arrested in September 1944 and tried in January 1945 for treason after degradation, Maurras was sentenced to life imprisonment and national degradation, shouting out: 'It is Dreyfus's revenge.'[54] In 1952 he made a deathbed conversion to Catholicism.

Maurras was the ideological mentor of the extremist French Right, exercising a pervasive influence far beyond the cohort of his outright disciples. However, his substitution of publication for action led some to part company with him and

---

[50] Ibid. 374–5; cf. 363–70, 387.   [51] Ibid. 403–9, 412–14.

[52] Ibid. 446; cf. 417, 441–8, 523–4. The Maurras 'divine surprise' article appeared in *Le Petit Marseillais*, 9 February 1941. In 1942, Laval offered the Pretender the post of Food Supply Minister. Pierre Milza, *Fascismes français, passé et présent*, 1987, 228–9.

[53] Quoted Weber, 468; cf. 461–71.

[54] Ibid. 475; cf. 474–6. De Gaulle's pre-war *La Discorde chez l'ennemi* was dedicated to Maurras but their nationalism took very different directions.

embrace fascism. Postponing to Chapter 8 a discussion of Georges Valois's fascist breakaway in 1925 (when we consider Extreme right-wing movements) we mention here its literary manifestations, exemplified in the indiscriminate nihilism of the novelist Drieu La Rochelle's 1934 assertion in *Socialisme fasciste*: 'We are against everyone. We fight everyone. That is what fascism is.'[55] Acknowledging *Action Française* as a forerunner, Drieu's pseudo-socialism and anti-Semitism went beyond nationalism to a fascist internationalism under the leadership of Nazi Germany, culminating in his enthusiastic collaboration after France's defeat and his suicide after Germany's defeat. The internal liberal democratic enemy was more alien to him than the foreign, German enemy. In charge of the influential *Nouvelle Revue Française*, Drieu was one of those—like Jean Cocteau and Jean Giono—who were fascinated by Hitler and were content to see French publishers' lists and bookshops purged of books that gave offence to the Nazis—the so-called 'Otto list'.

Céline's anti-Semitic pamphleteering reflected the same delirious nihilism and vociferous anti-parliamentarianism, asserting in 1937 that he far preferred Hitler to Blum. He conflated anti-Semitism with anglophobia, writing in 1938: 'The City, the secret service, the Jewish royal court of England have been responsible since Cromwell's time for all our failures and all our humiliations in every single sphere'.[56] Céline placed his widely admired literary talents in the service of the most genocidal racism, becoming the advocate of Nazi Germany and collaboration with Hitler before the outbreak of the Second World War. He was too extreme a pro-Nazi for the Vichy regime, fled France in 1945 but returned in 1951 thanks to an amnesty.

Robert Brasillach fared worse, being shot for collaboration in 1945, the court that sentenced him being reminded that as editor of the fascist politico-literary weekly *Je suis partout*, the epitome of intellectual fascism's anti-bourgeois and anti-Semitic proclivities, he had repeatedly called for the execution of his political enemies. The staff of this weekly came from *Action Française* but was even 'more coarse, more gross, more brutal, more aggressive' in the way its views were expounded.[57] After having intellectually worshipped Maurras, the latter broke with him in 1941 over Brasillach's excessively pro-German and Nazi stance.[58] It took several decades before the Extreme Right recovered from its discreditable guilt by association during the Second World War and it was left to others subsequently to pursue some of its 'nonconformist' themes.

---

[55] Quoted in Sternhell, 222. See also Pascal Balmand, 'Anti-intellectualism in French Political Culture' in Jennings, 166–70 and Winock, *Nationalisme*, 347–71 concentrating on Drieu's pro-fascist novel *Gilles*, 1939, about the Spanish Civil War.

[56] Quoted in Robert Gibson, *Best of Enemies*, 262 from *L'Ecole des cadavres*. See also Winock, *Nationalisme*, 377–91.

[57] Weber, 422; cf. 449–52, 508–9 and Milza, *Fascismes français*, 216–19.

[58] Schalk, 81–5, 97–9. Brasillach described the French Republic as 'a syphilitic strumpet, smelling of cheap perfume and vaginal discharge'. Quoted in R. Tucker, *The Fascist Ego: A Political Biography of Robert Brasillach*, 1975, 231. On the more circumspect fascism of Thierry Maulnier, who owed much to Sorel and Maurras, see Sternhell, 229–45, 251–2, 264–5.

COMMITMENT TO CATHOLIC ANTI-LIBERALISM:
ESPRIT AND URIAGE

The context in which the monthly *Esprit* came into existence in the 1930s—one of many 'nonconformist' publications that were started but the only survivor—was one in which bourgeois capitalism and liberal democracy seemed to be discredited and the Catholic Church suffered from guilt by association with what Emmanuel Mounier, *Esprit*'s founder-editor, memorably called the 'established disorder'.[59] He denounced the Church's embourgeoisement. Having lost most of the working class, it represented a reactionary minority whereas, following Péguy, Mounier wanted to associate Catholicism instead with a spiritual and societal revolution. This placed *Esprit* at loggerheads not only with *Action Française*, which attracted right-wing Catholic intellectuals, but also with the Christian Democrats, who since the Papal condemnation in 1910 of Marc Sangnier's *Sillon* and limited attraction of its successors *Jeune République* (from 1912) and *Parti Démocrate Populaire* (from 1924) occupied a Centrist posture. From its position on the Catholic Left, *Esprit* condemned the Christian Democrats as a timid compromise with bourgeois capitalism and parliamentarianism, a condemnation that it extended after the Second World War to their more successful emulators in the *Mouvement Républicain Populaire*. *Esprit*'s affinities were more with the thriving Catholic Action *Jeunesse Etudiante Chrétienne* (formed in 1912), with the *Confédération Française des Travailleurs Chrétiens* (started in 1919), as well as a minority of Catholic intellectuals. It also benefited from the Papal condemnation of *Action Française* in 1926 and the 1931 encyclical *Quadragesimo anno*'s anti-individualism, anti-capitalism, and anti-communism.[60] It was the loyal support of sections of the Roman Catholic subculture that gave *Esprit* greater staying power than its 1930s rivals.

Mounier's *Esprit* rejected both Marxist proletarian materialism and liberal bourgeois materialism, seeking what he called a 'Personalist' third way between Left and Right. He shared the fascist critique of parliamentary democracy and capitalism which he equated with plutocracy, roundly declaring in 1933: 'We hate liberalism, all liberalisms'—calling it the gravedigger of liberty. However, he did so from an explicitly Proudhonian federalist standpoint.[61] He rejected fascism's dictatorial statism, nationalism, colonialism, and anti-Semitism. He directly appealed to Péguy's philosemitism to oppose strongly French and Nazi exploitation of hostility to Jews. However, he refused to align himself with the defenders of democracy against fascism during the 1934 Stavisky riots and only offered critical support to the 1936 Popular Front government. Against predominant Catholic opinion, *Esprit* came out strongly for the Republic against Franco during the Spanish Civil War and condemned the 1938 Munich Agreement as ignominious

---

[59] *Esprit*, special issue March 1933 on 'Rupture de l'ordre chrétien et du désordre établi'. See also Michel Winock, *Histoire politique de la Revue 'Esprit', 1930–1950*, 1975, 30, 71–4, 157.
[60] Winock, *Histoire politique*, 24–5, 29–37.   [61] Ibid. 80. See also Sternhell, 277.

and dishonourable, predicting that it would not preserve peace or stop fascism. It led Mounier to abandon his previous pacifism.[62]

However, in 1940 Mounier was resigned—like most Frenchmen—to the durable defeat of democracy by totalitarianism, because unlike the few who rallied to de Gaulle in London, he regarded their act as desertion. In the belief that he could infiltrate Vichy thanks to some shared themes (anti-individualism, anti-capitalism, and anti-parliamentarianism), Mounier sought and secured the right to publish *Esprit*—under censorship. Separating the new state from the French nation, he neither condemned nor supported the Vichy regime but attempted to remake France along personalist lines by surreptitiously subverting the neo-clerical and reactionary improvizations of the so-called 'National Revolution'. *Esprit* was quickly forbidden to appear in August 1941 and in January 1942 Mounier and others were arrested owing to their Resistance contacts but released after a hunger strike and a period of house arrest owing to lack of evidence.[63] Rather than any active role in the Resistance, it was Mounier's influence on a much more ambiguous enterprise, the 1940–2 leadership training school of Uriage, that merits attention.

The Vichy regime needed both to indoctrinate new leaders with the Pétain-ist ideology to remobilize a people demoralized by defeat and to replace the republican elites, especially Jews and Freemasons, who were purged. 'A number of traditionalist intellectuals had been prophesying the collapse of modern society for decades, in 1940 they seemed to be vindicated by events.'[64] A cultural counter-revolution was attempted, inspired by neo-medieval spiritual values, that sought to inculcate Catholic dogma and respect for hierarchy through physical and doctrinal training. It can be seen as a response to the secular *Ecole Normale Supérieure* and anticipation of the post-war *Ecole Nationale d'Administration* but was an anachronistic reflection of the delusions of the anti-liberal and anti-democratic intellectuals of the 1930s. Apart from Mounier's influence and that of the conservative colonialist Marshal Lyautey, the Catholic military background of several Uriage activists, especially its head Dunoyer de Segonzac, was imparted to the enterprise. The latter had a 'quasi-mystical faith' in Marshal Pétain, whom he saw as a providential figure capable of playing the part of a twentieth-century Joan of Arc. Total and explicit submission to Pétain was required from all, while acceptance of traditional Catholic values was implicit.[65] Poetic expression was given to Catholic equivocation by Paul Claudel who wrote an ode to Marshal Pétain after France's defeat and then one to General de Gaulle after (another?) France's victory. Admittedly, a comparable versatility was shown by the French

---

[62] Winock, *Histoire politique*, 81–9, 95–107, 126–31, 175–7, 194–5. For a different emphasis, assimilating Mounierism to semi-fascism, see Sternhell, XV–XXI, 215–21, 274–81.

[63] Winock, *Histoire politique*, 207–8, 221–2, 235–7. See also Michel Bergès, *Vichy contre Mounier: Les Non-Conformistes face aux années 40*, 1997, 268–72; cf. 68–71 and Sternhell, 288–91.

[64] John Hellman, *The Knight-Monks of Vichy France: Uriage, 1940–45*, 1993, 8; cf. 3–12.

[65] Ibid. 119; cf. 19–21, 45–6, 84. See also Bernard Comte, *Une Utopie Combattante: L'Ecole des cadres d'Uriage, 1940–1942*, 1991, 132, 142–4.

Communist Party which was patriotic until the Nazi–Soviet Pact, defeatist until Hitler attacked Soviet Russia and then vigorously Resistant after 1941.

With a charismatic personality and monarchist views, Dunoyer de Segonzac attracted a galaxy of talented individuals including the future founder-editor of *Le Monde*, Hubert Beuve-Méry, the Jesuit admirer of Proudhon Henri de Lubac, the pro-corporatist economist François Perroux, Joffre Dumazedier who was active in the youth hostel movement, and the personalist philosopher and close associate of Mounier in *Esprit*, Jean Lacroix. Dunoyer de Segonzac was willing to accept 'a certain coordination of efforts' with Germany because 'There is a reciprocity that is built into the situation that we have not been able to avoid'.[66] As such, Uriage secured the support of Georges Lamirand, the Vichy Youth Minister, described as a 'brilliant orator', inclined 'agreeably to string together imprecise abstractions' but when Mounier's involvement was excluded at Vichy insistence and especially after the replacement of Prime Minister Darlan by Laval in 1942, Uriage changed from being loyally Pétainist to becoming militantly anti-German.[67] It was closed despite desperate efforts to secure a reprieve from Pétain and replaced by a fascist institution to train *Milice* leaders in anticipation of civil war, many of them ending up in German uniforms.[68]

Like Dunoyer de Segonzac, whose initial refusal to support de Gaulle led to his frosty reception in Algiers in early 1944, Beuve-Méry refused until late in the day to rush to the aid of a victorious Resistance. He supported Mounier's revival of *Esprit*, 'playing cat and mouse with Vichy censorship at the price of providing it with intellectual respectability'.[69] For 18 months he devoted himself to the role of training some 3,000 potential future national leaders. 'It seemed that for Beuve-Méry the postwar political struggle against a return to pre-war decadence was the highest priority; he thought it folly to have his elites killed to rid the country of the Germans when the Americans could do it. He needed the best and the brightest to transform France in accordance with Uriage ideals—to neutralize the threatened postwar American influence.'[70] This attitude—America as a moral and economic threat, albeit unlike that of Nazi Germany or Soviet Russia, not merely disliked but despised—was to be reflected in the neutralist policy adopted by Beuve-Méry's *Le Monde* after the Second World War. Its significance derived from his influence through a subculture with 'a strong sense of collective identity, an agenda, and extensive connections—particularly in administrative, religious and military circles. He represented the young Catholic intellectual elites who had been excluded during the Third Republic, had experienced a heady renaissance in the interwar period and had been catapulted to central roles under Vichy.'[71] Belatedly rallying to de Gaulle and the Resistance, they were intent on acquiring an insider role in the emerging Fourth Republic, filling a vacuum that pre-war politicians and Communists threatened to occupy.

[66] Quoted in Hellman, 119; cf. 82–4.
[67] Ibid. 170; cf. 36, 142–4, 166–9. Quotations from Bergès, 39–40.   [68] Hellman, 183–9.
[69] Jean-Noël Jeanneney and Jacques Julliard, *Le Monde de Beuve-Méry ou le métier d'Alceste*, 1979, 30–7.
[70] Hellman, 212.   [71] Ibid. 227; cf. 214.

Esprit was quickly revived after the war and rapidly increased its circulation. It was now much more political in content because while remaining committed to Péguy, it sought not just to deplore the degeneration of *mystique* into *politique* but to promote a new politics. However, this involved a rapprochement with the French Communist Party as part of a wider reconciliation of Christians with the working class and of intellectuals with a humanist Marxism. The PCF represented the heroic 'party of the proletariat', an ally in the purge of the old bourgeois elites and the replacement of what Mounier called 'a parliamentary democracy of the liberal and talkative type'.[72] While adopting a non-aligned attitude to the East–West cold war split, *Esprit* was especially fearful of American financial, military, and political domination, rejecting Atlanticist integration in NATO and supporting the fellow-travelling peace movements manipulated by the PCF.[73] *Esprit* was an early opponent of French colonialism, strongly opposing the Vietnam war. From 1947 it launched a series of articles under the heading 'Avoiding a war in North Africa' and denying that Algeria was part of France. We postpone until later in this chapter and Chapter 10 a discussion of French colonial policy but although *Esprit* sought to promote an egalitarian French Union, it courageously warned that failure to implement its ideals would lead to its disintegration.[74]

Beuve-Méry was able to impart Uriage values through the daily press just as Mounier's *Esprit* did in the monthly press. Before the Second World War, Beuve-Méry had been the Prague correspondent of *Le Temps* but resigned in protest against its censorship of his anti-Munich Agreement articles. He had warned the Czech President that France would leave his country in the lurch but was not believed. After serving in the army, he was responsible for the Uriage educational programme. When de Gaulle's Liberation government sought a replacement for *Le Temps*, which was expropriated for having continued publication for too long after the 1942 German takeover of the whole of France, Beuve-Méry was chosen as someone capable of editing a serious newspaper and expounding the government's foreign policy as its predecessor had done. He made clear to the MRP Information Minister who appointed him, that despite his Catholic predisposition, he would be independent of his and all other political parties. (In the event, Beuve-Méry only explicitly supported de Gaulle in 1944–5 and 1958 and Mendès France in 1954.)

While *Le Monde* inherited the appearance and a nucleus of journalists and readers from *Le Temps*, it was no longer the 'unofficial spokesman of the Quai d'Orsay'.[75] On the contrary, Beuve-Méry was opposed both to American capitalism and Russian totalitarianism, as well as campaigning against NATO in 1949–51 in favour of armed neutrality and hostility to German rearmament unless integrated into European defence. Nevertheless, *Le Monde* quickly doubled and then tripled the circulation achieved by the *Temps* and became the reliable newspaper of reference for the political class and intellectuals rather than of the business bourgeoisie. The latter attempted to promote rivals after failing in 1951 to buy out

---

[72] Winock, *Histoire politique*, 258; cf. 249–61, 290–4.   [73] Ibid. 272–3, 277–86.
[74] Ibid. 319–33.   [75] Jeanneney and Julliard, 80–1; cf. 48–58.

Beuve-Méry, prompting his wife to congratulate him on being worth his weight in gold. Right-wing leaders, like Antoine Pinay, were able to mobilize financial support for the ephemeral *Le Temps de Paris* in 1956 but despite its anti-Communist and pro-*Algérie Française* line, it failed to win readers. While *Le Monde*'s opposition to American hegemony was acceptable, its opposition to the Algerian War was to lead de Gaulle, on his 1958 return to power to say to Beuve-Méry: 'without me ... you would be hung.'[76]

THE LIBERAL COUNTER-ATTACK

Unlike *Le Temps*, the *Figaro* was allowed to reappear after the Second World War and it was in its columns that the liberal academic and journalist Raymond Aron took a different standpoint to Beuve-Méry on the cold war but a similar one on Algeria, albeit justified on expediential rather than moralistic grounds. Aron, as a quintessentially conspicuous public intellectual, was the most articulate and effective exponent of a liberalism that had been the focus of so much abuse from Left and Right. This partly explains his thirty-year choice of *Le Figaro* in preference to *Le Monde* as the outlet for his views; in addition, during the Fourth Republic the former was the journal of Establishment reference whereas the latter, as the mouthpiece of oppositional Left intellectuals, had little impact on government policy.[77] So, although it was more conservative than liberal, the *Figaro* commended itself to Aron's wish to exert political influence, although prior to the Second World War Aron had been a liberal socialist. In terms of his intellectual mentors, the later influence of Montesquieu and Tocqueville was anticipated by the Anglophile historian Elie Halévy, whose *Era of Tyrannies* condemned both fascism and communism as totalitarian and subjected Marxism to a liberal critique. So despite Aron's intellectual debt to Karl Marx and Max Weber, he asserted: 'My conclusions belong to the English school but I was formed above all by that of Germany.'[78]

During the Second World War, Aron was the de facto editor of *La France Libre* in London, which prepared him for his subsequent activity in journalism when he interrupted his academic career for ten years. A 1930s friend, André Malraux, appointed him director of his personal staff in the last two months of de Gaulle's 1945 government and after a happy year in 1946–7 writing for Albert Camus's *Combat*, he left for the *Figaro* as the cold war came to dominate international affairs and domestic politics. Much less active in the RPF than Malraux, who managed de Gaulle's provincial tours and rallies between 1948 and 1950, this stance still led to a break with his friend from the ENS, Sartre.

[76] Quoted ibid. 212; cf. 85–102, 169–98.   [77] Raymond Aron, *Mémoires*, 1983, 2.
[78] Quoted in Robert Colquhoun, *Raymond Aron*, II, 1986, 209; cf. 391 and I, 186–200. Aron called his 1944 collection of wartime essays *L'homme contre les tyrans*.

Although they had founded *Les Temps Modernes* together, Aron quickly left its editorial board in 1946 as their differences became evident, choosing opposite sides in the USA/USSR schism. The dissension was also philosophical, Aron having a better grasp of both the incompatible doctrines of Marxism and Existentialism before Sartre embraced and sought to combine them. Aron was steadfastly anti-Nazi during the 1930s and the Second World War, and anti-Stalinist thereafter. For his pains, Sartre attacked him as a pro-American warmonger, although Aron was circumspectly inclined to agree with Arthur Koestler: 'We are defending a half-truth against a total lie.' Never having himself shirked political commitment, Sartre's conception of revolution was castigated by Aron as rhetorical, romantic, and demagogic, while Sartre's fluctuating tactical flirtations with communism led Aron to assert that 'existentialism, while invoking commitment, seldom succeeds in committing itself' ... and that Sartre was 'a moralist lost in the jungle of politics.'[79]

Aron was a founder member in 1950 of the Congress of Cultural Freedom and for the next twenty years a leading contributor to its periodical *Preuves* and its British counterpart *Encounter*. Launched in 1951, *Preuves* was partly intended to counteract *Les Temps Modernes* but was from the start attacked not just by the fellow-travellers and Communists but also by *Esprit* and *Le Monde* as the mouthpiece of American capitalism and imperialism. When it was revealed that *Preuves* had been surreptitiously financed by the US Central Intelligence Agency, Aron remained convinced that he had fought the intellectually good fight. However, his main bombshell in the cold war was his 1955 *The Opium of the Intellectuals*. In his 1949 rebuttal of a work of Sartre's, Aron had already declared that the revolution being advocated was 'no more than the opium of the intellectuals'.[80] Dismissing as retrospective myths the concepts of Left, proletariat and revolution, Aron now woundingly wrote that French intellectuals 'have no wish to think seriously about the world or to change it; they merely wish to denounce it.' 'To the intellectual who turns to politics for the sake of diversion, or for a cause to believe in or a theme for speculation, reform is boring and revolution exciting ... the Frenchman is quintessentially the revolutionary in theory and the conservative in practice.'[81] By concluding his book with a section headed 'End of the Ideological Age?', Aron inadvertently prompted Daniel Bell and others to generalize an issue that had been posed by him interrogatively and only in relation to Marxism-Leninism. Aron was content to declare ironically: 'If the rest of the world were as sensible as Great Britain, the great debate would collapse from sheer boredom. Luckily, American senators, French intellectuals and soviet commissars will provide inexhaustible opportunities for dispute'.[82]

---

[79] Quoted in Colquhoun, I, 353; cf. 350–60, 407, 492 note, II, 343 and Aron, *Mémoires*, 715; cf. 720.

[80] Quoted in Colquhoun, I, 360. More generally, see Pierre Grémion, *Preuves: Une Revue Européenne à Paris*, 1989 and Pierre Grémion, *L'Intelligence de l'Anticommunisme: Le Congrès pour la liberté de la culture à Paris 1950–1975*, 1995. See also Drake, 88–91.

[81] Quoted in Colquhoun, I, 456, 462; cf. 458–9.

[82] Quoted in Colquhoun, I, 475; cf. Aron, *Mémoires*, 410–12.

In 1955, without giving up his journalism, Aron was appointed Professor of Sociology at the Sorbonne but he had already resigned his Chair in 1967, before mass education transformed it in 1968, although he was elected to a Chair at the Collège de France in 1970. In *The Elusive Revolution*, Aron expressed his indignation at the 'collective madness' or 'psychodrama' that a spasm of libertarian irrationality had provoked, leading temporarily to an 'abrupt disintegration of French society'.[83] It was a spectacular example of a familiar phenomenon: 'At heart deeply conservative, from time to time the French surrender to the illusion of completely changing the world at a stroke.'[84]

Having upset the Left by his reformist rejection of educational revolution, Aron aroused intense hostility on the Right by advocating Algerian independence when even *Le Monde*, *L'Express*, and *Esprit* were confining themselves to condemning repression and torture. Prevented from expressing these views in the *Figaro*, in 1957 Aron published *The Algerian Tragedy*, not wishing to repeat his previous mistake of remaining silent rather than calling for a French withdrawal from Indo-China. Attacked by the whole press (apart from *Le Monde*) which was aware of the truth but dared not print it, Aron quoted Montesquieu: 'Every citizen is obliged to die for his country; no one is obliged to lie for it.'[85] Avoiding moralistic criticisms, Aron, appreciating that 'the important thing was to convince the colonialists, not the anti-colonialists', emphasized that the war would not succeed and was not indispensable to French economic prosperity.[86] France's future was in Europe, not Algeria and because only a strong government could face the humiliation of conceding independence, Aron praised de Gaulle for what he called the 'heroism of abandonment'.[87]

The Fourth Republic had been discredited by its unsteady procession of weak governments and as Aron put it, 'Eventually, a country cannot obey those for whom it has contempt.'[88] Although he had supported de Gaulle's RPF, Aron was never a Gaullist without reservations and he argued after the 1958 installation of the Fifth Republic that 'the more the General insisted on the personal character of his legitimacy, the more he weakened the constitutional edifice he had himself established.'[89] In 1977, Aron parted company with the *Figaro*, after its new owner, the right-wing politician Robert Hersant and controller of an expanding press empire, intervened increasingly in editorial policy. Aron turned instead to the weekly *L'Express*.

Sartre and Aron personified the cold war schism between politically committed intellectuals but whereas Aron was isolated and ostracized between 1945 and 1975 when Sartre was the dominant figure, thereafter it was Aron's turn to exemplify the prevailing climate of opinion. By Sartre's death in 1980, liberalism was making a comeback and although it owed more to Thatcher and Reagan than Aron, it was no longer popular in intellectual circles to declare that it was 'better to be

[83] Quoted in Colquhoun, II, 335–7; cf. 4–6, 328–33, 339–42.
[84] Quoted in Colquhoun, II, 401.
[85] Aron, *Mémoires*, 366; cf. 360–79 and Colquhoun, II, 41–9.   [86] Colquhoun, II, 53.
[87] Aron, *Mémoires*, 386.   [88] Ibid. 381.   [89] Colquhoun, II, 70; cf. 72.

wrong with Sartre than right with Aron'.[90] In the years following his own death in 1983, Aron was belatedly recognized for his towering intellectual presence, reflected during his lifetime in a stream of influential books. In contrast with the many passionate partisan intellectuals and the dispassionate non-partisans, Aron was a dispassionate partisan in his demystification of the communist utopia. Events ensured that he has been retrospectively rehabilitated. He was a liberal rationalist, disenchanted with his century. His writings were characterized by their argumentative, anti-utopian appraisal of its illusions, mendacities, and brutalities. His legacy was in part perpetuated in the Institute named after him, headed initially by his protagonist the revisionist historian of the French Revolution François Furet, although there has been subsequent dissension leading to Pierre Rosanvallon's resignation as Director.

DECOLONIZATION AND THE INTELLECTUALS

Because French intellectuals have been more influential as opinion leaders with policymakers than their counterparts in other European countries, it is worth considering why, despite the violation of humanist ideals entailed by the efforts to preserve the French Empire in the mid-twentieth century, so many of them were reluctant to advocate decolonization. It was only belatedly that even liberal intellectuals acknowledged that far from extending human rights, these were being denied in France's colonies. Left-wing intellectuals were slow to recognize that colonial subjects were being exploited more brutally than the French proletariat and were more alienated because of the spurious substitution of their cultural identity by the imposition of a self-proclaimed superior foreign culture, albeit one that purported to have universal application.

In Chapter 10 we consider the post-Second World War replacement of the Empire by the French Union but our immediate concern is to explain why, despite its manifest failure, many intellectuals argued that colonial independence was not necessary because injustices were incidental not congenital, would be disastrous for the immature colonial peoples themselves and destructive of France's determination to retrieve her status as a world power. Risk falling under the domination of either Communist or Capitalist imperialisms, the colonized would be better advised to remain under a benevolent French wing. So in practice, it was easy for French intellectuals for all practical purposes to support a perpetuation of French imperialism rather than call for independence for the colonies.[91] Because the celebrated writers discussed also actively engaged in journalism, we shall also consider the specific impact of journalists in reorienting a public opinion that had imbibed under the Third Republic a belief in France's colonial vocation.

---

[90] Colquhoun, II, 577; cf. Aron, *Mémoires*, 720–1. More generally, see Jean-François Sirinelli, *Deux intellectuels dans le siècle, Sartre et Aron*, 1995.

[91] Paul Clay Sorum, *Intellectuals and Decolonization in France*, 1977, xiii, 67–8, 79, 83–4, 211–12.

It was Catholic moralists, whose views were reflected in *Esprit* and the weekly *Témoignage Chrétien* (to a lesser extent in the daily *Le Monde*), but whose most influential embodiment was François Mauriac because of his celebrity as a novelist, who in the 1950s increasingly criticized the betrayal of French values. They did so first in Indo-China, later in North Africa and in Algeria in particular, where the French army responded to terrorism with counter-terrorism and torture. Mauriac left the pro-colonialist *Figaro* in 1954 to publish a regular column in the weekly *L'Express* (whose editor Jean-Jacques Servan-Schreiber we discuss later) where he could expound his vehement views without restraint. Together with some Catholic intellectuals who, in January 1957, had founded a Committee for Spiritual Resistance, and others, he signed an open letter to the President of the Republic, printed in *Le Monde* on 22 March 1957, attacking methods of 'pacification' that had been defined as war crimes after the Second World War. Just before the fall of the Fourth Republic in 1958, Mauriac—together with Malraux and Sartre—signed a petition to the President of the Republic on the seizure of *The Question*, a book on torture in Algeria, calling in the name of the Declaration of the Rights of Man for an unequivocal condemnation of 'the use of torture, which brings shame to the causes that it supposedly serves'.[92] However, Mauriac became resigned to torture after de Gaulle's return to power as he alone could end the war on acceptable terms, without conceding power to the FLN Algerian rebels, which nevertheless proved unavoidable in 1962.

Camus also opposed torture but was unwilling to accept independence as the only way of ending the means being used to avoid it. He condemned the inhuman methods utilized by both sides as vitiating the ends they sought to serve. However, born in Algeria of settler stock, he was unable to abandon the million settlers to the political domination of terrorists. In response to a reproach by Moslem Algerian students for his defence of the rights of French Algerians, during a visit to Sweden to receive his Nobel Prize for literature, Camus—who had shifted from defending a pluralist autonomy to that of integration—made clear that he could not sacrifice his compatriots for the sake of his principles when faced with the agonizing choice. 'I have always condemned terror. I must also condemn a terrorism... that may one day strike my mother or my family. I believe in justice, but I will defend my mother before justice.'[93]

Sartre did not feel any need to confront Camus' dilemma. Sartre only became fully involved in the attack on colonialism in the mid-1950s, his analysis being dictated by his conflation of Marxism with Existentialism. While unoriginal and doctrinaire, his standpoint had the merit of simplicity: the only way of ending the atrocities necessitated by the protection of the colonial system was to abolish it comprehensively. Rebel terrorism was a legitimate response to systemic colonial violence and justified as necessary to stop it. This was taking the apology for revolutionary violence well beyond Sorel to that of Frantz Fanon, whose *The Wretched of the Earth* Sartre fulsomely prefaced in 1961, according to which all

---

[92] Quoted ibid. 120; cf. 51–4, 128, 165. [93] Quoted ibid. 137; cf. 61–4, 123, 130–1, 138–42.

the French were guilty and were fair targets for the regenerative violence of the oppressed.

As well as condemning the Camus standpoint as reactionary idealism, Sartre supported the anti-colonial activism of a former managing editor of his journal *Les Temps Modernes,* who decided that words were not enough. Francis Jeanson, a philosophy teacher, agreed in 1956 to help the FLN rebels in France and by 1960 was coordinating the activities of his antiwar movement with *Jeune Résistance,* an organization of those who had evaded call-up or had deserted. Sartre and Jeanson shared the view that supporting the FLN, with whom the aim of defeating impending French fascism was combined with seeking socialism (ignoring the FLN's primary commitment to nationalism) would provide 'the "shock therapy" necessary to awaken the Left.'[94] In September 1960, when some 20 members of the Jeanson movement were put on trial for treason, a Declaration of the Right of Callup Evasion in the Algerian War 'Manifesto of the 121' (to which 124 names were later added) was published, its signatories including André Breton as well as Sartre. (Between 1958 and 62, there were 67 manifestos prompted by the Algerian War, the 'Manifesto of the 121' in particular radicalizing the student leftism of the 1960s, culminating in 1968.)[95] Jeanson and his supporters did little to end the Algerian War—not their prime objective—and unlike the Extreme Right did not succeed in using it to cause the downfall of the Fourth Republic. By 1969, firebrand Jeanson had accepted appointment as head of the Chalon-sur-Saône culture and arts centre.

Raymond Aron changed his position from being pro-Empire in 1945 but from the start his realist views led him to give preference to economic modernization over retaining the colonies should they prove incompatible. By the early 1950s he had come around to the view that in Indo-China France was fighting a losing battle to prop up a regime without popular support. Britain had shown how the retreat from Empire could be profitable whereas France desperately clung on to its overseas sovereignty. He decided to make up for his discretion over Indo-China by sending the Socialist Prime Minister Mollet in 1956 a warning against pursuing a repressive Algerian policy, which he expanded in 1957 into *The Algerian Tragedy* 'which in terms of its impact both on government circles and on public opinion, was probably the single most influential writing on the Algerian problem.'[96] Not suffering from guilt by association with the Left and respected by conservative opinion thanks to his long association with the *Figaro,* he dispassionately demolished the case for resisting Algerian independence. Instead of squandering its resources on the war, which would be better employed in making the French economy capable of competing in the European Community, or in trying to solve Algeria's underdevelopment problem, despite the discovery of Saharan gas and oil, France should give up a guerrilla war it could not win without recourse to

---

[94] Paul Clay Sorum, 1977, xiii, 169; cf. 88–90, 127, 134–6, 143–5, 156–9, 166–78, 244. See also Sartre's Preface to Frantz Fanon, *The Wretched of the Earth,* 1961, 1967 English edn, 7–26. Sartre's 1960 play *Les Séquestrés d'Altona* had torture as a salient theme.

[95] Ory and Sirinelli, 205; cf. 196–208.   [96] Sorum, 197; cf. 183–5, 195–6.

an unacceptable total repression. Better to repatriate the French Algerians rather than persist in a policy that was historically condemned to fail. Although Aron was bitterly attacked at the time for his views, de Gaulle was to carry them into effect five years later.[97]

Two prominent non-Communist left-wing journalists can be picked out to illustrate how reformist intellectual anti-colonialism stopped short of outright anti-imperialism because of reluctance to accept the desirability and need for giving colonies their independence. Claude Bourdet, former Resistance leader, editor of the wartime *Combat* until captured in 1944, as editor of the daily *Combat* in succession to Camus from 1947 to 1950 and thereafter the founder-editor of the weekly *Observateur* (from 1954 *France-Observateur*) advocated a neutralist foreign policy and 'became the most vociferous of the critics of France's overseas policies'.[98] Having attacked cold-blooded torture in Algeria in 1951 and again in 1955—'Your Gestapo in Algeria'—he dubbed it 'the bestial crime above all others', repeatedly warning of approaching fascism.[99] However, he refused to support Jeanson and Sartre in approving desertion and aiding the enemy. Nevertheless, between 1954 and 1961, sixteen issues of *France-Observateur* and twenty-one issues of *L'Express* were confiscated to intimidate journalists by damaging these weeklies financially.[100]

The more moderate *L'Express* was founded in 1953 by Jean-Jacques Servan-Schreiber to promote the campaign of Pierre Mendès France to end the Indo-China war and modernize the French economy. Although he succeeded in rapidly making peace in Indo-China and increasing autonomy in Tunisia, ironically the Algerian revolt broke out on 1 November 1954 when Mendès France was Prime Minister and he declared that he would not accept secession from France of which it was an integral part. When he resigned from the Mollet government in May 1956, he did so because he then advocated giving Algeria independence. Servan-Schreiber, a former Free French fighter pilot like Mendès France, supported the effort to preserve a French Algeria and served there as a reserve officer. His best-selling book *Lieutenant in Algeria*, critical of the ineffectiveness of the 'pacification' campaign, was serialized in *L'Express* from March 1957. It caused an uproar and his indictment for demoralizing the army. General Paris de Bollardière, one of the few officers who rallied in 1940 to de Gaulle in London, under whom Servan-Schreiber had served in Algeria, resigned from his command and sent a letter of support for his book. Bollardière was adjudged guilty of insubordination and sentenced to sixty days in military confinement.

Although opposed to de Gaulle's return to power in 1958, Servan-Schreiber's *L'Express* favoured encouraging French soldiers to disobey illegal orders. This proved prescient when in April 1961 the four generals' seizure of power in Algeria failed because the conscript army refused to follow them, enabling de Gaulle to

---

[97] Ibid. 197–201, 204, 207–8.   [98] Ibid. 17; cf. 51, 65, 179–81.
[99] Ibid. 122; cf. 113,121, 148–9.
[100] Ibid. 147. See also Claude Estier, *La Gauche hebdomadaire, 1914–1962*, 1962, especially Chapter 6.

recover control.[101] After peace was made, Servan-Schreiber turned his attention first to promoting the presidential candidature of Gaston Defferre in 1963–4 and then to *The American Challenge*, a call to industrial arms against the satellization of European firms by American-controlled multinational corporations.[102] The end of decolonization meant that intellectual commitment was directed at new adversaries but we need to remember that there was a rival view, that the intellectual should concentrate on reaffirming timeless truths without being distracted by impassioned ideological controversy.

THE CASE AGAINST COMMITMENT

In 1927, a book appeared that caused an intellectual sensation by the polemical vehemence with which it attacked the subordination of the detached pursuit of truth to political passion by French writers, particularly those of a right-wing disposition. *La Trahison des Clercs* championed intransigent commitment to eternal, universal, abstract, rationalist principles, which Julien Benda claimed had been the standpoint of secular clerics since Socrates. While Benda had been an active Dreyfusard, he maintained that this was in defence of a universal principle of justice. He especially castigated writers like Barrès who had preached the superiority of the army and the sword over the intellectual and the academic gown. More generally, he pilloried old Dreyfusard friends like Péguy and Sorel, along with Barrès and Maurras, who in the wake of Nietzsche gave pride of place to courage and action over contemplative thought. Failure to defend absolute values by the intellectual elite was what constituted their betrayal, whether in support of collective interests like nationalism or to satisfy personal ambitions to achieve notoriety by pandering to public emotions.[103]

However, Benda's own ideological values were evident in his concern to deplore the attacks on liberalism, which we have seen was then particularly out of favour. He accepted that writers he admired like Voltaire and Hugo had achieved popularity in no small part thanks to their adopting a conspicuous political stance.

---

[101] Sorum, 105, 115–17, 150, 160, 165–6, 175, 189–90. See also Estier, 185–201.

[102] Jean-Jacques Servan-Schreiber, *The American Challenge*, 1967, 1969 English edn. On Servan-Schreiber's role in the Defferre campaign, having invented the mysterious 'Mr. X', see Georges Suffert, *De Defferre à Mitterrand: La Campagne Présidentielle*, 1966, 27, 33, 36, 63–8.

[103] Julien Benda, *La Trahison des Clercs*, 1927, 1965, 88–92, 112–15, 124–5, 137–49. Benda probably borrowed the notion of *Clerc* as an intellectual secular priest from Sorel's disciple Edouard Berth, used in his 1914 diatribe *Le Méfaits des intellectuels*. See Ray Nicols, *Treason, Tradition and the Intellectual: Julien Benda and Political Discourse*, 1978, 55; cf. 73–4 and Chapters 6 and 8 passim. More generally, see Robert J. Niess, *Julien Benda*, 1956 and Stephan Collini, *Absent Minds*, 279–87; cf. 25. A *clerc* is for Benda a secular cleric. For a convincing explanation of the enduring importance of French intellectuals in contrast to the situation in Britain and the USA in terms of the weakness of its universities, importance of the radical Left, hostility to liberalism and globalization, its anti-multiculturalist republican political culture, see Jeremy Jennings, 'Deaths of the Intellectual: a comparative autopsy' in Helen Small (ed.), *The Public Intellectual*, 2002, 123–8.

(In France, being an intellectual is almost synonymous with political commitment). Although he criticized the pacifism of a Romain Rolland for simply reversing Barrès's 'my country right even when wrong' into 'my country wrong even when right', Benda concentrated his fire mainly on the Right. While rejecting Nizan's total commitment to the Communist Party, in the 1930s context of fascist menace Benda justified his fellow-travelling signature of manifestos as a defence of eternal principles. After leading a precarious existence as a Jew during the German occupation of France, he justified the 1945 execution of Brasillach as exemplary punishment for an intellectual who had betrayed his clerical function even more than his country.[104] The artificial dichotomy between intellectual integrity and political commitment proved untenable. More than a Mounier, Benda was prepared to support, post-WWII many of the activities of the Communist Party, even though he preserved an intellectual distance from their doctrines, subordinating the single-minded pursuit of truth come what may to support for the masses and their political representatives.[105]

The contrast between the polarized political culture and the aspiration to intellectual universalism we have traced has been reflected in the tension between the rival temptations of indulging in an uninhibited partisan militancy and a fastidious preservation of personal integrity. The pull of commitment had been far greater than that of detachment when Catholicism and Communism in particular could command militant conviction. With the cooling of ideological controversy and the decreasingly divisive nature of French society, it has been less necessary to mobilize cultural support for political purposes. Whereas in the context of the cold war political culture, Sartre and Camus had shifted the emphasis in the theatre from the aesthetic to the politico-metaphysical, by the time Americanized mass culture made its impact, notably in the cinema and pop music, it proved more pervasive and enduring than an elitist Left's attempt to promote a counter-culture. However, before this state of relative calm and consensus was achieved in the late twentieth century, much turbulence had to be traversed.

Despite the congenital antagonism of Roman Catholicism and liberal secularism, a live and let live compromise had emerged by the end of the twentieth century in a religiously divided but reconciled society. Anticlericals no longer sought to impose secularism in the name of liberal neutrality, while the Catholics no longer sought to impose their religious dogma and justified their church schools on the grounds of the liberal right to freedom, albeit as an institutionalized rather than individual right. In 'a residually Christian society' in which the supernatural was no longer regarded as either natural or commonsensical, the French were content to settle for a 'regulated secularism'.[106] This does not mean that abortion, contraception, and euthanasia have ceased to be controversial but the liberal direction taken by French legislation is unmistakable. Despite the cultural

---

[104] Schalk, 45; cf. 33–43.

[105] Tony Judt, *Past Imperfect*, 50–1. See also Niess, *Julien Benda*, 192–6 and Rod Kedward, *La Vie en Bleu: France and the French since 1900*, 2005, 201–2, 364.

[106] Emile Poulat, *Liberté, Laicité: La guerre des deux France et le principe de la modernité*, 1987, 432; cf. 232–5.

shift that this has implied, it does not go as far as accepting multiculturalism as the Muslim headscarves controversy (in which intellectuals took an active part) was to demonstrate from 1989. However, the slow motion cultural revolution, with spasms of acceleration and retreat, has continued the long process of secularization in France without going to Anglo-American pluralist and permissive lengths. The fallout from post-Communism was more sudden if no less diffuse. After the ephemeral 1968 explosion of leftist ideologies and the recoil from the Soviet Union and Marxism-Leninism from the mid-1970s, many intellectuals abandoned political commitment, while others swung to the Right or settled for supporting a revived Socialist Party. French intellectuals were disinclined to follow George Orwell's stern 1948 advice that 'we should draw a sharper distinction than we do at present between our political and our literary loyalties.... When a writer engages in politics he should do so as a citizen, as a human being, but not *as a writer* .... Whatever else he does in the service of his party, he should never write for it.'[107] Such separation was foreign to French culture. However, Benda's 1927 call to avoid partisanship in favour of apolitical causes as well as absolute and universal values has been revived by Alain Finkielkraut in his 1987 *The Undoing of Thought*.[108] Nevertheless, France remained bitterly fragmented, despite despairing and defeatist calls to unity and identity. Furthermore, although the Left/Right dichotomy persisted, there were many Lefts and Rights, especially among committed intellectuals and in the fringe groups, which we explore in Chapters 8 and 9.

[107] George Orwell, 'Writers and Leviathan', an essay included in his *England: Your England*. See also Jeremy Jennings, '1898–1998: From Zola's "J'accuse" to the Death of the Intellectual' in *The European Legacy*, V, December 2000, 829–44.

[108] Alain Finkielkraut, *The Undoing of Thought*, 1987, 1988, Eng. edn. See also Christophe Prochasson, 'Intellectuals as Actors: Image and Reality' in Jennings (ed.) *Intellectuals in Twentieth Century France*, 67–8.

8

Adversaries: Polarized and Fragmented Party Politics of the Right

The normative emphasis on national unity has been the political counterpart of the 'refusal of the French to make friends when they could so easily make enemies'.[1] However, partisanship was not accompanied by loyalty to organized and disciplined political parties. When they were belatedly established, they were wracked by internecine tensions and schisms, often prompted by personality conflicts of ambition disguised as ideological dissensions. This was due fundamentally to the fact that in a conflict-ridden society craving unity, reluctance to accept the legitimacy of partisan divergence reduced their capacity to maintain effective organizations.

WEAK, FRACTIONALIZED, AND EVANESCENT PARTIES

Before considering the role of parties from the Third Republic, a retrospective glance is in order to place it in perspective. As we saw in Chapter 3, the Left/Right 'simplifying symbolism' originated in the French revolutionary representative assembly of the nation but such bipolarizations did not take hold as there was determined parliamentary resistance to acknowledging such a divisive duality.[2] The seating arrangements allowed shades of political opinion across the semicircular spectrum from the reactionary Right to the radical Left to be physically manifest in the Restoration Chamber. Governments drew their support from the Centre, which alone supported both the dynasty and the Charter, whereas the Ultra-Right was only loyal to the former and the Liberal Left to the latter. Political reality was a three-way split, complicated by shifting Right-Centre and Left-Centre alliances as political expediency dictated. So the scene was set for a multipolarized parliamentary-centred party system, whose unreliable support for government had to be secured by corruption and gerrymandering, practices that continued into the post-1848 era of manhood suffrage.

Restricting the suffrage to those deemed to have the rational capacity to vote, quite apart from itself being incapable of convincing definition, facilitated rather than prevented corrupt electoral practices and did not expand the numbers

[1] Brogan, 144.   [2] Gauchet, 'La Droite et la Gauche' in *Les lieux de mémoire*, III/I, 396, 402.

qualified to vote sufficiently quickly to provide support for too narrowly oligarchical a regime. The 1840s campaign against voting as the exclusive privilege of a few culminated in the 1848 Revolution's return to the manhood suffrage of the First Republic: direct elections, eligibility to vote at 21 and be elected from 25 but with a list system of voting, usually with 8 to 15 names. On 19 March 1848, Lamartine as head of the Provisional Government effusively declared that thanks to the inclusive nature of the election, 'there are no more proletarians in France'.[3] June 1848 class warfare was quickly to prove the contrary but the imprecision of political labels, despite symbolic identifiers like White versus Red or reactionaries-cum-moderates and radicals-cum-socialists, and the confusing diversity of lists prepared by newspapers or newly founded clubs for those unaccustomed to vote, meant that election to the Constituent Assembly was a hazardous exercise in democracy. The utopian celebration of a political pseudo-communion represented an anti-liberal aspiration that denied party competition *à l'anglaise* as both impracticable and undesirable.[4] It quickly ended in a Bonapartist presidency and imperial dictatorship based upon a name recognition that trumped the hopes of both monarchists and republicans. Personality carried the day with the disoriented, newly enfranchized public in the absence of organized political parties.

Recognizing their error belatedly, the 'social democrats' in 1849 selected candidates through departmental electoral committees, relying on the press, brochures, and songs to spread their propaganda, while the so-called 'party of order' distributed over half a million brochures, especially Thiers' *De la Propriété* attack on Proudhon.[5] Despite the rise in abstentions, the social democrats made gains in 1849–50, leading the Right in May 1851 to reduce the electorate by a third (essentially of workers, 57 per cent in the Paris area, 70 per cent in Lille, and 80 per cent in Roubaix). Louis Bonaparte prepared the ground for his December *coup d'état* by proposing restoration of manhood suffrage in November 1851, which was narrowly defeated.[6] Its restoration was combined, as we have seen, with administratively managed elections during the Second Empire, which taught the lesson that mobilizing the rural mass vote was an effective way of submerging would-be urban revolutionaries. However, notably at the local level and nationally in the 1860s, taking advantage of liberalization, an apprenticeship in democratic citizenship allowed new leaders, such as Léon Gambetta and Jules Ferry to emerge, who would lay the political foundations of the politics of the Third Republic. It was a wily liberal of the July Monarchy era, Duvergier de Hauranne, who in 1868 asserted that far from usurping the popular will and fomenting division, 'The only way of ensuring peace within a democratic society is to allow and promote as much as possible the formation of large political parties.'[7] His wise advice was not followed until the twentieth century.

---

[3] Rosanvallon, *Le sacre du citoyen*, 376; cf. 342–52, 373–9. See also Raymond Huard, *Le suffrage universel en France, 1848–1946*, 1991, 24–37.

[4] Rosanvallon, *Le sacre du citoyen*, 379–86.   [5] Huard, 46–8.   [6] Ibid. 51–9.

[7] Quoted ibid. 99 from 'La Démocratie et le droit de suffrage' in *Revue des Deux Mondes*, April 1868, 798; cf. 608–43, 785–821. More generally, see Sudhir Hazareesingh, *From Subject to Citizen: The Second Empire and the Emergence of Modern French Democracy*, 1998, especially the Conclusion.

After prolonged debates from 1870 to 1875, the Right resigned itself to manhood suffrage but gerrymandered the constituencies in favour of the rural areas for the Chamber of Deputies and ensured an even greater rural predominance in the Senate's composition. Gambetta and Ferry emphasized the reassuringly conservative character of the Third Republic they were seeking to establish. As Gambetta rhetorically declared in October 1877, democracy is 'a means peacefully to end all conflicts, resolve all crises and if universal suffrage functions in its full sovereignty, *no revolution is possible any longer* because there is no need to attempt a revolution, no *coup d'état* to fear, when France has spoken.'[8] Gambetta's assumption that enlightened party leadership, recruited by educational meritocracy, would overcome the handicap of a people ill-fitted to discharge their democratic responsibilities, meant that the task of popular education was urgent.

However, whereas in Britain extending the suffrage was channelled into a well-established party system, in France a mass electorate was confronted by shifting parliamentary groups that substituted their tactical intrigues for the preoccupations of their voters. The link between elections and the formation and survival of governments constituted by strong parties did not exist. Frequent changes in the electoral system—second ballot, list and (biased) proportional representation—were not the direct cause of the multiparty system that emerged. Despite the unifying importance attributed to the electoral system by Gambetta and his successors, 'it was not the only disruptive force, it was not the chief one, and it was not the oldest one. It merely allowed free play to the factions produced by the complexity of the nation's problems and the depth of its divisions.... Changes have neither affected the number and depth of the national cleavages nor allowed any system to be applied long enough to enable it to generate the forces that might correct its own excesses.'[9]

Party labels were not of great assistance to candidates, especially on the Right because they owed their election to their personal qualities and services rendered rather than to their national affiliations, which in any case often changed from one election to another. Significantly, they generally avoided using the term party in their names, except on the Left. The term 'Right' was disappearing by the time of the post-Dreyfus Affair 1902 election victory of the 'Bloc of the Lefts'; and by 1914 its representatives were preferring to call themselves 'Democratic Left', 'Republican Left', or 'Moderate Republicans', to distinguish themselves from the Radicals, Socialist Radicals, and Socialists (see Table 8.1).

Although no party could hope for a majority, 1899–1909 was a decade when three governments stayed in office for extended periods: Waldeck-Rousseau, 1899–1902, Combes 1902–5 and Clemenceau 1906–9. The Radicals in the Left-Centre occupied the centre of gravity of these coalition majorities. Party programmes made their appearance in the late nineteenth century but each candidate's personal *profession de foi* was more important. Parliamentary Groups were

---

[8] Quoted in Rosanvallon, 446; cf. 434–7, 444–5. Jules Ferry had already argued in similarly sweeping rhetorical vein in 1863, quoted ibid. 450; cf. 449. More generally, see Huard, 101–18.

[9] Peter Campbell, *French Electoral Systems*, 39, 44.

Table 8.1. Results of the 1902 Election to the Chamber of Deputies

'Party'	Votes number (000)	Votes (%)	Seats number	%
Conservative Right	1,188	14.1	83	14.4
Nationalists	1,195	14.2	62	10.8
Liberals	386	4.6	18	3.1
Moderate Republicans	2,501	29.7	175	30.4
Radicals	1,414	16.8	117	20.3
Socialist Radicals	853	10.1	75	13
Socialists	531	6.3	32	5.6
Revolutionary Socialists	344	4.1	13	2.3
Total	8,412	—	575	—

Source: Campbell, *French Electoral Systems and Elections since 1789*, 83.

officially recognized in 1910, by which time the Radical and Radical Socialist Party (1901) and the French Section of the Workers International, SFIO (1905) had been established but only the SFIO imposed strict voting discipline on its parliamentary party.

The turn of the century preoccupation with national decadence was fostered by a persistently falling birth rate and rural depopulation, increasing alcoholism and disease (notably tuberculosis and syphilis). This pervading pessimism favoured a revival of the Right, notably the *Action Française*, which, through to the 1930s, did its best to provoke panic by turning 'dismay into despair, disillusion into anger, disaffection into revolt and trouble into chaos'.[10] The sense of indecision, because France had lost the initiative internationally and suffered from an incoherent instability in domestic politics, led in the 1930s to bewildering reversals of traditional standpoints. 'Under stress, the pacifists turned warlike, and the nationalists opposed war; the Communists turned moderate and the moderates looked for extreme solutions; professed revolutionaries legally in power shunned disturbing reforms, while the defenders of order planned nihilistic campaigns of destruction and revolt.'[11] We explore these paradoxes in this chapter and in Chapter 9, examining separately the varied political postures within, as well as between, Right and Left, as they changed during and after WWII installation of the Vichy regime and the Fourth Republic's failure to remedy the party political weaknesses of the Third Republic. It was left to General de Gaulle's Fifth Republic after 1958 to create the institutional preconditions for a prolonged process of economic modernization, begun under the Fourth Republic at a remove from the stalemate of party politics. The reassertion of government authority meant that 'The state has promoted change by exploiting that very craving for security which had previously slowed down change'.[12]

It was not until 2002 that the mainstream French Right became largely united into a *Union pour un Mouvement Populaire* (UMP), while the French Left has

---

[10] Eugen Weber, *Action Française*, 296.   [11] Ibid. 295.

[12] Stanley Hoffmann in Hoffmann et al., *France: Change and Tradition*, 1968, 63.

remained split, although the Socialist Party may perhaps eventually succeed in uniting its mainstream components. However, this bipolarization involves excluding sizeable extremes to the National Front Right and Trotskyist Left. Midway through the twentieth century, the Communists on the Left and the Gaullists on the Right were sufficiently strong in popular support for André Malraux ringingly to declare to the Gaullist national party conference in 1949: 'There are us, the communists and nothing!' Despite its exaggeration, it had some plausibility. Since then, the Communists have been in steep decline so that their survival as a serious party is problematic because they have not found a way of replacing their discredited past with an attractive identity. Seeking to embody the nation state, the ex-Gaullists appear to have fared better than the protagonists of revolution but their submergence into the UMP has involved adopting in large measure the liberal conservative ideology of the 'Orleanist'/Giscardian Right-Centre of a 'modest state' integrated into the European Union. Before considering the new face of French party politics, we must first traverse the complex varieties of Right and Left parties that constitute a fragmented duality.

VARIETIES OF RIGHT: THE EXTREME RIGHT

Before the First World War, the Right was already deeply divided. The death of the ultra-reactionary Comte de Chambord in 1883, whose 'tutors had been told to teach him no history beyond 1788',[13] while resolving the Legitimist conflict with the Orleanists over issues like divine right and acceptance of the Revolution, did not prevent parliamentary royalism from shrinking to a few nostalgic aristocrats, despite the journalistic pyrotechnics of Maurras. Although the Right's voters were predominantly Catholic, some of its leading exponents like Maurras and Prime Minister and President Raymond Poincaré were vociferous secularists. The anti-Semitism of *Action Française* did not have the mass appeal of Drumont's *Libre Parole* but by 1906 he had lost his seat in parliament and his journal's sales were declining. In the absence of parliamentary parties capable of articulating and implementing the aspirations of those marginalized by the Opportunist and Radical Republic, recourse was made to extra-parliamentary direct action through leagues.

The prototype was the Patriots League. Started in 1882, by the mid-1880s it had under Déroulède's leadership (he was an effective populist poet and orator) argued that the parliamentary regime could not deliver a victorious return match against Germany and looked to General Boulanger as its Bonapartist-style champion, promising support for a takeover by *coup d'état*. Boulanger let the Patriots League down by an indecision induced in part by having been brought up to detest Louis-Napoleon's 1851 coup and disappointed the royalist Pretender, who financed him, by refusing to play the role of restoring the monarchy. The League's successors

---

[13] Zeldin, I, 398; cf. 399–401, 412–13.

were to confirm that while they could use a political or institutional crisis to mobilize protest, they could not succeed in bringing about regime change.[14]

The anti-Dreyfusard French Fatherland League having degenerated under the leadership of the literary critic Jules Lemaître and his Academician friends into an extension of his mistress's salon, Maurras and Léon Daudet broke away to assert an authoritarian nationalism, denied mass appeal by its anachronistic monarchism. What *Action Française* (AF) lacked in numbers it made up in its anti-parliamentary and anti-German vehemence. Although not directly implicated in the assassination of the First World War's most prominent and eloquent opponent, 'throughout July 1914, Maurras' attacks were steady and virulent, denouncing (Socialist leader) Jaurès as a traitor and a German agent, and rising to what could easily be taken as incitements to murder'.[15] The militant newsvendors of his journal often acted violently, the Catholic Democrat leader Marc Sangnier narrowly escaping in 1923 suffering a castor oil purge as practised by the Italian fascists. As well as daubing statues and disrupting lectures, plays and films of which they disapproved, the newsvendors rioted outside the Palais Bourbon in a 1925 protest against an attempt to form a Herriot government, the Radical leader narrowly escaping being thrown into the Seine. Given the fact that many of AF's newsvendors were students in the Paris Law Faculty, it is ironic that they showed an uninhibited inclination to break the law. Maurras was frequently sentenced to imprisonment for threats of murder (e.g. in 1925 against Jewish Interior Minister Schrameck who had cracked down on both AF and Communist violence) but until the Popular Front government of 1936 amnesties saved him from serving his sentence.[16]

The thuggish actions of the newsvendors were matched by the content of the propagandist newspaper which they hawked. It was often in financial difficulties, despite lots of small gifts and some large ones (e.g. from the perfume manufacturer François Coty) because of 'the costs of court actions, generally for libel or slander, sometimes for incitement to murder'....[17] It used the anti-Semitic *Protocols of the Sages of Zion* and when it was rapidly revealed as a forgery, a frequent AF contributor, the historian Jacques Bainville, cynically responded in 1921: 'So what?' Prejudices were as good as facts, an attitude that foreshadowed Vichy's anti-Semitic legislation, inspired and sponsored by AF associates.[18] Bainville campaigned for French occupation of the Rhur (which came in January 1922) and condemned British resistance to ruining Germany by reparations demands, accusing French governments of being subservient to foreigners: British, Jewish, Bolshevik, and German. Léon Daudet, then a deputy, helped secure the conciliatory Briand's resignation as Foreign Minister in 1921, while Bainville proudly asserted: 'We are the most reactionary country in the world. Let us, then, boldly become the leaders of reaction. In the Europe of today, this is the reason for our existence'.[19]

[14] Serge Berstein, 'La Ligue' in Sirinelli (ed.) *Histoire des droites en France*, II, 66–76 ; cf. Brogan, 184–9, 200, 206–10.

[15] E. Weber, *Action Française*, 91.   [16] Ibid. 142, 147, 160, 163, 180–2.

[17] Ibid. 190; cf. 188–91.   [18] Ibid. 201; cf. 195–200.   [19] Ibid. 121; cf. 119–20.

Although the AF shared Italian fascism's anti-parliamentary, anti-democratic, and anti-liberal standpoint, it rejected its statism and its pseudo-socialism. This is suggested by the trajectory of Georges Valois, who prior to the First World War, notably in his 1914 book *Monarchy and the Working Class*, tried to build an alliance between a Sorelian anarcho-syndicalism and a royalist nationalism on behalf of the AF. After a distinguished war record, he resumed his campaign for corporatist class collaboration but despairing of recruiting a mass working class following, he sought business financial support for a campaign to call an Estates General of French Production. But the business conception of corporatism was not what Valois sought: a synthesis of nationalism and collectivism rejecting both capitalism and socialism/communism, not merely preserve bourgeois privilege by establishing a conservative dictatorship on its behalf. When Valois decided to create an explicitly fascist movement in 1925, there was an acrimonious split from AF, with his mainly war veteran Blueshirts and the AF's newsvendors physically attacking each other in 1926, while their leaders slandered each other. Although his *Faisceau* movement, imitating Italian fascism, quickly collapsed in 1927 when his financial backers sided with AF, Valois popularized the idea of 'Neither Right nor Left' in his 1927 book on *Fascism*. Valois returned to his anarchist syndicalism from 1928, still calling in 1932 for a cultural revolution, and ended in the wartime Resistance, dying in the Bergen-Belsen concentration camp.[20]

Having lost such working class support as it had in 1925, AF lost much of its Catholic support with the Pope's condemnation in 1926 (on which we have already touched). In response to the AF's dislike of the 'Jewish Christ', a bishop justified the Pope's condemnation, declaring: 'if Maurras had his way, he would succeed in dechristianising Catholicism'.[21] The AF fell back on promoting corporatism in agriculture, which was more receptive and where it was well represented. With the right-wing conservatives Poincaré and Tardieu in power from 1926 to 1932, AF did not benefit from fear of the Left. It relied on attracting landowner-aristocrats, serving army officers, ex-servicemen, and doctors, the latter being 'propagandists as useful in their way as were commercial travellers'.[22] It held an annual May demonstration on Joan of Arc's Day. Unlike Valois' *Faisceau*, it survived and its newsvendors joined with the Fiery Cross ex-servicemen's organization in violently dispersing a November 1931 international disarmament conference, hailing its control of the Paris streets as a victory for the nationalist leagues over 'Anti-France'.[23] However, the 1934 Stavisky riots were to provide an opportunity to overthrow first the Chautemps and then the Daladier governments by street violence for the first time and threaten even the survival of the Republic.

What made the Stavisky scandal especially serious was that it exposed a network of complicity, involving parliamentarians, ex-ministers, senior officials, judges, and police, in which 'honest men were on good terms with fairly honest men, who were on good terms with shady men, who were on good terms with despicable

---

[20] Ibid. 205–211 and Sternhell, *Neither Right nor Left*, 61–2, 91–9, 105–18, 252. On Valois and the *Faisceau* see Robert Soucy, *French Fascism: The First Wave, 1924–1933*, 1986, Chapters 4–7.
[21] Eugen Weber, 254; cf. 253–5.   [22] Ibid. 266; cf. 265–7.   [23] Ibid. 301; cf. 300–3.

crooks'.[24] AF initiated the revelations exposing the alien swindler Stavisky's corrupt network, taken up by the rest of the press. Claiming that Stavisky had been 'suicided' and dubbing the deputies collectively as thieves, the scandal was exploited by riots directed against parliament in January 1934. After an especially violent riot in the proximity of the Chamber of Deputies on 27 January, Prime Minister Chautemps resigned despite retaining a parliamentary majority. This capitulation followed an AF-instigated street insurrection that had been handled indulgently, Prefect of Police Chiappe being in collusion with the Right. He was sacked by the new Prime Minister Daladier, despite Chiappe's popularity, apolitically achieved by 'introducing pedestrian crossings, cutting down the number of traffic accidents, vigorously supporting open prostitution and redesigning the shape of Paris *pissotières*.'[25]

Although Daladier secured a vote of confidence in defiance of the right-wing mob's 'patriotic violence', the death of fourteen people on 6 February and thirteen more in subsequent riots up to 12 February, led him to resign in favour of a national unity coalition headed by ex-President Doumergue. The fundamental question to be answered is why did the shaky Third Republic not fall to the violent onslaught to which it was subjected when it was so unreliably defended by a police and army of uncertain loyalty? The main reason was that the Extreme Right Leagues' leaderships were disunited; they could not agree either on a dictator or a restoration of monarchy and none was able to seize power on its own. While AF was happiest in polemics with rival pamphleteers, Colonel de La Rocque's more numerous Fiery Cross activists kept their disciplined supporters inactive in the street fighting.

The Leagues were as surprised by the way the riots had escalated as everyone else and had no plan to follow, even if they had succeeded in storming the Chamber of Deputies. The Right-Centre Doumergue government and its successors headed by Flandin and Laval took the wind out of their sails, despite the AF's belated efforts to coordinate all the Extreme Right apart from the Fiery Cross and the openly fascist movements. Shortly before the Popular Front came to power, the AF and its 1,000 strong newsvendor bully boy militia had been banned in February 1936 after a violent attack on Léon Blum, Maurras having earlier described him as 'a man to shoot down, but in the back', recalling Aragon's 1931 hate poem 'Fire on Blum' from the Extreme Left.[26] The affinity between the extremes was also reflected in the nonconformist rhetoric of Robert Aron and Arnaud Dandieu's New Order, declaring that they were half way between the Extreme Right and Extreme Left and anti-Centre.[27] The more hard-line AF activists broke away to form the Secret Committee of Revolutionary Action, ridiculed by nicknaming it the *Cagoule*. Financed by anti-Popular Front businessmen it provocatively

---

[24] Brogan, 660; cf. 653–65 and E. Weber, 320. See also Eugen Weber, *The Hollow Years: France in the 1930s*, 1995, 131–41, a book that provides a lively account of the period.

[25] E. Weber, *Action Française*, 325; cf. 322–31.

[26] Tony Judt, *The Burden of Responsibility*, 76, 80 and more generally, Eugen Weber, 332–67.

[27] Jean-Luc Pinol, '1919–58. Le temps des droites' in Sirinelli (ed.), *Histoire des droites en France*, I, 310.

bombed the headquarters of the peak Business Confederation and the emblematic UIMM metallurgical trade association. It collected arms but was broken up by arrests in late 1937.[28] Many of its conspirators ended up as Nazi collaborators, like the outright fascists to whom we now turn.

René Rémond is only the most distinguished of many French historians who into the 1980s treated French fascism as a foreign imported marginal phenomenon, which could be assimilated to Bonapartism of either a national-caesarist (Boulanger, La Rocque, and de Gaulle) or national-populist (Dorgères and Le Pen) kind. France was not receptive to fascism, he argued, because unlike Germany (but not Italy!) it was a First World War victor, whose ex-servicemen were inclined to pacifism after the previous bloodletting; the 1930s depression was relatively mild; it had a well-institutionalized democracy, not susceptible to youth upsurges, and seeking strong but not dictatorial leadership; the Radical Party retained much lower middle-class loyalty, while the reactionary Right was drawn to a clerical, militarist paternalism, and counter-revolutionary nationalism symbolized by Marshal Pétain and embodied in the Vichy regime, which Rémond nevertheless neglected.[29]

Because French historians had played down the French roots of European fascism, it was left to foreign historians to investigate the phenomenon from the 1970s. Of these, the most controversial was Zeev Sternhell, who emphasized the pioneering, pre-1914 role of French ideologists in preparing the post-First World War rise of fascism. He linked this with the crisis of elitist parliamentary democracy and a bourgeois, socio-economic reluctance to reform and modernize in response to the disruptive impact of industrializing mass society that prompted attacks from both Right and Left. Adopting the virulent attack on political and economic liberalism as the touchstone of these pre-fascist ideologues, he used their common terminology of revolutionary anti-capitalism to exaggerate the convergence of a reactionary authoritarian nationalism and the revisionist Marxism of a Sorel and a Henri de Man, neglecting the latter's rejection of militarism and imperialism.

Sternhell was perceptive in suggesting that because France had pioneered secularist democracy, it naturally provoked an early counter-attack from the Right. However, his retrospective reconstruction of teleological genealogies was too systematic, for example oversimplifying a Barrès evolution from Extreme Left to Extreme Right and ending up as a traditionalist conservative. Sternhell took advantage of the ambiguities of heterogeneous proto-fascist formulations to extend the breadth of its impregnation, tending to see it almost everywhere after French historians were stubbornly inclined to recognize it almost nowhere. Nevertheless, when the polemical dust settled, it came to be conceded that 'End of (nineteenth) century France saw the emergence of a new set of themes, an authoritarian

---

[28] Malcolm Anderson, *Conservative Politics in France*, 1974, 224–9, E. Weber, 397–402, and Pierre Milza, *Fascismes français, passé et présent*, 1987, 155–8.

[29] René Rémond, *Les Droites en France*, 4th edn, 1982, 203–37; cf. Pierre Milza, *Fascismes français* 16–21 and Philippe Burrin, 'Le Fascisme' in Sirinelli (ed.), *Histoire des droites en France*, I, 631–5.

and populist political culture, nationalist and anti-democratic, zenophobic, anti-Semitic and racist, with clear irrationalist tendencies. Rejection of society as a whole of conflicting interests, the choice of the nation as the basis of a closed and exclusive community: such was the soil without which fascism would have had no future.'[30] Even Rémond conceded in the case of the longest lived movement that 'It is true that *Action Française* cultivated in its supporters a predisposition to fascism; it is a fact that some disciples of Maurras went straight from the league to fascism'.[31] So Sternhell's forthright prosecution forced the French to face up to dealing with their domestic fascist potentialities less defensively.

Sternhell's stress on ideas rather than on events led him seriously to underemphasize the impact of the First World War mass mobilization for total militarization of civil society under authoritarian heroic leadership as a prelude to turning pre-fascist ideological potential into totalitarian fascist reality. The potent symbols of uniforms, flags, and marches, within a hierarchical framework, provided an anti-democratic and anti-market economy prototype. The victory of the Bolshevik Revolution in Russia provoked a fear that liberal democracy and bourgeois capitalism would not offer effective resistance to a Communist-led proletariat seeking a revolutionary alternative to parliament, private property and the 'divine right' employer. However, whereas liberalism, socialism, and communism were transnational, with a national dimension, the reverse was true of fascism. In Italy, where capitalism was weak and parliamentary democracy deadlocked, insurrectionary strikes in 1920 led to a provisional tactical alliance between conservative business and politicians with fascism, the former to hold on to power, the latter to acquire it. Mussolini in Italy showed the way to Hitler in Germany a decade later, as he brutally repressed his anti-capitalist radicals as well as all opposition, while subordinating his conservative-capitalist allies to fascist state control; although in the German case, it took the 1930s depression as well as political crisis to permit a Nazi takeover.

In France, where these conditions were not so severe in the 1920s and 1930s, and the army and police remained relatively loyal, Valois' imitation of Mussolini proved a fiasco. His *Faisceau* of Ex-Servicemen and Producers, launched on Armistice Day 1925 to utilize the wartime mystique, could not synthesize support from enough workers and businessmen to become a credible threat, although at its mid-1926 peak his movement had about 50,000 members.[32] A former member of *Faisceau*, Marcel Bucard, created *Francisme*, which never attracted more than 15,000 Blueshirt members between 1933 and 1939. It combined an admiration for Mussolini, from whom it received financial support, with the usual components

---

[30] Philippe Burrin, 'Le Fascisme', 630; cf. 605–29, Milza, *Fascismes français*, 22–47, 71–3, 88–92; and Winock, *Nationalisme, antisemitisme et fascisme en France*, 272–86. See Zeev Sternhell, *Maurice Barrès et le nationalisme français*, 1972; his *La Droite révolutionnaire, 1885–1914*, 1978 and especially *Neither Right nor Left: Fascist Ideology in France*, 1983, 1996 Eng. edn, especially 222–30, 259–68. See Michel Dobry (ed.), *Le mythe de l'allergie française au fascisme*, 2003. See also Robert Soucy, *Fascism in France: The case of Maurice Barrès*, 1972.

[31] René Rémond, *Les Droites en France*, 4th edn, 203.

[32] Philip Morgan, *Fascism in Europe, 1919–1945*, 2003, 54–8; cf. 20–8, 48–64. See also Milza, *Fascismes français*, 44–58, 93–108; and Burrin, 'Le Fascisme', 636–8.

such as corporatism. Bucard became a Nazi collaborator after France's defeat, when his movement was absorbed by the *Milice*.[33]

Fascism was not the most successful of the 1930s French nationalistic anti-liberalism and anti-parliamentary leagues. The Fiery Cross began life as an ex-servicemen's movement in 1927 but only became a mass movement after 1931 when Colonel François de La Rocque took over and especially from 1933 when the League of National Volunteers was established. Resolutely legalist and traditionalist, capitalizing on the 'fraternity of the trenches' and Catholicism for its support, it eschewed both totalitarianism and anti-Semitism. Demonstrating without rioting in February 1934, it was militantly anti-communist and anti-socialist. Forced by law to transform itself from a league into a party in 1936, the French Social Party by the end of the decade had about 700,000 members, despite losing some of the more extremist to Doriot's French Popular Party and outright fascist movements. Its Bonapartist posturing was in practice a bulwark against fascism, especially among the middle classes (which took over its motto: '*Travail, Famille, Patrie*'). In 1940–2, La Rocque supported the Vichy regime, then joined the Resistance and was deported by the Gestapo in 1943.[34]

By contrast, the former Communist leader Jacques Doriot, whose persuasive public and parliamentary oratory and months in jail had made him very popular, was the victim of rivalry with the PCF leader Maurice Thorez and for advocating a Popular Front strategy too soon. He left the PCF in 1935, attracting working class and unemployed support thanks to keeping his Saint-Denis power base until 1937. Although he won over some 100,000 members to his French Popular Party, discovery of his financial links with fascist Italy lost him support from 1938, PPF membership falling by 1942 to 30,000. Doriot's ignominious transition to fascism was completed during the war, where he fought on the Eastern front in a German uniform and aspired to be a French Fuhrer.[35]

While the Dorgères Greenshirt movement (discussed in Chapter 6) had certain affinities with fascism and its leader had advocated in 1933 'a Mussolini for France', he quickly became more reticent, championing instead an authoritarian and corporatist style of regime which came into existence in Vichy. He could not accept the subordination of the peasantry to industrialism, represented by fascism as well as liberalism or communism, and was too exclusively a peasant chief to become a national, cross-class leader. Despite his ardent support for Pétain, Dorgères was only involved until 1942 with the Vichy Peasant Corporation as its propagandist, because it preferred to rely on the agricultural organizations controlled by the rural notables. Dorgères helped to slow down the modernization process that was eliminating the peasantry but was no more successful than was Pierre Poujade (with whom he collaborated in the 1950s) in preventing it taking its toll among the shopkeepers and artisans.[36]

---

[33] Milza, 147–53; Burrin, 638–9.
[34] Winock, *Nationalisme*, 264–6; Milza, *Fascismes français*, 133–42.
[35] Winock, *Nationalisme*, 259–60; Milza, *Fascismes français*, 159–78, 253–6.
[36] Paxton, *French Peasant Fascism*, 155, 158; cf. 154–64. See also Jean-Michel Royer, 'De Dorgères à Poujade' in Jacques Fauvet and Henri Mendras (eds), *Les Paysans et la Politique*, 1958, 158–81. On the artisans and Vichy see Steven M. Zdatny, *The Politics of Survival*, Chapter 5.

VICHY: DEFEAT'S DIVINE SURPRISE OF REGIME CHANGE

While Italian fascism and German Nazism were both feared by the Extreme Right as military threats and admired as authoritarian examples to be copied, it was more a case of fashionable 'fascination than fascisation'.[37] Apart from the outright fascists in occupied Paris, the bulk of clerical conservatives who supported the Vichy regime wanted a state authoritarian enough to resist the subversive Left but not a totalitarian one that would interfere and impose collective action that they found repugnant. Protagonists of a largely self-sustaining civil society run by elites that had felt excluded from power by the parties, parliament, and administration of the Third Republic, they saw the defeat as a heaven sent opportunity to reassert control without going the whole Maurrasian way to reactionary renovation, much less adopt fascism as a form of government. Maurras himself was kept at arm's length as an impractical ideologue. In the context of the Occupation, this meant much more state control, thinly disguised as corporatism in agriculture and industry, to extract the resources demanded by the Germans.

Republican political and administrative personnel were purged, with particular rigour exercised against Jews and Freemasons. An August 1940 Law abolished Freemasonry as a secret society, civil servants being required to swear non-membership. Within a year, 14,600 former Freemason office holders had been excluded from the civil service. They were replaced by the defeated army and navy officers who also supplied ministers and Prefects, while notables who had been denied election by the voters were appointed to local office.[38] When Communist resistance developed from mid-1941, after the German invasion of Russia and ex-Socialist Vichy leaders Laval and Déat were wounded in August 1941, a State Tribunal was established with power to sentence to death. A conflict developed between the Justice Minister who wished to leave the task to the Germans and the Interior Minister who won the right for the French, so that hostages would not be chosen at random but from among communists. The Peasant Corporation and the 321 industrial Organization Committees became increasingly techno-bureaucratized. After the April 1942 installation of the Laval government and the November 1942 German occupation of the whole of France, dictatorship veered increasingly towards totalitarianism and by 1944 the fascists took control as the Vichy regime approached its death throes.

Despite the diversity of elites that came to power in defeat, it was not the traditionalists but the technocrats who most profited from a 'National Revolution' they had not created, while the fascists were confined to the roles of propaganda, anti-Semitism and repressing the Resistance being excluded from finance, foreign affairs, and defence. The reactionaries were fobbed off with promoting Catholic values. Only God was missing from the Vichy trilogy: 'Work, Family, Country'. However, in the matter of administrative centralization and capitalist

[37] Milza, 122; cf. 118–23.

[38] Stanley Hoffmann, 'The Vichy Circle of French Conservatives' Chapter 1, in *Decline or Renewal? France in the 1930s*, 1974, first appeared in the *Revue Française de Science Politique*, March 1956.

concentration backed up by coercive power, it was reforming technocrats who were in charge, as the regime was conceived as a response to national decline, decadence, decomposition, and defeat.[39] While the ideological need to restore the moral order by promoting family values, providing family allowances, restoring religious teaching in state schools and providing subsidies for Church schools, as well as the 'return to the land' theme popularized by Barrès and the novelist Jean Giono, pleased the traditionalists, the main structural reforms were in the state and economic spheres. The dysfunctional Third Republic governments, at the mercy of a parliament without a stable majority, were to be replaced by laws 'decreed' by Pétain, parliament having ceased to meet. The Council of State's legislative functions were expanded à la Napoleon, the role of Prefects reinforced, Regional Prefects created in 1941 and Secretaries General were established in all ministries to improve administrative coordination.

However, despite centralizing control, Vichy was too politically divided to establish a one-party state and far from reversing the Third Republic's revolving door governments, ministerial instability increased owing to the factional rivalries that plagued the regime. There were three major reshuffles in the second half of 1940 and two in each of years 1941, 1942, and 1943. In the first year alone there were four Foreign Ministers, five Interior and Education Ministers, and six Ministers of Industrial Production. Between 1940 and 1944, there were eight Ministers of Information and fifteen for the Radio.[40] While small business supported the regime's commitment to corporatism, industrial big business—mainly concentrated in the occupied zone and working with German contracts—was unenthusiastic. The Constitution that was to have been prepared by a consultative functionally representative National Council never materialized.

Drumont's zenophobic slogan 'France for the French', popularized by Maurras, was given lethal application against Jews by Vichy, although initially this was confined to draconian discrimination. An October 1940 Law, which defined a Jew of whatever religion as anyone having three grandparents of Jewish race, excluded Jews from elected and public office, from teaching and journalism. The 1871 Law granting Algerian Jews French nationality was abrogated and Prefects were authorized to intern foreign Jews in camps (facilitating their subsequent removal to German extermination). In 1941, Jews were restricted to 2 per cent of all professions, 3 per cent of secondary pupils and University students. Music, theatre, and cinema were closed occupations to Jews without special authorization and Jews were forbidden the Allier *département* where Vichy was located. In the Occupied Zone, Vichy through its Office for Jewish Affairs, sought to prevent the 'Aryanised' Jewish property falling into German rather than French hands. This

---

[39] Robert Paxton, *La France de Vichy, 1940–1944*, 2nd edn, 1997, 181–5, 189–90, 216–17, 274, 303–15. The English edition of this book first appeared in 1972 entitled *Vichy France: Old Guard and New Order, 1940–1944*. See also Andrew Shennan, *Rethinking France: Plans for Renewal 1940–1946*, 1989, Chapter 1.

[40] Paxton, *La France de Vichy, 1940–1944*, 243–4; cf. 238–41. On the 'restoration of moral order', see 192–212 and on the 'return to the land' 245–53. See also Richard Vinen, *The Politics of French Business 1936–1945*, 1991, especially Chapters 8–12.

Office was initially headed by Xavier Vallat, who had been very active in Extreme Right ex-servicemen associations in the 1930s and as a Deputy he was President of the Ex-Servicemen's Parliamentary Group. Appointed Ex-Servicemen Minister by Pétain, he was in 1942 replaced by the much more aggressive Anti-Jewish League's Louis Darquier (he assumed the additional name of de Pellepoix and in 1940 his organization was renamed the French Union for the Defence of the Race) who in 1944 was succeeded by a du Paty de Clam, son of the anti-Dreyfusard general of that name.

While Prime Minister Laval accepted the mass deportation to Germany of Jews, he appears to have tried unsuccessfully to confine it to non-French Jews. The process began with the deportation of 13,152 Jews on 16 July 1942 from the Paris Vel d'Hiv stadium. In all, some 76,000 Jews (two-thirds foreign) were sent to be exterminated. Of these only 2,564 returned from the concentration camps at the end of the war.[41] Many individual cases of French Jews being helped by their fellow countrymen (especially by Protestants, the most moving case being organized on a large scale and at great risk in the southern village of Chambon-sur-Lignon in the Haute Loire) surfaced after 1945. Nevertheless it was undoubtedly the case that from the October 1940 Vichy Jewish Statute drawn up by the former AF activist Raphaël Alibert, French official anti-Semitism preceded German pressure and in some respects went beyond its demands and administratively facilitated their satisfaction. In their desire to assert a semblance of sovereignty as well as to indulge their ideological connivance, French officials—and in particular Laval's associate Prefect of Police René Bousquet—rigorously implemented a systematic process of 'registration, despoliation, segregation, concentration, deportation'.[42]

As Stanley Hoffmann pertinently pointed out, Vichy's 'state collaboration' had much more ominous practical implications than the servile or ideological collaborationism of the unrepresentative French fascists. *Raison d'état* voluntary collaboration, based upon 'a mixture of resignation to and obstinate self-delusion about an untenable reality', led by 'a series of small Munichs' to involuntary collaboration, so playing into the Nazi Occupation's hands.[43] Opportunities for German exploitation of French factionalism were great because both the Pétainists and the enthusiastic collaborationists were divided, the latter ranging from journalists and intellectuals engaging in vindictive invective, to the anti-Communists and pacifists or the violent fascist militias in the Occupied zone. The Nazi Occupation used the latter to blackmail the Vichy regime into making increasing concessions, the 1940 Armistice agreement having explicitly committed the defeated French authorities

[41] Paxton, 1977, 219–27; cf. 212–14, 293. For a more detailed discussion, see Michael O. Marrus and Robert O. Paxton, *Vichy France and the Jews*, 1981, covering the roots of Vichy anti-Semitism, through the Vallat and Darquier periods of active anti-Semitism.

[42] Philippe Burrin, *Living with Defeat: France under the German Occupation, 1940–1944*, 1995, 1996, Eng. edn, 134; cf. 153–9 and Marrus and Paxton, 3–21; cf. 206–7, 270–3. On the Chambon-sur-Lignon story, see Philip Hallie, *Lest Innocent Blood be Shed*, 1978.

[43] Stanley Hoffmann, 'Self-Ensnared: Collaboration with Nazi Germany', Chapter 2, in *Decline or Renewal?*, 29; cf. 27–31, 44, first appeared in the *Journal of Modern History*, September 1968.

to 'collaborate' with the occupying victors. This led to the institutionalization of France's national nervous breakdown. However, despite numerous French overtures to play an active part in Hitler's New European Order against Britain, Hitler simply wanted a docile France to work for the German war effort, so French prisoners of war were not freed and the two-fifths of the country not occupied until 1942 was sealed off.[44]

When Hitler, having abandoned his attempt to cross the Channel, made clear he had no interest in making concessions to Vichy France, Pétain replaced Laval, the main proponent of maximum collaboration, with Admiral Darlan. This did not reverse the collaborationist policy but may have slowed it down until Laval returned to office in April 1942 under German pressure, having been kept in reserve in Paris to control Pétain by threatening to replace him. Pierre Laval had been a pre-First World War Socialist and the CGT's self-described 'manual lawyer' who defended prosecuted strikers. He was elected deputy in 1914 for the working class Paris suburb of Aubervilliers, of which he became Mayor in 1923 and remained so until 1944. In the 1920s, to satisfy his frustrated ministerial ambitions, he moved increasingly to the Right, holding office in several governments before himself becoming Prime Minister in 1931–2 and 1934–5. Having favoured a compromise peace during the First World War without being an outright pacifist and having voted against the Versailles Treaty, in addition to pursuing an alliance with Mussolini's Italy, Laval felt that geographical proximity necessitated a Franco-German rapprochement both before and after Hitler's advent. His disenchantment with parliamentary-dominated politics led him to favour authoritarianism and as early as 1937 he was advocating a national government headed by Pétain (who he had failed to persuade to join his government in 1935) intending him to be a figurehead behind whom he could control affairs.[45]

Defeat allowed him to revenge himself on the Popular Front parliament that had 'spewed me up'. By a mixture of tactical guile, deception and brutality, Laval, thanks to his awareness of the French public's urge to turn to a saviour in crisis and the pusillanimity of most of his parliamentary colleagues, pushed through not merely the suspension but the abolition of the Third Republic. He utilized the prestige of a Pétain, indifferent to constitutional matters, to achieve his purpose of having both Chambers indefinitely adjourned and securing the choice of Vichy as the capital of the Unoccupied Zone because Lyon was the fief of the Radical Edouard Herriot. He had himself appointed successor in the event of the aged Pétain's death, a position he lost on his removal from office in December 1940 on suspicion of seeking to replace Pétain sooner than that.

When Laval, at Hitler's behest, resumed as head of government in April 1942, he combined this with being Minister of Foreign Affairs, Interior and Information. He made an unsolicited offer to send French workers to Germany, replacing those going to the Eastern front, declaring, with Pétain's approval: 'I desire the victory of

[44] Paxton, *La France de Vichy*, 91–5, 100–3, 107–8, 111–23, 136.

[45] Geoffrey Warner, *Pierre Laval and the Eclipse of France*, 1968, 3–18, 24, 74, 80, 135–7, 142–58, 165–6, 254–9, 263–77.

Germany, for without it, bolshevism would tomorrow install itself everywhere.'[46] The logic of Laval's desire that France have a place in Hitler's new Europe meant that the disappointing response to the voluntary scheme led to it being made a compulsory one in September 1942. By the end of the year there were 320,000 French workers in Germany and 550,000 were working for Germany in France, despite the fact that in 1943–4 French officials significantly enforced this policy with much greater laxity than the transfer of Jews to Germany.

Because Laval was prepared 'to put all of France's resources freely at Germany's disposal', Hitler in April 1943 warned Pétain not to dismiss Laval because he alone was committed to Germany for better or for worse. In autumn 1940, before his dismissal by Pétain and rescue by Hitler, Laval, who knew that his reputation as an overconfident, slippery fixer made him unpopular, conceded: 'I have 80 per cent of the country against me and 90 per cent of the ministers.'[47] Things went from bad to worse in 1942–4, but Laval went on to the acrid end. He was extradited from his Spanish refuge to France where he was tried, sentenced to 'national degradation' and death, attempting suicide before being shot. (The public prosecutor and judge at Laval's trial had both served the Vichy regime.) He was a convenient conspicuous scapegoat on whom both the Right and Left could shift the blame for their own failings, a 1945 opinion poll showing that 78 per cent wanted Laval sentenced to death, while in a September 1944 poll 58 per cent thought Pétain should be acquitted.[48]

The Liberation purge which affected some 150,000 people in one way or another, led to more deaths and fewer imprisonments than in other occupied West European countries. Some 9,000 were killed without trial. Three quarters of the 124,613 tried were found guilty: 6,763 were sentenced to death but only some 1,600 executed; over 44,000 received various prison sentences. There was differential punishment of the elites. The unobtrusive techno-bureaucracy got off lightly but half the Prefects and members of the Council of State who had served as Prefects or ministers suffered. Ministers, journalists, and intellectuals were severely treated because they were more in the public eye and did not stand together as did the civil servants.

Black marketeers in general and grocers in particular fared well financially as did on a larger scale industrialists who had worked for Germany or profited from the spoliation of Jews. Investigation of business collaboration was more complex and took longer, so the cases were delayed and treated more leniently when passions had cooled. Louis Renault was an exceptional case; in contrast to Michelin who resisted industrial collaboration, Renault manufactured military vehicles for the German war effort, declaring: 'Only one thing counts, me and my factory'. He died in prison and his motor car company was confiscated and nationalized.

---

[46] Geoffrey Warner, 1968, 301; cf. 193–211, 299–302.

[47] Quoted in Burrin, *Living with Defeat*, 104; cf. 74, 79–80, 103–6, 113–15. Also Warner, 368; cf. 307–11, 361–74.

[48] Warner, 409; cf. 404–17 and Burrin, 'Vichy' in *Lieux de mémoire*, III/I, 331. On provincial life during the Occupation, see Robert Gildea, *Marianne in Chains: In Search of the German Occupation of France 1940–45*, 2002.

The Catholic Church quietly removed the most politically compromised bishops. The French Liberation armed forces were commanded by two Pétainists—de Lattre de Tassigny and Juin—and one Gaullist: Leclerc de Hauteclocque. The 569 parliamentarians who voted Pétain into power were declared ineligible but by 1953, René Coty, who was one of them, was elected second President of the Fourth Republic. In that year, by which time many Vichyites had resumed an active political role, a general amnesty was declared.[49]

For a while, de Gaulle's determination to restore French self-esteem and a semblance of national unity and to treat the Franco-French civil war as an interlude between Republics, seemed to suit the many who had an interest in maintaining a conspiracy of silence. They were content to forget if not forgive what had happened between 1940 and 1944, when 'many French people went half way or even all the way to meet the occupying power and its politics' because of 'constraint, material self-interest, personal compliance, and ideological connivance', with self-interest and intimidation predominating.[50] The facile oversimplification of 1940 comprehensive Pétainism switching to 1944 universal Gaullism ignores the shifting spectrum of public opinion as providential collaboration moved via prudential accommodation to outright hostility when the fortunes of war favoured the previously maligned Anglo-Saxons and Soviet Bolsheviks.

German exactions increased with their impending defeat. Struggling to survive a massive fall of a third in real wages, as the working population saw who was winning, they increasingly condemned the 1–2 million who favoured active collaboration and the 150,000 members of the collaborationist parties as guilty of treachery, although the purges mainly affected the small fry. Pétain continued to be respected even while the Vichy government became increasingly discredited and its propaganda could not compete effectively with the broadcasts of the BBC for the attention of the French public. 'Marshalism'—personal admiration for Marshal Pétain—was always much more extensive and enduring than 'Pétainism'—support for the Vichy National Revolution—still more than Collaboration with Nazi Germany.

The Catholic Church's role was especially significant, because of its affinity with Vichy's rechristianization programme and the elimination of its ideological enemies, which offered it an opportunity to retrieve a pivotal place lost under the Third Republic. 'While public opinion was evolving from hostile passivity towards active rejection, the Church remained unmoved, playing into the occupiers' hands through both its silence and its recommendations of obedience.'[51] The 'opportunist accommodation' which Vichy encouraged and which the Nazis welcomed at a time when nearly 4 million French people were working for the Germans (2.6 million in France and 1.3 million in Germany) in 1944—some 37 per cent of the male aged 16–60 population—was of major assistance to the German war

---

[49] Paxton, *La France de Vichy*, 369–89, 416–18, 421. For the Renault quotation see Burrin, *Living with Defeat*, 250; cf. 251–2. See also Annie Lacroix-Riz, *Industriels et Banquiers sous l'Occupation: La collaboration économique avec le Reich et Vichy*, 1999.

[50] Burrin, *Living with Defeat*, 175.

[51] Ibid. 225–6; cf. 117–89, 217–23, 432–3 and Henry Rousso, *The Vichy Syndrome*, 169.

effort against those that were fighting *inter alia* for the liberation of France.[52] The Vichy regime meanwhile actively opposed both the internal Resistance and the 'Free French' whom it vilified.

In his retrospective elucidation of *The Vichy Syndrome*, Henry Rousso has shown how from the 1970s, the rival myths that were substituted for the wartime reality and displaced the Dreyfus Affair as symbolizing Franco-French animosities, disintegrated as the urge to remember predominated over the compulsion to forget. A mendacious national pseudo-reconciliation based on 'official memory, which celebrates, selects, and censures in the name of the state', in any case suffered from a double split: between a divided Right, Gaullist, Conservative, and Pétainist, the latter perpetuated by the Extreme Right and a divided Communist and Socialist Left, as well as the semi-unanimist Resistancialist myth, championed especially by the Gaullists and Communists, excluding a few traitors, versus the semi-unanimist Pétainist myth of National Revolution to regenerate France. While the reservoir of symbolic memories was purged of 'unassimilable facts' by each, the Vichy apologists had most to hide: 'state collaboration, the French origins of Vichy anti-Semitism, and the deeply partisan, anti-Popular Front character of the regime, which was the source of deep and lasting divisions in French politics'.[53]

The return of the prisoners of war and the survivors of the Nazi concentration camps were largely ignored as colonial wars in Indo-China and then Algeria vied for elite and mass attention with the concern to rebuild the economy. Jean Dutourd's 1952 satire on black market grocers profiting from wartime scarcity, *Au Bon Beurre*, did not rattle political skeletons. However, French self-esteem was disturbed in 1971 both by the documentary film *The Sorrow and the Pity* that exposed the consoling myths of an undigested past that had not been looked in the eye and by President Pompidou's pardon, against the State Security Court and Justice Minister's advice, of former *milicien* and murderer Paul Touvier, concealed for decades by the Catholic Church in Lyon. Pompidou justified his decision by the need to forget the discordant past but his controversial action had the opposite effect to that intended, provoking thousands of newspaper articles between 1971 and 1976. Other films followed, making the seamy side of the Occupation much more familiar in the seventies and eighties, a particularly powerful impact being made by Claude Lanzmann's *Shoah* (1985) on the holocaust and Louis Malle's *Au Revoir les Enfants* (1987) about the deportation of Jewish children from the village of Izieu.[54]

While de Gaulle's war memoirs maximized the heroic role of the Free French, Robert Aron minimized the servile behaviour of Vichy France. It was left to an American historian, Robert Paxton, to provide the first balanced exposition of the unpalatable truth that was initially rejected both from the Left and especially the Right. He was later lionized, having in the interim prompted a polemical orgy of recollections by those involved on both sides, as well as numerous academic

---

[52] Burrin, *Living with Defeat*, 461; cf. 462–7.   [53] Rousso, 304, 302; cf. 297–305.
[54] Ibid. 116–26, 233–47. Stanley Hoffmann's review 'In the Looking Glass. Sorrow and Pity' is Chapter 3 in *Decline or Renewal?*

studies. From the 1980s it became the new textbook orthodoxy. Court cases followed belatedly, notably that of Maurice Papon, whose role in the deportation of Jews was exposed in 1981 by the *Canard Enchaîné*. In that year the newly elected President François Mitterrand paid his respects to the tomb of Jean Moulin— Resistance leader killed by the Gestapo after torture—to emphasize his later Resistance role after an equivocal Vichy record. The partisan utilization of Moulin as a consensus symbol had been ceremonially inaugurated in 1964 at the transfer of his remains to the Panthéon, when André Malraux in his epic apotheosis used him to legitimize 1960s Gaullism. Both examples confirm that 'The Panthéon was a place of oblivion as well as remembrance'.[55]

GAULLISM: INSTITUTIONALIZING HEROIC LEADERSHIP

General de Gaulle achieved at moments of national crisis a communion of 'Self and Nation which Barrès had sought and which so fascinated Malraux'. Through the heroic role he played in 1940 in personifying an idealized, undefeated France, after the 1958 establishment of the Fifth Republic, he reasserted the 'personalization of his power, which he refused to let become institutionalized'.[56] Recognizing no predecessors and dubious about his eventual successors, de Gaulle was sceptical on the score of substituting for the charismatic legitimacy which his response to national disaster had conferred upon him the flimsy and formal constitutional structures that had so often been found ineffective in France. The hero worship he enjoyed was unlike traditional or legal authority. 'Instead of recognition being treated as a consequence of legitimacy, it is treated as the basis of legitimacy' by those subject to it.[57] Anticipating de Gaulle, who attached cardinal importance to his unmediated relationship with the people, Max Weber stressed the importance of the plebiscite as the means of confirming what de Gaulle called the 'latent legitimacy' of his charismatic authority which persisted between the crises that necessitated its reassertion.[58] As we shall see, the personalized referendums on which de Gaulle relied for verification of the enduring direct, semi-mystical relationship with his countrymen, were to sustain his personal authority until 1969, when defeat in a non-crisis referendum, a forlorn attempt to revive a flagging heroic legitimacy, was interpreted as signifying that the will of the general was no longer synonymous with the general will. However, despite Malraux's desperate 1969 warning: 'There is no Gaullism without de Gaulle', the Fifth Republic calmly survived its founder to subside into the basis of an unheroic, routine political authority that successfully avoided the semi-stalemate that afflicted the latter-day Third Republic and too much of the Fourth Republic.

[55] Rousso, 95; cf. 83–93, 148–61, 180–4, 253–69.
[56] Stanley Hoffmann, 'Last Strains and Last Will: De Gaulle's *Memoirs of Hope*' in *Decline or Renewal?*, 265; cf. 266–7, 277.
[57] Max Weber, *The Theory of Social and Economic Organisation*, 1947, 386; cf. 359, 387.
[58] Charles de Gaulle, *Mémoires de Guerre*, III, 1959, 287.

'Routine authority is legitimate because of what it *is*, the heroic leader because of what he *does*.'[59] At a time of crisis, the collapse of legal authority may invite a personal assertion of authority to deal with the ensuing national emergency. To clean up the mess left by the inertia of the political class and military incompetence of a discredited and defeated Third Republic, two rival heroic military-cum-political leaders emerged in 1940 in Marshal Pétain and General de Gaulle as candidate national saviours. They were both political outsiders, the latter more than the former. They had been closely associated in their army careers. Pétain, the legendary First World War hero of the battle of Verdun, was de Gaulle's first commanding officer in 1912, who served under him at the start of the war. From the outset he never saw eye to eye with the Imperator about warfare: de Gaulle championing mobility and manoeuvre, Pétain's static strategy being symbolized by the Maginot Line. However, Pétain greatly admired de Gaulle's intellectual capacities so he asked him from 1921 to be his exponent as ghostwriter but was reluctant to acknowledge the latter's contribution, so he pigeonholed the resulting manuscript. When in 1938 de Gaulle self-confidently decided to publish in his own name the largely rewritten text as *France and Its Army,* it led to an acrimonious break with his former patron.

Having in the throes of defeat joined the Reynaud government in June 1940 as Under-Secretary of State for War, de Gaulle advised in vain against including Pétain because the latter notoriously wanted to make peace rather than war. De Gaulle later revealed that when his old leader succeeded Reynaud some two weeks later, he knew that it meant 'certain capitulation. I made my decision at once. I should leave the next morning' for England. Destiny decreed that helpless in its hour of disaster, 'it was for me to assume the country's fate, to take France upon myself.'[60] Sentenced to death for desertion to a foreign power, de Gaulle rebuffed a 1944 attempt by Pétain to secure a formal transfer of power to avoid civil war, convinced that he was quite capable of doing so on his own. He was helped in commuting Pétain's death sentence by the High Court's recommendation that it not be executed.

As a leader, de Gaulle was intransigent in his providential purpose but pragmatic in the tactical flexibility with which he pursued the one and adapted the other. 'Gaullism is a stance, not a doctrine, an attitude, not a coherent set of dogmas; a style without much substance—beyond the service of France and French *grandeur* itself never defined in content, only in context.'[61] Nevertheless, de Gaulle—temperamentally a born autocrat, fervent Catholic and army officer—was the most striking twentieth-century representative of a 'Republican Right' that

---

[59] Stanley Hoffmann, 'The Rulers: Heroic Leadership in Modern France' (which first appeared in 1967) in *Decline or Renewal?,* 86; cf. 71–2. See also Jack Hayward, 'Bonapartist and Gaullist Heroic Leadership: Comparing Crisis Appeals to an Impersonated People' in Peter Baehr and Melvin Richter (eds), *The History and Theory of Modern Dictatorship,* 2004, 221–39.

[60] De Gaulle's *Mémoires de Guerre,* I, 1954, 65, 74, quoted in Jean Lacouture, *De Gaulle, I, The Rebel, 1890–1944,* 1990, 207, 245; cf. 21–4, 74–86, 158–61, 189, 213–14.

[61] Stanley and Inge Hoffmann, 'De Gaulle as Political Artist: the Will to Grandeur' in *Decline or Renewal?,* 217; cf. 216–20.

had with reservations and unenthusiastically rallied to the Third Republic at the end of the nineteenth century. He was not a nostalgic reactionary but close to the nationalist mystique of a Péguy, with echoes of Michelet. It was his self-imposed mission both to rescue a Right that had disgraced itself under Vichy and to rebuild a discredited Republic that could reunify the nation and empower the state. The substantial posthumous consensus on his achievement, marked by the way his left-wing critics, such as François Mitterrand reversed their earlier condemnation, is his vindication.

The paradoxical result of de Gaulle's exertions and of the manipulation of the nation's historic memories was that this exceptional man, the apparently anachronistic personification of a vanishing French identity, took advantage of the exceptional circumstances of 1940 and 1958, to make an immense contribution to reducing the dissensions and instabilities that had bedevilled French history from the Revolution.[62] As a result, the defender of the grandeur of national distinctiveness contributed to its decline if not to its demise, a subject to which we return after having discussed in Chapter 10 de Gaulle's independent foreign and defence policy in which he self-confidently spoke for France in the relations between states. It is only then that we shall measure the full significance of de Gaulle's 1952 assertion that 'Every Frenchman has been, is or will be "Gaullist"'.[63] In retrospect, and taking all in all, most of those who rejected this or that action of a political protagonist deliberately seeking to be a solitary suprapartisan statesman, accepted him as the last of France's supreme historic national heros in a post-heroic age. As such, his legacy far transcended that of the succession of parties that, despite their formal labels were called Gaullist, but have abandoned many of the specific policies that he advocated.

Before turning to the partisan manifestations of the Gaullist phenomenon, let us examine how French public opinion has reacted to the General's characterization of their response to him. We are assisted by a comprehensive opinion survey conducted in connection with the 1990 conference for the centenary of his birth, 'de Gaulle in his century'. Asked whether they were Gaullist, 20 per cent said yes, 16 per cent no, 14 had no views and most significantly 50 per cent replied that it was a totally out of date designation. Furthermore, when asked whether the politicians who claimed to be Gaullist and supported his ideas were justified, by 3:1 they declared that they were unjustified in doing so, and a higher proportion— 68 to 18 per cent—maintained that they were hypocritical rather than sincere.[64] When asked what de Gaulle most represented for them 43 per cent said the 18 June 1940 broadcast appeal from London to carry on the war, 26 per cent replied the Liberation, and 15 per cent the founder of the Fifth Republic. The rest, such as the end of the Algerian War (7 per cent) were in single figures.[65] Asked

---

[62] Pierre Nora, 'L'historien devant de Gaulle' in Institut Charles de Gaulle, *De Gaulle en son siècle*, I, 1991, 173–7; cf. Maurice Agulhon, 'La "tradition républicaine" et le général de Gaulle', ibid. 192–3. See also Jean Charlot, 'Le Gaullisme' in Sirinelli (ed.), *Histoire des droites en France*, I, 656–9.

[63] Press conference of 10 March 1952, De Gaulle, *Discours et Messages, 1946–58*, II, 1970, 513.

[64] Institut Charles de Gaulle, *De Gaulle en son siècle, Sondages et enquêtes d'opinion*, 1992, 25–6.

[65] Ibid. 69.

Table 8.2. Approval of de Gaulle's actions, 1940–68[66]

	Approve (%)	Disapprove No (%)	Opinion (%)
Appeal of 18 June 1940	84	2	14
Refusal of any agreement with Marshal Pétain	54	19	27
Circumstances of his return to power in 1958	48	12	40
Independence of Algeria	64	18	18
Election of President by universal suffrage	88	3	9
De Gaulle's response to the May 1968 events	30	32	38

whether they approved his actions on a number of issues, Table 8.2 shows their response.

Taken in conjunction with the overall view that de Gaulle's action had been positive (84 per cent) with only 4 per cent judging it to have been negative, 12 per cent having no opinion,[67] it is clear that his memory is identified especially favourably with his wartime role and his institutionalization of presidential power by direct popular election. Continuing resentment, especially on the Right and Extreme Right, at his refusal to negotiate with Pétain, is recorded, while of those who still disliked the way in which de Gaulle returned to power in 1958 under pressure from an army-settler rebellion, the Communists are predictably the most numerous. Just as predictably, National Front voters were most hostile to his granting independence to Algeria; they were also disproportionately hostile to electing the President by universal suffrage but far outstripped by the Communists at the other extreme. On the one issue where disapprovals exceed approvals, de Gaulle's response to the May 1968 events, his support came especially from the old, the Right, and the less educated.[68] What these results do not mention is that de Gaulle's charismatic status was not continuous from 1940. For example, in September 1957, when asked who they would favour as Prime Minister, the uncharismatic Socialist Guy Mollet was chosen by 14 per cent, de Gaulle by 11 per cent, Pierre Mendès France by 9 per cent, and Antoine Pinay by 8 per cent.[69] So, a mere eight months before he took control, de Gaulle's public standing was very modest.

Asked how out of fifteen French historic figures ranked first, second, and third, the public would place them, de Gaulle came first and Pétain eleventh with Napoleon second, Joan of Arc fourth, Jules Ferry fifth and Clemenceau sixth.[70] While this reinforces de Gaulle's image as a charismatic leader, the leading expert on Gaullism, Jean Charlot, sought to play down its importance relative to its partisan expression, partly with a view to encouraging its propensity to survive its personification. He did so by showing that, for much of the Fourth Republic,

[66] Institut Charles de Gaulle, 1992, 73, derived from a table providing additional information.

[67] Ibid. 66.   [68] Ibid. 73–87.

[69] Roland Sadoun, 'De Gaulle et les sondages' in Institut Charles de Gaulle, *De Gaulle en son siècle*, I, 321; cf. 325.

[70] Institut Charles de Gaulle, *Sondages et enquêtes*, 33; cf. 36–9.

de Gaulle's return to power was not desired by a majority of the French people and during the Fifth Republic the gap between his popularity and that of his governments decreased, preparing the way for the partisan survival of Gaullism without de Gaulle under Pompidou, his Prime Minister from 1962 to 1968. Charlot argued that 'the Gaullist phenomenon was...the basis of a real change in the French political system: a change from a multiparty to a dominant-party system, with perhaps eventually...the prospect of a two-party system'.[71]

While Charlot's views were in one sense prophetic, with the Chirac-led 'Gaullists' forming the core of a predominantly united Right UMP party in 2002, its achievement has been at the cost of abandoning much of what de Gaulle stood for. The depersonalization and partisanization process began quickly under Pompidou and accelerated under Chirac. Significantly, when asked in 1990 whether when they were President they had been the head of a party majority or above party, 62 against 29 per cent regarded de Gaulle as above party, while only 28 against 55 per cent so regarded Pompidou.[72] The Right having become an appellation that dares to speak its name with pride, Chirac's UMP laid claim to the mantle of the General, which flattered only to deceive. De Gaulle had always believed that one could not both serve France and one's party. As he proudly declared at a Cabinet meeting after winning the struggle to impose direct election of the President in November 1962: 'I wanted to smash the parties. I alone was able to do it and alone in believing it possible at the time I chose. I was right against everyone. I declared war on the parties. I would not declare war on the party leaders. Parties cannot be won over but party leaders only seek to be won over'.[73] These words accurately convey de Gaulle's firmness of heroic purpose and flexibility in utilizing the infirmities of the politicians, unlike his successors who were the sort of party politicians he had manipulated with mastery. By 1969 the French signified to de Gaulle that they were tired of exhortation to heroic effort and content to return to humdrum politics.[74]

CATHOLIC POLITICAL ACTION AND THE RIGHT-CENTRE

It was under the Fourth Republic that Christian Democracy came to the fore as a political force, playing the pivotal role of the Radicals in the Third Republic as the Centrists who were virtually indispensable to 'Third Force' governments that were both anti-Communist and anti-Gaullist. Yet from its creation in 1944 until

[71] Jean Charlot, *The Gaullist Phenomenon*, 1970, 1971 edn, 17; cf. Chapter 2 especially. See also his *Le gaullisme d'opposition, 1946–1958*, 1983 and *L'UNR*, 1967.

[72] Institut Charles de Gaulle, *Sondages et enquêtes*, 172; cf. 173–4. More generally see Andrew Knapp, *Gaullism since de Gaulle*, 1994.

[73] Lacouture, *De Gaulle, III, Le Souverain, 1959–1970*, 1986, 1990 edn, 590–1; cf. II, *Le Politique, 1944–1959*, 1985, 1990 edn, 223–4, 235, 239, 545.

[74] On the 1969 referendum, see J. E. S. Hayward, 'Presidential Suicide by Plebiscite: de Gaulle's Exit, April 1969' in *Parliamentary Affairs*, XXII/4, Autumn 1969, 289–319.

it refused to follow de Gaulle into opposition in 1946, the Popular Republican Movement (MRP) had prided itself as being the 'party of fidelity' to de Gaulle. Thereafter, an enduring 'breach was opened between the party of Resistance Catholics and the Catholic leader of the Resistance',[75] who was scathingly to say of his erstwhile supporters that 'the sharks have swallowed the apostles' who had mobilized believers in aid of their political ambitions. While the MRP suffered a halving of its vote between 1946 and 1951, owing to desertions of its right-wing electoral clientele to the Gaullist RPF and the Conservative Right, it led to the exclusion of a takeover by the General until 1958, when the colonialist policy with which it had been closely identified caused the downfall of the Fourth Republic.

The MRP Ministers resigned from the Pompidou government in May 1962, following derogatory remarks about European integration. When the MRP opposed de Gaulle's October 1962 referendum on the direct election of the President as ending the prospect of a restoration of a parliament-centred democracy, it lost nearly half of its 1958 voters to the Gaullist UNR or to abstention at the subsequent election when the President dissolved the Assembly. Despite the MRP leader Jean Lecanuet's winning enough support to push de Gaulle unexpectedly into a second ballot at the 1965 presidential election, the Christian Democratic Party's demise was only postponed. In an increasingly bipolarized political system, in which Catholic fervour was receding and the rural support on which it had relied was declining, by the early 1970s it seemed that there was 'no future except as a ginger group within the Gaullist majority'.[76] Although the process was delayed by the success of the conservative Right in the person of Giscard d'Estaing at the 1974 presidential election, with the creation of the catch-all UMP in 2002, only a residual Right-Centre UDF survived in cohabitension with it. The post-Gaullist whale swallowed and partially digested most of the sharks that had eaten the apostles.

However, the pre-Second World War vicissitudes of an emerging Christian Democracy and the problems of a movement in which Left—inclined party activists had to coexist with a leadership in pursuit of their Right-inclined voters first need to be investigated. There had been a minority tradition within French Catholicism, represented under the July Monarchy by Lamennais and after his 1834 break with the Church by Lacordaire, continued in a diluted liberal form by Montalembert during the Second Empire, which had to await the papacy of Leo XIII (1878–1903) to secure a shift from royalism to the republic, reinforced by the second *ralliement* following the 1926 condemnation of *Action Française*. These shifts had been interrupted by Pope Pius IX's 1910 condemnation of Marc Sangnier's Sillon movement that from 1907 admitted Protestants and freethinkers to membership and sought to give explicit party expression to Christian Democracy, to which most of the French bishops were opposed.[77] Albert de Mun's

[75] Philip Wiliams, *Crisis and Compromise: Politics in the Fourth Republic*, 1964, 133.

[76] R. E. M. Irving, *Christian Democracy in France*, 1973, 233; cf. 242–3, 270.

[77] Ibid. Chapter 1. See also Caroline Ford, *Creating the Nation in Provincial France: Religion and Political Identity in Brittany*, 1993, 182–6.

attempt to create an explicitly Catholic Party in 1885 was crushed both by electoral defeat and the opposition of Pope Leo XIII, who was against linking the Church with the fate of the monarchists. De Mun in 1886 decided to promote Social Catholic Action by establishing the Catholic Association of French Youth (ACJF) which, assisted by the Pope's encyclicals, especially *Rerum Novarum* (1891), had by 1911 formed 150 farmers' branches, 118 friendly societies, 26 trade union branches, and 20 cooperative societies. Catholics also controlled most of the Scouting and Youth Hostel movements. However, until after the First World War, the ACJF was predominantly middle class, confirming in part Péguy's polemical assertion that 'It is no use hiding from the fact that, though the Church is no longer the official religion of the State, it has not ceased to be the official religion of the State bourgeoisie'.[78]

The national 'Sacred Union' promoted by the First World War and the 1919 electoral victory of the right-wing *Bloc National* allowed Sangnier and a few Christian Democrats to be elected deputies but it was not until 1924, in response to the Left's victory, that a small parliamentary group representing the Popular Democratic Party (PDP) was established, merging into the MRP after the Second World War. More significant was the development in the late 1920s and 1930s of Catholic Action organizations under the umbrella of ACJF, with the rapid recruitment of members to its agricultural, worker, and student branches, from which many of the post–Second World War MRP leaders came, via the Resistance. In 1919 the French Confederation of Christian Workers (CFTC) was established, recruiting especially among white-collar and women workers but although it too contributed towards the MRP activists, it did not succeed in preventing that party's rapid drift from Left-Centre to Right-Centre.[79]

During the Second World War, the Catholic Church not only survived intact but flourished thanks to the explicit support of almost all its bishops for the providential Vichy regime in the hope of rechristianizing a people decreasingly inclined to practice its nominal beliefs. Far from encouraging Resistance, the Church authorities condemned it as terrorism and supported corporatist institutions, although Cardinal Liénart (a First World War hero decorated for bravery at Verdun by Pétain) went further than many but not as far as Cardinal Baudrillart, Rector of the Paris Catholic Institute, who actively championed collaboration with the German Occupation. Archbishop Saliège was unusual, outspokenly condemning Vichy's state anti-Semitism by recalling Pope Pius XI's 1933 declaration: 'Anti-Semitism is inadmissible. Spiritually we are Semites'.[80] Priests of the Catholic Church individually suffered—153 were shot or died in concentration camps, over 300 were deported and as many imprisoned—but the future MRP leaders attacked the behaviour of the Assembly of Cardinals and Archbishops that had supported

---

[78] Gibson, *A Social History of French Catholicism*, 220, quoting Péguy's *Notre Jeunesse*, 1910.

[79] On the PDP, see Irving, 41–51. On Catholic Action, see William Bosworth, *Catholicism and Crisis in Modern France*, 1962. On the CFTC, see Gérard Adam, *La CFTC, 1940–1958*, 1964.

[80] W. D. Halls, *Politics, Society and Christianity in Vichy France*, 1995, 97; cf. 98–102, 107, 119, 137, 177, 200–8, 219, 253–7, 361–3, 369–79.

the Vichy regime. The Vatican stalled post-war sanctions against Vichyite bishops and eventually only three were induced to resign.

While the MRP 'movement' founded in 1944 deliberately avoided any reference to religion or party in its name, it did not succeed in distancing itself from its Catholic affiliations or partisan character. (It was not helped by Pope Pius XII's resounding silence during the war over Hitler's mass murder of the Jews but this did not become a controversial issue until the 1960s.) After an initial surge, the MRP retreated to the traditional Catholic areas of right-wing strength in Alsace-Lorraine, Brittany and a few enclaves in the south. Clinging to a 'third-way' doctrine between market liberalism and Marxist communism, it quickly became discredited as a party whose leaders were mainly concerned with securing and retaining office and whose policies generally sided with those of the government. This was not surprising as their leaders headed some and belonged to virtually all the Fourth Republic governments, including the last which handed over power to de Gaulle in 1958. The MRP brought down the governments of two leading figures—of the Right, Pinay in 1952, and of the Left, Mendès France in 1955—reflecting the fragility of Third Force parliamentary majorities struggling to cover the broad political spectrum between Gaullism and Communism. It not only lost the respect of Catholic intellectuals like Mauriac and Mounier; its membership fell from over 200,000 in 1946 to under 100,000 in 1950 and 40,000 in 1957.[81]

The MRP became especially identified with advocating European integration. Its most respected leader Robert Schuman's momentous role in creating the European Coal and Steel Community (ECSC), based on Franco-German reconciliation, is a matter to which we return in Chapter 10. It helped to compensate for the party's reactionary colonial policy represented by another MRP Prime Minister, Georges Bidault, who, despite a left-wing past under the Third Republic and in the Resistance, moved to the Right during the Fourth Republic and ended as a reactionary champion of *Algérie Française* in the Fifth Republic.

We have already seen that European policy was the issue that led to the resignation of MRP ministers in 1962 and to an MRP candidate, Lecanuet, retarding de Gaulle's 1965 re-election. Lecanuet attempted to revive the flagging fortunes of the MRP by rebranding it in 1966 as the Democratic Centre (CD) but his hopes were frustrated by the right-wing leader of the Independent Republicans (also created in 1966), Giscard d'Estaing, who was first to attract some of the CD's Right-Centre constituency and then in 1974 defeat the Gaullist candidate on the first ballot of the presidential election before winning the second ballot, founding in the process a broader based French Democratic Union (UDF) party which absorbed the CD.

LIBERAL CONSERVATISM

Although Orleanism as a political style and ideology might have appeared to die with the demise of the July Monarchy in 1848, it survived well into the twentieth

---

[81] Williams, 108; cf. Chapter 8 passim, Irving, Chapters 2 and 3, and Richard Vinen, *Bourgeois Politics in France, 1945–1951*, 1995, Chapter 10 passim.

century among an Anglophile political, financial, and intellectual elite who aspired to combine traditional social stability with modern economic development. It saw itself as occupying a reformist 'juste milieu' between revolution and counter-revolution but in practice maintaining order to preserve elite privilege took priority over promoting progress; its liberalism tended to be submerged by defence of the status quo. After the authoritarian interlude of the Second Empire, the Third Republic in its first decade brought together a liberal monarchist like Thiers and an opportunist republican like Gambetta in the elusive search for a French Whig-cum-Liberal Party able to attract the votes of the lower middle class but led by the upper middle class.

After Thiers's death in 1877 and until his own death in 1882, Gambetta sought to establish British-style government based on a stable partisan parliamentary majority. However, Thiers' overthrow by a monarchist parliamentary vote in 1873 was followed in 1882 by the defeat of the short-lived Gambetta government by the republican deputies that he was trying to turn 'into a party of government, whereas they were inescapably attached to their habits of opposition'.[82] They had preferred Jules Grévy to Gambetta as President of the Republic because he could be relied upon to allow parliament to usurp and monopolize popular sovereignty and block access to the premiership of forceful leaders like Gambetta and then Clemenceau. Just as the rivalry of the erstwhile allies Gambetta and Ferry prevented the emergence of a united parliamentary majority, so that between Ferry and Clemenceau led to the election as president of Sadi Carnot in 1887 'because of what his grandfather had done in 1793'.[83]

Like Gambetta, Ferry saw clericalism as the main enemy.[84] Religious belief was to be dissipated gradually by secular education. As Education Minister in three governments between 1879 and 1883, Ferry set about this task. While the Catholics would not accept that education could be neutral, the Radicals wanted a rapid elimination of Church influence. Their leader Clemenceau condemned Gambetta and Ferry as opportunists who found it tactically expedient to postpone the application of their principles.[85] The Gambetta legacy was most effectively continued by the Breton lawyer René Waldeck-Rousseau, who served as Minister of Interior in Gambetta's three month 'Great Ministry'. He combined liberal conservative moderation with firmness in implementation that was the hallmark of the 'Opportunism' that was a reproach popularized by the newspapers. Shorter on rhetoric than his flamboyant mentor, he was more successful in making the compromises that circumstances required. Less interested than his ally Ferry in education, he was more concerned with maintaining republican state control over subversive clericalism.

After piloting into law the 1884 legalization of trade union activity which others had prepared, Waldeck-Rousseau took a back seat, entering the Senate a decade later but remaining inactive until the Dreyfus crisis led him to head the 1899–1902 Government of Republican Defence. Waldeck-Rousseau had never

[82] Zeldin, *France*, I, 626.   [83] Brogan, *Development of Modern France*, 198; cf. 196–7.
[84] See Chapter 6 above.
[85] Brogan, 626–7; Pierre Barral, *Les Fondateurs de la Troisième République*, 1968, 128.

been favourable to nationalism and anti-Semitism, having as a lawyer in 1892 denounced Drumont as a base defamer. Primarily enraged by the procedural injustice of the Dreyfus Affair, he united the Republican Right-Centre with the Left, including in his government the Socialist Millerand which, as we see in Chapter 9, posed problems to the Left. He cracked down on the nationalist leagues and ordering the arrest of their leaders. In a Chamber of Deputies without Clemenceau and Jaurès, the less colourful Waldeck-Rousseau, respected as an acknowledged statesman, dominated proceedings. Remembered for the adoption of the 1901 Law on Associations, an undefeated Waldeck-Rousseau handed power to Combes in 1902, who carried through a much more abrasive anticlerical policy than his predecessor would have initiated.[86] He was, with Poincaré in 1928, the rare example of a Third Republic Prime Minister who left office voluntarily.

For a century from the 1890s, successive attempts at uniting the French Right failed because it consisted of a diversity of undisciplined parties and movements which only coalesced briefly in crisis when confronted by a resurgent Left. Some salient examples were those led by ex-Prime Ministers Jules Méline in 1898–1903 and Louis Barthou in 1911–14, ex-President Alexandre Millerand in 1924–6 and future Prime Minister Paul Reynaud in the late 1920s. Confusion was compounded by the fact that parliamentary groups and extra-parliamentary parties did not correspond in membership, which added indiscipline to dispersion. Leaders like Poincaré, Briand, Tardieu, and Laval had enemies as well as a network of friends across party lines. The weakness of the partisan Right was partially compensated by pressure groups such as Maurice Colrat's Association for the Defence of the Middle Classes (he was a political associate of Poincaré), Ernest Billiet's Union of Economic Interests or Jules Roche's League of Taxpayers. However, in conjunction with the main big business organizations (like the Steel Committee that became the UIMM), the farmers and ex-servicemen organizations, as well as the propagandist leagues and press, they exacerbated the fragmentation of the Right through what Colrat had called a 'unionized bourgeoisie',[87] rather than unifying it against the Left, which we see in Chapter 9 was also divided.

Prime Minister from 1896 to 1898, Jules Méline is identified especially with his 1892 protectionist tariff to safeguard French peasants from proletarianization as a consequence of cheap food imports but he was also seeking to protect the textile industry in his constituency. The Dreyfus Affair led to the break-up of Méline's 'governmental Republicans'. Raymond Poincaré formed his own Left Republican parliamentary group in 1899, accusing Méline of being 'the prisoner of a reactionary coalition... you only wish to see the danger of revolution at a moment when the reactionary peril is more menacing than ever.'[88] Poincaré's

---

[86] Pierre Sorlin, *Waldeck-Rousseau*, 1966.
[87] Gilles Le Béguec, 'Le parti' in Sirinelli (ed.), *Histoire des droites en France*, III, 36; cf. 14–43 and Gilles Le Béguec and Jacques Prévotat, '1898–1919. L'éveil à la modernité politique' in ibid. I, 235–40.
[88] Quoted in Malcolm Anderson, *Conservative Politics in France*, 37; cf. 34–7, 141.

liberal conservatism was in the spirit of Waldeck-Rousseau's pragmatism but he leaned more to the Right, moving from Prime Minister to President in 1913.

As wartime President he played an active role which led him in 1917 to call on a political opponent, Clemenceau, to take over as Prime Minister but they had differing views over the 1919 Versailles Peace Treaty, notably on how much Germany could be made to pay in reparations. Following the National Bloc's sweeping electoral victory in 1919, as Prime Minister from 1922 to 1924, Poincaré ordered the occupation of the Rhineland to enforce his reparations policy. He was recalled to office in 1926 as Prime Minister to deal with a run on the franc occasioned by the Left's financial mismanagement. 'The rich will pay' had been no more effective than 'Germany will pay' as a remedy to escalating public debt. Poincaré was able to reunite the Right-Centre and Left-Centre to 'save the franc' by producing a unified budget, increasing taxes, and making some economies, but the Left explained its failure and his success by the machinations of the '200 Families' who were deemed to control the Bank of France.[89]

Poincaré's successor, the abrasive would-be economic and political modernizer and disciple of Clemenceau, André Tardieu, three times Prime Minister between 1929 and 1932, failed to unite the Right in the 1930s and Paul Reynaud's inability to keep France in the war in 1940 exemplified the weaknesses of the mainstream Right that allowed Vichy's reactionary illiberalism to take over. Of the 80 parliamentarians out of 569 who voted against the demise of the Third Republic in July 1940 only 4 were from the Right and Right-Centre, although some were among the 17 who abstained.

With only a few maverick right-wingers being active in the Resistance—unlike the Christian Democrats, much less the Left—a weakened parliamentary Right was in 1946 split into six groups. It was only with the 1948 creation of the National Centre of Independents (CNI), which became the CNIP by confederation in 1951 with the Peasant Party (whose deputies numbered more professional lawyers than 'peasants') that electoral and parliamentary coordination of the conservative Right was achieved. Its architect was the CNIP's secretary-general, Senator Roger Duchet, who imaginatively started bottom-up with the local notables, receiving 7,500 responses from French mayors to a questionnaire which he followed up by personal contacts in a provincial tour. The resulting highly decentralized party structure avoided offering a doctrinal programme, still less one leader and party discipline in parliament.

However, a popular Prime Minister did emerge in the unlikely person of Antoine Pinay, former member of Vichy's National Council, who was fortunate not to be declared ineligible after the Second World War. His successful formula was to return to that of Poincaré in 1926: defending the franc by restraining public expenditure and floating a low interest loan without increasing taxes.[90] He only headed the government from March–December 1952 and bequeathed a

---

[89] Ibid. 51–5; cf. Brogan, 591–7 and David Watson, *Georges Clemenceau*, 269, 351–4.

[90] Anderson, 79–83, 232–9, Williams, Chapter 12, and Jacques Chapsal, *La vie politique en France de 1940 à 1958*, 1984, 341–52. See also Vinen, *Bourgeois Politics*, Chapter 13.

record budgetary deficit but his popularity was only rivalled during the Fourth Republic by Mendès France on the Left, who appealed for rigorous effort rather than Pinay's easy-going indulgence. Pinay's successor, René Mayer, who lasted as Prime Minister for less than five months, declared without irony of the thirty-six days before he was replaced that 'The best time in government is when one has been defeated and is a "caretaker" without fearing being overthrown. . . .'[91] This sums up the parlous state of Fourth Republic government.

The 'French Algerian' issue and the resurgence of de Gaulle divided the CNIP and discredited Duchet, who lost the post of secretary-general after the party's electoral defeat of 1962. His place on the liberal conservative Right was taken by Valéry Giscard d'Estaing's Independent Republican Party. It now served one's ministerial career to stick close to de Gaulle, unlike the Fourth Republic years when a deputy could reply to the intransigent General's assertion 'Without me you would not have been elected' with 'without you I would be a minister', but he should have admitted, quickly an ex-minister!

Despite his father's Extreme Right pre-war links with *Action Française* and the Fiery Cross, Giscard inherited the seat of his father-in-law in the National Assembly in 1956 and had an accelerated political career, serving in 1959 to 1960 with Pinay in the Finance Ministry before himself becoming Finance Minister from 1962 to 1965 and again from 1969 to 1974. In the interim, he had established the Independent Republicans as a loose federation in 1966. The Polytechnician Giscard freed the liberal conservative label from its identification with the protectionist policy of preserving a mass of micro, family firms, replaced by a competitive capitalism relying on industrial expansion under a new managerial elite. By his 'Yes, but' approach to support for de Gaulle, he prepared the way for opposition to the 1969 referendum that led to the latter's resignation. The ousting of Gaullism by Giscardism took until 1974, when Giscard defeated the Resistance hero and Gaullist standard bearer, Jacques Chaban-Delmas, on the first ballot of the presidential election, prior to winning on the second ballot.[92]

Having won power with the reassuring slogan of 'change without risk', Giscard was able to take over the Christian Democratic commitment to European integration. From his promotion of a directly elected European Parliament to his 2002–3 role in drafting a constitution for the European Union which his own countrymen rejected in a 2005 referendum, he gave practical expression to his liberal conservatism. In domestic policy he achieved relatively little, although he did increase the Opposition's ability to challenge legislation on grounds of unconstitutionality. His elitist liberalism, redolent of the Orleanist tradition, was condemned to compromise with the post-Gaullism of his first Prime Minister (1974–6) Jacques Chirac, 1974 accomplice and 1981 rival.

Giscard's pretentious 1976 ideological launching pad for a loose confederation of his own party with the CDS residue of the Christian Democrats and the conservative wing of the old Radical Party, the book was *Towards a New Democracy*.

---

[91] Quoted by Lacouture, *De Gaulle*, II, 448.   [92] Anderson, 259–67.

It was followed by their association in his Union for French Democracy or UDF.[93] However, Chirac's 1976 creation of the RPR post-Gaullist party and 1977 victory in the first election of a Paris Mayor since the 1871 Commune, heralded the subsequent domination of the mass party, dynamic ex-Gaullists over the cadre party, ex-Giscardians in the 1980s and 1990s, prior to the UMP dwarfing of the UDF in 2002, although Chirac's choice of Prime Minister, Jean-Pierre Raffarin came from the ex-Giscardians. It had been a long journey from fragmentation to relative consensus for the French Right. However, a menacing threat from the populist Extreme Right prevented the liberal and conservative Right from monopolizing mass support for introverted nationalism, the dilution of Gaullist extroverted nationalism creating the ideological space that the National Front has occupied since the 1980s.

THE POPULIST NATIONAL FRONT

While it is often the case that the extremes feed on and favour each other and the FN is at the forefront of anti-Communism, it was during a period in which the PCF was in steep decline that the FN made its spectacular break through. The exhaustion of the revolutionary impetus on the Left coincided with a re-emergence of a counter-revolutionary focus on the Right that had been buried prematurely. Xenophobia was discredited by its association with the defeatism and anti-Semitism of the Vichy regime, the authoritarian Right rallying after the Second World War to a Gaullist movement that repudiated such attitudes. However, while Gaullism's reassertion of national grandeur and power were attractive to the Extreme Right, it was repelled by key aspects of de Gaulle's policy when he returned to office in 1958. Decolonization was regarded as national betrayal, particularly when it came to Algeria. It was no accident that Le Pen, leader of the FN, was personally involved in the repression of the Algerian independence movement and has received strong support from areas—especially in south-east France—in which former Algerian settlers are concentrated. The Extreme Right also resented the process of economic modernization (begun before de Gaulle, but pushed further by him) that was destroying the peasant and small shopkeeper traditional society. There was always an important element of populist anti-capitalism and anti-technocracy in the French Extreme Right and once again Le Pen was associated with it, being elected a deputy of the small Extreme Right led by Pierre Poujade in 1956 after returning from Algeria. However, while bitterly opposed to de Gaulle, Le Pen did not take part in the movements that sought to overthrow de Gaulle by terrorism, carefully remaining within the bounds of the law. He devoted himself to unifying the highly fissiparous Extreme Right in the FN in 1972, but for a decade his attempts at making this a significant political force were miserable failures. What accounts for the transformation of 'France for the

---

[93] John R. Frears, *France in the Giscard Presidency*, 1981 and Valéry Giscard d'Estaing, *Towards a New Democracy*, 1976, 1977 Eng. edn.

French' xenophobia from a traditional phenomenon of political culture into an organized political movement capable of influencing policy?[94]

Clearly it could not just be a matter of the size of the immigration problem because France had for many years absorbed a particularly large number of immigrants. While the North African and black African element had increased at the expense of migration from other European countries, this also long predated the increase in electoral support for the Extreme Right in the 1980s. Because this resurgence coincided with the presence in power of the Left, it has been too readily assumed that it was in reaction to the Mitterrand presidency and Socialist governments that the FN was able to build up its spectacular increase in support.[95] Why was the RPR's and UDF's 'civilized Right' unable to capitalize on anti-Socialist sentiment? It was the failures of the centre-Right rather than of the Left that provided Le Pen with his opportunity for a political break-through. He used a wider range of appeals than the single issue of immigration, although he cleverly linked that with the issues of unemployment, crime, and the loss of national identity. The shift away from Gaullist nationalism and the pursuit of socially disruptive policies of economic modernization and exposure to international market forces meant that part of the Centre-Right's clientele felt abandoned. Furthermore, the process of liberalization and modernization within the Church meant that traditionalist Catholics also felt abandoned. While the FN cannot rival the main parties of the Centre-Right—especially the UDF—in attracting support from mainstream Catholics, it has appealed both to the ultra-traditionalist Catholics and to the dechristianized, who do not feel bound by the humanitarian and moralistic injunctions of the Catholic Church.

French extreme nationalism had always focused on the purported crisis of national identity, which gives it a popular appeal that transcends specific issues by those it includes and those it excludes from French France.[96] The rise of populism in France in its FN form is characterized by the attack upon elitist scapegoats (national technocrats and Eurocrats) and 'foreign' scapegoats, both Jewish financiers and media moguls, as well as the mass of impecunious North African immigrants, who are stigmatized as living off the home-grown French tax payers. It can draw upon diffuse support for its emphasis on issues that are at the forefront of public preoccupation. When asked in February 1995 what were the causes of the increase in populism in France, 60 per cent attributed it partly to unemployment, 45 per cent to a feeling of insecurity, 36 per cent to immigration and 33 per cent to corruption and financial scandals, while 32 per cent suggested religious fundamentalism. Among the other explanations, the crisis

---

[94] Nonna Mayer and Pascal Perrineau, *Le Front National à découvert*, 1996. See also Christopher Flood, 'National Populism' in Christopher Flood and Lawrence Bell (eds), *Political Ideologies in Contemporary France*, 1997, Chapter 4.

[95] Yves Gastaut, *L'Immigration et l'opinion en France sous la Ve Règpublique*, 2000.

[96] From a vast literature, one may mention Dominique Schnapper, 'The debate on immigration and the crisis of national identity' in *West European Politics*, 17/2, April 1994, Patrick Weil, *Qu'est qu'un français? Histoire de la nationalitè française depuis la Révolution*, 2002, and P. Weil, *La République et sa diversité: immigration, intégration, discrimination*, 2005.

of traditional parties and ideologies only rated 10 per cent and fears concerning European integration a mere 5 per cent.[97] The feeling of public despair at the incapacity of governments of both Left and Right to deal with mass unemployment accounts for the fact that in the presidential elections of 1995 and 2002 Le Pen, with the help of a quarter of the worker's vote, was able to first threaten and then overtake the Socialist candidate Jospin, as the second ballot contender against the victor, Chirac. The 2007 presidential election aroused fears of another upset of expectations of a run-off between the mainstream Right and Left. How had the fragmented Left fared meanwhile in the process of remaking partisan France?

[97] G. Le Gall, 'La tentation du populisme' in Sofres (ed.), *L'Etat de l'Opinion*, 1996.

9

Adversaries on the Left: Revolutionary Rhetoric and Reformist Realities

The divisions among the partisan Left, between Radicals, Socialists, Communists, and Anarchists, have been compounded by that between the industrial and political wings of fragmented working-class movements. Premature politicization and a lagging and partial process of proletarianization led to attraction by a bourgeois liberal democracy that assured their status as citizens but repulsion owing to their exclusion from the economic security to which they aspired. The dispersion of working classes condemned to find expression in a diversity of political parties compounded the distrust of a representative process in which leaders were regarded as substituting their priorities and interests for those of the led. In these circumstances, it is not surprising that following their post-revolutionary experience, there was an inclination to reject all government in practice, combined with a belief in an ideal government free from the disillusions to which they had previously been subjected.

Nevertheless, there was an obsessive, rhetorical appeal to revolution that mythologized the role of the working class that would redeem society of all its injustices and which delegitimized gradual and piecemeal reforms when these were proffered within a parliamentary democracy. Weak party and trade union organizations were supplemented by upsurges of a social and political militancy that demanded state intervention to satisfy neglected public needs but were allergic to sacrificing autonomy to institutionalized compromise. The abrasive coexistence between class warfare and political democracy, which goes back to 1848 and the Second Republic, looked for its resolution to a comprehensive revolution which the 1871 Paris Commune had shown to be unattainable by violence. Thereafter, the process of adapting to a situation in which revolution in France became a utopian project proved a painful one. The vicissitudes of an acceptance of reformist realities were characterized by an increasing divergence between the backward-facing strategic principles affirmed and the practices adopted to deal tactically with changing circumstances.

Although the Third Republic had been established despite efforts at a royalist restoration, it had first to defeat the Commune's attempt to establish a neo-Jacobin and proletarian dictatorship. The incorporation of revolutionary elitism first into Marxism and then into Leninism ensured that the Left would be divided—as had the Commune itself—between a Proudhonian, anti-authoritarian, and federalist socialism and syndicalism and a Blanquist,

authoritarian, and centralist communism. Marx's attempt to keep control of the
First International led to a split with the anarchists headed by Michael Bakunin
and was to be perpetuated in the conflicts between Jules Guesde and first Paul
Brousse and then Jean Jaurès for control of the Socialist movement and between
it and the anarcho-syndicalist trade union movement. In contrast to Blanqui's
catastrophism and Guesde's dogmatism, Jaurès adapted Marxism to accommodate a democracy that transcended the working classes and included the middle
classes that were turning increasingly for their political expression to the Radicals.
However, he was not able to bring the anti-parliamentary anarcho-syndicalists
within the bounds of a humanistic eclecticism. It would not survive the Bolshevik
Revolution's revival of Blanquism in the shape of a Marxism-Leninism which
split the Socialists in 1920 and the trade union movement a year later.[1] Before
discussing the momentous twentieth century severance between communism and
socialism and its consequences, we shall examine first three manifestations of
post-Commune anarchism that played an important part in the Left's dissensions
prior to the First World War and whose imprint has not been effaced.

ADVENT OF THE ANARCHIST OUTSIDERS

Proudhon's legacy to late nineteenth-century anarchism was a rejection of the
authoritarianisms of church, state, and capitalism. His influence was greatest
on Pelloutier-Sorel anarcho-syndicalism and on Brousse's municipal anarcho-
socialism, with far less influence than Bakunin on those anarchists who engaged
in terrorist action. We shall start by looking at Paul Brousse's trajectory from revolutionary to reformist, once he realized that revolution was no longer a practical
proposition.

A doctor by training (who pioneered the 'political surgery' when he became
a local councillor and deputy), Brousse was briefly a member of the First International but was expelled for siding with Bakunin against Marx in 1872. He
spent the next eight years in exile, mainly in Switzerland where he was a leading
propagandist on behalf of the Jura Federation brand of anarchism. Convinced
that calls for a general strike were futile well in advance of the demonstration
of its failure by the trade union movement in the first decade of the twentieth
century, Brousse was also convinced that the workers expected action not words.
So, he at first followed the Italian anarchist advocacy of 'propaganda by the deed'.
However, more than a decade before the French anarchist terrorist outrages of
the early 1890s, Brousse realized that recourse to individual acts of violence was
also unlikely to succeed, so pragmatically he fell back on his mentor Proudhon's
emphasis on communes as local organizations of anti-authoritarian politics. In

---

[1] On the nineteenth-century background to the Left's fragmented political culture, see George
Lichtheim's *Marxism in Modern France*, 1966, Chapter 1 and Tony Judt, *Marxism and the French Left*,
Chapter 2.

a non-revolutionary context, this meant concentrating on piecemeal, practical application of the anarcho-socialist programme. Ironically, in 1878 he was tried, imprisoned briefly, and then expelled form Switzerland for advocating in newspaper articles an extremist policy he was abandoning. The transformation from an anarchist into a 'Possibilist' took place in his 1879–80 Brussels and London exile and was complete by his return to France in 1880 following the amnesty for ex-Communards.

Brousse's advocacy of municipal socialism led him into bitter conflict with the Marxists for control of the socialist movement. Having engaged in polemics with Guesde over the Marx-inspired 1880 Minimum Programme of the nascent French Socialist Party, the ensuing struggle for control was provisionally won by Brousse in 1882. The expulsion of the Guesdists led to Marx's son-in-law Paul Lafargue's condemnation of Possiblism as a petit bourgeois, opportunist abandonment of collectivism. Brousse substituted his Municipal Programme for the Marxist Minimum Programme because it would give the workers experience in practical action by taking control—as the bourgeoisie had done earlier—where it was easiest to do so and enable them meanwhile to improve their material conditions such as housing. More generally, he championed the collective ownership and provision of public services as a way of satisfying the most pressing needs of the workers. Remaining committed to the class struggle but one waged by electoral means, it was Brousse's so-called Socialist Revolutionary Workers Party that dominated Socialist Party politics in the 1880s, not Guesde's French Workers Party or the Blanquist Central revolutionary Council. It achieved electoral success in the Paris Municipal Council (of which Brousse became President in 1905) and played a part in the anti-Boulangist campaign of late 1880s, unlike the Guesdist French Workers Party.

However, its weak trade union links resulted in a loss of working-class support that led to a 1890 split headed by former Communard Jean Allemane, destroying the Possibilists as a party. The rump eventually joined Jaurès' reformist wing of the united Socialist Party. The Allemanist 'workerist' concern to ensure party control over their representatives led them in 1891 to devise the requirement of a pre-signed resignation that elected members were to deposit with their local party organization, later imitated by the French Communist Party. Although a forgotten ancestor of French socialism, Paul Brousse's reformist strategy has since been shamefacedly practised even when shrouded in revolutionary posturing and pretence.[2] A century later, the democratic decentralist Socialist reforms of the 1980s, although less utopian in their ambitions, as would be expected from Interior Minister and Mayor of Marseille Defferre and Prime Minister and Mayor of Lille Mauroy, marked a belated reformist victory for the municipal socialism of the 1880s by increasing the scope of local economic interventionism. He also influenced the Fabian programme of gradual reform and municipal socialism that shaped the theory and practice of the British Labour Party.

---

[2] See the excellent book by David Stafford, *From Anarchism to Reformism: A Study of the Political Activities of Paul Brousse, 1870–90*, 1971. See also Zeldin, I, 753–6.

In the 1890s the spotlight on anarchist aspirations was first on the violent acts of 'propaganda by the deed' and then, when these had been successfully repressed, on the emergence of revolutionary syndicalism. The ground for these developments was prepared by the 1880s liberal legislation, notably the 1881 Press Law and the 1884 Trade Union Law, as well as increasing discontent with the social conservatism of the parliamentary politicians. A Parisian subculture in the illustrated press and cabarets exploited hostility not merely to state power but to bourgeois values generally, supplemented by the aggressive simplifications of the newspapers read aloud and discussed in cafés.

From 1895 to 1994, the most ideologically authoritative anarchist journal, until ended by his imprisonment, was Jean Grave's *Le Révolté*, which had abandoned 'propaganda by the deed' in the 1890s. He had earlier declared: 'Our propaganda among the people ought to show them that in a revolution, instead of stupidly going to the Hôtel de Ville to proclaim a government, we ought to go there to shoot whoever tries to set one up'.[3] Even more radical was the weekly *Le Père Peinard*, which achieved national notoriety and an estimated readership of 100,000. It was founded in 1889 by the future anarcho-syndicalist leader Emile Pouget, for which he edited *La Voix du Peuple* on returning from exile in England.

The journal of outsider anti-political and literary anarchism and nihilism was Zo d'Axa's *L'Endehors*, for which 'the style of one's life and one's art took precedence over their content, the act of rebellion over the cause'.[4] There were links with the avant-garde anarcho-Symbolist journals like *La Revue Blanche*, which in the 1890s attracted as contributors the future Socialist leader Léon Blum, the anti-anti-Semite Bernard-Lazare, and Julien Benda. All of them became ardent Dreyfusards, having been alerted to judicial injustice of guilt by association in the 1894 'Trial of the Thirty', in which nineteen anarchist theoreticians and artists were lumped together with eleven thieves, although the anarchists were acquitted after the prosecution's claims of conspiracy were successfully ridiculed.[5]

Aesthetic anarchists, such as Barrès, found rebellion a comfortable provisional pose in the late nineteenth century. The symbolist poets Mallarmé and Verlaine were attracted to anarchism by its form not its content, as an idealist 'insurrection against the rules'. However, they regarded books of poetry as more effective propaganda than bombs. Nevertheless, it became fashionable for *déclassé* intellectuals in search of a radical audience to associate with avant-garde anarchists as fellow-travelling outsiders. Unlike the anarcho-syndicalists who focused on collectively mobilizing workers, the anarcho-Symbolists concentrated on symbolic individual acts that they hoped would transcend the gulf between art and everyday life. When asked what he thought of Vaillant's bomb thrown in the Chamber of Deputies, the poet Laurent Tailhade replied: 'What do the victims matter if the gesture is beautiful.'[6] Vaillant's bomb was a deliberately non-lethal attempt to frighten

---

[3] Quoted in Brogan, 300; cf. 299–302.
[4] Richard D. Son, *Anarchism and Cultural Politics in Fin de Siècle France*, 1989, 17; cf. 14–18.
[5] Ibid. 22–4; cf. 17–18, 43, 47.   [6] Ibid. 234; cf. 181–3, 190–201, 211–17, 236, 241, 255–8.

the bourgeoisie and attract attention, both of which it was certainly successful in doing. Other acts, such as the 1894 assassination of President Carnot, were less clearly symbolic but the courageous way in which the anarchists faced death by the guillotine added to their public status as revolutionary heroes and selfless martyrs. In all, between 1892 and 1894, 13 attacks on symbols of authority, mostly with dynamite, killed ten people, with five anarchists being sentenced to death and three to life imprisonment.[7]

Bohemian Montmartre was the hotbed of anarchistic-inclined visual artists and a political cabaret subculture that was intermediary between the Left bank middle-class writers and proletarian Belleville, using derision to attack bourgeois morality. 'Montmartre functioned as a red-light district of the arts, where vice would be tolerated but geographically restricted. . . .'[8] Not formally absorbed by Paris until 1859, Montmartre retained its character as an artist's colony (attracting Van Gogh among others) and a focus for cabarets. Aristide Bruant sentimentalized the sub-proletariat of prostitutes and particularly the pimps, who achieved the ideal of not having to work for a living. In 1885, he followed Rodolphe Salis (who had published a newspaper from 1882 in association with his cabaret *Le Chat Noir*), printing regularly in *Le Mirliton* a song accompanied first by a Lautrec, and then a Steinlen, drawing. By their deliberate adoption of the picturesque, vernacular argot of the criminal underclass, these anarchistic cabarets (like Pouget, who thought that workers 'would be more willing to read a newspaper written as they spoke rather than one written as the bourgeois wrote'), 'emphasised the gulf that separated the formal language of the political elites from the subcultural idiom of the Parisian faubourgs in order to reinforce class conflict and promote working-class solidarity'.[9]

There was a crackdown on political cabarets from 1897 when Salis died and Bruant retired (they had been exempted from prior censorship), the latter drifting towards the anti-Semitic and national-populist Right. To avoid theatre censorship, plays were put on in subscription only playhouses. Although a Barrès 1894 play about parliamentary corruption aroused controversy, the biggest impact was made in 1896 by Alfred Jarry's 'pataphysical' obscene parody of political authority, *Ubu roi*. However, a greater anarchist threat to the Third Republic than either terrorism or derision was coming to the fore: the revolutionary syndicalist call for a general strike.

The industrial context in which anarcho-syndicalist ideas took hold in the trade union movement was one of increased militancy between 1880 and the First World War. 'Twice as many strikes took place in 1880–4 as in 1875–9 or in any previous period.' Thereafter, 'Each of the principal increases in strike activity was tied to an increase in the organisational capacities of labor'.[10] Unions often originated from spontaneous strikes, whose duration increased from an average of 7 days in 1875 to 21 days in 1902.[11] As the press concentrated on strikes, especially when

---

[7] Ibid. 237–61. [8] Ibid. 74; cf. 59–73. [9] Ibid. 100, 95; cf. 96–8, 147–54.
[10] Shorter and Tilly, 47.
[11] Gérard Noiriel, *Les ouvriers dans la société française: XIX–XXe siècle*, 1986, 99; cf. 104–8.

they resulted in violent confrontations with the army, workers were perceived by the middle classes predominantly in conflictual and threatening terms. The harsh and reactionary attitude of almost all employers gave the workers no hope of securing piecemeal concessions, while an ineffective and divided parliamentary socialism, whose leaders were almost entirely middle class, offered little prospect of supportive state intervention. The ghetto status of the working classes promoted an anti-political 'workerist' rationalization of exclusion, reinforced by the memory of the bloody class conflicts of 1848 and 1871. With the 1890s influx of anarchists into the trade unions, the scene was set for revolutionary syndicalism to become the opiate of the activist minority of French workers.[12]

The intellectual and organizational initiator of revolutionary syndicalism in France was the republican journalist Fernand Pelloutier. After being attracted to the Marxism of Jules Guesde, who had captured control of the first national trade union confederation, Pelloutier—whose thinking was suffused with the reading of Proudhon—decided that non-violent direct industrial action, rather than relying on a political party to win elections, would be the most rapid and effective way of achieving the replacement of capitalism by the free association of producers. In 1892, working with his fellow Breton journalist Aristide Briand, Pelloutier revived the Chartist 1830s idea of the general strike (emolliently called in Britain the Grand National Holiday), adopted in 1870s by the Bakuninists but abandoned by Brousse in favour of electoral action. Rejecting both the Blanquist attempt to seize power violently and the Guesdist indefinite postponement of the revolution until the conditions were ripe, Pelloutier presented the general strike as a legal, peaceful, and rapid way of demonstrating what Proudhon had called the political capacity of the working classes. Pelloutier optimistically believed that if the workers in the strategically vital sectors stayed at home for up to fifteen—later reduced to eight—days, the economy would grind to a halt without bloodshed. The workers would have achieved their own emancipation.[13] Briand quickly retreated to the position of using the *threat* of a general strike to exert pressure on government but as a minister in 1910 he was to use the call up of reservists and threat of court martial to repress a general strike.

To organize the general strike and deal with its aftermath, Pelloutier relied (as discussed in Chapter 6) on the local trades councils or *Bourses du Travail*, which functioned formally as labour exchanges but were also educational and propaganda institutions that provided practical help for workers and could collect funds to support them during a general strike. Following the 1884 abolition of the anti-trade union 1791 Le Chapelier Law, the first trades council was set up in Paris in 1887 with Possibilist support and in 1892 the increasing number of provincial councils led to their being federated. Pelloutier became General-Secretary of the Federation of Trades Councils in 1895, the year in which the General Confederation of Labour or CGT was established to unite the workers

---

[12] V. R. Lorwin, *The French Labor Movement*, 1954, 36–9.

[13] Jeremy Jennings, *Syndicalism in France: A Study of Ideas*, 1900, 11–18, 22 and Jacques Julliard, *Fernand Pelloutier et les origines du syndicalisme d'action directe*, 1971, 61–89, 124–5, 206–8, 304–7.

organized in centralized industrial unions rather than territorially federalized in autonomous local councils.

The CGT did not—until unified with the Trades Councils in 1902—support the general strike, so there were polemics between them until Pelloutier's early death in 1901.[14] Victor Griffuelhes, who became the first General-Secretary of the unified trade union movement in 1902, was not in favour of a strong organization, fearing (like Robert Michels and his 'iron law of oligarchy') that it would lead to embourgeoisement and the failure to create a classless society. The anarchist Pouget's fiery journalism stressed that the class war would be fought between minorities, with the parliamentary socialists like Briand traitorously ready to use the army against the workers. Industrial sabotage, ranging from working to rule and go slows to outright machine smashing, were tactics advocated by Pouget but were opposed both by an opponent of the general strike like Jaurès and a supporter like Sorel.[15]

In an earlier article on 'General Strike and Revolution', republished in his 1902 *Etudes Socialistes*, which refuted in advance the hopes placed in this mobilizing myth by Sorel in his *Reflections on Violence*, Jean Jaurès argued that three preconditions were necessary for it to succeed. It had to be used in support of a specific objective that aroused worker enthusiasm and could be quickly implemented, such as the 8-hour workday, unemployment insurance, or old-age pensions; it had to win public support; it must be non-violent, otherwise it would lead not to bourgeois capitulation but to many years of reactionary repression. Instead, the general strike's advocates were trying to lead the proletariat into unintentional revolutionary action, mistaking 'a tactic of despair for a revolutionary method' because 'there is only one sovereign method to achieve socialism today: legally win a majority.'[16] Sorel's associate Hubert Lagardelle responded by rejecting 'parliamentary cretinism' and 'governmental socialism' as based on counter-revolutionary democratic fictions but unlike Sorel he believed that the general strike would eventually succeed. Disillusion led Lagardelle, via advocating regionalism in the 1920s and planning in the 1930s, to end as a Vichy Minister of Labour in the 1940s.[17]

In 1906, the Amiens Charter of the CGT represented the commitment to anarcho-syndicalism of the united trade union movement. Carried by 803 votes to 8, after a motion proposing an understanding with the recently unified Socialist Party was defeated by 724 votes to 34 and 37 abstentions, it declared its independence of all parties. Asserting the existence of an economic class struggle, trade unions sought to improve wages and reduce working hours but their ambition was to achieve the 'complete emancipation' of the workers by dispossessing the capitalists. The general strike was 'the means of action and ... while unions today are resistance groups, in the future they will be responsible for production and

---

[14] Julliard, Chapter 4 and Fernand Pelloutier's *Histoire des Bourses du travail: Origine, institutions, avenir*, 1902, with a Preface by Sorel.

[15] Jennings, *Syndicalism in France*, 8–9, 24–38, 44–50.

[16] Jean Jaurès, *Etudes Socialistes*, 1902, 121; cf. 97–120.

[17] Jennings, 86–99, 110–13; on Sorel 56–7.

distribution, the basis of social reorganization'.[18] Opposed by the reformist leader of the Printers' Union, Auguste Keufer, these tactics demonstrated their ineffectiveness, the CGT losing its conflicts with the governments of Clemenceau and Briand. The supreme fiasco of the general strike was the failure in 1914 to use it to prevent French involvement in the First World War. Thereafter, the Bolshevik Revolution led to a split in both the Socialist Party and the CGT, to which we shall return later. First, we must consider the opposite end of the left-wing spectrum, the so-called Radical and Radical Socialist Republican Party.

Before we bid farewell to the anarcho-syndicalist strand in the French Left, its resurgence in May 1968 showed that it had not disappeared but remained recessive and capable of reviving unpredictably. Sparked by student unrest, in which Daniel Cohn-Bendit was to emerge as the most articulate exponent, it rapidly escalated into an all-out attack on institutional authority. Not merely the Gaullist Fifth Republic but the control of employers in the factories became the target of what became a short-lived revolutionary political and social crisis. However, the communist control of the CGT ensured that the occupation of the factories did not lead to a pursuit of workers control but was switched to a successful demand for substantial wage increases, while political control was reasserted by calling a general election that submerged the activist minorities in the democratic mass vote. It was Trotskyist movements that subsequently established themselves as the non-libertarian voice of the Extreme Left.

RADICALS: PIVOTAL PARTY OF THE THIRD AND FOURTH REPUBLICS

The Radical Party's use of the term 'radical' has been derisively said to derive from 'radish', being red outside and white inside. Radicals acquired a reputation for not translating their doctrines into deeds because 'they were constantly allying with their supposed enemies, temporising, compromising and muddling through'.[19] While this was true of the latter part of the Third Republic, notably of Edouard Herriot, it was not true of Clemenceau, Combes, or Léon Bourgeois. As Mayor of Montmartre in 1870–1, Clemenceau failed in his efforts to avoid a bloody confrontation between the Thiers government and the Paris Commune, his future Republican rival Jules Ferry siding with Thiers. This gave rise to an intense personal enmity between the champions of a Radical versus an Opportunist Republic. The Extreme Left in the first decade of the Third Republic was led initially by the 1848 Socialist leader Louis Blanc but Clemenceau, elected Deputy in 1876, became in 1877 Secretary of the committee uniting the Republican opposition to President MacMahon. Leading the opposition to the Ferry and

---

[18] See the full text in John Gretton, *Students and Workers*, 1969, 168. On the reformist syndicalism of Keufer, see Jennings, Chapter 4.

[19] Zeldin, I, 683; cf. 691.

the Opportunists, he was determined to divide the radical from the conservative Republicans.

From 1880, Clemenceau, as Deputy for Montmartre, propounded a comprehensive Radical programme involving, beyond anticlerical education provision, abolition of the Senate, communal autonomy, election of magistrates and the abolition of the death penalty, progressive income and inheritance taxes, reduction in working hours, and the recognition of trade unions, which brought him close to the reformist socialists on issues that had been abandoned by the Gambetta of the 1869 Belleville programme. (In 1882 Clemenceau and the Radicals voted with the Right to cause the downfall of the Gambetta government.) To promote his programme, he launched a newspaper, *Justice*, but his dependence for financial support on a financier involved in the Panama scandal led to the loss of his seat in parliament in 1893. His attempt to set up a Radical Party, the Republican–Socialist alliance, was a complete failure, not assisted by his abrasive debating style and extremist reputation, which earned him more enemies than friends and frequent duels.[20] The Radicals remained dispersed until 1901 and Clemenceau was excluded from office until 1905.

As we have seen earlier, Clemenceau's ministerial ambitions, animosity to Ferry and desire for radical constitutional revision led him to promote the career of General Boulanger as War Minister and block the election as President of Ferry in favour of the mediocre Sadi Carnot in the wake of the 1887 Grévy resignation. When Clemenceau realized that Boulanger was encouraging some of the extreme anti-system Radicals like Rochefort to foment a *coup d'état*, he broke with him and when Boulanger's campaign was assisted by election in numerous constituencies, Clemenceau introduced the law forbidding this potentially plebiscitary practice. The legacy of Clemenceau's attempt to counteract Opportunist conservatism at all costs was combined with his switch of constituencies from radical Montmartre to rural Var and the abandonment of his Radical programme. More generally, 'Boulangism dealt a blow to working-class urban Radicalism, especially that of Paris, from which it never fully recovered. The receding tide of Boulangism left many of the constituencies which had been firmly Radical in the hands of the Socialists; Radicalism began to appear more as a rural, and above all, a southern affair.'[21] Radicals now joined governments of the Right-Centre and Left-Centre, acquiring an enduring identification with provincial, small town new notables, more concerned with preserving the status quo than with promoting change.

Discredited by the Panama scandal, Clemenceau went into the political wilderness until resuscitated by his energetic Dreyfusard journalistic campaign. Although no one could have been said to have replaced 'the Tiger', the statesman-like Léon Bourgeois emerged as a much more consensual personification of Radicalism. He corrected the Third Republic's calculated conservatism with something of the generous social fraternalism of the early Second Republic. Bourgeois

[20] David Watson, *Georges Clemenceau*, 63–78; cf. Chapter 4 and Odile Rudelle, *La République Absolue*, 70–6.
[21] Watson, 10; cf. 104–13 and Rudelle, 164–93, 205–32, 248–55.

had been a sub-Prefect and Prefect from 1876, becoming Paris Prefect of Police in 1887 at the age of 36. Elected Deputy in 1888—receiving 48,000 votes to Boulanger's 16,000—he became a minister in the same year, serving in turn as Interior, Education, and Justice Minister until becoming Prime Minister of the first wholly Radical government in 1895–6.

Instead of Clemenceau, the redoubtable polemicist, Bourgeois formulated the conciliatory doctrine of Solidarism that offered a justification in terms of 'social debt' for social reform paid for in part by a progressive income tax, a Radicalism reconciling social liberalism and liberal socialism. This helped him to secure the support of socialists like Jaurès. He ordered the reopening of the Paris Trades Council (which had been closed in the panic following anarchist terrorism), but the life of his government was cut short by Senate opposition to his tax proposals, leading them to refuse to vote the military budget. Not a fighter like Clemenceau, Bourgeois resigned, later playing a part in the creation for the Radical Party in 1901 and becoming a pioneer champion of the 'Society of Nations' that was established after the First World War as the League of Nations.[22]

The Welfare State legislation he favoured was only slowly enacted, partly because of the fiscal conservatism of many of his fellow Radicals. The factory regulation of working women and children was slowed up by Senate opposition to improvements in the 1874 Law fixing a minimum age of 12 and appointing 15 inspectors. An 11-hour maximum working day for women, and children from 16 to 18 was decided in 1892, with a 10-hour day for those aged 13–15. A general 10-hour workday 1900 law was ineffectively implemented but prepared the way for the 1919 8-hour workday. From 1891, a Labour Office collected working conditions statistics but an 1892 law on voluntary industrial arbitration was little used and Millerand's attempt to make it compulsory failed. Four laws dealing with industrial injuries insurance were passed between 1898 and 1902 but Senate opposition prevented a pensions Bill becoming law until 1910. Trade union objection to compulsory pensions contributions was an additional factor, considering that their ability to collect subscriptions and offer friendly society services would suffer as a result.

Following the Combes government's concentration upon anticlericalism, which confirmed the pertinence of Herr's comment that a Radical was 'a conservative who doesn't go to mass',[23] Clemenceau, now a Senator, made his ministerial début aged 63 in the 1905 Sarrien government. An apocryphal story claimed that asked by the Prime Minister what he would take (as refreshment) he replied 'the Interior' and this was the post he got![24] He quickly became embroiled with a violent 1906 strike in the Northern coalfield following an explosion in which some 1,100 miners were killed. After a personal attempt at conciliation, the death of a soldier led him to send in 20,000 troops. He ordered the arrest of Griffuelhes, General

---

[22] J. E. S. Hayward, 'The Official Social Philosophy of the French Third Republic: Léon Bourgeois and Solidarism', in *International Review of Social History*, VI/I, 1961, 19–48. On the slow advance of social welfare legislation in the next paragraph, see Zeldin, I, 666–9.

[23] Quoted in Goldberg, *Jaurès*, 394.   [24] Watson, 171 note.

Table 9.1. Results of the 1906 election to the Chamber of Deputies

'Party'	Votes		Seats	
	Number (000)	%	Number	%
Conservative and Extreme Right	2,572	29.2	107	18.6
Moderate Republicans	1,238	14.0	67	11.7
Left Republicans	704	8.0	52	9.0
Independent Radicals	692	7.9	39	6.8
Socialist Radicals	2,515	28.5	239	41.6
Independent Socialists	205	2.3	18	3.1
Socialists	877	10.0	53	9.2

Source: Slightly modified from Campbell, *French Electoral Systems and Elections since 1789*, 84.

Secretary of the CGT, on the eve of a May 1 demonstration in favour of the 8-hour working day, having concentrated 40,000 troops in Paris. Perhaps understandable as a precaution in the context of the concurrent general strike agitation, this characteristic overreaction provoked general industrial unrest amounting in 1906 to nearly 10 million days work lost, 'almost double that of any other year before 1919'.[25]

Nevertheless, the elections that followed in the same month as the May 1 demonstration and strikes resulted in a major advance of the left-wing candidates (who generally stood down in favour of the best placed Left candidate on the second ballot) of both the Socialist Radical and Socialist parties (see Table 9.1). However, as the Socialists would no longer support a Radical-led government that repressed strikers, and Clemenceau attacked Jaurès for condoning CGT extremism, the Radicals had to turn to the Conservative Republicans of the Centre-Right, thus paradoxically shifting the parliamentary majority to the Right. This meant that the Radicals gave increasing priority to the wallets they kept on the Right over their hearts on the Left, a crucial factor in shaping public policy. 'From 1906 to the fall of the Third Republic the Radicals became the centre of gravity of political France',[26] but its right wing often voted with the Conservatives and its left wing with the Socialists. Lacking a clear political orientation, despite their impressive public support, 'Between 1900 and 1939 no radical was ever President of the Republic, and there was a radical Prime Minister for only a quarter of this period'.[27]

Clemenceau, who had dominated the 1905–6 Sarrien government, shortly before becoming Prime Minister in October 1906 explained that 'For an honest man, when he enters the government, the time of criticism and of pure idealism is behind him. His first duty is to set limits to his aims. Henceforth he has to take account of circumstances... In order to achieve those parts of his programme that are immediately applicable, he must compromise with the customs and habits created by the very system he wants to change.'[28] Having frankly acknowledged

[25] Ibid. 174; cf. 172–6 and Zeldin, I, 705.   [26] Watson, 178; cf. 176–81.
[27] Zeldin, I, 715–16; cf. 714, 719–24.   [28] Quoted in Watson, 182.

the constraints of politically realistic action, his government had several notable features. As well as symbolically appointing the Dreyfusard General Picquart as Minister of War, he chose an Independent Socialist, Viviani, as the first ever Minister of Labour and another, Briand, as Education Minister. The Radical Joseph Caillaux was appointed Finance Minister to implement the commitment to introduce an income tax, the government programme also including the institution of a maximum 10-hour workday and old-age pensions. Clemenceau combined the premiership with the Ministry of the Interior and so responsibility for maintaining order. In conjunction with his declaration that 'The real France is founded on property, property, property',[29] this was quickly to bring him once again into collision with the trade unions.

The 1907 flashpoint was the issue of whether public employees could join trade unions affiliated to the revolutionary syndicalist CGT. Minister of Education Briand, former advocate of the general strike, denied primary schoolteachers this right and sacked the Teachers Union General Secretary. Others wished to go further and ban the CGT. Clemenceau refused to do so on the ground that however repugnant its leadership, he would not condone denying the aspirations of the proletariat and its representatives, even though the CGT only represented a minority of the unionized workers, themselves a small minority of the working classes. In refusing to do so, he placated the left wing of his own party and despite the 7-hour speech by Jaurès attacking the renegade Briand (who argued that he was avoiding schools proselytizing for revolution), Clemenceau secured a comfortable Left-Centre majority which supported him until 1909 with increasing help from the Right-Centre. He continued to repress the violent industrial unrest (especially of 1907–8) that over the lifetime of his government resulted in '104 years in prison sentences, 667 wounded workers, 20 dead workers and 392 dismissals'.[30] Clemenceau also dealt firmly with rural riots in the South (supported by the CGT), provoked by the collapse of wine prices due to overproduction, but they stopped once the prices to the producers recovered.

Much of parliamentary debate in 1908–9 was devoted to the Income Tax Bill being piloted by Finance Minister Caillaux. 'Between 1872 and 1907 no fewer than 65 bills were moved to introduce some form of income tax' and Caillaux's proposal of a higher rate for the rich was denounced as a class struggle tax.[31] Votes of confidence were necessary to persuade reluctant Radicals to support contentious clauses and in March 1909 it was approved only to be blocked in the Senate until Caillaux secured its adoption in 1913, with low rates and generous exemptions for peasants and state bondholders. It was finally implemented in 1917 to finance the war.

It was Clemenceau's pugnacity that led to his defeat in 1909 on a conflict over foreign policy with Delcassé and he was not to return to office until 1917 to lead

---

[29] Quoted in Goldberg, *The Life of Jean Jaurès*, 363; cf. 364 and Watson, 183–4.

[30] Calculations quoted in Goldberg, 368 from Edouard Dolléans, *Histoire du Mouvement Ouvrier*, 1939–53, II, 145. See also Watson, 187–90, 200–5 and Goldberg, 354–7, 364–7 and Jacques Julliard, *Clemenceau briseur de grèves*, 1965

[31] Zeldin, I, 711; cf. 712.

France to victory. Joseph Caillaux became the most prominent Radical leader until his defeatist attitudes towards Germany before and during the First World War as well as the scandal of his wife's murder of the editor of the *Figaro* in 1914 over embarrassing revelations of private correspondence and a prolonged anti-Caillaux campaign, led to his being discredited. He was arrested in 1918 and imprisoned for treason, a process in which Clemenceau's vendetta against him played an active part. Caillaux subsequently re-emerged as a Radical Senator who opposed the Popular Front government in 1936–7 and voted for Pétain in 1940.[32]

We deal with Clemenceau's role in the First World War and the peace settlement in Chapter 10 but after the wartime suspension of class conflict he secured the 1919 passage of laws on the 8-hour working day and collective bargaining, although the latter quickly petered out because most agreements made in 1919 were not subsequently renewed by the employers. It was left to renegade Socialist Millerand to repress the 1920 strikes, Clemenceau having suffered the humiliation of losing the presidential election to the pale Deschanel, who died after going mad shortly afterwards; he was replaced by Millerand, backed by the right-wing parliamentary majority.

The new leader of the Radical Party in 1919 was Edouard Herriot, who personified the educational meritocracy that the Third Republic raised to prominence from the lower middle classes as propounded by Gambetta. After studying at the *Ecole Normale Supérieure*, he taught in Lyon before becoming its Mayor in 1906, a post he held for the next fifty years, apart from a Vichy parenthesis. He came to the fore in national politics at a time when the Radicals lost half the deputies elected in 1914 and when he was unable to exercise real authority over the undisciplined parliamentary party. So, he became accustomed to making compromises to keep a catch-all party together by allowing its representatives to lean Right or Left as expediency required, or portfolio-pursuing ambitions dictated. He shifted the extra-parliamentary party to the Left-Centre, turning down an offer to joining the Poincaré government in 1922 and preparing for the 1924 elections in alliance with the Socialists, who only accepted an electoral Cartel of the Lefts but refused to join a government that they would not control.[33] The canker of the Herriot government's weakness was thus lodged in the fruit of victory, although its failure had wider causes. The Socialist leader Léon Blum was in 1936 to receive the same half-hearted 'support without participation' from the Communist Party, like the rope supporting the hanged man.

The Radical Party left-wing successfully insisted that Herriot refuse to form a government until Millerand—the de facto leader of the defeated *Bloc National*—had resigned as President of the Republic. Herriot made some symbolic gestures such as diplomatic recognition of the Soviet Union, the transfer of the remains of Jaurès to the *Panthéon* and amnesty for Caillaux. He was subsequently hampered

[32] Jean-Denis Bredin, *Joseph Caillaux*, 1980. See also Watson, 196, 205–6, 279, 287–9, Weber, *Action Française*, 104–10 and Brogan, 450.

[33] Serge Berstein, *Edouard Herriot ou la République en Personne*, 1985, 15–105, 112–16, 139–40, 148–51.

in his financial policy by Caillaux whose financial orthodoxy, in alliance with the business interests, led to a refusal to subscribe to state loans and a flight of capital, especially when Herriot at Blum's suggestion proposed a capital levy. This was rejected by the Senate, leading to Herriot's 'falling to the Left', blaming the 'wall of money' for his defeat. He should have devalued the franc, as Poincaré did in 1926 to 'save' the sinking currency, and while resenting the financial and political assistance Poincaré received that he had been denied, he joined his government as Minister of Education. This displeased the Left of the party, led by his former Lyon pupil Edouard Daladier but until the 1936 Popular Front the Radicals favoured governing with the Right after electoral alliances with the Left while the 'war of the two Edouards' continued.

Following Daladier's 1934 resignation in the context of the Stavisky riots, Herriot joined a Right-Centre 'truce government' to restore order. Herriot neither supported nor opposed the Radicals joining the 1935 Socialist-Communist alliance in preparation for the 1936 elections and was marginalized by Daladier, his centrist tactics not being suited to a situation polarized between anti-fascism and anti-communism. He accepted the 1938 Munich Agreement appeasing Hitler and though he was against the 1940 armistice, as President of the Chamber of Deputies, he did not vote on the abolition of the Third Republic. Removed as Mayor of Lyon, he was placed under house arrest, interned, and handed over to the Germans in 1943, having rejected earlier invitations from Churchill and Roosevelt to leave France. He objected to de Gaulle's refusal to resurrect the Third Republic but his election as President of the National Assembly from 1947 to 1953 symbolized a return to government by Assembly and to centrist politics under the Fourth Republic, following the exclusion of Communists from government.[34]

The Socialists and MRP were not strong enough to sustain a 'Third Force' against both Gaullists and Communists, so they had to secure the support of the Radicals and even Conservatives, resulting in uneasy and ephemeral coalition governments. Great skill was required to keep such divergent politicians together in what amounted in practice to a Third Farce. Henri Queuille had served frequently as Minister of Agriculture during the Third Republic and as a de facto minister with de Gaulle in 1943–4. He then held ministerial office without a break from 1948 to 1954, including thirteen months in 1948–9 and four months in 1951 as Prime Minister. His conciliatory, non-partisan, and unpretentious political style secured a measure of stability at the cost of immobility, personifying the tactics of indefinitely postponing controversial issues, achieving survival through inaction.[35]

Edgar Faure received his first ministerial appointment from Queuille but was a close associate and future Finance Minister of the most impressive Radical leader of the Fourth Republic, Pierre Mendès France, whom he succeeded as

---

[34] Serge Berstein, 1985, 129–299 and Francis de Tarr, *The French Radical Party from Herriot to Mendès-France*, 1961, Chapter 3.

[35] De Tarr, 159–67, Williams, 36–7, and Chapsal, 277–82, 291–4. For a sympathetically informed view of the ministerial class of the Fourth Republic by a senior civil servant, see Louis Franck, *697 Ministres: Souvenirs d'un Directeur general des prix 1947–1962*, 1986.

Prime Minister in 1955. (Determined to cling to office, Edgar Faure once asked for twenty votes of confidence on a single day.[36]) Condemned to improvise to survive by seeking support from the Right, Faure characteristically responded to the reproach that he was a political weathercock by saying: 'I have not changed my position; it is the direction of the wind that has changed.' His opportunistic dissolution of the National Assembly led to his expulsion from the Radical Party in December 1955 by the supporters of Mendès France. De Gaulle turned to Edgar Faure in 1968 to sort out as Education Minister the university unrest of that year, which he did with typical ingenuity.

The most memorable of Fourth Republic Prime Ministers was Mendès France. Converted to Radicalism at sixteen by hearing a Herriot speech, he had his nose broken by *Action Française* thugs before becoming a Deputy in 1932 and a junior minister in Blum's short-lived second Popular Front government. Escaping from Vichy arrest in 1941, he served in the Free French Air Force before being appointed National Economy Minister by de Gaulle in 1944 but he resigned in 1945 when his economic austerity proposals were not accepted. His subsequent warnings were ignored. In 1953 he was only narrowly rejected as Prime Minister but helped by the press campaign of Servan-Schreiber's *L'Express* he came to power in 1954. In a little over seven months, he ended the Indo-China War, secured the rejection of a proposed European Army and curbed the influential alcohol lobby.

Although the outbreak of the Algerian War occurred during his premiership, this issue led him to resign from the Mollet government in 1956 when it chose a policy of repression that he believed would result in Algerian independence. Remembered for his assertion 'To govern is to choose', his problem was that the leaders of the Fourth Republic preferred to avoid having to choose. His attempt to modernize the Radical Party in 1955–7 failed: 'Prudence and guile, not decision and discipline led Radical politicians to success' and his failure marked the end of the Radical Party as an influential actor in French politics.[37] It split in the Fifth Republic into two insignificant Left and Right Radical parties, marking the break point of the increasing bipolarization that rendered their habitual centrist manoeuvres redundant.

SOCIALISM: FRAGMENTATION, UNITY, AND DUALITY

The movements that advocated socialism after the defeat of the Paris Commune remained for the rest of the nineteenth century diminutive in membership, factionally fragmented and bedevilled by sectarian ideological disputes. They were incapable of achieving either reform or revolution over which they endlessly argued, so it is not surprising that most workers shunned all the squabbling

---

[36] John D. Huber, *Rationalizing Parliament: Legislative Institutions and Party Politics in France*, 1996, 52. More generally on Edgar Faure, see de Tarr, 167–85.

[37] Williams, 131; cf. 126–30 and de Tarr, Chapter 8.

factions. Even though hopes of a conspiratorial insurrection did not survive Blanqui's death, a Blanquist movement did, while Proudhonism was perpetuated in
anarcho-syndicalism. However, the new doctrine that made an increasing impact
was Marxism, thanks in particular to the 1876 conversion of Jules Guesde and his
emergence as a prominent political leader after being imprisoned for six months
in 1878 for organizing a banned International Workers Congress in Paris. In this,
he was seconded by Marx's son-in-law Paul Lafargue.

A ruthless authoritarian who was convinced that workers could not be represented by leaders of their own class, Guesde was an unremitting party organizer,
journalist, propagandist, and dogmatically self-righteous ideologist in the cause
of raising revolutionary consciousness. Convinced that revolution was imminent
because wages were bound to fall, even though they were rising (an immiser-
ation thesis that was propagated by the Communists in the twentieth century
with even greater implausibility), Guesde perpetuated revolutionary rhetoric long
after reformist practice had superseded its relevance. Nevertheless, the Guesdists
laid the basis in the 1880s and 1890s of the first centrally organized, disciplined
national political party, the French Workers Party, class-based, with solid bastions
particularly in the industrial North.[38]

As we have seen, Guesde quickly came into conflict with Brousse, who accused
him of seeking personal dictatorship in the name of the proletariat over the new
party, whose 1880 Minimum Programme Guesde had drawn up with Marx in
London. While the reformist proposals: a 6-day workweek and 8-hour workday,
a minimum wage law linked to the cost of living and equal wages for women,
combined with a call for arming the people, were not at issue, party democracy
and decentralized organization were. The pragmatic emphasis upon practice over
doctrinaire theory led to the defeat of the Guesdist collectivists.

It was only in the 1890s, when the Guesdists adopted the piecemeal reformist
tactics of the Possibilists, that they ceased to be dismissed as Impossibilists waiting
indefinitely for a supposedly inevitable revolution. They now proposed contest-
ing local elections as preparations for class war. Standing for election in 1892
on a moderate programme of an 8-hour workday, free medical services, and
a minimum wage for local authority workers, Guesdists won a majority on 26
commune councils, thanks to alliances with other Socialist parties. At the 1893
parliamentary elections, six Guesdists—including Guesde in the textile town of
Roubaix—were elected with Radical support, as were eleven Socialists from other
parties and twenty Independent Socialists who refused to join any of the rival
Socialist parties, least of all the Guesdists who were determined to exert extra-
parliamentary control over their deputies.[39]

It was from among the Independent Socialists in parliament that the Socialists'
most spellbinding orators emerged: Millerand, Viviani but above all Jaurès. He
began his parliamentary career as an Opportunist but whereas the bulk of the
Opportunists turned Right, Jaurès turned Left. After he lost his seat in 1889, he was

---

[38] Zeldin, I, 745–51; Moss, 81–91, 105–6, 113.
[39] Aaron Noland, *The Founding of the French Socialist Party, 1893–1905*, 1956, 5–32; Moss, 111–20.

converted to an eclectic, moralistic socialism by Lucien Herr, which incorporated a partial, non-determinist Marxism into a humanistic, cross-class democratic republicanism, based on the legacy of the French Revolution. This conversion took place in a context of class conflict, the first French celebration of 1 May with a strike to secure the 8-hour workday, called by the Second International, leading to a bloody confrontation in the textile town of Fourmies. State-supported employer resistance to the trade unions led to lockouts and political strikes. Jaurès was actively involved in a 10-week coalminers strike at Carmaux over the dismissal of the Socialist Mayor from his post. He attacked this act as a violation of democracy and as a result of arbitration the Mayor was reinstated and most of the miners re-employed, Jaurès going on to win a by-election in 1893. In 1895 he was involved in the Carmaux glassworkers lockout, provoked by an employer determined to break the trade union with the support of the Prefect, which led to the establishment of a glass producing cooperative in nearby Albi.[40]

Although these events—demonstrating the alliance between state officials and capitalist employers—were calculated to make Jaurès pessimistic about the potential for social reform, he joined the other deputies of the Socialist Union in supporting the 1895–6 Radical government because of Léon Bourgeois' fiscal and social reform programme. He regretted the Prime Minister's decision to resign in the face of Senate intransigence, despite the Deputies having voted him their confidence. After Socialist victories in 150 communes in the 1896 local elections, including control of Bordeaux, Dijon, Lille, and Marseille, a celebratory banquet was held at St Mandé at which Alexandre Millerand expounded the Socialist Minimum Programme. To reinforce the Socialist Union of most Socialist and a few Socialist Radical deputies that had met weekly since 1893, Millerand set out the conditions that candidates in the 1898 parliamentary elections would have to meet if they were to receive second ballot endorsement as the best placed Socialist candidate. These were the attainment of power by election, followed by the gradual socialization of the means of production, distribution, and exchange.

Unity was assisted by the evolution of Guesdists and Blanquists towards reformism. Under the pressure of their involvement in the democratic process locally and nationally, they were in practice abandoning their doctrinal dogmatism. Like Jaurès and Millerand, they accepted that the state should be used rather than smashed and that revolution was no longer on the agenda.[41] However, in 1898–9 the Dreyfus and Millerand Affairs were to postpone the process of socialist unification by opening up a period of polarizing polemics.

In January 1898, in response to Zola's *J'accuse* the Socialist deputies declared their neutrality, partly because of their fear that they would not be re-elected in 1898 owing to the surge of anti-Semitism sweeping public opinion. Jaurès—notably persuaded by Herr and Péguy—nevertheless became convinced of Dreyfus' innocence and played a decisive part in the Dreyfusard campaign, as we saw in Chapter 6. Jaurès declared that 'without contradicting our principles ... we can, while continuing our revolutionary struggle, retain our sense of compassion; we

---

[40] Goldberg, 62–3, 71–2, 98–107, 140–50.   [41] Ibid. 174–67; Noland, 40–1, 46–60.

are not required, for the sake of socialism to abandon humanity'.[42] He was rebutting Guesde's view that proletarians should not bother with an intra-bourgeois conflict.

Despite Socialist gains, increasing their deputies from thirty-seven to forty-two, Jaurès was defeated at Carmaux and Guesde at Roubaix, while Drumont was elected in Algiers. Although the Socialists formed a Vigilance Committee out of fear of a possible military *coup d'état*, Jaurès and Guesde quickly parted company over the issue of whether Millerand should join the Waldeck-Rousseau government of National Defence. Millerand had been elected as a Radical in 1885, and became an Independent Socialist in 1891. In the absence of the defeated Jaurès and Guesde, he was the spokesman of the Socialist Group in the Chamber of Deputies and secured its support in June 1899 for his entering the government in his personal capacity.

Jaurès, Brousse, and the majority of the Socialist Deputies joined the Left Bloc supporting the Waldeck-Rousseau government but the Blanquists and Guesdists resigned from the Socialist Parliamentary Group, accusing the majority of deviation from the pre-1890s class struggle position to which they now retreated. Guesde's manifesto asserted: 'Party of opposition we are, party of opposition we must remain, entering Parliament and other elective assemblies as though we were in an enemy state, only in order to fight the enemy class and the political groups that represent it.'[43] At the December 1899 Congress of all Socialist Organizations, at which a power struggle took place with Guesde, Jaurès characteristically sought to reconcile tactical ministerial participation with strategic class struggle but the Congress compromised, accepting such participation only in exceptional circumstances. In the context of abrasive industrial conflict, with strikes increasing from well under a million workdays lost in 1899 to over three million in 1900, the new French Socialist Party was immediately driven by an anti-ministerialist extra-parliamentary party and a pro-ministerialist parliamentary group leading to a 1901 split specifically over the refusal to expel Millerand, with the Guesdists establishing the Socialist Party of France. Jaurès played a crucial role in the Left Bloc's support for the Combes government from 1902 to 1905. Although he did his best to save Millerand from expulsion on the ground that the Socialist Party should be a broad church, the ex-minister was now voting too often with the Right to avoid exclusion in January 1904.[44]

Jaurès was re-elected Deputy in 1902 and from 1903 edited his own newspaper, *L'Humanité*. (It became the property of the Socialist Party in 1906 and at the 1920 split it was taken over by the Communist Party.) A key doctrinal duel was fought at the 1904 Amsterdam Congress of the Second International between Jaurès and Guesde, which the latter won and duly exploited by calling for unity talks based on the Amsterdam principles. The resulting 'Pact of Union' produced

---

[42] Article of 10 August 1898 that formed part of his 1898 book *Les Preuves*, included in *Oeuvres de Jean Jaurès*, VI/I, 'L'Affaire Dreyfus', 466; cf. 93–9, 405–11, 451–725. See also Noland, 63–8 and Goldberg, 217–30, 239–40.

[43] Quoted in Goldberg, 257; cf. 250–65 and Noland, 89–138.

[44] Noland, 148–58. See also Zeldin, I, 686–7, 765–7 and Sorlin, 461–78.

a compromise tilted in an anti-reformist direction. Only in 'exceptional circumstances' could Socialist Deputies join a Left Bloc. Jaurès chose unity, leading to a break with Briand and others who drifted to the Right in 1905 when Rouvier replaced Combes as Prime Minister. It was especially difficult for Socialists to offer support; as Clemenceau caustically declared: 'It is not a government: it is a board of directors'.[45]

The new 1905 Socialist Party, French Section of the Workers International, had 46,380 members, 36 Deputies, and 1,500 commune councillors. It reaffirmed the reformist St Mandé Programme but insisted that Socialist Party Deputies must act in conformity with the tactics decided by the party's annual conference. At the 1906 general election, the party programme was: proportional representation; election of judges; free education; a progressive income tax; one-day-off weekly; an 8-hour workday; the nationalization of the Bank of France, insurance companies, and oil refineries; trade union rights for government employees; replacement of the standing army by a militia. The new party modestly increased its representation.[46] Both the Socialist Party and the CGT were handicapped by the fact that the working class was a minority in a population dominated by the peasants and the self-employed, so Jaurès did his best, especially in the pages of *L'Humanité*, to promote cooperation between equals, avoiding Guesde's desire to subordinate the trade unions to the party.[47] We shall postpone until Chapter 10 the fatal efforts of Jaurès to prevent the First World War.

Socialists, including Guesde, served as ministers in the wartime 'Sacred Union' governments and the CGT substantially increased its membership. Blum, the disciple of Jaurès who emerged as the Socialist leader after the First World War, did not hold ministerial office until he became Prime Minister of the Popular Front government in 1936, but as chief of the ministerial staff to the Socialist Minister of Public Works, Marcel Sembat, he was from 1914 to 1916 initiated in to the workings of government. Prior to the war, Léon Blum had devoted himself primarily to literary criticism and his legal work in the Council of State. However, he had been won over in 1893 to socialism by Lucien Herr, while the Dreyfus Affair led from 1897 to a close friendship with Jaurès. These two dominant personalities shaped Blum's political views and conduct for the rest of his life, especially Jaurès' eclectic attempt at reconciling materialism and idealism, democratic gradualism and proletarian revolution, patriotism, and internationalism.

From an Alsace Jewish family, Blum felt particular affinity with Dreyfus and as a public lawyer profound outrage at the fraudulent nature of his condemnation, so he assisted Zola's defence lawyers at his trial. Having helped Jaurès raise the funds to found *L'Humanité*, Blum withdrew from active involvement in Socialist in-fighting because he was not happy with the Guesde-leaning compromise struck in 1905, even though Jaurès was in effective command, especially from 1908. He devoted himself instead to his theatre criticism and the Council of State, as well as publishing books on marriage and on Stendhal... until the outbreak of war

---

[45] Goldberg, 335; cf. 319–20, 326–30, 340, 553; Noland, 159–84.
[46] Goldberg, 353–4; Noland, 186–7.   [47] Goldberg, 390–3; cf. 362.

abruptly brought him back to active politics and assumption of the post-Bolshevik Revolution vacant leadership of the Jaurèsian remnant of a sundered Socialist Party.[48]

Before doing so, Blum utilized his 1914–16 experience to publish articles that in 1918 appeared as a book, *Letters on Governmental Reform*. At a time when Clemenceau was providing a demonstration of the need for strong political leadership, Blum, using British practice as his model, emphasized the need for a Prime Minister in control of both the executive and legislature, free of other ministerial duties. This would require a Cabinet Office staff, disciplined political parties, and a reduction in the legislative dominance of parliamentary committees if government instability was to be avoided.[49] It was only when Blum became Prime Minister in 1936 that he was able to introduce some of the non-socialist modernization of government measures he had proposed, the parliamentary political class being resistant to creating the institutional preconditions of effective leadership.

Faced with a Socialist Party that was from 1917 shifting away from a patriotic reformism towards revolutionary pacifism, Blum, as an eloquent disciple of Jaurès, emerged into prominence as a conciliator, possibly capable of preserving the unity of a polarized party. Refusing an electoral alliance with the Radicals, the Socialist Party lost thirty-four seats at the 1919 election despite increasing its vote, with the 'Blue Horizon' Chamber of Deputies as a result. Having rejected Jaurès' attempts to persuade him to be a candidate in 1902 and 1906, Blum was elected in 1919, quickly becoming secretary and spokesman of the Socialist parliamentary group and leader of the party's Right-Centre.

In a context of industrial unrest, in which old syndicalist hands like Griffuelhes and Sorel saw the Russian Soviets as the realization of their aspirations, the CGT in 1920 stumbled into a general strike that failed. The Socialist Party, likewise under the pressure of a mass of young, naive new members, moved first to abandon the Socialist Second International and then to accept the Soviet-imposed 21 Conditions for admission to the Communist Third International. These required repeatedly purging the party and Members of Parliament of reformists and subordinating parliamentarians to the party according to a military-style discipline dubbed democratic centralism. Party cells would be established in trade unions and cooperatives; propaganda among the troops would be undertaken; its press subordinated to party control and required to propagate proletarian dictatorship, anti-imperialism, and anti-colonialism. Party programmes required approval by the Communist International, whose decisions would be binding. Anyone not accepting these conditions should be expelled. Believing that the Russian Revolution heralded a Europe-wide swing to Communism, these demands were uncritically swallowed by most Socialists.

Faced with these draconian conditions and in the knowledge that his views would be supported by only a minority of a party about to opt for Bolshevik-style

---

[48] Joel Colton, *Léon Blum: Humanist in Politics*, 1966, Chapter 1 and Jean Lacouture, *Léon Blum*, 1979 edn, 11–127.

[49] Colton, 39–40; Lacouture, 132–4.

Communism, Blum made the speech of his life at the Tours Congress of December 1920, explaining that an ideological gulf separated democratic socialists from dictatorial communists. He maintained that socialists were not divided over seeking revolution but on the nature of the party that would wield power after the revolution. He attacked Leninism as the revival of Blanquism, the mobilization of herd-like mass violence by a conspiratorial advance guard for permanent not temporary dictatorship. Blum declared that nevertheless, theoretically, he accepted 'the impersonal dictatorship of the proletariat', exercised 'in virtue of a fiction to which we all agree' by a Socialist Party purporting to represent the whole proletariat.[50] Despite his efforts to avoid the fratricidal split, it took place under remorseless pressure from Moscow. A despairing Guesde said of the conditions: 'They are at once everything I have recommended all my life and what all my life I have condemned', while Marcel Sembat disconsolantly declared in retrospect: 'The Congress of Tours was the second assassination of Jaurès.'[51]

Although the Communist Party initially took over three quarters of the Socialist Party's members, fifty-five of the sixty-eight deputies, and most of the mayors and commune councillors stayed with 'the old Home'. The Socialist representatives were increasingly bourgeois who had never set foot in a factory. Its Guesdist General Secretary Paul Faure emphasized that the Socialists remained a doctrinaire party of class struggle and revolution rather than reform, while its parliamentary leader Blum perpetuated the Jaurès emphasis upon short-term reform in the service of long-term revolution in almost daily front page articles in *Le Populaire*, the Socialist replacement for the lost *L'Humanité*.

Having persuaded, with difficulty, the party to give 'support without participation' to the 1924 Herriot government, Blum was indirectly the cause of its fall by persuading the Radical Prime Minister to propose a capital levy which was rejected by the Senate majority (including some Radicals). The subsequent failure of six short-lived Left-Centre governments denied Socialist support led Blum in 1926 to formulate his distinction between the exercise of power and the conquest of power. While reassuring the party activists that the ultimate revolutionary objective was to transform capitalism into socialism, he argued that rather than waiting indefinitely for a revolutionary situation to mature, its parliamentary leaders should be willing to lead a government to carry out reforms within the framework of the existing political and economic institutions. This ingenious semantic compromise was ten years later to achieve its purpose of persuading the extra-parliamentary protagonists of Marxist orthodoxy to accept with enthusiasm a reformist Popular Front government led by Blum.[52] Meanwhile, the Socialists refused to share in Radical-led coalition governments as the unreal argument continued between reformists unable to reform and revolutionists incapable of

---

[50] Quoted from the full Blum speech in Annie Kriegel, *Le Congrès de Tours (Decembre 1920): Naissance du Parti Communiste*, 1964, 128–9; cf. 101–36. More generally see Lichtheim, 34–46, Judt, 122–51 and Annie Kriegel, *Aux Origines du Communisme Français*, 1969.

[51] Guesde quoted by Williams, 88 and Sembat by Colton, 54; cf. 50–3 and Lacouture, 152–68.

[52] Colton, 71–3, 138; cf. Lacouture, 193–5, 197–9.

carrying out a revolution. Some revisionist neo-Socialists broke away in 1933, their leaders ending up as fascist supporters of the Vichy regime.

It required the insurrectionary Stavisky riots of February 1934 to persuade Blum of the need to support Radical Prime Minister Daladier by joining his government to save parliamentary democracy from the threat of a right-wing dictatorship, but despite this offer and a vote of confidence Daladier resigned. However, before the Left could unite against the fascist threat from abroad as well as in France, it was necessary for Moscow—fearing Nazism in Germany—to give the green light to the French Communist Party (PCF) to offer collaboration between parties and trade unions in June 1934. Although a 'United Action Pact' was signed in July, Blum was naturally wary, having earlier been described by the Communist leader Thorez as a 'repugnant reptile, jackal, lackey of the London bankers, spy, mad warmonger'; while a previous Communist General-Secretary had declared: 'We are close to the Socialists, like the hand is close to the chicken to be plucked',[53] using the tactics of 'union at the base' to undermine their leaders. In the context of worldwide depression and of aggressive fascism, under activist pressure from within his own rank and file, Blum agreed to work politically in a defensive alliance with a conciliatory PCF, while the Socialist and Communist trade unions prepared to merge in a reunified CGT in March 1936.

On 14 July 1935, a mass Rally of nine organizations—including the Socialist, Communist, and Radical parties, both trade union confederations, the League of the Rights of Man, and the Vigilance Committee of Antifascist Intellectuals—pledged to work for a Popular Front, whose electoral programme was published in January 1936 after protracted negotiations. As well as calling for dissolution of the fascist leagues and support for the collective security through the League of Nations, it proposed a deliberately modest economic programme. Only the Bank of France and armaments firms were to be nationalized. An unspecified reduction of the work week without reduction of wages, pensioning off older workers to provide jobs for the young, a public works programme, and a much more progressive income tax, were its salient features.[54] On the strength of this programme, the Popular Front won a composite parliamentary majority (Table 9.2).

The Communists doubled their 1932 vote and increased their representation from eleven to seventy-two thanks to the electoral alliance, while the Socialist vote actually fell slightly but modestly increased seats won. The Right held its own in votes and seats, the main losses being suffered by the Radicals and Right-Centre owing to the polarization that occurred.

Blum had been convalescing from being brutally beaten up by a royalist student mob in February 1936, so he took no part in the election campaign. Nevertheless, as leader of the largest party in a Popular Front that on paper had a majority of 376 deputies to 214, Blum—vilified and execrated by the Right—was called upon by President Lebrun to form a government. The customary one-month interval

---

[53] Quoted in Lacouture, 204, 244; cf. Colton, 99–109.
[54] David Thomson, *Democracy in France: The Third Republic*, 1946, Appendix 2, 253–7.

Table 9.2. Results of the 1936 election to the Chamber of Deputies

Party	Votes (000's)	Seats
Communists	1,469	72
Socialists and	1,997	147
Dissident Socialists		51
Radicals	1,955	106
Right-Centre and	4,234	76
Right		138

Source: Georges Dupeux, *Le Front Populaire et les Elections de 1936*, 1959, 139.

before the electoral victor assumed office proved to be a cataclysmic parenthesis, underlining the pressures from capital and labour that the incoming government would face. As a result of panic due to loss of confidence despite the Left's reassurances, a speculative flight of capital had started well before the election and within a week after it, the Bank of France recorded a drop of 2.5 billion francs in its gold reserves. The consequent run on the franc in September forced a 29 per cent currency devaluation, with resulting inflationary price increases. From 14 May a series of sit-down strikes by workers restless for change and impatient with the slowness of the post-electoral political process took place. They remained in occupation of their workplaces, locking out their employers in an unprecedented strike movement that took everyone by surprise, pleasant or unpleasant. On the selfsame 14 May, the PCF Politbureau informed Blum that they would support without participating in his government but while the Communists exploited to the full the spontaneous factory occupations they had not initiated, a conspiracy theory explanation is not in order.

On 27 May the leader of the Socialist left wing, Marceau Pivert, published a notorious article in which he proclaimed that in the context of nearly two million workers engaged in sit-down strikes, 'Everything is possible and quickly'.[55] This was to misinterpret the workers' aspirations, which were to assert their wish to be treated with respect by their employers and for improvements in their wages and conditions of work, not to demand revolution. Rejecting Pivert's call on 6 May that he should take office immediately after the election with the argument: 'Do you think that in our place the fascists would hesitate for a moment?' Blum responded: 'No, but that's just the point, we are not fascists'.[56] He was supported by the Communist *L'Humanité*, which in a 3 June editorial asserted 'Everything is

---

[55] For the full text of Pivert's article see *Léon Blum chef de gouvernement 1936–1937*, 1967, 178–80. For Leon Trotsky's June 1936 claim that 'The French Revolution has begun!' see his *Whither France?*, 1936, 1974 (ed), 131–6. More generally, see Daniel Brower, *The New Jacobins: The French Communist Party and the Popular Front*, 1969.

[56] Irwin M. Wall, 'French Socialism and the Popular Front', in *Journal of Contemporary History*, III, 1970, 6; cf. 5–7.

not possible' and on 11 June the Communist leader Maurice Thorez memorably declared: 'It is necessary to know how to end a strike.'[57]

Giving priority to preserving an anti-fascist alliance that required not frightening the Radicals, the Communists deliberately rejected the opportunity to fulfil the anarcho-syndicalist hope of using a widespread strike for revolutionary purposes. Instead they supported the piecemeal reformism of Blum and Léon Jouhaux, General-Secretary of a reunited CGT, who negotiated the 7 June Matignon Agreement with the employers' representatives. In exchange for ending the sit-down occupation of the factories, the employers leaders conceded a general and substantial wage increase ranging from 7 to 15 per cent, the institutionalization of collective bargaining, with elected shop steward in workplaces with more than 10 employees.[58] Later in June, laws providing for 2 weeks holiday with pay and the 40-hour workweek, as well as for collective bargaining, were passed, thanks to continuing strike pressure. The electoral victory and strikes had combined to ensure an unprecedented change in the daily lives of French working people.

Léon Blum's government innovated in various ways, notably by the inclusion of three women in junior ministerial education and health posts at a time when they could not sit in parliament or even vote. The CGT leader, Jouhaux, turned down the offer of a post, being committed to the separation of trade unionism and holding political office. After its early achievements, thanks to the strikes, the Blum government encountered pressure on the overvalued franc, so despite its initial unrealistic rejection of both deflation and devaluation, in September the franc was devalued, too late to lay the blame on its predecessors. While it still retained its impetus, the Popular Front government nationalized the Bank of France and extended the age of compulsory education to 14, together with many other lesser reforms. Although only 4 per cent of French workers were covered by collective bargaining agreements in 1934, there was a spectacular increase in their number from 35 to 2,336 by December 1936, covering most workers' employment and minimum wage rates.[59] Related to this change was the consecration of the concept of 'most representative trade unions' as having negotiation rights and the temporary increase of CGT membership from a million to nearly five million. However, the employers—who felt they had been betrayed by their leaders at Matignon—often did not honour these agreements and took an early opportunity not to renew them. They also replaced their conciliatory representatives as part of an organizational change in the General Employers Confederation, with a much more intransigent leadership now that their fear had abated.

In 1935 Blum had already modified his idea of 'exercising power' to the defensive notion of 'occupying power' to avoid fascism. But with the Senate's opposition—led by its Finance Committee Chairman Caillaux, who attacked Blum as a 'Lilliputan Roosevelt'—to his demand for increased powers of economic

[57] Julian Jackson, *The Popular Front in France: Defending Democracy, 1934–8*, 1988, 10, 88, 95–6; cf. Chapter 3 and Colton, 154, Lacouture, 288–94.

[58] Colton, 147–55. For the text of the Matignon Agreement, see Jackson, 305–6.

[59] Ibid. 164–5; cf. Chapter 6.

crisis intervention, Blum resigned in June 1937.[60] Via a 'pause' in reforms announced in February 1937, the final months were downhill all the way as the Radicals deserted him and the Popular Front disintegrated. Blum was reproached from the Left for expiring without a fight. The 'occupation of power' had been the prelude to capitulation. Having described the 1938 Munich Agreement with Hitler as prompting in him a 'cowardly relief and shame', he felt compelled by the pacifist majority of the parliamentary party, led by General Secretary Paul Faure, to support it,[61] heralding the defeatism that in 1940 led so many of them—including Faure—to accept the Vichy regime.

In July 1940, Blum witnessed at Vichy the disintegration of the Socialist parliamentary party—ninety voted for Pétain, thirty-five against, and six abstained—and the abolition of the Third Republic, followed in September by his arrest and political trial, postponed until February 1942, for demoralizing the country and leaving it unprepared for war. (*Before* the trial, Blum, Daladier, and General Gamelin were sentenced by a separate Court of Political Justice, to life imprisonment, confirmed by Pétain in October 1941.) The aim was to exonerate the army for defeat, blamed on the politicians of the Third Republic. Thanks in part to Blum's skill, in his element as a lawyer-politician, the trial turned into a fiasco for the Vichy regime, which by a reversal of roles was itself pilloried and humiliatingly forced to suspend proceedings in April 1942.[62] Before he was deported to Buchenwald, where he spent the last two years of the war, Blum was able to advise Daniel Mayer on the organization of a clandestine Socialist Party in Occupied France and urge de Gaulle to acknowledge that 'The negation ... of political parties is equivalent to the negation of democracy.'[63] He returned to France in 1945 as a national hero but when de Gaulle offered him a ministerial post Blum said he would devote his remaining energies to his party newspaper, *Le Populaire*, faced on the Left by a Communist Party that had overtaken it in membership and prestige as well as seats in the Constituent Assembly.

The Socialists were not idle during the Vichy period, playing an active part in Resistance organizations and in planning for liberation. Within a consensus that the future should be inspired by socialism as the mystique to overcome the prewar stalemate, Mayer, under the auspices of the Committee for Socialist Action, made a major contribution through its study commissions to the March 1944 Programme of the National Council of the Resistance. It received the support of all the left-wing parties and movements, notably the emphasis on national economic planning and nationalization of major industrial and financial institutions. Paradoxically, despite providing the largest intellectual input into post-war reform,

[60] Ibid. 274–6; cf. *Léon Blum chef de gouvernement*, 34–5, 166–73, 222–4, 253–4. A favourable view of the Popular Front government's economic policy is given by Pierre Mendès France, ibid. 233–40. For an evocatively illustrated account centred on the press campaign against the Popular Front government, see Louis Bodin and Jean Touchard, *Front Populaire* 1936, 1961, See also Lacouture, 194–303, 411–15.

[61] Lacouture, 427–8; and Colton, 316–19.

[62] Colton, Chapters 13–15 and Lacouture, 444–78.

[63] Letter of 15 March 1943 to de Gaulle, quoted in Colton, 436; cf. 433–6 and Lacouture, 491–2.

once the Liberation arrived, the interest in policy reform 'appeared to evaporate. The main concerns of the (Socialist) party in the period 1944–6 were either tactical or doctrinal'.[64] After de Gaulle resigned, the Socialists were sandwiched between the Communists on the Left and the MRP on the Centre-Right in Tripartite governments. The compromises that ensued led the neo-Guesdist Guy Mollet to win control of the Socialist Party from Daniel Mayer, who represented the Jaurès-Blum wing.

The Socialists lost electoral support in 1946, winning only 17.9 per cent of the vote compared to 28.6 per cent for the Communists and 26.3 per cent for the MRP. This followed Mayer's replacement by Mollet, who played the old Guesdist anti-revisionist and anti-bourgeois card, as well as blaming Mayer for the decline in the party's fortunes. However, although the pre-First World War emphasis on Marxist revolutionary orthodoxy and workerist class struggle was still popular with the rank and file, it was blatantly anachronistic after the Second World War when only the Communists could convincingly claim to be the main working-class party. When in 1947 the Communists voted against the Ramadier government's wage freeze policy and supported CGT strikes, the Socialist Prime Minister—with Blum's support but violating the party's insistence on the inclusion of the Communists in any government with Socialist participation—did not resign but simply replaced the Communist ministers.[65] Against Mollet's wishes, the Social-ist Party then approved what in practice amounted to the replacement of Left-Centre tripartism with a Right-Centre Third Force, revealing that the Cold War polarization internationally could not be prevented from having a dramatic impact on the Socialist party's domestic alliances. When the Communists demon-strated that they were more the party of the East than of the Left, the Socialists showed that they were more the party of the West when a choice had to be made. As a result, they were 'prisoners of their conservative partners', becoming like the latter-day Third Republic Radicals 'the gravediggers of a (Fourth) Republic, less because they misrepresented the French people than because they represented them all too well'.[66]

Mollet abandoned in practice his pseudo-Marxist rhetoric and in due course became Prime Minister in 1956, only to yield to Algerian settler–military pressure in the conflict that had broken out in 1954. This war (which we shall deal with in Chapter 10) led in 1958 to the downfall of the Fourth Republic, with Mollet serving in de Gaulle's government that took over. In the 1960s the Socialist Party seemed to be in long-term decline but the 1970s saw the rejuvenation of the non-Communist Left in which François Mitterrand, a late and calculating 'convert' to socialism, played a crucial part. He substituted for the party's habitual ideological soul–searching a clear-headed, pragmatic pursuit of power, couched in phrases to please its activists. Becoming First Secretary of the Socialist Party in 1971, he

[64] Andrew Shennan, *Rethinking France*, 86; cf. 85–92. For a summary of the National Council of the Resistance programme, see Thomson, *Democracy in France*, 257–9. For more detail on the period, see Bruce D Graham, *The French Socialists and Tripartisme, 1944–1947*, 1965.

[65] Graham, *The French Socialists and Tripartisme*, 213–19, 230–2, 260–4.

[66] Williams, 102; cf. 90 and Chapter 7 passim.

realized that a reviving party, buoyed by an increasing service sector, white-collar electorate, could come to dominate an alliance with the Communist Party, relying on a shrinking working-class and suffering guilt by association with a discredited Soviet Union.

Narrowly defeated in the 1974 Presidential Election and despite the Communist deliberate abandonment of the 1972 Common Programme which led to the electoral setback of the 1978 general election, Mitterrand was elected President of the Republic in 1981. The Socialist-dominated Mauroy government that secured an unprecedented overall Socialist parliamentary majority was able to admit four Communist ministers, who 'entered on their knees'. Before returning in the final chapter to the post-1981 fortunes of the Socialists, we must examine how the Communist Party lost the dominant position it had enjoyed on the Left when the Socialist Party split in 1920, until its Soviet model finally disintegrated seventy years later.

COMMUNISM: THE SECULAR DECLINE OF A SECTARIAN PARTY

'If it had been said of the early Christians that they awaited the coming of the saviour and instead got the church, it may be said of the French proletariat that it expected the Revolution and instead got the Communist party.'[67] Lichtheim pinpointed the French Left's longing for the fulfilment of the Jacobin promise of 1793, which made Leninism and the Russian Revolution attractive because, via the Blanquist features of the failed 1871 Commune, it 'incorporated the heritage of the French Revolution at its most dictatorial'.[68] The Bolshevik Revolution would fulfil the hopes that had not been achieved by a pioneering French Revolution. Although the French Communist Party (PCF) took twelve years to Bolshevize the party that emerged from the 1920 split by successive purges of those who had misunderstood the Moscow-dictated objectives, 'The real faith of the Communist *militants* after 1920 was syndicalist. In so far as the working-class member of the French CP had a vision of the future, it was the old anarcho-syndicalist dream of a factory without bosses, a society without exploiters, and a nation without a state. That this utopia had not by any means been realized in the USSR was a circumstance of which he remained in ignorance.'[69] The party did its best to keep its members in ignorance. The result was 'the French Communist party—a Stalinist apparatus with an instinctively syndicalist mass following'[70]—a would-be totalitarian organization that triumphed over its overtly liberating revolutionary purpose.

The context in which this paradoxical achievement occurred was the 'total' First World War. It generated a discredit of the prospect of peaceful prosperity

[67] Lichtheim, *Marxism in Modern France*, 68.
[68] Ibid. 10; cf. 11, 17, 71 and François Furet, *Le Passé d'une illusion: Essai sur l'idée communiste au XXE siècle*, 107–32, 390–5, 441–3, 495–6.
[69] Lichtheim, 70.   [70] Ibid. 179.

governed by liberal, political, and economic values and institutions in favour of a pervasive violence, prompting fear and public passivity that encouraged the reciprocal extremisms of communism and fascism. Lenin and Mussolini had shared a pre-war hatred of parliamentary reformism and bourgeois capitalism and in their different ways they used the world war to take advantage of weakened political systems in 1917 and 1920–22 respectively, as Hitler did a decade after his failed *putsch* of 1923. A perceptive historian, Elie Halévy, as early as 1914, was privately anticipating the anti-liberal consequences of the war and by 1938 when his *Era of Tyrannies* was published, he recognized the totalitarian affinities of Stalin, Mussolini, and Hitler despite the contrast and conflicts between fascism and anti-fascism which dominated national and international politics in the 1930s.[71] Although Halévy was not alone in his prophetic judgement, it was not accepted as the unwelcome reality until well after the Second World War.

George Orwell, whose satire *Animal Farm* was the most trenchant critique of Bolshevism, convincingly asserted that 'Nothing has contributed so much to the corruption of the original idea of socialism as the belief that Russia is a socialist country and that every act of its rulers must be excused if not imitated'.[72] As we have already mentioned, the fellow-travellers excused their crimes, while the party slavishly followed their twists and turns. As the French Section of the Communist International, the PCF interpreted proletarian internationalism as unswerving subservience to the party line decided in Moscow. When the Bolshevization of the party was completed in 1932, it was in effect led by a tandem of the overt General-Secretary Maurice Thorez and the covert local agent of the Comintern, Eugen Fried. Thereafter, it acquired and retained long after the death of Stalin the reputation of being the most Stalinist of Western Communist Parties. One of the party's veteran leaders and its presidential candidate in 1969, Jacques Duclos, had twenty years earlier declared in a sycophantic speech: 'To be Stalinist, such is the ambition of everyone of us, comrades. But perhaps we should be modest, knowing all that we must do to impregnate ourselves completely with Stalin's teachings. Instead of presumptuously proclaiming: "We are Stalinists", we would be nearer the mark if we said: "We are trying and will try, with more energy than ever, to be Stalinists"'.[73] This grovelling attitude was reflected in the party's adamant denial of the authenticity of Kruschev's leaked secret report to the 1956 Soviet Twentieth Party Congress denouncing Stalin.

In the mid-1930s, Thorez followed the Soviet instruction to promote a Popular Front and shed its sectarian identity, using the anti-fascist campaign and the 1936 elections and strikes to achieve specific reforms as stepping stones for its longer term aim of controlling both the political and industrial Left. After the

---

[71] Furet, *Le passé d'une illusion*, 86–8, 269, 284, 288.

[72] George Orwell, Preface to the Ukrainian edition of *Animal Farm* in his *Collected Essays, Journalism and Letters*, III, 1978, 405.

[73] Quoted in André Barjonet, *La CGT: Histoire. Structure. Doctrine*, 1968, 128–9 note. See also Irwin M. Wall, *French Communism in the Era of Stalin: The Quest for Unity and Integration, 1945–1962*, 1983, 99–103; Alfred J. Rieber, *Stalin and the French Communist Party, 1941–1947*, 1962 and Sudhir Hazareesingh, *Intellectuals and the French Communist Party*, 275–83, 288–91.

Table 9.3. The French Communist Party and public opinion, 1966–70

Why people vote Communist	January 1966 (%)	January 1970 (%)
Establish a Communist regime	9	5
Oppose the government	18	20
Express general discontent	45	53
No reply	28	22

Source: Sondages, 1970, 36–7.

setback of the August 1939 Ribbentrop-Molotiv Pact that made nonsense of its previous anti-fascism, the PCF retrieved its tarnished credentials by its prominent role in the Resistance, emerging from the Second World War as one of the three strongest parties but the most disciplined and with a propaganda apparatus that outdistanced all the others. (Its oft proclaimed 75,000 wartime martyrs was at least double the correct figure, a transposition of the habit of doubling the number of mass demonstrators.) Like Catholic Action, the PCF had proliferated specialized satellite or 'front' mass organizations to attract not merely workers but farmers and housewives to create a counter society within and against bourgeois society. In an attempt to approximate to a Soviet-style totalitarianism without the comprehensive police and political control, the PCF sought to absorb all aspects of party members' activities within the ramifications of the party. Party life replaced private life, so to be purged from the party meant virtual exclusion from all one's activities and loss of all one's friends.

Nevertheless, the relative stability of a nucleus of leaders was accompanied by a high turnover of membership, of the order of 10 per cent annually. So the PCF has been compared to a railway station, with a constant stream of people coming and going. However, one should distinguish between long-standing stationmasters like Maurice Thorez and Georges Marchais and the season ticket holders and the day trippers. The Communists were 'the only Fourth Republican party to retain their pre-war leadership',[74] its propensity to self-perpetuation being a function of its unconditional alignment on the USSR. Combined with the Blanquist cell structure, adopted by the Bolsheviks because of its suitability for clandestine action, it became a technique for imposing hierarchical centralized domination. It also led a purportedly revolutionary party to an introvert imperviousness to changing circumstances that contributed to an inertial incapacity to adapt to a non-revolutionary context and secular decline during the Fifth Republic.

Until the Socialist revival of the 1970s, the Communist Party continued to dominate the left of the political spectrum because although it defended working-class interests ineffectively, there seemed to be no viable alternative. As Table 9.3 shows, the bulk of Communist support was derived from negative factors rather than a desire for communism. The fact that the Communists in 1968 used their control

---

[74] Williams, 80; cf. Chapter 6 passim. See also Jean Elleinstein, *LePC*, 1976.

over the CGT to secure wage increases and end the factory occupations rather than allow the Extreme Left to exploit the problematic revolutionary potential of the student-led unrest was eloquent testimony that the PCF had become a party of protest that had abandoned its revolutionary pretensions.[75] Once an alternative party of the Left emerged that could mobilize public discontent in favour of economic and social reform, the hollowness of its revolutionary rhetoric was exposed and retro-communism was becoming a redundant, residual communism. An unconvincing mid-1970s attempt at a change of tactics and terminology under the guise of 'Eurocommunism' proved an ephemeral exercise in disassociating itself from Leninism.

The exposure of Soviet concentration camps and the collapse of Marxist intellectual hegemony in the 1970s were the prelude to the PCF's 1980s humiliations: loss of electoral support, loss of its sense of direction, and loss of influence on French society and even over the CGT trade union in the 1990s. Having treated historical determinism as the sole tribunal, communism was condemned by it to disappear as a major political actor in France in favour of market democracy. In 2002, supreme humiliation, the Communist presidential candidate was outdistanced by two Trotskyist candidates, showing that it was no longer effectively playing its oppositional function of spokesman for the discontented Left. It was obsolete, without the prospect of revival in a deindustrializing society with a shrinking manual worker constituency of potential support.[76] In addition, as Mitterrand declared as early as 1976, 'My great, historic luck was the unbelievable mediocrity of the Communist leaders.... One can manipulate them at will.'[77]

The lack of consensus, which had been a continuing theme of analyses of French politics since the French Revolution, was replaced by late twentieth-century ideological convergence. Government had been stabilized and the adversarial partisan culture had succumbed to a fatalist collective abdication to forces beyond French control. However, before we discuss these developments as they relate to the end of French exceptionalism and the despair at not having a plausible alternative to encroaching Americanization, we shall in Chapter 10 consider an imperial vocation that gave way until the end of the twentieth century to a Franco-German led European substitute for a receding national identity.

[75] A judiciously inconclusive discussion of the eight main explanations of the May 1968 events is provided in Philippe Bénéton and Jean Touchard, 'Les interpretations de la crise de mai-juin 1968', *Revue Française de Science Politique*, XX/3, June 1970. For a perceptive personal view, see Raymond Aron, *The Elusive Revolution*, 1969.

[76] Quoted in Franz-Olivier Giesbert, *Le Président*, 1990, 1991, 30.

[77] For a prophetically opinionated analysis of the French Communist Party by a leading actor in May 1968, see Daniel Cohn-Bendit, *Le Gauchisme: Remède à la maladie sénile du communisme*, 1968.

10

Embattled Nation: Politicized Army, Imperial Decolonization, and European Integration

Force has been a major factor in forging the French state, expanding its power and consolidating its hold over a nation all too inclined to civil discord. So the character and role of the army's officer corps, the role of the colonial army and the impact of three wars against Germany from 1870 to 1945 upon a European integration based upon Franco-Saxon reconciliation will be the salient themes of this investigation of an embattled France. They reflect an interaction between resigned continuities and unexpected changes, characterized by prolonged immobilities and sudden accelerations. These factors have conditioned France's introvert ability to maintain internal order and her extrovert efforts to assert a distinctive international role as ambitions have had to be adjusted to diminishing capacities.

AN ARMY IN POLITICS

Three sources of recruitment to France's officer corps have in succession predominantly shaped its composition as well as reflecting changing French nineteenth-century society. Despite the Revolution's anti-elitist legacy of the citizen nation-in-arms, the army was led by a changing three-fold combination of aristocrats in the style of the Old Regime, based on inherited family military service traditions; of bravura wartime-made men who fought their way to prominence in the revolutionary and Napoleonic wars from modest origins; of techno-meritocrats based on training notably through St Cyr and the *Ecole Polytechnique*, who increasingly displaced the first two categories. However, prior to the First World War, aristocrats were particularly present in the general staff and cavalry, fighters who rose through their actions in the colonial troops and the infantry, while the techno-meritocrats were especially to be found among the artillery and engineers.[1] Although the July Monarchy abolished special preference for the nobility and junior army officers were increasingly promoted from the ranks, generals often continued to owe their advancement more to their social status than to their military prowess. This was also reflected in the importance of active

---

[1] Christophe Charle, *Les Hauts Fonctionnaires*, 136, 141, 143.

or retired generals in parliament and in the diplomatic service. Between 1816 to 1825 and 1830 to 1870 the Ministers of War were either Generals or Marshals, while for thirty-one out of the forty-four years from 1871 to 1914, all the War Ministers were generals.[2]

Until the Dreyfus Affair at the end of the nineteenth century, 'The army tended to be an isolated community, hostile to the bourgeois values of civilian society, sensitive to criticism of military affairs in the press, and insistent on autonomy in military matters. In fighting for self-regulation, military officers did not believe themselves to be seeking political power; on the contrary, what they sought...was the isolation of the army from what was felt to be the corrupting and divisive effects of politics.'[3] This was reinforced by the Third Republic's denial to military personnel of the right to vote in 1872 or to stand for parliamentary election, to belong to political parties and to speak or write for publication without the minister's approval. The exchange of semi-autonomy for political neutrality led to a separation but not subordination of the army to government. The Boulanger crisis and then the Dreyfus Affair, however, led to the assertion of political control as War Ministers General Galliffet in 1899–1900 and then General André purged the officer corps of anti-republicans and ended promotion by co-optation. Ironically, Boulanger had been an untypical Republican General; most of the officer corps were royalist rather than Boulangist. As we saw earlier, André's use of confidential reports from Freemasons in dealing with promotions led to his resignation in November 1904 and that of Prime Minister Combes in January 1905.

The army had been used in the 1851 *coup d'état*, by Louis-Napoleon having in advance appointed Bonapartist officers who would follow him rather than the parliamentary leaders, so that the army obeyed the orders of their commander-in-chief to overthrow the Republic. After the 1871 civil war, one of those 1851 leaders, now Prime Minister Thiers, resisted universal conscription, which he feared would 'put a rifle on the shoulder of every Socialist'.[4] Conscription had been systematic from 1798 but with exemptions. Napoleon made compulsory military service literally into a lottery. 'Every canton of France was responsible for a certain number of recruits. The lots were drawn annually, and the youths with numbers higher than the required contingent were exempt. So were married men, priests, and those who could afford to pay for a substitute to serve in their stead.' Unsurprisingly, 'there ensued a great many religious vocations, and the rate of marriages among eighteen-year-olds increased considerably.'[5] Military service was regarded as an obnoxious imposition, prompting frequent evasion or desertion, exacerbated by its inegalitarian impact. 'The long term of duty (six years after 1818, eight years after 1824, seven years between 1855 and 1868, five years until 1889) meant that comparatively few men were inducted yearly: 10 per cent or less of the age group subject to the draft.'[6] Although substitution was ended in 1873, dispensations increased for the educated middle-classes until 1905 when

    [2] Christophe Charle, 151; cf. 139–40 and Estèbe, *Ministres de la République*, 127–33.

    [3] John S. Ambler, *Soldiers Against the State: The French Army in Politics*, 1968, 9; cf. 25 and Goguel, *La Politique des Partis*, 158–9, 171.

    [4] Quoted by Brogan, 117.   [5] Eugen Weber, *Peasants into Frenchmen*, 292.

    [6] Ibid. 292; cf. 293–7.

every physically fit youth served for the same time—two years, extended to three years in 1913. It says something of the physical state of French manhood that in 1872, of the men aged 20 called up, one-third were too infirm or deformed for military service,[7] so nominally universal conscription was still clearly not comprehensive.

The anti-republican views of the top military brass are reflected in the 1887 Memoirs of General du Barail, who, recalling his role in the 1851 coup, disingenuously declared: 'I had no political opinions whatsoever.... I nourished against Republican institutions that instinctive antipathy which is deep in the soul of every soldier,' asserting more generally: 'By its motto alone the Republic is the negation of the Army, for liberty, equality and fraternity mean indiscipline, lack of obedience and negation of hierarchical principles.'[8] Gambetta's confidential 1876–8 enquiry into the political attitudes of army officers revealed that 70 per cent of generals were varieties of anti-republican and only 9 per cent republican, although they fared better among the more junior officers.[9] Nevertheless, while we have seen that the National Guard were actively involved in the 1830, 1848, and 1871 insurrections, by contrast the regular army acquired between the end of the Napoleonic Wars and the Second World War a professional ethic of obedience to government as the legitimate civil authority. A purely defensive view of the role of the army developed on the Republican Left, ranging from the moderate Jules Simon's wishful thinking in 1867: 'We want to have an army of citizens which will be invincible at home and incapable of waging war abroad',[10] to Jean Jaurès 1910 New Army rejection of anti-militarism in favour of a militia-based military.

The outbreak of the First World War revealed a contradiction between the defensive posture of the French army and its offensive-centred doctrine identified with Marshal Foch. Although the French soldiers fought bravely in 1914–18 (unlike the Second World War), despite massive casualties, war weariness, mutinies, and defeatism were only surmounted in 1917 by calling on Clemenceau to galvanize the war effort and the appointment of Pétain as the Commander-in-Chief. Clemenceau was single-mindedly committed to winning as an interventionist War Minister as well as Prime Minister. In announcing the German defeat in 1918, Clemenceau proudly reminded the Chamber of Deputies that he was the sole survivor of those who in 1871 had protested against a defeated France's loss of Alsace-Lorraine. As for the assassin of Jaurès (who had sought to prevent the outbreak of war) he was not tried until the shock of his crime had dissipated and then acquitted.[11] In the context of the 'Sacred Union' proclaimed by President Poincaré, killing Jaurès was a patriotic crime to be exonerated.

---

[7] Zeldin, *France*, I, 304.   [8] Quoted by Ambler, 29, 33.

[9] Ambler, 31–2 drawing on François Bédarida, 'L'armée et la république: les opinions politiques des officiers français en 1876–1878' in *Revue historique*, July–September 1964, 119–64.

[10] Quoted by Bury, *Gambetta's Final Years*, 61; cf. Richard D Challener, *The French Theory of the Nation in Arms, 1866–1939*, 1965, 68–74, 276. On anti-militarism in the CGT, see Jennings, *Syndicalism in France*, 39–41, 137–8.

[11] Brogan, 528; cf. Book 9 passim.

Denis Brogan forthrightly wrote of the catastrophic collapse in 1940: 'The military defeat of France was not simply a product of inertia, incompetence, archaic military doctrine, national divisions on the Right and Left, moral decay. It was a disaster; it was in some ways a disgrace.'[12] The Commander-in-Chief General Maxime Weygand, who refused to carry on the war in North Africa and championed an armistice in order to prevent the army disintegrating and public anarchy, revealed his anti-republican colours in writing to Marshal Pétain in June 1940; 'The old order of things, that is to say a political regime of Masonic, capitalist and international compromises has led us to our present straits. France wants no more of it.'[13] Where Weygand threatened disobedience to impose acquiescence in defeat, de Gaulle accused Pétain of outright treason, being in turn sentenced to death in absentia. Faced with the choice, almost all French officers sided with Pétain, who represented both dominant military values and formal legality. Many senior political and administrative posts in Vichy were held by officers. 'With the help of Admiral Darlan, the opportunistic, ambitious and fiercely Anglophobe vice-president of the cabinet after February 1941, the government and administration were flooded with admirals.'[14] The loss of 20,000 killed and 2 million prisoners of war had led to a national nervous breakdown in 1940 of which unscrupulous military leaders took advantage to reorient France in a reactionary direction.

Commanders in the colonial empire were placed in severe predicaments. Thus in Syria, fighting between Vichy French troops and Gaullist troops led to the death of over a thousand of the former and some 800 of the latter. At the Liberation, the Vichy commander pleaded that he had only obeyed orders but was condemned with the words: 'At the grade you hold and in the functions you fulfill, one is judge of the orders he receives.'[15] When the Allies landed in North Africa in 1942 some 700 French and 500 Americans were killed before the Vichy troops ceased fighting. In the confusion, the Vichy commanders in Tunisia did not know 'whether duty required them to fight the Americans, the Germans, neither or both.'[16]

The German occupation of the Vichy zone in November 1942 led to the elimination of the French army in France but the Toulon fleet commander scuttled his ships to prevent the Germans taking them over. The struggle for power in North Africa between Generals Giraud and de Gaulle was won by the latter who was far more than a soldier and showed it by outmanoeuvring his rival. The French armed forces were never to recover their role as the supreme, symbolic embodiment of national patriotism, and the end of conscription by President Chirac meant that both militarism and anti-militarism disappeared, allowing pacifism to assume a greater place than it had previously occupied. When terrorism replaces invasion as

[12] Brogan, x, Introduction to the 1964 edn. On the demoralized post-First World War French army and pacifist population, see Eugen Weber, *The Hollow Years: France in the 1930s*, 1995, Chapter 1. The finest French meditation on the Capitulation of 1940 in its immediate aftermath is Marc Bloch's *L'étrange défaite*, 1957. One of France's finest French historians who served in the army in both world wars, Bloch was shot as a Resister in 1944.

[13] Quoted by Ambler, 60; cf. 58–63.   [14] Ibid. 71; cf. 66–73.   [15] Quoted ibid. 75.

[16] Ibid. 76. More generally, see Général de Gaulle, *Mémoires de Guerre*, 3 volumes, 1954–9.

the main threat, people look to the police rather than to the army for protection. However, before considering the post-Second World War rearguard role of the army in fighting colonial wars in Vietnam and Algeria, as well as overthrowing the Fourth Republic and bringing de Gaulle to power, we must first look back at the nineteenth century process of colonial expansion.

EXTENDING THE EMPIRE

Although a Colonial Ministry to administer the Empire was only separated from the Navy Ministry in 1894, post-Napoleonic imperialism was the result of political decisions in the cases of Algeria (1830), Cochin China (1859), Tunisia (1881), and Madagascar (1895), despite the fact that 'The extension of the French Empire in the nineteenth century was partially the result of uncontrolled initiative on the part of colonial military commanders'.[17] They used their freedom of action to extend control especially in West Africa, New Caledonia, and Indo-China. A series of proconsuls emerged such as Thomas Bugeaud, who was forced to retire as a colonel because he had rallied to Napoleon in 1815. Retrieving his position in 1830, as a Deputy he presciently opposed the colonization of Algeria because 'sooner or later, we shall have to leave it whether we like it or not'.[18] After brutally repressing the 1834 unrest in Paris, he went on to 'pacify' Algeria as Governor General and Commander-in-Chief from 1844 to 1847, where he consolidated the French hold. Marshal Hubert Lyautey made his reputation in Morocco, developing his influential views on 'the social role of the officer'. This went well beyond conquest through a fusion of forceful military and paternalistic functions, ranging from territorial administration through education and health, economic development, and public works. As early as 1897, Lyautey was condemning 'the vice of our institutions, of this omnicompetent, *incompetent, unstable* and *irresponsible* parliamentarism', and following the 1934 Stavisky riots he successfully threatened to lead a march on parliament unless Prime Minister Daladier resigned.[19]

Assertive colonial generals like Gallieni in Madagascar and Indo-China, Lyautey in Algeria, Morocco, and Indo-China, usually used colonial service as an outlet for ambitions that might otherwise have been directed against the government and regime in France. However, they left 'a legacy of independence and occasional disobedience of governmental authorities'[20] that influenced a non-colonial General de Gaulle in 1940 and then threatened to overthrow him in 1960–2 after having in 1958 installed him to state power. Nevertheless, politicians did not fully

---

[17] Ambler, 10; cf. 11.

[18] Quoted in Douglas Porch, *The French Foreign Legion: A Complete History*, 1991, 72; cf. 71–83. See also Pinkney, *Decisive Years*, 141–5.

[19] Quoted in Ambler, 33; cf. 37–8, 47–8, 186, 190–1. See also Girardet, *La Société Militaire*, Chapter 8 passim.

[20] Ambler, 222; cf. 310–11.

share the military view that retention of the colonies was an integral imperative of French national identity, conflating nationalism and colonialism. Confusion was compounded by the fact that Algerians were treated as French nationalists but not citizens.

The post-Napoleonic French Empire began and ended in Algeria: in 1830 to associate a failing Bourbon monarchy with military glory and in 1962 to free the Fifth Republic from a war that could not be either won or lost militarily. Prior to the Third Republic of the 1880s, there was no consistent colonial policy and public indifference prevailed towards what seemed to be a series of disparate improvizations. Most economists like Say and Bastiat followed their British counterparts in condemning colonialism in the name of free trade, culminating in the 1861 Cobden-Chevalier Treaty. Furthermore, unlike Britain, France was a country of immigration not emigration, so that in 1870 half of the 200,000 European settlers in Algeria were not of French origin.

The protagonists of colonialism were more militarist and religious than commercial, although the Chambers of Commerce of the ports of Bordeaux, Marseille, and Nantes were ardent advocates. The promotion of international prestige and the civilizing mission combined the efforts of Catholic missionaries (who also acted as couriers, translators, and negotiators for French traders), and those on the secular left like Gambetta and Ferry who sought to spread humanist values, ending ignorance and superstition, to enlighten backward peoples. France saw itself as an anti-slavery liberator, not an exploitative conqueror. Twenty-two new religious missionary orders were founded between 1816 and 1870 and continued thereafter, opening the way to military and settler occupation, which in turn promoted proselytization.[21] Gambetta argued in 1878 that 'Algeria ought to be governed like the rest of France, because she is a French land *par excellence*. ... The principle which should direct our labours, regulate our decisions and govern all our reflections is the principle of assimilation'.[22] Gambetta's plea that this principle should be extended to all French overseas territories, with Africa and Asia after 1870 playing the role of Algeria after 1830, was to dog subsequent French colonial policy. This was because the French never accepted that they should implement the inordinate implications of assimilation. The disjunction between rhetoric and reality was pursued by Ferry and his successors.

As well as putting the classic mercantilist case for acquiring sources of raw materials and protected markets, Prime Minister Jules Ferry asserted that France

[21] Raoul Girardet, *L'Idée Coloniale en France, 1871–1962*, 1972, 4–16 and Marc Michel, 'La colonisation' in Sirinelli (ed.), *Histoire des droites en France*, III, 125–40.

[22] Quoted in Bury, *Gambetta's Final Years*, 70; cf. 62–80, 215–17. See also Raymond F. Betts, *Assimilation and Association in French Colonial Theory, 1890–1914*, 1961 and Alice L. Conklin, *A Mission to Civilize: The Republican Idea of Empire in France and West Africa, 1895–1930*, 1997, especially the Introduction. 'The attraction of this policy of assimilation was that it appeared to satisfy at the same time the desires both to dominate the colonial peoples and to liberate them: their absorption would be their liberation.' (Sorum, *Intellectuals and Decolonization in France*, 23.) On the manner in which 'the colonial policy of assimilation as the only way to combine liberalism and centralism' worked out subsequently, see ibid. 185; cf. 23–4, 29, 34, 59, 107, 184, 191 and Alfred Grosser, *La IVe République et sa Politique Extérieure*, 1961, 250.

could not be another Belgium or Switzerland. 'She must also be a great country, exercising over the destinies of Europe all its influence, she should spread this influence throughout the world, and carry wherever she can her language, her customs, her flag, her weapons, her genius.'[23] Ferry's adventurist policy was opposed by Clemenceau, Déroulède, and Rochefort as a costly diversion of resources away from the prime objective of revenge on Germany and retrieving the lost provinces of Alsace-Lorraine. Déroulède contemptuously declared: 'I have lost two sisters and you offer me twenty servants.'[24]

Although the colonies accounted for less than 10 per cent in pre-First World War French trade and foreign investment, public expenditure on the colonies nearly doubled between 1789 and 1885 and had nearly tripled by 1902. The colonial lobby was very active, a former Under-Secretary of State for the Colonies establishing a Colonial Group of ninety-one in the Chamber of Deputies that more than doubled in its predominantly Right-Centre membership by 1902. Firms with colonial business interests set up the French Colonial Union in 1893 and in 1894 the first fully fledged Ministry of the Colonies was established. In 1889 the Colonial School was created to train colonial officials but favouritism in senior appointments still accounted for four-fifths of the total. Pro-colonial chauvinists saw Britain rather than Germany as the main rival, the 1898 Fashoda confrontation between a French attempt to get a foothold on the Nile (to link her West and East African colonies) with a British force under Kitchener, ending in a French humiliating withdrawal. Another colonial confrontation in the decade before the First World War in Morocco promoted Germanophobia above Anglophobia. Nevertheless the French continued polemically to contrast their civilizing, cultural emphasis with the exploitative capacity and greater colour prejudice attributed to the British, despite looking to the British alliance against the German threat.[25]

Before the outbreak of the First World War, it was already being argued that colonial troops would help make up the deficiency in numbers of the French army. When war came, a million colonial soldiers and workers made a massive contribution to the war effort, 205,000 being killed.[26] The interwar years were characterized by the repression of early manifestations of Indochinese and North African nationalism and Leninist Third International ineffectual anti-imperialist incitement. The French Communist Party advocated Algerian independence until 1935, when it switched to a Popular Front policy of improving native rights within an 'Overseas France' regarded as an indivisible part of the Empire without which

[23] Ferry's speech in defence of his record when his government fell on 11 April 1885, quoted in Girardet, *L'Idée Coloniale*, 50; cf. 25–62. Paul Leroy-Beaulieu's *De la colonisation chez les peuples modernes* appeared in 1874. A close friend and future biographer of Ferry, the historian Alfred Rambaud, published in 1885 a translation of J. R. Seeley's influential colonialist apologia, *The Expansion of England*.

[24] Quoted by Girardet, *L'Idée Coloniale*, 68; cf. 302 note and more generally Brogan, Book V on 'France Overseas'

[25] Girardet, 68–99 and Brogan, 322–6, 391–5, 399–401. For an earlier example of acrimonious Anglo-French colonial rivalry verging on war over Syria—the notorious 'Eastern Question'—see Bury and Tombs, *Thiers*, 63–79.

[26] Girardet, 118–19; cf. 99–102 on Colonel Mangin's 1910 book *La force noir*.

France could not claim to be a great power. This was despite a fact-finding report commissioned by the 1936 Blum government which stated that 'the budget of Indo-China was supplied by three well-springs: gambling, opium and alcohol', all state-controlled; that French officials imposed a 'monthly alcohol quota for each village' and in Cambodia 'opium dens were closed for not having purchased their monthly quota' but the Popular Front government failed to end such exactions.[27] Nevertheless, the former Governor General of Indo-China and several times Radical Minister for Colonial Affairs, Albert Sarraut, asserted in popular books that French humanist colonialism involved the strong French acting with fraternal solidarity to help the colonized weak.

At the apogee of French colonialism, with expanding trade and numerous propagandist books and films, the 1931 Paris Colonial Exhibition, which attracted thirty-four million visitors, prompted Colonial Minister Paul Reynaud to invoke the 'white man's burden' and prepare a toast to Kipling, regretting that France did not have the same devotion to their Empire as did the British![28] However, the post-Second World War colonial decolonization of the British Empire did not arouse such heated soul-searching and violent confrontations as the end of French imperial domination, a subject to which we shall return.

UNHOLY COLONIAL WARS, IMPERIAL RETREAT
AND NEOCOLONIALISM

France emerged from the Second World War in 1945 only to be plunged into two successive revolutionary wars from 1946 to 1962, in which the guerrilla and terrorist tactics of their antagonists led in response to the development of psychological warfare, torture, and summary execution tactics that exerted almost unbearable tensions between French elevated principles and debased practices. Following Vichy–Gaullist rivalry for control of the Empire (which was used as a springboard for the Allied invasion of France and the Normandy landings, as well as the embarrassing fact that the French liberation forces were mainly colonial Africans), French leaders had to consider whether colonial nationalist aspirations could be appeased while clinging on to their desire to perpetuate imperial domination.

The January 1944 Brazzaville Conference was responsible for encapsulating the French refusal to face frankly the choice between accepting the nationalists' demands for eventual independence and reasserting the indissolubility of the French Union. De Gaulle, despite suggesting a semi-federal system that concentrated most power in Paris but was unpopular with the colonial Governors

---

[27] Quoted in Panwong Norindr, 'The Popular Front's Colonial Policies in Indochina: Reassessing the Popular Front's "Colonisation Altruiste"' in Tony Chafer and Amanda Sackur (eds), *French Colonial Empire and the Popular Front: Hope and Disillusion*, 1999, 233; cf. Chapter 12 passim.

[28] Michel, 143–4; cf. Girardet, *L'Idée Coloniale*, 117–49. For a corrective to the oversimplified contrast between French and British colonial administration, see Véronique Dimier, *Le gouvernement des colonies, regards croisés franco-britanniques*, 2004.

General, came down against independence or self-government, as did his Fourth Republic successors. 'Federalism was a particularly attractive slogan because it concealed the crucial issue...of sovereignty....It could be used to disguise independence or to disguise continued domination by France. The apparent consensus for federalism, therefore, was to a large extent only a verbal illusion.'[29] Thereafter, French practice was to assert the integrity, inalienability and individuality of 'the Republic' and to condemn any concessions of sovereignty as abdication and abandonment. A new style pseudo-egalitarian mystique was quickly subsumed under an old-style inegalitarianism, despite a warning by the Francophile future President of Senegal, Leopold Senghor, that the French Union would only succeed if it was based upon a relationship of equality. Under the guise of assimilation, a uniform and unequal association—a caricature of the British Commonwealth—was all that was made available within a diverse union of '100 million Frenchmen', a slogan, not an accurate description or one destined for durability.[30]

The 1946–54 Vietnam War prepared the pitting of the French Army against the Fourth Republic, whose destruction was a consequence of the Algerian War. A key role was played in 1946 by a Gaullist High Commissioner in Vietnam, Admiral Thierry d'Argenlieu, who encouraged by the reinstalled local French administration and the colonial lobby, inaugurated the policy of forcing the hand of governments in Paris. They were reduced to being spectators, validating retrospectively illegal acts they had not authorized, although MRP leader Bidault was a willing facilitator as Foreign Minister or Prime Minister from 1944 to 1948, until he was replaced by a more European-orientated Robert Schuman. In 1956, General Navarre, who had led France to the decisive 1954 defeat of Dien Bien Phu, when French casualties were 1,500 dead and 10,000 prisoners, applied the Maurrasian distinction between the legal and the real country, with the army representing the latter. He advocated that the parliamentary charlatans embodying republican legality should make way for a 'great surgeon'. This view was shared by the Gaullist plotter and future Prime Minister Michel Debré, who asserted in 1957: 'A legal Government might well be illegitimate; an illegal authority legitimate.'[31]

General Paul Ely, who helped de Gaulle to play the role of 'great surgeon' in the 1958 crisis by resigning as Chief of Staff of National Defence (a post to which he was reappointed later in 1958 by de Gaulle), sententiously proclaimed that the army in revolt had shown 'with the highest discipline, profound respect for a "genuine legality"', when in fact it had left the country no alternative other than civil war or de Gaulle.[32] Although he had never been particularly popular among his fellow officers, they found it convenient to refer to his 1940 example of choosing to place national honour above obedience as a traditional military servitude. However, the public protest against torture and summary executions, leading to the incarceration and resignation of General Paris de Bollardière from

---

[29] Sorum, 192; cf. 191–4. Institut Charles de Gaulle, *De Gaulle en son siècle*, VI, 1992, 18–19, 25–6, 247. See also Martin Shipway, 'Reformism and the French "Official Mind": the 1944 Brazzaville Conference and the Legacy of the Popular Front' in Chafer and Sackur (eds), Chapter 6.

[30] Gordon Wright, *The Reshaping of French Democracy*, 1950, 142–50, 201–5, 213–15, 242–3.

[31] Quoted in Ambler, 118; cf. 119, 132, 223–5, 246.   [32] Ibid. 119; cf. 121, 267, 269.

his command in Algeria, might be considered a better expression of national honour than most of his peers, who lived in introspective isolation from civil society.[33]

The lessons that the French theoreticians of colonial war learnt from their adversaries were fourfold. First, since the East–West stalemate made nuclear war improbable, the armed forces should concentrate on dealing with colonial subversives. Secondly, the main enemy was international communism, using anticolonial nationalism as preliminary to a Third World War in which the fate of Western civilization was at stake. Thirdly, the main objective was not so much a military victory as to win over the colonial populations, the struggle for whose support would be decisive. Fourthly, the French army should adopt the organizational, indoctrination, and propaganda manipulative methods used by its opponents. While 'neither the French government nor the majority of French officers were willing to turn the whole of Algeria into a totalitarian state...the army would have to focus its new political and ideological leadership, not only on the Algerians, but on the French government and the metropolitan French population as well'.[34]

Owing to the equivocation and procrastination of most Fourth Republic politicians, colonial wars contributed directly or indirectly to the downfall of sixteen out of its eighteen ephemeral caretaker governments. Treated in Algeria as subjects not citizens in 'a country run by and for Europeans', subjected to rigged elections and repression, the Liberation was a lost opportunity to achieve an accommodation with the reformists. This left the way open for alienated revolutionaries to combine with an alienated army and settlers to destroy first the Fourth Republic and then French Algeria as the bulk of the French people, led by de Gaulle, sought to avoid France itself being Algerianized. It has been pertinently pointed out the 'Algeria's status as an integral part of the French Republic has always been, to some extent, both juridically and politically a fiction, the realities of which were observed by verbal make-believe, wishful thinking, or deliberate falsification, from the middle of the nineteenth century to well beyond the end of the Second World War'. Dorothy Pickles went on to argue that 'The difference between "colonialist" and "anticolonialist" was the difference between those who clung to the fictions of assimilation and those who wanted to make it a reality. The mistake of too many French politicians and administrators was that they did not recognize quickly enough that assimilation had ceased to be a possible road for even moderate nationalist opinion', so that France was condemned either to wage an interminable war or to concede independence.[35]

Before independence was attained, much blood was shed and intense arguments exchanged. The messianic, anti-imperialist revolutionaries were personified by two assimilated Martinique-born intellectuals from Fort de France, Aimé Césaire and Frantz Fanon. A Communist deputy and mayor in the Caribbean who

---

[33] Quoted in Ambler, 145; cf. 143–7, 300–16.   [34] Ibid. 169; cf. 180–207, 334–6, 341–3.
[35] Dorothy Pickles, *Algeria and France: From Colonialism to Cooperation*, 1963, 18, 51; cf. 57, 195–8. On de Gaulle's exclusion of assimilation as too late and integration as a 'hollow formula', see Charles de Gaulle, *Mémoires d'Espoir*, 1970, 51–2.

resigned from the party in 1956, Césaire was a poet-politician who combined a Marxist conception of a colonized proletariat with a lyrical desire to respond to white racism by restoring cultural negritude to end the dehumanization of both the colonizer and the colonized. Fanon, who joined the rebel FLN in 1957, emphasized violent self-assertion against the colonizers as part of a global class struggle. This involved the rejection of Western values by an alienated peasantry that replaced the failed revolution by the alienated proletariat; a sanguinary political romanticism that, we have seen, was endorsed by Sartre and other Left intellectuals.[36]

Humanist moral protest against torture, racism, electoral fraud, illiteracy, unemployment, and poverty, which together led to colonial insurrection was expressed by the Left Catholic periodical *Esprit*; the first article revealing the practice of torture by Jean-Marie Domenach appearing in December 1954, followed by Claude Bourdet in *France-Observateur* and François Mauriac in *L'Express* in January 1955. 'Although the French had used torture in Madagascar (in 1947), Indo-China and Morocco, and indeed in Algeria before 1954, in Algeria it now became a daily, routine occurrence . . . .'[37] These anti-colonialist intellectuals sought to reform the colonial system rather than ending it, although by the end of the 1950s they accepted that Algerian independence was unavoidable. As in Vietnam, they were worried that France was leaving the field open to the rival Soviet and American imperialisms.

More effective in undermining the colonialist case than polemical passion aimed at arousing French opinion against the Algerian War was the disillusioned detachment of the realists. In 1956, the journalist Raymond Cartier, in the mass circulation *Paris-Match*, argued that compared to the expanding European market, the preservation of protected colonial markets was a burden not worth carrying for Frenchmen. Realistically, 'Politics is the art of adapting to the events that can no longer be directed.'[38] More influential on the elites was Raymond Aron's *Algerian Tragedy*, which argued that not only was the Empire unprofitable, it had been condemned from the 1945 pseudo-victory. France could prosper without the French Union and should negotiate Algerian independence. Aron recalled in 1958 that Governor General Bugeaud had declared in 1840 that he had 'always considered Algeria the most baleful present the Restoration had made to the July Revolution.'[39]

Because of the 'discrepancy between what the politicians said in private and their public declarations', Aron was attacked from the Right as a defeatist traitor, while those on the Left were embarrassed that someone they regarded as right wing was being more forthright than they were.[40] Although successive

---

[36] Girardet, *L'Idée Coloniale*, 211–19. On the advocacy by Césaire and Senghor (who became President of Senegal from 1960 to 1980) of negritude as a rejection of the loss of authenticity resulting from a policy of assimilation, see Sorum, *Intellectuals and Decolonization in France*, 212–23 and Aimé Césaire, *Discours sur le colonialisme*, 1955.

[37] Drake, *Intellectuals and Politics in Postwar France*, 113; cf. 108–14 and Sorum; 26, 30–1, 78–9, 94–5, 118.

[38] Quoted in Sorum, 202; cf. 203–4 and Girardet, *L'Idée Coloniale*, 228–32.

[39] Quoted in Colquhoun, *Raymond Aron*, II, 61.   [40] Drake, 117; cf. 115–16; Michel, 155–8.

French governments held on to the illusory assumption that a settlement short of complete independence could be negotiated and accepted by the settlers, the no-win military deadlock continued despite Minister Resident in Algeria Lacoste's repeated prediction that victory was only the 'last quarter of an hour away'. As a result, a deadly dialectic of terrorism and torture continued, increasing Algerian unity and French disunity.[41] 'A whole machine of deception has been built up, which reaches from the police officer who uses torture, via the judge who accepts the results of the interrogation as valid evidence to the Prime Minister who either issues a denial or says nothing.'[42] Meanwhile public opinion was shifting: in January 1958, 27 per cent thought Algeria would become independent, increasing to 57 per cent by December 1959 and 69 per cent in May 1961. The increasingly acrimonious debate over who was demoralizing the French army and people was preparing the way for the 1958 army-settler insurrection against an indecisive regime unable to resolve the Algerian predicament to their satisfaction.

A key figure in the outcome was General Jacques Massu, whose Tenth Paratroop Division was given full police powers in Algiers in 1957, where hundreds of people were being killed. Thousands of suspects were 'interrogated, often tortured, and sometimes executed without a trial'.[43] Massu justified the army dirtying its hands to extract information to save lives; in terms of restoring order he did win the 'Battle of Algiers'. On 13 May 1958 'Massu faced a settler rebellion which was not directly of his making; yet he was in full agreement with its intent, and, rather than repress it with violence, he preferred to become an insurgent himself', assuming headship of the insurrectionary Algiers Committee of Public Safety.[44] Helped by Generals Ely and Salan to secure a bloodless change of Republic by mobilizing military pressure on Paris, and by a member of the Defence Minister's staff Léon Delbecque and former Governor General Jacques Soustelle to steer the crisis towards de Gaulle as the saviour of the situation, Massu was the man of the hour. However, the unconditional Gaullist had a year later realised that de Gaulle was moving towards Algerian independence and after an incautious press interview he was recalled to Paris and relieved of his command.[45] Massu had become a victim of the strong government he had helped to restore. Nevertheless, in May 1968, when de Gaulle was uncertain how to deal with the

[41] Pickles, 39–41.

[42] Vidal-Naquet, *Torture: Cancer of Democracy*, 135; cf. especially Chapters 1–2. See also Sorum, 119–29 and Ambler, 236–40.

[43] Ambler, 181; cf. 184–5, 240 and Vidal-Naquet, Chapter 3, who particularly emphasizes the role of Colonel Bigeard.

[44] Ambler, 262; cf. 261–7. For the most reliable of many accounts of the 1958 overthrow of the Fourth Republic, see Philip Williams, 'The Fourth Republic: murder or suicide' in *Wars, Plots and Scandals in Post-war France*, 1970, Chapter 7.

[45] Ibid. 270–1; de Gaulle, *Mémoires d'Espoir*, 86; cf. Chapters 2 and 3 on Overseas and Algeria. De Gaulle recalled what he said to the generals in Algeria: 'You are not the army for the army. You are the army of France. You only exist by her, for her and at her service' (ibid. 83). On de Gaulle's evolving Algerian policy, see also *De Gaulle en son siècle*, VI, 143–81, Alfred Grosser, *French Foreign Policy under de Gaulle*, 1967, Chapter 3, and Sorum, 27–9, 38, 103, 165–8 and 207–8.

student-prompted general strike in Paris that threatened the Fifth Republic, he went to Baden-Baden in Germany where Massu, as Commander of the French forces stationed there, encouraged him to reassert his authority, backed if necessary by the armed forces..., which proved unnecessary.

Before then, the attempted Paris 1961 putsch led by four prominent generals but whose driving forces were five colonels with 'more to gain and less to lose', shattered the myth of army unity. The putsch quickly collapsed thanks to the loyalty to de Gaulle of the bulk of the 400,000 troops stationed in Algeria, especially the 150,000 conscripts, who responded to de Gaulle's broadcast appeal. The rebels consisted mainly of the 18,000 parachutists and 30,000 Foreign Legionaries, some 3 and 5 per cent respectively of the total forces in Algeria. They were the elite troops with a strong *esprit de corps*, who had borne the brunt of the fighting in Indo-China and Algeria, where they had suffered heavy losses.[46] The Legionnaire parachutists were the hardcore of the insurrection, fearing that the loss of Algeria would lead to their dissolution—which it did not—although they reluctantly left their legendary headquarters at Sidi-bel-Abbès in 1962.

The myth and mystique of the Foreign Legion, which was used as a proto-praetorian guard in 1958 and in 1961, belong to a tradition of employing mercenaries. The French Revolution had combined the use of foreign legions of ideological sympathizers with conscription, but after the 1830 Revolution the present Foreign Legion was improvized in March 1831 to serve outside France, especially in Algeria. It was a way of getting rid of the many troublesome foreign revolutionaries who had taken refuge in France after the failure of their attempts to emulate her example. It subsequently fashioned, out of a variety of unpromising destitutes, misfits, and undesirables, an elite corps of mercenaries ready to die to expand and then preserve the French Empire.[47] After the loss of Algeria, the Foreign Legion's headquarters was moved to Aubagne, near Marseille, allowing them to be used by de Gaulle to support ex-colonial regimes in Mauretania (1963), Gabon (1964), Djbouti (1967), and Chad (1968), a 'military assistance' policy that was continued by his successors.

In April 1962, de Gaulle called a referendum to approve his Algerian conclusion to France's painful decolonization, receiving the support of 91 per cent of the votes. Surviving the OAS threats to his life, he was able to overcome the parties who sought to dispense with him now that the Algerian imbroglio had been resolved. With another successful referendum in October 1962 on the direct election of the President and the dissolution of the Assembly, de Gaulle turned the tables on his opponents. Algeria achieved independence but de Gaulle's hope that interdependence would continue, did not materialize. Most French settlers left Algeria, only some 18,000 choosing to remain. Ironically, since then French governments have been concerned to limit Algerian immigration into France. Did his French Community fare better?

[46] Ambler, Chapter 12.
[47] Porch, especially xiii–xxiii. P. C. Wren's mythmaking *Beau Geste* and two subsequent novels did much to promote the Foreign Legion in the twentieth century.

De Gaulle's intention in 1958 was, in line with France's ambitious 'millenary vocation of influence and expansion', to develop with 'privileged partners' in Africa 'cooperation' which would replace past domination.[48] However, the French Community, despite being approved in referendums by massive majorities in all the former Black African countries except Guinea, quickly evolved by 1960 away from a French-dominated 'federalism' to confederalism and then independence. A multilateral 'Community' was replaced by some 200 bilateral contractual agreements between France and some 20 African states because although 'lip service was paid to equality' it was unacceptable as, if implemented, 'French policy could be determined by a majority of African states'.[49] Clientelist relations between France and her junior 'partners' of a one-sided kind developed, with military and monetary guarantees (through the 'franc zone') being supplemented by public aid through grants rather than loans and educational cooperation through the provision of teachers to preserve and develop the use of the French language. Provision was made for prior consultation with Paris before taking major foreign policy decisions and defence assistance against internal and external threats was facilitated by on the spot French military bases. In this way, many of the 'common functions' that the Community was to have retained under de facto French control—defence, currency, education—were perpetuated on a bilateral basis.[50] These were managed on de Gaulle's behalf by the Secretary-General of the Community, Jacques Foccart, who became in 1961, after its demise, Secretary-General for African and Madagascan Affairs.

From 1959 until 1974 (when Giscard d'Estaing replaced Pompidou as President of the Republic), Foccart, based in the Elysée, pulled the strings of French post-colonial policy thanks to a network of personal relations with the African heads of state, based upon mutual trust. He ran a virtual mini-ministry as part of the President's 'reserved sector'. An import–export businessman, he had joined the Resistance, achieving the rank of Lieutenant-Colonel before going in 1944 to London as a member of the Gaullist intelligence service. After the war, he became active in the Gaullist RPF movement, and by 1954 he had become its Secretary-General. He was active in preparing de Gaulle's return to power in 1958, thereafter combining his African functions with intelligence work and looking after de Gaulle's personal security, especially at times of crisis like 1961 and 1968. De Gaulle saw him briefly each evening, valuing his advice on party matters as well as African affairs.

The former French colonies being unprepared for independence, Foccart assisted de Gaulle in propping them up, including the preservation of internal order through helping them organize their police and intelligence services and sending in French troops when necessary. The Ministry of Cooperation was confined to routine matters, while Foccart each week coordinated the

[48] De Gaulle, *Mémoires d'Espoir*, 45; cf. 43–4, 65, 73–5, 113, 137.

[49] Grosser, 55; cf. Chapter 4 passim.

[50] Jean-Claude Gautron, 'La politique d'aide et de coopération de la France en Afrique francophone' in *De Gaulle en son siècle*, VI, 256–64; cf. Martial Ahipeaud and Yves Morel, 'La coopération monétaure et financière entre les Etats de la zone franc en Afrique et Madagascar (1958–1969)', ibid. 271–91.

Africa-related work of the Finance, Foreign Affairs, and Defence ministries. He helped select ambassadors and gave them directives without going through the Foreign Ministry. He regularly and frequently received African ministers visiting Paris. Foccart was thus the pivot of de Gaulle's African 'cooperation' policy and largely preserved this role under President Pompidou, who continued to act the feudal sovereign towards his African vassals while Foccart provided advice and assistance.[51]

Giscard, as President, removed Foccart as part of his determination to dismantle the Gaullist networks that not only provided unofficial sources of information but secured kickbacks, with some of the African grants in aid returning to the successive 'Gaullist' parties as illicit funding that survived into the Chirac 1980s and 1990s. However, he kept on Foccart's deputy René Journiac to take advantage of the personal relations he had developed with African leaders. Giscard continued a strongly interventionist policy, not merely in former French colonies but also in the former Belgian Congo, because in Africa, with a small number of troops, one could still play the role of a great power. Elsewhere, French Polynesia was militarily valuable as the location of the Pacific Experimental Centre where France exploded her nuclear bombs after she lost the use of the Sahara.

The short-circuiting of the Cooperation Ministry continued during the Mitterrand presidency. As Interior Minister in 1954, Mitterrand had asserted that in Algeria 'the only negotiation is war', but by 1957 he was advocating a more decentralized autonomy 'for without Africa there will be no History of France in the Twenty-first century'.[52] As President of the Republic from 1981 to 1995, he persisted with the neo-colonial policy of his predecessors. In place of the Foccart-Journiac system, Mitterrand relied upon a Third Republic-style Freemason network, linking his friend Guy Penne with African leaders, supplemented by his journalist son Jean-Christophe Mitterrand, who was quickly nicknamed 'Papamadit' (Daddy told me). This highly personalized form of control not only meant that French management of neo-colonial relations was conducted on the African rather than European model; it lent itself to a state corruption which it is estimated accounted for at least 40 per cent of the French aid provided. The state oil company ELF was an important channel for providing funds both for African leaders, notably Gabon, with kickbacks for French political parties, of the Right pre-1981 and of both Left and Right thereafter.

While educational and military cooperation in kind rather than in cash ensured that some aid did materialize, there was little effective control over the bilateral programmes involved and these declined in the 1980s and 1990s. This continuity with pre-independence malpractices has been challenged in the context of French unwillingness to continue to carry the financial burdens in a region where increasingly the costs of influence far exceed the benefits of perpetuating post-imperial pretence. Already under the second cohabitation of 1993–5, Prime

---

[51] Samy Cohen, *Les conseillers du Président: De Charles de Gaulle à Valéry Giscard d'Estaing*, 1980, 147–62.

[52] Quoted in Sorum, 100, 189. See François Mitterrand, *Présence française et abandon*, 1957, 237.

Minister Balladur had halved the value of the French African franc. The Overseas Cooperation budget having regularly declined since 1992, in February 1998 the Jospin government merged 'Overseas Cooperation' with the Foreign Ministry, a junior minister being attached to the latter, symbolizing the low priority now attached to it.[53]

Despite the decline in economic and military terms of the colonial legacy, it has been rejuvenated culturally and rhetorically since the 1960s through the multilateral Francophone movement. The 1961 initiative came from outside France: Quebec seeking to preserve its identity by asserting a French Canadian culture against the majority English language culture of both the rest of Canada and the USA. Although de Gaulle was not keen to institutionalize the francophone phenomenon, his visit to Quebec in 1967, marked by his speech provocatively proclaiming 'Long live free Quebec', not only encouraged the secessionist movement but indirectly various cultural organizations based upon the French language.[54] In 1970 an Agency for Cultural and Technical Cooperation was established in Paris, financed mainly by France and Canada (who were rivals for leadership) involving twenty-eight member and four associate states, with Quebec separately represented. Although it was then decided to hold francophone summit meetings, the first did not take place until 1986. Only in 1991 was a Permanent Francophone Council set up to coordinate activities between summits, with a secretary-general appointed in 1997, suggesting a gradual institutionalization not marked by a sense of urgency. Annual meetings of francophone Foreign Ministers are occasionally supplemented by meetings of Sports and Education Ministers, while since 1997 the International Assembly of French Language Parliamentarians has acquired consultative status.[55] Post-colonial Algeria has steered clear of Francophonia.

Francophonia is a heterogeneous, geographically dispersed conglomerate in both membership and purpose. By 1997 it had associated 50 states or governments in only 30 of which was French an official language, and by 2006, designated Francophone Year, 63 states belonged to the International Francophone Organization, covering 175 million French speakers. Only 14 per cent of their trade is conducted between them, mainly between France and Africa. For France, francophonia is a tool of foreign policy, being especially useful diplomatically in the United Nations and for North–South dialogue. For Canada, Belgium, and Switzerland, it allows expression to important minorities of their populations. For the developing member countries, it offers a source of assistance and a forum for asserting themselves politically. Thus in 1989 President Mitterrand announced at the Dakar summit that France was renouncing claims for debt on thirty-five of the poorest countries, many of which were African.

The francophone institutions were not involved in dealing with the major African crises of the late twentieth century. Their specific function is to resist the

---

[53] Marie-Christine Kessler, *La Politique Etrangère de la France: Acteurs et processus*, 1999, 306–67.

[54] Ibid. 411–13. See also Sylvie Guillaume, 'Le general de Gaulle et le Québec' in *De Gaulle en son siècle*, VI, 509–17.

[55] Kessler, 413–16.

linguistic advance of Anglo-American English. In 1986, the Chirac government designated a minister for francophone affairs without resolving turf wars with the Foreign Affairs and Cooperation ministries and since then it has frequently shifted in its location within the French governmental system. A related manifestation of French cultural ideology was the 1994 Toubon Law that irritatingly sought to impose the use of the French language by all French institutions. The Constitutional Council quickly struck down the articles banning the use of foreign terms as infringing the Declaration of Rights (article 10: protecting freedom of communication of opinion). It has deservedly been the subject of much derision, more symbolic of an assertion of French cultural superiority than effective in practice.[56] Rather than this rearguard action to preserve a residual manifestation of an imperial hegemony, it is to Europe and Franco-German relations that we must turn for the focus of a future-oriented foreign policy.

FRANCO-GERMAN RELATIONS: FROM HEREDITARY ENMITY TO CONCERTED AMITY

The Third Republic was born out of defeat by Bismarck's Prussia and died owing to defeat by Hitler's Germany. French diplomacy prior to the First World War was dominated by the belief that a Franco-German conflict was inevitable, so alliances were developed with Britain and Russia. Even Jaurès, who played down the military threat and hoped for peace, nevertheless rejected anti-militarism and advocated reliance upon the 'armed nation', that is a territorial militia capable of fighting defensive war against a potentially aggressive pan-Germanism. In the atmosphere of nationalist war hysteria of 1913, his old friend Péguy appealed to Jacobinism in declaring : 'In time of war, there is only one policy—the policy of the National Convention. That means Jaurès in a cart and a drum-roll to drown out his powerful voice.'[57] So in 1914, when Jaurès—hoping for reciprocity from the German Social Democrats—persuaded the French Socialists to call for a general strike against war, he was assassinated. His party eulogised him but then supported the war he had strived in vain to prevent.

Having sustained massive losses, France emerged in 1918 as a victor with a defeatist mentality, more inclined to pacifism than the nationalistic vociferations of its ex-servicemen associations implied. The Versailles Peace Treaty—the first major international agreement not written in Latin or French, with English now on equal terms with French—secured the return of Alsace-Lorraine but not the annexation of the Saarland, a pretension that would arise again after the Second World War. The French hope of dismembering Germany into its pre-Bismarckian

---

[56] Ibid. 416–38. See also Dennis Ager, '*Francophonie' in the 1990s: Problems and Opportunities*, 1996. French has been particularly losing ground to English in Europe as is German to English in France, despite official efforts to the contrary.

[57] Quoted in Goldberg, *Jaurès*, 442; cf. 386–8.

disunity was rejected. Clemenceau bitterly said to British Prime Minister Lloyd George: 'Within an hour of the Armistice, I had the impression that you had become once again the enemies of France'.[58] He had to settle for a fifteen-year military occupation of the Rhineland and an Anglo-American guarantee of France's frontier with Germany.

As part of its policy of permanently weakening Germany, France insisted on tough reparations, the popular slogan being 'Germany will pay'! German inability to pay led to occupation of the Rhur from 1923 to 1924, until the Herriot government ended a policy that provoked German hostility without securing financial reparation, proving to be a politically costly failure. The *Action Française* historian-journalist Jacques Bainville's verdict on the Versailles Treaty was that it was too soft in its severity and too severe in its softness.[59] When Hitler came to power, the AF adopted an ambivalent policy, sympathizing with his anti-Semitism and anti-communism but fearing the threat to France. In the 1930s the French Right was myopically more preoccupied with the enemy within France than the foreign enemy. This led after defeat to uneasy collaboration, while Pierre Laval's failure to secure a pre-war reconciliation with Hitler (who regarded France as Germany's mortal enemy), led him to wholehearted collaboration.

Despite Hitler having made his intentions clear in *Mein Kampf*, the French Right generally hoped that a precipitate acceptance of defeat would result in a Bismarckian peace. Instead they were subjected to a Carthaginian peace. As early as 1936, Marshal Pétain had revealed to the Italian Ambassador his stereotypical Anglophobia. 'England has always been France's most implacable enemy.... France has two hereditary enemies, the English and the Germans but the former are older and more perfidious. That is why I should incline to an alliance with the latter, which would guarantee absolute peace in Europe, especially if Italy joined in that alliance ... a better distribution (sic) of British colonies would make it possible to provide wealth and work for all'.[60] The head of the Vichy regime's choice of allies from 1940 to 1944 is clearly anticipated in these remarks, made well before defeat could be claimed to have imposed its preferences. The octogenarian 'hero of Verdun' brought into the Reynaud government to bolster belligerency was already resigned to defeat. Pétain's choice of Prime Minister from 1941 to 1942, Admiral Darlan, was—like many naval officers—anti-British, because of historic and colonial rivalry. Such was the background to the declaration in Pétain's speech on 30 October 1940, a week after meeting Hitler at Montoire: 'I am today setting out along the road of collaboration'.[61] Both sides were disappointed because it did not lead to France declaring war on Britain over Anglo-French hostilities in the French colonies, or to the 'magnificent opportunity' that Laval discerned in 1940, or even to an improvement in the Occupation conditions.[62]

[58] Quoted in Robert Gibson, *Best of Enemies*, 247.

[59] Weber, *Action Française*, 544; cf. 115–20, 276–86, Goguel, 217, 220–55, and Brogan, 546–7, 570–80.

[60] Quoted in Philippe Burrin, *Living with Defeat*, 61; cf. 34, 85.   [61] Quoted ibid. 4.

[62] Warner, *Laval*, 234; cf. 235–43.

Pétain and the Commander-in-Chief General Weygand had opposed France's entry into the war and were defeatist. Together with Admiral Darlan they chose an armistice rather than capitulation for political rather than military reasons. They did not want to carry on the war by withdrawing to North Africa as urged by de Gaulle and Reynaud among others. The contrast between Pétain's comforting broadcast to the French people on 17 June 1940 accepting defeat and de Gaulle's little heard intransigent BBC broadcast from London a day later rejecting it, could not have been more stark. Nevertheless, 'Both were symbols of the divorce of the army from the Third Republic, which Pétain condemned for bringing forth defeat, de Gaulle for resigning itself to the armistice.'[63] Despite the stringent terms—occupation of three-fifths of the richest and most urbanized parts of France, the French to pay the occupation costs, 2 million prisoners (1.5 million transferred to Germany) to be held until peace was signed, requisitioning of French property at will—the armistice was initially popular. The prime concern was an end to fighting, so a quick German victory was widely desired, inducing friendly resignation. It was assumed that Britain would speedily be defeated and that France should reach an accommodation with a German hegemony that would last indefinitely. Many bankers and industrialists were keen to ingratiate themselves with the German authorities, while the Communist newspaper *L'Humanité* called for fraternization with the Germans.[64]

'The leaders of Vichy were neither proud nor perspicacious enough to choose, as did de Gaulle, to continue the struggle alongside England, but nor were they modest or cautious enough to adopt a policy of minimal involvement with Germany, from which they could extricate themselves in time' should its dominance cease.[65] They comprehensively failed to achieve their objectives: minimizing the looting of French resources, reasserting French sovereignty in non-military matters, retrieving her international status and ensuring the regime's post-war survival. They settled for an equivocal policy of non-belligerence, not going to war with Britain but providing arms and bases for Germany. Their failures were partly due to the fact that despite Pétain's popularity, the Vichy leaders were both mediocre and divided, notably between politicians like Laval and generals like Weygand, as reflected in their exchange: 'All parliamentarians are scoundrels.... All military men are cretins.'[66] Their successive sell-outs to the Germans demonstrated that they were willing to settle for little when put under pressure. As a result the German Occupation costs were inflated into 'legalized extortion', the demarcation line between the occupied and non-occupied zones was used as a noose, tightened and relaxed as and when required and Laval was held in reserve should Pétain be insufficiently pliable. Through making successive concessions, 'the leaders of the French state allowed themselves to be sucked into the spiral of satellization'.[67] In a comparably weak position, de Gaulle never allowed this to happen in dealing with his Anglo-American allies.

[63] Ibid. 10; cf. 5–14 and Warner, *Laval*, 159–84.   [64] Burrin, 12, 19–30, 77–8.
[65] Ibid. 66; cf. 80–1.   [66] Quoted ibid. 76; cf. 69–74.
[67] Burrin, 131; cf. Warner, *Laval*, 217; cf. 213–31, 254–73.

After the December 1940–April 1942 interlude when Admiral Darlan was head of government, marked by undeclared naval and colonial armed conflict with Britain, the Germans imposed his replacement by Laval, who was modestly also Minister of Foreign Affairs, Interior, and Information. Darlan remained head of the vestigial French armed forces, while Pétain was reduced to the largely ceremonial role of head of state, having already accepted that he needed German approval for any reshuffle of ministers.[68] The November 1942 Allied invasion of North Africa led to confusion, with Vichy ordering its troops to resist (they quickly surrendered) but refusing to declare war on 'Anglo-Saxon aggression' because Hitler refused to treat France as an ally. The Germans responded by occupying the whole of the country and attempting to seize the French fleet in Toulon but three battleships, seven cruisers, and an aircraft carrier were scuttled. Laval acquired dictatorial powers from Pétain and lucidly declared: 'If the Germans are beaten, General de Gaulle will return. He will be supported and I have no illusions about this, by 80 or 90 per cent of the French people and I shall be hanged. There are two men who can save our country at the present time, and if I weren't Laval, I would like to be General de Gaulle.'[69]

Although, by the end of 1942, Vichy retained the fiction of sovereignty, it had lost control of all metropolitan France, its African Empire and what remained of its armed forces. By 1944, 2.6 million French people were working for the Germans in France and some 1.3 million in Germany, in all 37 per cent of the male population between ages 16 and 60. French industrialists and bankers were developing links with senior partner German firms and envisaged sharing the future European market. 'After November 1942, the confusion of French and German interests was justified in the name of a "European revolution" which, through a transposition of the twofold internal struggle against democracy and communism to the continental level, became first and foremost a struggle against common enemies.'[70] In 1943–4, this attitude was increasingly confined to the pro-fascist Right as the majority adoption of opportunistic accommodation shifted towards passive or active resistance.

From 1944 to 1946 when de Gaulle returned to power in France, his initial attitude was to revert to the post-First World War position of Bainville and seek the dismemberment of Germany. For France to re-establish itself as a world power, Germany had to be kept weak. By the time he resumed power in 1958, his approach was entirely different. This was because meanwhile a democratic Federal German Republic had become an enthusiastic partner in the Fourth Republic's project of European integration and France could aspire to mobilize a revived German strength to assert a world role it could not sustain on its own. As early as his September 1946 visionary Zurich speech, Churchill had pointed the way: 'The first step in the recreation of the European family must be the partnership

[68] Warner, 286–90.   [69] Quoted ibid. 352; cf. 319–57.
[70] Burrin, 412; cf. 462 and Chapters 15–18 passim.

between France and Germany. In this way only can France recover the moral and cultural leadership of Europe.'[71]

While Georges Bidault was Foreign Minister from 1944 to 1948, French policy towards Germany continued to be based upon nationalism, not reconciliation. It should be disarmed militarily, economically, and politically, without a central government, separated from the Rhur and Rhineland (to be placed under international control) and forced to pay reparations. However, the onset of the cold war, with the Berlin Blockade of March 1948 forcing the French to abandon playing off the Soviet Union against the 'Anglo-Saxons', meant that Soviet Russia replaced Germany as the main enemy. The change in policy was exemplified by the replacement in July 1948 of Resister Georges Bidault by fellow Christian Democrat Robert Schuman, who had served briefly in one of Pétain's governments. Nevertheless, 'Stalin did as much as Schuman to reconcile France and Germany.'[72]

However, the person who changed the conceptual context in which France's 'German problem' could be practically approached was Jean Monnet. He persuaded Schuman that the way to end nationalist war between the two countries for ever, at a time when the American government was pressing for German rearmament directed against the Soviet threat, was to pool sovereignty over the industrial sinews of war, coal, and steel, by creating a supranational authority. 'As a bilateral problem, Franco-German relations were insoluble. The Schuman Plan broke out of the impasse not by reaching a deal between France and Germany but by pointing beyond them both to a common goal and larger context, that is, a United Europe.'[73]

THE FRENCH ROAD TO A FRANCO-SAXON EUROPEAN UNION

Of three crises in Franco-German relations during the Fourth Republic, the first—hostility to the 1948 amalgamation of the three zones of occupation as a preliminary to the creation of the Federal German Republic, and the third, namely, the 1950–4 attempt to create a EDC to make German rearmament acceptable—were defeats for France. Only in the second of the crises, the 1950 concern to circumscribe reviving German industrial dominance through the ECSC was French policy partially successful, thanks to what is know as the Schuman Plan although its real architect was Monnet. More significantly, the ECSC provided the model for the EEC and the future progress of European integration. Whereas for Schuman, the ECSC was primarily a short-term solution to a Franco-German problem, for Monnet it was a strategic step towards a supranational European Union.

In the late 1940s cold war context, the American priority to achieving German economic recovery as part of the Marshall Plan for Western Europe, with the

---

[71] Quoted in Robert Gibson, *Best of Enemies*, 299.

[72] Irving, *Christian Democracy in France*, 166; cf. 159–65.

[73] François Duchêne, *Jean Monnet: The First Statesman of Interdependence*, 1994, 374–5; cf. 199 and Jean Monnet, *Mémoires*, 1976, 107, 336.

prospect of a German addition to Western defence, meant that French leaders had to overcome their propensity to dwell upon past wounds and enduring fears. Their wish to cling onto their British ally as a countervailing power came into collision with its reluctance to accept the integration with Germany that was indispensable in the post-war international context. This reluctance could only be compensated by relying upon the USA, unlike Britain an active supporter of European unification. 'The Schuman Plan, though a shift from Britain to Germany, was in fact a transfer of insurance from Britain to America. America was far more of a counterweight to Germany than Britain could be.'[74] Monnet's close 'Anglo-Saxon' affinities, which led de Gaulle to describe him caustically as a 'great American', admirably fitted him to steer France away from indulging nationalistic retrospective resentments towards supranational aspirations.

Monnet's personality did not prepare him to be a conventional political leader, hence his need of Schuman. Monnet was a poor public speaker who relied upon behind-the-scenes manipulation; repelled by party politics, he shunned elected office, preferring to conspire in the public interest as he had done in the General Planning Commissariat, over whose destinies he presided from 1946 to 1952.[75] An outsider, exemplified by his incomparable transatlantic network of elite contracts, he became a perfect insider until de Gaulle's return to power. During the Fourth Republic, Monnet not only knew where decisions were made; he knew intimately the people who made them. As the capacity to decide within and outside France, was dispersed, only someone who could be trusted by a network of influential friends could play the crucial role of unobtrusive coordinator of coordinators in matters of high public policy. His strength was not in originality of ideas but as a persuader of those in a position to act effectively.

Monnet worked closely with the astute German Chancellor, Konrad Adenauer, as well as with Robert Schuman. The latter only became French when aged 32 (his part of Lorraine having been annexed by Germany in 1871) and Schuman served in the German army in the First World War. This led some French nationalists to dismiss him as a *Boche*. Adenauer and Schuman both came from close to the Franco-German frontier and were especially sensitized to the explosive potential of French attempts to annex the coal-rich Saarland. (They tactfully excluded it from the Schuman Plan negotiations and following a 1955 referendum the Saar quietly returned to Germany. Monnet had after the First World War already acknowledged that French annexation was doomed to fail.)[76] Despite the bitter opposition of the Gaullists and Communists, as well as the reservations of the 'Third Force' parties, Monnet and Schuman pushed through a supranational policy which meant that 'France lost its freedom to do as it liked along with everyone else'.[77] Only in this way would West Germany, Italy, and the Benelux take part...and Britain refuse to join. To prevent opposition from the protectionist

---

[74] Duchêne, 204; cf. 189, 383.

[75] Ibid. Chapter 5 on Monnet's role as Planning Commissioner. See also Monnet, *Mémoires*, Chapter 10.

[76] Monnet, *Mémoires*, 106–7; cf. 374–5 and Duchêne, 190–7, 219, 372.   [77] Duchêne, 205.

French steel interests, seeking to preserve their traditional cartel privileges, from blocking reform in alliance with nationalists the key decision was rushed through in 1950. The negotiations were conducted personally by Monnet with Schuman's support, short-circuiting the Foreign Ministry diplomats who could not be relied upon to transcend habitual short-sighted national self-interest. The ECSC Treaty was ratified by the National Assembly in December 1950 against hostile Gaullist and Communist votes. However, Monnet acknowledged that without the pressure exerted by the American government, he would not have been able to pull off his spectacular achievement.[78] In August 1952, the ECSC's High Authority was established in Luxembourg, presided over by Monnet.

Meanwhile, the outbreak of war in divided Korea—having ominous analogies with divided Germany—led to US pressure for the creation of a European army including German forces alongside NATO. Once again Monnet swung into action, persuading Prime Minister René Pleven that the French government should make a proposal on the model of the ECSC and in October 1950 an unenthusiastic Pleven secured the National Assembly's approval. Only German troops were to be fully integrated into the European Army, the other five countries retaining national forces, essential in France's case for its colonial war in Indo-China. Warning of political difficulties ahead came in 1952 when the Pinay government only signed the EDC Treaty 'on the tacit condition that no immediate attempt should be made to ratify it' and his government fell in December 1952 because he was about to do so.[79] Monnet, in proposing the EDC to Pleven, wrote that despite the USA's leadership, she 'will not develop the political vision of which the world stands in need. I think that is our task.'[80] So, the Schuman and Pleven Plans would require an overarching supranational European Political Community to provide a federalist framework. This was blocked by Georges Bidault, who replaced Schuman as Foreign Minister in 1953. He also stalled ratification, the prospect of which (together with the Dien Bien Phu defeat) precipitated the fall of the René Mayer government in 1954.[81]

Having ended the war in Indo-China, Mendès France (Mayer's successor) presented the EDC Treaty for ratification, losing three Gaullist ministers as a result. While adopting a formally neutral stance, he made clear his major reservation: 'the axiom of French policy must be to stick to Great Britain'.[82] It was defeated by 319 votes to 264, the combination of the Gaullist, Communist, and half the Socialist and Radical opponents saluting their victory by singing the *Marseillaise*! Ironically, four years after launching and then rejecting the EDC project, the French National Assembly approved the German Federal Republic's entry into NATO, Britain rewarding recourse to intergovernmentalism as against federalism by giving Western European Union a military guarantee it had refused the EDC.

Not accepting the major setback, the Belgian Foreign Minister Paul-Henri Spaak agreed with Monnet that if the latter (who was completing his term of office

---

[78] Ibid. 218; cf. 199–225, 398–9. See also Monnet, *Mémoires*, Chapters 12 and 13.
[79] Duchêne, 233; cf. 226–35, 253.   [80] Quoted ibid. 228; cf. 234.   [81] Ibid. 253–5.
[82] Ibid. 255; cf. 256 and Grosser, *La IVe République et sa Politique Etrangère*, 312–19, 326.

as ECSC President in February 1955) would prepare a relaunch of the European federalist project, Spaak would play the politico-diplomatic role of Schuman for the ECSC. However, the keenest supporter of a European Common Market, which had vital German support, was the Dutch Foreign Minister Johan Beyen. He persuaded Spaak and Monnet that this was the best way to pursue the supranational European venture and it was duly proposed in April 1955 and approved at the June Messina conference, despite French reluctance.[83] Thereafter, Monnet concentrated on promoting Euratom (a nuclear energy community) and incessant lobbying through the Action Committee for a United States of Europe. He exercised a decisive influence on French approval of the Rome Treaty establishing the Common Market thanks especially to his influence over the Socialist leader and Prime Minister from 1956 to 1957, Guy Mollet, despite the distraction of the Algerian War.[84] However, the Mollet government had fallen by the time the Rome Treaty was ratified in July 1957 and France's financial difficulties made it unlikely that it would be able to implement its provisions. Paradoxically, it was the return of de Gaulle in 1958 that allowed France to honour its signature and rescued the European Economic Community (EEC) from suffering the fate of the European Defence Community (EDC).[85]

De Gaulle was categorically opposed to supranationalism, which he equated with 'the submission of France to a law that was not its own.'[86] He was in favour of the systematic cooperation of European nation states but rejected British membership of the EEC because it refused to abandon its Atlanticist orientation in favour of a Continental 'European Europe'. For him, 'At the heart of the problem and at the centre of the Continent is Germany.'[87] He accepted that Adenauer's Germany was not Hitler's Germany and that close Franco-German intergovernmental bilateral cooperation could become the foundation and the model for the joint political and economic activities of the six EEC states. He had reluctantly to accept that Adenauer was not willing to substitute the protection of France's recently acquired atomic bomb for more substantial American-guaranteed security against the Soviet threat and the prospect that the Atlantic Alliance might eventually secure the reunification of Germany.

Assisted by the fact that de Gaulle's Foreign Minister, Couve de Murville, had been French Ambassador in Bonn, intergovernmental links between officials of both countries were developed. In September 1962, during an official visit to Bonn (then the pre-unified German capital) de Gaulle asked Adenauer

[83] Duchêne, 262–83; cf. Monnet, 469–73.

[84] Duchêne, 287–92; cf. 292–306 on Euratom negotiations and Monnet, 484–9.

[85] Alain Peyrefitte, *Le Mal Français*, 1976, 53–6; cf. Grosser, *La IVe République et sa Politique Extérieure*, 345–9.

[86] De Gaulle, *Mémoires d'Espoir*, 184; cf. 196–9. At a 9 September 1968 press conference de Gaulle declared: 'Although a member of the Common Market, we have never agreed to a so-called "supranational" system for the Six which would submerge France in a stateless entity, and which would have no policy other than that of the overseas (US) protector'. Quoted by Guy de Carmoy in Waites, 368.

[87] De Gaulle, *Mémoires d'Espoir*, 186; cf. 203–5, 233–7 for de Gaulle's assessment of the readiness of Britain to choose a 'European (i.e. non-American) Europe'. For a polemical and partisan account of the 1963 French rejection of British entry into the EEC, see Nora Beloff, *The General Says No*, 1963. For a somewhat more balanced view see John Newhouse, *De Gaulle and the Anglo-Saxons*, 1970.

whether he was ready for political union with France, to which the German Chancellor acceded....but not until others joined them. Adenauer also pressed for a written agreement, to which the French Foreign Ministry quickly responded with a memorandum that set out the contents of what became the January 1963 Elysée Treaty: coordination of foreign policies, defence cooperation, promoting the teaching of each other's language, and developing youth exchanges. The historic reversal of France's alliances is symbolized by de Gaulle's high-handed rejection of British EEC entry (desired by the other five EEC members) at a 14 January press conference and the signature of the Franco-German treaty on 22 January at the price of a preamble, on which the Bonn Parliament insisted, to reiterate Germany's Atlanticist alliance.[88] This German reservation demonstrated that Britain was not the only American Trojan Horse within the European fold.

In the short term, there was little coordination of Franco-German policies, de Gaulle's reassertion of nationalism being precisely what Adenauer sought to free Germans from because of their recent past. De Gaulle pursued French interests ruthlessly, an example of his 'ultimatum strategy'[89] being his 1963 imposition of a Common Agricultural Policy that helped ease financially the modernization of the French peasantry by extending French protectionism to the European Community and dominating the EEC budget into the twenty-first century. By reorienting European integration away from supranationalism towards intergovernmentalism, de Gaulle ensured that the major decisions made in Brussels were usually not taken by the Brussels Commission as Monnet had hoped, on the model of the ECSC High Authority.

The prospect that on 1 January 1966 many EEC matters would be decided by a qualified majority vote, as provided for in the Rome Treaty, led to the boycott of the EEC's activities for six months in 1965, the 'empty chair' tactic having been suggested by Foreign Minister Couve de Murville. Following de Gaulle's re-election as President of the Republic in December 1965 (being forced into a second ballot by anxious farm voters at the prospect of losing generous EEC subsidies) France secured the so-called 'Luxembourg compromise' by which whenever a member state considered that very important national interests were at stake, it could exercise a veto. As a result, until the European Single Act of 1986 twenty years later, *all matters* required a unanimous vote in the Council of Ministers, a victory for the Gaullist conception of European integration.[90]

---

[88] See Jacques Bariéty, 'De Gaulle, Adenauer et la genèse du traité de l'Elysée du 22 janvier 1963' in *De Gaulle en son siècle*, VI, 353–64 and Hans-Peter Schwartz, 'Le president de Gaulle, le chancelier fédéral Adenauer et la genèse du traité de l'Elysée', ibid. 364–73. See also Hans Stercken, 'Une Europe européenne sans préambule!', ibid. especially 377–8 and Hans-Peter Schwartz, 'La politique allemande du general de Gaulle: ruptures ou continuité?', ibid. 407–10.

[89] Alfred Grosser, *French Foreign Policy under de Gaulle*, 84; cf. 65–80 on Franco-German relations. On agricultural policy, see Alain Guyomarch et al., *France in the European Union*, 1998, Chapter 5.

[90] Testimony of Couve de Murville in *De Gaulle en son siècle*, II, 110–11. More generally, see Jack Hayward, 'La Cinquième République et l'intégration communautaire' in François d'Arcy and Luc Rouban (eds), *De la Ve République à l'Europe*, 1996, 27–35.

Just before the June 1965 EEC crisis came to a head, Prime Minister Pompidou sought pragmatically to defuse the confrontation, anticipating his presidential attitude from 1969 to 1974, through piecemeal integration that sought to bypass the Monnet and de Gaulle institutional approaches. 'What can the goal of a European policy be? Federation? Confederation? Let us not quarrel over words. In any case, no one can claim ... that all the conditions have been met for a true federation ... with a single government, a common parliament, one foreign policy, one military policy, and one financial, economic and social policy. At the present stage, there is no possibility other than to encourage a gradual *rapprochement* among the European states which will lead them little by little to harmonize their policies....'[91] Pompidou sought to counterbalance a stronger Germany by favouring the entry of Britain into the EEC on 1 January 1973, assisted by the ardently pro-European Prime Minister Edward Heath. This proved to be a parenthesis, as faced with post-Heath British government's recourse to the brake and not the accelerator, Pompidou's successor Valéry Giscard d'Estaing returned to close Franco-German cooperation based upon a personal relationship with Helmut Schmidt that matched the de Gaulle–Adenauer collaboration and the subsequent Mitterrand–Kohl decisive duo of the 1980s and early 1990s.

Underpinning these summit personal relations between the leaders in France has been an Interministerial Committee for European Economic Cooperation (SGCI) that was established in 1948 by Schuman. The creation of the ECSC and then the EEC gave it increased importance in preparing the French position in routine matters as well as major issues when they arose. The hub of French EU interministerial communication and coordination continues to be located in the SGCI, which is the arena in which day-to-day coordination procedures are organized, meetings held, and information circulated. Precisely because de Gaulle and his successors feared that the national interest would not be properly defended if French ministers and officials colluded piecemeal with their EU counterparts, the SGCI became a watchdog centrally supervizing—in so far as it could—the complex process of intercommunication within the French administration and with Brussels. The maze of Brussels committees struggling to achieve consensus has increased the unpredictability and complexity of the coordination required among the French actors. In addition, joint Franco-German pre-negotiation increased, not only between the heads of government and foreign ministers but between officials in the other ministries.[92] This has been important, particularly because France has been concerned conspicuously to initiate rather than respond to European policies and Germany has not wished to appear too assertive, usually preferring to play a supporting role.

Although President Giscard championed a confederal European Community, reflected in his role in the creation of the six-monthly intergovernmental European Council to curb the power of the European Commission, he also pushed

---

[91] Quoted in Jack Hayward, *The One and Indivisible French Republic*, 243; cf. 244.

[92] See Christian Lequesne, *Paris-Bruxelles: Comment se fait la politique européenne de la France*, 1993 and Douglas Webber, *The Franco-German Relationship in the European Union*, 1999.

for the direct election of the European Parliament in 1976 and the establishment of the European Monetary System (EMS) in 1979, forerunner of Economic and Monetary Union (EMU) achieved under the leadership of Mitterrand and Kohl and of the Euro, achieved under Chirac's presidency. The EMS owed a great deal to the close friendship of Giscard and Chancellor Schmidt, both of whom had previously been Finance Ministers, while EMU was assisted by the President of the EU Commission Jacques Delors' good standing with Chancellor Kohl, allowing him to sustain the momentum behind the Franco-German negotiations. His efforts were structurally sustained by the institutionalized links between the two countries: central banks, finance ministries, and above all Mitterrand—Kohl summits.[93]

As French Finance Minister (1981–4), Jacques Delors had—in alliance with Prime Minister Mauroy—played a crucial part in persuading President Mitterrand in 1983 to give priority to keeping France within the EMS rather than letting the franc float outside it. This was a momentous decision, involving the sacrifice of domestic socialist policies to the prerequisites of continuing the process of European integration. However, it also underlined the fact that, unlike other issues, in the sphere of financial policy, the German Bundesbank carried great weight in pushing for a stringent Stability and Growth Pact. By 2003, it was ironically to prove too difficult for either Germany or France to meet its conditions, so that the sanctions for which it provided were not enforced by the European Commission despite the lamentations of the European Central Bank.

The disappearance of the Soviet Union and the end of the cold war, leaving the USA as the single dominant world power, compelled French policymakers, as a matter of national self-respect, to fall back even more upon the attempt to create a European countervailing power. As confederalist François Mitterrand put it: 'France is our fatherland but Europe is our future'. With Britain continuing to refuse to choose between its American ally and its European partners, France turned increasingly to its former hereditary enemy who had now become its virtual hereditary friend. Particularly in the context of an enlarged European Union, in which its influence was being diluted, the temptation was great to fall back on a Franco-German hard core, as envisaged in 1994 by the German Christian Democrats Karl Lamers and Wolfgang Schäuble, to achieve an ever closer bilateral union.[94]

Whether this is merely a mobilizing utopia, to be used to frighten reluctant EU partners into accepting Franco-German initiatives, or whether it heralds a disintegration of the European project into concentric circles or case-by-case cooperation, remains unclear after the French rejected by 55 per cent in a referendum

---

[93] Kenneth Dyson and Kevin Featherstone, *The Road to Maastricht: Negotiating Economic and Monetary Union*, 1999 and David Howarth, *The French Road to European Monetary Union*, 2000. On federalist Jacques Delors, see Charles Grant, *Delors: Inside the House that Jacques Built*, 1994 and Georges Ross, *Jacques Delors and European Integration*, 1995. See also Epilogue.

[94] Karl Lamers and Wolfgang Schäuble, 'Réflexions sur une politique européenne', *Revue des affaires européenes*, in I, 1995, 12–14. For a comprehensive and detailed review, see Alistair Cole, *Franco-German Relations*, 2001.

the minimalist draft EU Constitution prepared by a Convention presided over by Giscard d'Estaing. What is clear is that France's political leaders remain resolutely committed to their conception of a 'European Europe' predicated on French preferences that cannot hope to prevail without German support. However, the weakening of Franco-German influence in a European Union of twenty-five members has led to disenchantment with an organization France can no longer steer, and seems to be taking not a social market but a free-trading liberal, British direction. As a result, there is a feeling both among the elite and general public, despite adopting a distinctive attitude over the Iraq War and resisting acquiescence in American hegemony, that France is no longer able to sustain the status as a world power after which it nostalgically hankers. De Gaulle's assertion that 'Europe is the means for France to become again what she has not been since Waterloo: the first in the world'[95] has proved to be an illusion in pursuit of an anachronism. The 2005 French referendum rejection of the European constitutional treaty marked the French electorate's decision to opt out of a leaderless integration process that France no longer controlled.

[95] Quoted in Alain Peyrefitte, *C'était de Gaulle*, I, 1994, 159. For succinct studies of how Franco-German reconciliation was subsumed into European integration, see Julius W. Friend, *The Linchpin: French-German Relations, 1950–1990*, 1991 and its successor by the same author, *Unequal Partners: French-German Relations, 1989–2000*, 2001. For another good general review, see Alistair Cole, *Franco-German Relations*, 2001.

11

Diluting French Political Culture with European Social Liberalism

In the Introduction we found ample confirmation of René Rémond's assessment that 'By projecting their own various likes and dislikes onto the American political scene, (the French) formed a distorted impression of the reality, once coloured by the concerns of French politics. Everyone had an America of their own making',[1] compulsively and narcissistically compared with a rival universalist model with which it was incompatible. As earlier chapters have demonstrated, liberalism encountered deep-seated hostility across the political spectrum in France. Even among those who had been attracted by the arguments of a Constant or a Tocqueville, 'By the middle of the nineteenth century this intellectually important, though ultimately impotent school of liberalism had given way to a distinctive French doctrine called 'republicanism ... the least precise and most widely invoked concept in the French political lexicon. ... '[2] Committed to state action rather than civil society or individual initiative, to law rather than contract, centralization not decentralization, to social cohesion not uninhibited competition and to a state-created common culture, the 'Republic' carried with it the ancient virtue of association with the citizens of an idealized Roman Republic committed to the public good rather than despised Carthaginian commercialism. A predominant illiberalism, liberal pluralism suffering guilt from its Anglo-American associations, held the field from most of the mid-nineteenth to the mid-twentieth centuries in France.

Despite being obsessively invoked as the lowest common denominator of an increasingly individualist society, increasingly 'the Republic' was a resonantly hollow shell, emptied of the collectivist content and capacity for national mobilization that had symbolized a different founding myth from that of the pluralist-federalist American Republic. Especially from the 1970s, the divergent but mutually supporting illiberal faces on the Communist Left and the Catholic Right were showing advanced symptoms of exhaustion, leaving an opportunity—in the more stable institutional and prosperous economy of the Fifth Republic—for a bourgeois liberal revival to occupy the vacant space. Rivals as setting the shape of things to come, the ideological cold war between Marxism and Liberalism turned decisively in the latter's favour thanks to the discrediting of repeated claims of

---

[1] Rémond, *Les Etats-Unis devant l'opinion française*, II, 698.
[2] Mark Lilla, 'The Legitimacy of the Liberal Age', Introduction in Lilla (ed.), *New French Thought: Political Philosophy*, 1994, 8; cf. 9.

capitalism's imminent and inevitable demise and the association of Marxism with the conspicuous failures of Communist regimes to live up to their pretensions. Nevertheless, because it was so foreign to their political culture, 'Few French thinkers consider themselves to be liberals in an unqualified sense, and fewer still in an American or British sense'.[3] Ironically, it did not help those bold enough to fly the liberal flag, that during the 1980s French liberal revival, American liberalism and British liberal socialism were retreating before neo-conservatism.

A FALSE DAWN: RELAUNCHING THE LIBERAL CRITIQUE OF FRENCH POLITICAL CULTURE

The French revival of interest in Tocqueville provides a touchstone in locating the liberal intellectual counter-attack upon the continuities of a political culture that seemed incapable of resolving its crises by making the changes required by modernization and a commitment to liberty as the pivotal means and purpose of public policy. Tocqueville's writings had continuously been of interest in America and Britain in the late nineteenth and early twentieth centuries, so it had to be repatriated from there. Pride of place goes to Raymond Aron, whose belated interest in Tocqueville after 1950 was in part associated with his preoccupation with the need to contain communism and its Marxist-Leninist proponents, Aron having himself been particularly interested in Marxist thought from the 1930s. The fact that Aron ceased to be an intellectual outsider in the 1980s and that periodicals like his own *Commentaire* and *Le Débat* founded by Pierre Nora and Marcel Gauchet set the new intellectual fashion, exemplified the liberal comeback, while even the Left Catholic *Esprit* became a friendly critic, not an unfriendly one, like its founder Mounier.

In the 1960s, Aron's political sociology was reinforced by direct encounter with the American social science of Stanley Hoffmann, who moved from Sciences Po in Paris to Harvard University, and by Michel Crozier who from the late 1940s spent extended periods in America. Both of them drew heavily on Tocqueville in their critique of France as a stalemate society by implicit or explicit comparison with the USA. The anthropologist Louis Dumont took up Tocqueville's ideal type contrast between traditional hierarchical societies and modern egalitarian societies in his conceptually influential *Homo Hierarchicus* of 1966, *Homo Aequalis* of 1977 and *Essays on Individualism* of 1986. From the 1970s, historians François Furet and then Pierre Rosanvallon reconsidered post-revolutionary history from the Tocqueville standpoint of correcting its illiberal features while preserving its democratic impetus. They drew their inspiration more from his *Old Regime* rather than *Democracy in America*, which was especially prized by Crozier. In the 1980s, Laurent Cohen-Tanugi, an international business lawyer, drew on his two-year experience at the Harvard Law School, Wall Street, and Washington, to sing the

---

[3] Mark Lilla, 1994, 15; cf. 16.

praises of a flexible self-regulating civil society compared with rigid, hegemonic state regulated France. His book *Le droit sans l'état* was described in Hoffmann's preface as 'the most Tocquevillian of books on the USA since Tocqueville'.[4]

The American-oriented, liberal revival also had economic and political manifestations. Jean Monnet, who played a pivotal part in promoting French post-war economic modernization as well as European integration as a way of exerting external pressure to perpetuate and extend the American propensity to persistent change, had close links with Britain and the USA from the First World War and was attacked for his 'Atlanticism' not least by de Gaulle. Through the mid-1960s Fourth Plan's emphasis on the use of economic planning to achieve 'a less partial idea of man', Jacques Delors imparted a Social Catholic emphasis to the regulation of the market economy which he later furthered as President of the European Community Commission. Between these two ventures, Delors devised the New Society social programme of the Chaban-Delmas 1969–72 government, marking a forlorn attempt to give the policies of the Gaullist Right a liberal socialist orientation.

A more specifically social democratic emphasis upon the role of civil society rather than state action was developed by Michel Rocard, who became socialist Prime Minister from 1988 to 1991, with limited success. The most penetrating critique attempting to combine eclectically the early manifestations of the liberal upsurge was made by an intimate of de Gaulle, whom he served as minister before doing so with his successors Pompidou and Giscard. It achieved its impact through a 1976 best-seller, *Le Mal Français*, in which Alain Peyrefitte drew upon his political and ministerial experience as an informed insider to deliver a devastating critique of the French system of government. We shall return to most of these exponents of the need to adopt liberal reforms, commencing with Raymond Aron.

Aron described himself as a 'latter-day descendant' of the liberal tradition personified by Montesquieu in the eighteenth century and Tocqueville in the nineteenth century.[5] Unlike those who concentrated on industrialization, class struggle, or capitalism, Tocqueville's focus on democracy was more relevant to the late twentieth century. In *Democracy in America*, Tocqueville had sought to 'answer the question: why is American society liberal?' and in the *Old Regime*: 'why does France, in the course of her revolution towards democracy, have so much trouble maintaining a political regime of liberty?'[6] Owing to a decisive

---

[4] Hoffmann, Preface to Laurent Cohen-Tanugi, *Le droit sans l'état: Sur la démocratie en France et en Amérique*, 1985, vii. More generally on the post-Marxist resurgence of liberalism, see Eric Fassin, 'Good Cop, Bad Cop: Modèle et contre-modèle américains dans le discours libéral français depuis les années 1980' in *Raisons Politiques*, February 2001, special issue on 'Le moment tocquevillien'.

[5] Raymond Aron, *Main Currents in Sociological Thought*, I, 1965, 259. He added the Anglophile historian Elie Halévy as a twentieth protagonist of the French liberal tradition. Halévy has been described as the neglected 'missing link between Alexis de Tocqueville and Aron' in an interesting biography from a liberal perspective, see Nicholas Baverez, *Raymond Aron: Un moraliste au temps des idéologies*, 1993, 99; cf. 101, 156.

[6] Aron, *Main Currents*, 185; cf. 183, 192.

failure to synthesize aristocracy and democracy that Britain had achieved, the post-revolutionary French were less fortunate; 'in the absence of political liberty, they did not succeed in acquiring that sense of solidarity indispensable to the health of the body politic'.[7] Tocqueville had shown how 'American society can provide not a model but a lesson to European societies by showing them how liberty is safeguarded in democratic society'.[8] Aron was the first person to receive the Tocqueville prize, from Alain Peyrefitte (other recipients including Louis Dumont in 1987 and François Furet in 1990) and from 1979 until his death in 1983 he headed the editorial team publishing a new edition of Tocqueville's works, being succeeded by Furet. Appropriately, Aron and Tocqueville moved centre stage simultaneously, although neither of them would have been pleased with the debased economistic liberalism that came to the fore, imitating more of America's acquisitive vices than its dynamic civil society virtues.[9]

Stanley Hoffmann described Aron as 'a coolly fervent Liberal' who was his model, 'mentor and friend'.[10] Especially indebted to him for his views on international politics, after 1956 Hoffmann combined Aron's historical sociological approach, acquired from him in the early 1950s, with a Tocquevillian melding of the interaction between French political culture and centralized institutions culminating in an authoritarian style of government.[11] Because, like Aron and Crozier, Hoffmann examined French democracy with a demi-American detachment, it was natural that he should present his 'Paradoxes of the French Political Community' to a seminar series at Harvard, followed by a Sciences Po colloquium in the years 1959–61, in which they took part. Reacting against Herbert Luethy's indiscriminately hypercritical *The State of France* (1955), which contrasted France's convulsive surface political instability and economic backwardness with the steady continuity and accretion of absolute state power, Hoffmann developed two influential concepts: 'stalemate society' and 'Republican synthesis'. Although he disagreed with his friend Michel Crozier 'about whether the "stalemate society" was, as I thought, a thing of the past, or, as he believed, still the bane of France', he admired and shared his analysis of France's style of authority as first formulated in an issue of *Esprit* to which he also contributed.[12] In fact, Hoffmann's scrupulous analysis was more inconclusive, asserting that 'The old integrating forces of politics have been *dis*integrated and the new integrating factors in society have not broken through.'[13]

Crozier's 1957 article on 'France land of command' anticipated his 1963 *Bureaucratic Phenomenon* discussion of crisis leading to change within a culturally determined routine style of authority acquired in childhood, shared by superiors and their subordinates. Responding like Hoffmann to Luethy's onslaught on French immobilism, Crozier attributed self-perpetuating deadlock to those having

---

[7] Aron, 1965, 210; cf. 217.   [8] Ibid. 193.   [9] Mélonio, 279–85, 389.

[10] Stanley Hoffmann, 'A Retrospective on World Politics' in Linda B. Miller and Michael Joseph Smith (eds), *Ideas and Ideals: Essays on Politics in Honor of Stanley Hoffmann*, 1993, 8–9; cf. 66–7.

[11] Hoffmann, 'To Be or not to Be French', ibid. 33–4; cf. 186.   [12] Ibid. 37.

[13] 'Paradoxes of the French Political Community' in Hoffmann et al. (eds), *France: Change and Tradition*, 1963.

decision-making power not knowing and those who know having no power. 'Fear of face-to-face relations' led to a crisis that had to be dealt politically because 'We cannot conceive of a conflict, a discussion, any direct relationship, without it being mediated by politics'.[14] In his article entitled 'Politics first!' in the same issue of *Esprit*, Hoffmann anticipated his stalemate argument by discussing the 'vicious circles' that afflicted both French politics and society because despite the 'absurd' claims on the French Right to be in favour of anti-statist liberalism, it was not practised. What prevailed, as Tocqueville had summed up the Old Regime with the formula 'rigid rules, but flexibility, not to say laxity, in their application', persisted in closed shop 'group immobilism in a society where protectionism was general and institutionalized', leading to a 'disposition towards partial impotence'.[15]

Both Hoffmann and Crozier were preoccupied with how to avoid national decline by modernizing French illiberal political culture and practices. Hoffmann argued in 1967 that while accepting Crozier's model of routine authority, the Third and Fourth Republics had been a caricature of it because passive political leaders, out of the imperative of self-preservation, had allowed events to impose unwelcome decisions upon them. It was necessary to complete it with a model of crisis authority, which Hoffmann formulated as 'heroic leadership' of which de Gaulle was the contemporary personification, a leader able to break out of the vicious circle of immobilism, while Pétain had sought to prop up the stalemate society.[16] Although the heroic leader apparently overcame the challenge of May 1968, there was a 'return to a more routine-like authority' symbolized by de Gaulle's referendum defeat in 1969 and his resignation.[17]

Crozier had in 1964 sensed the coming attempt at cultural revolution with intellectuals as the main agents of change but in *The Stalled Society* of 1970, whose title was explicitly inspired by Hoffmann, he criticized reliance on crisis to bring about change as dysfunctional when the need for change was accelerating. He did not share Hoffmann's willingness to accept a heroic leader's imposition of change without choice but gloomily acknowledged the prevailing 'absolutist conception of authority without which it is impossible for a Frenchman to imagine the successful undertaking of even the most trivial collective action ... the French are terrified of situations where they are likely to be dependent, but at the same time

[14] Crozier, 'La France terre de commandement' in *Esprit*, XXI, December 1957, 789; cf. 782–90. More generally, especially for the American influences on Crozier's analysis, see the very perceptive article by Pierre Grémion, 'Michel Crozier's Long March: the Making of *The Bureaucratic Phenomenon in Political Studies*', XL/I, March 1992, 5–20. For Crozier's retrospective reflections, see his 'Comment je me suis découvert sociologue' in *Revue Française de Science Politique*, XLVI, February 1996, 80–95.

[15] Hoffmann, 'Politique d'abord!' in *Esprit*, 1957, 816; cf. 815–17. The Tocqueville quotation is from *The Old Regime*, 67.

[16] Hoffmann, 'The Rulers: Heroic Leadership in Modern France', a revised version of a 1967 publication, included in Hoffmann, *Decline or Renewal? France since the 1930s*, 1974, 68–86, 99–100. This book is dedicated to Michel Crozier and Jean-Marie Domenach. The final chapter 'The State: For What Society?' is a fascinating commentary on the problems that preoccupied both Hoffmann and Crozier, with allusions to their agreements and disagreements.

[17] Ibid. 103–7. More generally see ibid. Chapter 6 on 'Confrontation in May 1968'.

they are incapable of conceiving of a collectivity that has no strong authority. As a result, they cannot support (more precisely, put up with) the very authority they consider to be indispensable'.[18] In desperation he concluded that 'The only way to avoid explosions is to have the courage to provoke controlled crises'.[19]

Hoffmann refused to treat the problem so melodramatically. He agreed that in France 'the state is often faced with forces that can cooperate neither with it nor with one another. Yet we have to remember that if this picture were the whole truth, the changes in French society could be explained only by assuming the state is neither so indispensable nor so much a cause of paralysis as Crozier's analysis suggests'.[20] State ambitions had played an important part in bringing about change after 1945, but 'while the state has incited French society to change, French society has only rarely forced the state to change, and pressures for change internal to the state have been almost non-existent'.[21] So for Hoffmann politics should be given priority over the organizational constraints which Crozier emphasized and had led him to become increasingly modest in his reform aspirations.

By 1987, when he published *Etat modeste, Etat moderne*, Crozier acknowledged that the old stalemate state was obsolete and that the 'modernizing state' had been compelled to accept the requirements of a competitive industrial society. However, an impersonal rule-bound French bureaucracy was 'completely disconcerted by the new changes it must make, which goes against all its instincts, questions its structural logic, its reasoning processes and even its legitimacy'.[22] Increased government activity was not sustained by increased efficacy. Crozier was concerned to 'transform the megalomaniac "state" not by attacking the indispensable administrative elites but by making them through cultural change agents of social change'.[23] Despite his pleas for pluralism, his 1984 book *The Trouble with America* had indicated that although he still felt that he had two homelands, France and an idealized America of 'unlimited social progress', he felt that the rationalist dream had dwindled into 'empty rhetoric' in a country that had 'lost its bearings'.[24] 'The United States of today is no longer the America Tocqueville described. Its voluntary associations have ceased to be the mainstay of a democratic constitution on the move but are now simply a means of self-defence for various interests' was

---

[18] Michel Crozier, *The Stalled Society*, 1970, 1973, 94–5; cf. 80, 90–2. Chapter 7 is devoted to 'The Meaning of the May 1968 Crisis'.

[19] Ibid. 168; cf. 176.

[20] Hoffmann, *Decline or Renewal*, 471–2. In his Preface Hoffmann says of Crozier's theory that it is 'so powerful it sometimes seems to explain everything', viii.

[21] Ibid. 454; cf. Stanley Hoffmann, 'La société française en question' in Francis Pavé (ed.), *L'Analyse Stratégique. Sa genèse, ses applications et ses problèmes actuels: Autour de Michel Crozier*, 1994, 30–8.

[22] Michel Crozier, *Etat modeste, Etat moderne: Stratégie pour un autre changement*, 1987, 96; cf. 44–6, 57–8, 91–7.

[23] Ibid. 212; cf. 216–19, 237–8. However, by 1995, in *La Crise de l'intelligence: Essai sur l'impuissance des élites à se réformer*, 186, Crozier favoured abolishing ENA, a view shared by some of its leading products such as former Prime Ministers Laurent Fabius and Alain Juppé, for whom ENA was a scapegoat for the French state's failings.

[24] Michel Crozier, *The Trouble with America*, 1984, xvii–xviii.

his disenchanted verdict, concluding 'Nobody would dare use the American case today as the laboratory for the future'.[25]

With François Furet we return to the liberal perspective on the past in his *Interpreting the French Revolution*, which reoriented the previously Marxist-dominated view, linked with the presupposition that the successful Bolshevik Revolution was the legitimate successor of the Jacobin glorious failure at ruthlessly enforcing the 'general will'. As an ex-Marxist and Communist, Furet had shared that cult, with which he became disenchanted as Aron had with Germanic philosophy of history. They both reacted against the totalitarian phenomenon, proudly asserted in 1925 by Mussolini but condemned by liberal democrats as common to both fascism and communism, just as Tocqueville had reacted against the authoritarian Second Empire. A revolutionary messianic dogma, discredited by association with communism, that had exercised such a hold on the French imagination, with Lenin's successors exercising proletarian dictatorship modelled on the bourgeois dictatorship which Robespierre had briefly wielded, was ripe for demolition.

Significantly, the essay 'De Tocqueville and the problem of the French Revolution' first appeared in a 1971 collection in honour of Raymond Aron, whose 1955 *Opium of the Intellectuals*, together with the Soviet repression of the 1956 Hungarian uprising, played a crucial part in Furet's abandonment of communism and his focus on revolutionary ideology and its exhaustion. While Tocqueville had not proffered a general theory of political change, his sociocultural explanation of how the liberal demand for individual rights, rejecting the 1688 'English strategy' for protecting them, had in France led through political absolutism to servitude. In his reconceptualization of French post-revolutionary history with Jacobinism reinterpreted in the light of Bolshevism, Furet influentially liberalized its legacy as a non-unanimous foundation for the French Republic. This became the core of Furet's new orthodoxy that achieved its widespread consecration during the 1989 bicentenary celebrations.[26] Coinciding with the collapse of the Communist central-eastern European regimes, a cavalcade of French Tocquevillians went east to teach lessons in liberalizing democratic transition.

While the USA was both liberal and democratic, Britain was more liberal than democratic and France more democratic than liberal as well as being more revolutionary, so it seemed superficially to have affinities with the Soviet Union. In particular, Furet's *Le passé d'une illusion* linked the French sympathy with Soviet Russia and anti-Americanism with the hatred of the bourgeoisie which had united so many from the Catholic, traditionalist Right to revolutionary Communism on the Left and was compounded by bourgeois guilty self-hatred for having substituted an avaricious, sordid market society for public spirited citizenship. The USA was doubly damned through its identification with capitalism and bourgeois society. Furet perceptively contrasts capitalism's 'homeland par

---

[25] Ibid. 85, 145.

[26] François Furet, *La Gauche et la Révolution au milieu du XIXe siècle: Edgar Quinet et la Question du Jacobinisme, 1865–1870*, 1986, 13, 17. See his 'The French Revolution is over', Part I of *Interpreting the French Revolution*, 1978, 1981 and more generally Mélonio, 290–3, 297 and Sunil Khilnani, *Arguing Revolution: The Intellectual Left in Postwar France*, 1993, Chapter 6.

excellence, the USA, which does not have a bourgeoisie but a bourgeois people, which is totally different', with the French Revolution's creation of 'a bourgeoisie without a capitalist spirit'.[27] Even when France had rapidly become, thanks to affluence and economic modernization, a comprehensively bourgeois society, devotion to self-interest and moneymaking, an unashamed source of pride in America, was normatively repudiated even when practised with hypocritical zeal by the French. So, at least 'in principle', the French bourgeoisie appeared to be its own worst enemy, overt self-scapegoating masking uninhibited egotism in practice.

While the French communists, who had 'transferred revolutionary legitimacy from Paris to Moscow', ignored both Soviet reality and the social changes that were rendering revolution unattainable in France, backward-looking 'gaullists and communists were at the end of the road, each being in its own way the victim of modernisation'.[28] Gaullism's institutional legacy was the Fifth Republic but at the price of effacing the anachronistic attempt to perpetuate French exceptionalism.[29] Assisted by the disintegration of French communism, President Mitterrand's achievement in the 1980s was 'to have buried the socialist idea at the very time that he led the socialists to office'. As for the champion of civil society, 'Michel Rocard, the socialist closest to the centre, the least socialist', he would not be able to 'fill the empty space left by the decomposition of communism and gaullism'.[30] Furet concluded that 'the image of Revolution had perennially provided the means of cementing their political unity around their conflicts' in France but now 'Its citizens argue about the distribution of the national wealth, not over the legacies of national history'.[31]

Pierre Rosanvallon shared Furet's anti-Jacobin view of French state–society relations. They launched with others the Saint-Simon Foundation in 1982, an influential think tank reflecting upon how France's problems could be dealt with by broadly social liberal solutions. They went on in 1988 to publish (with the journalist Jacques Julliard) a book significantly subtitled '*The End of the French Exception*', commissioned by the Foundation and they worked together in the Raymond Aron Centre of Political Research to promote his liberal approach, Rosanvallon succeeding Furet at his death in 1997 as the Director of the Centre.[32] In the 1970s he was a leading economic expert for the de-confessionalized CFDT trade union (after having been a leader of the Young Christian Student movement)

---

[27] François Furet, *Le passé d'une illusion: Essai sur l'idée communiste au XXe siècle*, 1995, 23–4; cf. 27–36, 391–5, 443 and Furet 'La France Unie' in François Furet, Jacques Julliard and Pierre Rosanvallon (eds), *La République de Centre*, 1988, 32, 61. For most of the 1980s and early 1990s, Furet was a Visiting Professor at Chicago University.

[28] Furet, 'La France Unie', 21, 30.

[29] Ibid. 19–21, 52. See also Christian Saint-Etienne, *L'Exception Française*, 1992, 26–9 and the excessive *L' Etat mensonger*, 1996.

[30] Furet, 'La France Unie' 42' 49–50.   [31] Ibid. 53, 55.

[32] For a succinct intellectual autobiography up to Rosanvallon's decision to wind up the Saint-Simon Foundation in 1999, see 'Entretien avec Pierre Rosanvallon' in *Raisons Politiques*, February 2001, 49–62.

defending its commitment to workers control, also advocated by Rocard's leftist PSU.

He switched to historian of ideas and institutions in the 1980s when he became convinced of the exhaustion of the social democratic capacity to deal with the challenge to the Welfare State of neo-liberalism, Rosanvallon publishing critical analyses of the revived liberal 'negation of the social'. Nevertheless, he rejected reliance upon the state as the sole way of achieving 'collective solidarity' and substituted for the quarrel over nationalization versus privatization the need to 'redefine the frontiers and the relations between state and society'.[33] As he put it in 1988, despite the revival of interest in civil society (to which we return in discussing the roles of Delors and Rocard) the political dilemma was that 'the separation of the political system and civil society is a condition of individual liberty but this productive separation permanently threatens to become negative distance. That is why their opposition is continuously both advocated and denounced.'[34] Having rejected purely market solutions or reliance on the state (explicitly following Proudhon in 'asserting the irreducibility of the social to the political'), Rosanvallon focused upon 'the increasing interpenetration between the state and civil society in a world of networks and organisations', whether public or private.[35]

Drawing upon contrasts with British liberalism, for which his 1985 *Le Moment Guizot* prepared the way, and American pluralism that Tocqueville had described, Rosanvallon argued that whereas in Britain the seventeenth-century individualist revolution had led to self-government in the state and a self-reliant civil society, in France the Revolution illiberally democratized a state absolutism that subordinated a decorporatized civil society, allowing no intermediaries between citizens and government. 'French society ceaselessly oscillated between the idealism of social fusion in the nation and the apocalyptic vision of a divided society in which any conflict is suspected of leading to civil war.'[36] As he put it in 1994, the tension between British consensual monarchical liberalism and French dissensual republican democracy meant that while 'there is *both* a Jacobin and a British spirit in French institutions', the former regrettably predominated over the latter, reflecting 'the illiberalism of French political culture'.[37] Consequently, France adopted 'a radical anti-pluralism, prompt to identify all particularities with abominated privileges and all local identities as dangerously divisive', leading to the systematic neglect of civil society.[38]

---

[33] Pierre Rosanvallon, *La crise de l'Etat-providence*, 1981, 1983 Revised edn, 111; cf. Chapter 3. See also his *L'Age de l'Autogestion*, 1976.

[34] Pierre Rosanvallon, 'Malaise dans la représentation' in Furet et al., *La République de Centre*, 159; cf. 135–6.

[35] Ibid. 181; cf. 175.   [36] Ibid. 168; cf. 162–7.

[37] Pierre Rosanvallon, *La Monarchie Impossible: Les Chartes de 1814 et de 1830*, 1994, 7, 180; cf. 174–9 and Pierre Rosanvallon, *L'Etat en France de 1789 à nos jours*, 1990, 96–9.

[38] Pierre Rosanvallon, *Le Peuple Introuvable: Histoire de la représentation démocratique en France*, 1998, 39.

By 2004, when he published *Le Modèle Politique Français. La société civile contre le jacobinisme de 1789 à nos jours*, Rosanvallon was nevertheless arguing that 'French singularity is more accentuated in the way the country sees itself than how it works in practice'.[39] Despite his desire to assert that there has been a neglected surreptitious pluralization of French society, he has to admit that rather than the bottom-up self-managed associations advocated by the 'Second Left' in the 1960s and 1970s, it is the administratively financed and controlled top-down 'appendages of the state' that have since flourished; while regarding both the New Society Delors changes of 1969–72 and of the Rocard government in 1989–91, 'the reforms actually adopted have been well short of the intentions proclaimed and the proposals made'.[40] The gap left by the partial retreat of the would-be sovereign state has not been sufficiently filled by an expansion of civil society associations, while international market economy inroads have been only partially contained by the advance of European integration.

While historian Rosanvallon compared France's state model with Britain, lawyer Cohen-Tanugi followed Crozier in turning to the USA for the model of a countervailing self-regulating civil society and in regarding France as rigidly bureaucratized. Because liberalism is foreign to the French political system, he bluntly posed the question: 'is France ready for what would be for her a cultural revolution, the coming of liberal democracy, historically rejected both by revolution and by reaction'.[41] While detecting a slow evolution in the 1980s of French society towards autonomous self-regulation, Cohen-Tanugi regarded it as relatively passive. It was faced by an 'omnipresent albeit not omnipotent state and a marginalized juridical system' by contrast with a dynamic, innovative, and competitive USA, although like Crozier, he accepted that American reverential legalism had gone too far.[42] Cohen-Tanugi frequently refers to Tocqueville's *Democracy in America* chapter on 'The legal spirit in the US', arguing that his analysis of enduring Franco-American contrasts remains relevant because, along with federalism and local self-government, judicial review secures the reconciliation of liberalism and democracy. Whereas American judicial power derived from the reaction against royal absolutism, French subordination of the judiciary had been a response to obstructive intervention by the *parlements*. State pre-eminence over law in France has meant that there is a cavalier disregard towards respect for the rule of law.

Whereas in the USA, society is the engine of change, in France, while multiplying regulations, the state administration deals with implementation problems by 'closing its eyes to illegalities that it has itself helped create' and the jurists of the Council of State too often give priority to the requirements of discretionary administrative action over citizen rights.[43] Tocqueville had recognized

---

[39] Pierre Rosanvallon, *Le Modèle Politique Français: La société civile contre le jacobinisme de 1789 à nos jours*, 2004, 12. For a review of this book, see Jack Hayward, 'Testing the Limits of French Statism' in *European Journal of Political Theory*, IV/3, 2005, 301–7.

[40] Rosanvallon, *Le Modèle Politique Français*, 425; cf. 420–1.

[41] Cohen-Tanugi, 194; cf. 5–8, 15, 193–5, 205–6.   [42] Ibid. 8; cf. 23, 196.

[43] Ibid. 54; cf. 25–7, 41–9, 68, 87, 101–6.

that American reliance upon enlightened self-interest had allowed all to share in pursuing the mythical general interest but in France this was an exorbitant state monopoly. The American legal system offered better protection of rights than had its French counterpart, including competitive regulation of the market economy, underpinned by a pluralism that did not restrict society by trying to ensure that everything should start and end with the state.[44] Although the French Constitutional Council and the overriding European Court of Justice have introduced an important element of judicial review, French governments and public opinion have only in part accepted this liberal constraint on democracy.

ANTI-STATIST REFORMIST SOCIALISM

If the liberals had been voicing their criticisms in the political wilderness, what of the reformist socialists who directly influenced government policy and actually held ministerial office? They were less inclined to make explicit comparisons with the USA but by drawing on some of the liberal critiques, the transatlantic references were implicit. Revulsion against the Jacobin *dirigiste* state and in favour of a reinvigorated civil society was prominent in minorities on the Social Catholic and trade union Left, championed by Jacques Delors and by the political New Left and its leading protagonist Michel Rocard, who were friends and rivals from 1958 when Rocard left the unreformed Socialist Party. They were both marked for life by their immense admiration for Pierre Mendès France, from whom they acquired a disposition not to place partisan loyalty above commitment to the purposes it purported to serve.

Delors' starting point was Mounier's *Esprit* and its Social Catholic moralistic critique of a decadent bourgeois society opposed to modernization and defence of the 'established disorder'. More specifically, it involved a threefold rejection of (*a*) an authoritarian political culture based on what Crozier had called in his 1957 *Esprit* article the denial of face-to-face relations between government and social groups; (*b*) an excessive individualism especially manifested in consumer society excesses; and (*c*) 'the inability of a capitalist society fundamentally to change human relations and give everyone equality of opportunity'.[45] His values were those of the Catholic Young Workers Movement, which he carried with him into working with the CFTC trade union, after rapidly abandoning the Christian Democratic MRP in 1946 because it was not being faithful in political practice to its principles, acquiring in the process a lifelong allergy to political parties.

Seeking to combine reflection and action, in 1952 Delors joined the *Vie Nouvelle* Catholic education movement and by 1959 he had helped steer it leftwards, and had established a monthly *Cahiers Citoyen 60*. It was associated with a network

---

[44] Ibid. 116–32.

[45] Jacques Delors, *Changer*, 1975, 35; cf. 8, 32–4, 53–4, 106, 111, 140, 286 and Jacques Delors, *Mémoires*, 2004, 15, 35–7, 41–3, 69, 78.

of clubs that by 1965, when Delors was required to give this work up because of his official position in the Planning Commission, had acquired about 5,000 members. He sought to render his official and unofficial activities compatible by writing under the pseudonym of Roger Jacques but his identity was not concealed by this transparent subterfuge. (Inspector of Finance Michel Rocard chose the pseudonym Michel Servet.) Unlike the more technocratic and statist Jean Moulin Club, *Citoyen 60* drew its socialist inspiration from the anti-elitist and anti-statist, bottom-up approach of Proudhon, although it was willing cautiously to collaborate with those seeking a more participatory, civil society-oriented democracy.[46]

Having begun his professional career in the Bank of France in 1944, Delors was drawn from 1953 into giving economic advice to the left-wing minority that was converting the CFTC by 1964 into the CFDT, working especially with its Research and Economic Action Bureau which he headed from 1957 and writing for the journal *Reconstruction*. From 1959–1961, he was nominated by the union to the Economic and Social Council, which enabled him to extend his range to a more 'democratic' concerted economic planning. It led to his appointment to the Planning Commissariat by Commissioner Pierre Massé who was struck by his report on the Fourth Plan's priorities which stressed the need to develop public services and non-market consumption, reinforced by his masterminding of the 1961 CFTC so-called Bonety Report advocating a national incomes policy.

Delors was becoming a reformist social engineer, not only called upon—thanks to his trade union and official planning links—to resolve major industrial disputes but to propose negotiating structures that would overcome the difficulties of achieving face-to-face relations in situations of conflict. Appointed social adviser to the Planning Commissioner by Massé in 1962 to undertake this extension of Monnet's ambitions to modernizing and consensualizing socio-industrial relations, Delors recalled in his Memoirs that his 1960s 'years at the Plan were the best time of my professional life'.[47] The socio-economic opening up and modernization of French society from 1985 to 1994 was to be pursued by Delors as President of the European Commission, national economic planning having meanwhile fallen into disrepute. However, in 1964, Delors was one of the planners in a forward look to 1985 that posed the need to 'confront America' by changing French attitudes to avoid economic decadence by promoting European integration. In 1968 he was part of an elite group with Crozier seeking to end France's 'stalemate', Delors' handiwork being evident in the chapter on labour relations that foreshadowed his role during the 1969–72 government.[48]

---

[46] Delors, *Changer*, 66–7; cf. 38–40, 61–3, 72–3, 76–8, 330; Delors, *Mémoires*, 39, 66.

[47] Delors, *Mémoires*, 47; cf. 45–56, 60–1, 66, 71–2, 86, Delors, *Changer*, 81–95; Hervé Hamon and Patrick Rotman, *La Deuxième Gauche: Histoire intellectuelle et politique de la CFDT*, 1982, 135–8, 345. On the decline of planning's credibility from the Sixth Plan (1971–5), see Jack Hayward, *The State and the Market Economy: Industrial Patriotism and Economic Intervention in France*, 1986, 174–7, 222.

[48] Claude Alphandéry et al., *Pour Nationaliser l'Etat*, 1968, 110–11; cf. 126–8. See also Commissariat Général du Plan, *Réflexions pour 1985*, 1964, 12–13.

His major part in Prime Minister Chaban-Delmas's 1969–72 reformist government was prompted by the May 1968 crisis, in which he took no part. In its wake,
some social changes might be possible as a result of the cultural shake up that
it symbolized, despite the large reactionary right-wing parliamentary majority
elected to restore stability. Following de Gaulle's 1969 resignation, the Left did
badly, the Defferre-Mendès France tandem securing the derisory vote of 5 per cent
at the ensuing presidential election, while further left, Rocard had to be content
with 3.5 per cent. The conservative-minded President Pompidou having chosen
as Prime Minister a dynamic Gaullist modernizer with a Resistance record for
two, whose public image of sympathy for social justice might forestall further
industrial strikes, Delors felt that with Chaban-Delmas, who had the courage to
take political risks, and had led a Gaullist faction into the Mendès France 1954–5
government, he could join his New Society venture provided certain preconditions
were accepted.

This took the form of a letter on 18 June 1969 to the Prime Minister setting
out his conception of the social policy to be carried out. In addition to specific
proposals, it emphasized the need for a Crozierian change in the style of social and
occupational relations. First, decentralization and regionalization of the state was
a prerequisite of facilitating economic and social initiative and change. Second,
a consensual 'Modernization Code' should be negotiated to promote a 'network
of contractual relations'. Third, at the level of the firm, an authoritarian management would need to overcome 'the refusal of face-to-face relations' with trade
unions by collective bargaining to facilitate changes such as the gradual reduction
in working hours and to diminish strikes. Fourth, to promote social solidarity,
social transfer payments should be redistributed away from agriculture and a
chaotic health system towards helping the poor, the old, and the handicapped.[49]
Acceptance of his policy conditions led to Chaban-Delmas being attacked bitterly for carrying out a left-wing programme with a right-wing parliamentary
majority.

Together with the more liberal modernizer, Simon Nora, who had been on
Prime Minister Mendès France's staff, and whom Delors replaced as head of
Chaban-Delmas's staff in 1971, Delors drafted Chaban-Delmas's September 1969
New Society policy declaration that was based on a Hoffmann-Crozier analysis
of what the latter called in his 1970 book the stalemated society. (The label
'New Society' was Chaban's own, inspired during a visit to the USA by President Johnson's 'New Frontier' slogan.) In contrast with the 1981–4 Mauroy
government in which he was Finance Minister, committed to changing to an
entirely different society, Delors, like the Chaban-Delmas government, was more
realistically devoted to improving existing society, although even this proved too
much for Pompidou. The President was irritated by the hyperactive and popular
Prime Minister undermining his pre-eminence, by his liberalization of broadcasting (a government spokesman *inter alia* replacing the interventionist Minister

---

[49] For the full text of Delors's letter to Chaban-Delmas, see his *Changer*, 333–9. See also Jean Bunel
and Paul Meunier, *Chaban-Delmas...*, 1972, 19–26.

of Information), modest 1972 Regionalization Law and most fundamentally by
the ambitious Delors-driven social reformism that he feared would destabilize
traditional hierarchy and be a distraction from promoting wealth-creating big
business. Ironically, the Delors strategy of social change also met with reticence
from the trade unions—even his own CFDT that was moving leftwards—so that
he had to compromise with business to promote his industrial training programme in the 1971 Law, introduce an incomes policy first in public enterprise
and institutionalize collective bargaining, what was dubbed by *L'Express* 'social
delorism'.[50]

The heroic attempt at releasing the brakes on France's stalled society was
doomed to failure above all because it was trying to reform without enough
reformers. The receding May 1968 crisis encouraged the belief that the unwelcome
changes proposed could be diluted or rejected. Chaban-Delmas clearly did not
have the wholehearted support of either his own ministers or of his parliamentary
majority. He was undermined by the President's staff and the extra-parliamentary
party who claimed that they spoke for the 'silent majority' of public opinion.
The failure to do more than tinker with regional reform in 1972 prompted a
Crozieran warning that it would not be possible 'much longer to evade the
uneluctable choice between increased centralisation, which can only guarantee the
rationality of decision at the price of increased administrative authoritarianism
and local irresponsibility whose social cost is incalculable, and a decentralisation
that involves important risks of irrationality in the present feeble state, in terms
of men and skills, of local representative structures but which, in the long run,
seems to be a precondition of an effective local contribution to economic development and regional planning'.[51] Chaban's attempt to retrieve the situation by
putting a vote of confidence to the National Assembly, carried overwhelmingly on
23 May 1972, was met by President Pompidou curtly demanding his resignation
on 5 July.

Having turned down an offer from Mitterrand to find him a seat in parliament in 1965, Delors decided to accept his invitation to join the Socialist Party
in 1974, as had many from the New Left, led by Rocard, and from the CFDT.

---

[50] Bunel and Meunier, 73–89, 99–117; cf. 42, 48–9 and Charles Grant, *Delors: Inside the House that
Jacques Built*, 1994, 30–5. Simon Nora represented the elitist 'new Saint-Simonians' who put their trust
in promoting industrial society and were well represented in the Jean Moulin Club (discussed later)
by contrast with the Delors *Citoyen 60* club (ibid. 39, 43). Nora, in line with his 1967 report on public
enterprises, was able to begin the process of divesting 'the government of the burden of financing the
deficits of public enterprises which sheltered from the market test of efficiency behind their public
service vocation.' (Jack Hayward, *The One and Indivisible French Republic*, 225; cf. 224.)

[51] Pierre Grémion and Jean-Pierre Worms, 'La concertation régionale, innovation ou tradition' in
Aménagement du Territoire et Développment Régional, 1968, 60. See also Bunel and Meunier, 172–
7, 180–3, 208–15 and Serge Berstein and Jean-Pierre Rioux, *The Pompidou Years, 1969–1974*, 1995,
2000 Eng. edn. 22, 33–5, 39, 48–50, 68–9. On the Pompidou minimilization of Chaban's intended
regional reform, see Hayward, *The State and the Market Economy*, 156–7. For Pompidou's scathing
views on the New Society programme, see Alain Peyrefitte, *Le Mal Français* 1976, 94–100. See also
Delors, *Changer*, 97–113, Delors, *Mémoires*, 74–85, 101–3 and the dismissive comments on the New
Society Government by Stanley Hoffmann, *Decline or Renewal?*, 183–4.

He remained a fish out of water and was lucky to be elected to the European Parliament in 1979 owing to his lowly place on the party list, but was chosen as chairman of its economic and monetary committee. Nevertheless, conscious of how few socialists had any experience of government, Mitterrand not only actively involved the reassuring Delors in his presidential campaign but surprised him by preferring to appoint him Finance Minister rather than to the less prominent post of Secretary-General of the Presidency or Planning Commissioner he personally desired. He did so partly because 'The more Mitterrand used Delors, the less he had need of Rocard. Alone of the socialists, Delors could put Rocard in the shade, where Mitterrand wanted him'.[52] Mitterrand's political skill fascinated Delors, replacing Mendès France as his political role model. 'He taught me everything in politics'.[53] However, Delors as Finance Minister and Rocard as Planning Minister opposed 100 per cent nationalization of major industries and (not as many) banks, reflecting their anti-statism, but they were overruled by Mitterrand and the majority of the Mauroy government,[54] despite Delors threatening resignation.

Delors (supported by Rocard) failed to persuade President Mitterrand either to devalue or float the franc or to pursue an austerity economic policy—despite provocatively calling in November 1981 for a 'pause' in costly reforms that symbolically and calculatedly recalled Léon Blum's retreat from the Popular Front's unsustainable ambitions.[55] However, the decisive battle in 1982–3, which he won with the support of Prime Minister Mauroy while Mitterrand wavered, was whether France should accept the liberal economic implications of remaining within the EMS or continue to pursue a socialist policy, floating the currency to meet the run on the franc. Mitterrand's choice of the European, liberal alternative was the moment of truth at which the socialists abandoned their programme, although future Prime Minister (in 1997–2002) Lionel Jospin at the time sought to disguise it as a 'parenthesis'. Mitterrand tried to persuade Delors to become Prime Minister in March 1983 but would not accept his condition that he also take over control of monetary policy from the Finance Ministry, considering that this would make Delors too powerful.[56] Nevertheless, Mitterrand was able in 1994 to secure the post of President of the European Commission for Delors, which was to extend the logic of the 1983 policy choice. Because the 1983 economic crisis had shown that France could not cope with its difficulties without recourse to the European Community, it should seek to steer its activity through a man committed to pressing it forward and with the skill to do so.

---

[52] Quoted in Grant, 45; cf. Delors, *Mémoires*, 126–7.

[53] Quoted in Grant, 55; cf. 41–4; cf. Delors, *Mémoires*, 138–9.

[54] Pierre Favier and Michel Martin-Roland, *La Décennie Mitterrand*, I, 123–6; cf. Jacques Attali, *Verbatim*, I, 1993, 75–7, 115, 120.

[55] Ibid. 409–10 and Delors, *Mémoires*, 148–9.

[56] Favier and Martin-Roland, I, 428–30, 438–9, 443, 450–3, 467–83, 488–9, 498–50. See also Grant, 50–60; Delors, *Mémoires*, 159, 168 and the succinct account in Jack Hayward and Vincent Wright, *Governing from the Centre: Core Executive Coordination in France*, 2002, 67–8; cf. 78–9.

Having succeeded in making the liberal market economy reluctantly acceptable to the Socialists, from 1985 Delors' aim was not only to complete the European Common Market but to make it an integrated social market economy. 'The free market calls for solidarity. So I tried to translate my favourite formula: competition that stimulates, cooperation that reinforces, solidarity that unites' in his preferred achievement of the single internal European market by 1992 as a stepping stone to federalist economic and political unification.[57] Delors had to fight hard to include a 'social chapter' in the 1992 Maastricht Treaty, which extended European Community regulation to cover consultation of workers and equal opportunities in the labour market, recalling his 'New Society' efforts twenty years before. Against British government opposition (and opt out) Delors—faithful to Mounier—passionately argued that in contrast to the USA, European, Christian, and social democratic values necessitated counterbalancing individualist competitiveness with social solidarity.[58] His daughter, Martine Aubry, as Employment and Solidarity Minister from 1997 to 2000 in the Jospin government, pushed through the reduction in the work week from 39 to 35 hours but in a more *dirigiste* manner than her father would have done.

Delors sought to pacify those who opposed what they called the menace of a European super state by appealing to the Social Catholic principle of subsidiarity, which Pope Pius XI had in a 1931 encyclical invoked to defend individuals and families against totalitarian states. Delors had frequently mentioned it in speeches before but in 1992 he secured its inclusion in the Maastricht Treaty, confining European Community activities to those that member states could not adequately undertake. Nevertheless, because it could be used to argue diametrically opposed cases on what should be done at which level and because 'Subsidiarity was too arcane an idea and too ugly a word to capture the public imagination', it failed to stem the increasing tide of intergovernmentalism and Euroscepticism.[59] The European Commission could no longer play the Monnet role of elite integration by stealth. By the end of 1993 Delors melancholically recognized: 'I became the symbol of an idea of Europe which is in the process of vanishing'.[60] In 1994, when he was coming to the end of his presidency of the Commission, he refused to stand as Socialist candidate in the 1995 French presidential election despite his popularity and likelihood of winning because he felt that he was too centrist for his party; he would not be able to rely on its support to carry out the reforms he believed to be indispensable. In France, there was not the Left-Centre unity between the latterday legatees of Social Democracy and Christian Democracy that had enabled him to succeed partially and for a while in the European Community.[61]

Michel Rocard, Delors' rival for leadership of the 'Second Left', would not have allowed such scruples to stand in the way of his presidential ambitions but his

---

[57] Delors, *Mémoires*, 223; cf. 228 and Grant, 66–70. For two excellent general reviews of his role as European Commission President, see Helen Drake, *Jacques Delors: Perspectives on a European Leader*, 2000 and the insider view of George Ross, *Jacques Delors and European Integration*, 1995.

[58] Grant, 86–7, 238, 261, 269.   [59] Ibid. 221; cf. 203, 213–14, 217–20, 269.

[60] Ibid. 269; cf. 232–4.

[61] Delors, *Mémoires*, 20–6, Grant, 252–5, 258–9; and Favier and Martin-Roland, IV, 1999, 596–9.

party no longer wanted him as its candidate. Despite the convergence of their views, they were culturally, ideologically and by career background poles apart, even though they were both socialists with long-standing membership of the CFDT trade union with its civil society not statist focus. A secular Protestant not a non-clerical Catholic, intellectually indebted to Marx not Mounier, who did not come up the hard way like Delors but was an ENA trained Finance Inspector, Rocard only came to reformism via being a revolutionary. Whereas Delors never overcame his viceral suspicion of politics as amoral and fatally susceptible to a 'Jacobin' statism, Rocard wholeheartedly accepted that collective action meant exercising government power as the principal means of achieving autonomous civil society ends. Out of economic realism they both accepted accommodating the prerequisites to achieve social purposes, not merely adopting American anti-trust action to promote competition. They were de facto liberal socialists who dared not speak their name because of the guilt by association that even a regulated socio-liberalism connoted in France, especially on the Left. A lack of ideological legitimacy meant that neither Delors or Rocard could convert their popularity outside the Socialist Party and pioneering role in the New or Second Left into political leadership of the mainstream non-Communist Left. In 1995 and 2002, it was Lionel Jospin who stood on a semi-social democratic platform in the presidential elections, having in 1997–2002 carried out in part, as Prime Minister, a reformist Rocardian programme without Rocard.

While Rocard's strategic trajectory was from the enfeebled social democratic SFIO to a liberalized socialism via an anti-statist leftism, he was always in a non conformist minority, consistent with his French Protestant culture. To that Protestant upbringing is attributed a self-righteous and stiff-necked personality inclined to a virtuous, vehement preaching, symbolically reflected in the choice of a heterdox Protestant martyr, Michel Servet, for his pseudonym and practically by unease with congenitally dirty party politics by contrast with disinterested civil society. Although he refused to follow him in the uncompromising unrealism with which he rejected the Fifth Republic, Rocard was drawn to Mendès France as a conviction statesman characterized by his moralistic economic rigour in contrast both with Mollet and Mitterrand. His prominent role in the miniscule Socialist student movement led to collaboration with the more numerous Catholic students, opposition to the Algerian War helping to win them over to the Left so that 'the first generation of Rocardians would be Catholic'.[62] Like Delors, he helped bridge the religious divide, although they both encountered lifelong suspicions from the obsessively anticlerical Left.

Having followed the classic *cursus honoram* of Sciences Po and ENA, Rocard chose the Inspectorate of Finance on the advice of Simon Nora (Delors' future partner in the Chaban-Delmas New Society team) but before taking up his post, he did his military service in Algeria, provoking controversy by a 1959 report on the inhumane displacement of the local population that could have cost him his official career. He joined the so-called Unified Socialist Party or PSU created in

---

[62] Jean-Louis Andréani, *Le Mystère Rocard*, 1993, 57; cf. 11–60.

1960 but in the early 1960s he combined this with his duties in the 'holy of holies' of the Finance Ministry, the Treasury Division (in what was to become its Forecasting Section) and with membership of the *Club Jean Moulin*. Named after the Resistance hero, it drew upon Mendèsists, Left Catholics, Left Socialists, and ex-wartime Resisters, mainly from senior public sector administrators and educators, acting not in defence of the discredited Fourth Republic but of a republican utopia to be created. Their aim was not merely to modernize the Left (as indicated in one of its collective publications—in this case jointly with Delors' *Citoyen 60*—in 1965 called *Un parti pour la gauche*) but to change French politics, bypassing the traditional parties and relying on support from social movements.

Michel Crozier wrote the December 1963 Manifesto of a group of associations, including the Lyon *Cercle Tocqueville* and *Citoyen 60*, after joint meetings organized by the *Club Jean Moulin*, calling for decentralization and democratic planning extended to a federalist European state.[63] Rocard served his intellectual apprenticeship in the club (alongside his technocratic training in the Treasury) on which Crozier exercised an important influence, abandoning his earlier Marxism for Crozierian piecemeal reformist change that Rocard openly espoused from the mid-1970s and the Socialist Party shamefacedly adopted from the mid-1980s. (Crozier's Centre for the Sociology of Organizations shared accommodation with the *Club Jean Moulin*.) While the club was the crucible in which such elements were fused, Rocard abandoned it in 1966 because after its campaign (in association with Servan-Schreiber's *Horizon 80* organization) to impose Defferre's presidential candidature on the SFIO, had come the decision to join Mitterrand's Left Federation, which Mollet dismissed as attempting to create an 'American-style Democratic Party'. This context prompted Rocard to look instead to the PSU as the unlikely instrument for achieving an innovative neo-reformism against Mitterrand's backward-looking 'Union of the Left' strategy.[64]

Although he because national secretary of the PSU in 1967, Rocard could not be said to have controlled a mini-party, locked in interminable ideological disputes between modernists, Maoists and Trotskyists, 'ungovernable... often on the brink of paralysis, even of disintegration' if this did not imply a measure of integration.[65] Leading opponent of a merger with Mitterrand's Left Federation, Rocard became the spokesman of the PSU at its 1967 Congress for a CFDT-inspired programme of workers control in firms and a Counter-Plan in opposition to the official Fifth Plan as a national medium-term economic policy.[66] Rocard's breakthrough had come a year earlier at a Grenoble colloquium, when his advocacy of a Girondinist decentralization incorporating a bottom-up approach

---

[63] For the text of the Manifesto that appeared in *Le Monde*, 17 December 1963, see Georges Suffert, *De Defferre à Mitterrand*, 1996, Appendix 1, 150–4; cf. 19–37, 50–4.

[64] Andréani, 75–100 and Clare Andrieu, 'Le Club Jean Moulin...1958–70' in C. Andrieu et al., *Associations et Champ Politique: La loi de 1901 à l'épreuve du siècle*, 2001, 560–75. More generally, on difficult party-association relations in France, see Andrieu, 'La concurrence des légitimés partisane et associative', ibid. 25–45. On the content of Club Jean Moulin's publications, see Bernard Rettenbach, 'La conception de la démocratie selon le club Jean Moulin' in Edmond Lipiansky and Bernard Rettenbach (eds) *Ordre et Démocratie*, 1967, 113–74.

[65] Andréani, 80; cf. 85.   [66] Hamon and Rotman, 171; cf. 13, 166–9, 176–7.

to social change, was subsequently published with the striking title *Décoloniser la Province*, a Jean Moulin-style collective effort which he wrote up and popularized. Although the brochure invoked what he was not yet calling civil society and was couched, despite its provocative rhetoric, in the regionalizing terms of technocratic economic changes rather than cultural regionalism, the explicitly anti-Jacobin formulation made clear his commitment to an alternative decentralist, bottom-up political culture in conjunction with the CFDT.[67] However, in 1982 it was Minister of the Interior Gaston Defferre, who had begun the decolonization of French Africa, long-standing Mayor of Marseille, in conjunction with Prime Minister Pierre Mauroy, long-standing Mayor of Lille, who carried through a decisive decentralist shift of power in provincial France but the main beneficiaries were the local and regional political leaders not the civil society associations.

May 1968, an apparent civil society explosion that subverted state *dirigisme*, led by students (one of whose leaders was Jacques Sauvageot of the PSU) and workers, prompted Rocard's PSU to improvize tactically to exploit a seeming revolutionary situation. As Crozier had presciently pointed out in his 1964 *Bureaucratic Phenomenon*: 'To obtain a limited reform in France, one is always obliged to attack the whole "system", which is thus constantly called into question.... Reform can be brought about only be sweeping revolution. Reformers, in any case, cannot succeed without counting on the pressure generated by revolutionary or quasi-revolutionary movements'.[68] This helps explain the political schizophrenia of Rocard, a tactical would-be revolutionary but non-violent anarcho-Marxist, while strategically still being a prudent reformist. In a minority, Rocard struggled to cope with the verbal leftist extremism of a PSU, 42 per cent of whose members had joined it in 1968–9. He won 3.5 per cent vote, in the 1969 presidential election, at which all left-wing candidates were eliminated on the first ballot. He missed the rejuvenation of the Socialist Party in 1969 and then 1971, not grasping the significance for its future of Mitterrand's taking control, while the PSU remained suicidally locked in dogmatic ideological disputes, declining in disunity. The PSU rejected the 1972 Common Programme between the Socialists and Communists, hoping to outflank them on the Left by calling for workers control.

'Rocard's itinerary is that of a generation which thought in 1968 that everything was possible, rebounded from it and ended up in the Socialist party'.[69] At the 1973 general election Rocard lost the Assembly seat he had won in a 1969 by-election against de Gaulle's last Prime Minister Couve de Murville. He resigned as head of the PSU, returned to the Finance Ministry and, realizing that his overambitious PSU strategy had failed, prepared to rejoin the Socialist Party. His opportunity

---

[67] Andréani, 443–8, 471, 519–20. *Décoloniser la province* was published anonymously in 1967 on behalf of the Comité d'initiative of the Rencontre socialiste de Grenoble. See also Yves Mény, *Centralisation et décentralisation dans le débat politique français [1945–1969]*, 1974, 475–502.

[68] Crozier, *The Bureaucratic Phenomenon*, 287; cf. 196.

[69] Andréani, 279; cf. 107–42, 525–7. On Rocard's PSU period, see Jean-François Bizot, *Au Parti des Socialistes*, 1975, Chapter 6, Appendix 2 on 'socialisme autogestionnaire', 470–80.

came at the 1974 presidential election. Rocard joined in Mitterrand's campaign and, after the *Assises du Socialisme* in October, promoted by CFDT leader Edmond Maire, Rosanvallon and others, led a third of the PSU into the Socialist Party despite his continuing reservations about the statist Common Programme. As we saw earlier, Delors also joined the Socialist Party in 1974. Delors had briefly belonged to the PSU (more a cause group than a party aspiring to governmental power) but his unequivocal and consistent reformism meant that their personal relations were 'always characterized by an ambiguous complicity-rivalry. Until 1981, complicity predominated' but thereafter with Delors as powerful Finance Minister and allied with Mitterrand while Rocard was consigned to the weak Planning Ministry, rivalry between the former working class, Catholic trade unionist, and the bourgeois, Protestant politician for leadership of the 'Second Left' poisoned their dealings.[70]

They were both 'outsiders' but unlike Delors Rocard was explicitly a challenger to Mitterrand as leader of the Socialist Party that the latter had rebuilt. Rocard aroused party activist animosity through by-passing the party, appealing directly to civil society associations and the voters generally through the mass media and acquiring an enduring popularity as measured regularly by opinion polls. At the 1977 Party Congress, Rocard explicitly distinguished the Left's two cultures: Jacobin and doctrinaire Marxist versus his Second or New Left based on contract, decentralization and workers control. However, Rocard's uneasy combination of elitist, summit social democracy and mass participatory democracy—locally and in factories—had dwindled from a utopia of comprehensive change into piecemeal improvements that capitalism could accommodate. For his pains he was attacked as 'Rocard d'Estaing' (evoking affinity with Giscard d'Estaing) a right-wing deviationist assimilated to the 'American Left... whose function has been to hasten the Americanisation of French society and avoid any revolutionary outcome of the crisis of advanced capitalism'.[71] The latter diatribe was due to Jean-Pierre Chevènement, sometime ally of Mitterrand, who had caustically described the former's faction as trying to create 'a fake Communist Party with real petty bourgeois'.

Seeking to replace rather than succeed Mitterrand, Rocard counter-attacked on the night of the Socialist defeat at the 1978 general election, blaming Mitterrand's style, the 'archaic' invocation of a rupture with capitalism and declaring one should 'speak more truthfully, closer to the facts'.[72] However, he was outmanoeuvred by the man he dubbed a 'loser' who went on to win power in 1981. Denying accusations that he wanted to convert the Socialist Party into an American Democratic Party, Rocard failed to win control of the Party at the 1979 Metz Congress, which led him to abandon his effort to replace the Mitterrandist Jacobins in favour of a less isolated synthesis between the two cultures. Thereafter,

---

[70] Andréani, 566; cf. 144–57, 681–2, Grant, 21–2, 25, Delors, *Mémoires*, 42, 118–19, and Hamon and Rotman, 270–8

[71] Andréani, 161; cf. 160, 465–6.

[72] Ibid. 353; cf. 349–92, 533–6. On Mitterrand's view of Rocard see Jacques Attali, *Verbatim II 1986–88*, 512, 521, 532 and *Verbatim III 1988–91*, 10, 65, 492, 599, 664.

he was a prisoner of the wily Mitterrand. Whereas Rocard admitted in his 1979 Metz motion and speech that the 'rupture with capitalism' would take 150 years, because 'The economy cannot be changed by decree', Mitterrand blithely promised that it could be achieved in 100 days, using Delors—who was closer to Rocard—as a reassuring, plausible counterweight.[73]

Admitting that he had 'dreamed too much', Rocard nevertheless remained an unrepentant Keynesian and replaced public ownership with public control over the means of production and finance. He reluctantly recognized that the 'third sector' of social movement voluntary associations would remain marginal, even though as Planning Minister in 1981–3 he established an Interministerial Delegation for the Social Economy. This was even more true when as Prime Minister he represented the government in dealing with social movements trying to cope with superior market forces and needing more state support than his piecemeal reformism could offer. His failure to achieve solidarity through social dialogue and contractualization in a Delors-style reconciliation between state, market and civil society, meant that by the time of his 1982–3 Interim Plan and even more of the Mitterrand policy U-turn of 1983, 'the Rocardian economic model is increasingly synonymous with "social liberalism"' of a Keynesian kind.[74] While this temperate social capitalism attracted some elite support, the Socialists increasingly lost their working class support, especially as Rocard's Finance Minister (imposed by Mitterrand) adopted a monetarist 'strong franc' policy. As early as 1981, Edmond Maire and the CFDT had chosen 'resyndicalization' as against working closely with the Socialist government, just as it had refused to collaborate with the Chaban-Delmas Government despite Delors' role in its industrial relations policies. Even their civil society friends remained suspicious of Socialist governments—for good reason. Under the smokescreen of Crozierian-type slogans of 'better state' not 'less state', Rocard was increasingly resigned to getting into step with a globalized market capitalism rather than changing it.

By 1981, Rocard was speaking of 'remaking France into a nation of entrepreneurs' and in addressing 'the challenges of the 1980s' a year later he denied that France faced a short-term crisis from which it could revert to its indulgent practices. This was unrealistic because 'We are not in the throes of a crisis but rather in a gigantic process of change.... We are moving towards a new state of world affairs where the rate of economic growth will be low or non-existent, where the quantitative aspects of social protection will stagnate, where international competition will be keener and keener, and where instability and even insecurity will become more general'.[75] Although his innovative state-region and public enterprise planning contracts survived the National Plan's retreat, by the

---

[73] Andréani, 533; cf. Grant, 41–5, 59, 81–2. Crozier published a book in 1979 entitled *On ne change pas la société par décret*. Having influenced Rocard from 1960s Club Jean Moulin days, Crozier described himself in 1990 as a 'radical Rocardian' and in 1991 claimed that, like the Chaban-Delmas government, the Rocard government would be remembered for its reformist impetus (ibid. 262).

[74] Andréani, 546; cf. 473, 476, 497–9, 538–44, 553, 561.

[75] Commissariat du Plan, 8 September 1982, mimeo, 2–3. See Jack Hayward, 'Changing direction and Socialist Crisis Mismanagement', Chapter 10 in *The State and the Market Economy*.

time he became Prime Minister, while officially he maintained that 'Just because France accepts the constrained choice of an open economy it does not mean that this (Tenth) Plan is liberal', he was often heard privately saying that because of uncertainty 'Pluriannual planning is the final expression of poetry'.[76] Nevertheless, before he left office in 1991, Rocard carried through the General Social Contribution tax to prevent the bankruptcy of the Social Security system and (revenge for 1981) facilitate partial privatization of public enterprises. A promoter of modernizing social liberalization, Rocard was 'a hope, a promise, without ever managing to achieve either of them'.[77]

By the end of the 1980s, the collapse of Soviet centralized state planning along with the Soviet Union meant that the US-dominated world market economy had become the unavoidable context of French public action. Having earlier helped to promote acceptance of competitive markets as a counterweight to state power, Rocard was now forced to champion public services as an indirect help to the competitiveness of firms. As his speechwriter euphemistically put it in September 1990: 'Historical evolution has led us from an administrative conception of social justice to a sort of tempered capitalism. This naturally poses more doctrinal problems to the socialist tradition than to the liberal tradition'.[78] Coupled with the assertion of the democratic primacy of public opinion, these references to liberal capitalism provoked an outcry form the Jacobin Left, reasserting the primacy of the party activists. Rocard's brand of liberal socialism, which seemed economically unable to attain its social ambitions, has since remained anathema not merely to most of those inside the Socialist Party but has shared in the wider rejection of liberalism on the Right as well as on most of the trade union as well as the political Left. This was spectacularly demonstrated in the debate leading to the French rejection of the European constitutional treaty in May 2005.

If Rocard achieved less than he had promised before he held office, Alain Peyrefitte contradicted his actions as minister even before leaving office. He had been a vehemently illiberal Minister of Information in the Pompidou government from 1962, systematically interfering in radio and TV broadcasts, which only ended when Chaban-Delmas rejected 'the voice of France' (Pompidou dixit) standpoint and secured a measure of autonomy for them. Peyrefitte lost office seeking to impose competitive selection of students, as Minister of Education during the May 1968 events, but became secretary-general for the post-Gaullist UDR party in 1972

---

[76] Attali, *Verbatim III*, 194; cf. 193–5 and Andréani, 571; cf. 564, 570.

[77] Jean-Marie Colombani, *De la France en général et de ses dirigeants en particulier*, 1996, 184; cf. 181–91. By the end of the 1990s, the yield from the CSG increased from 1.1 to 7.5 per cent of earnings 'permitting corresponding reductions in the more regressive payroll taxes'. Jonah D. Levy, 'France. Directing Adjustment' in Fritz Scharpf and Vivien Schmidt (eds) *Welfare and Work in the Open Economy*, II, 2000, 315.

[78] Quoted Andréani, 560; cf. 184–5, 265, 494, 608–11. The speechwriter was Guy Carcassonne, whose negotiating skills played a crucial part in the survival and achievements of the Rocard government. On budgetary matters in 1988–91, see John Huber, *Rationalizing Parliament: Legislative Institutions and Party Politics in France*, 1996, 149–75.

before holding several ministerial posts in the 1970s, ending as a repressive Justice Minister, accused by Rocard of seeking to 'domesticate justice'.

However, in 1976 he published *Le Mal Français* (which sold over a million copies), a vigorous liberal critique of French political and administrative practice as pilloried by Michel Crozier and Stanley Hoffmann. The legacies of the Counter-Reformation and the Revolution had meant that France was 'neither truly despotic, nor truly liberal', reluctant to accept decentralizing and competition-promoting reforms, a country in which 'Every Frenchman is a potential rioter'.[79] In 1976, Peyrefitte also used research by Crozier and others in support of decentralization proposals but resistance to change once again demonstrated that even his literary talents and political contacts could not succeed.[80] Although it was under the Socialists, with Defferre's 1982 reforms that significant decentralist change came, Peyrefitte's legacy on the Right was reflected in the 2003 constitutional amendment formally incorporating decentralization of the Republic and the extension of the powers of *départements* and regions in the 2004 Law, pushed through by Prime Minister Jean-Pierre Raffarin against the Jacobin-like son of Michel Debré, Speaker of the National Assembly Jean-Louis Debré.

WHY 1980s ASSOCIATIONAL LIBERALISM PETERED OUT

France did not experience the two historic Anglo-American civil society victories over the state: the English Civil War followed by the 1688 Revolution and the American War of Independence. Instead, it suffered the anti-liberal backwash of the Counter-Reformation and of Marxist Communism, although the latter was never in political control in France and has left few after-effects.[81] We have seen how the liberal endeavours since the pre-revolutionary years and during successive regimes have failed fundamentally to modify the stifling state domination of society because the pluralist, Anglo-American anti-model has proved instinctively repugnant. It remains to consider why the most recent reaction against state *dirigisme* since the 1980s has once again been defused. Over and above the specific circumstances, choices and compromises that were made, there has been a deep-seated rejection of the reciprocal relationship between state and society. A strong state is more readily achieved not be systematically subordinating a weak territorial and functional civil society but by empowering and sustaining the local institutions and voluntary associations Tocqueville had

---

[79] Alain Peyrefitte, *Le Mal Français*, 1976, 431, 376. On the bold Chaban-Delmas liberal reform of the Peyrefitte-style control of radio and TV that partly precipitated his downfall, see Bunel and Meunier, 184–95. On the failure of regional reform, ibid. 172–7, 180–3 and Peyrefitte, *Le Mal Français*, 451–3, 456. See also the obituary by Thomas Ferenczi, 'Alain Peyrefitte, un intellectual en politique', *Le Monde*, 30 November 1999, 16.

[80] Alain Peyrefitte et al., *Décentraliser les Responsabilités: Pourquoi? Comment?*, 1976.

[81] Ernest Gellner, *Conditions of Liberty: Civil Society and Its Rivals*, 1994, 193–5.

investigated and described in Britain and America. The French have in practice been unwilling to accept this, distrusting liberalism out of a fear of freedom as a source of insecurity for the weak and an instrument of market domination by the strong.

The most searching analysis of why, in late twentieth-century France, the attempts to reduce state intervention have misfired because civil society is unable to fill the space liberated has been provided by Jonah Levy's appropriately entitled *Tocqueville's Revenge*. Because, since his day, the capitalist market economy had become an even more powerful countervailing force to the state's interventionist proclivities, it has been necessary that they be made 'consonant with market, social, and territorial realities'. However, 'French authorities have found that taking the state out of the economy does not suffice to put other actors in and may even jeopardise the state's withdrawal over time'.[82] Because habits contracted over the centuries have fostered a state-society stalemate, 'Although national leadership has actually encouraged societal and local actors to assume key responsibilities handled previously by Paris, these non-state actors have proved incapable of rising to the occasion'.[83] This is not always true as the Employers Association MEDEF, led by Ernest-Antoine Seillière, has had some success in pursuing a pro-business agenda until his resignation in 2005.

So, it was not because the French have ignored alternatives to pervasive and rigid state control. Whether it was the cultural subversion symbolized by May 1968 or the economic subversion of globalization, the view that the old order was no longer viable became prevalent. Neither the monetarist macro economic orientation taken by the Socialists after 1983 nor the nominal neo-liberalism of Chirac and Balladur which did not go far beyond clientelist privatization, involved a conversion to Anglo-American market liberalism. Nor did the Delors-Rocard-CFDT 'belief that French society harboured tremendous potential for self-organization and collective action' prove feasible either in the workplace or in society generally.[84] 'Associational liberalism offered the ideal formula for a France that wanted to break with its discredited *dirigiste* past, but that feared and rejected an Anglo-Saxon future'.[85] Still, it amounted more to popular rhetoric than reality. Decentralization was recentralized by activist direct administrative intervention under cover of 'a variety of duplicitous practices, including the transfer of underfunded programmes and extortionate pseudocontractualisation procedures.'[86] 'The result is a proliferation of phantom programmes, which are often little more than glossy brochures and one-person offices'.[87]

Similarly, despite the attempt to empower France's feeble trade unions by the Socialists, they were obliged—like the Delors-inspired Chaban-Delmas government—to resort to top-down state intervention. Where in 1969–72 this

---

[82] Jonah D. Levy, *Tocqueville's Revenge: State, Society and Economy in Contemporary France*, 1999, 3, 284; cf. 286–90.

[83] Ibid. 11–12; cf. 235.   [84] Ibid. 75; cf. 57–76.   [85] Ibid. 86; cf. 8.

[86] Ibid. 231; cf. 230–2.

[87] Jonah D. Levy, 'Territorial politics after decentralisation' in Alain Guyomarch et al. (eds), *Developments in French Politics 2*, 2001, 100; cf. 94–9.

was done by increasing the statutory minimum wage and by formal national agreements, 'in fact largely drafted and imposed by the government' covering 'training, maternity leave, job security, early retirement, unemployment benefit, and working conditions', under Mitterrand maximum weekly working hours were for a start unilaterally reduced to thirty-nine.[88] By 1993, Minister of Labour Martine Aubry restricted by law the right of employers to sack workers and when she returned to office after 1997 reduced the statutory work week to 35 hours. To contain increasing unemployment, governments reduced working life so that 'By the age of 60, less than a third of the French labour force is still employed'.[89] 'Powerless to attack the root causes of unemployment, the government is reduced to making it as painless as possible through a combination of pseudojobs for the young and early retirement for the aged'.[90]

However, the budgetary cost of such policies has proved unsustainable, with the result that the weak trade unions have been increasingly left to the mercy of employer-imposed Anglo-American style flexibility and job insecurity, compounded by the threat of delocalization of firms. Motivated partly by wishing to remain at arm's length from problems they cannot resolve, government action tends to be 'more market-conforming than past state intervention, or at least conceived as a temporary measure to ease the transition to a more market-regulated system'.[91] However, Levy concludes that France remains 'a state whose reforms are either half-hearted or rejected; and a state that is unable to resist the demands for protection or compensation for the various losers of market competition', which applies to failed industrial national champions even more than to redundant employees.[92] Confronted by demands that he thought legitimate but could not satisfy because of economic constraints, Prime Minister Jospin couched his de facto social liberalism in the formula: 'yes to the market economy, no to market society'.[93]

The outsider's pessimistic assessment of France's predicament has been shared in more obsessive and impassioned fashion by much insider journalistic and pamphleteering commentary on France's relative decline. Not merely has the reality of national cultural, linguistic, military, economic, and political standing fallen but the consciousness of the widening gap between flattering self-perception and stern reality has become incontrovertible. Anti-France susceptibilities might not simply be provoked by foreign comparisons but were often home-grown. To take one of the more intelligent and early examples of French exasperated reaction against their own national pretensions, Nicolas Baverez's *La France qui tombe* will serve. Faced with US world domination and Britain's increasing EU policy preponderance, an EU which France had hoped to utilize for her ends, ritualistically clinging to the Franco-German axis was as pointless as responding to US unilateralism with its own, when it did not have the strength to make its posturing

---

[88] Levy, *Tocqueville's Revenge*, 237; 238–40.   [89] Ibid. 252; cf. 249–54.
[90] Ibid. 257; cf. 240–1.   [91] Ibid. 284; cf. 246, 290.   [92] Ibid. 292; cf. 278–9.
[93] Etienne Schweisguth, 'Declin et recomposition des cultures politiques' in S. Berstein (ed.), *Les cultures politiques en France*, 398–402, 407–9.

effective. Having lost control of public expenditure, devoted disproportionately to transfer payments (22.5 per cent of GNP) and the civil service (14.5 per cent of GNP), the French 'social-socialist model' remained devoted to the 'sanctuarisation of the public sector'.[94] It accounted for 9 million people, as against a 15.5 million private sector, 12 million receiving transfer payments and 24 million inactive, of whom half were pensioners, whose number would inexorably increase. Unable to count on the state's strength to give them a sense of their own strength, French citizens feel disempowered and disoriented, abandoned to an insecure fate.

Bavarez repeatedly calls for 'shock therapy' to overcome the stalemate that earlier liberal analysts of the French predicament had detected but he is unduly optimistic about the mass of his fellow countrymen when he claims that what is missing to avoid a retreat into introvert protectionism and denial is not the public demand for drastic reform but the supply of political leaders to carry it out.[95] Some on the Right may hope that Nicolas Sarkozy, elected head of the UMP in 2004, who has not concealed his attraction to British and American practices, will provide more deftly the shock therapy administered by Margaret Thatcher to Britain in the 1980s. Be that as it may, welfare state reforms have so far been too little and too late, transferring too many of the escalating costs to posterity in rising national debt. The French Left has condemned itself to its present stalemate, half retrospectively clinging nostalgically to a better yesterday, while the other half aspire ineffectively to a better, liberalized tomorrow that dare not speak its name unambiguously, having described its 1983 'U-turn' as (Jospin *dixit*) a 'parenthesis'.

Nevertheless, circumstances may impose change even if the willingness to propose or accept it is absent. Yet liberal intellectuals like Crozier, who regarded America as their second homeland, have shed much of their admiration owing to its inability to live up to its ideals, which partly accounts for prevailing despair at finding any alternative way out of France's incapacity to perpetuate its unviable national exceptionalisms. Socialist solutions are a spent force, transnational capitalism is obnoxious and third ways relying upon civil society are unconvincing. Still, if the bulk of opinion leaders do not know what they are for, apart from preserving what they can of the past, they know what they are against.[96] 'Liberalism, there is the enemy!' American-led economic liberalism, the spearhead of modernization pressures, mediated by a competition-promoting EU, encounters an unimpaired hostility. Whether it is to defend traditional or recent *droits acquis*, the state protection against social insecurity in the name of solidarity or defence

[94] Nicolas Baverez, *La France qui tombe*, 2003, 78, 85, 123.

[95] Ibid. 22, 133–4. From the flurry of 'declinist' publications in mid-2005, one of the briefest and best is by Maurice Lévy, 'Sur le déclin, exactement' in *Le Monde*, 29.7.05. For a more optimistic assessment of the forces of progress versus stagnation, see Jacques Marseille, *La Guerre des deux Frances: Celle qui avance et celle qui freine, 2004*.

[96] Raymond Boudon, *Pourquoi les intellectuels n'aiment pas le libéralisme*, 2004. For an authoritative and splenetic example of the anti-liberal standpoint in terms of an international capitalist conspiracy, see Pierre Bourdieu, *Contre-feux: propos pour servir à la résistance contre l'invasion néo-liberale*, 1998. For a counterblast and defence of liberal socialism see Jacques Julliard, *Le malheur français*, 2005, 124–32; cf. 42–5, 54–7, 61.

of national champion firms from foreign takeover, the enemies from without and from within are feared as imposing humiliating repugnant priorities and values. There is an uneasy coexistence between the assertion of anti-liberal principles and the reluctant acceptance of liberalizing, un-French practices. This was reflected in the virulently anti-liberal 'No' campaign against the proposed EU constitutional treaty in May 2005. Two kinds of shamefaced modernization are on offer: a liberal socialism of the Left and a social liberalism of the Right. Ideologically exhausted, France seemed to be resigning itself to *la pensée unique*, a semi-consensus that has not been willed and cannot inspire a mobilizing enthusiasm for the effort of national reassertion on behalf of a state that has lost its capacity to direct and a sense of direction.

Until the Muslim challenge relaunched the secularist issue in France, a weakened Catholic Church had accepted that it was not synonymous with but an important component of a plural French culture. An increasing liberalization of Christian religion into a private matter has meant that attitudes traditionally identified as foreign and Anglo-Saxon have quietly become widely accepted. It was no longer necessary to choose between republican citizenship and the community of believers. 'The values of Protestantism [notably individualism, tolerance, secularism] seem actually to have become those of society as a whole—so much so that the notion of the Protestantization of French society has practically become a cliché.'[97] Ironically, an offensive religious fundamentalism having been reinvigorated in US politics, this has become yet another way of alienating France from American values and practices, intolerance having crossed the Atlantic. Nevertheless, the French commitment to the secularist neutrality of its public institutions—especially the educational matrix of common citizenship—has shown itself still capable of a defensive intolerance to preserve what remains of its national identity. The retreat from Catholicism as symbolizing national identity and the army as embodiment of national patriotism has led to sport (notably football imported from Britain) becoming the mass weekly celebration of both identity and patriotism.

While the focus upon nation-centred history, still more a reliance upon collective memory based upon selective amnesia, sacrifices French would-be universality to a defensive particularity, the increasing agreement about fundamentals—religious, political, institutional, and economic—has blurred most of the cleavages that accentuated its distinctive features. If Franco-French conflicts are less significant in prompting the need to reassert national identity against home-grown scapegoats, foreign counter-identities can still be mobilized to perform the repellent function of anti-France both within an integrated Europe and between it and the American-dominated world beyond it. The French elite problem is that, even with German support, it cannot mobilize a disunited European Union

---

[97] Pierre Birnbaum, *The Idea of France*, 264; cf. 210–12, 220–1, 242. See also Jean Bauberot, *Le Protestantisme doit-il mourir? La Différence protestante dans une France pluriculturelle*, 1988 and André Encrevé, *Les Protestants en France de 1800 à nos jours: Histoire d'une réintegration*, 1985. See also William Safran, 'Ethno religious Politics in France: Jews and Muslims' in *West European Politics*, May 2004, xxvii/3. 423–51 98.

against a domineering US counter-identity and has no other enemy to compel it to unite.

The French vote against the European constitutional treaty in the 2005 referendum reflected the rejection of over half the Socialist voters of the market-compatible social liberalism of Delors and Rocard. While the better-educated, secure middle-class professional classes predominantly voted in favour (as well as the retired, with memories of the Second World War), the bulk of the working classes, lower-middle classes, farmers, the unemployed and insecure voted against. The latter did so in alliance with the nationalist Right, which made up the other half of the negative vote. The theme of the propaganda against the treaty was that it consecrated market liberalism, which had since the 1957 Rome Treaty been a pivotal feature of European integration, although—as we recalled earlier—Delors never failed to combine 'competition that stimulates, cooperation that reinforces, solidarity that unites'. The Delors package of competition with solidarity proved unacceptable as supposedly antithetical to an unrealistic public that wished nostalgically to cling to its social and economic protections and benefits but shunned the costs and exposure to increased competitiveness that alone could fund them. The 1983 rejection of a 'rupture with capitalism' by the socialists in favour of an open European market that Delors had secured as Finance Minister before implementing it as European Commission President was again in question. Furthermore, what a majority of the French voters rejected was a project inspired by a French initiative and led by a former French President of the Republic, signifying that an elitist France of both Left-Centre and Right-Centre was no longer able to play the modernizing role in which it had taken pride and had enabled it to conflate its European strategy with national reassertion. Jacques Chirac had from 1995 presided over the loss of impetus and then the bankruptcy of the French capacity to lead others in a direction it determined. All the Fifth Republic Presidents have flaunted a Louis XIV 'Court politics' complex but Chirac, more than his predecessors, had lacked the reformist ability to resolve low-politics internecine conflicts, dismissed as a distraction from the high politics pursuit of international glory.[98]

The 2007 presidential election campaign was dominated by two candidates who had both supported the European constitutional treaty and represented the liberal socialist wing of the Socialist Party (Ségolène Royal) and the liberal wing of the UMP Right (Nicolas Sarkozy). So, more as a result of external pressure than from popular choice and despite the vociferous hostility of the extremes of Left and Right, elite liberalism is once again making an attempted comeback, persuasively presented by populist mass communication.

---

[98] Franz-Olivier Giesbert, *La Tragédie du president, Scènes de la vie politique 1986–2006*, 2006.

Epilogue: Confronting the National Identity Crisis

What imparts to modern French political history its dramatic asperity is the intermittent clash between its elevated principles and its frequently dubious practices, between its ideals and interests, its rhetoric and reality. Consequently, generalizations are at the mercy of incessant contradiction by countervailing plausibilities. Their perpetual tension provides the dynamic of a society that is liable to render prediction particularly hazardous and subject to prompt refutation. The French are capable, in rapid succession, of plumbing unfathomable depths as well as attaining stupendous heights. So, it is not a country likely to leave the close foreign observer indifferent to the shifting spectacle that combines arresting alarms and excursions with a grip on some profound and enduring essentials of human existence. It is an exaggeration to claim that 'France has always been Europe's political laboratory'[1] if this ignores that it has itself borrowed from others, notably Roman Law for its state and Roman Catholicism for religion, before later influences from Italy, Britain, and Germany. Nevertheless, the impassioned conflicts that have provided its political history have exercised a powerful attraction. It is partly for this very reason that the loss of its standing as an enviable model for others has been felt as a devastating disfigurement of the nation's self-esteem. Preoccupation with memory and national identity reflects the resulting loss of self-confidence and obsessive and excessive concern with relative national decline when contrasted with the inordinate expectations cultivated by implicit comprehension with grandiose past achievements.

The belated disinterring of some of the country's more discreditable past activities, such as the Napoleonic revival of slavery after its abolition by the French Revolution and definitive abolition by the Second Republic, colonialism's more uncivilized aspects, notably in Algeria from the early 1830s to the late 1950s, or its behaviour during the German Second World War Occupation, have produced ambivalent responses, reflecting both denial and guilt. A convenient way of resolving the problem was to assert that the 'real France' was not to be identified with a posited 'anti-France', notably in the case of the Vichy regime. Claiming to represent national authenticity, Marshal Pétain had forthrightly declared in September 1940 that national defeat would nevertheless allow France to return to its true identity. 'There is no possible neutrality between good and evil, order and

---

[1] George Lichtheim, *Marxism in Modern France*, 1966, 163.

disorder, France and anti-France.' De Gaulle had peremptorily reversed the roles of what constituted France and its negation. Evasively, in October 1977, former right-wing Prime Minister Edouard Balladur asked: 'During the Occupation, was France in London or Vichy?' while Socialist Prime Minister Lionel Jospin asserted that 'Vichy was the negation of France, in any case the negation of the Republic'.[2]

By the twentieth century, 'the Republic' come to embody a set of values constitutive of a secular political culture aspiring to achieve consensus and institutionalization, even when threatened by a multiculturalism based upon inadequately assimilated immigration.[3] Nevertheless, the rule of law in principle continues to be belied by its systematically tolerated infringements (*l'état de droit* all too often being in practice an *état de passe droit*) and nominal equality is contradicted by a multitude of increasing inequalities. Despite lip service to equality, France has systematically institutionalized educational, cultural, social, economic, and political inequality. What has caused unease bordering upon desperation is that the norm has become blatantly incredible. It is the coexistence of the reality of inequality and the official republican principle that has exposed the hypocrisy of past pretence. The legitimizing myth cannot any longer be sustained when inequality is coupled with insecurity. The French state may continue to rock and roll alarmingly, it has not sunk. The successive Revolutions, Empires, and Republics imparted dynamism to French politics, even if they each in turn succumbed to immobilism. Although national pride requires that the impulse to change, advocated in principle, and postponed for as long as possible in practice, should be presented as coming from within the country, it is—and there is the rub—decreasingly a matter of national choice.

Will it require a major crisis to break the hold of immobilisms that mean that decisive reforms can only be carried out in the face of extreme necessity? Both the Left and the Right are predisposed to prevent indispensable changes whose urgency is understood but cannot be explicitly admitted, still less carried out. The political system operates as an organized hypocrisy, the 'French model' being defended by those unwilling to create the conditions for both its honest application and its survival in an inhospitable international environment. To do so would require 'upsetting "sheltered" France to improve the prospects of "exposed" France.'[4]

It took the Second World War to shake France out of its economic lethargy half a century ago and the Algerian War to give it stable political institutions. Membership of the European Union has not yet persuaded the majority of French people that its state is often the problem rather than the solution to its problems. France's friends can only hope that in the early twenty-first century it will

---

[2] All three quotations are from Julian Jackson, *France: The Dark Years, 1940–1944*, 2001, 150, 631–2.

[3] For an admirably succinct analysis of the significance of 'the Republic' in France, see David Howarth and Georgios Varouxakis, *Contemporary France*, 2003, 4–13. They point out that all French parties other than the National Front are accepted as Republican because it alone is judged not to accept the consensual national values.

[4] Jacques Marseille, *Du Bon usage de la guerre civile en France*, 2006, 172; cf. 167–71. See also his *La Guerre des deux France*, 2004 and Franz-Olivier Giesbert, *La Tragédie du président*, 2006, 359–62.

not require such dramatically severe crises to impart the necessary impetus to remake France, enabling it both to shake off its paralyzing self-doubt and its nostalgic illusion of selfless superiority. Can one conclude on a more optimistic note? Perhaps, after a prolonged period of institutionalized dualism in which the sanctified 1789 principles were systematically violated, all too often experienced as intolerant liberticide, inequality, and fratricide, the French may come to accept that recently adopted individualist and pluralist practices are permitting them personally to enjoy more freedom from social and state control, greater sex and age equality, more fraternity within France, and between it and other countries. If these affirmations are at least partially true, they mean that France is closer to the unfulfilled promise of 1789 than ever before, without the need to move on to a Sixth Republic.

Index

England/Britain/UK and USA are not listed because references to them are so frequent as to be not particularly helpful.